THE NINTH PANCHEN LAMA (1883–1937)

A LIFE AT THE CROSSROADS OF SINO-TIBETAN RELATIONS

FABIENNE JAGOU

Translated by
REBECCA BISSETT BUECHEL

ÉCOLE FRANÇAISE D'EXTRÊME-ORIENT
PARIS

SILKWORM BOOKS
CHIANG MAI

978-616-215-016-6

Published in 2011 by

École Française d'Extrême-Orient
22, Avenue du Président Wilson
75116 Paris cedex 16, France
http://www.efeo.fr

and

Silkworm Books
6 Sukkasem Road, T. Suthep
Chiang Mai 50200 Thailand
info@silkwormbooks.com
http://www.silkwormbooks.com

Cover photograph: Portrait of the Ninth Panchen Lama hanging in the prayer room of Tashilhunpo monastery in the Tibetan settlement of Bylakuppe, Karnataka, India (1995), by Patrick Jagou.

THE EFEO-SILKWORM BOOKS SERIES is an innovative new series of research work on Asia, a collaboration between the École Française d'Extrême-Orient (EFEO) and Silkworm Books to translate French publications for an English-language readership. *The Ninth Panchen Lama (1883–1937)* is the first publication in the EFEO-Silkworm Books Series.

Typeset by Silk Type in Adobe Text Pro
Printed in Thailand by O. S. Printing House, Bangkok

10 9 8 7 6 5 4 3 2 1

THE NINTH PANCHEN LAMA (1883–1937)

CONTENTS

ACKNOWLEDGMENTS

This book represents the culmination of research that Professor Pierre-Etienne Will from the College de France kindly consented to direct. May he find here the expression of my sincerest gratitude for his standards of excellence, intellectual rigor, and sense of history he so ably imparted. An equally warm thank you goes to Mr. Fernand Meyer, director of research at France's Centre National de la Recherche Scientifique, whose open-mindedness, infinite patience, and fine scholarship contributed decisively to the accomplishment of this work, as well as to Ms. Anne Chayet, director of research at Centre National de la Recherche Scientifique, for her enthusiastic encouragement and precious advice. This study could simply never have existed without the confidence that the late Yonten Gyatso, researcher at the Centre National de la Recherche Scientifique, and Tashi Tsering, director of the Amnye Machen Institute in Dharamsala, placed in me. My intellectual debt to them is truly vast given the knowledge they shared and the orientation they lent to the inquiry.

The documentation that I had access to in Taiwan, China, and India would have been far more limited without the assistance of many individuals. In Taiwan, Zhang Junyi, professor at Taipei's Zhengzhi University, helped me take my first steps in Academia Sinica. In China, Li Pengnian, employee at Archive Number Two in Nanjing, and Ran Guangrong, history professor at the University of Sichuan in Chengdu, guided me through the recesses of the archives there. In India, Lobsang Shastri, head of the Tibetan Works and Archives at the Library of Tibetan Works and Archives in Dharamsala, enabled me to consult a number of essential Tibetan documents. My immense appreciation goes to all of them, in addition to the library staff at these institutes as well as the staff at the India Office in London and Stanford University's Hoover Institution on War, Revolution and Peace in California.

In the same way, I would like to thank those who allowed the use of their private libraries, especially Katia Buffetrille, cultural anthropologist and Tibetologist, and Françoise Aubin, director of research at the Centre d'Études des Relations Internationales in Paris.

I am exceedingly grateful to the numerous people who consented to be interviewed. They did not hesitate to delve into their past and contribute their time to this effort. Particularly notable are the testimonies of the late Kachen Jangpa Thubten, disciple of the Ninth Panchen Lama and abbot of the Tashilhunpo monastery in Bylakuppe, India, and Yéshé Dorjé, former bodyguard of the Ninth Panchen Lama. Ngachen Darba Hutuktu's facilitation with the interviews in South India was likewise invaluable.

Further, I would especially like to thank the official and private associations who generously gave funds without which this work would not have been possible: The French Ministère de l'Éducation, de la Recherche et de la Technologie, the French and Chinese (People's Republic of China) Ministries of Foreign Affairs, Taiwan's Mongolian and Tibetan Affairs Commission, and the Chiang Ching-kuo Foundation for International Scholarly Exchange, as well as the Institut National des Langues Orientales in Paris.

Franciscus Verellen, director of the École Française d'Extrême-Orient (EFEO), Yves Goudineau and François Lachaud, former vice-directors, Valérie Liger-Belair, administrative chief, Astrid Aschehoug and Géraldine Hue from EFEO Éditions, and Jacques Leider, my colleague in charge of the EFEO office in Chiang Mai, were most supportive and helpful in working with me on this English edition and I thank them very sincerely.

Without the graciousness of Rebecca Bissett Buechel, my patient translator, this English version would have never come into being. I am extremely grateful. Alex McKay and Peter Zarrow were also very helpful in reviewing certain parts of the English manuscript. And finally, but not least, the enthusiasm of Trasvin Jittidecharak from Silkworm to publish this book in English and the thorough copyediting of the final manuscript by Lisa S. Keary also earned my undying gratitude.

Lastly, I truly hope that the Chinese and Tibetans who so aided in this research will, in turn, give their opinions on this work, which reflects a Western view of their history. If this study may in some way help enhance their understanding of their own past and serve to find ways to live in mutual peace, then my dearest aim will have been achieved.

PREFACE

The controversy arising in May 1995 regarding the selection of the reincarnation of the deceased Tenth Panchen Lama (in which Chinese authorities took into custody the child chosen as the Eleventh Panchen Lama by the current Fourteenth Dalai Lama and imposed their own choice on the Buddhist community, all the while cloaking the affair in dubious historical arguments) has made it all the more urgent to clarify the tormented history of relations between China and Tibet at the beginning of the twentieth century. Indeed, the flight of the Ninth Panchen Lama from Tibet and his exile and death in China directly opened the door for Chinese Republican, and then Communist, control over the Tenth Panchen Lama, who passed away on January 28, 1989, with repercussions even today over the polemical selection of his successor.[1]

An earlier study, which I conducted for a postgraduate degree at École des Hautes Études en Sciences Sociales, revealed that the Ninth Panchen Lama's flight was not only the most intense episode in his life, but that it had a determining effect on the history of contemporary Tibet.[2] Due to the audacity of the flight and its final destination, both Indian and American authors have characterized the prelate as an opponent to the Thirteenth Dalai Lama's regime.[3] Yet their analyses differ greatly when describing the man himself. While the American scholar Melvyn C. Goldstein is reluctant to position himself on the Ninth Panchen Lama's temperament, his analysis shows the Panchen Lama to be very determined to set up the independence of his province and ready to re-examine the very foundations of the Tibetan political system. Parshotam Mehra, on the contrary, portrays the Panchen Lama as being "weak and timid," "gullible," "far from sure of his ground," as opposed to the Thirteenth Dalai Lama whom he considers a "clever, astute manager and manipulator of men," knowing how to handle people and turn circumstances to his benefit. All the accounts from travelers and explorers who met the Panchen Lama in person describe him as courteous, benevolent, detached from ambition, and solely focused on Buddhist philosophical study.[4]

Chinese authors, when analyzing the particular actions of the Ninth Panchen Lama, invariably conclude that he was a "great Chinese patriot." They feel that his actions "contributed to the unification of the Motherland." More recently, Jiang Ping recognized the Panchen Lama's preponderant role in the spread of Tibetan Buddhism. Before him, Shi Dongchu, a Taiwanese historian, had also analyzed the importance of the religious role the Panchen Lama played by examining the funeral orations given upon the death of the prelate. Following the example of continental Chinese, he recognized that the Buddhist work accomplished by the Ninth Panchen Lama in China contributed to unification and peace.[5]

Such a divergence in the analyses of Western and Chinese authors can, in part, be explained by the respective sources of information used. One group uses documents from the British government and the other group from Chinese government archives. Admittedly, though, the British sources used by both Goldstein and Mehra do not prevent them from having diverging opinions of the Ninth Panchen Lama.

Chinese authors show particular interest in the years that the Panchen Lama spent in China, neglecting the causes for his departure from Tibet and the reasons he failed to return. On the other hand, Western researchers have tended to be unacquainted with the activities of the Panchen Lama in China.

The contradictions in these points of view left me wanting to know more. An initial look at the available works in Parisian libraries offered no new elements to the question.[6] No biography of the Ninth Panchen Lama in any language was referenced there. Moreover, other sources concerning the Panchen Lama that were mentioned were press articles inaccessible from Paris.

As for the English translation of the work by the Tibetan historian Shakabpa Wangchuk Deden, it is silent on the fourteen years spent by the Panchen Lama in China. In general, the Tibetan sources translated into English were insufficient. Learning Tibetan (in addition to knowing Chinese) turned out to be indispensable to delving deeper into the subject.

The exile of the Ninth Panchen Lama in China took place during the Republican regime. Faced with the dearth of information on his life during this period, it became necessary first to go to Taiwan to consult the Nationalist government's archives. The correspondence of the Foreign Office of the Qing dynasty (1644–1911) found at Academia Sinica revealed nothing more than a few partial bits of information about the period of the Panchen Lama's life up to 1923, when he was still residing in Tibet.[7] I discovered that most of the documents concerning the Mongolian and Tibetan Affairs Commission, which was created by the Republican government in 1928, are currently located in Nanjing in the People's Republic of China.

From the outset, research undertaken in China in 1992 and 1993 turned out to be problematic due to the political situation in Tibet, since all requests for historical documents covering this country are considered suspicious. For the Chinese, Tibet represents such a sensitive topic that it precludes them from having any objectivity on the issue. In this context, research in China proved to be a real obstacle, which explains why it was necessary to spend a year in the field before obtaining any significant results. Only tenacity and patience allowed me to bring together a great number of documents that until then had been unexploited, study them firsthand, and present them herein.

First of all, there are two hagiographies written by disciples of the Ninth Panchen Lama entitled *Banchan da shi quanji* (Complete Works of the Great Master Panchen) and *Banchan da shi dong lai shiwu nian dashiji* (Main Events during the Fifteen Years the Great Master Panchen Spent in the East), both published in Chongqing in 1943. Their respective authors, Liu Jiaju (Kelzang Chönjor) and Chen Wenjian, who remains unidentified, retrace the prelate's life from 1923 to 1937. Kelzang Chönjor was both secretary and interpreter to the Panchen Lama and wrote his work based on day-to-day notes taken during the prelate's lifetime. He chose to divide his text into two parts. First, he chronologically relates the events and actions of his master; second, he compiles the teachings, political speeches, and correspondence of the Panchen Lama. Chen Wenjian wrote a chronological biography of the Panchen Lama inspired by Kelzang Chönjor's notes. We must also note a journal published in 1935 by Buddhist and lay Chinese and compiled by Chen Yisun, entitled *Banchan dong lai* (The Panchen Came to the East), telling about the trip made by the Panchen Lama from Shanghai to Hangzhou in 1934.

Various documents from governmental bodies such as the Mongolian and Tibetan Affairs Commission, Chinese State Council, Nanjing Tibet Office, Lhasa China Office, and the Panchen Lama's offices in Beijing, Nanjing, Chengdu, Xining, Dartsédo, and Shenyang added a wealth of specifics to the two hagiographies mentioned. These telegrams, letters, and reports mainly involve the organization of the Panchen Lama's offices, the titles that the Republican government bestowed on him, and the negotiations surrounding his return to Tibet. However, it must be pointed out that at the Number Two Historical Archives in Nanjing simple consultation of the catalogue of documents was forbidden. Even though the support of Professor Ran Guangrong from the History Department at Sichuan University was invaluable in bypassing the ban on examining certain documents, it was not sufficient to bestow the liberty of choosing directly from their catalogue.

There are most probably other sources on the subject that were inaccessible for this research effort. I should also highlight the fact that a great number of the documents consulted at the Number Two Historical Archives have since been published in two collected works listed in this present volume's bibliography: *Jiu shi Banchan yuanji zhiji he shi shi Banchan chuanshi zuochuang dang'an xuanbian* (Compilation of Documents Preserved in the Nanjing Archives Concerning the Death of the Ninth Panchen Lama and the Enthronement of the Tenth Panchen Lama) and *Jiu shi Banchan neidi huodong ji fan Zang shouzu dang'an xuanbian* (Compilation of Documents Preserved in the Nanjing Archives Regarding the Activities of the Ninth Panchen Lama in China and the Obstacles to His Return to Tibet), both compiled by the Second Historical Archives of China.

To this selection of sources we can add articles from the press covering the period from 1921 to 1940 in magazines such as *Meng Zang yuebao, Meng Zang shibao, Kang Zang yuebao,* and so forth, which dealt with the Chinese Nationalist government's relations with Tibet and Inner Mongolia and informed their readers of the Panchen Lama's activities at that time. Most of the magazines were published in three languages: Chinese, Tibetan, and Mongol. Some were published by the Mongolian and Tibetan Affairs Commission, others by the Sichuan authorities. Consulting them is difficult since they are not grouped together in one place.

At the library of Stanford University's Hoover Institution on War, Revolution and Peace, I was able to consult the national daily newspapers *Dagong bao* and *Zhongyang ribao,* although the library's collections unfortunately had gaps.

With *Dagong bao* I focused on the period from 1917 to 1939 and with *Zhongyang ribao* from 1930 to 1940.

For his part, the Ninth Panchen Lama had similarly created his own magazine, *Xichui xuanhua shi gongshu yuekan*, to spread, among other things, his political speeches and religious teachings. Published monthly from 1935 to 1937, it was edited and printed in Xining, but it is impossible to conclusively determine who actually directed the work.

All in all, studying these documents from China revealed only two points of view: that of the Chinese Nationalist government and that of the Ninth Panchen Lama and certain members of his entourage (filtered by Chinese authorities). Consequently, research on Tibetan documents and interviews became imperative.

Conducting research among the Tibetans proved to be just as trying. Tibet remains very Buddhist in its culture and Tibetans find it natural to test the patience and motivation of a researcher as a sort of safeguard. Earning their trust can be no easy task. In any case, such an inquiry would have been clearly impossible had it been undertaken by a Chinese-speaking Tibetan or a Tibetan-speaking Chinese, due to the political divergence that places the respective researchers largely in opposition.

One trip to Tibet and two to the exiled Tibetan communities in India allowed me to assemble primary documents, the majority of which had never been previously consulted. These documents revealed themselves to be of a very different nature from those found in China. First, I had to determine whether a Tibetan version of the Panchen Lama's biography actually existed. According to Tibetan tradition, at the death of every great spiritual master a biography is written by the main disciples. It is to serve as testimony and example for future generations. Scholars can find all kinds of interesting information in these documents whether of a historical, geographical, religious, or anthropological nature. The complete works are usually made up of several volumes. The events and actions of the master are contained in the first volume (*rnam thar*), and the teachings and correspondence are in the following ones (*gsung 'bum*).

At the time of writing the French version of this book, the first volume of the Ninth Panchen Lama's biography seemed to have disappeared or to have been destroyed. Lokesh Chandra, editor of *Materials for a History of Tibetan Literature*, mentions the existence of a biography and a five-volume compilation of the prelate's words housed in the Densapa collection (Densapa was a well-known bibliophile from Sikkim).[8] However, he specified that Densapa never obtained the first volume.[9] As for the archivists from Tashilhunpo monastery in Tibet, they clearly indicated to me that the first volume of the complete works of the Ninth Panchen Lama had been destroyed, which at the time I legitimately doubted. In this way, despite research efforts and numerous leads in Tibet during sojourns to the great monasteries of Kumbum, Labrang trashikhyil, and Tashilhunpo, where the Ninth Panchen Lama had resided, and in India during visits to the Tibetan exile communities in Dharamsala, Himachal Pradesh, and at the Tashilhunpo monastery in the state of Karnataka, this first volume could not be located. Much later in 2004 while the French version of this book was being printed, I managed to find it, thanks to the late Gene Smith—to whom I am sincerely grateful.

My first plan was to use the document for this English translation, but upon reading it, I quickly realized that, on the one hand, the document brought new approaches to research on the modern period in general and on the Ninth Panchen Lama's life in particular, but on the other hand, the use of the text required caution as it was published so long after the prelate's death. In fact, two biographies of the Ninth Panchen Lama were suddenly available in 2003. The first relates the life of the prelate in Tibet from his selection in 1888 to 1941, the date of the return of his corpse to Tashilhunpo. It was written by one of the Panchen Lama's disciples and is dated 1945. The second retraces the entire life of the Ninth Panchen Lama (1883–1941). Its writing began after the Chinese State Council gave its authorization, following the death of the Tenth Panchen Lama in 1989, and its authors are members of the Historical Research Committee of Tashilhunpo.[10] It is dated 1996, the year after the debate surrounding the selection of the Eleventh Panchen Lama, and was thus naturally subject to strict monitoring by Chinese authorities.[11] Consequently, I have deliberately chosen not to use this source, leaving to future generations the task of completing, developing, and contradicting this present volume.

The printing blocks of the Ninth Panchen Lama's biography corresponding to volumes two, three, four, and five have been preserved at the Tashilhunpo monastery in Tibet. It was thus possible to acquire a recent print of them, giving an exhaustive collection of the Ninth Panchen Lama's spiritual work. Only one political speech is found in this compilation.[12] Any correspondence exchanged between the Thirteenth Dalai Lama and the Ninth Panchen Lama has been edited out. However, this document was published in 1973, right in the middle of the Chinese Cultural Revolution when all Tibetan publications were prohibited from print, which makes it dubious and could explain why no correspondence was incorporated in these volumes.[13] Another possibility is self-censorship.

If we focus on the biography (in two volumes) and writings (in five volumes) of the Thirteenth Dalai Lama, which were duly written and indexed according to tradition, we can see that a selective choice was made. These documents contain much information on the selection and enthronement of the Ninth Panchen Lama and on the various meetings that took place between the two prelates; however, the content of their conversations is never revealed. The correspondence contained in this work is equally frustrating. It contains just a few letters written between 1915 and 1922, and excludes all the letters exchanged between the Thirteenth Dalai Lama and the Ninth Panchen Lama after the latter fled Tibet. Following his departure, the Panchen Lama disappears completely from the Thirteenth Dalai Lama's biography; that is to say, after 1923. We can also suppose that because of its polemical nature, the correspondence exchanged between the Thirteenth Dalai Lama and the Ninth Panchen Lama was better suited to the Tibetan administrative archives than to the spiritual work of the

Thirteenth Dalai Lama. Thus, a useful resource was the biography of Phabongka Rinpoche, a great spiritual master from the Kham region of Tibet sent by Reting to the Ninth Panchen Lama in 1936, since it brought to light new elements surrounding the Panchen Lama's plan to return to Tibet.

After studying these biographies, it seemed appropriate to complement them with an analysis of Tibetan administrative documents from that time. There again, new complications arose given that the archives in Lhasa are still closed today and no one knows exactly what they hold. What remained to be checked was the document collection preserved by the Tibetans in exile in India. Those who fled in 1959, leaving suddenly for the journey to India, attempted to preserve the main part of their archives. These collections were often saved in dire circumstances, most often carried over the Himalayas on the backs of those escaping on foot. While the majority of these texts concern Buddhist philosophy, a small number of official documents were preserved in the Library of Tibetan Works and Archives (LTWA) in Dharamsala. Such is the case of two original administrative documents that were miraculously preserved, and which genuinely elucidate aspects of the Ninth Panchen Lama's flight. Without them, the only other official Tibetan texts available are Chinese versions of documents produced by the Tibetan Council of Ministers. The translations from Tibetan to Chinese were done at the time by members of the Mongolian and Tibetan Affairs Commission, and those from Tibetan to English by the British officials sent on missions to Lhasa by their government. Due to their biased nature, these translations must be used prudently.

Aside from these Tibetan sources and the newspaper *Yul phyogs so so'i gsar 'gyur me long*, written in Tibetan and published in Darjeeling by Tharchin, a pastor from Kinnaur in Himachal Pradesh, who diffused them throughout the Himalayan region from 1925 to 1950, the only path left to explore were testimonies, both written and oral.[14]

After the Chinese Cultural Revolution, many offices were created across China and in each of the three main Tibetan regions—Ü-Tsang, Kham, and Amdo—under the auspices of the "Political Consultative Conference," which had the official goal of gathering accounts of direct testimony about the past. In the case of the Tibetans, the former Tibetan government officials agreed to do this in exchange for a salary, and the Chinese testifying about Tibetan events did likewise. Nine volumes of approximately three hundred pages each were written and published in Tibetan between 1982 and 1986 for limited diffusion (*neibu*) solely for the region of Central Tibet under the title *Bod rang skyong ljongs rig gnas lo rgyus dpyad gzhi* (Materials on the Culture and History of the Autonomous Region of Tibet). The articles published in these volumes are of unparalleled historical value. Their content, which comprises an indispensable source for understanding Tibetan history during the first half of the twentieth century, must obviously be subject to caution due to the circumstances surrounding their creation.

In actual fact, the primary objective of the "Political Consultative Conference" was to detect possible sympathizers who might be likely to enroll in the

Chinese Communist Party, especially among the individuals who had belonged to the Republican government and had made amends. Since no one was taken in by this tactic, the testimonies were often merely political cant. One proof of the uncomfortable conditions of these interviews is that today certain Tibetan authors will go as far as renouncing their articles, claiming to be just editors, for instance, even if their declarations were in no way detrimental to the Tibetan cause.[15] However, it was possible to use certain articles that contain oral testimony from eyewitnesses, whether from the Chinese who had lived in Lhasa, such as Liu Shenqi, the Chinese interpreter at the Lhasa China Office in 1940 or Tibetans themselves, including Kugo Ngawang Riktröl, an official of the Lhasa government; W. T. Serga, an inhabitant of Kardzé and a witness to the events after the death of the Ninth Panchen Lama; Yéshé Dorjé, bodyguard to the Ninth Panchen Lama; and Kachen Jangpa Thubten as well as Kachen Lakpa Dorjé, monks who had begun their philosophical studies under the guidance of the Ninth Panchen Lama.

The selection of Chinese and Tibetan sources available made it necessary to verify the British sources cited by Parshotam Mehra and Melvyn C. Goldstein. In effect, the India Record Office in London is packed full of documents translated from Chinese or Tibetan into English, which leads to another question: how did such supposedly confidential information, such as the many letters exchanged between the Thirteenth Dalai Lama and the Ninth Panchen Lama, fall into the hands of the British envoys?

For this volume, establishing a factual biography of the Ninth Panchen Lama became the first necessary step. I decided to ask three broad questions: Why did he leave Tibet? What were his activities in China? Why did he never return to Tibet? Beyond the chain of events, it remains difficult to understand the motivation of the Tibetan prelate without taking into account the Tibetan and Chinese political, economic, and religious contexts during that period. In Tibet, did his influence harm the construction of a new, centralized state? In China, had the Republican government appropriated him in order to benefit their policy towards Tibet and Mongolia? Had the Ninth Panchen Lama manipulated the Chinese government, and, if so, to what end? Had he become a pawn in the diplomatic game among Britain, China, and Tibet? Finally, from a more general point of view, is it possible to say that the Ninth Panchen Lama betrayed his country to the point of compromising its independence? I will try to respond to these many questions throughout this volume.

The first part of the book presents the economic and structural causes behind the flight of the Panchen Lama. Wishing to strengthen the sovereignty of his country, the Thirteenth Dalai Lama had decided to develop a standing army. In furtherance to this effort, he levied a contribution on Tashilhunpo monastery to finance one quarter of the military budget, and also to provide *ulag*, a form of taxation that involved providing free labor and transport animals to assist traveling officials. The Panchen Lama refused to pay, claiming it was impossible to raise the required amount. The legal battle that ensued is described and the insolvency of the Panchen Lama's estate is demonstrated. Finally, the institutional role of the Panchen Lama is examined in relation to that of the Thirteenth Dalai Lama.

Part 2 of the book shows how the Panchen Lama encouraged the renewal of Buddhism in China through his transmission of a great number of teachings and the establishment of associations and Buddhist institutes. The willingness of the Panchen Lama to set up chaplain-donor relations with Chinese officials is likewise brought to light. At first, the prelate associated with Chinese warlords. Then he became acquainted with the Republican leaders and espoused their political agenda. He especially adopted Sun Yat-sen's "Three Principles of the People," of which he offered a re-reading from a Buddhist perspective. He turned into an ambassador of Chinese values, which he propagated in Inner Mongolia and along the Tibetan border. In Inner Mongolia, he mediated several times on behalf of the Mongol princes in their attempt at autonomy. Along the Tibetan border, he created local offices and published a specialized magazine aimed at communicating the Chinese Republican government ideals to Tibet. In return, he expected China to help put into place a modernization program in Tibet that he himself had drawn up. The motivation of each party involved is analyzed.

Finally, part 3 explains the aborted return of the Panchen Lama to Tibet from the point of view of various actors involved: the Panchen Lama and his entourage, the Tibetan administration in Lhasa, the Republican Chinese authorities, and the British government. It concludes with an investigation into the role of the Panchen Lama's entourage who were endeavoring to create an independent state in Kham after the prelate's death, which occurred on December 1, 1937. The final chapter describes the twists and turns in the lengthy transfer of the prelate's remains to the reliquary at Tashilhunpo in Tibet.

NOTE ON TRANSLITERATION

The Tibetan in this book is rendered in simplified phonetic spellings. I have adopted the Tibetan and Himalayan Digital Library (THDL) transliteration system. However, I have retained more commonly used phonetic spellings for some proper names such as Tashilhunpo for Trashi Lhünpo (bKra shis lhun po), Reting for Radreng (Rwa sgreng), Shigatse for Shikatsé (gZhis ka rtse), and Kashag for Kashak (bka'shag), as well as for certain Tibetan names, e.g., Thubten for Tupten (Thub bstan). Some of the THDL romanized terms that diverge from more commonly used phonetic spellings include Gyeltsé (Gyantse), Kyégudo (Jyekundo), Kardzé (Ganze), and Cinpa (Jinpa).

Appendix G provides a list of all Tibetan phonetic names and terms used herein and their orthography based on the T. V. Wylie system (1959). In the case of author names cited under the Wylie system, radical letters are capitalized to preserve the Tibetan orthography of the written language, for example, Don khang sKal bzang bDe skyid.

Pinyin transcriptions have been employed for Chinese names and words, with the exception of more familiarly known spellings such as Chiang Kai-shek, Kuomintang, and Sun Yat-sen, which follow the Wade-Giles romanization system.

In transcribing Mongolian proper nouns, when a term or name has a conventional spelling in English it is retained, e.g., Genghis Khan, rather than Chinggis Khaan.

PROLOGUE

At the beginning of winter, on December 22, 1923, Lozang Chöki Nyima (1883–1937), the Ninth Panchen Lama—the highest Tibetan hierarch after the Dalai Lama—suddenly left his monastery, Tashilhunpo, in the utmost secrecy.[1] Leaving the Tibetan province of Tsang, he rode out on a white horse, accompanied by a few of his monks, hastening towards Tibet's desolate northeast. As soon as news of his flight reached Lhasa, Tibetan government ministers had them followed by one thousand troops, headed by the minister of finance, Lungshar, and escorted by General Tsogo.[2] But the government troops were quickly out-distanced by the Panchen Lama and his men, who were able to take small, snowy, frozen mountain trails inaccessible to the troops.

Legend has it that cranes flew along leading the way for the fleeing party. Snow fell continually, hiding their horses' tracks. Lungshar and Tsogo lost the runaways in the mountains. Lungshar abandoned his search leaving it up to Tsogo to capture them and bring them to the capital. Little did he know that General Tsogo was actually a disciple of the Panchen Lama. So, when the general and his soldiers got very close to the spiritual master, contrary to expectation, Tsogo had the troops halt and rest a day or two. When they took to the road again, the Panchen Lama and those with him were already long gone. The general then, in turn, stopped the pursuit and returned to Lhasa. He was later demoted for having failed this mission.

Immediately, the people of Tsang hailed the success of the Panchen Lama through song:

Our Master is a god,
His horse is a bird.
After having put a golden saddle on the bird
He has flown off into the sky.[3]

They also celebrated the failure of the Tibetan army, singing:

Lungshar, the so-called accountant,
Made an error in his accounts and returned.
Tsogo, saying he is a hunting hound,
Has returned sniffing the ground.[4]

Sanctions quickly fell on the inhabitants of the province of Tsang. The monastery of Tashilhunpo, including all its goods and subjects, were seized and placed under the jurisdiction of the Tibetan government.[5] The officials who had not fled with their master were relieved of their functions. Others, among those who then tried to leave, were brought to Lhasa, the capital, and imprisoned. The Tibetan government also named a new general administrator (*kyabying dzasa lama*) for the monastery as well as some officials to assist him in the task. The new administrator was Drékang Khenchen Lozang Tenzin who officially took charge of running the monastery as of February 1924, and who from then on managed its holdings, including the private residence of the Panchen Lama as well as his lands and subjects.[6] Neither the Panchen Lama's family nor his goods were spared. Those closest to him were forbidden to join him and imprisoned.[7] The districts of Gampa, Lhatsé, Namring, and Phüntsoling, the lands of Shétongmön shimükang,[8] Tanak Rinchentsé, Lènlunrab, and the pastures and farmland of Gyeltsé, where the Panchen Lama retained usufruct, were also confiscated by the Lhasa government.[9]

Having no viable choice but to continue on into exile, the Panchen Lama and his entourage crossed the villages of Narthang and Bodong gangjong, and the river Tsangchen tchuwo.[10] They advanced on Tibet's high plateau which, at an average altitude of four thousand meters, is comprised of an arid and rocky desert sliced by east-west running mountain chains whose summits reach six thousand meters, and where an unsurpassedly severe continental climate precludes human beings or even trees from remaining for long. They managed to cross the Tibetan border and enter the Chinese province of Gansu. According to legend, despite the fierce cold and snow, they traveled what usually requires an entire month in just one week. However, their journey became worse and worse with their supplies running dangerously low. The Panchen Lama was reduced to sharing his own roasted barley flour (*tsampa*) spoonful by spoonful with his entourage. Soon even this was finished. Faced with no more supplies, the Panchen Lama led an offering ceremony. The next day, nomads arrived with an abundance of roasted barley, yaks, and butter. The travelers attributed the arrival of this godsend to the supernatural powers of their master and his ceremony of the day before. Food was no longer a problem. For a number of days they continued to wander through the province of Gansu. They then got lost in the desert. Once again, provisions were low and had to be rationed. In the village of Mage, the Panchen Lama gave a Buddhist teaching and the inhabitants thanked him with an offering of one hundred beasts of burden. But their roaming through Gansu continued.

Later, they met with the entourage of Jétsun Dampa (1870–1924), the great reincarnated master from the Republic of Mongolia who warned the Panchen Lama against going to Mongolia, as it had been undermined by Russia's presence. In the meantime, a large number of officials from Tashilhunpo monastery had left Tibet seeking to join their master. But as the winter was stormy with constant snowfall, the passes in northern Tibet were blocked. The group of dissident officials decided to leave Tibet by way of the south. From there they reached Calcutta via Darjeeling, and then they sailed for Shanghai or Hong Kong. Lozang Gyeltsen, a favorite of the Panchen Lama, was among them.[11] He finally arrived in Hong Kong on March 20, 1924. From there he contacted the local Chinese authorities and informed them of the Panchen Lama's departure from Tibet, explaining that he would like to locate him. He also told the Chinese authorities that the Panchen Lama wished to come to China.[12] Up until then, no Chinese official had noted the presence of either the Panchen Lama or his entourage in Gansu Province.

Having been informed of the situation on March 25, 1924, Cao Kun, the president of the Chinese Republic, gave orders to his local officials, notably Ma Qi, commander of a battalion from Qinghai and Ningxia stationed at the border of Gansu and Qinghai.[13] Ma Qi was commanded to determine the entourage's whereabouts and escort the "touring living Buddha" to Beijing as soon as possible.[14]

The rupture between the Thirteenth Dalai Lama and the Ninth Panchen Lama seemed absolute. Having been received by Chinese authorities, the Panchen Lama would soon find himself closely entwined with the projects of the Republican government, especially with its international policies. After a fourteen-year exile, he died prematurely at the age of fifty-four, never having had the opportunity to see his native land again.

RUSSIA
KAZAKHSTAN
MONGOLIA
Heilongjiang
Harbin
Changchun
Jilin
Shenyang
Liaoning
KOREA
KYRGYZSTAN
Urumqi
Beijing
Hohhot
Tianjin
Xinjiang
Hebei
Shanxi
Gansu
Shandong
Ningxia
Taiyuan
Jinan
Xining
Lanzhou
Zhengzhou
Hangsu
Qinghai
Xian
Nanjing
Shanghai
Henan
TIBET
Amdo
Shaanxi
Hubei
Anhui
Hangzhou
Wuhan
Shigatse
Tsang
Sichuan
Chengdu
Nangchang
Zhejiang
Lhasa
Kham
Changsha
Jiangxi
Fuzhou
Taipei
Guizhou
Hunan
NEPAL
Fujian
BHUTAN
Guiyang
TAIWAN
Guandong
INDIA
Kunming
Guangxi
Guangzhou
BANGALADESH
Yunnan
Hongkong
Nanning
Macao
VIETNAM
MYAMMAR
LAOS
N
THAILAND
0
800 Kilometres

PART ONE

TIBET

(1883–1923)

When the Panchen Lama fled Tibet and went to China, the faces of both political and religious life in Tibet changed. After being recognized as a reincarnated master and receiving the corresponding education, the prelate found himself caught between, on the one hand, the loyalty he owed the Gélukpa Buddhist order and, on the other, the incipient nationalism that was being introduced by the Thirteenth Dalai Lama, which made the Tibetan government less tolerant towards self-sufficient monastic entities such as Tashilhunpo. Since the Thirteenth Dalai Lama and the Panchen Lama maintained the appearance of good relations, we do not know for sure whether an actual disagreement ever took place between them. As for the last representatives of the Qing Empire, as well as the Chinese Republicans and the British, they did not miss the opportunities offered by the situation to achieve their own ends, especially taking advantage of the two clerics' lack of experience in international politics. The Manchu agents, and even more so the Chinese Republicans, chose to side with the disciple rather than the master, in the hopes of staking claims on a Tibet that was endeavoring simultaneously to liberate itself and to attain status as a recognized sovereign state.

LEFT: Portrait of the Ninth Panchen Lama hanging in the prayer room of Tashilhunpo monastery in the Tibetan settlement of Bylakuppe, Karnataka, India, 1995, courtesy of Patrick Jagou

BELOW: Ninth Panchen Lama in India, 1906, courtesy of the Library of Tibetan Works and Archives

ABOVE: *Thangka* depicting Tashilhunpo monastery in Shigatse hanging in the Tashilhunpo monastery, Bylakuppe, Karnataka, India, 1995, courtesy of Patrick Jagou

BELOW: Ninth Panchen Lama and his entourage in India, c. 1906, courtesy of Ngachen Rinpoche, reincarnated master of Tashilhunpo monastery, Bylakuppe, Karnataka, India

ABOVE: Ninth Panchen Lama and Chiang Kai-shek at the opening ceremony of the Chinese parliament, 1931, by Bosshardt-Dephot, in *L'illustration: Journal universel*, Hebdomadaire-Paris, France

BELOW: Ninth Panchen Lama in an airplane, from the collection of Elliot Sperling, courtesy of *Lungta*, a publication of the Amnye Machen Institute, Dharamsala, India

ABOVE: *Thangka* depicting the Ninth Panchen Lama, in Kelzangpel (sKal bzang dpal), *Thang gé gyu tsel* (Thang ga'i sgyu rtsal), Sichuan meishu chubanshe

LEFT: Portrait of the Ninth Panchen Lama, c. 1930s, courtesy of a Tibetan residing in Taipei

BELOW: Ninth Panchen Lama and his entourage together with an assembly of Chinese lay Buddhists, c. 1930s, courtesy of Tashi Tsering, director of the Amnye Machen Institute, Dharamsala, India

1

CHILDHOOD

The Panchen Lama's birth and early years occurred in the midst of great political turmoil in Tibet. British India and Imperial Russia were both vying for a foothold in the country, which had been weakened by the early deaths of four consecutive Dalai Lamas. Tibet's spiritual and temporal leader, the Thirteenth Dalai Lama, was just seven years old when the Panchen Lama was born.

POLITICAL CONTEXT AT PANCHEN LAMA'S BIRTH

In 1855–56 the Gurkhas from Nepal attacked Tibet. The Tibetans tried to resist but were defeated. They were obliged to pay an annual tribute and forced once again to submit to trade restrictions that the Gurkhas had previously imposed in 1792, after their earlier invasion. During this second attack, the Manchus had not come to help the Tibetans as they had in 1792, enforcing a *de facto* protectorate that had linked the two countries ever since the Manchu and Tibetan armies had conjointly driven out the Jüüngar (Dzungar) from Tibet in 1720. This defeat by the Gurkhas was a painful humiliation for upper-class Tibetan society as well as for the government milieu. The absence of imperial Manchu troops revealed one of Tibet's most visible deficiencies at that time: the inability to mobilize an army.

The fact of the matter was that the Manchus were actually too busy to help the Tibetans, since they themselves were subject to the threat of encroaching Western powers, combined with their own volatile domestic situation. It was in the mid-nineteenth century that Western powers had imposed the opening of Manchu ports to international trade, with the ensuing integration of their empire into a world order conceived of and organized by European powers. After signing the Treaties of Nanking (1842), Tianjin (1858), and Peking (1860–61), the Western powers benefited from numerous rights and privileges in China. Among other things, they were granted concessions and reduced customs on imports. China's internal situation was unsettled due to an increase in population that had outgrown its agricultural production capacity, which at the time was behind in technological innovations. This led to a seemingly unstoppable economic imbalance. Due to these factors, popular uprisings abounded: Taiping (1851–64), Nian (1851–55), and later the revolts of Yunnan (1856–73) and present-day Xinjiang (1870–75), obliging the Chinese state to undertake various reforms, including one that concerned its army.

New regional military divisions were given the task of handling any insurrections and reinforcing the empire's borders. In the southwest province of Yunnan where Franco-British rivalry was rampant, and to the north in Central Asia where Russo-British competition was appearing, Chinese military forces managed to control the revolts and stabilize their bases.[1]

For seventy years, from 1806 to 1876, the year of the Thirteenth Dalai Lama's birth, there had been a succession of four Dalai Lamas, none of whom reached his majority. Tibet had thus experienced successive regencies, with all their associated intrigue, feuding, administrative negligence, and general degradation of the country.

The weakness of Tibet's defense system, in addition to the power vacuum linked to the regency system, left the country vulnerable to British and Russian scheming. The British, present in India since the end of the eighteenth century, had progressively advanced towards the Himalayan region. In 1816 they extended their protectorate to Nepal, in 1846 to Kashmir and Ladakh, in 1861 to Sikkim, and in 1865 to Bhutan, whereas Tibet continued to remain closed to them. As for the Russians, by the end of the nineteenth century they had taken a vast amount of territory ranging from the Caspian to present-day Xinjiang, including Turkmenistan and Pamir as well as the cities of Tashkent, Samarkand, Bukhara, and Khiva. Their expanding presence and their need to put down any sign of revolt in India forced the British to maintain a local army and to create buffer states such as the Punjab. Moreover, persistent rumors, on top of the recent Russian encroachment into Outer Mongolia, led the British to suspect the Russians of plotting with the Tibetans. From then on, the Tibetan plateau became the object of a struggle for influence between two powers, each hoping to make Tibet a buffer zone.

With an average altitude of four thousand meters, Tibet towers over the Chinese province of Xinjiang and Central Asia to the north, China to the northeast and east, Ladakh and Kashmir to the west and India, Nepal, and Burma to the south. Nearly the same size as Western Europe, it covers more than three million square kilometers. The highest mountain range on earth lines the borders of this immense expanse of land. To the south and from east to west lies the powerful Himalayan barrier separating Tibet from India, Nepal, Sikkim, Bhutan, Burma, and China. To the west, the Karakoram Range and to the north the Kunlun Mountains demarcate the border with Xinjiang and Mongolia. To the east, Tibet is divided from the Chinese provinces of Yunnan and Sichuan by north/south mountain ranges furrowed by all four of the largest rivers in Asia: the Yangtze, Mekong, Salween, and Yalong. For the British and the Russians, Tibet and its strategic position were of the highest priority.

The Eighth Panchen Lama, Lozang Pelden Chöki Dragpa Tenpé Wangchuk (1855–1882), while surviving his childhood and adolescence (unlike the Ninth, Tenth, Eleventh, and Twelfth Dalai Lamas), passed away at a relatively young age. Little interested in the bustle of secular life, he fulfilled the traditional image of the Panchen Lama as being solely focused on spiritual issues and Buddhist philosophical study, keeping far from the preoccupations of worldly affairs. Thus the Dalai Lama was left as the sole spiritual and temporal ruler of Tibet. The Eighth Panchen Lama preferred to dedicate his time to Buddhist philosophical study and to scrupulously accomplishing his responsibilities. According to Tibetan tradition, ever since the Fourth Dalai Lama (1589–1616) chose the Fourth Panchen Lama, Lozang Chöki Gyeltsen (1567/70–1662), the relationship of master and disciple that linked the two men has been transmitted from reincarnation to reincarnation. Due to this special relationship, it was the responsibility of the Eighth Panchen Lama to identify the reincarnation of the Twelfth Dalai Lama (1856–1875), see to his religious vows, and give him his religious name. This is how in 1878, the Eighth Panchen Lama gave the name Thubten Gyatso to a young child located in the Dakpo region, having recognized him, two years earlier, as the reincarnation of the deceased Twelfth Dalai Lama. This child, the Thirteenth Dalai Lama (1876–1933), was enthroned in the Potala Palace in Lhasa one year later on June 14, 1879.

TITLE AND LINEAGE OF THE PANCHEN LAMAS

According to legend, Shérab Senggé (1382–1445), founder of the first Tantric Gélukpa school, pointed his finger towards a mountain indicating where the Tashilhunpo monastery would later be constructed, while traveling to Narthang from Samdrubtsé, the city that would later be called Shigatse.[2] At that moment, he is said to have made a prediction: "A white-haired man, Gédun Drub, will teach here."[3] In 1447 Gédun Drub (1391–1474), a man in his late fifties with white hair and the nephew and disciple of Tsongkapa (1357–1419), founded a monastery at Shigatse in the Tsang region that he named Tashilhunpo.

During a dream it is said that Gédun Drub received a revelation of the name Tashilhunpo (lit. "Auspicious Mountain"). He then fulfilled Shérab Senggé's prophecy with the help of financing from Phyongyépa Pèljor Zangpo, governor of Samdrubtsé.[4] Assisted by monks from the city, he began construction of the first building and commissioned a large statue of Buddha. In 1448 the finished statue arrived for installation in the building. Inside the metal bust, Gédun Drub placed the most precious objects he possessed: a silver statue of Amitābha, one of the five transcendental Buddhas of Saṃbhogakāya, and the skull of Shérab Senggé encrusted with precious stones. Shérab Senggé was one of his two spiritual masters, the other was his uncle Tsongkapa. In the lower part of the metal bust, he put mantras (esoteric phrasings), customary dhāranī (incantations), and excerpts from the Vinayapiṭaka (Buddhist scriptures primarily pertaining to the rules of monastic life for monks and nuns in their respective communities), as well as the monk's robes of Tsongkapa. Gédun Drub then consecrated his life to the development of this new monastery, of which he would later become abbot and founder of three colleges of logic: Thösam Norbuling, Kyilkang Lèkshéling, and Shartsé Samtènling.[5]

Since his scholarly achievements spread his fame beyond the Tsang region, he was given the name Panchen Gédun Drub by his disciples and by those around him. *Pan* is an abbreviation of the Sanskrit word *paṇḍita,* which means "erudite" and in Tibetan the word *chen* means "great." At the time, the word *panchen* prefaced to Gédun Drub's name indicated that he was a great scholar. Ever since, the title "Panchen" has been connected to the monastery of Tashilhunpo, and all of the ecclesiastics that have succeeded Gédun Drub to the abbot's throne have been referred to as "Panchen."

Gédun Drub's career turned out to be a determining factor in the establishment of the Gélukpa school in Tsang. He passed away in 1474 at the age of eighty-three, and from that time on, the Dalai Lamas were bound to the abbatial seat of Tashilhunpo. Later, other ties would further unite the Dalai Lamas to what would become the Panchen Lamas.[6]

In 1476 Gédun Gyatso (1476–1542) was born in Tsang and was recognized shortly afterwards as the reincarnation of Gédun Drub by the Gélukpa school. Gédun Gyatso took his monk's vows as a novice (*gétsul*) and as a fully ordained monk (*gélong*) with Lungrik Gyatso, the abbot of Tashilhunpo from 1478 to 1487. He studied at Tashilhunpo and then left for Drépung monastery where he completed his Buddhist training. The new abbot of Tashilhunpo, Panchen Yéshé Tsémo (1487–1510), invited Gédun Gyatso to his monastery, which he accepted. From 1510 to 1517, at the request of the abbot, Gédun Gyatso took charge of Tashilhunpo and with this role, the title of "Panchen." Later, he returned to Drépung where he also became abbot. He died in 1542 at the age of sixty-six.[7]

Sönam Gyatso (1543–1588), who was recognized as the reincarnation of Gédun Gyatso, also went to Tashilhunpo to study. He was offered the position of abbot of the monastery, but he refused since he was already in charge of Sera and Drépung. By 1569 he was famous throughout Tibet and Mongolia, and in 1575 Altan Khan (1507–1582), head of the Mongol Tümed tribe, invited him to teach in Mongolia. At first, Sönam Gyatso declined. But Altan Khan persisted with such a profusion of gifts that, in the end, Sönam Gyatso relented. He left Drépung in 1577.[8] Officially Sönam Gyatso set out for Mongolia but, due to unfavorable weather, it took him a year to arrive. He was accompanied by a number of noblemen and monks, among whom was a child named Lozang Chöki Gyeltsen. This child would later become the Fourth Panchen Lama, although the first to be officially recognized during his lifetime.

Upon arrival in Hohhot, then capital of Mongolia, Sönam Gyatso met Altan Khan who had converted to Buddhism and now favored the Gélukpa school. Sönam Gyatso gave teachings to the prince and his people, and in return he received presents, protection, and the Mongol title "Dalai" from Altan Khan. "Dalai" is the Mongol word for the Tibetan term "Gyatso" which means "Universal

Ocean." To Altan Khan, this title was given to honor his master's erudition and wisdom, considered vast as the ocean.

Gédun Drub and Gédun Gyatso, the two previous incarnations of Sönam Gyatso, received the same title posthumously, as the first and second Dalai Lamas. Sönam Gyatso became the Third Dalai Lama. While all had studied at Tashilhunpo, the privileged relationship of master to disciple between the Panchen and Dalai Lamas had not yet been born. It was not until the cultivation of a close relationship between the Fourth Panchen Lama and the Fourth Dalai Lama that this would take form.

In 1589 Yönten Gyatso (1589–1616), great grandson of Altan Khan, was born in Mongolia. Representatives from the three great Gélukpa monasteries in Lhasa (Drépung, Ganden, and Sera) were to recognize him as the reincarnation of Sönam Gyatso, who had died in 1588. Yönten Gyatso was brought to Tibet in 1601 at the age of twelve, escorted by Mongols and Gélukpa emissaries. Shortly after his arrival in the capital, he was enthroned as the Fourth Dalai Lama.

Panchen Lozang Chöki Gyeltsen, abbot of Tashilhunpo since 1601, went to see the Fourth Dalai Lama who was studying at Drépung monastery, where the Panchen would give him many teachings.[9] A master-disciple relationship (*yabsé*, lit. "father-son") was thus established between the two men, never to be broken from then on.[10] Accordingly, in 1607, the master, Panchen Lozang Chöki Gyeltsen warmly welcomed his disciple, the Fourth Dalai Lama, to Tashilhunpo. Nine years later, upon the death of the Fourth Dalai Lama, the abbot of Tashilhunpo joined in the search for his reincarnation.

Ngawang Lozang Gyatso (1617–1682) was recognized as the reincarnation of Yönten Gyatso by Panchen Lozang Chöki Gyeltsen, and in 1622 he received the title of Fifth Dalai Lama. Panchen Lozang Chöki Gyeltsen conferred the preliminary vows of a novice monk on Ngawang Lozang Gyatso in 1625 and those of an ordained monk twelve years later.[11] In this way, he perpetuated the relationship between master and disciple that had been established with the Fourth Dalai Lama.

In the Tibetan Buddhist tradition, the disciple must honor his spiritual master, particularly by giving him offerings. It is thus probable that the Fifth Dalai Lama lavished gifts on Panchen Lozang Chöki Gyeltsen. After 1642, when the Dalai Lama was enthroned at the Shigatse Fort as spiritual and temporal leader of Tibet with the support of the Qoshût Mongols, his generosity towards his master increased considerably.

The Fifth Dalai Lama and Güshri Khan (1582–1656), head of the Qoshût Mongol tribe and protector of the Gélukpa school, first gave Panchen Lozang Chöki Gyeltsen the land of the Shang Ganden Rabgyé[12] and Engön monasteries, as well as the Dragkü, Sagampa, Cenlung, Ngachö, and Shikasamdrubtsé valleys. Under the regency of Sönam Rabten (1642–58), he would give the Lèn, Dam, Tsédong, Dorling, Gyangdochö, Shé, Narthang, Tsongdü, Lakhuk, and Dargyé valleys.[13]

Next under the regency of Trinlé Gyatso (1660–68), the Fifth Dalai Lama and Prince Tenzin Dalé Gyelpo, the grandson of Güshri Khan, would give him the Tobshi valley. Finally, under the regency of Lozang Thutob (1669–75), the Fifth Dalai Lama and Tenzin Dalé Gyelpo would give Panchen Lozang Chöki Gyeltsen the Rongtso, Gyelchen, and Tsé valleys, as well as the Ngapa Lama lands[14] located in the Shigatse area.[15]

These gifts had a sectarian significance. Most of the lands that the Fifth Dalai Lama and Güshri Khan had given to the young incarnation belonged to the monasteries of the Karma Kagyüpa school of Tibetan Buddhism. This was a direct consequence of earlier events when Karma Tensung Wangpo, the prince of Tsang who supported the Karmapas, brought his troops to Lhasa in 1605 and expelled the Mongol escort of the Fourth Dalai Lama stationed in the city. Upon Karma Tensung Wangpo's death, six years later, his son, Karma Püntsok Namgyel, succeeded him, and inherited territory comprised of Tsang, Ngari, and a large part of Ü. In 1618 he attacked and took Lhasa, setting up two military camps there. He cracked down on the Gélukpa monasteries in the region, nearly proscribing them. But the Mongol troops that had been expelled from Lhasa by Karma Tensung Wangpo in 1605 returned to help the Gélukpas. In 1620 they attacked and defeated both of Karma Püntsok Namgyel's military camps. In the subsequent explosive situation, Panchen Lozang Chöki Gyeltsen played the role of mediator. He negotiated the retreat of the Mongol troops in exchange for authorization to reopen the Gélukpa monasteries.

At the death of Karma Püntsok Namgyel in 1621, his son Karma Tenkyong Wangpo succeeded him. No sooner was he in power than he undertook new attacks against the Gélukpa's members and goods, and proclaimed his sovereignty over Tibet, eventually forbidding Tibetans and Mongols to follow the teachings of the Gélukpa masters. Through these measures, the Karmapas once again confronted the Gélukpas. In other parts of Tibet, the situation turned out to be just as chaotic. In the northwest, Tsogt, a Mongol chief, was supporting the Sakyapa school, and to the east, the King of Beri, who was a follower of the Bön religion, was persecuting monks from the monastery of Litang, which had been founded in 1580 by the Third Dalai Lama.

Faced with this anarchical situation and seeking to restore order, the Fifth Dalai Lama's entourage called on the Qoshût forces led by Güshri Khan. In 1639 Güshri Khan first marched towards Beri in Kham, where the fighting lasted from mid-1639 to mid-1640. Then he moved to Tsang, conquering it and taking Shigatse in 1641. During these battles, Panchen Lozang Chöki Gyeltsen left Tashilhunpo temporarily for security. Güshri Khan definitively defeated the Karmapa in 1642. Next Güshri Khan invited the Fifth Dalai Lama to Shigatse, handing over to him spiritual and temporal power over Tibet. Although Güshri Khan was in a commanding position with his Qoshût troops established in Central Tibet, he decided not to intervene in Tibetan civil affairs, but reserved the military power for himself by creating the position of regent (*dési*). In this way, he transformed Tibet into a unified whole, a situation which had not existed since the reign of Changchub Gyeltsen (1302–73). He also gave the entire Tsang region to the Fifth Dalai Lama.[16]

Thanks to the generosity of numerous actors, including his disciple the Fifth Dalai Lama as well as Güshri Khan and various regents, Panchen Lozang Chöki Gyeltsen found himself the head of a monastery with a considerable domain.

In contrast to his predecessors, Panchen Lozang Chöki Gyeltsen already belonged to a line of *tulku* (reincarnated lamas) when he was named abbot in 1601. In 1583 he had been recognized as the reincarnation of Ensapa Lozang Döndrub (1505–1566), the abbot of the small monastery Ensa in Tsang that belonged to Sönam Chöki Langpo (1439–1504).[17] Originally from Ensa, Sönam Chöki Langpo had studied at Ganden monastery. He then settled down in his village's monastery, which was of the Sakyapa school. Under his influence, the monks of the monastery embraced the principles of the Gélukpa school. Their reputation for seriousness was such that they were allowed to continue their studies at Tashilhunpo. As for Sönam Chöki Langpo, he had been declared the reincarnation of Kédrub Gélèk Pelzang (1385–1438), who had been one of Tsongkapa's closest disciples in 1407. In this way, the abbatial seat of the Ensa monastery was attached to the *tulku* line that, besides Panchen Lozang Chöki Gyeltsen, included Ensapa Lozang Döndrub (1505–1566), Sönam Chöki Langpo (1439–1504), and Kédrub Gélèk Pelzang (1385–1438) among its ranks.[18]

In his capacity as abbot of Tashilhunpo, honored by the greatest of his time, such as the Fifth Dalai Lama, Güshri Khan, and so forth, Panchen Lozang Chöki Gyeltsen could legitimately be considered a Panchen Lama. "Lama" is a Tibetan term literally meaning "supreme," "unequaled," "he who holds himself highest." It translates into Sanskrit as "guru," which means "weighty," "great," and by extension, "venerable master." In Tibet, a lama is a master of Buddhist philosophy who is respected, even venerated, by his disciples for the quality of his dharma teaching. Attributed with such moral authority, he often directs the spiritual affairs of one or more monasteries, as was the case of Panchen Lozang Chöki Gyeltsen, or Panchen Rinpoche, since he belonged to the line of the *tulku* from Ensa. While the word *rinpoche* characterizes an extremely erudite lama with high spiritual accomplishments, Tibetans generally use the word to designate *tulku* who are, by definition, reincarnated lamas.

By these frequent generous offerings, coupled with the veneration attributed to Panchen Rinpoche Lozang Chöki Gyeltsen, the Fifth Dalai Lama created a *de facto* new line attached to the monastery at Tashilhunpo.[19] Consequently, Panchen Rinpoche Lozang Chöki Gyeltsen is often considered the veritable first Panchen Lama. However, given the fact that he was already the third reincarnation of the *tulku* from Ensa, others consider him as the Fourth Panchen Lama.

Today, two numbering systems are commonly used by the Tibetans. One begins with Kédrub Gélèk Pelzang, disciple of Tsongkapa and the other with

Panchen Rinpoche Lozang Chöki Gyeltsen. The Tibetans tend to use the second method, while the Chinese have adopted the first. Thus, the incarnation the Tibetans refer to as the Sixth Panchen Lama is known as the Ninth Panchen Lama by the Chinese. However an increasing number of Tibetans opt for using "Ninth Panchen Lama" in the place of "Sixth Panchen Lama." Because of this, the literature has a tendency to use the numbering beginning at the time of Tsongkapa. Here we have chosen this numbering style for clarity in the presentation, although logic would designate Lozang Chöki Nyima as the sixth master of the reincarnated line to hold the title Panchen Lama. Following the Buddhist tradition, the two lines of the Panchen Lama can be traced to the time of Buddha Śākyamuni (see Appendix A for the complete lineage of Panchen Lamas, including the two numbering systems).[20]

When Panchen Rinpoche Lozang Chöki Gyeltsen was recognized as the first Panchen Lama, the line of the Ensa Tulku was interrupted and a new one created. Kédrub Sangyé Yéshé (1525–1590), who had been the disciple of Ensapa Lozang Döndrub (1505–1566) and tutor of the First Panchen Lama, became the first Ensa Rinpoche.

The title of "Panchen Lama" was probably not formally given to Panchen Rinpoche Lozang Chöki Gyeltsen. But, for sure, the responsibilities of the abbot of Tashilhunpo, with its numerous offerings of land given by the Fifth Dalai Lama, along with the veneration accorded to the position, would make Lozang Chöki Gyeltsen the first authentic Panchen Lama, a title which acknowledged an already existing situation. Beyond the title, the corresponding function of the Panchen Lama was still to be defined. From the end of the eighteenth century, this situation would give rise to a range of interpretations of the Panchen Lama's role, as much from the Chinese as from the British side, both hoping to turn things to their advantage.

Additionally, the Fifth Dalai Lama's actual motives remain open to speculation. Today it is difficult to say whether the land offered by the Fifth Dalai Lama to his spiritual master, the Fourth Panchen Lama, a surface area equal to the province of Tsang, was a genuine gift from disciple to master or a conscious political act. This gift of land enabled the Fifth Dalai Lama to keep a potential rival, whose celebrity could be intimidating, far from the affairs of Lhasa. In a more general light, this gift placed the Gélukpa in charge of Tsang once and for all, pushing the Karma Kagyüpa from this province.

BIRTH AND RECOGNITION

At the end of the nineteenth century, the Eighth Panchen Lama, inspired by study, became especially interested in the Sakyapa doctrine, even though his lineage, like that of the Dalai Lamas, belonged to the Gélukpa school. Some monks from his monastery complained to the Tibetan government, which also followed the Gélukpa order, requesting that the Panchen Lama be brought into line. On his side, the Eighth Panchen Lama endeavored to identify those who had denounced him, and discovered the origin of the complaint to be his own mother. According to Tsybikov, a Russian traveler in Tibet from 1899 to 1902, this woman, known for her cantankerous and aggressive character, was in the habit of taking those around her to court, with the result that the Eighth Panchen Lama is said to have declared "Oh, how nice it would be to have a mother unable to speak!" Aside from this anecdote, it would seem that some of those who complained conspired against him to the point of wishing to assassinate him. Thus when, on August 28, 1882, the Eighth Panchen Lama died at his monastery, Tashilhunpo, some said his mother had poisoned him.[21] On September 5 the abbots of the monastery requested that the Thirteenth Dalai Lama write a prayer for a swift return of his reincarnation. The regent, Gyeltsab Tatsag Rinpoche (r. 1875–86), composed the prayer, since the Thirteenth Dalai Lama was only six years old at the time. He sent the prayer to all the monasteries and the government administrative centers of Ü and Tsang, so that the lay people and monks could recite it. The prayers were to be made as soon as possible.[22]

Six years later, on January 4, 1888, Zala Nominhan Lozang Döndrub, the general administrator of Tashilhunpo, brought three children to Lhasa. A special delegation of monks from the monastery had found these children who were considered potential reincarnations of the Eighth Panchen Lama. He introduced them to the Thirteenth Dalai Lama who was at his summer palace, the Norbulingka. Two of the children were from Lamo[23] and Tobgyel,[24] located in the province of Tsang, while the third was from the village Brum gasha in the Dakpo region.[25] The Thirteenth Dalai Lama began the last tests for the selection, undoubtedly with the help of his regent, or one of his two tutors, given his young age of eleven. Based on the test results, he designated the child from Dakpo as the reincarnation of the Eighth Panchen Lama.[26] Could this child, who came from the same region as the Thirteenth Dalai Lama, knowingly have been chosen at the expense of those born in Tsang? In accordance with the custom established since 1792 by the Manchu emperor Qianlong (r. 1736–95), the choice had to be confirmed by drawing lots, which led to a ceremony celebrated on February 26, 1888. A description of the ritual, as found in a biography of the Thirteenth Dalai Lama, states:

> Demo Hutuktu,[27] Wenshi,[28] the Manchu imperial resident in Tibet, Lozang Döndrub, general administrator of Tashilhunpo as well as a large gathering met at the Potala where all the monks were reciting prayers. In a special ceremonial room for this purpose, a Manchu secretary arranged pieces of paper, on which the names of the children and their birthplace had been written, in front of a golden urn. The monks fell silent. The Manchu official bowed and placed the pieces of paper in the urn. The monks began praying once again, and when they

> had stopped, Wenshi, the Manchu official residing in Tibet, knelt down and took the golden urn in his hands shaking it three times. The piece of paper with the name from Dakpo then flew out of the urn. Those participating thus had the certitude that the one whose name came out of the urn was the emanation of Buddha Amitābha.[29]

After drawing lots to confirm the Thirteenth Dalai Lama's choice, Samdrub Gyatso, the child from Dakpo, was officially declared the Ninth Panchen Lama. The same day, the Thirteenth Dalai Lama ordained him and gave him the religious name of Jétsun Lozang Chöki Nyima Gélèk Namgyel.[30] His mother took nun's vows.[31]

The search for and recognition of the Panchen Lama corresponded perfectly to the customs followed for the reincarnation of great Gélukpa masters. However, the steps leading to the identification of the Panchen Lama warrant a closer look.

During the year 1883, a delegation of monks from Tashilhunpo had scoured the country looking for the reincarnation of the Eighth Panchen Lama. Certain indications guided their work. At the end of 1882, a mushroom is said to have suddenly grown on one of the pillars of the chapel where the body of the deceased Eighth Panchen Lama lay, enshrined in a reliquary. The oracles of Tashilhunpo combined the two syllables of the word *kasha* (*ka* means "pillar" and *sha* is the word for "mushroom") deducing that the Ninth Panchen Lama would be reborn in a village phonetically close to Kasha.[32] Other auspicious signs appeared orienting their search towards the region of Dakpo where abundant harvests and prolific herds had been reported that year.[33]

In 1882 Damchö Tsomo, a young woman from the village of Brum gasha was expecting a child. Her status was very modest, for she was only a servant living on the lands of the aristocratic family she worked for. Indeed, according to Dakpo Rinpoche, she had been born deaf and dumb.[34] The inhabitants of the household where she worked had taught her to read and write, and she managed to communicate with gestures and written notations.[35] According to the late Kachen Jangpa Thubten, a monk from Tashilhunpo, she was said to have stopped speaking the day of the child's conception (or birth), so as never to reveal the identity of the father.[36] The first hypothesis, that she was born deaf and dumb, seems more plausible. Indeed, it does appear the Ninth Panchen Lama's mother was unable to speak until her death. Thus, the wish stated previously by the Eighth Panchen Lama had been, in a manner of speaking, accomplished.

On February 19, 1883, Damchö Tsomo gave birth to a son that she named Samdrub Gyatso.[37] It is also said she gave birth to twins.[38] The twin of Samdrub Gyatso, or his younger brother,[39] was to be recognized as the reincarnation of Tséchokling Rinpoche.[40] Quickly several rumors about the child sprang up, soon turning into legend, as is the tradition in Tibet regarding all-important religious figures. One such story says that, one day, while Damchö Tsomo was pregnant, she went to get some water. Near the well, she tripped and fell to the ground. The bucket fell from her hands and its rim was damaged, leaving a mark on the stone. One month after his birth, the child, who went with his mother everywhere, was with her near the well. He is said to have immediately recognized the mark left by the bucket, and to have placed his foot on it, carving its imprint into the stone. From then on the villagers considered the little Samdrub Gyatso an exceptional being.[41]

Other legends developed surrounding the father of Samdrub Gyatso. According to Kachen Jangpa Thubten, the expectant mother is said to have had a dream of a white man (an occidental, according to Jangpa Thubten) while she was taking care of the sheep. Nine months later, she miraculously gave birth to a child.[42] But, according to David Macdonald, Tibetans confided in him another story in which the father was a great Buddhist master from the Dakpo, the same district where the Thirteenth Dalai Lama was born. Surprising physical resemblances noted between the Ninth Panchen Lama and the Thirteenth Dalai Lama suggested kinship.[43]

When the Panchen Lama was enthroned in 1891, the Manchus fueled rumors by conferring the title of sixth rank prince (*fuguo gong*) on the child's maternal grandfather rather than on his father, as stipulated in the rules given by the Qianlong Emperor.[44]

Generally, the Tibetan legends surrounding the Ninth Panchen Lama exalt his miraculous birth and tend to conceal the moral indiscretions of his father. The Tibetan government did not reveal the details about the Panchen Lama's father to the British until 1914. At that time, Shédra Peljor Dorjé, prime minister (*lönchen*) from 1907 to 1919, passed on the minutes of a trial to Charles Bell, the British civil political officer in Sikkim, in which the Ninth Panchen Lama is cited:

> A complaint from Tashilhunpo was lodged in Lhasa declaring that the father of the Panchen Lama had been assassinated, that the general administrator had tried to bring the government of Lhasa under his influence through black magic, and that he had also tried to rob the Panchen Lama of his powers. The Panchen Lama ordered a detailed investigation to be undertaken when asked whether the affair should be examined. According to his wishes, Minister Sarchyung as well as other civil servants were asked to examine the veracity of the facts. It was discovered that the Panchen Lama's father was having an affair with the wife of the Panchen Lama's head attendant. This woman wished to poison the Panchen Lama's mother so she could marry the Panchen Lama's father. However, that day, the Panchen Lama's mother did not eat, as she felt unwell. She offered the poisoned food to her husband who ate it and fell sick. Some servants who ate the leftovers also fell ill. The scraps of the meal were eaten by a dog that then died. The life of the Panchen Lama's father and that of his servants were saved thanks to Kusho Badu-la, an excellent doctor.

> The results of the different inquiries indicate that the wife of the head attendant was the poisoner, although she tried to accuse her own daughter. Thus, she was sentenced to exile and to prison. The Panchen Lama's father was given the same sentence for having had a romantic relationship with this woman. Then, the head attendant, who was a very powerful man with more influence than the general administrator himself, persuaded the general administrator to order the Phüntsoling, district governor, where the Panchen Lama's father had been imprisoned, to assassinate him in his cell. The Panchen Lama's father was found dead from a blow to his head with a club. The investigators also found that the general administrator had written spells destined to bring members of the Lhasa government under his influence and had placed them under their pillows. Moreover, they realized that the general administrator had tried to take away the Panchen Lama's powers and make them his. All the guilty were condemned to a fine or demoted. The money from these fines was subsequently given to the Panchen Lama.[45]

Charles Bell does not give the date of the trial. Hugh Richardson suggests that it was some time between November 1903 and July 1904 because, according to him, Sarchyung Tséten Wangchuk Dorjé (1857–1914), the minister in charge of the investigation, was posted in Lhasa during that time.[46] Luciano Petech dates Sarchyung Tséten Wangchuk Dorjé's mission from 1904 to 1914, but notes that he was absent from Lhasa from February to May 1906 and from 1910 to 1912.[47] Logically, this trial, in which the minister participated, must have taken place sometime between the beginning of 1904, or the end of 1903, and February 1906, or between May 1906 and 1910, or between 1912 and 1914.

The minutes of the trial lead one to question certain aspects of the monastic life at Tashilhunpo, including the relations maintained between the monastery and the Tibetan government, which will be examined in the following chapter, as its importance to later events will become clear. Whatever the case, the Tibetan government never revealed the name of the Panchen Lama's father (a certain Tagrin) until 1923 when the master fled Tashilhunpo.[48] These rumors, legends, and documents can lead one to think that Samdrub Gyatso, the Ninth Panchen Lama, was born as a result of the love of an aristocrat with loose morals and the servant Damchö Tsomo.

THE EARLY YEARS

On February 4, 1889, the recently recognized Ninth Panchen Lama left his palace on the roof of the Jokhang temple in Lhasa. As the seven-year-old made his way to his monastery, we can easily imagine the scene, as it would have unfolded.

The young Panchen Lama, protected by a considerable entourage, heads towards Tashilhunpo.[49] Leaving Lhasa, these remarkable travelers follow the road towards the west along the Brahmaputra River. Next they cross the Kangpa pass, snowy at this time of year, which marks the border between the provinces of Ü and Tsang. They go through the city of Rinpung, turning northwest to follow the Surong River bed, and then, once again, the Brahmaputra. A long line of pilgrims crowding the side of the road holds out incense and white offering scarves to the young master. All show their piety and respect, displaying a reverential, joyful attitude. Around the bend the young Panchen Lama can see the imposing fort of Shigatse. A defensive structure, possibly the model for the architects of the Potala in Lhasa, this edifice houses the administrative offices where Shigatse's two district chiefs live. It seems to watch over the city, whose inhabitants have decorated their houses to celebrate the master's return. Juniper burns on the flat rooftops above the recently whitewashed walls. To the southwest of the fort, about a kilometer away, a nine-storey building, built for displaying the giant Buddhist appliquéd wall hangings during religious festivals, simply peels off the sky.[50]

The procession continues, but the child cannot see his monastery, hidden behind the peak of Makpönri (lit. "General Mountain"). Still, he knows he is approaching from the powerful sound of the horns and conchs that the monks are blowing to their very last breath. Suddenly, he sees five temples with golden roofs, lined up from east to west, where the body of his predecessor lies in a mausoleum laden with gold and jewels, in addition to the monastic buildings' crimson walls.[51] Today, auspicious symbols traced on the ground in chalk lace the path leading to his palace. Finally, the young Panchen Lama steps into the monastery enclosure and takes the footpaths that wind between the walls concealing the three colleges of logic from passing pilgrims. To finish, he catches sight of his palace, called the Ganden Tönpo or Ganden Podrang, between the mausoleums of the Fourth and Fifth Panchen Lamas. Entering, he discovers a small apartment divided into two parts. The first room, with no roof, is exposed to the sky. The second, covered, is raised up from the first. Latticework separates the room from the reception space.[52] Through a window the Panchen Lama can make out the golden roofs of his other two palaces—Kungyabling and Déchen Kelzang—located a kilometer or so outside the monastery. He learns that he will live in the first from August to October, and in the second from March to May.[53] Another palace attached to the monastery, surrounded by luxuriant vegetation, catches his attention. It is Dékilingka where his mother, who has come with him, will live.[54]

Did the Tibetan prelate realize then, at the age of seven, the extent of the responsibilities that would be his from that moment on as the abbot of a vast monastic complex, whose main building, Tashilhunpo, sheltered thirty-five hundred monks (not counting those who lived in the 230 other monasteries that belong to Tashilhunpo), and whose lands covered an area of 300,000 sq km?[55]

On February 1, 1892, the Ninth Panchen Lama was enthroned at Tashilhunpo where he made his novice vows under the regent Demo Hutuktu.[56] The Thirteenth Dalai Lama, who was then only fifteen and had not yet been ordained, would not have been qualified to supervise the Panchen Lama's vows, and so was not present at the ceremony. As of that day the Panchen Lama was to begin a long course of study aimed at taking him to the highest levels of spiritual realization. Ngachen Létog Lopa, his oldest tutor taught him reading and writing. He had him memorize the basic Buddhist texts and initiated him into the art of debate. He taught him the five main sciences: grammar, logic, Buddhist philosophy, arts, and medical techniques; and the five secondary sciences: composition, poetry, lexicography, astrology, and theater. The Panchen Lama also received Tantric initiations, and showed himself especially talented in logic, a subject he adored.[57] He had to pass the same exams as the ordinary monks, but at a younger age since, according to Tibetan Buddhism, he would benefit from knowledge acquired in previous incarnations.[58]

Each year on the second, third, and fourth days of the first month of the lunar calendar the monastic exams for the title of *kachen,* unique to Tashilhunpo monastery, took place in his presence. At these occasions, all the monks gathered in the paved courtyard in front of the big assembly hall. Eighteen monks competed in debates on philosophical subjects with the abbots of the colleges of logic. The first day, six of them would be questioned on a variety of subjects. On the second day, six others would go through the same questioning, and the final six on the third day. The first-ranked *kachen* would later occupy the post of abbot for the three colleges of logic and then as abbot for the Tantric college, each post being held for six years. The normal procedure was for the Panchen Lama to choose the abbots for the Tashilhunpo colleges himself from those monks who had passed their *kachen* exam. In the absence of the Panchen Lama or while he was too young (the case of the Ninth Panchen Lama at the time), the Dalai Lama (or the regent) would appoint the examiners.[59]

In order to round off the Panchen Lama's education, the Thirteenth Dalai Lama appointed Reting Rinpoche as his junior tutor, and on April 26, 1896, Reting joined the Panchen Lama at Tashilhunpo.[60] Until at least April 1902, the Panchen Lama devoted his entire time to studying inside his monastery. Then at the age of nineteen, he went to Lhasa to make his monk's vows under his spiritual master, the Thirteenth Dalai Lama. He was accompanied by Reting Rinpoche, his junior tutor, and his inner circle. Upon arriving at his destination, the Panchen Lama settled into his palace on the Jokhang roof. On May 11, 1902, the festivities commenced. The Thirteenth Dalai Lama, who was twenty-six at the time and residing at the Norbulingka, made his first visit to the Panchen Lama. The master and disciple met at the Potala. Then nine days later, the Thirteenth Dalai Lama met the Panchen Lama again with the members of his entourage. Finally, on May 22, the Panchen Lama took his monk's vows in front of the statue of Buddha in the Jokhang, in the presence of all the representatives of the Gélukpa school: the Dalai Lama, the abbots of the three main monasteries, Ganden, Drépung, and Sera, and those of the Ganden colleges, Shar and Tsé. During the following days, the ministers, members of the private residence of the Dalai Lama,[61] officials of Tashilhunpo, abbots and reincarnated masters, as well as the Manchu imperial resident in Tibet filed past, one by one, to pay homage to the spiritual and temporal head of Tibet and to his disciple. On June 9 all the ceremonies were completed, and the Panchen Lama said goodbye to the Dalai Lama, who offered him gifts, gave him advice, and suggested he return in two or three years. Everything seemed to be going well between the two men.

Two days later, the Panchen Lama set out for the return to his monastery in Tsang.[62] There, monastic life took its course. The thirty-five hundred monks from the three colleges of logic awoke daily at two or three in the morning to participate in the offering ceremony. They would crowd into the main hall of the monastery where they would sit cross-legged in rows perpendicular to the Panchen Lama's throne, which towered above the assembly. They were divided into two groups. The first two rows in the center faced each other. Then on each side, the next row sat with their backs turned to the preceding one to then face the third one and so on. The temperature inside the great hall would be icy. All the monks wore their monastic robes, whose detailing signified their affiliation to Tashilhunpo: the long hat perpendicular to their line of vision instead of parallel as at the other Gélukpa monasteries, the carefully formed fold on each side of their skirts in place of, for example, the two folds on the left side at Sera, their pleated capes yellow, as opposed to red at the other Gélukpa monasteries, including monks from the Panchen Lama's private college.[63]

Rapidly settled in, they would be ready to recite their prayers. Those lucky enough to benefit from material help from donors might light their text with lamps of yak butter, while the poorer ones would light a stick of incense and blow on the glowing end to use it for a sliver of light. During the first offering ceremony of the day, the monks received a bowl of tea and butter to which they could add grilled barley flour that they would have brought with them. The morning continued with two other offering ceremonies following the first. Next, the monks would return to their quarters and begin studying their Buddhist texts in their cells. In the afternoon, two services would be organized in each college's prayer hall. In the evening, the monks would debate philosophical subjects in the courtyard of their college well into the night.[64]

The Panchen Lama often attended the daily debate classes. For this, he would dress in simple robes and cover his head with his *zen* (cape), so as not to bother the monks in their intense intellectual effort. Since his well-cared-for garments spread a pleasant and characteristic perfume, the monks immediately sensed that he was present. They would then double their efforts to satisfy their master, who would encourage them in their studies by rewarding the best debaters.[65]

For the first twenty years of his life, the Panchen Lama divided his time between study and religious practice under the benevolent guidance of his two tutors who trained him for his duties. Although we have no concrete proof, he probably passed his exams well. Even upon close inspection, nothing stands out to suggest the dramatic adventures that would later disrupt the life of this peaceful abbot of Tashilhunpo.

2

FLIGHT FROM TIBET

The Panchen Lama left Tashilhunpo, on December 22, 1923, accompanied by a few monks.[1] Shortly thereafter, Muchawa, the Shigatse district governor, informed the Tibetan government of the event via Gyeltsé's telegraph.[2] He also inspected the monastery.[3] There he found a letter (we don't know exactly where), which the Panchen Lama had left for the attention of the abbots of the four colleges and the officials of his monastery. In the letter the Panchen Lama briefly outlined the reasons for his departure:

> Orders were issued to all Jongpoens [district governors] of Tsang Province that they must supply free transport, and so forth, to the officials of the Lhasa government, against the prevailing custom. Moreover, I have been asked to make contributions for the upkeep of the Tibetan army, but the nobles and subjects were unable to take the responsibility of meeting these demands. For these reasons, the subjects of the Tashilhunpo government were disappointed and became dissatisfied. You are all aware of these facts and these things have made it quite impossible for us to live in peace. I should have made further representation, but it would have created a difficult position for His Holiness. I am, therefore, leaving Tashilhunpo for a short period to make it easier for His Holiness the Dalai Lama. I am going to see whether I can secure anyone to mediate between us, with the assistance of the dispensers of gifts in Kham and Mongolia whither I have dispatched messengers. It is quite impossible for me to make the annual contributions to meet the military expenses and I am compelled to proceed to an unknown destination to try to raise funds from the Buddhists who may be inclined to help me voluntarily ...[4]

The Panchen Lama's reasons for leaving Tashilhunpo are clearly stated in his letter; that is, to try to raise money abroad in order to make the necessary tax payment that had come calling at his monastery door. In any case, his intention to go to Mongolia was evident as early as January 1924. While crossing the province of Gansu with his entourage, he is said to have met the chamberlain of Mongolia's highest spiritual authority, the Buddhist master Jétsun Dampa (1870–1924), as previously noted, who was actually on his way to meet him.[5] The chamberlain strongly advised the Panchen Lama against going to Outer Mongolia, as hostile Russians were already stationed in the region.[6]

Seven months later, in July 1924, the Panchen Lama reconfirmed the reasons for his departure in a letter he addressed to the Thirteenth Dalai Lama via telegraph from Chamdo:

> Tashilhunpo and the lesser monasteries, which are under my jurisdiction, have greatly suffered and the few poor peasants working on the lands belonging to these monasteries have become destitute owing to the new taxes and unprecedented call for free labor. Again, to pay the enormous tax known as one quarter of the army expenditure with no land as a means from which the money could be obtained and which none of the other subjects had to pay, caused us great anxiety. Moreover my poor and unsophisticated servants had to endure great hardship and cruelty so that there was no peace of mind either ... externally or internally and they suffered great indignity ...[7]

The Tibetan originals of these two letters attributed to the Panchen Lama have still not been found. David Macdonald, the British trade agent in Gyeltsé, translated the first letter into English just after its discovery by Muchawa, while F. M. Bailey, the British political officer in Sikkim, translated the second one eight years later.[8] Two fragments of the first letter were published in Tibet, but without the original it is impossible to say if they are accurate. In any case, they are close enough to the English translation preserved at the India Office Library in London.[9]

Even if these documents do suggest that the issue of taxes was the cause for the Panchen Lama's departure, the turbulent events during the years preceding 1923 that both the Thirteenth Dalai Lama and the Ninth Panchen Lama experienced, raises reasonable doubts about the tax issue as the Panchen Lama's sole reason for leaving Tibet. Several other factors must be weighed in, including the military invasion of Tibet both by the English and the Chinese, the Thirteenth Dalai Lama's two periods of exile, the Manchu Empire's fall, the Chinese Republic's emergence, and the modern world's sudden appearance on the Tibetan plateau. Moreover, the fact that the Panchen Lama sought a mediator between himself and the Dalai Lama reveals the possible existence of a disagreement between master and disciple. In fact, it is also plausible that the Panchen Lama underestimated the forces that would come into play when he jeopardized the unique "father-son" model, particularly over such a worldly issue as taxes, while also having virtually no firsthand knowledge of the outside world.

THE DALAI LAMA'S POLITICAL AWAKENING

At the turn of the century, the situation in Tibet seemed peaceful and far from the reach of any upheaval. The young Panchen Lama had begun his philosophical studies at Tashilhunpo and the Thirteenth Dalai Lama was readying himself for his role as spiritual and temporal head of Tibet. But things were different outside Tibet. Manchu power had completely crumbled after Japanese attacks. Japan had annexed the Ryukyu Islands in 1879 and Korea had opened to Japanese trade in 1896. In 1894 and 1895, Chinese and Japanese forces would clash at China's expense. With the Shimonoseki Treaty (1895), China recognized the independence of Korea and ceded Taiwan, the Pescadores Islands, and the peninsula of Liaodong to Japan. The revised treaty of November 1896, acceded under the influence of the Western powers of Germany, France, and Russia, favored a Sino-Russian rapprochement that cost China its control over Manchuria.[10]

As for the British in India, they once again became interested in Tibet after multiple violations by the Tibetans of the commercial treaties of 1886 and 1890 signed between England and China.[11] Besides, and not without reason, the British witnessed Russian stratagems in Tibet in the person of the Buriat monk Dorjieff, an emissary of the Tsar, and his close association with the Thirteenth Dalai Lama.

Agvan Dorjieff (1854–1938), like many young Mongol monks, had studied at Drépung monastery where he had obtained the title of doctor of philosophy (*géshé larampa*) in 1888, and in 1898 he traveled to Tibet and around China before returning to Russia.[12] Given that his biographers enjoyed enhancing the mystery surrounding his motives as well as the people behind his movements, it is difficult to say if he was acting on his own initiative, as an emissary of the Thirteenth Dalai Lama, or for Tsar Nicolas II.[13] All the same, in 1889 he became the debating companion (*tsenzhab*) of the Dalai Lama and received the title of abbot (*kenchen*), as well as a seal. Then he returned to Russia.[14] His presence in Lhasa and his various travels awakened suspicions in the British concerning Russian plans for Tibet. In 1903 a British mission led by Colonel Francis Younghusband (1863–1942) prepared to enter Tibet. Once they reached the Tibetan border, the British negotiated fiercely with members of the Tibetan government to open roads and commercial trading posts. They withdrew as winter approached—their own intransigence having made negotiations impossible.

In springtime 1904 Colonel Younghusband deliberately crossed into Tibet, leading five thousand well-trained soldiers in an attack against the Tibetans, who were armed only with archaic weapons and protected by "magic charms."[15] Talks began between the two parties. The defeat was severe, with the destruction serving as a territorial marker.[16] In addition, the invaders, without precedent, passed Gyeltsé and quickly headed for the Tibetan capital in order to negotiate directly with the Thirteenth Dalai Lama. In view of their advance, the Dalai Lama took the precaution of naming Méru Lozang Gyeltsen, the Ganden Tri Rinpoche, to the post of regent and left for Outer Mongolia.[17] From this moment on, the Thirteenth Dalai Lama found himself hostage to conflicts that surpassed him and which put many things at stake besides British commercial interests: the borders between the British-Indian and Chinese empires, the liquidation of the Manchu heritage by the victorious Chinese Nationalists, and the reorganization of the entire political and economic map of the Far East. Amidst this grand turbulence—even if it had only involved confronting the young Chinese Republic's pertinacious will for integration—the Dalai Lama's claim to independence in 1913 had no real chance of being heard. His hasty departure several years earlier was to be the prelude to an extended period of exile, which would introduce him to not only Outer Mongolia, but to China and British India as well.

During his absence, the British would negotiate, without Manchu intervention, with Ganden Tri Rinpoche the surrender of Tibet. Following these negotiations, on September 7, 1904, the Convention of Lhasa was signed. Under its terms the Tibetans would ratify two treaties agreed on between China and Britain in 1886 and 1890, and were forced to open two new markets: one at Gyeltsé, in the province of Tsang, and the other in Gartok in Ngari, in addition to the one in Yatung that had been established earlier under the 1890 agreement, but which had not actually been operationalized. Moreover, the Tibetans had to commit to obtaining Britain's consent before negotiating with other countries, and had to pay a war indemnity.[18]

With the Convention of Lhasa, the Russians saw the establishment of a British protectorate in Tibet, and so decided to expand the territories under their control. Tibet found itself at the center of a rapidly mutating world where alliances were being shaken. In 1907 the Russians gave the Japanese a part of Manchuria as well as part of Korea; in exchange, they pursued their interests in Outer Mongolia with no opposition and continued advances into the Buddhist regions that the British, after their raid on Lhasa, seemed to be threatening from the south. Yet in 1908 the Russians and British still managed to sign a treaty involving Persia, Afghanistan, and Tibet. This treaty outlined their respective spheres of influence and included their mutual promise to "respect the territorial integrity of Tibet and to abstain from all interference in the Tibetan internal administration." In the text, both Russia and Britain recognized the sovereignty of China over Tibet and committed themselves to not entering into negotiation with Tibetan authorities without prior consultation with the Chinese government.[19]

The Thirteenth Dalai Lama's exile and the recognition of Chinese suzerainty over Tibet by two great powers actually pushed the doors wide open for Qing control over the Tibetan government. Thus, conscious of the vulnerability of their southwest border after the British troops attained Lhasa, the Qing decided without delay to place the Kham region under its control. With this objective, Zhao Erfeng (d. 1911), the high official in charge of Sichuan and Yunnan border affairs, was ordered to militarily "pacify" this area. Little by little, as the troops advanced, despite resistance from the locals, Tibetan cities and districts were progressively incorporated into the Chinese administrative structure.[20]

In Central Tibet, the Manchus recalled the imperial resident Youtai, who was accused of incompetence for not participating in the Tibeto-British negotiations and for allowing the Convention of Lhasa to conclude without Beijing's approval. In his place they appointed Zhang Yintang as Chinese governor of Tibet (*fu doutong*).[21] These measures prompted the Thirteenth Dalai Lama, who had been traveling for several years in Outer Mongolia and in the Tibetan region of Amdo, to accept the invitation that was extended by the Guangxu Emperor (r. 1875–1909) and Empress Dowager Cixi (1835–1908) to come to Beijing. Along the way, the Dalai Lama stopped at Mount Wutai where he led numerous religious ceremonies, and was visited by the foreign diplomat A. Izvolsky, the Russian minister of foreign affairs, and W. W. Rockhill, then American minister to China.[22]

On August 3, 1908, the Thirteenth Dalai Lama arrived in Beijing where he stayed at the Yellow Temple (*Huang si*).[23] During his sojourn, he took care of many religious and temporal duties related to his title, and met more foreign diplomats. Most importantly, he met the emperor and Empress Dowager, and requested they withdraw their troops from Kham. However, he was only able to achieve a promised reduction in the number of Chinese soldiers, and no official document was signed regarding this topic.[24] On November 28, 1908, the Thirteenth Dalai Lama left Beijing and headed for Kumbum monastery, where he stayed for several months before continuing on to Central Tibet.[25] He finally returned to the Potala Palace in Lhasa on November 11, 1909.

Less than two months later on January 3, 1910, Zhao Erfeng's troops arrived in Lhasa. The Thirteenth Dalai Lama named as regent Ngawang Lozang Tenpé Gyeltsen, the Ganden Tri Rinpoche at the time, and once again fled.[26] Faced with few options, this time he headed towards India. The Chinese sent troops in his pursuit, but to no avail. Once in India, the Thirteenth Dalai Lama was welcomed and helped by the British.[27] There he met with Lord Minto, the viceroy of India.[28]

In Lhasa, despite resistance from the local population, Zhang Yintang put in place and imposed the political and administrative order of the Manchus.[29] Tibetan ministers that had signed the Convention of Lhasa were relieved of their functions. Zhang Yintang also suggested that a larger group of Manchu officials participate in Tibetan administrative dealings, that communication lines be built, and that Chinese schools be established in Lhasa.[30]

At the beginning of 1912, Chinese troops still occupied the Tibetan capital. Once the Chinese Republic was proclaimed, the Thirteenth Dalai Lama from exile in India encouraged the Tibetans to double their efforts against the occupiers. He officially declared that the Sino-Tibetan relationship had been broken in 1910 when the Manchurian army invaded Tibet. This relationship, according to the Tibetans, was one of "chaplain to donor" between the Dalai Lama and the Manchu emperor that had existed since the seventeenth century. In an unexpected turn of events, Manchu troops, deprived of authority with the fall of the Manchu Empire, laid down their arms. The Thirteenth Dalai Lama was able to enter Lhasa on January 3, 1913. After this long period of violence and political trauma, the Dalai Lama quickly and firmly regained power over the situation. He remunerated or punished officials according to whether they had held their positions during the Manchu occupation.[31] After dealing with his staff, he then went about reforming Tibet's political, economic, and social systems.

During his various periods of exile, the Dalai Lama met several foreign political figures with whom he shared ideas. He was also able to observe firsthand the economic situation of the countries he had traveled through and to compare them to that of Tibet. These encounters catalyzed his resolve to begin reforms that would modernize his country. Moreover, his exile made him aware that only an efficient defense system could guarantee Tibet's sovereignty, and could prevent the humiliation of future exile. With this in mind, on January 8, 1913, the Thirteenth Dalai Lama issued a proclamation that was circulated to all districts explaining the lessons learned from the Manchu occupation of 1910 and announcing five new measures: (1) the safeguard and conservation of Tibet's Buddhist institutions, (2) a ban on trade, loan businesses, and bartering by monastery officials, (3) heightened control on officials collecting taxes as well as a ban on certain corporal punishments, (4) the creation of a well-equipped and well-trained army, and (5) the authorization to cultivate vacant land as well as a tax exemption for peasants for a period of three years.[32]

Next he set himself the task of defining the status of Tibet on the international scene and, accordingly, of normalizing his relations with China. He urged the British, with whom he held a good rapport from his stay in India, to arrange a tripartite conference where they would play the role of mediators.[33] The British paid close attention to the Thirteenth Dalai Lama's request as the advance of Manchu troops up to Lhasa and their interference in Tibet's internal affairs had threatened the border of their empire. Moreover, the Chinese had ignored British protests to the Chinese minister of foreign affairs regarding the violation of the Sino-British Convention of 1906, and refused to consider Tibet as an independent country.

On January 11, 1913, Outer Mongolia and Tibet mutually recognized each other's independence. The two nations signed a treaty concerning religious and cultural exchange in addition to the free circulation of traders from one country to the other. They also promised mutual assistance in case of danger coming from domestic or foreign elements.[34] Some months later, the Chinese recognized the autonomy of Outer Mongolia while the Russians accepted Chinese suzerainty over the same land. Mongolia thus acquired the unusual status of an autonomous country that was a Russian protectorate and a Chinese suzerainty.[35]

The signature of these two treaties put into question the Anglo-Russian Convention signed in 1907. From then on the British feared Russian advances in Tibet and the ensuing threat to their empire. As far as the Chinese were concerned, they were hoping to sign an accord directly with the Thirteenth Dalai Lama. The spiritual and temporal leader of Tibet refused and proposed that China participate in a tripartite conference to be held in India. The British were able to convince the Chinese to attend this conference, which took place in Simla, the British-Indian summer capital.

After the Dalai Lama's return to Tibet on January 6, 1913, Zhang Yintang, the then vice-military governor stationed in Lhasa, and Lian Yu, the imperial resident, were expelled from Tibet along with other Chinese officials.[36] The new Chinese Republican government named Lu Xingqi to replace the two senior officers. But the Tibetan authorities refused to authorize his entry into Tibet. Lu Xingqi was thus forced to handle his assignment as a Chinese government official from

Calcutta, and used a network of minor figures to communicate with the Panchen Lama.[37] The first exchange of letters between them, which was intercepted by the British, concerned the acceptance by the Panchen Lama of gifts and a title given by Yuan Shikai, the president of the Chinese Republic.[38] The next letter is said to have expressed the will of the Panchen Lama to be represented at the Simla conference. His request was apparently turned down by the government of Beijing and also refused by Charles Bell.[39]

On July 3, 1914, the British and the Tibetans signed the Simla Convention, but since the Chinese did not ratify it, it was not considered applicable under international law, although it did function as the basis of Tibet's relations with British India.

At the beginning of the Thirteenth Dalai Lama's reign in 1895, the Tibetan army comprised six regiments spread over the territories of both Ü and Tsang provinces. Two regiments were stationed in Ü, while four were in Tsang: one in Tsangkul Dzong, one in Shigatse, one responsible for Gyeltsé and Tökul Dzong, and one in Dingri.[40] Each of these regiments was organized in the following way: one general (*dapön; daibeng*) for two battalions (*rushok; rubeng*), who directed two company commanders (*gyashok; jiabeng*). The two company commanders led five section leaders (*dingshok; dingbeng*) who, in turn, commanded twenty-five soldiers (*cushok*).

Originally this army was probably no more than a sort of Praetorian Guard, supplemented by local militia raised in a quasi-feudal manner. The date of its formation remains difficult to determine. One author suggests the date of 1642 for its creation and 1750 for its organization and deployment in the field.[41] Another one states that the regular Tibetan army's formation dates from 1792 and that one thousand soldiers were stationed in Ü and twelve hundred in Tsang shortly after 1846.[42] Given that in 1642 the Hoshuud tribe was charged with the defense of Tibet, it seems unlikely that the Tibetans felt the need to create their own army at that time. The dates of 1750 or 1792, therefore, seem more realistic.

At the beginning of 1912, a single regiment was comprised of 527 soldiers and officers. The Tibetan army, which had six regiments, thus totaled approximately 3,160 soldiers and officers, who were badly equipped and spread over two provinces in Central Tibet (Ü and Tsang).[43] From his exile in Darjeeling in Sikkim, the Thirteenth Dalai Lama decided to name a defense minister. He appointed Trimön Norbu Wangyel and Champa Tendar, two of his staff still in Lhasa, to secretly recruit soldiers and buy arms and ammunition from the Chinese soldiers who had been stationed in Lhasa since 1910. Next he named the hero of the battle of Cagzam, Labzang Tadul (better known as Tsarong Shape), as commander-in-chief of the Tibetan army, who was joined by Trimön Norbu Wangyel and Champa Tendar in Lhasa in January 1912.[44] The Tibetan resistance took form, and in August 1912 it defeated the Chinese soldiers stationed in Lhasa who, before fleeing to China, left close to a thousand weapons that were then used to equip the Tibetan army.

As soon as the Dalai Lama had returned to Lhasa in January 1913, he made the decision to establish a powerful Tibetan army to ensure the independence of his country. He sought to accomplish this by first setting up new rules for drafting conscripts. Previously the government only recruited soldiers when needed. These would be chosen from those living on government lands, which served as a kind of reservoir of conscripts. The government lands reserved for conscription were called "military lots" (*makang*). Certain regions such as Dakpo, Kongpo, and the three provinces of Kham, Amdo, and Ngari had been exempt from conscription, which mainly operated in Ü and Tsang.[45] From 1913 things would change and a new rule was instituted. Concerning Ü, it was decided to systematically recruit one soldier from every two military lots. In Tsang, the ratio was established at one soldier for every four military lots. The immediate objective was to enlarge the regular military count by one thousand soldiers.[46] As this was an additional contribution of men, the Tibetan government exempted each soldier's family from paying for his food and equipment, a provision that had been required in the past. It took care of those expenses through the budget allocated to what had become a regular standing army.

For the Tibetan government, rapidly equipping its new four thousand strong army was a priority. Up until then, the only weapons Tibetan soldiers had consisted of bows and arrows, a few rifles made by Muslim artisans in Lhasa, and the weapons abandoned by the Chinese during their hasty departure in 1912.[47] This equipment was more than outdated. That is why, strengthened by the new relations he had made with the representatives of the British government in India (including Charles Bell, the political officer in Sikkim), the Thirteenth Dalai Lama requested their aid. As a first step, the British supplied five thousand rifles and half a million cartridges, but refused to exceed this.[48] Concerned about maintaining good relations with China, the British gave numerous reasons for their limited aid. Their arms and positions in India barely covered the needs of their own army, they said, and hastened to add that Chandra Shumshere, minister of Nepal, opposed their supplying weapons to Tibetans for fear they would attack his country.[49] To get around these obstacles, Tsarong, the second commander of the Tibetan army, asked Charles Bell to provide him with an export license so he could buy old rifles in Calcutta, but the British authorities refused him.[50] Short of alternatives, the Tibetans had to resort to importing arms from Japan.[51]

As for the soldiers' training and drilling, the Thirteenth Dalai Lama and his government, conscious of their lacunae in this subject, decided to test the value of several foreign methods starting in 1914. One regiment was placed under the authority of a British instructor, another under a Mongol trained in China, a third under a Mongol trained in Russia, and finally one under a Japanese ex-soldier. A parade and military maneuvers were organized in order to allow the government to choose a model that best suited its army. The British model was eventually chosen. Numerous Tibetan military officers were selected and sent to Quetta in the northwest of present-day Pakistan, Shillong in present-day

Assam, and to Gangtok in Sikkim. They were to be trained by British instructors so they could, in turn, train their own units of Tibetan soldiers.[52] The Tibetan army saw its ranks and arms grow. At the same time, these soldiers also received superior training and practice. However, to create an army worthy of its name necessitated the input of significant funds.

Initially taxes paid in kind (grain) as well as in cash were raised from the soldiers' families as well as those living on lands that were required to provide conscripts and support the troops. Yet the supplies obtained proved to be insufficient, while in the meantime, sporadic conflicts began to occur on the Sino-Tibetan border in 1918, obliging a major portion of the troops to be stationed in Kham, putting a strain on local granaries there.[53] Once again, the Tibetans looked for a source of funding from the British. This time, they tried to impose customs duties on articles imported from India. The British refused to allow this, since they judged it to be in contravention of the terms of the Simla Convention signed in 1914. Instead, they proposed that equivalent customs duties be imposed on goods that the Tibetans imported from China, an idea flatly rejected by the Chinese.[54]

It was probably at this time that the Thirteenth Dalai Lama decided to raise a special tax designed to finance the expanding Tibetan army. He informed the Panchen Lama that Tashilhunpo would have to take responsibility for paying one quarter of the army's total budget.[55] To justify his decision, the Dalai Lama used supporting evidence that in 1791 Tashilhunpo had paid a quarter of the necessary military expenses to repel the attacks by the Gurkhas from Nepal.

In addition to the military tax, the Dalai Lama is said to have required the Panchen Lama to reimburse back payments corresponding to the Anglo-Tibetan wars of 1888 and 1904 and the Sino-Tibetan one of 1912–13.[56] Out of the 108,000 measures of grain (*kel*) used by the Tibetan government in military operations since 1888, the Panchen Lama's debt would have thus amounted to 72,000 measures.[57] The Dalai Lama seemed convinced that the Panchen Lama could handle financing a quarter of the army's budget plus pay this debt, considering the supposed wealth of Tashilhunpo monastery. After all, wasn't the Panchen Lama building a monumental gold statue of Buddha Maitreya?[58]

The description of the statue the Panchen Lama was constructing provided by Alexandra David-Neel, the French explorer who was in Shigatse in July 1916, would tend to support the Thirteenth Dalai Lama:

> I saw the huge image [of the future Buddha Maitreya] placed in a hall with galleries that allowed the devotees to circle around it on the ground floor on a level with the feet and successively ascending the first, second and third galleries, up to its belt, its shoulders and its head. Twenty jewellers were setting the enormous ornaments that were to adorn the gigantic Maitreya. They were re-setting the jewels presented by the ladies belonging to the nobility of Tsang, the mother of the Tashi Lama at their head ...[59]

Despite what appears to involve a significant expense, calculating the actual income of Tashilhunpo at the time would provide a broader picture of the financial condition of the Panchen Lama's monastery and its ability to meet Lhasa's monetary demands.

REVENUE OF TASHILHUNPO

Over the centuries, successive Dalai Lamas and their governments had offered a great amount of land to the Panchen Lamas. In the seventeenth century, at the time of the Fifth Dalai Lama (1617–1682), the Fourth Panchen Lama had received extensive tracts of land, as we saw earlier. Later, the sovereign Lhazang Khan, great grandson of Güshri Khan who reigned over Central Tibet from 1706 to 1717, granted the Fifth Panchen Lama (1663–1737) the valleys of Drubrultsang, Tashi Dzong, Lukdong, Tsar, Korlam, Dongkar,[60] Rinchentsé, Gyelchung, Léu, Zurbuk, Pagrong, Öyug, and Ramding. He also gave lands to the Tashilhunpo colleges of Thösam Norbuling and Kyilkang Lèkshéling. The Seventh Dalai Lama (1708–1757) gave the province of Ngari to the Fifth Panchen Lama, who is said to have refused, explaining that his monastery possessed enough land to fulfill the needs of his monks. Legend has it that soon after, Pholhané Sönam Tobgyé, "sovereign" of Tibet from 1728 to 1747, offered the lands of Dzongka,[61] Kyirong,[62] and Ngari Korsum (Mangyül, Gugé, and Pureng) to the Fifth Panchen Lama, who returned them.[63] In 1731 records state that he offered the district of Nakartsé to the Fifth Panchen Lama, who again refused his offer.[64] Certain sources suggest that the Yongzheng Emperor (r. 1723–36) had already offered the lands of Dzongka, Kyirong, and Ngari Korsum to the Panchen Lama in 1728. The Qianlong Emperor is said to have also offered the districts of Lhatsé, Phüntsoling, and Namring several times.[65] Yet it is also said that the Fifth Panchen Lama ended up accepting them only after the insistence of the Manchu imperial resident stationed in Tibet.[66]

According to Luciano Petech, the Fifth Panchen Lama probably became landowner of the districts of Lhatsé, Phüntsoling, and Namring in 1728.[67] According to S. C. Das, the Yongzheng Emperor sent an official to Tibet to establish the border between Ü and Tsang. At this time, the imperial resident seems to have proposed suzerainty to be held by the Fifth Panchen Lama for all of the Tibetan provinces from the Kangpa pass to Mount Kailash. Using the pretext of his age and doubts of his capacity to take charge of such responsibilities, the Fifth Panchen Lama is said to have declined the offer. Hiding behind an imperial edict, the imperial resident apparently insisted, to the point that the Fifth Panchen Lama could no longer refuse. After having consulted Pholhané, and in agreement with him, he is said to have accepted the ownership of the lands extending to the west of Panam, including the districts of Lhatsé, Phüntsoling, Namring, Dzongka, Kirong, and Ngari Korsum. In compensation, he reportedly returned holdings such as Phakri, Gyeltsé, Yarbroktso, and other domains to Pholhané.[68]

Yet no formal proof attributing land ownership of these six districts to the Fifth Panchen Lama can be found in his biography, or in local monographs and contemporary works on geography, or in *The Veritable Records of the Qing Dynasty*. It seems highly unlikely that these properties belonged to the prelate, particularly as there is no evidence that Yongzheng offered them to him. Nor does it seem credible that Yongzheng would have donated lands that were not his. We must note that where nature created, and the Tibetans themselves recognized, four geographical regions (the Changthang plateau in the north/northwest; Central Tibet comprising the provinces of Ü and Tsang to the south; Kham, to the southeast; and Amdo, to the northeast), the Manchus only distinguished two regions: Inner Tibet (*Qian Zang*) and Outer Tibet (*Hou Zang*).[69] According to the Manchus' understanding of the distribution of powers in Tibet, they mistakenly believed that the Dalai Lama governed Inner Tibet while the Panchen Lama ruled Outer Tibet.[70]

Whatever the case, the attribution of the districts of Nakartsé, Panam, and Namring to the Fifth Panchen Lama remains debatable, since, as we will see, these lands became the object of bitter dispute when the Tibetan government and the Panchen Lama began negotiations for the prelate's return to Tibet in 1934.

According to a Tibetan study published in 1983, at the beginning of the twentieth century, it is estimated that Tashilhunpo covered an area of approximately 300,000 sq km and included 230 affiliated monasteries, as previously noted.[71] Yet W. G. Surkhang's estimate from the land registers completed in 1740 shows Tashilhunpo's land holdings at slightly more than two thousand lots (*kang*).[72] The differences in these estimates, in all probability, revolve around two different ways of assessing Tashilhunpo's properties. First, a *kang* was a plot of land on which a determined quantity of grain could be sown. This quantity of grain was expressed in a measurement known as *kel*, which was the quantity of grain held in a standard container called *'bo* (or *kharu*).[73] All the approved containers were marked with a government stamp.[74] One *kel* equaled approximately 27–33 British pounds of grain (one British pound being the equivalent of 453 grams), that is, between 12.2 and 14.9 kilograms.[75] Depending on how it was measured, a *kang* equaled approximately nine to eleven British acres (a British acre equaling 4.047 square meters).[76] This means a lot could total between 3.64 and 4.45 hectares. If we consider the estimate of Tashilhunpo's lands of 2,000 *kang* as presented by Surkhang, the monastic domain would measure approximately 73–89 sq km, a far cry from the figure of 300,000 sq km cited in the 1983 Tibetan study.

At the time of the Ninth Panchen Lama, the provinces of Ü, Tsang, and Ngari were made up of some fifty districts.[77] Today what is called the Tibet Autonomous Region (TAR), which comprises Ü, Tsang, and Ngari provinces, covers 1,221,000 sq km.[78] Consequently, the average area of a single district would have been around 24,400 sq km. According to M. C. Goldstein, the Tashilhunpo lands extended over ten districts.[79] This figure seems to be confirmed by the Tibetan study published in 1983, which indicates that the Tashilhunpo domain was composed of three districts, five domains (*shika*) equaling a surface area of five districts, sixty-eight small lots (*shika chung*), and twenty-six pastures (*brokwa*).[80] Thus, admitting a count of ten districts each with an average size of 24,400 sq km, the monastic lands of Tashilhunpo would have covered an area of approximately 244,000 sq km, close to the figure of 300,000 sq km. We can then suppose that the two thousand lots (73–89 sq km) mentioned by Surkhang refer only to the expanse of land attached to the Panchen Lama's private residence, rather than to the entire monastery. It does seem very unlikely that 230 affiliated monasteries could exist on only 80 or 90 sq km. In any case, with probably ten districts, the territory controlled by the Ninth Panchen Lama comprised one-fifth of Central Tibet and accordingly must have ensured significant revenue.

Nevertheless, the income from these lands remains extremely difficult to evaluate, as no author has mentioned any specific amount. The only data available come from Ran Hongling, professor at Chengdu's Southwest University for Nationalities. He indicates, without any source citations, that the income from Tashilhunpo's monastic land holdings was distributed as follows: 67 percent was generated from agricultural production, 21.6 percent was from livestock, and 11.4 percent came from trade and crafts.[81] Unfortunately, he does not reveal a monetary figure for Tashilhunpo's income, which suggests that these percentages might be estimates; neither does he mention offerings from devotees, which the monastery surely received.

One possible method for arriving at a rough estimate of Tashilhunpo's income consists in evaluating the number of monks the monastery was able to feed and board. According to several sources, the monastic population at the beginning of the century varied between three and four thousand monks.[82] During field interviews, it emerged that the Tashilhunpo monks received larger food portions than those at other large Gélukpa monasteries. According to different interviewees, a Tashilhunpo monk received between 32 and 38 measures of grilled barley flour per year.[83] This calculates to approximately 246–292 kg, which means a daily ration of 670 to 800 grams, depending on local eating habits. In comparison, a monk from Ganden received ten measures a year, or three times less than his Tashilhunpo counterpart. So, if the number of monks living at Tashilhunpo was from three to four thousand, the quantity of grilled barley flour the monastery needed to produce annually to fulfill their needs would have amounted to approximately 730–1,168 tons (96,000–152,000 measures of flour or 49,485–95,597 measures of grain, for an average value of 72,500 measures of grain).[84] But the agricultural production of the monastery also had to feed the subjects living on the land, and include a reserve of grain needed to sow the fields the following year. Supposing that three to four thousand subjects depended on Tashilhunpo, that means tripling the figure obtained for feeding the monks alone by including the grain reserve and the foodstuffs for the subjects, leading us to an estimated agricultural revenue for the monastery of about 217,500 measures or 2,800 tons of barley. Of course, such an estimate is used only to obtain a working assumption rather than a precise number, especially when it is known that production measures and capacity varied from one region of Tibet to another.

Narratives by travelers visiting Tashilhunpo at the beginning of the twentieth century provide some clues of the monastery's holdings. Tsybikov, a Russian who traveled to Tibet at the beginning of the century, describes the roofs of Tashilhunpo's temples and stupas as "made of copper plates covered with gold," with the Fifth Panchen Lama's stupa "particularly opulent."[85] Giuseppe Tucci also underlined the wealth of the monastery, saying that its "chapels were vying with each other in the wealth of their ornaments, in their display of gold, precious and semi-precious stones, in the bulk of their statues ... The abbots' mortal remains were enclosed in huge mausoleums laden with gold and jewels.[86] As for Alexandra David-Neel, who lived at Tashilhunpo from July 17–26, 1916, her impression was that a "barbaric splendour reigned in the temples, halls and palaces of the dignitaries. No description can give an idea of it. Gold, silver, turquoise, jade were lavishly used on the altars, the tombs, the ornamented doors, the ritualistic implements and even on mere household objects for the use of wealthy lamas."[87]

In summary, the monastic lands of Tashilhunpo probably extended over 300,000 sq km, while those of the Ninth Panchen Lama's private residence covered about 80 sq km. The agricultural production of the monastic lands could be estimated at approximately 2,800 tons of barley per year.[88] To the agricultural income must be added that from livestock, trade and crafts, not counting offerings from the faithful and donors. All of this made up a considerable amount of wealth, which impressed many travelers.

DECREES OF 1917 AND 1923

In 1916 the period of tax exemption that had until then been instituted by the Thirteenth Dalai Lama expired. Shortly thereafter, a decree dated the year of the Fire Snake (1917) imposed new taxes on Tashilhunpo. The original text of this decree cannot be found, but it is cited by Dönkhang Kelzang Dékyi, and a later decree, dated 1923, refers to it.[89]

The decree of the year of the Fire Snake imposed an extraordinary tax (*gyelchak légyor*) on herds in the Gyeltsé district consisting of one horse for every one hundred horses possessed and one beast of burden for every three hundred beasts of burden in a herd.[90] In addition to this tax, the subjects living on the lands of Tashilhunpo within the district of Gyeltsé were to provide one-seventh of their total number of horses and beasts of burden.[91] The 1923 decree states in its introduction that twelve ordinances (*tsatsik*) comprised the 1917 decree. It indicates that these ordinances not only imposed an extraordinary tax on the subjects of the Gyeltsé, but that a tax on the herds in Gyeltsé was also imposed and was collected for British use (*cinko raluktsa shak*).[92] Moreover, the decrees ordered peasant taxpayers from all the districts of Tsang to provide a crossing *ulag*; this included those on the lands of the Ninth Panchen Lama's private residence. The term *ulag* refers to various types of corvée labor. The "crossing *ulag*" (*sadzong lamtok*) consisted in facilitating the transport of officials from the Tibetan government (or members of their family), as well as British envoys or imperial Manchu residents and their goods, provided an official permit (*lamyik*), affording access to this service, was held. It included necessary horses, beasts of burden, food for the travelers and animals, fuel, and servants.[93]

One reason the Thirteenth Dalai Lama may have decided to impose the crossing *ulag* on Tashilhunpo is that, at the time, some Tibetan troops were stationed in Tsang, particularly in the districts of Tsangkul Dzong, Shigatse, Gyeltsé, Tökul Dzong, and Dingri. These troops were ready to push back possible attacks on Tibet's south and southwest borders. In this capacity, they were called to move across Tashilhunpo lands. Yet, only the crossing *ulag* would allow them to cover their needs and expenses as they traveled. It thus became vital for the troops that Tashilhunpo provide this *ulag*.

Apparently, the Thirteenth Dalai Lama's decision to impose the crossing *ulag* on the subjects living in Tsang was preceded by a special mission sent to Tashilhunpo. The members of this mission belonged to the Tax Inspection Commission (*babshi lékung*) based in Lhasa and attached to the Ministry of Finance. If the term *bab* literally means "tax," then taken in this context it would qualify as "large untaxed tracts of land," with the term *shi* meaning "exam" or "inspection" and *lékung* meaning "commission" or "bureau." The Tax Inspection Commission was specifically in charge of verifying that the aristocrats and abbots had not seized lands since the 1830 land registry when, for example, a landowner with no descendants passed away. In this particular case, the commission was empowered to confiscate any such lands, so as to give them to other more legitimate people or require the abusive landowner to settle the tax.[94] In practical terms, Lungshar, the minister of finance overseeing the Tax Inspection Commission, sent employees to Tashilhunpo, including an attendant of the fifth rank (*drönyer*) who was assisted by a few lay officials of the ninth rank. There they created a local branch to inspect the monastery's lands.[95]

In January 1918 Chinese troops would again try to cross Tibet's eastern border. They came up against trained Tibetan soldiers who not only defied them, but also engaged in a counter-attack and advanced all the way up to Dergé. The Chinese, outflanked, asked for mediation from the British. A tripartite arrangement was subsequently made on August 19, 1918, between Britain, China, and Tibet, which fixed the border at the upper Yangtze River, leaving the territories of Dergé and Dzayül under Tibetan control.[96] However, skirmishes revealed how important it was to have troops stationed permanently in Kham and Amdo, in addition to those in Central Tibet. This reinforced the Dalai Lama's theory that new revenue was needed to maintain the soldiers. That is why, on January 25, 1921, the National Assembly (*tsokdu*) decided to increase the number of conscripts from five hundred to one thousand per year in order to achieve a force of seventeen thousand soldiers.[97] The government also confirmed and reinforced the content of the twelve ordinances from the 1917 decree, which it announced on August 2, 1923.[98]

The Tibetan government sent Secretary Samkhar Ngawang Shényen and Minister of Finance Lungshar to investigate the situation of the Shigatse lands; first, because of difficulties encountered by the subjects living in the Tsang districts and on the lands of the private residence at Tashilhunpo, and secondly, because of the government's concern with the tax on herds from Gyeltsé collected for British use, the crossing *ulag*, and the extraordinary tax concerning the subjects of Gyeltsé. After the investigation, Lungshar and his colleague brought back requests to the government on behalf of the officials of Tashilhunpo, copies of various documents, and a written proposal for a resolution. Upon examining these different documents, the government decided that the twelve ordinances from 1917 remained valid. As for the crossing *ulag*, the office of the Tibetan Council of Ministers informed the prime minister that the requests and copies of the documents presented by the representatives of Tashilhunpo's private residence were contrary to the content of the order of 1917. To clarify certain issues, Lungshar and Tenpa Dargyé, the high ecclesiastic attendant, were once again appointed to carry out a counter-investigation.

After receiving the requests and replies from those involved, the government made a number of decisions. It declared that the private residence of Tashilhunpo had to provide the crossing *ulag* on Tsang lands according to the measures set during the Tibeto-Gurkha War of 1791, which were confirmed in a 1793 decree and the respective 1830 land registry. The government stated that according to the 1793 decree and a particular, but unspecified, law, all the subjects of the Tsang districts had to provide transport *ulag* for one district (*dzongkyel*), in addition to one-sixth of the sojourn *ulag* (*satsik*).[99]

It also mentioned a letter stamped with a seal (*bukdam gochen*) and dated 1855 in which it was clearly indicated that in case of war, civil disturbance, or flooding, all the subjects of Tashilhunpo's private residence were required to pay the entire crossing *ulag*. It pointed out that during the war between Nepal and Tibet in 1855, a letter from Minister Shédra stipulated that Tashilhunpo had to provide the soldiers' salaries, horses, and beasts of burden within the framework of the transport *ulag* for one district. It claimed to have proof that on that occasion the monastery did provide *ulag*. Relying on the 1791 and 1855 precedents (both during wars with Nepal) and citing an ordinance from 1915, Lhasa now required Tashilhunpo to supply the transport *ulag* and pay a special tax (*makdön*) composed of matches, saltpetre, ammunition, and horses in order for the soldiers based in Dingri to maintain the upkeep of their regiment.

In addition, the government made reference to an ordinance from 1707, confirmed in 1717, showing that the subjects of the other three great Gélukpa monasteries (Drépung, Ganden, and Sera) had to equally honor the transport *ulag* for one district. The government further stipulated that the private residence of Tashilhunpo had to follow the Dalai Lama's orders and that no tax exemption was to be given in the various ordinances applying to all aristocratic, governmental, or monastic lands. It emphasized the fact that, in the future, an army would have the role of protecting Tibet. Thus, according to the government, as Tibet was a country giving great importance to religion, regardless of the number of plots of land Tashilhunpo possessed, its subjects had to comply with the transport *ulag* following government orders, which themselves would be decided as circumstances arose. The government further underlined the fact that Tashilhunpo subjects could no longer cite earlier documents to avoid paying their due taxes.

Moreover, Lhasa claimed to have proof that the Tashilhunpo private residence had usually refused to meet its obligations to provide food for important governmental representatives, such as Manchu imperial residents in Tibet during their inspections, as well as various unexpected travelers. It reproached them for actually breaking the law by creating local laws stamped with their own seals exempting all the Tsang districts from the crossing *ulag*. It also accused Tashilhunpo administrators of having made their own tax calculations on taxes that had been raised on their lands since 1793 for no specific purpose. The government further declared illegal the fact that Tashilhunpo had not paid a regular military tax (*makchok*); the text, however, gives no further details of this tax. Similarly, citing the 1923 decree confirming that of 1917, the Tibetan government ordered Tashilhunpo's private residence to supply transport *ulag* for the districts within its monastic lands in Tsang. For all the revealed irregularities, the government condemned the Tashilhunpo private residence and required payment of fourteen fines, amounting to 110 ounces (*sang*) of gold, and demanded it to settle its debts, totaling 1,965 ounces of silver and 3,325 Nepalese coins.

PANCHEN LAMA'S REACTION TO THE EXTRAORDINARY TAX

To say that the Panchen Lama and his officials were taken aback by the government's monetary demands is an understatement. Heated arguments ensued between Lhasa and Shigatse. At Tashilhunpo, disbelief and a feeling of false accusation permeated the entire monastery complex, particularly the private residence, in all likelihood. The Panchen Lama and his officials had to have felt intense enmity at being ordered to not only provide transport *ulag* across all of Tashilhunpo's monastic lands but to also pay "back taxes" in addition to financing a large chunk of the army's military budget; they certainly found it unfair that the Tibetan government grounded a legal precedent on an event going back to 1791 to require the tax payment.

By August 1923 the Panchen Lama knew he would have to contribute annually the equivalent of one quarter of the national defense budget, representing approximately 37,500 British pounds.[100] This is the equivalent of about 2.5 million Tibetan *sang*, the local currency at the time.[101] He would also have to pay the backdated debts corresponding to the Anglo-Tibetan wars in 1888 and 1904, and the Sino-Tibetan one from 1912–13, totaling approximately 27,000 measures of grain, i.e., 405,000 *sang*.[102] In addition, he would have to supply transport *ulag*, especially for the movements of the four regiments based in Tsang, and pay 110 ounces of gold in fines as well as settle the debts arising from all the irregularities found by the government investigators.

The transport *ulag* collected annually by a regiment of 527 men passing through a particular district could equal 9,876 to 10,596 beasts of burden, 816 to 1,164 horses, 34,860 ounces of silver for salary needs, and 13,560 measures of grain.[103] In this way, the annual contribution to the national defense budget and the payment of back debts corresponding to previous wars amounted to nearly 3,000,000 *sang* compared with 3,262,500 *sang* of probable annual revenue of Tashilhunpo (indispensable to the survival of the monks, the subjects, and the provision of grain seed for the following year). It would seem, thus, that the Panchen Lama did actually find himself incapable of meeting the global sum of these payments.

This was, without a doubt, the reason that as early as 1917 a heated debate coupled with a judicial battle began between the officials of Lhasa and those of Tashilhunpo, who refused to accept the debt, since according to them they had not been required to pay it during the previous centuries.

The only tangible evidence available on the subject of the legal dispute between Lhasa and Shigatse appears in a document from 1923, containing the stated position of officials from Tashilhunpo's private residence concerning the extraordinary tax imposed in 1917.

According to this document, which comes from Lhasa, the officials from Tashilhunpo admitted that during the war of 1791 against the Gurkhas, their monastery had, in fact, supplied the crossing *ulag* for travelers, servants, soldiers, and ministers. This situation is said to have been enacted into law by a decree in 1793, which stated that the tax-paying peasants who worked on government lands had to furnish the total sum of the sojourn *ulag* on one lot and three-quarters of the transport *ulag* for one district, while the subjects living on the lands of the Tashilhunpo private residence had to pay the remaining quarter.

Officials from Tashilhunpo claimed that they no longer had to pay the crossing *ulag*, nor raise troops, nor create garrisons since, according to them, the 1793 decree had become obsolete. To demonstrate this, they referred to a document (*shébam*) dated 1872 in which the crossing *ulag* was not mentioned. Due to this fact, according to them, everyone was aware that aside from exceptional circumstances, and following a century-old custom, Tashilhunpo provided neither the sojourn *ulag* on a plot of land, nor the transport *ulag* for one district.

They also cited an order (*kashok*) from 1916, exempting Tashilhunpo from the transport *ulag*.[104]

Beyond the legal aspects, it is difficult to assess the validity of Tashilhunpo's arguments due to a lack of available documents. To better understand the Panchen Lama's reluctance to pay these taxes and contributions, it is worth investigating the institutional position of Tashilhunpo within the context of Tibet as a whole.

The institution of the Panchen Lamas occupied an especially important place in Tibet's history because of the unique relationship linking it to that of the Dalai Lamas. During their lifetimes, the two prelates were often brought into an alternating master-disciple relationship. Moreover, upon the death of the master, the disciple was directly involved in the process of locating and recognizing the deceased's next reincarnation.

In less than three centuries, the Panchen Lamas saw their political role grow, almost against their will.[105] With their spiritual reputation equaling, perhaps at times surpassing, that of the Dalai Lamas, they were constrained to take a growing part in the political life of Tibet insofar as they were solicited more and more by both the Manchus and the British. While the two foreign powers' motivations certainly differed, each was seeking a way to take advantage of the two heads of the Gélukpa. The premature death of the Sixth, Ninth, Tenth, Eleventh, and Twelfth Dalai Lamas and the intrigues of unscrupulous regents would amplify this phenomenon. In this way, down to the beginning of the twentieth century, Tashilhunpo enjoyed relative autonomy made possible by the remoteness of Shigatse from Lhasa (a ten-day walk or seven days on horseback separated the capital of Tsang from that of Ü). Its relative autonomy was further bolstered by the expanse of arable land on Tashilhunpo's monastic domain that guaranteed it enough agricultural production to affirm its economic power, as well as the tax exemption it seemed to benefit from, and the esteem held and caution used by foreign powers towards the line of the Panchen Lamas. At the beginning of the twentieth century, the monastic condition was such that it acquired a substantial administration. But could it be called a "government?"

The Tashilhunpo administration, inasmuch as I have been able to piece it together, and that of the Tibetan government in Lhasa were each divided into two main branches, one in charge of religious affairs and the other overseeing civil affairs, including military affairs, in the case of the Tibetan government. In both cases, the religious branch was composed exclusively of monks. But the civil and military branches of the Tibetan government were administered by lay people who worked in close collaboration with the monks, whereas the comparable branch at Tashilhunpo was mainly run by monks.[106] In fact, the civil and military branches in Lhasa had all the characteristics of a true government. Together, they were led by a prime minister (*silön*) at the head of a cabinet made up of four ministers (*kalön*), who themselves, in turn, supervised the ministers of finance, justice, defense, and so forth. The equivalent branch at Tashilhunpo was organized like an administrative service. In particular, it was not placed under the authority of a Council of Ministers (*kashag*). In the translations of letters written by the Panchen Lama, both David Macdonald, the British trade agent in Gyeltsé, and F. M. Bailey, the British political officer in Sikkim, describe Tashilhunpo's general administrator as "prime minister."[107] Obviously this title didn't correspond to the reality of the situation since there were no other ministers at the head of the "Department Concerning the Base" (*shökor lékung*), one of two departments comprising Tashilhunpo's administration, the other department being the "Department Concerning the Summit" (*tsékor lékung*). Another fundamental difference distinguishing the Tashilhunpo administration from that of the Tibetan government was that although Chinese sources indicate that Tashilhunpo had an army, British and Tibetan sources never mention its existence.[108] It seems, then, that the Chinese authors confused the regular army regiments administered by the Tibetan government stationed in Tsang with a Tashilhunpo army. Finally, all the officials of the Tibetan government were recruited from all over Tibet, while those at Tashilhunpo were chosen solely from among the local people.

The administrative framework of Tashilhunpo was, therefore, not comparable to that of the Tibetan government, except for having a two-branched overall structure.[109] Also, the Tibetan government exerted control on the province of Ü through the intermediary of district governors who administered each of the fifty-three districts (*dzong*) making up Central Tibet. It is left to be determined whether the Tashilhunpo administration's authority exerted itself over the districts heads in the province of Tsang. According to Chinese sources, in 1899 the Panchen Lama led Tsang.[110] Some years later, the British confirmed this interpretation. For example, Charles Bell affirmed that the Panchen Lama's power extended over three districts, without citing which ones.[111] On their side, David Macdonald and Frederick Williamson, who sojourned in Shigatse from July 2–9, 1934, indicate that all officials of the province of Tsang were appointed by the Panchen Lama, except for those who were placed at strategic points such as Gyeltsé.[112] But we also know that in 1915 the Tibetan government named a civil governor (*cidzong*) to Shigatse in charge of supervising the two district heads (a monk and a layperson) already acting in that capacity.[113] At about the same time, between 1913 and 1917, Lhasa had created new governor-general (*cikyab*) posts placed at each border town: Chamdo in 1913, Dergé in 1914, Hor in 1916, and at Gromo and Lhokha in 1917. Indeed, it seems likely that the aim of the governor appointed to Shigatse was to take back administrative control of the region. His title, *cidzong* (lit. "general-governor of the district"), unique in all Tibet, and different from the title of governor-general, confirms the special character of his task. The nomination of this figure probably fell into a general policy by the authorities in Lhasa of specifically taking back control of the administration of Tashilhunpo.

In the end, Tashilhunpo benefited, more often than not, from having relative political autonomy with respect to Lhasa that was derived, as previously noted, from its long distance from the capital, its economic self-sufficiency, its *de facto* tax exemption, and the esteem and caution the Manchus and British had displayed towards the lineage of the Panchen Lamas. Although Tashilhunpo had a number of important positions, the monastery's administration did not belong to a government nor did it have an army under its control. It is thus possible to affirm that the Panchen Lama was not the temporal leader of a sovereign nation (Tsang) claiming its independence. However, managing the monastic lands as they saw fit and having inherited a several century long autonomous situation, it is understandable that the Panchen Lama and the members of his administration would be hostile towards the authoritarian measures taken by the Tibetan government—measures that seemed to put this autonomy in question. Given such conditions, and knowing that the Panchen Lama and those around him found themselves unconcerned by the budding nationalism initiated by the Dalai Lama, their refusal to pay the crossing *ulag* on their lands and to finance one quarter of Tibet's military expenses seems less surprising when one perceives them as possible tactics to consolidate a sovereign country.

RELATIONS WITH THE DALAI LAMA

Several incidents prior to the Panchen Lama's refusal to pay the crossing *ulag* and to finance one-quarter of Tibet's military expenses may have, it seems, tarnished the prelate's relations with the Thirteenth Dalai Lama. In January 1904, for instance, the Panchen Lama invited the Thirteenth Dalai Lama to come to his monastery to bless it. In a letter dated January 23, 1904, his master replied:

> Recently, I received your letter and have taken note. In this letter you ask whether I can find time to take a pilgrimage to Tsang. As I have the heavy responsibility of both religion and politics, I must administer the political and religious affairs on a daily basis. In addition, according to recent reports, war is soon to break out. The other side may attack as soon as the temperature is milder. If I go to Shigatse, it will be difficult for me to stay informed of events and to run operations. Also, I am now praying to remove obstacles. So, it is impossible and inopportune to delay these practices. As soon as I have obtained a result, that is to say, at the end of this year, or the beginning of next, I will go on a pilgrimage to Tsang.[114]

In the Tibetan Buddhist tradition, when a spiritual master is not satisfied with the behavior of his disciple, he expresses this by refusing his requests. In this case, however, nothing apparently justified such an attitude on the part of the Dalai Lama towards his disciple. It simply seems that the Dalai Lama had valid reasons not to leave Lhasa. In fact, as we have seen, a few months later, troops under Colonel Younghusband entered Tibet and forced the Thirteenth Dalai Lama to go into exile in Outer Mongolia. It was then that the Manchus decided to temporarily relieve the Dalai Lama of his duties and provisionally name the Panchen Lama in his place.[115] But the Panchen Lama refused to accept the post, explaining to the Qing emperor that the Thirteenth Dalai Lama alone was able to appoint officials to the government, given his role both as spiritual and temporal leader of Tibet.[116]

After the British reached an agreement with Tibetan authorities in October 1905, Captain Frederick O'Connor, the new British trade agent in Gyeltsé, went to Tashilhunpo where he met with the Panchen Lama. Bonds of friendship grew between the two men. According to the British, Captain O'Connor invited the Panchen Lama to come to Calcutta to meet the Prince of Wales upon recommendation by Lord Curzon, the viceroy of India (1899–1905). The Panchen Lama hesitated and said he must get Beijing's authority before accepting. But the captain convinced him of the pointlessness of this step.[117] Moreover, he assured him of support from the British army in the event of Manchu reprisals. O'Connor would later be censured for giving this assurance without authority.[118]

Captain O'Connor is said to have come with thirty soldiers to Tashilhunpo to deliver the invitation from Lord Curzon. This, it would seem, made it difficult for the prelate to decline, at least according to a report written by one of the Panchen Lama's followers and addressed to the imperial resident in Tibet describing the threatening presence of the soldiers surrounding Captain O'Connor.[119]

The Panchen Lama arrived in Calcutta in January 1906 at the age of twenty-two. He was received by Lord Minto, the new, recently named viceroy of India. During their interview, the Panchen Lama again asked, but in vain, for support from the British army against potential Manchu reprisals. He was then invited by Thubthob Namgyel and Ugyen Wangchuk, the monarchs of Sikkim and Bhutan respectively, to meet with them. He also spoke with the Prince of Wales and visited a British army barracks, and attended a military parade in Rawalpindi, alongside all four of the statesmen: the viceroy of India, the maharajah of Sikkim, the king of Bhutan, and the Prince of Wales.[120] He took advantage of his trip to India to make some pilgrimages, after which he declared himself "particularly pleased to have been able to visit the sacred Buddhist sites that he had known about through texts and *thangkas*."[121]

On February 9, 1906, the Panchen Lama returned to his monastery. He had reason for worry. For one thing he had rejected the Qing offer to assume the position of the Thirteenth Dalai Lama, who was in exile in Mongolia. For another, his apparent sympathies with the British invaders and his activities in India could seem suspicious to the Tibetan government. In order to limit possible detrimental effects, he undertook two parallel projects. Through the intermediary of his attendant, he addressed a report to the Qing emperor, explaining the reasons for his voyage to India while also inviting Charles Bell, the British political officer in Sikkim, to come to visit him at Tashilhunpo. Bell accepted his invitation, with approval from his own government. He went to Shigatse and stayed one week at the monastery in November 1906. During their meetings, the Panchen Lama is said to have confided his fears.[122] He asked Bell to renew the commitment given by Captain O'Connor that the British army would step in if needed, but Bell could promise nothing.[123]

The Qing emperor concluded that the Panchen Lama had acted against his will and that the British had forced him to go to India.[124] The Tibetan government seems to have suspected the Panchen Lama of soliciting aid from the British to gain independence for Tsang. In effect, if we are to believe Bell, the Panchen Lama wanted to divide and weaken Tibet.[125] Nevertheless, in the absence of the Thirteenth Dalai Lama, the Tibetan government took no sanctions against him.

In June 1909 the Thirteenth Dalai Lama was making his way back from exile. As he approached Chugoringmo, near Nakchu, the Panchen Lama's attendant is reported to have been waiting for him and gave him offerings, which the Thirteenth Dalai Lama accepted.[126] On August 1, 1909, the Panchen Lama sent one of his officials to Chugoringmo to welcome his spiritual master. Since the meetings with the Panchen Lama's emissaries went well and the Dalai Lama had accepted their offerings, the disciple could conclude that his spiritual master held no ill will towards him as a consequence of his visit to India. The next day the Panchen Lama came in person to meet the Thirteenth Dalai Lama. He was invited into a tent where refreshments had been prepared for his arrival. The master and disciple settled in under the tent and conversed for a moment, in complete privacy. No reference exists as to the content of their conversation. At the end of the day, the Panchen Lama and his entourage returned to Nakchu where the Dalai Lama followed on August 3. Along the way, an extremely large number of monks and lay people and an honor guard lined the road to the door of Shab monastery.[127] When the Dalai Lama entered the room where the Panchen Lama was waiting for him with the abbot Drubkhang Rinpoche, the two men made prostrations to the Thirteenth Dalai Lama and gave him offerings. The next day, members of the Panchen Lama's entourage made offerings to the Thirteenth Dalai Lama and invited him to a reception they had prepared in his honor. Did they have things to atone for?

On August 15, 1909, the Panchen Lama left for his monastery, escorted by officials while the Dalai Lama and his party headed for Lhasa.[128] Their meetings seemed to have taken place with no particular incident. Their relationship of master and disciple seemed to remain intact, despite the Panchen Lama's visit to India; so the case was closed, at least in appearance.

In mid-November 1909, the Dalai Lama returned to the Potala in Lhasa. In January 1910 he had to flee to India in the face of threats from Zhao Erfeng's troops, which were advancing from the east. While passing near Tashilhunpo, he could have planned to stop. According to Chinese sources, the Dalai Lama feared the Panchen Lama could not guarantee his security, which is why he did not visit Tashilhunpo.[129] Tibetan sources claim that the Thirteenth Dalai Lama invited the Panchen Lama to leave with him, but the master of Tashilhunpo refused the offer.[130] Neither of these two statements is mentioned in the biography of the Thirteenth Dalai Lama by Purchok Yongdzin Tulku (Phur lcog yongs 'dzin sprul sku).

The Qing emperor once again assumed the right to depose the Dalai Lama and proposed to proceed with another drawing of lots. In the meantime, he named the Panchen Lama provisionally to the seat of the Dalai Lama. The Panchen Lama categorically refused and advised Lian Yu, the imperial resident in Tibet, to return the title to the Dalai Lama.[131] In January 1911 the Panchen Lama, nevertheless, went to Lhasa (for the third time in his life, now aged twenty-eight). According to W. D. Shakabpa, he had no other choice, given the collaboration between his own officials and the Manchus.[132] Ya Hanzhang, on the other hand, claims the Panchen Lama accepted the invitation to come to Lhasa by Lian Yu, who is said to have insisted so much that the Tashilhunpo abbot could not refuse.[133]

Upon arriving in Lhasa, the Panchen Lama first stayed in the palace located on the roof of the Jokhang. He then moved into the Norbulingka, the Thirteenth Dalai Lama's summer palace. It is at that time that he is said to have committed a huge error in protocol by sitting on the throne of his spiritual master, ostensibly because there was no other seat prepared for him in the room.[134] The Panchen Lama is said to have multiplied such blunders by showing himself in public with Lian Yu, who accompanied him to society events and to the theater. During the butter lamp festival, the two men sat in their palanquins and went around in procession, as was the habit of the Thirteenth Dalai Lama, only to be booed by the population of Lhasa.[135]

Apparently Lian Yu had created the entire scheme. Some time later, the Panchen Lama confided to Macdonald that Lian Yu had deliberately prepared the room at the Norbulingka in such a way that he had been forced to sit on the throne of his spiritual master, while actually preferring to die than act against the interests of the Dalai Lama.[136] But, in the minds of the Tibetans in Lhasa, the error had been committed and a satirical song ran through the streets of the capital:

The bird known as magpie
Has a body that is half black and half white
After the great cuckoo bird arrives,
They will slowly be able to have discussions.

According to M. C. Goldstein, the magpie with black and white feathers represents the Panchen Lama, whose behavior was open to criticism. The cuckoo, considered by Tibetans as the king of birds, would be no other than the Dalai Lama.[137]

In March 1911 the Panchen Lama returned to his monastery in Tashilhunpo where he undertook the construction of a monumental statue of Maitreya, the Buddha of the future. Perhaps he felt ashamed of his recent conduct because in the Tibetan Buddhist tradition a long pilgrimage or a large scale offering (here, the statue of Maitreya) generally possessed expiatory qualities for a faithful penitent. Looking at available sources, it is difficult to determine whether the Panchen Lama had been manipulated by Lian Yu or whether he had acted willingly. Faced with the ambiguous conduct of his disciple, would the Dalai Lama remain indulgent towards him?

At the beginning of 1912, it seems that the Panchen Lama feared sanctions, because he sent two emissaries to give an oral message to Charles Bell, who retransmitted it to his government advising them that:

> Lhasa is mistrustful of the Panchen Lama and his administrators from Tashilhunpo. The administrators in Lhasa consider the Panchen Lama to be pro-Chinese. In addition, a garrison of three hundred Chinese soldiers has been set up in Shigatse. The Panchen Lama fears that if he opposes them, the Chinese will sack his monastery.[138]

In response to the Panchen Lama's request for advice from the British, Bell used the pretext of neutrality to avoid giving him an answer. Nevertheless, the master of Tashilhunpo continued to inform Bell of the development of the situation, explaining:

> The Tibetan soldiers arrived in Shigatse to fight the Chinese soldiers. I sent the head of the Muslims, the representative of the Nepalese and an emissary of Tashilhunpo to try to conciliate the two parties. The fight began suddenly and I left for Kangwa Dzong with a group of people. It lasted two or three days after my departure. And then, my representatives at Tashilhunpo, in accordance with my instructions, settled matters amicably between the parties, and the Chinese returned home.[139]

Confronted with the lack of cooperation from the British, the Panchen Lama invited Thubthob Namgyel, the maharaja from Sikkim with whom he had cultivated a friendship since his trip to India in 1905, to come visit him in Kangwa Dzong. He wanted to ask him to intercede on his behalf with the British, because he wished to import arms and ammunition from Calcutta to defend his monastery.[140]

When the Panchen Lama learned about the return of the Dalai Lama to Lhasa, which had been freed from the presence of Manchu soldiers, he hastened to undertake two related actions. First, he tried to convince the British to plead his case and that of his officials if the Dalai Lama were to punish the behavior they had exhibited during the Manchu occupation, as can be seen from the message that David Macdonald sent to the secretary of His Majesty's Government in India, after having received a call from the Panchen Lama:

> He now, therefore, earnestly hopes: that the British government will move the Dalai Lama not to take action against himself and his officers; that failing this, this government will guarantee for those whose lives are threatened safe conduct to India.[141]

In addition, the Panchen Lama asked that the British accord him an escort of fifty soldiers and asked them to be present when he went to meet his master.[142] But the British refused to reply to his requests. It seems clear that the Panchen Lama felt guilty about making blunders while in Lhasa. If, as he confirmed to David Macdonald, the Dalai Lama had nothing to reproach him for, he would not have needed to make such requests to the British.

The Panchen Lama's second move was to begin to approach his spiritual master similar to the way he had following his inappropriate trip to India. He thus sent an emissary to give homage and offerings to the Thirteenth Dalai Lama. Then he went personally to meet his spiritual master at Ralung monastery and once again made offerings. The master and disciple stayed in the monastery seven days, sharing meals and taking walks together. Their meetings, it is said, were cordial. The whole week, members of the Panchen Lama's entourage made prostrations before the Dalai Lama. According to W. D. Shakabpa they recognized the behavioral errors that they made during the Chinese occupation and sought to make amends.[143] Pleased with the outcome of the meeting, the Panchen Lama set off to return to his monastery. He stopped off in Gyeltsé on July 19, 1912. There he informed David Macdonald, the British trade agent, that his visit to Ralung had been a success and that all the disagreements had been ironed out. But he also said that the Dalai Lama had warned the officials from Tashilhunpo against repeating their unacceptable actions.[144]

It is true that the Panchen Lama seems to have lacked good judgment both when he accepted an invitation to India by the British invaders, and again when in Lhasa he associated with Lian Yu, the Manchu imperial resident during the Dalai Lama's exile. Should such transgressions be put down to political immaturity (he was twenty-two while in India and twenty-eight in Lhasa)? It does seem obvious that the Manchus and the British were manipulating the Panchen Lama heavily to their advantage, and then in an instant did not hesitate to abandon his calls for help once the Dalai Lama began moving closer towards British India. By proposing to the Panchen Lama that he take the place of the Dalai Lama each time the Tibetan leader went into exile, the Manchus played the disciple off against the master. Since the Dalai Lama had left the country without naming a true regent, their game was much easier.[145] Indeed, the head of the Gélukpa school, the guardian of the Ganden throne that the Dalai Lama had designated to rule affairs in his absence, had no experience whatsoever in political matters.

Beyond appearances and international stakes, the amicable outcome of the meetings in Ralung, described by W. D. Shakabpa as well as in the biography of the Thirteenth Dalai Lama by Purchok, shows once again that the master administered no punishment to the Panchen Lama. However, other means would enable him to show his disapproval.

It seems, in effect, that the Thirteenth Dalai Lama did not try to humor his disciple. According to Kachen Lozang Döndrub, a monk at Tashilhunpo during the time of the Ninth Panchen Lama, and Dakpo Rinpoche, a monk from Drépung monastery, the prelate, who was a keen enthusiast of debating, often invited skilled debate masters to Tashilhunpo. This is how Coné, who was a *géshé* (learned teacher), and Samlo, a master of the Labrang trashikhyil monastery in Amdo, as well as Özer Dorjé, former abbot of the Gomang college of Drépung, would come regularly to teach at Tashilhunpo. The Panchen Lama had built a preferential relationship with Özer Dorjé, whose great erudition he admired. He wished that Özer Dorjé would spend some time at Tashilhunpo, but completely unexpectedly, the Thirteenth Dalai Lama called the debate master to Lhasa.[146] After this scheduling issue, the Panchen Lama is said to have harbored some bitterness towards the Dalai Lama.

The Panchen Lama then requested teachings from his master, but the Thirteenth Dalai Lama rejected his request saying he should try asking again the following autumn. A short time later, the Dalai Lama entered a meditative retreat for three years. At the end of his three-year retreat, on March 17, 1918, the Panchen Lama requested authorization from the Dalai Lama to undertake pilgrimages to Nepal, Kailash, and Tsari. Once more the reply was negative.[147]

If, in actual fact, the Panchen Lama's pretext was to expiate past faults, he had decided on his pilgrimage after the new tax laws for Tashilhunpo outlined in the 1917 decree took effect. It turns out that the Dalai Lama, while not judging on mere intent, held doubts regarding the motivation of his disciple and his close associates, even though the Panchen Lama's letter to the Dalai Lama confirms that his construction of the Maitreya statue did represent expiatory goals. In accordance with the Tibetan Buddhist tradition, the Panchen Lama had erected this statue to accumulate positive karma destined to counteract his past behavior, cause for negative karma. His master encouraged him in this undertaking rather than authorizing him to go on pilgrimage in Nepal. In appearance, the relationship of master and disciple between the two men seemed strong. But, by his refusal, the Dalai Lama showed that he suspected that the Panchen Lama was using the pretext of a simple pilgrimage to Nepal to flee Tibet and avoid the new tax.

The next year, the Panchen Lama again requested teachings from the Thirteenth Dalai Lama, who again refused him. The Panchen Lama then proposed that the Thirteenth Dalai Lama come to Tashilhunpo to bless the just-completed Maitreya statue, but the spiritual and temporal leader of Tibet declined the invitation. In fact, according to the British, the Panchen Lama wished to speak to the Dalai Lama about the extraordinary tax that was recently imposed on his lands.[148] Finally, on November 21, 1919, the Dalai Lama informed the Panchen Lama that he would receive him.[149]

According to Purchok's biography of the Thirteenth Dalai Lama, in November 1919 the Panchen Lama set out for Lhasa. On November 21, twelve riders met him as an escort. Next the officials of the Tibetan government welcomed him in Kyitseluding. And finally, the Panchen Lama arrived at the Norbulingka where he bowed before the Dalai Lama. The master and disciple rejoiced at their reunion in the Gépèl Kangzang palace. The Panchen Lama presented the mandala offering and offerings of the "Three Jewels" to his spiritual master.[150] The officials of the fourth rank who had accompanied him followed suit, honoring the Dalai Lama in turn. Shortly afterwards, the Dalai Lama and the Panchen Lama attended a military parade of 350 soldiers.

In the days that followed, the two men met often. They spoke about religion, politics, and shared meals together.[151] However, nothing indicates that they brought up the thorny issue of the Tashilhunpo taxes during their meetings. On February 10, 1920, the Panchen Lama had one last visit with the Dalai Lama before leaving the Tibetan capital. He made another mandala offering and presented offerings of the "Three Jewels." After having a last meal together and a long discussion, the Dalai Lama handed the Panchen Lama a salutation scarf along with some gifts. On his return to Tashilhunpo, the Panchen Lama was escorted by 281 soldiers. At Kyitseluding, a chamberlain presented him with a salutation scarf and welcomed him at Gampasharmé.[152]

Once again, it seems that the Thirteenth Dalai Lama had forced himself to maintain appearances while underlining again the unacceptable behavior of some officials from Tashilhunpo. It is difficult to say whether the organization of a military parade of soldiers and the soldiers sent to escort the prelate home was meant to enhance the prestige of the Panchen Lama, to reassure him, or to intimidate him.

While it is clear that the Panchen Lama took initiatives liable to tarnish his relationship with the Thirteenth Dalai Lama, in the tradition of Tibetan Buddhism, it is inconceivable that master and disciple be in conflict, because this would give both of them serious karmic consequences. Thus, wouldn't the Panchen Lama and the Dalai Lama take pains to pass the blame to their respective associates, for acts that could otherwise create disharmony between them? At this level of study, it is difficult to establish what part of the responsibility lies on their respective entourages, but the ambitions of those close to the Panchen Lama appear in broad daylight further down the road. If, in the Tibetan Buddhist tradition, a dispute between "ordinary" master and disciple were already serious, a quarrel between the Dalai Lama and the Panchen Lama would put into doubt the legitimacy of their lineages and their complementarity. Moreover, since the Thirteenth Dalai Lama had recognized Samdrub Gyatso as the Ninth Panchen Lama, it would be practically impossible for him to renounce the Panchen Lama without discrediting himself. With the moral obligation to safeguard their relationship at all costs, so as not to compromise the future of their respective lineages, the Dalai Lama and the Panchen Lama would use Buddhist rituals at their disposal for one to express discontent and for the other his remorse.

If the Ninth Panchen Lama and the Thirteenth Dalai Lama stayed on personal good terms in spite of everything, then logically it is impossible to affirm, as certain Western and Chinese authors have hastily done, whether the cause of the Panchen Lama's departure lay in the degradation of their relationship.

It is clear that the inflexible attitude of the Panchen Lama and that of the members of his administration concerning the extraordinary tax put the Thirteenth Dalai Lama and the Tashilhunpo abbot in difficulty. Did this problem affect the master-disciple relationship that bonded them? In the Tibetan Buddhist tradition, the disciple owes absolute devotion to his spiritual master, and in no case should he criticize him or see his faults. What happens, then, in this precise case? The correspondence between the two prelates exchanged after the Panchen Lama's departure reveals their feelings on this subject. In the letter left at his monastery just before his flight from Tibet in 1923, the Panchen Lama wrote:

> His Holiness has always shown me kindness. The investigating officers listened to the advice of evil-minded persons and made it very difficult for His Holiness to grant my requests.[153]

In response, on January 26, 1924, the Dalai Lama wrote:

> As regards the free supplies and transport asked for from the subjects of the Tashilhunpo government,[154] they have agreed to supply the same and the demands are in accordance with the existing agreements. I have therefore issued orders that these should be complied with and there is no cause for complaint. The investigating officers have not shown any favour to any party by myself, especially as we are both on most friendly terms. In connection with the payment of one fourth of the total military expenditure in Tibet, it may be mentioned that it is in accordance with former custom, but as the Prime Minister did not make the payment for a number of years, the amount accumulated and could not be paid at once ... This time, the Tashi Lama has gone secretly on the pretext that the two things mentioned above caused him trouble and listened to the advice of evil persons.[155]

In July 1924, the Panchen Lama replied:

> Although it is impossible for Your Holiness to entertain any ill intentions toward me, being teacher and pupil, yet as I had written to Your Holiness many times before, some of the ignorant and mischievous officials of Your Holiness who have an axe to grind have been creating estrangement and inconvenience between us ... Although I tried many times to obtain a personal interview so as to lay before Your Holiness the real state of affairs as it is in my mind and obtain Your Holiness's true advice as to what is the best thing to be done to help towards paying this new army expenditure tax. This again the abovementioned ill-minded officials of Your Holiness with the purpose of frustrating amicable settlement concocted many difficulties in the way.[156]

To conclude, two years later, on June 12, 1926, the Dalai Lama went further:

> You say, and I think so, too, that some evil-minded subordinate, who did not wish that the teacher and pupil should remain on good terms, must have reported against and caused trouble for Labrang, that it was not convenient for you to come and lay your grievances before me in person, to clear my mind and take my advice ... In order to make permanent the secular and religious rule of Tibet, it was found expedient to assess and collect extra taxes. This measure has affected all the landlords, the Government and the monasteries—a fact which is well known to you—and it was not especially adopted in order to put the Labrang into trouble. It is no new thing for a Government to call for reports from its subordinates with regards to new taxation. These reports the subordinates base on their experience. If anyone has said anything untoward between the teacher and the pupil I would not have taken notice of it. Whatever cause for complaint the Labrang might have, we could have gone into it at our leisure. But, instead you have left suddenly without any reason. It is not possible that you could have become disloyal to me. In all probability you have been swayed by the reports of one or two servants, who do not understand things.[157]

Upon reading these excerpts, it is clear that the two prelates were trying to save appearances at all costs while conforming to Buddhist principles. This is why, in order to safeguard their relationship, the Panchen Lama took pains to clear the Thirteenth Dalai Lama and to accuse the government officials in Lhasa of all wrongdoing. At the same time, adopting a paternalistic attitude, the Dalai Lama himself does his utmost to preserve the dignity of the Panchen Lama and to blame his associates while also defending his own government.

The true reasons that pushed the Panchen Lama to leave Tibet remain obscure. The prelate affirmed that he left to seek the necessary funds to pay the extraordinary tax. But the sanctions that the Tibetan government laid on him for his refusal to pay the tax certainly had a determining effect on his decision. We must thus question whether the Panchen Lama's departure was planned in advance (which would make the first hypothesis plausible) or was caused by fear (which would validate the second).

PREMEDITATED DEPARTURE OR HURRIED FLIGHT?

In order to try to understand the motives behind the Panchen Lama's departure, I began by studying a document originating from the Tibetan government. This piece of writing, conserved at the Library of Tibetan Works and Archives (LTWA) in Dharamsala in northern India, is a copy of a poster, which, according to Tashi Tsering, historian and director of the Amnye Machen Institute in Dharamsala, would have been posted on the surrounding wall of Tashilhunpo monastery shortly after the departure of the Panchen Lama. It is rectangular in form (108 cm x 54 cm) and contains thirty-four lines. It lacks a date, signature, and seal, making its authentication debatable. It is written in the spoken language used by the inhabitants of the province of Tsang in Tibetan cursive calligraphy. Once more, members of Tashi Tsering's research team kindly transcribed this document into printed characters so that I could use it. Here are the most significant passages:

> The Panchen Lama has left in secret towards the north of Tibet. A hundred or so armed monks have fled with him ... Certain people say that, without a doubt, the Panchen Lama could no longer stand the Tibetan government....
>
> Others say: "There is another reason." When the Dalai Lama left for China, Mongolia, and India, the Panchen Lama and Lozang, his favorite, offered gifts to the two Manchu imperial residents in Tibet, Lian Yu[158] and Zhang Yintang,[159] and requested the Manchu emperor to hand the spiritual and temporal powers of Tibet to the Panchen Lama. A favorite of the Tashi Lama called Tségrön went to Beijing in China. Everyone knows that he informed all the foreign representatives. It is said, therefore, that [the Panchen Lama] left in secret because he felt guilty and feared that an investigation [would] be done by the Tibetan government. When the Dalai Lama went to India, Lian Yu invited the Tashi Lama to come to Lhasa. There, all of the Dalai Lama's thrones had been thrown out and replaced by those of the Tashi Lama. Seeing this, the monks and lay people were shocked and cried torrents of tears....
>
> The Tashi Lama's father, Rimshi Tadrin la and other ministers took on bad behavior. After the father Tadrin la was arrested and put in prison in Lhatsé, the Tashi Lama wrote a sealed letter in which the following phrase was written: "Must kill." Although the Tibetan government received this document, no investigation was undertaken.
>
> According to the Buddhist tradition, disciples must respect their masters from whom they have requested teachings. This law must not be violated. The Tashi Lama did not piously respect the Dalai Lama Rinpoche. Secretly fleeing, the Tashi Lama, his ministers, and his servants have trespassed religious discipline and civil law....
>
> Some say that the Tibetan government should examine all these reasons. Others say that, recently, when civil war erupted in Tibet, the private residence of Tashilhunpo did not contribute its payment for the soldiers' salaries. [The Tibetan government] pushed it to do so, but the Ninth Panchen Lama did not do it. This is why, without a doubt, [the Panchen Lama] left in secret.

Reading this text, the predominant feeling is that the Panchen Lama fled. While this text clearly represents an anti-Panchen Lama perspective that may or may not have been widespread, there were other opinions more favorable to the Panchen Lama.

For instance, we can look at the vocabulary used to describe the departure of the Panchen Lama in original and secondary sources. In the text just presented here, the author uses the term "left secretly" (*sangpheb*) twice and "left in secret" (*sangcölcé*) twice. In his view, Purchok, the biographer of the Thirteenth Dalai

Lama, used the expression "left towards China as if he were fleeing" (*lobur cölthab tagur gyacok cibgyurdzé*). In a later Tibetan study, Shakabpa used the phrasing "left secretly" (*sangphep*). In Tibet, many levels of language (ordinary and honorific) are used depending on the social rank that each possesses regarding the person they are speaking with. For example, a religious person will readily use the verb *cibgyurdzé* (introducing the notion of a trip on horseback) or less frequently the verb *phep* to designate trips by a fellow monk. As for lay people, such as members of the Tibetan government and historians, they are obliged to use the honorific verb of movement *phep*, which designates the voyage of a great religious master. So, the choice of the verbs *cibgyurdzé* and *phep* to describe the departure of the Panchen Lama does not indicate a value judgment on the part of the Tibetan authors, because they are used in a systematic way. In both cases they mean "leave." However the addition of adverbs "hastily" or "secretly" changes the meaning.

In the British documents contemporary to the event that translate the correspondence between the Ninth Panchen Lama and the Thirteenth Dalai Lama, the authors specify in the case of the disciple: "I am leaving Tashilhunpo for a short period" and that of the master: "The Panchen Lama has gone secretly," "you departed secretly," "you have left your monastery," and "you have left Shigatse." Moreover, the terms "secret departure," "your departure," and "run away" appear in the vocabulary of the Thirteenth Dalai Lama translated by the English. Finally, in the Chinese administrative sources at that time we see the expression: "The Panchen Lama intends to go to China" (*Banchan da shi ni jiang lai Hua*). Examining the vocabulary used by the different actors, it seems that the expression "leave secretly" is the most frequently used.

After having studied the form of the original sources, we can move on to their content. The letter that the Panchen Lama left at his monastery just before his departure in 1923 and that which he wrote to the Thirteenth Dalai Lama in July 1924 show that he felt the dispute between the Tashilhunpo administration and the Tibetan government in Lhasa was insoluble. Indeed, in his own phrasing in two separate instances:

> With regard to the troubles of the Tashilhunpo Government and their subjects, I have submitted representations to His Holiness the Dalai Lama on several occasions, but my requests have not been granted.[160]

> Your Holiness informed me that even to have just a personal interview would place both the teacher and the pupil in an awkward position. Therefore not knowing what to do, leaving a note to Your Holiness asking for permission to be transmitted by the Shigatse-Chizong, I set forth and I did not ask for permission beforehand as it might again make things awkward and this is the real reason and please do not be offended with me.[161]

It seems that the only solution left for the Panchen Lama was to leave Tibet. Equally, it seems that he had methodically organized his departure, based on the following excerpt from the letter he left behind for the attention of the Thirteenth Dalai Lama when he departed from his monastery:

> I may state here once and for all that I have no desire to do anything against the wishes of His Holiness the Dalai Lama or that will be injurious to our prestige. The letter which I have addressed to His Holiness should be at once forwarded, so as to make matters clear to him.[162]

Such a message could unlikely have been written in haste, since the Panchen Lama specified that he was "leaving Tashilhunpo for a short period." He further took care to organize the operations of his monastery in his absence:

> After due consideration I have appointed the Acting Prime Minister and the Abbots of the four Colleges to carry on the administration during my absence:[163] First of all, you should see that the customary ceremonies are performed in the Tashilhunpo and other monasteries as usual. You should also see that the Lamas of the different monasteries receive their rations; and that the monks study all the religious books and preach the religion, and that they do not neglect the subject of disputation; and above all, you should see that all the monastic rules are duly observed. Finally, you should discharge your duties faithfully and treat the poor subjects and monks with all consideration and help them in every way possible. You should keep careful accounts of all receipts and expenditure from land tenure, etc., and apply the balance for the observance of religious ceremonies. You should carry on your duties appertaining to the spiritual and temporal powers after due consultations; but if you cannot decide any big question, you should refer the matter to me for orders. You should discharge the duties of your responsible position without fail and leave nothing undone. I hereby command all the monks and laymen, who are subjects of the Tashilhunpo Government, to obey the orders of the Acting Prime Minister and Council and discharge theirs duties faithfully. Let all noblemen and peasants bear these instructions in mind and act accordingly.[164]

Indeed, it is likely that the Panchen Lama had time to prepare his departure in the sense that, at that time, it did not seem as if he was directly threatened, at least if we believe the contents of a letter that the Thirteenth Dalai Lama sent him in January 1924:

> I have not once used any force to exact the payment. On the other hand, out of compassion, I agreed that the payment should be spread over several years and reduced the amount as much as I could. This fact is known to all the wise men.

Nonetheless, in reading another passage of this letter it seems that the Thirteenth Dalai Lama was annoyed at not having been consulted by his disciple and that he reproached him for leaving Tibet:

> Having heard of your secret departure I have been deeply grieved at the news because our relations had been friendly and I was your teacher. Remembering the fact that you and I were born as a father and son (i.e., teacher and disciple), it is not right for me to treat you just as I pleased; but there is a custom prevailing among the high-class people that the elder should advise the younger. You did not consult me in the matter and I do not know the real reasons for your departure and what the end will be ... But you must have been misled by your followers who had previously caused mischief. As sins cannot be washed away by water and mental sorrow cannot be removed by the hands, why are you disappointed? ... I request you to think over the conversation we had at our previous meeting; and if you read the correspondence that has passed between us, you will understand everything. You have written to me frequently saying that there is no other protector to whom you can go for assistance and protection. In view of the correspondence and the conversation we had at our meeting, it is not understood why you departed secretly unless you have found yourself at fault....
>
> It is not understood why you have left your monastery in which you should now be sitting in meditation. You seem to have forgotten the sacred history of your predecessors and wandered away to a desert where there are no people—like a butterfly that is attracted by the lamp light—and thus bringing trouble to yourself. Such conduct does not do credit to your predecessors and if you had only taken the trouble to consult your teacher "Lhopa," he would have given you sound advice. But you did not consult him and ran away with your sinful companions who resemble elephants and followed the wrong path. Although you are a holy person, if the fruits of your deed ripen, there is no doubt that you will suffer great hardships ... It is mentioned in many religious books that you and I and all the holy persons should strive to work for the benefit of all living beings. It is difficult to believe that a person who thinks of himself only and who is not freed from the three sins [i.e., anger, pride, and ignorance] should be regarded as a Lama or Buddha. As selfishness is a great evil in this world, the wisest course to adopt is to repent and turn back from the wrong path.[165]

The Thirteenth Dalai Lama thus reproached the Panchen Lama for his stratagem of taking flight, ironically a stratagem that he himself had used when faced with serious difficulties both in 1904 and 1910.

We see that lacking arguments, the Dalai Lama calls on the precepts of Tibetan Buddhist tradition to bring his disciple back onto the path to his monastery. Yet the Panchen Lama had requested private interviews with his master only to be refused, for which he claimed the Lhasa incarnation had been badly advised by his officials. So, who are we to believe? The master who reproaches his disciple for not having consulted him? Or the disciple who claims that his demands for meetings were rejected? The letter of the Dalai Lama contains perhaps an element of response to these questions. By sending Lungshar, the finance minister, to the Panchen Lama to persuade him to return to Shigatse, the Dalai Lama chose a competent spokesperson to deal with the recalcitrant prelate about the tax dispute. However, when we learn that Lungshar was accompanied by one thousand soldiers, it puts into doubt the peaceful intentions of the Dalai Lama and of the Tibetan government.[166] On the other hand, the fact that the Panchen Lama had "Lungshar hot on his heels" clearly describes a flight.

The key to the enigma resides, perhaps, in the testimony of the late Kachen Jangpa Thubten, who, at the time, was a monk at Tashilhunpo. By his account, in the autumn of 1923, the Panchen Lama sent an offering of incense to the Thirteenth Dalai Lama. The master and the disciple would have understood each other: *pö*, the Tibetan term meaning "incense," also means "change of residence." In return, the Dalai Lama is said to have offered a white horse to the Panchen Lama. In this way he was implicitly giving his authorization to leave Tibet.[167] We should point out that the monastery of Kumbum has kept a stuffed white horse, which is supposedly the one which the Dalai Lama had offered to the Panchen Lama and which he took when leaving Tibet. Moreover, according to Jangpa Thubten, on the evening of the Panchen Lama's departure, the Dalai Lama is said to have had the monks in Lhasa organize a great offering ceremony. In his entourage, no one knew the reason why. Thus we might conclude that the Dalai Lama was aware of the Panchen Lama's departure. But, if he had known, it would have been impossible to have publicly given his opinion since it would have discredited the members of his own government.

The most appropriate expression to describe the action of the Panchen Lama at dawn on December 22, 1923, seems to be a "premeditated secret departure." It is yet to be determined whether it was the Panchen Lama himself or his associates who made the decision to leave. As a general rule, in the Tibetan Buddhist tradition, a spiritual master chooses his journeys according to requests of a religious nature that he might receive, knowing that the individual or the monastery inviting him would take charge of his travel expenses. In this case, the Panchen Lama had received no invitation from abroad. This would, therefore, seem more like a decision made by his entourage.

Would the Panchen Lama have accepted the measures of his entourage in order to solicit possible donors and raise enough funds to pay the extraordinary tax or to escape imminent sanctions by the Tibetan government, or both?

At present, it is difficult to respond to that question. Chapters 3 and 4 examine the activities undertaken by the Panchen Lama during his exile, which can perhaps provide elements of a response. Whether the Dalai Lama was informed or not, it is more probable that the main reason for the Panchen Lama's departure lies in the dispute between Tashilhunpo and the Tibetan government concerning the extraordinary tax imposed on the Panchen Lama's monastery. The basis for the abbot's departure probably does not lie in a supposed quarrel between himself and the Dalai Lama because, until the end, the two prelates took pains to preserve their master-disciple relationship and consistently blamed each other's entourage for the problems that emerged. Can we affirm, as some Indian,

American, and Chinese authors have done, that the Panchen Lama had a plan to create a genuinely independent Tsang (with the help of the Chinese or others), the existence of which would harm Tibet's cohesion?[168] It is hard to say at this point, but we will look at this question in the following chapters.

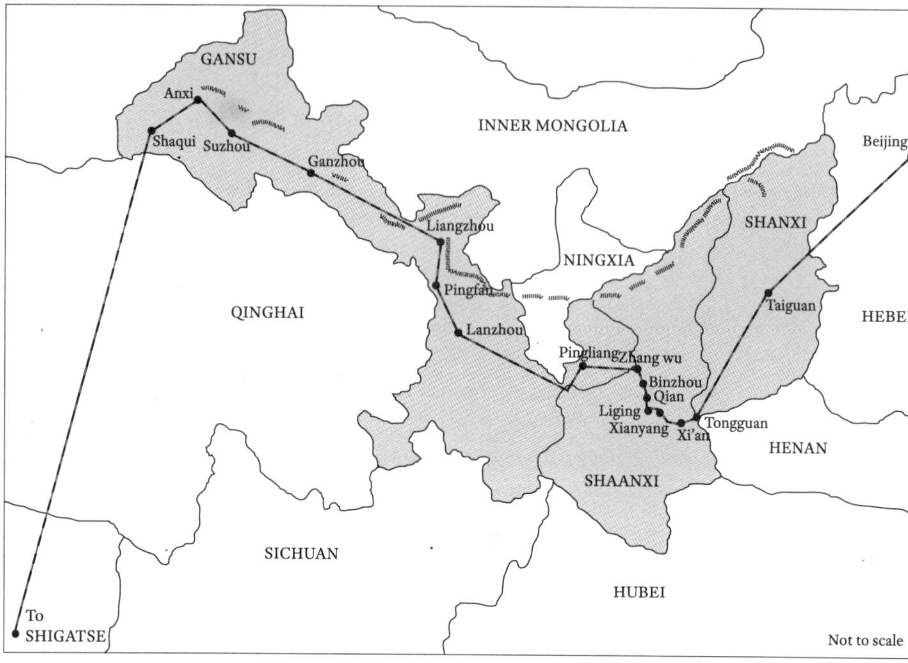

Route of Panchen Lama from Shigatse to Beijing (1923–25)

PART TWO

CHINA
(1924–1935)

The Panchen Lama headed east after leaving Shigatse in 1923. In Inner Mongolia and China, he continued his religious activities. He was well received by the Mongolian and Chinese Buddhist world, especially since he was the guardian of numerous esoteric teachings. He was thus able to develop chaplain-donor relationships not only with Mongol princes, but also with warlords and members of the Republican government. These encounters initiated the Panchen Lama into politics. The prelate adopted Sun Yat-sen's "Three Principles of the People" and accepted a mission to spread Chinese Republican values in Inner Mongolia and on the Sino-Tibetan border. In return, he expected China to help him put into place a program he had developed for the modernization of Tibet.

3

RELIGIOUS AFFAIRS

When the Panchen Lama arrived in China, Buddhism was enjoying a revival in the center and south, while it seemed moribund in the north. The lineage of esoteric teachings of which the abbot of Tashilhunpo was the holder captured the interest of an inner circle of initiates who desired to revive Chinese Tantric Buddhism, which had been lost for years.

Many had been discouraged from entering monastic orders during the period 1911–28. The local reality showed that a combined effect of three factors was responsible for this. The first of these factors was the strict laws put in place by the government in the north, notably, stricter control on the activities and goods of the monasteries. The second factor was the climate of violence imposed by the warlords, whose soldiers did not hesitate to occupy abandoned monasteries. And, the third one involved the hostility of public opinion caused by the behavior of certain, little-educated monks with loose morals.[1] It seems this phenomenon was particularly centered in northern China. Illustrating this decay are H. Welch's photos in his work from that time showing dilapidated and abandoned monasteries. Yet he also points out that between 1864 and 1912, groups of lay Buddhists, who had stayed active in the region of Jiangsu until the installation of the Republican government, had undertaken repairs and renovation of Buddhist places of worship that had been destroyed by the Taiping rebellion in Nanjing and its surroundings.[2]

STATE OF BUDDHISM IN CHINA (EARLY 1900s)

Yang Wenhui, a lay Buddhist, is considered the main initiator of the Buddhist monastic renaissance that began at the end of the Qing, some of which Welch captured in his photographs. Yang's activities ranged from republishing Buddhist texts to the creation of a school for monks, to the opening of Buddhist associations.[3] However, the monastic community itself did not remain inactive. The restrictive measures taken by the Chinese government towards monks, particularly a requirement to register with the Department of the Interior, forced some of them to change their behavior. Some created schools within their monastery where classes in Chinese writing, math, philosophy, and even English were taught to the monks. This way they cut short the northern government's plan to transform the majority of monasteries into public schools and thus managed to avoid the seizure of their monasteries' goods. Others, responding to criticism, founded seminaries that gave more rigorous religious teaching. Seventy-one seminaries were opened in the Chinese Republic from 1911 to 1928, and in 1936, forty-five were still active. Yet their function seems to have remained marginal since only a total of seventy-five hundred students attended.[4]

Under pressure from Chinese public opinion, a reformation movement in monastic life was born. At the head, the monk Taixu (1889–1947) initiated a failed attempt to form a national Buddhist association, following which lay people and clergy opened three short-lived associations, but their dissolution occurred shortly after their creation. Additionally, Taixu had the desire to reform the monastic community, since he judged the behavior of the monks to be the origin of the recent decline in Chinese Buddhism. Between 1915 and 1947, he wrote up no less than seven versions of a proposal to reorganize the community of monks, known as the Sangha. And yet none of them was adopted or applied by those concerned.[5]

After its foundation in Nanjing, the Republican government pronounced itself in favor of better control and heightened protection of monastic property, promulgating laws to this effect in January and then in December 1929. It obliged each abbot to declare his monastery's goods to the authorities and to submit all transfers of capital, patrimony, and so forth for government approval. The government believed that in this way it could protect the monasteries against unscrupulous individuals' greed by ensuring that everything belonged to the monastic institution rather than to the abbot. In case of fraud, the government claimed the right to depose the abbot.[6] Curiously, the government took no measures to control ordinations. The laws put into effect by the Republican government were reinforced in 1931 and confirmed in 1933 by Chiang Kai-shek (1887–1975), who forbade armed soldiers and warlords to lodge in the monasteries.[7] Nevertheless, these laws must not have been strictly applied in northern China, since John Blofeld witnessed, as late as 1931–32, Feng Yuxiang soldiers staying in monasteries.[8]

The softening of the Republican government's policies regarding Buddhism, the incapacity of monks to create a national congregation, and the failure of reformers favored the development of associations by Buddhist lay people. These associations, which appeared especially in the region of Nanjing, gave monks the funds they needed to restore monasteries. The associations participated in charity causes such as the construction of hospitals for orphans, but one of their main missions was the printing and distribution of Buddhist texts. With this aim, these Buddhist associations undertook the restoration of the printing presses that had been attacked by the Taiping. Then they researched Buddhist texts in what remained of the monasteries' private libraries. In this way, the printing and distribution of Buddhist texts in the 1930s had actually become a prosperous activity, which, from Nanjing and the surrounding region, enabled Buddhism to extend throughout central and southern China. Numerous printing presses specialized in this activity. All varieties of Chinese Buddhism were soon represented, such as the schools of Tiantai, Huayan, and Lü, where the study of texts predominated, as well as those that emphasized meditative practices, including the school of Chan for which meditation was the central practice and the Pure Land (Jingtu) school whose adepts gave priority to recitation in the name of the Buddha Amitābha.[9] Buddhism thus benefited from a resurgence of interest in central and southern China.[10]

At the beginning of the twentieth century, lay Buddhists, accompanied by monks, had gone to Japan to study Tantric Buddhism with the masters of the Shingon school in order to renew this tradition, which had been lost in China. Upon their return, they contributed to the diffusion of Buddhism in Japan and China. Japanese masters and monks were invited to Republican China and certain ones earned much success and esteem. But while they founded a dozen monasteries in Shanghai, their action did not have widespread impact.

Other Chinese lay Buddhists became interested in the esoteric path taught by the Tibetan masters with the same aim of reviving Chinese Tantric Buddhism. Since the monks residing in the Tibetan monasteries in Beijing in the Palace of Eternal Harmony (*Yonghe gong*) and the Yellow Temple (*Huang si*) seemed lax in their respect for monastic discipline and appeared to have abandoned the transmission of the Tantric texts, these lay Chinese Buddhists felt the necessity to invite Tibetan masters to China. This is how, according to Fafang, a Chinese monk and disciple of Taixu, the Tibetan masters first came to China in the middle of the 1920s.[11] For instance, the abbot of Riwoché monastery in Amdo, the Gara Lama, also known as Nuona Lama in Chinese literature (1865-1936), arrived in Beijing in February 1924, but his dubious reputation preceded him. He was said to have escaped from prison in Lhasa where he had been held five years for unclear reasons.[12] That same year, Köncho Chungné (1883–1944), holder of a *géshé* degree, went to Beijing after the Thirteenth Dalai Lama had named him abbot of the Palace of Eternal Harmony.[13] Finally, Géshé Dorjé Tsipa (Duojie Jueba), a monk from the Kham region who had studied many years in Lhasa before going to teach in Mongolia, traveled to Beijing in 1925.[14]

Responding to the requests of lay Buddhists, the Panchen Lama visited Beijing in 1925, after which he devoted much of his time and energy to religious activities. Although it is tempting to attribute an "angelic" role to the Tibetan masters, rigorous analysis of the religious activities of a classic *tulku* is essential for an understanding of the relationship of chaplain to donor, a determinant characteristic of Tibetan Buddhism.[15] In Tibetan texts, this relationship is designated by the expression *chöyön* (or *yönchö*), a contracted form of the two terms *chöné* and *yöndag*. *Chöné* (S. *dānapati*) literally means "donor."

In the Buddhist tradition, it is said that to obtain enlightenment, one must accumulate wisdom and merit. The accumulation of wisdom means developing the comprehension of the vacuity of all things, while the accumulation of merit is accomplished by the regular practice of donations, offerings, and by developing such qualities as love, compassion, generosity, ethics, patience, and so forth.

Buddhists, who try to live their lives according to the instructions left by Buddha Śākyamuni, put all their trust—the expression being "to take refuge"—in the "Three Jewels" (Buddha, Dharma, and Sangha), which they venerate. They compare Buddha to a doctor who is capable of saving everyone from sickness and suffering, whereas the Dharma (the teachings of Buddha) is linked to the treatment prescribed by a doctor, and the Sangha (the community of nuns and monks) represent the nurses who administer the sick with care and affection. According to Buddhists, making offerings to the Three Jewels is thus extremely beneficial. The disciples who adhere to this practice accumulate great merit and significantly increase their chances of attaining enlightenment.

In Buddhism, there are many ways to make an offering to Buddha. In general, disciples arrange a small altar in their homes where they place a representation of Buddha, either a statue or a painting. There each day they place seven traditional offerings consisting of a cup of water, some food, flowers, incense, perfume, a lit candle (that corresponds to the offering of light), and a little bell (representing the offering of music.) Ordinarily, Tibetan Buddhists symbolize these offerings by seven copper bowls that they fill with water in the morning and empty at night. Other types of offerings are providing for the material needs of monks and nuns or helping in the construction of monastic residences to support the religious community in their efforts.

In actual fact, devotees consider that from among the Three Jewels, the Dharma is the most important since only through its application can disciples liberate themselves from samsara (the cycle of conditioned existence), and thus achieve enlightenment. Contributing to the printing or publishing of Buddhist texts or being associated with a Buddhist teaching organization are acts which, when done with the proper motivation, would qualify as significant offerings to the Dharma.

According to Buddhists, giving gifts to a lama to facilitate his Dharma teaching under the best possible conditions is an even higher offering. We must remember that the sole purpose of the lama in Tibetan Buddhism is to liberate all beings from suffering and to lead them to full enlightenment. Without the lama, a worthy ambassador of the Buddhas in the phenomenal world, there is no Dharma. Thus, making an offering to a lama means in essence honoring the Dharma. Continued over time, this act is doubly interesting. On the one hand, it allows the lama to overcome material constraints and so devote his life to "turning the Wheel of Dharma," that is, to teaching the doctrine and making it accessible, and on the other hand, it gives disciples the opportunity to practice their generosity and accumulate much merit. If their means do not allow them to offer material donations to their lama, the disciples also have the possibility of serving and/or protecting him. In any case, they must respect their teacher and act according to the instructions of the Dharma that the lama teaches. Of course, they are free to decide the level and the frequency of their donations. They only give donations to the lama they feel gives teachings that benefit the community and enable them to fight against their own suffering. If the teachings given by a lama do not, or no longer, correspond to the disciples' expectations, the disciples are free to leave. In doing so, they deprive the lama of their donations, which could force him to end his religious activities. When a lama gives a high quality teaching and his disciples feel its worth, and when on top of that he behaves in conformity with the words of Buddha that he teaches, then the donations flow and his monastery will have a prosperous period.

The main mission of the lama is to teach the Dharma, expecting nothing in return. The disciple is free to make offerings to help with the spread of the doctrine to help alleviate suffering in the world, and thus accumulate merit with a view to reaching enlightenment. This being the case, the disciple enters the role of donor when the lama who teaches the Dharma accepts the donations and finds himself chaplain. When circumstances require, the disciple must do all he can to protect the Dharma, and thus the lama as well. In an extreme case, if the donor is a head of state that uses force to protect the chaplain, he enters a category called "universal monarchs" (S. *cakravartin,* lit. "master of the wheel") and commits to everything that will "turn the wheel of Dharma" to maintain the equilibrium of the world (Tib. *korlö gyurwe gyelpo*).

The great monastic entities that developed in Tibet would never have seen the light of day without the help of local aristocrats who created a chaplain-donor bond with the most famous lama of their region. Because of this, each monastery in Tibet has its protector(s). A wealthy donor participates in the foundation of a monastery by giving, for example, a part of his lands to the lama. Later, the donor continues to give offerings, particularly during the major Buddhist ceremonies that occur annually. In return, the monks of the monastery perform rituals and recite prayers for the benefit of the donor's family, as well as remembering births and deaths as they arise.

Thus, in Tibetan Buddhism the chaplain-donor relationship must be considered in addition to the classic relationship between master and disciple.

THE PANCHEN LAMA'S RELIGIOUS ACTIVITIES

During his fourteen years in exile in China, the Panchen Lama developed three types of religious activities. He gave Buddhist teachings and initiations, he opened offices and philosophically oriented schools, and he participated actively in the search for the reincarnation of the Thirteenth Dalai Lama. Two hagiographies enumerate the Tantric initiations the Panchen Lama gave to the public. Their large number (nineteen) does not necessarily mean that the Panchen Lama gave them more importance than standard teachings; it simply confirms that their more spectacular nature led to better publicity. The nineteen ceremonies consisted of nine Kālacakra[16] and nine long life initiations (five Amitāyus,[17] three Tārā,[18] and one uncertain), as well as one Bhaiṣajyaguru initiation.[19] Our sources also describe two teachings of guru yoga,[20] a commentary on "taking refuge,"[21] and an explanation on the meaning of the mantra *om mani padme hum*.[22] They also mention many other teachings without specifying the theme. Among all these ceremonies that the Panchen Lama led, the Kālacakra initiations in Beijing and Hangzhou had particular impact. The importance that these ceremonies held for the local lay Buddhists is highlighted in the two hagiographies as well as in Chinese newspapers. Indeed, the descriptions given by Liu Jiaju, Chen Wenjian, and several Chinese journalists reveal the names of the Panchen Lama's donors, where the ceremonies took place, and the number of attendees. Two initiations will serve as examples in our analysis.

At the beginning of October 1932, the Panchen Lama went to Beijing.[23] In doing this, he was accepting the invitation of the lay Buddhist associations and Duan Qirui, a Chinese warlord and the ex-president of the Peking government, that had requested a Kālacakra initiation from him at the beginning of 1932.[24] The newspaper *Dagong bao* published numerous articles on the subject of the prelate's arrival and twice announced the date of the ceremony.[25] On October 14, the Panchen Lama began the preliminary rituals and prayers and from October 21–24, 1932, he gave his ninth Kālacakra initiation in China, with the official aim of curbing the Japanese invasion and of promoting peace. The ceremony took place in the Hall of Supreme Harmony, where a platform covered with red carpets and an altar had been prepared. The choice of this room, which is located in the palace of the same name in the heart of the Forbidden City, is of symbolic value since many other important events were held there, including the enthronement of the new emperor, as well as New Year, winter solstice, and longevity celebrations, among others.[26] The doors to the east and west were decorated, while a Republican flag and Buddhist banners adorned the main door. Well before the opening of the ceremony, which took place at 1:00 p.m., the faithful, who had been seated on the ground, flocked inside. Several thousand people overflowed from the room into an adjoining space. According to the newspaper *Dagong bao*, the attendance ranged from sixty to seventy thousand people. Chinese belonging to the warlord sphere of influence such as Duan Qirui, Wu Peifu,[27] Sun Chuanfang,[28] and Zhang Xueliang,[29] as well as journalists and Mongol celebrities such as Prince Demchüg Dongrub[30] and the Changkya Hutuktu,[31] and Chinese and Tibetan lay Buddhists and foreigners were all present for the initiation.

On the platform above the banners of red and yellow silk, the monks and the Mongols sat to the right of the altar, the notables to the left. The Panchen Lama, surrounded by ritual objects, conducted the ceremony from the center facing the main door. His words were translated into Chinese by a monk seated at his side. Each day, at the end of the ceremony, students of all nationalities questioned the prelate and Tibetans prostrated before their master, requesting his blessing. Chen Wenjian, one of the biographers of the Ninth Panchen Lama, deplored the behavior of the Chinese students, who were not attentive, and argued and conversed well into the night. At the end of the initiation, Xiejian, an official appointed by the Minister of Education Dai Jitao, offered the Panchen Lama salutation scarves on which the following lines were embroidered: "May the Wheel of Dharma often be turned. Today is a big day for Buddha."[32] Chen Wenjian noted that this event was without precedent in China and that the ceremony was grand.[33] Indeed, this ceremony celebrated by the Panchen Lama was to be the only Kālacakra initiation ever given in Beijing. It got wide coverage in the newspaper columns of *Dagong bao*.

In the spring of 1934, the Panchen Lama decided to accept the numerous requests he had received to give a Kālacakra initiation in Hangzhou. According to Chen Wenjian and Liu Jiaju, the prelate had been invited by the abbot of the Lingyin Temple, whom he had already visited in April 1925, and by the Chinese monk Taixu whom he had just met. According to the newspaper *Zhongyang ribao*, Dai Jitao and Wang Yiting were the ones that had invited the Panchen Lama.[34] Yet according to Chen Yisun, the Panchen Lama was invited by Gao Erdeng and Chen Yisun himself, two members of the provincial government of Zhejiang.[35] It also seems that members of lay Buddhist associations in the Nanjing area, impressed by the quality and force of the Beijing initiation they had attended, insisted that the prelate come teach the Kālacakra in their region.

Accompanied by his attendant Lozang Gyeltsen as well as twenty or so people from his entourage and more than forty servants, not forgetting ten or so members of the Republican government (themselves each with twenty or so servants), the Panchen Lama arrived at the train station in Hangzhou on April 26, 1934.[36] Members of the Mongolian and Tibetan Affairs Commission were responsible for organizing the reception.[37] Lay people, such as Sun Chuanfang, the warlord military governor of Zhejiang Province and Xia Chao, the civil governor of the same province, and many monks gathered on the platform of the station to the sound of military music to greet the Panchen Lama. According to Chen Yisun, as the Panchen Lama stepped off the train, complete confusion erupted. Everyone wondered how to receive the Buddhist master before whom, according to Tibetan custom, one must prostrate as a sign of respect. Finally, some chose to shake his hand, others stayed sitting, and yet others expressed words of welcome. Only the few Tibetans present in the crowd gave salutation scarves to the prelate. Then, the representatives of the different associations gave speeches, while the monks from the Lingyin Temple recited prayers.[38] Hundreds, maybe thousands, witnessed the scene. Chen Yisun quotes the number of ten thousand, while Chen Wenjian, always the optimist, estimates twenty thousand.[39]

Several days earlier the newspapers in Hangzhou had proclaimed the Panchen Lama's arrival. *Zhongyang ribao*, in particular, had published a front-page article on the subject on April 16, 1934, followed by several related articles continuing through April 21. In its columns, one of its journalist wrote of the exceptional nature of the Kālacakra and highlighted its link to Tantric Buddhism, praising the beneficial effects the average attendee can procure from such an initiation, particularly in terms of happiness for oneself and one's family, the elimination of obstacles, suffering, illness, and so forth. The journalist's stories indicated that on April 28, 1934, preliminary religious practices would be held prior to the ceremony.[40] Such publicity could only have served to attract a crowd and transform the arrival of the Panchen Lama into a significant local event.

From May 13–15, 1934, the Tibetan prelate conducted his seventh Kālacakra initiation for world peace since leaving Shigatse. The ceremony was celebrated in the prayer hall of the Lingyin Temple where a large altar was prepared and hangings in the form of the Kālacakra emblem were displayed.[41] Mixed with the religious locals who formed a compact crowd were those who had come especially from Tibet and Mongolia to receive the words of the master.[42] According to Chen Wenjian and Liu Jiaju, the gathering numbered in the tens of thousands of people (they give the figure ninety thousand, which according to their habit would most likely be an overestimate). Among the attendees were Duan Qirui and Dai Jitao.[43] The Panchen Lama spoke in his native tongue, translated into Chinese by Liu Jiaju. More than the preceding ones, this seventh Kālacakra initiation seems to have impressed those present. This initiation particularly touched Yéshé Dorjé, who participated in the ceremony as a bodyguard of the Panchen Lama. I was able to meet this witness face to face in Chengdu in November 1992. He still remembered the spiritual force of the teaching. The participants were captivated, he told me, and it was a challenge for him to contain the overflow of the compressed mass of people.[44] Several lay attendees, one of whom was Chen Yisun, would write descriptions that were then assembled into a collection entitled *Banchan dong lai* (The Panchen Came to the East), published in Hangzhou in 1935. Everyone claimed to have been particularly struck by the initiation and by the welcome given to the Panchen Lama. As for the newspaper *Zhongyang ribao,* it gave a long commentary on the event in the days that followed. This Kālacakra was filmed and shown in 1955 to the monks at Tashilhunpo in Tibet. One of them who saw the screening confirmed to me the great number of people in attendance and the remarkable solemnity emanating from the film.[45]

MOTIVES FOR PROPAGATING BUDDHISM IN CHINA

Several driving mechanisms were behind the Panchen Lama's level of religious activity in propagating and diffusing the Buddhist doctrine in a country he did not know. Before examining these, it is important to keep in mind the following points: (1) the flourishing state of Buddhism in China in the years 1920–30; (2) teaching Buddhism and conferring initiations are the main activities of a master in Tibetan Buddhism; (3) a Tibetan master only teaches upon receiving a request from those interested; and (4) within Tibetan Buddhism a relationship of "chaplain to donor" coexists with that of "master to disciple."

As in Tibet, where the majority of teachings are given at the request of disciples, in China the Panchen Lama was frequently solicited by the Mongols, and thus logically gave teachings there in response to multiple invitations. His actions in Inner Mongolia cannot be called proselytism, since the entire country was already won over to the cause of Buddhism.[46] Through the teachings and initiations that the prelate gave in the Yangzi basin, which were first requested by the clergy of the Longchang and Lingyin temples and then by the lay people, the Panchen Lama undeniably contributed to the development of Buddhism in the Republic of China at that time, his host land.

In accepting to teach Buddhism and open himself up to the maximum number of auditors and disciples, the prelate was conforming to the bodhisattva ethic, like any Buddhist master. He was also multiplying his occasions to locate chaplain-donor relationships, possibly to build up a network of new patrons. Was this second motive really his? Was he looking for donations? Was he "hunting for offerings?"

When the Panchen Lama first met with the warlords during the period December 1923, the year he fled Tashilhunpo, to 1926, it seemed that he was trying to raise funds that would allow him to pay the tax required by the Tibetan government. In doing so, he was following the Tibetan tradition where the master receives donations in exchange for the transmission of Buddhist texts. From 1926 on, the Panchen Lama's motives would evolve in line with his circumstances. For instance, parallel to his Buddhist teachings and transmissions of Tantric initiations, he opened offices and founded associations and Buddhist institutes, as a way to perpetuate over the long term his philosophical teachings in the field.

According to Tibetan Buddhist tradition, the Panchen Lama is the emanation of Amitābha, of whom Amitāyus is the reflexive form and is considered the Buddha of eternal life. It is natural that a Tibetan master, who is considered the manifestation of this divinity, would develop affinities with it and deepen his knowledge of it to the point of specializing in its associated rituals. Also, it seems that in China, Amitābha had been assimilated by the Taoists early on as a long-life divinity whose elixir they looked for ardently. Thus, Amitābha rapidly gained a privileged place in the popular fervor towards Buddhism. The growing importance of the prelate's cult gave birth to Buddhist schools like the school of Pure Land, which placed him at the center of their doctrine. The fact that the Panchen Lama, a living representation of Amitābha, was solicited by Chinese followers devoted to the cult of this divinity, is, in this way, quite logical.

Numerous masters gave Kālacakra initiations, but those of the Panchen Lama were more particularly linked to the Kālacakra from the point of view of the lineage transmission, and to the future of Buddhism. According to Buddhist tradition, one year after achieving enlightenment, Buddha appeared as the Kālacakra deity in Dhānyakaṭaka in the south of India, while at the same time he taught the Sutra of Wisdom (*Prajñāpāramitā*) at Vulture Peak. The king of the mythical kingdom Shambhala, which is said to be located to the north of Tibet near the river Sītā, attended this teaching before returning to his kingdom. There the teaching of Kālacakra was transmitted from king to king. In 966 Chilupā, an Indian master, went to Shambhala and received this initiation. Upon returning to India, he transmitted Kālacakra to Nāropa who, in turn, transmitted it to Atīśa, who taught it to Potowa. In 1026 the Kālacakra teaching was translated into Tibetan and transmitted in Tibet. Tsongkapa, the founder of the Gélukpa school, received it and transmitted it to his two main disciples, Gyeltsab Darma Rinchen (1364–1432) and Kédrub Gélèk Pelzang (1385–1438), who was the first in the line of Panchen Lamas, according to one lineage enumeration. Dating from this moment, the Kālacakra initiation was linked to the Panchen Lamas, and then from Lozang Chöki Gyeltsen (1567/70–1662) to the monastery of Tashilhunpo.

According to legend, the twenty-fifth king of Shambhala will be a reincarnation of the Panchen Lama. He will accede to the throne in approximately three hundred years from now in AD 2327 and will reign one hundred and some years. One year before the end of his reign in AD 2425, barbarians will attack his kingdom and will endanger the transmission of Buddhist teachings. But the warriors of Shambhala will end up the victors in this war and Buddhism will once again be diffused for eighteen thousand years. In this case, the Panchen Lama's enthusiasm in transmitting the Kālacakra initiations is explained by the fact that the Buddhist disciple that receives it is assured a rebirth in the kingdom of Shambhala. There, not only will he continue to practice this initiation, but he will be under the protection of the twenty-fifth king of Shambhala, that is, the last Panchen Lama, when the war breaks out.[47]

The Ninth Panchen Lama revealed himself to be truly one of the main guardians of the Kālacakra initiation. During the first half of the twentieth century, consecutive Kālacakra practices were given each day by the monks of the Tantric college at Tashilhunpo to which he belonged. Moreover, every year in April a giant mandala made of chalk was traced on the roof of the Palace of Omniscience while the Panchen Lama gave the great initiation of Kālacakra in the Palace of the Virtuous.[48] It seems natural, therefore, that during his exile in China the Panchen Lama continued to confer the Kālacakra transmission, for which he was the guardian of the lineage. On the other hand, due to his absence from Tashilhunpo, the transmission of the teaching was interrupted within his monastery after 1923.

In Tibetan Buddhism, the Kālacakra initiation belongs to the family of the *Anuttarayogatantra*. These are the highest Tantric teachings, the most complex, and the most secret. The master transmits them to a handful of selected disciples depending on their spiritual realizations. For those not yet ready, this initiation would nevertheless leave a positive imprint in the mind of the listeners, allowing them to practice more easily in a later life. Why then did the Panchen Lama transmit it nine times to thousands of people, the majority of whom were lay people largely ignorant in Tantric matters? The Panchen Lama must have been following the aim he had given himself at his departure: to honor his debts with the Tibetan government. In that capacity, he would have been looking for a means of connecting with future donors and their favors. Allowing it to be heard one way or another, particularly through the press as was done in Beijing and Hangzhou, the strong attraction of the lofty teaching on peace was sure to assemble a large audience. In this way the Panchen Lama increased his chances of meeting new donors in the crowds of attendees. He could also take advantage of these large gatherings to find supporters who could help him return to Tibet, and through the power of the Kālacakra let his cause be known to a larger audience. This was likely the case, showing how the Tibetan prelate seemed to possess the art of revealing the conjunction of religious and political messages, putting one at the service of the other.

Finally, the possibility that through the Kālacakra, the Panchen Lama may have simultaneously been following altruistic goals, as befitted his ecclesiastical position, cannot be excluded. In this way, the initiations helped the Panchen Lama's efforts to promote peace in the world. In fact, the prelate was an indefatigable ambassador for peace. At the beginning of the 1930s, faced with the attitude of the Japanese, the chaotic state of China, and the international political situation, certain Chinese feared an explosion of a second world war. Not long after the Kālacakra initiation in Hangzhou in May 1934, the Panchen Lama met the head of an association for peace in the world, which had been created in China ten years prior. The members openly feared another world war would break out and asked the prelate to pray for peace. He accepted, heartily approving the association's action, and encouraged the head to continue his efforts.[49] The Panchen Lama let nothing stop him. By increasing the number of Kālacakra initiations he gave, he undoubtedly felt that he was contributing to the stability in the world.

ATTENDEES AND DONORS

Whatever his motives were, the Panchen Lama recruited his patrons from a broad swath of society—the warlords and their allies (Duan Qirui, Sun Chuanfang, Zhang Zuolin, Zhang Xueliang), the heads of the Mongol leagues (the Prince Demchüg Dongrub, and to a lesser extent the Princes Darhan, Tüsheet, Jasaqt, Sönam Rabten, Abaga, and so forth), and also among the Chinese Republicans (Dai Jitao, Shi Qingyang, and Wang Yongbin, among others).[50] His most loyal donors were, based on the evidence and by order of appearance, Duan Qirui, the Prince Demchüg Dongrub, and Dai Jitao, not to mention the cohort of anonymous lay people who offered according to their means.

The religious activities of the Panchen Lama were not terribly important to some of the warlords because, on the one hand, Buddhism was dying out in the regions where they held sway, such that demand was weak, and, on the other hand, their warlike character probably did not predispose them to listening to a philosophy turned towards peace of mind. Only a few written sources make reference to the contact between the warlords and the Panchen Lama.

We do know that in April 1925 the prelate went to Shanghai to give teachings, following an invitation from Sun Chuanfang, the warlord of Zhejiang who was a practicing lay Buddhist. In October 1926 the Panchen Lama went to Fengtian for more than three months, where Zhang Zuolin, the local warlord, received him and became his disciple.[51] The prelate returned to Fengtian in June 1929 at the request of Zhang Xueliang, the son of Zhang Zuolin, who wanted him to celebrate a funeral oration in memory of his father, the warlord of Manchuria assassinated by the Japanese. The Panchen Lama returned to Fengtian during trips he made to Inner Mongolia from September 1929 to April 1930 to meet again with Zhang Xueliang, who had also become his disciple, and one last time from February to April 1931 to give Buddhist teachings there.[52] And that's it. The participation of Duan Qirui, the ex-president of the northern government, and Wu Peifu, who was head of the Zhili clique, as well as Sun Chuanfang and Zhang Xueliang at the Kālacakra initiation held in Beijing in October 1932 seems to have concluded the Panchen Lama's cycle of religious activities destined to attract the warlords.

The warlord Duan Qirui was an especially fervent Buddhist. Prior to the arrival of the Panchen Lama in China, he directed a Sino-Japanese association researching Tantric Buddhism. He took this activity so seriously that his contemporaries had nicknamed him "Śākyamuni!"[53] It is likely that during their first meeting in March 1925, Duan Qirui became a disciple of the Panchen Lama, given that he had invited the Tibetan prelate to come to teach the Kālacakra in Beijing. Conforming to tradition, Duan Qirui probably financed all or a part of the master's trip and helped with the organization of the ceremony. In Tibetan Buddhism when a disciple solicits the visit and teachings of his spiritual master, he is expected to arrange financing for his travel, take care of the logistics of the event (rental of the venue, publicity, translators, etc.) and see to his needs during his stay. The facts show that Duan Qirui did indeed make a donation of 2,000 yuan to the Panchen Lama on this occasion.[54] In 1934 Duan Qirui also participated in the Kālacakra in Hangzhou.

The Tibetan prelate received an unequaled welcome from the Mongol princes, whose families had been Gélukpa Buddhists for several centuries. He was able to multiply the number of Buddhist teachings and Tantric initiations he gave thanks to both the respect he showed for the local clergy and the strong spiritual expectations of the population and the princes. During the four years he spent in Inner Mongolia out of his fourteen years in exile, he conferred five Kālacakra initiations. Each of these attracted thousands of the faithful. The initiation of July 1932, which took place on the lands of the Üjümücin Banner of the Shilingol

League, probably at the initiative of Prince Sönam Rabten, seems to have been the most important.

The great Mongol masters, such as Kanjurwa Hutuktu, crossed the steppe for several days before reaching the ceremony. Once there, they were cared for by the organizers and brought to yurts that had been reserved for them. The initiation took place in the open air in the middle of pastures on a platform upon which a throne had been set. The Panchen Lama was surrounded by thousands of monks and lay people sitting cross-legged on the grass. The teaching was at times inaudible, but the attention of the audience was acute. All felt that if they managed to catch the ringing of the bells, the rolling of the drums, or the clinking of the cymbals in the ritual, they would receive the blessing of the initiation.[55] The faith of the Mongols was sincere and the ceremony was a success, we are told.

During three long trips that the Panchen Lama took through Inner Mongolia, the princes Darhan, Tüsheet, Jasaqt, Azaihuoqin, Abaga, Sönam Rabten, and Demchüg Dongrub gave him their complete hospitality.[56] Prince Demchüg Dongrub was the main Mongol benefactor of the Panchen Lama. He was the head of the Western Sünid Banner of the Shilingol League. A graduate of the Beijing Institute of Mongolian and Tibetan Studies, he succeeded his father as the head of the Sünid Banner in 1919. In November 1931 the Panchen Lama arrived on his lands and stopped to give Buddhist teachings. Since the Panchen Lama had no monastery in Inner Mongolia, Prince Demchüg Dongrub proposed to the heads of the other leagues that they build one for him. Soon tree trunks coming from Amdo were transported to the Yellow River. From there, they were floated down the river and taken to Prince Demchüg Dongrub's lands where the monastery was to be built. The plans were drawn up by an architect originally from Beijing, while the Chinese labor came from the province of Shanxi.[57] Once the construction was complete, the three colleges of logic, Tantrism, and medicine of this monastery, which was named the "Monastery of the Panchen Lama" would welcome 159 monks.[58] Through his gesture, Prince Demchüg Dongrub showed himself to be one of the main Mongol donors to the Panchen Lama. But he was not alone. After the Panchen Lama taught at the Wangjie Suoma Temple on the lands of Prince Demchüg Dongrub, the monks offered their monastery to him. The prelate accepted this gift and renamed Wangjie Suoma, the abbot of the monastery, Gajin Qingpi, which is derived from another name for the monastery: Gajin Temple.[59] Later in August 1933, Prince Demchüg Dongrub also offered the Panchen Lama the Bayanqota monastery, also known as Ganden chöling püntsok gön. According to Chen Wenjian, the Panchen Lama was emotional when he accepted this latest gift from the prince on September 10.[60]

Dai Jitao (1890–1949), who was Sun Yat-sen's secretary in 1912 and the vice minister for foreign affairs for the Canton government as well as minister of education from 1928 to 1938, was also, in most people's opinion, a fervent Buddhist.[61] In fact, he is said to have attended most of the teachings given by the Panchen Lama in Inner China and had often sponsored them, becoming over time one of the most generous donors to the Tibetan prelate. Dai Jitao participated in the organization of the prelate's teaching in Pukou in June 1931, as well as at the Bhaiṣajyaguru initiation also given in Pukou in spring 1933, and at the Kālacakra initiations in Hangzhou in May 1934 and at Kumbum in September (or October) 1935. At the Bhaiṣajyaguru initiation, Dai Jitao financed the printing of one thousand booklets for the attendees that contained the words of the medicine Buddha.[62] It seems that the Kālacakra initiation in Hangzhou could not have taken place without the active support of Dai Jitao.[63]

At the beginning of 1927, the Panchen Lama met Puyi, the deposed Qing emperor, while he was celebrating the New Year in Shenyang. However, nothing gives evidence that Puyi became either his disciple or his donor.

As for Tibetan donors of the Panchen Lama, few written Tibetan testimonies exist except for that of Phabongka Rinpoche (1878–1941), a respected figure in Tibetan Buddhism. The biographer Lozang Dorjé notes that Phabongka Rinpoche met with the Panchen Lama in the Tibetan province of Kham in January 1937. There, the prelate gave a long life initiation attended by Tibetan nomads, and Phabongka Rinpoche is said to have been very impressed by the ease with which the Panchen Lama ran the initiation.[64] Later, Phabongka Rinpoche's appreciation for the quality of the Panchen Lama's teachings spread across Tibet. It has been handed down to our day several times by Tibetan masters as well as disciples of Phabongka Rinpoche living in exile.[65]

PANCHEN LAMA OFFICES AND ASSOCIATIONS

The work of the Ninth Panchen Lama represented in the hagiographies of Liu Jiaju and Chen Wenjian seems to have been considerable. But once the great assemblies, the official receptions, and banquets were finished, enthusiasm subsided and the Buddhist messages of the Panchen Lama ran the risk of being forgotten. That is why the prelate created various religious organizations—evidence of his effort to spread Buddhism in China—while his disciples tried to gather together the texts of their master's teachings. Following the example of Taixu, the Chinese monk reformer,[66] the Panchen Lama founded associations and opened offices (*Banchan banshichu*), whose activities remain vague.[67]

On May 25, 1934, after the Kālacakra initiation in Hangzhou, the Panchen Lama encouraged Wu Tiecheng, mayor of the city, and Duan Qirui, former president of the northern government, as well as a number of local lay Buddhists to found the Association of Enlightenment Studies (*Puti xuehui*).[68] The goal of this association was to develop the spread of Tibetan Buddhism by translating the main religious texts into Chinese, and also by promoting their publication and putting in place an infrastructure to invite Tibetan masters to give teachings. The Panchen Lama also suggested that his Chinese audience create an Institute of Mongolian and Tibetan Studies (*Meng Zang xueyuan*) placed under his spiritual guidance and under that of the Changkya Hutuktu, with the goal of increasing knowledge of Mongolian and Tibetan cultures.[69] In the end, he convinced the Chinese to take care of the financing of the association and of the institute.[70] The Institute of Mongolian and Tibetan Studies opened its doors mid-June 1934,[71] and the statutes of the Association of Enlightenment Studies were registered in May 1935.[72] In July 1935, while in Amdo, the Panchen Lama made a donation of 2,000 yuan to the association, whose inauguration was set for November 12.[73] During a meeting organized after the ceremony, he was named president of the association while the Gara Rinpoche and the Chinese master Yinguang became the vice presidents,[74] Duan Qirui the administrator, and Wang Yiting and Qu Wenliu, two lay Buddhists from Shanghai, the managers.[75] One year later the Association for Enlightenment Studies opened a branch on Mount Wutai where the responsibility for the translation of Tibetan texts was given to the monk Nenghai, one of the three young Chinese who had left to study in Lhasa after taking the course at the Buddhist Institute of Tibetan Studies created by Taixu in 1924.[76]

On the fringes of the Panchen Lama's Association of Enlightenment Studies and the Institute of Mongolian and Tibetan Studies, other schools whose aim was the study of Tibetan Buddhism were created at the beginning of the 1930s, such as the Association for Tantric Buddhist Studies (*misheng xuehui*) in Wuhan, the Association for Kham and Tibetan Studies (*Kang Zang xuefa tuan*) in Chengdu, and the Tantric Buddhist Institute in Beijing (*Beiping mi Zang yuan*).[77] The Sino-Tibetan Philosophical and Religious Seminary, branching from the World Buddhist Institute in Chongqing created by Taixu in 1932, was entrusted to the monk Fazun in 1934.[78]

The near simultaneous creation of these schools seems to indicate that they responded to a true spiritual need in the field and on the part of the sponsors; for each of the schools found its place and was not in competition with the others due to their distance from one another. In putting these facilities and this fixed framework at the disposal of new lay disciples, the Panchen Lama hoped to nourish their faith towards him. Although it is reasonable to think that these associations were also intended to print the Panchen Lama's teachings—the transcriptions of which have reached us today from other sources.

One of the final tasks of the Panchen Lama was to find the reincarnation of the Thirteenth Dalai Lama, whose death was announced on December 17, 1933. The Chinese government made every effort to organize funerary ceremonies led by the Panchen Lama.

SEARCH FOR THE DALAI LAMA'S REINCARNATION

The prelate was informed of the Dalai Lama's death while he was on the lands of the Yeke Juu League, and thus officiated where he was. He ordered monks from all of the Tibetan monasteries to perform ceremonies and offerings, and to pray that the Thirteenth Dalai Lama would reincarnate quickly. In his absence, he asked the Changkya Hutuktu to lead the ceremonies in Beijing in honor of the spiritual and temporal head of Tibet.[79] At the same time, he wrote a prayer that he dedicated to his deceased master expressing the wish that this prayer be distributed to all Tibetan monasteries and recited by the monks.

At the beginning of January 1934, the Panchen Lama arrived in Nanjing, where Shi Qingyang and Dai Jitao, who had invited him, were waiting.[80] The Chinese government made 50,000 yuan available for a memorial service for the Thirteenth Dalai Lama, the preparations for which were entrusted to the Mongolian and Tibetan Affairs Commission (*Meng Zang weiyuanhui*). More than eight thousand people were invited, among whom were representatives of the government, the Nationalist Party as well as numerous political figures. The ceremony took place on February 14 under the spiritual guidance of the Panchen Lama. It was held in the Ningyuan Pavilion on the education ministry's premises and, according to protocol, lasted from 8:00 a.m. to 5:00 p.m. The choice of the venue obviously underlines the influence of Dai Jitao as disciple and donor to the Panchen Lama. At the end of the day, the prelate began a three-day prayer and recitation session reserved for the religious community.[81] The funeral ceremony headed by the Panchen Lama then ended with those prayers.

It is not surprising that the Panchen Lama led memorial ceremonies for the Thirteenth Dalai Lama in Nanjing rather than in Lhasa, since the dispute between him and the Tibetan government had not yet been smoothed over.

Parallel to this ceremony, the Panchen Lama had begun the search for the Thirteenth Dalai Lama's reincarnation throughout Tibet. He so informed the Tibetan government.[82] From their side, the government and the Tibetan clergy had also begun to assemble their own search team. This is why Kétsang Rinpoche and Lozang Gyatso arrived at the Kyégu döndrubling monastery where the Panchen Lama was residing on February 12, 1937, having come from Lhasa. The two clergymen, appointed by the Tibetan government to conduct the search, requested the help of the prelate in order to do their search in the best manner possible for all Tibetans. A few days later, they confided their worries to him since trouble had broken out in Qinghai and the roads were unsure. They asked him to intercede with the Republican government on their behalf. The Panchen Lama agreed to send a telegram to Ma Bufang, the military governor of Qinghai Province, who took reassuring measures.[83]

At the beginning of May 1937, the two clergy investigators appointed by the Tibetan government made another request for help from the Panchen Lama. They wished to know where, according to him, the reincarnation of the spiritual and temporal head of Tibet was located, in addition to the names of different children he had pre-selected. The Panchen Lama agreed to cooperate with the Tibetan authorities; having conducted his own search, he had chosen three children born in Amdo. The prelate then decided to assign two members of his entourage, Tséchokling Rinpoche and Wangdü Norbu (his vicar), to give help to the clergymen from Lhasa. The two teams joined their efforts in Xining and chose two children from the three that the Panchen Lama had pre-selected as potential reincarnations of the Thirteenth Dalai Lama.[84] Finally, according to an article from the *Times*, dated July 22, 1937 (confirmed sixty years later in a letter from the Fourteenth Dalai Lama addressed to Jiang Zemin, president of the People's Republic of China, dated October 11, 1995), one of these two children would become the Fourteenth Dalai Lama.[85] Accordingly, Tibetan history upheld tradition, with the Ninth Panchen Lama discovering the Fourteenth Dalai Lama.

PANCHEN LAMA'S INFLUENCE

The religious activity of the Panchen Lama in China was considerable. It benefited from circumstances favorable to the development of Buddhist studies and, more particularly, to Tantric teachings. However, little information enables us to measure the continuity of this effort. Kelzang Chönjor (aka Liu Jiaju) seems to have been the only member of the Panchen Lama's entourage to translate and transcribe some of the teachings transmitted by the prelate in China. In addition, the work accomplished by the Panchen Lama's associations and offices remains vague. Few, in fact, hardly any, of the transcriptions left today seem to originate from these associations and offices. And yet, it is undeniable that the Panchen Lama fulfilled his functions as a Buddhist master and aided in the spread and renaissance of Buddhism in modern China.

The Tibetan tradition sees a religious master as a link in the diffusion of Buddhism. A teaching is, therefore, transmitted from master to disciple. Then, the disciple, once having accomplished the attendant spiritual realization, can, in turn, teach it. In any case, the disciple refers to and affirms the teaching's transmission lineage. Yet, seeing the transcriptions of the teachings transmitted by the Panchen Lama, it seems that the prelate (or his translators) omitted to mention who his masters were. Chinese sources remain silent on this matter for the first forty years of the Panchen Lama's life. Tibetan writings gathered at Tashilhunpo monastery would help to elucidate the mystery of the teachings the Panchen Lama received and identify his masters. The entire spiritual work of the Panchen Lama could then be better known. Unfortunately access to Tashilhunpo's holdings is restricted by Chinese authorities.

The Panchen Lama had, parallel to his religious work, quite a significant political presence. From a Tibetan point of view, it was not unusual to consider that the second was not in contradiction to the first. And, in fact, could reveal the very use of the Buddhist "skillful means" and the bodhisattva's obligation to adapt to situations and individuals. In any case, it cannot be denied that the Panchen Lama admirably transformed the situations he found himself in favorably, all the while accomplishing (or was it in order *to* accomplish?) the actions reserved, by the doctrine, for an authentic spiritual master.

It remains unclear at this point whether the Panchen Lama's religious influence was intended to build a cadre of donors to assist with the extraordinary tax imposed on Tashilhunpo by Lhasa or whether it was intended to meet other aims.

4

CHINESE AND ASIAN POLITICS

Abbots of Tibetan monasteries are usually little involved in politics inasmuch as they do not participate in directing public affairs and rarely take initiatives in this domain. The only action taken of a political nature is to accept the requests of foreign disciples who wish to receive a Buddhist teaching, which could call for travel and possibly invitations by local political leaders—perhaps even interviews with them. If local leaders do not come forward (which is always a possibility), the spiritual master is not offended and travels to other places, responding to requests of a spiritual nature as they arise. Should a political leader invite the religious dignitary to give a teaching, his gesture opens up the possibility of creating a new chaplain-donor relation and to increasing the protection that goes hand in hand with it.

It is clear that the behavior of Tibetan prelates has not been neutral, however, in the sense that accepting the protection of a political leader could potentially provide a kind of "certificate of good morals," and could be seen as supporting a political leader's policies. Over the centuries, following their religious duties, Tibetan ecclesiastical dignitaries have tended to let their officers get involved in the public affairs of their region. However, few have taken any striking political positions. The facts show that they restricted themselves to an essentially passive political role, at least in appearance.

When we observe the Panchen Lama's behavior in China, we can see that in his case his involvement in the political sphere quickly surpassed that of his counterparts who remained in Tibet.

PANCHEN LAMA'S POLITICAL OUTLOOK

On January 27, 1925, the prelate distinguished himself with a talk in favor of the "union of the five nationalities" and "national reconstruction" that he gave in Beijing during a preliminary meeting to the first National Reconstruction Conference (*shanhou huiyi*) to which the prelate had been invited.[1] The Panchen Lama took advantage of the opportunity to criticize in the strongest terms the far from glorious behavior of certain high Chinese officials. On February 1, the first formal day of the conference, the prelate cautiously sent his attendant Lozang Gyeltsen to represent him, and to read a statement regarding his opinion of what he believed to be some rather unscrupulous officials of the Republican government. In the meantime, the Panchen Lama himself preferred to transmit a Green Tārā initiation at Mount Wutai in Shanxi Province.[2]

The content of the prelate's statement, which contained more than a simple dressing down of officials' behavior, would have been somewhat surprising for the informed observer, whether Tibetan or Chinese. In it the Panchen Lama underlines the importance of the "union of Inner China with its peripheries, which could allow the construction of a true nation."[3] At the same time, he openly reproaches the Republican government for speaking about a union, but doing nothing serious to put it into place, and especially for neglecting to resolve obstacles hindering it. What were his motives for such an approach?

Remembering the relation of "chaplain-donor" and considering his surprising position concerning the subject of the union of Inner China with Tibet and Mongolia one could be tempted to think that the Panchen Lama was acting in a calculated way and was expressing "politically correct" views with the prosaic goal of creating a chaplain-donor relationship, as well as to draw himself the material support and protection from the Republican government that he lacked. This was no doubt partially the case, as will be later confirmed. But at the same time, we see him taking the risk of publicly disapproving of the behavior of Chinese officials. We can therefore ask ourselves: What pushed him to react this way? When and how did the Panchen Lama come to be involved in politics?

If the Panchen Lama's participation at the National Reconstruction Conference in 1925 contains vocabulary borrowed from Sun Yat-sen, in particular the expressions "union of the five nationalities," "national reconstruction," "union of China and its peripheries," "saving China" and "project for a new Chinese Nation," it is not until 1929 that we see the Tibetan prelate officially declare himself in favor of the political program of Sun Yat-sen, the founder of the Chinese Nationalist Party. In a letter from the Panchen Lama to Yan Xishan, the director of the Mongolian and Tibetan Affairs Commission, dated January 24, 1929, the prelate writes: "The Chinese Republic is a true country. The principles and political guidelines and instructions passed on by Sun Yat-sen must be applied on the entire Chinese territory."[4]

A bit later, on May 5, 1931, the Panchen Lama gave a speech in Nanjing during the opening ceremony of the National People's Convention (*Guomin huiyi*) in which he encouraged attendees "to clearly understand and recognize that the 'Three Principles of the People' were revolutionary ideas perfect for safeguarding China and the world."[5] The Panchen Lama seemed convinced of Sun Yat-sen's political direction, to the point of defending his policy. But we do not know how the Panchen Lama became aware of the "Three Principles of the People." The prelate neither spoke nor read Chinese, or, if he did, he had only a cursory knowledge of the language, and no translation of the "Three Principles of the People" from Chinese into Tibetan seems to have been available at that time.

A Buddhist Reading of the "Three Principles of the People"

The Panchen Lama publicly declared his admiration for Sun Yat-sen on May 9, 1934.[6] That day, he had gone to the Lingyin Temple in Hangzhou to give a Kālacakra initiation. During the opening ceremony, he gave a speech in which he praised President Sun Yat-sen who "devoted his entire life to the community with no selfish thoughts, no grasping of the ego." He further clarified his opinion, stressing that "the eminent Chinese president Sun had initiated a revolution, founded the Republic of China, and taken pains to make the nation prosperous and the people happy through his pure heart." The prelate advised the attendees present at the ceremony to "follow in the footsteps of the president, to honor his heart, and consider the prosperity of the country and the well-being of the people as their first task."[7]

As a master of Buddhist philosophy, the Panchen Lama probably found in Sun Yat-sen's thought ideas that were close to his own, which he could easily accept. Sun Yat-sen's goal was to save China, which was, at the time, subject to Western imperialist powers. According to Sun, China suffered not only from political domination and economic pressure from the West, but also from insufficient demographic growth that made it vulnerable. He believed that there were two methods available for resisting the imperialists. The first consisted in awakening the people's national consciousness, putting democracy into place, and assuring the welfare of the people; the second involved using force. Sun advocated the first method, which contains the essence of the "Three Principles of the People," namely, nationalism, democracy, and the well-being of the people.[8] Sun Yat-sen's idea was simple. To save China, it was necessary to increase births and to resist political domination and pressure from foreign powers. To do this, he was going to put into place a project to edify the nation based on the "Three Principles of the People."

In his speech on May 9, 1934, the Panchen Lama observed that "a deep examination of these principles of the president and Buddhist doctrine reveals that they are identical, exactly like two sides of the same thing . . . they are similar and complementary. . . . no divergence exists." He further stated that whichever point he examined in the "Three Principles of the People," he found the "quintessence of Buddhist ideals." The Panchen Lama emphasized that the president's main principles "aim at eliminating the suffering of the people and at bringing happiness to the greatest number possible, while the Buddhist doctrine supports these ideals of equality and elimination of suffering." Moreover, Sun Yat-sen's "will of liberating the country and the people is also a Buddhist idea."[9]

In fact, the Panchen Lama seems to have found an endless source of political inspiration in the "Three Principles of the People" on which he could draw abundantly and which he used to his own advantage. It remains difficult, however, to determine whether he really understood Sun's political thought or if he contented himself with pronouncing discourses prepared by his assistants (there is no evidence of transcriptions of the prelate's speeches into Tibetan, except for one).[10] In any case, the Panchen Lama expressed opinions that were to influence his conduct in the field and, furthermore, his destiny.

"Union of the Five Nationalities"

During the initial period of wandering that followed his departure from Tibet and which brought him into contact with the warlord milieu from 1924 to 1926, the Panchen Lama had occasion to understand the state of provincial China and the troubles besetting it. The nearly anarchical situation that he observed firsthand seems to have inspired the subject of his first political discourse in early 1925. At that time, the prelate developed an idea that would become the leitmotif of his political action: union. The Republican revolution aimed to resolve conflicts, reestablish order, pursue national reconstruction, and to put into place reconstruction projects based on the "Three Principles of the People." But these would not be possible without the prior condition of achieving the union of Inner China and its peripheries. In other words, the "harmonious coexistence of the five nationalities" (*wuzu gonghe*) would need to be achieved. The logical sequence of arguments the prelate used to arrive at this conclusion was first, the need to build a new Chinese nation, which would not be possible unless the sporadic regional conflicts ceased; second, the regional conflicts could only end when one understood their underlying origins and eradicated them; and finally, to eradicate the underlying origins of regional conflicts the people of the five nations would have to unite their forces, defending and mutually protecting each other. We can guess that the Panchen Lama borrowed the idea of the "union of Inner China and its peripheries" from Sun Yat-sen as a means to defend the Tibetan cause.

Sun Yat-sen, who was ephemerally the president of the Chinese Republic following its founding in 1912, declared that from that moment on the Chinese nation (*Zhonghua minzu*) would be characterized by "national unity" (*minzu tuanjie*). He defined the new state's territorial limits as the borders of the deposed dynasty. Thus, the Uighurs, Mongols, Tibetans, and even Manchus were included in the Chinese nation. According to Sun, the five major nationalities that peopled the Chinese nation were henceforth to live in a climate of harmonious coexistence. He announced that they would soon have equal rights (*yi lü pingdeng*) thanks to the establishment of an autonomous local system (*difang zizhi*).[11] "Equality," as Sun understood it, meant nothing more than "eliminating the inequalities that had been put in place by the Manchus." He resumed the discourse of the revolutionaries that held the Manchus responsible for the oppression of the Han, Uighur, Mongol, and Tibetan peoples to whom he promised "equality" from then on. However, it was not until January 1924 that he finally gave his views on how this "equality" would benefit the five nationalities.[12]

Sun Yat-sen made a distinction between the "nation" that was born of natural forces, historical evolution, and race (*minzu*) on the one hand, and the "state" (*guojia*) created by military intervention, on the other. According to him, the nation-race is composed of individuals who share the same blood, way of life, language, religion, and customs. He added that if the criterion of blood, of heredity is innate, the four other criteria are acquired over time. He felt that the Uighurs, Manchus, Mongols, and Tibetans could easily adopt the mores of the Han population. To assimilate these four nationalities into China, he would facilitate their access to Chinese culture, and, if needed, he would force the more reluctant ones to adopt Chinese ways and customs, religion, and language with which they had no affinity. In this way, Sun conceived it possible to give "equality" to the Han, Uighurs, Manchus, Mongols, and Tibetans.[13]

In addition, conscious of the scale of the task, Sun Yat-sen defined two indispensable preliminary phases to the creation of a constitutional government. The first phase was a "military phase" (*junzheng*) whose aim was to end the practices inherited from the Manchu dynasty and that influenced the republic even after 1912. This would necessarily be followed by a second phase called the "supervisory phase" (*xunzheng*), which would be aimed at training the people and having them participate in the nation's political life. Once all the sub-prefectures had become autonomous, a constitutional government could be established. Sun specified that local autonomy must inculcate a national consciousness on the part of the new citizens of the republic rather than fostering separatism. But he did not indicate what policies he planned to use in Tibet and Mongolia. Among Sun's inner circle, certain revolutionaries and reformers were partisans of independence for Tibet and Mongolia. They considered, in effect, that it was preferable to use them as buffer states than to allow them to become hotbeds of domestic unrest.[14]

Today, we may conclude that Sun Yat-sen's version of "equality before the law" did not actually provide the same equality for everyone, since, in an obviously ethnocentric fashion, it blindly allied itself to a policy of assimilation into Chinese culture. In that way, the peoples in question would undergo forced conformity justified by the logic of "union." The Panchen Lama would push this logic of pure equality to the letter in order to distance himself from ethnocentric interpretations of it. According to the prelate, the "harmonious coexistence of the five nationalities" could only exist when "the people of the five nationalities are neither superior nor inferior; neither far nor close [with respect to Inner China]; neither poor, nor rich; neither aristocratic nor commoner; where all is equitable; where the whole territory is administered; where each person benefits from civilization."[15]

In substance, the five nationalities could not cohabit or live in harmony unless they benefited from the same rights and were treated in the same way. Of course, given his ecclesiastical post, the Panchen Lama extolled respect for religious beliefs that was so important to the Tibetans, as well as the Mongols and Uighurs, and which had been included in the Chinese Republic's constitution. He publicly declared his opinion on this subject twice, in 1931 and 1935.[16] Taking this stance had significance.

It must be remembered that on the high plateau, the Tibetans continually mix religious practice with daily life, such that Buddhism is assimilated into their culture. As a result, in defending religious liberty, the Panchen Lama was implicitly working in favor of difference, in favor of respect by the Republican government for the cultural uniqueness of the different peoples—Uighurs, Manchus, Mongols, and Tibetans—who were invited to join the "union of the five nationalities."

In January 1929 the Panchen Lama for the first time expressed his opinion regarding the place of Tibet in the "union of the five nationalities." He had just spent five years in China and Inner Mongolia. At the end of a long religious voyage in which he had crisscrossed Inner Mongolia, he observed that the Chinese Republic had been destabilized for seventeen years, the causes of which lying in the pressure of the warlords and foreign powers. He spoke with full knowledge of the facts and did not content himself with simply repeating Sun Yat-sen's opinions. On the one hand, the Panchen Lama had witnessed conflicts between opposing warlords and he knew what they were capable of. On the other hand, he had seen the British army of Col. Francis Younghusband attack Tibet in 1904, and he could not ignore the Russian and Japanese division of Manchuria in 1907 as well as Russia's control of Outer Mongolia since 1924. For him, the foreign threat was not simply theoretical. In commenting on the effects this instability had had on the Chinese Republic, he said,

> The compatriots of the five nationalities are unconcerned with one another to the point that dissension reigns everywhere and, in addition, they do not share the same fate. Given that Tibet is located far to the west, the situation is even more tragic.[17]

In evoking the term "Chinese Republic," the Panchen Lama directly evokes Sun Yat-sen. What matters for him is that the Chinese Republic consists of the "union of the five nationalities." He declares this again and again. In 1931 the prelate had noted that the Han, Manchus, Mongols, Uighurs, and Tibetans had formed one single Chinese people ever since the 1911 Revolution.[18] In 1932 he remarked that "the Chinese Republic exists thanks to the contribution of the five nationalities."[19] And again in 1933, he argued that the five nationalities had formed "one family" since the beginning of the Republic.[20]

Status of Tibet

Concerning Tibet, specifically, did the Panchen Lama have other choices besides affirming that his country was an integral part of the "union of the five nationalities" that formed the Chinese Republic? His reasoning was that previously Tibet belonged to China and, therefore, there was no reason for that to cease, or for Tibet to refuse to participate in the union with the other nationalities. This point of view was reaffirmed in 1931 in a speech entitled "Tibet is Part of China's

National Territory"[21] and again in another speech he gave in 1933, in which he invokes historical ties, demonstrating that at the time of imperial China, Tibet and China held very close relations based on the chaplain-donor roles that existed between the Dalai Lama and the emperor, and additionally between the Panchen Lama and the emperor.[22] The Panchen Lama continues, saying that the situation had changed in 1911, and, thus for historical and geographical reasons,

> the Tibetans wanted to abandon China and tried to establish their independence, although in reality this was impossible. If China lost Tibet, it would be like a car that lost its wheels. That is why the union between Tibet and China is doubly profitable, while their separation harms both parties.[23]

In a letter to Yan Xishan, the director of the Mongolian and Tibetan Affairs Commission, the prelate explained why Tibet had initially wanted to separate from China after the fall of the Manchu Empire and pursue independence:

> At the end of the Qing dynasty and at the beginning of the Chinese Republic, a minority of Chinese and Tibetans acted in their own interest. They did not look at the general situation, but fought one against the other. In the end, the Dalai Lama fled to India, while at the same time, a pro-British clique was formed and gave the opportunity to surrounding countries to invade Tibet. During the revolution of 1911, Chinese soldiers and officials stationed in Tibet were chased out and Sino-Tibetan relations progressively deteriorated. Moreover, the imperialists attempted to manage Tibet's economic and cultural affairs. They incited Tibetans to declare independence for their country and exhorted them to send armies to Xikang where their incursions went all the way to the Sichuan border. Having humiliated, pillaged, and raped, complaints against the imperialists were made throughout the region and many went hungry. The pro-British clique instigated these events. When these people destroyed Sino-Tibetan relations, they were not looking after Tibet's interests, but acted without thinking... In addition, they used arms to oppress monks and the people, and they raised heavy taxes.[24]

In 1930, the Panchen Lama would add the following to the same subject:

> China and Tibet had always collaborated. From a historical view, Sino-Tibetan relations had been established for several hundreds of years... Who would have believed that a small group of malicious men, inspired by selfish feelings, would have fomented such a plot! All of them kept up the discord at the expense of the Dalai Lama and insidiously harmed Sino-Tibetan relations to the point that the Dalai Lama allowed himself to be pushed around and to even act against the will of the Chinese central government... Yet, the malicious people... incited a small group of men to appropriate, by any means, political power and crush people with taxes. Nothing stopped them. When they encountered powerful imperialists, they

> immediately changed policies. They demanded armed men; they flattered them and ended up subjugating them. They relied on the imperialist forces to protect them and willingly served them. Witness to these events, I was devastated.[25]

It is clear that the Panchen Lama did not appreciate the British, which only confirmed their own assumptions! The reasons are simple. First, the prelate had difficulty forgetting their armed intervention in 1904, which had, for all intents and purposes, discredited them in the eyes of the Tibetan population. Next, in October 1904, the Panchen Lama received a visit from Captain O'Connor, the British trade agent in Gyeltsé, and a bond of friendship had grown between the two men. However, it seems that this "bond of friendship" did not have the same weight for each man. On his side, the Panchen Lama felt the relationship was one of chaplain-donor, identical to a dozen other such relationships he had created during his life as abbot. But what did Captain O'Connor know of the chaplain-donor relationship? The misunderstanding worsened when the trade agent invited the Panchen Lama to go to India to visit the viceroy of the British colonial empire. Accepting this invitation, the Panchen Lama thought to benefit from British protection. Unfortunately for him, each time he requested their aid over the next five years, especially the help of their army, they refused him, citing only nebulous reasons. Suffering at least three rejections from their side, it is conceivable the Panchen Lama would harbor some resentment towards them. He became all the more bitter when after 1910 he had occasion to see that the British did not treat all Tibetan dignitaries the same way. In effect, when the Thirteenth Dalai Lama fled to India at the beginning of 1910 and stayed until the end of 1912, the British gave him protection, which would progressively spread to the Tibetan government in Lhasa.

The Panchen Lama attributed the responsibility for his hasty departure from Tashilhunpo to those he named as the "pro-British clique," who had obtained power in the Tibetan government. He accused them "of crushing the people with taxes." In 1929 he said:

> The people of Xikang and of Tibet who live under this reproachful authority feel anger, but dare not show it. I have witnessed such a situation; my pain is intense. That is why I have left everything to come to the East as the representative of monks and lay Tibetans.[26]

At the beginning of 1931, the prelate came back to this same point and stated that he had been witness to the supposed atrocities of the "pro-British clique" and "was devastated," which is why he came to Inner China.[27] At the end of 1931, he further lamented that the situation had changed following the revolution:

> Since then, no province has had peace and the border regions suffer this influence. The situation in Tibet is even more unstable. I left behind my powers to come east because there I was undergoing testing and danger.[28]

And lastly in 1933, the Panchen Lama further explained that:

> Dissension [had] formed between the Han and the Tibetans, healthy relations progressively disintegrated ... I could not stay and do nothing because the sufferings of the people of Xikang and of Tibet are from day to day more and more intolerable. Consequently, knowing the moral prestige of the government, I went east to Inner China.[29]

It seems rather excessive, in my opinion, to claim, as the Panchen Lama did, that the Tibetan government had become infiltrated by the British. Nevertheless, the question merits further examination. In defense of the prelate, it is worth recalling the 1923 decree in which the Tibetan government placed a tax on the Gyeltsé herds, the proceeds of which were for British use. As for the taxes allotted to finance the regular Tibetan army, we know that they too existed, thanks, in part, to the British for helping strengthen Tibet's military powers.

We can deepen our understanding of the Panchen Lama's views on the "union of the five nationalities" by examining the period prior to 1911. While Tibet benefited from a *de facto* independence during the period 1912–49, before that it had, strictly speaking, enjoyed the status of a "nation." Tibet was, in other words, a community comprised of a group of humans settled on a specific land by its will to live together and form an entity, who were characterized by the consciousness of their cultural and historical identity. It is more difficult to affirm that Tibet was a "state," since despite the Tibetan nation possessing a government, its power was not representative due to its theocratic nature. Although, it is equally true that myriad governments, led by dictators, monarchies, and so forth, are also not representative. Perhaps more pertinently, between the thirteenth century and 1911, Tibet's history shows it lacked sovereignty in the sense that its defense system relied mainly on the support of foreign "protectors," such as the Mongols or the Manchus.

The propensity of the Dalai Lamas and Panchen Lamas to create chaplain-donor relations with the Manchu emperors is the origin of a serious misunderstanding that has existed between China and Tibet for centuries.[30] The Tibetan term *chöyön* means "chaplain-donor" and has no translation in Chinese. If the fact of placing oneself under the protection of a donor is a natural act for a Tibetan chaplain, the same role signifies something else in the mind of a Manchu donor, especially when it involves the emperor. In the eyes of the Manchus, placing oneself under political protection and accepting Qing titles and seals amounts to accepting the donor's authority and to establishing a relationship of vassal to suzerain. In this way, each time a Dalai Lama or a Panchen Lama believed he was setting up the chaplain-donor role with the Manchu emperor, in reality, as the Chinese powers saw it, he submitted himself as a vassal. In this way, China has claimed suzerainty over Tibet for several centuries. Convinced of their right, Chinese leaders, whether Manchu emperors or presidents of the republic, affirm in all good faith that China holds suzerainty over Tibet. According to this logic, Tibet is part of China. For in accepting military support, Tibet accepts its vassal status.

It seems that on their side, over the centuries, the succession of Tibetan leaders made use of this misunderstanding as it suited them, and rejected it when they deemed the military protection had overstepped its bounds. What is so intriguing in the case of the Panchen Lama is to see a Tibetan prelate of his rank taking a public position normally stated by Chinese dignitaries. Yet would it be shocking to proclaim that until 1911 Tibet had had the status of a nation without sovereignty and that it had placed itself under the protectorate of the Manchu dynasty, if facts prove this to be true? On the other hand, it is surprising to note that the Panchen Lama's thinking went well beyond that of Sun Yat-sen regarding the membership of Tibet in the "union of the five nationalities."

Sun Yat-sen died without leaving any clear policy guidelines for either Tibet or Mongolia. Some of his associates were in favor of independence for the two nations. The Panchen Lama accorded the Republican government the right to claim Tibet's inclusion in the "union of the five nationalities," in part, to better fulfill his responsibilities toward what he called the "weak peoples." We will also see how this stance translates into action in terms of the relationship between the Panchen Lama and the Republican government. In any case, to affirm the inclusion of Tibet in the "union of the five nationalities," the Panchen Lama needed either a huge dose of courage, foolhardiness, cynicism, or treachery, depending on whose side we place him.

To encourage Mongolia and Tibet to rally behind the "union of the five nationalities" and actually achieve such a union, the Panchen Lama proposed three tangible measures: (1) promote peace, (2) invite the people in question to participate in the political life of the union and communicate the virtues of Sun Yat-sen's policies (especially the concept of equality, while also emphasizing the importance of morality), and (3) put in place development projects appropriate to each region, designed and financed by the Republican government.

In substance, the prelate considered that one of the Republican government's responsibilities was to help peripheral regions develop their economies, whereas Sun Yat-sen had left no specific instructions regarding this domain. The Panchen Lama's argument rested on a strict interpretation of the "Three Principles of the People." In 1931 he declared that he understood that "asking the Chinese government to help weak peoples conformed to the 'Three Principles of the People.'"[31] He made reference to a passage from the Sun Yat-sen's work that stated:

> We must help the weak and little peoples and oppose ourselves to the great powers of this world ... Before the development of China begins, let us commit ourselves today to raising the fallen and helping the weak.[32]

The Panchen Lama thus felt that there must not be two standards, and that the "benevolent measures" proclaimed by the Chinese government should profit China as well as Tibet and Mongolia, because during his travels through

China he was able to observe the budding beneficial effects of the economic development born of the national reconstruction project. The prelate also could not keep himself from comparing what he had seen in Mongolia and Tibet with the situation in China, which had opened to industrial progress. Several times he deplored "the pitiful situation in which the Tibetan people live, crushed by the taxes of the pro-British clique" and "the continually increasing suffering endured by the Tibetan people."[33] He added that:

> Mongolia and Tibet are two weak peoples with backward cultures ... [and] are regions where one never knows in the morning what the evening holds due to the development of the international situation and the imbalance of powers.[34]

Did the right recognized by the Republican government to insist that the peripheral regions adhere to the "union of the five nationalities" go along with the responsibility to ensure their economic development and guarantee their people a standard of living comparable to that of Inner China? As of 1929 the Panchen Lama warned Yan Xishan, director of the Mongolian and Tibetan Affairs Commission, on this subject:

> If the Chinese government neglects the peripheral regions, long-lasting peace cannot be expected, even if Inner China moves from the "supervisory phase" to the "constitutional phase."[35]

In concrete terms, beyond declarations of good intentions, what was the Panchen Lama expecting from the Republican government? He hoped that the Chinese leaders would clearly explain their intentions regarding the peoples in the peripheral regions, in order to gain their trust and facilitate their adherence to the union, and that a real project of construction would be put in place that took into account their differences. As a first step, the prelate set out to inform them of what he considered to be the "true situation of Tibet and Mongolia" and to request their help. In service of this dual goal, he wrote to Yan Xishan in 1929 and Chiang Kai-shek in 1930. Then, confronted with the feebleness of their responses, he himself conceived of a development project, which he later put forward to them with the hope of securing their support for it.

An outline of this project can be found in a speech that the prelate gave before Ma Hongkui, military governor of Ningxia, and the members of his government in January 1935.[36] Later in March 1935, the Panchen Lama raised the issue of this project again in a letter addressed to Huang Musong, the Chinese emissary to Tibet.[37] And he did so yet again in May 1935 during remarks he made in Xining in the presence of the local military chief Ma Bufang.[38] From these, the goals of the Panchen Lama development project emerge: to facilitate communication between regions in order to meet the needs of the people, to promote and develop education, and to instruct the people on the need for modernization.

This position contains nothing radical, since all these objectives are found in Sun Yat-sen's third principle of the people, that of "well-being." But in the immediate term, the Panchen Lama felt that his project must contribute to consolidating national defense in order to make up for the delays in the peripheral regions.

To reinforce the defense of the border regions, the Panchen Lama envisioned three steps for actualizing the goals of his development project. The first step consisted in constructing communication lines. Regarding this he said:

> The development and the economy of a region depend entirely on its roads. If I go back to Tibet, I would build roads for bus lines ... Politics and communication lines are inseparable.... In all the important districts, I would [also] set up radio transmitters and post offices.

His second step was to develop education:

> Tibet is a Buddhist land and many Tibetans are studying Buddhist philosophy. They do not feel concerned by politics. That is why those governing cannot understand the present national nor international politics nor the incredible development of technology. At the same time they do not see the threats that are present in their community. Now that I am returning to Tibet, I plan to create schools, to raise the level of education of the people, to encourage the young to take initiatives and open up to the outside world.

The third step consisted in promoting modernization initiatives:

> The Tibetan people advocate isolationism. They do not seek out contacts. They do not have their own means to modernize. That is why foreigners eye Tibet looking for opportunities. Presently, I am looking for competent men from different fields of modernization to accompany me to Tibet. Moreover, I strongly hope that in China men who are competent in art and technology and endowed with noble aspirations will go to the border regions to help the people there begin to modernize. Conversely, I will send young Tibetans to study technology in Inner China. [39]

The question of defense for the border regions seemed to seriously worry the Panchen Lama since he warned the Republican government about it several times through various public speeches. In 1931, for example, he said, "If Tibet is invaded by imperialists, it is as if our own door was destroyed by others. Inevitably, when the lips are gone, the teeth are exposed to cold."[40] Shortly thereafter in the same year, he further commented that the situation in Outer Mongolia should serve as a potent warning:

> All soft talk and gifts coming from a foreigner conceal a hidden agenda. We must not, therefore, be taken in. This region is subjected to pressure from powerful neighbors. The falcon does not let the deer out of his sight.[41]

In 1933 the prelate stated further that Mongolia and Tibet were extremely important for China's foreign relations because they act like buffer zones to the country's northwestern neighbors: Japan and Russia abut Mongolia, while Tibet borders British India. He renewed his warnings, telling members of the Republican government that if they could not find a way together to protect Tibet and Mongolia efficiently, then one day they would be invaded by foreign countries "which would be as cruel as cutting the hands and feet from a man. The situation in Outer Mongolia is proof of this today."[42]

To secure a center-periphery balance favorable to a harmonious relationship among the five nationalities and to ensure the economic development and modernization of Mongolia and Tibet, such that its peoples would no longer live in misery, the Panchen Lama believed strongly in the need for education and skills building. He believed that if the northwest inhabitants could read, then they could understand the current crises and better use raw materials and livestock, as well as improve hygiene, industry, and communication networks, so as to "cultivate each one's talents in the fields that would help the northwest catch up, being guided by the southeast provinces until they reach the same level."[43] The prelate made economic development a main topic of concern and repeatedly proclaimed: "From now on, throughout the country, may everyone, high and low, make it a point to make up for the delays! Without changing that, we cannot improve the situation!"[44]

Morality and Politics

Mixing politics and religion seemed natural for the Panchen Lama in the sense that each was at the service of mankind. He affirmed this many times. In a speech that he gave in September 1931 in Inner Mongolia, he pointed out that: "Perfecting the self goes back to practicing to attain enlightenment. [Let us] unite together through the force of religion. [Let us] use this force to protect our territory against national catastrophes." Later in his speech, the Panchen Lama reiterated this point saying:

> [Let us] unite the hearts of men through the strength of religion and safeguard the national territory through this powerful teaching, to pray to the Three Jewels, to bless the crowds, to care for the physical and mental health of each one.[45]

In 1932 he declared:

> The selfish imagine that politics consists in leading people, but it is more effective to exert a virtuous influence on people's thought through religion. We obtain better results ... Politics is nothing more than building a happy world where people live in peace.[46]

And in 1934 the Tibetan prelate said further:

> Politics and religion are complementary and are easily well-suited to each other.... On a small scale, we can liberate each being; on a large scale we can appease the politics of the entire world [through religion]. In this case, not only happiness and prosperity of the nation are assured, but peace and happiness for all humanity will follow ... I want my compatriots to study the true principles [of Sun Yat-sen] carefully, apply the policy through the virtues of the Buddhist law, and diffuse the doctrine of Buddha through the strength of politics.[47]

The Panchen Lama did not hesitate to disapprove of the activities of the members of the Republican government that diverged from this policy. As early as 1925 in his first speech, he clearly called those to order whom he felt had disregarded moral principles. For the prelate, sporadic regional fighting and the sacrifice of soldiers, along with the dilapidation of the state's gold had its origin in, among other things, "the selfishness of high officials drunk on their powers and the injustices they commit." According to Buddhist tradition, selfishness begins with the grasping of the self and in the ignorance of the illusory character of "I," which believes itself eternal, autonomous, self-made. This ignorance leads to obsessive desire to control, to possess all objects (or people) seeming pleasant to the all-powerful "I." It also leads to the development of hate, of violent rejection of all objects (or people) who seem unpleasant to the "I," and in the end creates general egoism, egocentrism, egotism, and so forth. The Panchen Lama advised members of the incriminated Republican government to "heal the illness of their grasping for the self, to correct themselves, to repent." He felt that if they adopted, as a basic principle, sincerity and the elimination of the grasping for the self, then national reconstruction would be easier to put in place.[48]

Shortly thereafter, the prelate reinforced his moral message and criticism of certain Chinese politicians, taking the parable of the rainbow, which is well-known to Buddhists, and affirming that:

> Emptiness cannot be grasped ... There are those who after the rain look at the seven-colored rainbow. They love the rainbow to the point of wanting to grasp it, but what is left in their hands? Emptiness! Today, numerous are those taking part in politics. Some express one opinion, the others express another, but no one really examines the causes of what is bad. They only produce empty words on a piece of paper. That is exactly like the one who admires the rainbow and hopes to grasp what is empty, but ends up obtaining nothing.[49]

The Panchen Lama used the occasion of the first National Reconstruction Conference to warn members of the Republican government who proclaimed the "harmonious coexistence of the five nationalities," but who, in fact, delayed applying it. In 1925 he noticed that in practice there was discrimination against certain territories and that the laws were "neither equitable, nor just, nor impartial" towards the people, and that the time was not right "for achieving union" of the five nationalities. The Panchen Lama would go even further in his discourse on morality in politics during a talk he gave on May 5, 1931, at the opening ceremony of the National People's Convention held in Nanjing. He warned Chinese politicians that before wishing to exercise their authority by telling others what they must do, before claiming to govern their country, they should mend their ways, and first control themselves. He summed up his thought in a short, powerful, succinct phrase: "to liberate the country, one must liberate oneself." The prelate's reasoning was that if one desires to liberate the country, then one must begin by the liberation of self, which first requires practicing good. To practice good, however, one first needs pure thoughts. The desire for pure thoughts consists in devoting oneself to reflection, which, in turn, means testing the nature of things. For the prelate, "those who test the nature of things achieve ultimate truth."

When evoking the possibility of liberating oneself, the Panchen Lama was naturally referring to a Buddhist notion. "Liberation" in this context consists in unchaining oneself from samsara, the cycle of conditioned existences by the force of karma, the supposed origin of all suffering. According to Buddhism, to achieve liberation from samsara, one must start by becoming aware of the "ultimate truth," the vacuity of all things, the empty character of autonomous existence, self-produced in a fusion of objects and beings belonging to the phenomenal world. Only the one who, by applying the teachings handed down by Buddha Śākayamuni, has acquired the deep and definitive conviction, based on his own existence, that phenomena exist, yes, but in a web of causes and conditions—that they are empty of all form of autonomous, self-produced existence—only such a person can truly claim to be liberated. Obviously, the Panchen Lama did not require as much for Chinese politicians!

Concerning the practice of good to liberate oneself, he told them, "If we do not work nor train ourselves toward the achievement of our own perfection, how can we help others when meeting a great number of difficulties?" In discussing the necessity of nurturing pure thoughts, the prelate went on to quote Confucius, whom he judged more accessible to their cultural reference. He urged the officials to "devote themselves to reflection in order to have a correct view of things, to be able to clearly distinguish true from false, good from bad." He also gave them an example that concerned them directly. He explained that if one clearly understands and recognizes that the "Three Principles of the People" are perfect revolutionary principles for safeguarding China and the world, then one will not be afraid to brave perils and to sacrifice oneself for their application. However, if one does not manage to sincerely believe in these principles and put them into practice ardently, then "we will fear the dangers and the sacrifice." The Tibetan prelate then invited the officials to "test the nature of things," and proposed that they "inform themselves attentively, to analyze and examine all phenomena whatever the moment and the place they are in." He concluded by pushing them to ask themselves: "Why has China reached this state of poverty and weakness today?"[50]

Promoting Peace

During the Panchen Lama's exile in China, the centrality of morality to politics remained one of his favorite subjects. Nevertheless, other subjects were dear to him as well. In his discourses, the term "peace" appeared regularly and the Panchen Lama never missed an opportunity to expound upon it. Logically, he believed that to achieve the "harmonious coexistence of the five nationalities," the people had to make peace.

Already in 1929 the prelate had developed three strategies for achieving peace. The first one involved favoring the union of China with its peripheries to achieve the "harmonious coexistence of the five nationalities" and together resisting the infringements of the great neighboring powers. The second entailed working to ensure that China could support and lead the Tibetan people so they could rule themselves autonomously (here the prelate insisted on the concept of equality between the different nationalities). And as a final strategy, the prelate wished to protect and diffuse the Tibetan religion to make the true essence of Buddhism contribute towards world peace. Two years later, his thoughts on the subject were further detailed. "All conflicts can be resolved through Buddhism," he said. "On the one hand, Buddhism can help in the appeasement of world wars, and on the other it can bring a huge contribution to world cultural heritage." The Panchen Lama then went on to declare himself ready to give "new momentum comeback to the teaching of the Yellow Hats [Gélukpa], to safeguard the national territory, to eliminate the suffering of the people, to send out a call for peace."[51]

When the Tibetan prelate asked the Republican government for a plan of resistance against the Japanese who were threatening to invade, he admitted to praying "for the eternal stability of the nation, the end of combats, and the complete elimination of suffering."[52] During the same year, he took stock of his actions since his arrival in China and claimed to have always cherished the values of peace. Similarly, he wished for the resolution of conflicts between the nationalities, adding that he endeavored "to harmonize the feelings between the Mongols and the Han through compassion."[53] In 1935 during another self-assessment, he said:

> At each place I have stopped, I had the occasion to organize Buddhist ceremonies; to spread the virtuous principles of the Chinese central government; to expose the "Three Principles of the People" in great detail; to advise monks, lay people, leaders, and officials of each of the Inner Mongolia banners to eliminate dissension among the nationalities.[54]

Most certainly the Panchen Lama acted in coherence with these religious convictions during his entire exile and became an indefatigable defender of peace. As evidence shows, his praise of the virtues of peace was not sufficient to convince Mongolia and Tibet to rejoin the union. To lead the people of these nations to recognize the good intentions of the Chinese government, the prelate decided to explain to them the advantages of equal rights within the republic. As his partners in dialogue seemed little receptive and unprepared for this kind of message, the Panchen Lama created an easier parallel for them in a speech that he gave in May 1934. As he put it:

> The cardinal virtue of he who governs the country under a clement sky consists in paying particular attention to peace, to being certain to follow a peaceful path and take care to preserve equality within the people ... Each of the paragraphs of the program of the "Three Principles of the People" of Sun Yat-sen mentions equality within the people, in particular, equality between individuals, equality between nationalities within the country, equality from an economic point of view, equality from a political point of view.

To further impress upon the minds of his audience, the Panchen Lama discussed his interpretation of equality, which, for him, must reign between the government and the people. For this, he took inspiration from a meditation well-known to Buddhists called "Exchanging and Equalizing Self with Others" that is attributed to Buddha Śākyamuni and was transmitted by the masters Mañjuśrī, Śāntideva, and Nāgārjuna. Ensuing from this Buddhist thought, the Panchen Lama adopted the reasoning that the government and the people cannot be separated. Further,

> They are beneficial to one another. The government depends on the people and their production. If there are no people, a nation cannot be built. This logic of interdependence, thus, explains that the people truly bring great benefit to the government. The government must bear in mind this benefit and take care of the people. It should not oppress, nor disregard the "barbarians." It must take upon itself to be beneficial, in turn, to the people. On the other hand, the people benefit from the government's protection. This explains the great benefit of the government towards the people. The people must keep in mind this benefit and, in turn, support the government. This is the path of mutual equality.

Then the Panchen Lama delved into the heart of the subject and examined equality between the nationalities. He began with the principle that "the five great nationalities of China wish to be treated in an equal manner, without taking into account their distance [from the center]." From there, he developed his idea:

> Today, in everything, mankind gives great importance to his private interest and very little to collective interest, not looking further than his own "I." Due to the

> intense nature of this self-grasping, thoughts of attachment and aversion towards our friends and enemies arise in our minds. Likewise we experience attachment towards those we love and to those who are close to us, and aversion towards those we hate and who are our enemies. And we are not considerate towards those who are in the middle (who are neither friend nor enemy) ... Those who are quarrelsome are that way spontaneously. They are selfish and want immediate pleasure. They do not worry about the suffering of those who founded the nation. The fact is therein. One single selfish thought destroys the merit brought by loyalty, filial piety, love, faith, and peace ... As a general rule, the selfish person holds resentment; he is incapable of feeling love. He is afraid of losing his body. He constantly worries and doubts. He does not pay attention to his faith. Whatever happens, that is the result of selfish grasping. If this attachment to the self arises, equality, then, cannot become a reality. The principle of equality must not only apply to material goods or social position. Above all, one needs a steady heart. If attachment to self is not eliminated, if a pure spark does not rapidly appear in our heart, "equality" will then remain merely a pious vow.

At this stage in his discourse, the Panchen Lama made a declaration in the form of a prophecy:

> If equality of material goods and social positions has already been established, but if it stems from a motivation that is impure and shortsighted, it will be an impossible equality to maintain. On the contrary, envy and jealousy for those in high positions and an even less equal world will arise from such "pseudo-equality."[55]

Does not what the prelate described in the 1930s correspond to what we have since seen in countries where the dictatorship of the proletariat degenerated into totalitarian regimes, controlled by small groups who misappropriated the principles of equality proclaimed by the Marxists, turning it to their own personal benefit?

The Panchen Lama explained that while common sense tells us that equality includes fidelity, filial piety, and so forth, it sidesteps the notion of the distribution of wealth. Equality was an important point for the prelate. He felt that the rich must save the poor, and the scholarly must teach those who are not, so that each person will have access to knowledge. It was indispensable that each person offers his material belongings, his knowledge, and his talents as a means to contribute to the development of the nation and the people. In order to act for the benefit of the greatest number and apply the theory of equality to material goods, the prelate urged his audience to follow the path of the compassionate heart. This meant that people should mutually help one another. If one acted only for one's own interest, happiness would be destroyed for eternity. The principle of equality involved everyone working together and helping each other with an unwavering heart. For the prelate: "If the principle of saving the nation and the great law of compassion of the Buddhist doctrine to free beings indeed match, then we can affirm that the heart of men can be pacified and beings can be united."[56]

It is clear that the Panchen Lama's thought contains the ingredients of a politically engaged Buddhism, one that focuses on internal transformation (before governing, it is necessary to govern oneself), discernment (which enables understanding situations with patience), equality (which leads to participation), compassion (which prepares union), love for the other (whether he belongs to the center or to Tibet or Mongolia), non-violence (which allows for peace), peace (which allows for the development of democracy), material development (which encourages happiness when accompanied by proper motivation), and interdependence of nations (which leads to universal responsibility).

The Panchen Lama's speeches, whether or not they were prepared by secretaries or members of the Republican government, reveal the basis of his thought to be a Buddhist rereading of the "Three Principles of the People," in which the prelate seems to have deeply believed. For him, such a union constituted the Chinese Republic. To achieve a Republican revolution, it was necessary to achieve the union of China with Tibet and Mongolia, that is, the "union of the five nationalities." Mongolia and Tibet were an integral part of the union of the nationalities. To obtain the adherence of Mongolia and Tibet to the union of nationalities and achieve the "harmonious coexistence of the five nationalities," it would be necessary to promote peace, explain to the respective peoples the importance of the concept of equality and participation in the political life of the republic, and to promote development projects specific to their needs that the Chinese Republic would implement. Mongolia and Tibet, as well as the other peripheral regions, would have to receive the status of regional autonomy, benefiting from support from the Republican government. Furthermore, to be credible, political programs could not afford to neglect the factor of morality that needed to be embedded in social policies.

In any case, the Panchen Lama developed his political thought very early on and stayed faithful to it till the end of his days. It is with this state of mind that he traveled to the warlords and the princes of Inner Mongolia from 1924 to 1931.

THE WARLORDS

After leaving Tashilhunpo, we do not know whether the Panchen Lama planned from the outset to go at some point to Beijing, then the capital of China, or if circumstances led him there. The facts remain that the first official figure that the Panchen Lama met was Lu Hongtao, the warlord from Gansu.[57] From this meeting on, the Panchen Lama found himself with no other option than to follow him. As the prelate crossed the province of Gansu and passed through Ganzhou, Liangzhou, and Pingfan, at each step military officers greeted him warmly and offered him their protection. Some gave him an escort of one hundred soldiers.

On May 8 (or May 9), 1924, the Panchen Lama arrived in Lanzhou where he was welcomed by thousands of people seeking his benediction. He settled into the monastery in Leitan and decided to stay for a while. During his sojourn, Lu Hongtao provided for his needs and that of his entourage. The warlord gave the prelate 300 yuan a day. Either because the Panchen Lama was still reluctant to go to Beijing or because he had stayed too long in Lanzhou, on July 16, 1924, Cao Kun, president of the Chinese Republic, gave him the title "Faithful Orator Devoted to the Propagation of Values" (*Zhizhong chanhua*).[58] This was one that Yuan Shikai had already attributed to him on May 1, 1913.[59]

The warlords Lu Entai, Hu Jingyi, Lu Zhenhua, and Yan Xishan took turns escorting the prelate to Beijing. He followed them since he lacked money and supplies. His hasty departure from Tashilhunpo had left the Tibetan prelate without his usual resources, and his survival depended on the goodwill of those he met. The warlords' motivations for assisting him remain unclear. Did they even know who he was? And yet, it seemed that all of them sought to find favor with the Panchen Lama, who, in turn, believed he was helping rein in the passions of these cynical ruffians.

After Cao Kun was nominated as head of the Republican government, the head of the Zhili clique, Wu Peifu, militarily controlled northern and central China, and was trying to unify the entire Chinese territory through the use of force. Wu, however, ran up against other divisions of the Beiyang army who were vying with him in their efforts to control northern China and the Beijing government. Then at the end of 1924, Feng Yuxiang, one of Wu Peifu's lieutenants, and Zhang Zuolin, the warlord of Fengtian, created an alliance against Wu Peifu.[60] According to his biographers, the Panchen Lama sent a telegram requesting that the fighting stop. Zhang Zuolin is said to have immediately replied that he was ready to give concessions to Wu Peifu and hoped to reach a peace agreement. Then other warlords, including Feng Yuxiang, are said to have taken the same attitude as Zhang Zuolin and offered to assist the Panchen Lama. Faced with the fierceness of the battles, the Panchen Lama is said to have sent telegrams to all branches of the Chinese government explaining the Buddhist law of cause and effect and the importance of being vigilant.[61] Biographers note that the Panchen Lama intervened again to try to bring peace between Zhang Zongchang, a lieutenant of Zhang Zuolin, and Qi Xieyuan, Wu Peifu's lieutenant, who fought each other in January 1925.[62] The prelate similarly intervened between Sun Chuanfang, another of Wu Peifu's lieutenants, and Feng Yuxiang's lieutenant Lu Yongxiang.[63] It seems that the warlords had overestimated the effects of the Panchen Lama's pacifying actions, because if the January 31, 1925 issue of *Dagong bao* said that Sun Chuanfang suddenly left the front, in the next day's edition it explained that the warlord's retreat was part of a military strategy.

In November 1925 the Panchen Lama began calls for peace to calm the warring passions of these men.[64] Briefly, the alliance between Feng Yuxiang and Zhang Zuolin broke when Zhang took control of the Beijing government. Sun

Chuanfang and Feng Yuxiang united to fight Zhang Zuolin. Wu Peifu then came back on the military scene supporting Zhang Zuolin. Feng Yuxiang and his allies were conquered. They fled to the Soviet Union, while Zhang Zuolin and Wu Peifu took control of northern China. However, since they were unable to establish a truly new government, a regent cabinet under military power was set up instead.[65] Obviously they took no account of the prelate's advice.

If the Panchen Lama's biographers emphasized his role as a pacifier, the biographers of the warlords do not speak of him at all.[66] In fact, the warlords obeyed the law of the strongest and did not bother themselves with mediators to reach a negotiated peace. It is clear that during the prelate's trip from Gansu to Beijing, he was confronted with a civil war situation, but his influence and any tangible results he may have obtained remain difficult to evaluate. The Panchen Lama's biographers certainly exaggerated the pacifying effects of his actions. Nevertheless, such actions on his part would correspond with his position as a religious leader and also with his political ideas.

The fact remains that nearly a year after the warlords' provisions of material support the Panchen Lama had still not reached Beijing. On January 15, 1925, the northern government contacted Beijing with a "pressing" issue, but did not provide any specific details. Duan Qirui, the new president of the republic, who was a fervent Buddhist and a donor of the Panchen Lama, sent a small group of men to Taiyuan. The group was comprised of Duan Hongye, his oldest son, Thubzang Norbu, a representative of the Mongolian and Tibetan Affairs Commission, Tukwen Rinpoche (Tuguan Hutuktu), and the Changkya Hutuktu. Their mission was to escort the Panchen Lama to Beijing.

Ngawang Lozang Chöden (1891–1957), the Changkya Hutuktu, who belonged to a *tulku* lineage close to the Qing emperors, was born in the Tibetan region of Amdo. In 1893 he was recognized as a *hutuktu*, a reincarnation of the Buddha Śakyamuni.[67] Ngawang Lozang Chöden was enthroned in Baruun monastery[68] in 1897, and became deputy director of the Office of Lama Seals at the Ministry of Rites at the age of fourteen in 1904, taking charge of this department two years later. He traveled extensively in Inner and Outer Mongolia to spread the Buddhist doctrine. In 1912 he responded to an invitation by the Republican government and went to Beijing. On this occasion, he was able to meet Yuan Shikai who is said to have insisted that he protect Buddhism, and to have suggested that the problems in Mongolia and Tibet could be resolved through religion.[69] Yuan Shikai bestowed on Ngawang Lozang Chöden the titles of "Omniscient Saint Full of Virtue and Compassion" (*Guanding pushan guangci*) and "Great Enlightened Savior" (*Hong ji guangming*). Following a sojourn at his monastery in Amdo, the Changkya Hutuktu returned to Beijing in 1919, at which time he received the title "Guest Who Devotes Himself to the Propagation of Values" (*Zhaoyin chanhua*). From Beijing, Ngawang Lozang Chöden moved towards the south of China. He taught Buddhism in Nanjing, Shanghai, and Hangzhou. After a return to Beijing and a new trip to Mongolia, he was then present in Taiyuan in 1925.

From Taiyuan, the Panchen Lama and the Changkya Hutuktu traveled in palanquins decorated with thick yellow silk and five-colored banners.[70] The magnificent, solemn procession entered Beijing on January 20, 1925.[71] The Panchen Lama was lodged in the Yingtai Palace of the Forbidden City. Once there, the organization of his daily life fell into place. The minister of finance allotted him 400 yuan per day and even gave him a yellow car!

In Beijing the Panchen Lama became a sort of voluntary hostage of the authorities. After the first National Reconstruction Conference, he met twice with Duan Qirui. On March 2, 1925, they attended a banquet together, and on the March 13 they discussed Mongolian and Tibetan issues. The Panchen Lama seemed to maintain good relations with Duan Qirui's government, since the minister of Mongolian and Tibetan affairs requested the Ministry of Finance to pay the expenses for receiving the prelate, which amounted to 30,000 yuan.[72] In the autumn of the same year, it gave him the title "World Savior Who Propagates Orthodoxy" (*Xuan cheng ji shi*) and a golden seal.[73] We do not know if the Panchen Lama transmitted teachings to Duan Qirui, nor do we know Duan Qirui's intentions towards the Panchen Lama.

The relationship established between Sun Chuanfang and the Panchen Lama seems clearer. For the prelate, the invitation from Sun Chuanfang meant an opportunity to build a new chaplain-donor relation. That is why the Panchen Lama went to Shanghai on April 29, 1925.[74] Afterwards he went to the Lingyin Temple in Hangzhou where he gave Buddhist initiations. In this way, the Panchen Lama first began giving Buddhist teachings and initiations to the warlords. But Sun Chuanfang soon began to show off his strength, demonstrating what he could bring to the prelate by bringing him on a visit to a military garrison and military exercise session.[75] The behavior of Sun Chuanfang towards the Panchen Lama could explain the nature and particular consideration that he and others of his ilk had for the prelate. The lives of the warlords were constantly threatened due to incessant wars. Because of the excessive danger in their lives, it seems that one of their unexpressed goals was to acquire supernatural powers, such as exceptional longevity through Tantric initiations. This seems to be confirmed by the attendance of numerous warlords and their allies, such as Duan Qirui, Wu Peifu, and Zhang Xueliang, at the Kālācakra initiation, one of the strongest Tantric initiations in Tibetan Buddhism, that was conferred by the Panchen Lama in the Hall of Supreme Harmony in the Forbidden City in Beijing in October 1932.

In 1927 Zhang Zuolin proclaimed himself "Supreme General of the Chinese Military Government" for having vanquished the expeditionary forces of the Kuomintang. However, he then had to retreat prior to the advance of the KMT's northern expeditionary armies.[76] A year later in June 1928 he died when the Japanese army deliberately blew up a train he was on. His son Zhang Xueliang asked the Panchen Lama to recite prayers for his father (Zhang Zuolin and the Panchen Lama had met in October 1926), confirming the special relationship established between the warlord and the Tibetan prelate. It seems that Zhang Xueliang wanted to continue this relationship. In September 1929, when he succeeded his father as head of the local clique, he sent Li Shaobai to the Panchen Lama to invite him for a visit. The Panchen Lama agreed and decided to spend the winter in Shenyang. In this way, the two men consolidated their relationship as chaplain-donor.

On November 22, 1929, the Panchen Lama encouraged the Republican government to end the reign of the warlords in order to spare human lives. He also advised Yan Xishan and Feng Yuxiang to cease combat and to spare the people further suffering.[77] Indeed, although the northern expedition had ended, the authority of certain warlords had extended across several provinces. Moreover, when Chiang Kai-shek decided to end the united front created between his party and the Comintern, the Nationalist Party broke into two groups. One was referred to as the Left Wing and remained in favor of the long-standing alliance with the Communists while the other, the Right Wing, abandoned this union. Members of the Left Wing of the Nationalist Party, such as Li Zongren, Zhang Fakui, and Wang Jingwei allied themselves with the warlords Yan Xishan and Feng Yuxiang against the Chiang Kai-shek government. With their support, Yan Xishan, the military governor of Shanxi, took control of the Beijing government in September 1930.[78]

In July Chiang Kai-shek launched numerous offensives against the warlords, both in northern and southern China. By September 1930 he had stabilized his bases in Shandong. Yan Xishan requested the support of Zhang Xueliang but was refused. As a result, Yan Xishan retreated to Shanxi. Then, when Chiang Kai-shek had vanquished Feng Yuxiang, Zhang Xueliang joined him. Thanks to the cooperation of Zhang Xueliang, the warlord of Fengtian, Chiang Kai-shek took Beijing and emerged as the victor in this fight for something close to control of all of China.[79] After the defeat of Feng Yuxiang, the Panchen Lama went to Shenyang where he gave numerous Buddhist teachings to Zhang Xueliang in April 1931.[80]

This last episode ended the relations that the Panchen Lama had maintained with the warlords. We could say they met in an opportunistic way, each seeking their own benefit from the other. The Panchen Lama undertook to find new donors who could help him free himself from the debt he had with the Tibetan government. As for the warlords, heedless of Dharma precepts, they were nevertheless interested in the Tantric initiations given by the prelate because they hoped that therein they would find magical powers that would make them invincible. During the period he frequented the warlords, the Panchen Lama tried, no doubt, to promote values of peace with them. But warlike tendencies were so anchored in their daily lives that they could not follow the prelate's advice to any significant extent. However, it seems that the Panchen Lama did have a deeper influence on two of the warlords: Sun Chuanfang and Duan Qirui. Sun Chuanfang took vows as a Buddhist two years after meeting the Tibetan prelate, and Duan Qirui eventually left the political scene to devote his life to Buddhist studies.[81]

THE PRINCES OF INNER MONGOLIA

In Inner Mongolia two political currents arose in the 1920s.[82] One espoused the ideas of the Chinese Nationalist Party. Its partisans created the Mongol Nationalist Party in October 1925 with the agreement of Sun Yat-sen, who saw it as a way to increase the influence of his party.[83] They wished to eliminate princely privileges and put in place a Republican framework, while, at the same time, benefit from their status as an autonomous region within the Chinese Republic. They were led by Buyantai and supported by the warlord Feng Yuxiang. Buyantai was a Mongol from the Qorcin Banner of the Josutu League.[84] Holding a degree from the Institute for Mongolian and Tibetan Studies in Beijing, he joined Sun Yat-sen in Shanghai in 1918. Sun Yat-sen named him member of the executive committee in 1924. Buyantai became president of the new Mongol Nationalist Party in March 1925, and organized a Mongol revolutionary army.[85] The sympathizers of the other political current also wanted to obtain the status of an autonomous region within the Chinese Republic, but while still preserving princely privileges. They favored a vibrant Mongol culture and rejected assimilation into Chinese culture. They were led by Prince Demchüg Dongrub, Mongol chief of the Western Sünid Banner of the Shilingol League.

In 1928 the Mongols tried to negotiate with Chiang Kai-shek the status of an autonomous region for Inner Mongolia after the dissolution of the Mongol Nationalist Party and the creation of the Republican government in Nanjing.[86] But Chiang Kai-shek refused and divided the territory of Inner Mongolia, creating four separate regions—Chahar, Jehol, Ningxia, and Suiyuan—that were superimposed on the domains of the leagues and banners.[87] Some months later, faced with the lack of results from Buyantai's dealings with the Republican government, Unenbayin, an advisor to the Mongolian and Tibetan Affairs Commission, went to Nanjing to protest against this measure and demanded autonomous regional status for Inner Mongolia.

Unenbayin was born in 1896. A Mongol from the Qorcin Banner of the Josutu League, he was the first Mongol to graduate from the University of Beijing, receiving his diploma in 1926. He taught at the Institute of Mongolian and Tibetan Studies in Beijing and assisted the director of the Mongolian and Tibetan Affairs office. Like Buyantai, he was part of a progressive establishment advocating for an autonomous Inner Mongolia inside the administrative structure of the Chinese Republic, under the condition that the Mongol culture be respected and preserved.[88] While Unenbayin expected a positive response to his proposal, Chiang Kai-shek chose instead to elevate the "Special Regions" to the rank of provinces on August 29, 1928. Unenbayin thereupon decided to establish the Office of Affairs of the Allied Leagues and Banners of Mongolia (*Menggu ge meng qi lianhe zhu Jing banshichu*) in Nanjing where he could more easily work for the Mongol cause, while the Chinese authorities reorganized the Mongolian and Tibetan Affairs Commission.[89]

It is in this context that the Panchen Lama traveled tirelessly throughout Inner Mongolia. At the beginning of 1927, the Tibetan prelate was the guest of Prince Darhan, then Prince Tüsheet, both from the Qorcin Banner of the Jerim League. In June 1928 he went to the estate of Prince Jastu also from the Qorcin of the Jerim League. In November of the same year he visited the lands of the Üjümücin Banner, and then those of Prince Abaga. By April 1929 the Panchen Lama was crossing the territory of Abaga and Eastern Sünid, and by June he had arrived in the region of Prince Demchüg Dongrub, chief of the Western Sünid. In August the prelate returned to the Abaga lands, crossing the area of the Üjümücin from west to east. He then passed through the estate of the Eastern Qocit and the Western and Eastern Üjümücin Banners as well as those of the Qorcin. Finally, in April 1930 he traveled to the province of Liaoning, and then returned to Inner Mongolia to stay with Sönam Rabten, chief of the Western Üjümücin.[90] Throughout his travels, the prelate spent the essential part of his time giving Buddhist teachings. His activities were, however, not restricted to the religious realm.

On November 1, 1930, the Panchen Lama wrote to Chiang Kai-shek through the auspices of the Mongolian and Tibetan Affairs Commission. In the letter, written in his native tongue with a salutation scarf attached, he told the Chinese leader:

> You have invited me twice already, but at those times China was undergoing never-ending calamities. The circumstances were not favorable. I was thus constrained to stay temporarily in Mongolia. I have been devastated by the schism in the five nationalities. Several times, I have tried to advise the Mongol people through religious precepts, so that they will turn to the Chinese central government and not succumb to the talk from other parties.[91]

The Panchen Lama obviously wanted it known for the record that he had tried to convince the Mongols to participate in the "union of the five nationalities."

Several months later on May 5, 1931, the Panchen Lama met Chiang Kai-shek in Nanjing during the National People's Convention that celebrated the creation of the Nanjing government.[92] At this occasion, the prelate gave a speech entitled "I Hope the Inhabitants of the Country Know Tibet."[93] Among the eight sessions that comprised this meeting, one was about the development of the Mongol culture. The Panchen Lama took part in it and gave another speech entitled "Before Governing the Country, One Must First Govern Oneself," in which he focused on, among other things, the importance of Mongolia and Tibet as buffer states protecting China from its powerful neighbors—the British Raj and Russia. The prelate emphasized the critical situation the Mongol and Tibetan peoples found themselves in "due to the evolution of the international situation and the imbalance of forces," and he encouraged the Republican government to put in place a large-scale development project capable of improving their standard of living, while preserving their culture. The purpose of such a project was to also guarantee the "sovereignty" of the two nations faced with the aggressive impulses of the Russians and British.[94]

OFFICIAL POLITICAL ACTIONS

On July 1, 1931, while in Nanjing, the Panchen Lama received from Chiang Kai-shek the title of "Great and Glorious Master Panchen Who Protects the Country and Propagates its Values" (*Huguo xuanhua guanghui da shi*).[95] This date is important. From then on, the Panchen Lama, in effect, began a cycle of activities that were officially part of the political system of the Chinese Republic. He had in this way just obtained recognition and material support from the Republican government, which had appreciated his action in the field and, by placing him under its protection, had become his donor. In exchange, he accepted a two-pronged political role.

First, the prelate saw himself as given the task of ambassador, responsible for spreading the Republican government's policies, especially its "values," in the peripheral regions. This involved no contradiction for him, especially since such government policies were built on the basis of the "Three Principles of the People," which, as we have seen, he supported. As for the "values" handed down from Sun Yat-sen, they were sufficiently close to his own that he was able to appropriate them without difficulty. Second, the prelate had the duty of informing the government of the situation in the peripheral territories as he witnessed it, which he had done previously with the hopes of convincing Republican leaders to release funds to help the economically weaker peoples.

On July 8, 1931, the Panchen Lama left Nanjing for a trip that took him all the way to Heilongjiang, where he decided to stop in Hulunbuir. As he approached the city, located near the border of the Mongolian People's Republic, its inhabitants came to pay homage to him. On September 5, 1931, he gave a speech in which he reminded the Mongols that in the past they had maintained good relations with the Chinese:

> Let us remember that Sino-Mongol relations are closely linked. Since the dynasties of the Qin and the Han where their exchanges were cordial, until the dynasties of the Tang and the Yuan where they were closer still, the influence of Chinese culture on Mongols allowed the two peoples to deepen their relations. In the past, the Chinese and the Mongols mutually helped each other. This way, in the past, ancestors, grandfathers, or fathers lived together on good terms. Later the descendants, sons, and grandsons lived in harmony . . .[96]

The Panchen Lama used the situation of the Mongolian People's Republic as an example, warning his audience to be wary of foreigners. He exhorted them to rally to the "union of the five nationalities" and concluded his speech with the words: "[Let us] unite together to resist the enemy and lay down the cornerstone of the country." From Hulunbuir the Panchen Lama telegraphed the Mongolian and Tibetan Affairs Commission to order the Sünid and Üjümücin Banners to prepare for his arrival on their lands and to ensure his protection, as the area had become dangerous for him.[97] It seems that the Tibetan prelate was a victim of an attempted kidnapping by individuals who wished to take him to the Mongolian People's Republic by force, but the Hailar authorities had managed to thwart the plan. Who would have wanted to kidnap him?

Existing sources offer three possible hypotheses, but among them, none is conclusive. The first hypothesis speculates that the plotters were from the Mongolian People's Republic. Remember that on December 29, 1911, the territory had come under Russian control. In 1924 the Jétsun Dampa, the "Sovereign of Outer Mongolia," had died, and the birth of the Mongolian People's Republic was proclaimed. In 1930 certain members of the new Mongolian People's Republic are said to have contacted the Panchen Lama, asking him to help them defend their northern border against a massive influx of Russians, since they believed the prelate was at the head of a powerful army. Others, more radical, had imagined an invasion of the Mongolian People's Republic from Manchuria and Inner Mongolia. The management of the operations, aided by Japanese forces, would have been given to the Panchen Lama since, according to the plotters of this intrigue, only he could rally all the Buddhist Mongols against the pro-Soviet Mongol Revolutionary Party. On the other hand, the plotters would have allowed the search for the reincarnation of the deceased Jétsun Dampa in order to put the incarnate on the throne.[98] The Panchen Lama had declined their invitation, which meant that they might have attempted a kidnapping, so that his presence could serve their cause.

The second hypothesis implicates the members of the old Mongol Nationalist Party (1925–27) of Inner Mongolia. These figures were violently anti-clerical, to the point that in July 1929 they considered the Panchen Lama a "mortal danger for the Mongols."[99] Some of them, such as Fu Mingtai and Merse (Guo Daofu), were originally from Hulunbuir. They, therefore, had a direct interest in eliminating the Panchen Lama from the local political scene, as his actions hindered their policies.[100] The third hypothesis points to the Japanese, who at the time had just invaded the two northeast provinces of Jilin and Liaoning, shortly after the "Mukden Incident."[101] It is possible, though not likely, that they might have desired to bring the Panchen Lama to their side to support their policies in Inner Mongolia.

On October 12, 1931, Unenbayin managed to put a proposed law (*Menggu meng bu qi zuzhi fa*) to a vote before the Chinese National Assembly that would redefine the organization of the Mongol leagues, tribes, and banners. This law would also have established relations with Chinese districts and provinces (Articles 5–9). It sought to reform the administration of each league (Articles 10–21) as well as that of the banners (Articles 22–35). Additionally, it would have imposed the creation of an assembly for each league, whose members would be elected for a mandate of one year (Articles 17–18). These representatives of the people would, in turn, choose permanent members (Article 19). The decisions made at the assembly would then be ratified by the Chinese State Council (Articles 20–21).[102]

For Unenbayin, this law marked the first step of the integration of Inner Mongolia into the Chinese Republic. However, it was unacceptable to Prince Demchüg Dongrub and to the other heads of the leagues and banners, because their privileges and powers would have devolved to a council elected by the people. Dissatisfied with the law's content, the Mongol princes decided to ignore it and establish their autonomy without the help of China. They chose Prince Demchüg Dongrub as their head.[103] At the beginning of 1932, when the Panchen Lama was still residing at Prince Demchüg Dongrub's estate, the prelate temporarily ceased his activities so that he could be near Prince Demchüg Dongrub for any support he might be able to provide. On February 5, 1932, the Japanese invaded the northeast border province of Heilongjiang with no resistance. Indeed, Chiang Kai-shek, who took it upon himself to eradicate the bases for Communism in Jiangsu, had ordered Zhang Xueliang not to fight against the Japanese. From then on, the Japanese were able to occupy the three Manchurian provinces of Jilin, Liaoning, and Heilongjiang. On March 1, 1932, the Japanese founded the state of Manchukuo and placed Puyi, the last Qing emperor, at its head.

The Panchen Lama returned to the lands of the Ulanqab League as well as to those of the Sünid and Üjümücin Banners of the Shilingol League. At Bat Khaalga monastery under the Darhan Banner of the Ulanqab League, he invited his audience to take an oath of resistance against the Japanese.[104] On March 4, 1932, the Tibetan prelate sent a telegram to the Chinese central authorities requesting that they prepare a plan of resistance against the Japanese. In his message, he reminded them of his own activities on the ground: "During these last five months, the princes and people have forbidden use of the roads to better welcome me during my long trip. I have been propagating the guidelines of the Chinese central government policies."[105]

On April 14, 1932, the Panchen Lama received a new title from the Chinese government, that of "Emissary in Charge of Spreading Values in the Western Region" (*Xichui xuanhua shi*).[106] Theoretically, the task associated with this title ended his mission in Inner Mongolia since propagating values on the Western frontier would essentially entail travel through Amdo, Kham, and Ü-Tsang. Nevertheless, from July to September 1932 the Panchen Lama remained at Bat Khaalga monastery where he intensified his religious activities.[107] Then he went to Suiyuan where Fu Zuoyi, governor of the province, welcomed him.[108] During the Kālacakra ceremony in Beijing, he met Prince Demchüg Dongrub and the Changkya Hutuktu, and spoke extensively about the situation in Inner Mongolia.[109]

In December the same year, Prince Demchüg Dongrub again went to Nanjing where he requested that Chiang Kai-shek not divide Inner Mongolia and that he renounce the incorporation of the Mongol leagues and banners into Chinese provinces. According to the prince, Inner Mongolia occupied a strategic position for protecting China from Japan. He added that China's interests alone would be insufficient to motivate the Mongols to fight side by side with the Chinese, and that to resist the Japanese invasion, his compatriots needed a strong national consciousness. Prince Demchüg Dongrub's request for obtaining autonomy for Inner Mongolia fell on deaf ears. Chiang Kai-shek refused to consider it.[110]

At around the same time, the Panchen Lama went to Nanjing at the request of members of the numerous local lay Buddhist associations that had attended the Kālacakra in Beijing. He was said to have been impressed by the associations' quality and strength as well as that of the Republican government, which insisted on giving him the seal of "Emissary in Charge of Spreading Values in the Western Region."[111]

On December 21, the Tibetan prelate received journalists at the Overseas Chinese Hotel in Nanjing in which he assessed his action in Inner Mongolia:

> These last years, the affairs of State have become more and more complex. Foreign incursions have been deeper and deeper ... The situation is unstable. Ever since the upheaval last autumn with the Manchuria incident, the Mongols are restless ... They recognize the virtues of the Chinese central government and cry bitterly. All the princes and dukes of the leagues and banners are united to defend the country ... So quickly, ten years have passed since I left Tibet to come east ... I have traveled continuously between Mongolia and Inner China and have been unsparing in my efforts to diffuse the virtuous policies of the government.[112]

Two days later, the Panchen Lama expressed himself in similar terms during a meeting to welcome officials who had come to receive him in Nanjing:

> I am leaving the capital to head west because of the present situation. But this does not mean I am giving up my interest in the political affairs of the center. As the Mongols have been destabilized, the moment has come to spread the values in the whole region of Mongolia, east and west, so that each prince and each duke of the leagues and banners knows the basics. I spoke about the relations between the Han and the Mongols using metaphors and I presented the general policies of the Chinese central government as well as its will to protect the Mongol people. Our Mongol compatriots have understood. They were very moved and said: "We vow to sincerely defend the country and support the Chinese central government."[113]

On January 21, 1933, while participating in the commemoration of the fifth anniversary of the founding of the Mongolian and Tibetan Affairs Commission, the Panchen Lama gave a speech in which he provided a summary of his work on the propagation of values in eastern and western Mongolia. The Tibetan prelate particularly emphasized his efforts to spread the Chinese central government's policies, since he was worried about Japanese and Russian influence in Mongolia. He spoke of the "harmonious coexistence of the five nationalities" as a "determined and achievable project," and his plans to spread those values to the western regions.[114]

Despite his declarations about his plans to travel to westward, the Tibetan prelate could not restrain himself from returning to Inner Mongolia in February 1933. This change makes one think he considered his mission there unfinished. Although officially assigned by the Chinese government to go propagate their values in the western regions, he went where his conscience called him.

Leaving on February 7, the Panchen Lama first stopped in Beijing where he was welcomed by Zhang Xueliang, and on February 17 he arrived at Bat Khaalga monastery.[115] In March 1933, while residing in Inner Mongolia, he became alarmed at the progression of Japanese troops that were invading the province of Jehol. Fulfilling his mission as an informant, he sent a telegram explaining the situation to the Chinese authorities, and encouraged them to reinforce their border defense. According to the prelate, "each prince and each duke has respected the general guidelines of the Chinese central government policy. One after another they vowed to take arms and dedicate themselves to the country to chase out the Japanese tyrants."[116]

In the field, the advance of Japanese troops increasingly frightened the Mongols who, deprived of an army, were unable to resist. The unrest of the Mongols reached a peak on May 3, 1933, when the Japanese took half of Jehol Province and annexed it to that of Xing'an, which they had created in March of the same year.[117]

The lands of the Üjümücin and Sünid Banners in the Shilingol League bordered those provinces that had been colonized by the Japanese. The Panchen Lama, who affirmed his wish to calm the climate of war and assure the Mongol princes of the Republican government's support, envisaged teaching Buddhist doctrine on the lands of these two banners. Shi Qingyang, the director of the Mongolian and Tibetan Affairs Commission, tried to dissuade him, because according to him the prelate would expose himself to too much peril. Indeed, rumor had it that the Japanese and Emperor Puyi wanted to send a representative to "invite" the Panchen Lama to go to Changchun to teach Buddhism. Other rumors had it that the Japanese were ready to send ten planes to kidnap the Tibetan master. Finally, the director of the Sino-Japanese Tantric Buddhist Research Association took the opportunity to send greetings to the Panchen Lama, which added to the confusion.[118] The recommendations of Shi Qingyang were ultimately in vain. The Panchen Lama, more persistent than ever, went to the lands of the Shilingol League in spite of the danger.

On May 31, 1933, the Chinese and Japanese governments signed the Treaty of Tanggu. The Chinese government recognized Japanese presence in Manchuria and Inner Mongolia. It declared that the eastern part of Suiyuan Province, the northern area of Chahar Province, and the eastern territory of the Yeke Juu League were "demilitarized zones" (*fei wuzhuang qu*).[119] The Republican government put forth no resistance to the Japanese troops and committed to nonintervention in these zones.

That is why one month later in June 1933, Prince Demchüg Dongrub, persuaded that only a united Mongol front would allow them to resist the enemy, assembled the heads of the other banners and held a large meeting in Bat Khaalga monastery to determine the best tactical way to defend western Mongolia.[120] He contacted each of the chiefs one by one, and had little difficulty convincing them to attend the meeting. In addition to wishing to repel the Japanese troops, each of the meeting's members had his own reasons for participating. Several were experiencing pressure from ex-warlords who wanted to take their territories; for example, Yan Xishan, the warlord from Shanxi, had been harassing Yönden Wangchuk, head of the Ulanqab League whose land seemed sufficient for feeding his soldiers. Some were trailed by their local warlord, making it difficult for Prince Demchüg Dongrub to freely communicate with them. Others were openly forbidden from attending. Fu Zuoyi, the ex-warlord of Suiyuan, for instance, prevented Altan Ocir, the head of the Yeke Juu League, from traveling to the meeting. Altan Ocir was, therefore, secretly contacted and gave his support to the movement.[121]

Following this first meeting of the Movement for the Autonomy of Inner Mongolia (*Nei Mengu zizhi yundong*) of which Prince Demchüg Dongrub had taken the lead, the Mongol chiefs demanded the creation of an autonomous government of Inner Mongolia, which would be under the direct control of the Chinese Republican government.[122] In other words, they would no longer accept answering to the provincial governments of Chahar and Suiyuan created by the Republican government in 1928 to stifle the budding Mongol autonomy movement.[123] This request was obviously rejected.

On his side, the Panchen Lama left Bat Khaalga monastery on July 1, 1933, and arrived on the lands of Prince Demchüg Dongrub the following month on August 7. From there he wrote a long telegram to the Mongolian and Tibetan Affairs Commission, explaining in detail the results of the journey he had undertaken to the leagues and banners of western Mongolia. The Tibetan prelate was continually wooed. A certain Suzuki came to visit him on Prince Demchüg Dongrub's lands on September 4, 1933. On September 7, representatives from the provincial government of Gansu offered sacred texts to the Bat Khaalga monastery.[124] The same day, Lozang Gyeltsen, the Panchen Lama's attendant, arrived from Beijing at Prince Demchüg Dongrub's estate, while Lozang Tsültrim and Kelzang Chönjor went to Bat Khaalga monastery. Fu Zuoyi requested Buddhist representatives, one of whom was a certain Liu Deng, to also go to Bat Khaalga monastery. Finally, the governor of the Shanxi provincial government sent both Shi Huayan, the general administrator from the region responsible for clearing lands for cultivation, and Dingwang Dorjé, the director of the Office of the Panchen Lama in Suiyuan, to show friendship to the prelate at the request of Prince Dörben Keüked.[125]

On September 24, 1933, the Japanese occupied Dolonnor, then Jiaotou bao in Chahar Province. Their spies infiltrated the ranks of the leagues and banners. They ran over the lands of the Shilingol League and then advanced on the lands of the Üjümücin League. They tried to get close to Prince Sönam Rabten.[126] According to Fang Fanjiu, the Mongol princes immediately called the Mongol chiefs of all the leagues and banners, including those living in Nanjing and Beijing, to come to the first of several meetings to be held on September 28, 1933. These meetings would attempt to put into place an autonomous government in Inner Mongolia, despite the refusal of Nanjing to do so.[127] Chen Wenjian and Liu Jiaju, however, indicated that this first meeting would be held on September 11 in the Bat Khaalga monastery in the Darhan Banner of the Ulanqab League. At the time, the Panchen Lama was staying on the lands of the Üjümücin Banner. The princes noted that they had learned from Prince Demchüg Dongrub, himself, that the structure of the autonomous government of Inner Mongolia would be decided then and there. As the Mongol chiefs had not yet planned to meet, the autonomous government of Inner Mongolia would have to be organized later. In any case, Prince Demchüg Dongrub had confided in the Panchen Lama on September 19, 1933. In response, the Tibetan prelate sent two representatives, his attendant Lozang Gyeltsen as well as Kelzang Chönjor, to Chiang Kai-shek's headquarters in Nanchang in Jiangxi to inform him of the developments regarding the Inner Mongolia situation.[128]

On September 28, 1933, not long before leaving Prince Demchüg Dongrub's estate to head towards the Ulanqab League lands, the Panchen Lama telegraphed the director of the Mongolian and Tibetan Affairs Commission asking him to request the Republican government to send high officials to Inner Mongolia to undertake negotiations with the Mongols who were about to create an autonomous government.[129] In addition, he invited the Mongol princes to interviews in which he advised them to wait until the arrival of representatives from the authorities in Nanjing before creating their government, but without success.

One Mongol prince who was opposed to the autonomy of Inner Mongolia is said to have requested that the Changkya Hutuktu come and accomplish his mission as "Emissary in Charge of Spreading Values in the Mongol Leagues" (*Meng qi xuanhua shi*), a title given to him by the Mongolian and Tibetan Affairs Commission in April 1932. The Buddhist master left Mount Wutai and headed for Beijing on October 2. After crossing Taiyuan, he arrived in Beijing. There he met two obstacles. The excessive cost of the trip prevented him from continuing. The Changkya Hutuktu is said to have then requested the princes of the leagues to finance him, but they refused.[130] The Mongols rejected his mediation outright. Mongol students and intellectuals had demonstrated against him in Nanjing, and apparently even threatened him if he acted against the political aspirations of the Mongol people.[131]

Whatever the case, the first meeting to establish an autonomous Inner Mongolia government took place at Bat Khaalga monastery on October 9, 1933. The members of the future government were designated. Prince Yon of the Ulanqab League and Prince Demchüg Dongrub were included.[132] Their first mission consisted in preparing the organizing principles of the autonomous government.

Four days later, the members of the future Mongol government, under Japanese pressure, hastened to develop this law.[133]

A second meeting was held at Bat Khaalga monastery on October 15, 1933, in which 116 Mongols, representing the various leagues and banners, attended. The designated head of the autonomous Mongol government, Prince Yon, along with all the other princes had invited the Panchen Lama several times to come and preside over the meeting. Prince Yon first sent the prelate a telegram on October 11. Then the representatives of the government went personally to see him on October 14.[134] It is probable that the Mongols felt the Panchen Lama, independent of his personal convictions in favor of the five nationalities, would better be able to defend their interests due to his good relations with the Chinese authorities. Yet, nothing indicates that the Tibetan prelate was present at the monastery by October 15. His biography fails to clearly indicate whether he actually accepted this role. On October 15, Prince Yon notes in his opening remarks that he had invited the Panchen Lama to preside over the meeting when the Tibetan master was staying on Prince Dörben Keüked's estate. In addition, we know that on November 2, the Panchen Lama was staying at Bat Khaalga monastery, but the date of his arrival remains difficult to determine.

In any case, Prince Yon, who led the session, read out loud three times the organizational law of the government. This law specified that the autonomous government of Inner Mongolia would stay under the direct control of the Chinese central government. The autonomous government would manage its internal political affairs within the territorial limits of Inner Mongolia, while the Chinese central government would take care of military affairs and foreign relations. The autonomous government would be composed of a department of political affairs, a judicial commission, and an advisory department. The organizational law proposed by Prince Yon was approved by the majority of the members at the meeting, and the "Autonomous Mongol Government" was officially created that day.[135]

On October 19 the members of the new government met for the third time in order to put into place its administrative structures. The key measures they took concerned a working budget and the creation of an army. They decided that each league and banner would contribute 320,000 yuan to the annual budget of the autonomous government. In addition, each league had to furnish one thousand soldiers and one thousand horses to create a Mongol guard. The next day the members of the Mongol Office in Nanjing called a press conference. They announced that the major part of Inner Mongolia had been occupied by the Japanese, and that the leagues and banners of Shilingol, Üjümücin, and Yeke Juu had been pushed to the brink of disaster. The members of these leagues had the feeling that if they didn't organize themselves, they would be unable to resist the Japanese invasion, which is why they requested that the Republican government recognize Inner Mongolia as an autonomous region.[136]

On October 20, 1933, the Republican government sent two representatives, Huang Shaohong, the minister of the interior, and Zhao Pilian, the deputy director of the Mongolian and Tibetan Affairs Commission, to negotiate with the Mongols.[137] They asked the Changkya Hutuktu to accompany these two representatives. At the announcement of this news, various Mongol associations in Nanjing opposed the mediation of the Changkya Hutuktu. Members of the Association of Compatriots of Inner and Outer Mongolia (*Nei Wai Meng lü Ping tongxiang hui*) in Beijing rejected his intervention on the pretext that he was hostile to the establishment of an autonomous government. In the same way, members of the Association for the Safeguard of Mongolia (*Menggu jiuji hui*) let it be known that the task of monks was not to interfere in domestic politics, but to recite prayers and honor Buddha. They added that the comments made by the Changkya Hutuktu did not reflect those of the Mongol people and that in no case could this Buddhist master know how to represent them to the Chinese government.[138]

A fourth meeting was held at Bat Khaalga monastery on October 21, where the Mongols officially elected members of their autonomous government by yelling out the names and having the attendees approve or reject them. Prince Yon was elected president. Prince Demchüg Dongrub became the director of the department of political affairs. E'erheseqinzhamubala and Babaoduo'erji would direct, respectively, the judicial commission and the advisory department. The autonomous government would have its headquarters in Tianchi, on the lands of the Dürben Quqet Banner of the Ulanqab League.[139] The same day, the representatives of the Republican government, Huang Shaohong and Zhao Pilian, arrived in Beijing. They met with the governor of Chahar Province and with the Changkya Hutuktu.[140]

On October 24, 1933, members of the Mongol Autonomous Government met for the fifth time. They prepared to welcome Huang Shaohong and Zhao Pilian. The Panchen Lama, who had been residing at Bat Khaalga monastery since mid- to late-October, participated in the discussions. He gave a speech to the Mongol princes during which he asked them not to make an irreversible decision before the two Chinese officials arrived. He advised them to opt for the status of regional autonomy so as to benefit from the support of the Chinese government. Faithful to his political convictions, he said to them:

> The reason I have sojourned in Inner China and near the Mongol border for ten or so years now, and why I have not returned to Tibet is that I pray for a sincere union, the coexistence and prosperity of the five nationalities. My humble self begs you to be full of concern and to strive for this sought-after goal. If so, I will not be the only one happy.[141]

When the time was ready the Mongol Autonomous Government sent representatives to welcome Huang Shaohong and Zhao Pilian to Suiyuan, while the Panchen Lama left the task of greeting them to a member of his entourage.[142] Arriving at Bat Khaalga monastery on October 31 (or November 10), 1933, the two representatives of the Republican government are said to have honored the holiness of the site by prostrating to the representations of Buddha. When the Panchen Lama, who had left the monastery to go to the Yeke Juu estate on November 4, came back, he asked them to pray for the happiness of the nation.[143] Parallel to these pious actions they led heated negotiations with the members of the Mongol Autonomous Government to whom they transmitted the decisions taken by the Chinese State Council. According to the Chinese, the Mongolian and Tibetan Affairs Commission was to become either the Ministry of Border Affairs (*bianwu bu*) or the Ministry of Mongolia and Tibet (*Meng Zang bu*). In either case, this department would be administered directly by the Chinese State Council. The provinces and districts already existing in Inner Mongolia would be kept. The Mongols living in these provinces would need to create a commission of political affairs for the Mongol Region, whose mission would be to manage domestic affairs, and to found a Mongol assembly, which would be controlled by the Ministry of Border Affairs. The Chinese State Council would administer military and foreign affairs. Finally, a military academy would be created in a place chosen by the Republican government.

The members of the Mongol Autonomous Government rejected these proposals and instead put forth their own. According to them, the Mongol Autonomous Government would be the highest body in Inner Mongolia. It would be run directly by the Chinese State Council and would be funded by the Republican government. Under the administration of this autonomous government, the organization of leagues and banners would be maintained. The existing districts or political offices would disappear with none others created. The taxes imposed on Mongol pasture, which had been collected by the provincial governments, would be collected by the autonomous government. The clearing of Mongol lands for cultivation would be forbidden. Taxes on cropland would be collected by two officials who belonged, respectively, to the autonomous government and the provincial government in question, before being shared equitably between the two governments. The Mongol Autonomous Government would create offices in each village to replace those previously founded by the provincial governments. In the case of legal disputes between a Mongol and a Han, the Mongol Autonomous Government would send an emissary to represent the Mongol before the court.[144] Discussion among the members of the autonomous government and the two representatives from the Republican government were bitter. Even after each side had outlined their projects over the course of about ten days, points of divergence remained, according to the Panchen Lama's biographer.[145]

On November 17, 1933, while the representatives of the Republican government were just about to leave Bat Khaalga monastery, Prince Yon proposed mediation by the Panchen Lama, which they accepted.[146] As it turns out, the negotiations were interrupted without the prelate having the opportunity to intervene, and Huang Shaohong and Zhao Pilian left for Suiyuan. On November 19 the two Chinese representatives presented a project to the authorities of Chahar and Suiyuan that they intended to publish in Nanjing, but it was completely different from the one they had put forward to the Mongol princes. The key points of this project were establishing two autonomous Mongol governments. The Shilingol and Chahar Leagues would fall under the jurisdiction of one. The Üjümücin Banner and Yeke Juu and Alashan Leagues would be administered by the other. These two autonomous governments would be under the Chinese State Council. They would manage Inner Mongolia's internal affairs and would receive monthly subsidies from the Chinese central government. The provincial government would give rulings in cases of judicial conflict.[147] The provincial authorities of Chahar and Suiyuan raised no objection regarding the proposal and seemed to accept it.[148] Yet neither the provincial authorities nor the two Chinese representatives suspected to what extent this project was inadequate, considering the Mongol desire for self-determination.

Shortly after the death of the Thirteenth Dalai Lama, which occurred on December 17, 1933, the Panchen Lama decided to go to Nanjing, at the invitation of Shi Qingyang and Dai Jitao to perform a ceremony in honor of his deceased spiritual master. Accompanied by an entourage of about sixty people, he left Bat Khaalga monastery on January 16, 1934, and headed towards Nanjing.

On their side, the Mongols did not give up. They sent Unenbayin, the director of the Office of Mongol Leagues and Banners, to Nanjing to submit directly to the Chinese State Council a new project called "The Eight Governing Principles for Mongol Autonomy." Curiously enough, this report received approval from Chiang Kai-shek on February 28, 1934, which seemed to indicate that the Republican government had relaxed its position. According to the report, an autonomous policy would be established for a Mongolian commission to administer the territories of the Shilingol, Ulanqab, Yeke Juu, Tümed, Alashan, and Ejin Gol Leagues, and the Chahar tribe. It would be based in the province of Chahar, and would come under the direct jurisdiction of the Chinese State Council. Financing would come from the Chinese central government. All the members of the commission would be Mongol. However, one executive official would be named by the Republican government, who would act as an advisor or mediator in cases of conflict between the commission and the provincial governments. The Chahar tribe would become a league. The powers of the heads of leagues and banners would be kept intact. Unless the head of a league or a banner opposed, the conversion of pasture into cropland would cease. A percentage of all taxes collected by the provincial governments on the croplands of the leagues and banners would be given to the heads of each league. The creation of governing districts on the lands of the leagues and banners would cease unless circumstances required it. And, in that case, the approval of the heads of the leagues and banners would be necessary.[149]

On April 23, 1934, Prince Yon from the Ulanqab League was named president of this newly founded commission, while Prince Demchüg Dongrub became director of the Office of Political Affairs.[150] However, numerous obstacles arose as soon as they wanted to put the commission in place. In actual fact, the subsidies given by the Republican government turned out to be insufficient. Moreover, the Mongols were confronted by illegal doings on the part of the governors of the provincial governments of Shanxi and Suiyuan, who were Yan Xishan and Fu Zuoyi, respectively. Indeed, the two ex-warlords refused to hand over the specified portion of the taxes on cropland to the Autonomous Commission of Mongolia. In addition, they did not agree to the withdrawal of their troops from Mongol land. Finally, they managed to divide the autonomous commission of Prince Demchüg Dongrub by creating another autonomous commission of Suiyuan.[151] From then on two autonomous commissions would oppose each other on the territory of Inner Mongolia: that of Chahar Province, headed by Prince Demchüg Dongrub, and that of Suiyuan Province presided by Fu Zuoyi. The government of Nanjing decided to withdraw its support from Prince Demchüg Dongrub and encourage Fu Zuoyi. Disappointed by the behavior of the Republican authorities, Prince Demchüg Dongrub turned towards Japan.

In Nanjing the heat was apparently overwhelming to the Panchen Lama, so he decided to go to Beijing. But there as well, the temperature was unbearable and he wished to go further north—to Inner Mongolia, for example! Indeed, the head of the Yeke Juu League invited him to come to his estate. On August 11, 1934, the prelate left Beijing and headed towards the lands of the Yeke Juu League. On the way, he stopped in Suiyuan where Fu Zuoyi welcomed him at the station. Then, he crossed Baotou and arrived on the lands of the Yeke Juu on August 17, 1934. He then traveled from the Jasaq Banner to that of the Otoq, then to the Qanggin Banner. On September 7, 1934, he conferred a Tantric initiation at the Anfu monastery on the lands of the Qanggin Banner. During this initiation, many visitors came up to him predicting the deterioration of the situation in Inner Mongolia. For his part, Prince Yon from the Ulanqab League sent a delegate with his greetings to the Panchen Lama—a delegate who later returned to the Bat Khaalga monastery on September 15. Two days later, Yan Xishan had presents brought to the Tibetan master, who had clearly become the object of favor seeking. Then Prince Yon himself came with a letter from Prince Demchüg Dongrub. In it, Prince Demchüg Dongrub requested advice from the Panchen Lama who, in response, encouraged him one last time to rally the Mongol banners together under the goal of the "union of the five nationalities."

Things proceeded as if Yan Xishan, Fu Zuoyi, and Prince Demchüg Dongrub, whose interests diverged, were rivals in attracting the consideration and approval of the prelate.

In October 1934, while still sojourning in Inner Mongolia, the Panchen Lama declined to fulfill the requests of the princes of the league (notably those of Prince Demchüg Dongrub), because he had turned to other projects. It seems he had decided to move towards Tibet. On November 9, he left the Qanggin Banner to go to that of Otoq, near the village of Ningxia. Immediately, the governor of Ningxia Province invited him to propagate values in his province. Prince Demchüg Dongrub then went there to ask him for a teaching. The Panchen Lama once again refused him.[152] It is likely that the prelate did not share the radical views of autonomy of his Mongol disciple and that he would have preferred to see him adhere to the "union of the five nationalities." Had he begun to feel manipulated by the prince who was using him to plead the Mongol cause to the Republican government? In any case, by refusing to give his teaching, the Panchen Lama punished the prince in the traditional way that Buddhist masters often show their disapproval.

From that point on, the Panchen Lama dedicated a major part of his time to negotiating conditions for his return to Tibet, preparing the logistics of his trip, and putting together a development project befitting his country. He only occasionally devoted himself to the official task of "Emissary in Charge of Spreading Values in the Western Region."

THE REPUBLICAN GOVERNMENT

The Republican government's relationship with the Panchen Lama was, on the surface, characterized by opening official offices, granting titles, and providing support for the development of his projects, but in reality officials maintained a certain distance. Meanwhile, the only contact of a political nature that the northern government had with the Panchen Lama turned out to be rather limited, represented by little more than the granting of a title.

The preparatory meeting for the first National Reconstruction Conference held on January 27, 1925, to which the Panchen Lama had been invited, was convened for the purpose of determining ways to achieve the unity of the Chinese nation. It was organized at the initiative of Feng Yuxiang, Zhang Zuolin, and Duan Qirui. But even before Sun Yat-sen arrived in Tianjin on his way to Beijing to participate in the meeting, Duan Qirui had announced the organization of his government. On January 27, the preparatory session of the first National Reconstruction Conference was held in the absence of Sun Yat-sen and the representatives of his party. The Panchen Lama, who was present, gave his first political discourse in which he took the risk of criticizing the injustices committed by certain high Chinese officials, as well as their selfishness and their ambitions for power.

No doubt fearing the reaction of the Chinese authorities, the prelate preferred to stay away from the official opening of the convention on February 1 and take care of religious activities on Mount Wutai. He sent his attendant Lozang Gyeltsen to read a prepared statement for the occasion. In it, the Panchen Lama outlined his thought on and justification for the union of China with Mongolia and Tibet as well as the "union of the five nationalities," all the while emphasizing the shortcomings of the system and the incompetence of many of the current politicians. Nevertheless, the Chinese authorities did not seem to hold it against him since in August 1925 Gong Xinzhan, minister of the interior and Kunzang Norbu, the director of the Ministry of Mongolian and Tibetan Affairs (*Meng Zang yuan/Meng Zang bu*) gave him the title of "World Savior Who Propagates Orthodoxy" (*Xuan cheng ji shi*), as well as a golden seal.[153] This episode, at the time, concluded the relations between the northern government and the Panchen Lama.

At the beginning of 1928, the Nanjing government showed interest in Tibetan and Mongol issues by reforming the Mongolian and Tibetan Affairs Ministry and creating a commission of the same name. On April 21, 1911, in the last days of the Qing, the Office of Mongolian and Tibetan Affairs (*Meng Zang shiwu chu*) had been created by the minister of the interior. It replaced the old Qing Ministry Ruling the Outer Provinces (*Li fan yuan*) and was organized under a different structure.[154] On July 24, 1911, this office became the Department of Mongolian and Tibetan Affairs (*Meng Zang shiwu ju*).[155] It was placed under the direction of the premier (*guowu zongli*). On May 18, 1914, the Department of Mongolian and Tibetan Affairs was transformed into the Ministry of Mongolian and Tibetan Affairs.[156] It fell under the jurisdiction of the president (*da zongtong*).[157] However, repeatedly raising the status of the office over more than a decade, while also increasing the number of its officials whose duties were to manage Mongolian and Tibetan Affairs, failed to lead to any definitive policy.

This changed in January 1928 when the Mongolian and Tibetan Affairs Commission was founded. This administrative entity was made up of an office of general affairs, an office of Mongol affairs, an office of Tibetan affairs, a section of advisors, an administrative section, an office for publishing and translation, an office of inspection, a commission for education, and so forth. It was responsible to the Chinese State Council, and was equal in rank to the other ministries.

The Mongolian and Tibetan Affairs Commission officially opened its doors on December 27, 1928. The next day, Chiang Kai-shek, wishing to establish his authority in Inner Mongolia, named Yan Xishan to head it. Yan was the military governor of Shanxi Province adjacent to Inner Mongolia on its northwest border, and favored the rapid colonization of Mongol lands. On January 5, 1929, he published the "Program for Actions of the Mongolian and Tibetan Affairs Commission and the Steps for its Implementation" as well as a "Timetable of Work to be Accomplished by the Mongolian and Tibetan Affairs Commission During the Supervisory Phase." Its multiple goals were to include: (i) examining the existing administrative systems in Inner Mongolia and Tibet, (ii) modifying those systems so as to transform these nations into autonomous regions under the control of the Republican government, (iii) stimulating participation of the population in the country's politics, (iv) ensuring public security, (v) monitoring foreign relations, (vi) overseeing financial management, (vii) developing communication networks, (viii) founding educational structures, (ix) reorganizing the judicial system, (x) developing local industry, and (xi) protecting Buddhism.[158]

The Republican government thus attached itself to a warlord whom it promoted to the rank of high central office and whose policy towards Inner Mongolia was in line with its own. However, since the means proposed by the Mongolian and Tibetan Affairs Commission to put regional autonomy into place did not correspond to the aspirations of the Mongols, the actions undertaken by the Republican government in Inner Mongolia met with systematic opposition.

While waiting to designate a more effective spokesperson in Inner Mongolia, the Mongolian and Tibetan Affairs Commission decided to turn their attention to Tibet, even more so since the Panchen Lama had already created an office in Nanjing, which had not yet been officially recognized by the Republican government. In addition, the commission had received a letter signed by the prelate, dated January 24, 1929, whose content required a response on their part.

In this letter the Panchen Lama discussed the historical links between China and Tibet. He deplored the increasing hold that the British imperialists had on Tibet's economic and cultural affairs, and accused pro-British Tibetans of promoting views of independence for the sole aim of personal gain. According to the prelate, this group had imposed themselves at the head of the country during the Thirteenth Dalai Lama's exile in India. He felt that the dealings of this faction contributed to the decline in Sino-Tibetan relations. He further stated that he, himself, doubted the viability of a Tibet outside the circle of the five nationalities, and, therefore, he advocated that Tibet rally to the union in order to better resist pressure from the British. In this regard, he requested help from China and called for respect and equality between the different nationalities. The Panchen Lama also expressed his delight at the establishment of the Republican government after the internal troubles that had agitated China with the associated loss of authority of the northern government. He called for applying Sun Yat-sen's political instructions and industrial projects in Tibet, and warned the Republican government that if Tibet, Xikang, and Qinghai were to be excluded from economic development, lasting peace could never be achieved between China and Mongolia and Tibet.[159]

On February 28, 1929, the Republican government officially recognized the creation of the Office of the Panchen Lama in Nanjing (*Banchan zhu Jing banshichu*), whose headquarters were at 13 Qiwang Street.[160] This office in the Chinese capital became the locus through which passed all correspondence exchanged between the Panchen Lama and the Mongolian and Tibetan Affairs Commission. Although the Panchen Lama named Lozang Gyeltsen and Zhu Funan, respectively as director and deputy director, this office was under the supervision of the Mongolian and Tibetan Affairs Commission.[161]

This is how, on November 8, 1930, the Office of Civil Affairs of the Republican government received a letter from the Panchen Lama dated November 1, addressed to the attention of Chiang Kai-shek. In this letter, which was written in Tibetan and translated into Chinese by a member of the Mongolian and Tibetan Affairs Commission, the prelate opened with praise for Chiang Kai-shek and his merits. Then he requested an interview with the Chinese leader. He expressed his concern regarding the reluctance of the Mongols to follow the "union of the five nationalities," and also pointed out the existence of historical links uniting China and Tibet, while deploring the behavior of a handful of "selfish and devious" Tibetans who, acting at the expense of the Thirteenth Dalai Lama, sought to weaken Sino-Tibetan relations. He advised the Republican government to watch out for the representatives sent to Nanjing to negotiate Tibet's status with authorities in Lhasa, who were, according to the Panchen Lama, in the hands of the imperialists. He stressed the deplorable conditions in which the Tibetan people lived, and suggested that Chiang Kai-shek should not be content with only one version of the facts when trying to resolve the Sino-Tibetan disagreement, but that he take into account the Panchen Lama's perspective on this issue. The Tibetan prelate described his own ordeal of not knowing how best "to protect the Motherland and eradicate the suffering of the people of Xikang and Tibet." He stated that, although his compatriots called for his return to the country, the absence of cooperation between the Chinese and Tibetans would only serve to worsen the situation and, from a moral perspective, block him from returning home. To conclude, the Panchen Lama implored Chiang Kai-shek "to manage Tibetan affairs equitably."

It would seem that the behavior of the prelate, who had been traveling tirelessly throughout Inner Mongolia, as well as the tone of his letters and speeches must have finally caught the attention of Chiang Kai-shek, because a few months later the Chinese leader invited the Panchen Lama to participate in the opening ceremony of the National People's Convention that was to take place in Nanjing on May 5, 1931.[162] The religious dignitary traveled by train from Shenyang, the capital of Fengtian, where he had been residing for three months after leaving Inner Mongolia. He made a weeklong stop in Beijing where he met with a large number of lay Buddhists.[163] Once in Nanjing, the Panchen Lama and the members of his entourage were taken to a residence specially prepared for them at government headquarters.[164] On May 5, Chiang Kai-shek received the Tibetan ecclesiastic who attended the convention's opening ceremony at his side.[165]

On June 12, 1931, Dai Jitao sent a request to the Government Assembly that the Panchen Lama be given the title "Great and Glorious Master Panchen Who Protects the Country and Propagates its Values" (*Huguo xuanhua guanghui da shi*).[166] Less than two weeks later on June 21, the Mongolian and Tibetan Affairs Commission proposed that the prelate be given the title "Emissary in Charge of Spreading Values in the Western Region," with the mission of spreading Sun Yat-sen's "Three Principles of the People" and the orders of the Chinese government, in addition to energizing the monks and lay Buddhists in those regions. Regarding questions pertaining to how government policy would be carried out, the Panchen Lama was to seek advice from the Chinese central government or the provincial authority concerned, but was not to "intervene directly" in regional affairs. The Mongolian and Tibetan Affairs Commission would provide the prelate with the necessary resources to set up offices in the Xikang and Qinghai provinces. Each office would consist of an administrative division, a propaganda division, and a religious affairs division. The Panchen Lama would be assisted in his duties by two advisors named by the Nanjing government. He would send employees in charge of propaganda to their related provinces, and he would form a guard, the head and members of his choosing, but whose military instructor would be appointed by the Chinese authorities. The Republican government would also provide him with arms, ammunition, and cars, as well as 30,000 yuan a month, of which half would be allocated for the expenses of running the office and the other half for expenses associated with the guard. A yearly salary of 200,000 yuan would be paid to the Panchen Lama and his entourage.[167]

On July 1, 1931, during a ceremony celebrated in Nanjing in the government building known as the Hall of Rites, Chiang Kai-shek officially gave the prelate the title "Great and Glorious Master Panchen Who Protects the Country and Propagates its Values." A yearly allowance of 120,000 yuan went along with the role.[168] In this way, the Republican government gently adopted this zealous and unexpected ambassador of Sun Yat-sen's principles, and tried to channel his actions in the field for the benefit of Chinese government policy. By according the Panchen Lama an allowance, they hoped to make him feel indebted to them, and thus receptive to their orders. They let the prelate leave on July 8 for Inner Mongolia. Adorned with his new title, he seemed to take to heart his duty as "propagator of values."

In March 1932 the Chinese State Council received a telegram, dated the fourth and signed by the Panchen Lama, in which the concerned prelate insisted that the Republican government give him the means necessary to resist the Japanese who were encroaching on Inner Mongolia.[169] Rather than providing a response, the Mongolian and Tibetan Affairs Commission sent the prelate's attendant Lozang Gyeltsen (who at the time was director of the Panchen Lama's bureau office in Nanjing as well as director of the commission's Office of Tibetan Affairs) to Inner Mongolia to give the Panchen Lama the seal on which his title of "Great and Glorious Master Panchen Who Protects the Country and Propagates its Values" was engraved in Chinese and Tibetan.[170] Some days later, the Republican government decided to accept the Mongolian and Tibetan Affairs Commission's earlier proposal and confer a new title on the Panchen Lama, that of "Emissary in Charge of Spreading Values in the Western Region." The official act of bestowing this title was published on April 14, 1932.[171] On April 30, 1932, the government officially declared that the headquarters of the office attached to the duty associated with this new title would be based in Xiangride (Xiang'erde) in Qinghai.[172]

In giving the Panchen Lama the new title of "Emissary in Charge of Spreading Values in the Western Region" the government was prodding him to leave Inner Mongolia. Indeed, the Mongolian and Tibetan Affairs Commission considered the mission of the Panchen Lama in Inner Mongolia to be finished, since it had appointed the Changkya Hutuktu "Emissary in Charge of Spreading Values in the Mongolian Leagues."[173] It seems that in the field, the prelate was too zealous in his promotion of the values and the "union of the five nationalities," as well as the defense of the borders (political ideas in which he resolutely believed) to the point of disturbing Chinese politics. Chiang Kai-shek, who was preoccupied with the Communist threat, seems to have decided to abandon Inner Mongolia to the Japanese—thus bending, if not breaking, the principle of the "union of the five nationalities." It is, therefore, probable that the Republican government judged cumbersome, even risky, the posturing that the Panchen Lama took in favor of Inner Mongolia, and decided to call him back, all the while trying not to upset him, since he could still be useful to them in pleading other sensitive causes, such as those of Chinese interests in Tibet.

Nevertheless, the Panchen Lama persisted in staying in Inner Mongolia and pursuing his politico-religious agenda. Henceforth, the Republican government multiplied their stratagems to convince him to willingly return to Nanjing. They invited him to attend the Third Plenary Session, where a ceremony had been organized in his honor in connection with awarding him the seal of "Emissary in Charge of Spreading Values in the Western Region." They also invited him to the commemoration of the fifth anniversary of the founding of the Mongolian and Tibetan Affairs Commission. The Panchen Lama, little accustomed to the subtleties of Chinese politics (given his extended stays in Mongolia and his distance from the corridors of power), let himself be convinced and agreed to return to Nanjing, all the more willingly given the fact that, at the same time, he had numerous invitations from local Buddhist lay associations.

The director of the Mongolian and Tibetan Affairs Commission and the Republican government ministers received the Panchen Lama in Nanjing for the start of the Third Plenary Session. On December 21, 1932, the interim president Lin Sen accorded him an interview, in which the prelate expressed his thoughts on returning to Tibet.[174] Next, on December 25, 1932, the Panchen Lama, wearing a jacket and robe of yellow silk with thick-soled red and yellow ankle-boots (as planned the day before by the Mongolian and Tibetan Affairs Commission), was invited into the Hall of Rites. There, Zhang Ji, who represented the interim president, had the Tibetan prelate take an oath and gave him the seal of "Emissary in Charge of Spreading Values in the Western Region."[175] Once the ceremony ended, Dai Jitao offered him two pictorial representations, one of Tsongkapa, the founder of the Gélukpa school and the other of the Panchen Lama himself, whom Dai Jitao considered as his own spiritual master.

A few days later on January 21, 1933, the Mongolian and Tibetan Affairs Commission received the prelate at the ceremony commemorating the fifth anniversary of its founding. There the Panchen Lama gave a speech entitled "The Link Between the History of Tibet and the Five Nationalities," during which he once again gave a long and thorough historical discourse on the links uniting China and Tibet, justifying, in his own way, his departure from Tashilhunpo. He also gave a report on his work spreading values in Inner Mongolia and announced his intention of going, as soon as he could, to the western regions, all the while not missing the opportunity to lay out his defense of the "union of the five nationalities" and to invoke his concern about the future of Tibet and Inner Mongolia.[176]

It is difficult to gauge how the speech was received by the members of the Mongolian and Tibetan Affairs Commission. However, we can imagine their reaction when they discovered that the Panchen Lama, who left Nanjing on February 7, 1933, had headed back to Inner Mongolia instead of going to the western regions, as he had previously announced to the press.[177] Despite the surprise the Panchen Lama had just given them, Republican government officials hastened to put in place an Office of the Emissary in Charge of Spreading Values in the Western Region, hoping this would encourage the prelate to take care of his new duties. Indeed, for the Chinese authorities, the only way of getting the Panchen Lama out of Inner Mongolia would be to provide him with a credible pretext to go to the western regions. The creation of this office in Xiangride in Qinghai may have been just such a pretext.

The State Council described this administrative entity in Xiangride as an "office" (*bangong*).[178] Yet this appellation remained the subject of discussion. In effect, although the Chinese State Council had ruled long before in favor of the creation of the office being called "Office of Decentralized Administration" (*xingshu*), the minister of political and military affairs intervened in a letter addressed to the Chinese State Council dated December 31, 1932, requesting a modification of the term *bangong* to *xingyuan*, meaning "private office."[179] Under the pretext that the two emissaries in charge of the propagation of values (the Panchen Lama in the western regions and the Changkya Hutuktu in Mongolia) were both ecclesiastics aided in their duties by monks, the minister of political and military affairs emphasized in his letter that the two offices must be different from existing administrative structures.[180]

The Mongolian and Tibetan Affairs Commission, who had received a copy of this letter, informed Lozang Gyeltsen of it. The Panchen Lama's attendant immediately telegraphed his reply to the commission. He preferred that the name "Office of Decentralized Administration" (which would become *gongshu* in his vocabulary) be maintained since the Republican government had officially appointed the Panchen Lama "Emissary in Charge of Spreading Values in the Western Region."[181] In addition, he informed the Panchen Lama of the problem, who then directly contacted the Mongolian and Tibetan Affairs Commission. The Tibetan master also wished to keep the name "Office of Decentralized Administration" (*gongshu*) despite the opposition demonstrated by the members of the Thirteenth Dalai Lama's office in Nanjing. In reality Lozang Gyeltsen had told him, probably inaccurately, that the request for the modification of the name originated with representatives of the Thirteenth Dalai Lama![182] In the end, the name remained unchanged. In correspondence to the Chinese State Council, the office is named "Office of Decentralized Administration."[183] Later the nomenclature of "private office" (*xingyuan*) would designate the closest associates of the Panchen Lama, that is, the people who assisted him in his duties related to the "Great and Glorious Master Panchen Who Protects the Country and Propagates its Values" and the "Emissary in Charge of Spreading Values in the Western Region."

On April 23, 1933, the office in question had still not been created.[184] The Chinese State Council undertook to speed up its opening, since the Panchen Lama, who was once again in Inner Mongolia, was far from inactive. On March 16, 1933, the prelate addressed a telegram to the members of the Nationalist Party, the government of the Republic, the Military Affairs Commission, all the ministers and all the commissions, as well as the staff headquarters, in an effort, presumably, to increase his chances of being heard. In his letter he expressed concern over the Japanese occupation of Jehol Province and asked that "those who are far from the battle field ... or who give orders ... require [their] armies to reinforce the defense [of Inner Mongolia] and maintain [its] borders." At this, he expressed indignation at the tragic events these individuals were faced with in the field.

His testimony could have only embarrassed the Chinese authorities, because it accused them indirectly of doing nothing to save Inner Mongolia. If the Republican government approved of the innocuous work of the propagation of values undertaken by the Panchen Lama in Inner Mongolia, the seriousness of the problems the prelate revealed and the complicated and expensive solutions he requested, including a significant increase in reinforcements, put them in an uncomfortable situation. More than ever the Chinese State Council felt the urgency of having to get the Panchen Lama back in line, and sending him as quickly as possible to the western regions where his actions would be less likely to interfere with Chinese interests.

With this aim in mind, on May 27, 1933, the Chinese State Council issued to the Mongolian and Tibetan Affairs Commission an immediately effective directive. The general contents of the directive were that the Office of the Emissary in Charge of Spreading Values in the Western Region would answer directly to the Chinese State Council, and as its mission would manage all the affairs relating to the propagation of values in the western regions. This work would be divided into two divisions: the first, dedicated to the administration of general affairs, would distribute, recopy, and archive all documents received and sent and would be responsible for the accounting and management of daily purchases, while the second division would be responsible for propaganda and administer all activities related to the propagation of values.[185] The Emissary in Charge of Spreading Values in the Western Region would ensure the general management of the office, and would be assisted by four secretaries, of whom two would be named directly and two others upon recommendation by the head of state. The emissary would be expected to surround himself with expert advisors. Two directors, who would be appointed directly by the head of state, would each run the two divisions. Four to six department heads would be chosen upon the recommendation of the Panchen Lama, and eight to twelve department employees would be named by their hierarchical superior in each department.

The Mongolian and Tibetan Affairs Commission transmitted this directive to the Panchen Lama who then sent a copy to each of his offices. The prelate's offices waited for word from the Republican government to act.[186] From then on, when the Panchen Lama addressed the Chinese Nationalist government in written correspondence, he would sign it "Emissary in Charge of Spreading Values in the Western Region." Such correspondence would be sent to his office in

Nanjing, which, in turn, would transmit it to the Mongolian and Tibetan Affairs Commission who would forward it to the Chinese State Council.

The offices created by the Tibetan master in Beijing, Xining, Shenyang, Nanjing, and Dartsédo from 1925 to 1930 would progressively become annexes of his Office of Decentralized Administration. In this way, the Republican government would gradually appropriate the "maverick" of values. Nonetheless, in August 1933, the Panchen Lama still persisted in his actions in Inner Mongolia. He sent a confidential telegram to the Mongolian and Tibetan Affairs Commission in which he entreated the Republican government to send military reinforcements to the Mongols who were on their last leg. The commission forwarded his message to the Chinese State Council accompanied by the following comments:

> We have just received, this instant, a telegram from the Panchen Lama, Emissary in Charge of Spreading Values in the Western Region, dated the thirteenth and sent from Pangjiang [the domain of Prince Demchüg Dongrub]. The Panchen Lama therein describes the results of the trip he recently took to the Western Mongol leagues and banners to spread the virtuous principles of the Chinese central government, to reassure the Mongol people, and to make each head of the banners understand the great principles, so they can unite and resist foreign aggression. He asks the Chinese central government to send military reinforcements there to protect the national borders. In addition to having replied to the Panchen Lama congratulating him, we have copied and archived the original telegram. We here transmit it to you hoping you will thoroughly examine it.
>
> Respectfully, to the President of the Chinese State Council,
> Wang Jingwei

In spite of (or perhaps because of) the more or less neutral tone of the commission's note, the Chinese State Council would ignore the Panchen Lama's request and leave the Mongols, as we have seen, to battle alone against the Japanese. The absence of a Chinese reaction to Japanese aggression led the Mongol princes to try to take their destiny in their own hand by setting up an autonomous government and by envisaging the creation of an army. When the director of the Mongolian and Tibetan Affairs Commission received another telegram from the Panchen Lama asking the commission to send Chinese officials to encourage the Mongols not to reject the idea of the "union of the five nationalities," the authorities in Nanjing would finally pay serious attention to the messages from the prelate.[187]

First, on October 18, 1933, the Republican government praised the Panchen Lama in an official decree:

> The Great and Glorious Master Panchen Who Protects the Country and Propagates its Values, the Emissary in Charge of Spreading Values in the Western Region,

> faithful to the Nationalist Party and to the country exhibits great loyalty to the government. Already named propagator of values, summer and winter he travels relentlessly and tirelessly. He explains the will of the Chinese central government to the high officials. He stimulates the faithfulness of the people. His good advice spreads far and wide. The atmosphere in the border regions is harmonious today. The country continues to encounter difficulties, because there are many enemies at the borders. Therefore, it is necessary to push aside the danger and stabilize the border situation. The government thinks of the commendable actions accomplished by the Panchen Lama with concern and makes sincere homage to him. The government particularly praises the Panchen Lama in order to highlight his great merit.[188]

Two years later, the Republican government seemed to follow the advice of the Panchen Lama and, as we have seen, decided to send Huang Shaohong and Zhao Pilian to attempt to convince the Mongols to stay within the framework of the "union of the five nationalities." Dispatching two officials was clearly easier for the government than sending an army to support the Mongol princes. Taking this step, while refusing to provide military support, revealed that the government did not actually have the means to deploy troops on this front. In the following weeks, as the Panchen Lama played a predominant role in the negotiations that were embroiling the Mongol princes and the two Chinese representatives, the Republican government judged it opportune to call him back to Nanjing. Coming up against the pro-independence determination of the Mongols, it became clear to the government that the negotiators it had sent would not be able to reach an agreement, despite the commitment of the prelate who had been sparing no effort to help. At worst, leaving the Panchen Lama to act at will in Inner Mongolia ran the risk of seeing him become increasingly involved in China's border politics, which they perceived as interference. Thus, they settled the issue of Inner Mongolia's separatist ambitions in their style by "dividing and conquering" through the creation of two autonomous political commissions, favoring the one headed by a prior warlord who had been won over to the Chinese cause.

Cleverly taking advantage of the death of the Thirteenth Dalai Lama and of the chagrin it apparently caused his disciple, Dai Jitao and Shi Qingyang, the then director of the Mongolian and Tibetan Affairs Commission invited the Panchen Lama to Nanjing to participate in the funeral rites. The Panchen Lama's pain was such, however, that he initially ignored the invitation and refused to eat, to the point that his health deteriorated. Later, Kelzang Chönjor met him at Baruun monastery and encouraged him to come to Nanjing. This time, the Panchen Lama accepted.[189] He arrived in the Republican capital on January 22, 1934.[190] Why did the prelate accept this invitation to Nanjing? Wasn't his place at the Thirteenth Dalai Lama's funeral ceremony in Lhasa? Other factors concerning the Republican government seem to have influenced this decision.

On February 2, 1934, when President Lin Sen received the prelate for an interview something unexpected occurred. The Panchen Lama and Kelzang

Chönjor and the two monks who were accompanying him prostrated before the president, and then the president proceeded to do the same! Next, the Panchen Lama offered Lin Sen a salutation scarf, which he immediately offered back conforming to Tibetan custom. After this exchange, a conversation between the two men began, with Kelzang Chönjor acting as translator. After exchanging typical niceties, the Tibetan master assured the Chinese president of his support for the border peoples. As for the Chinese president, he congratulated the Panchen Lama for having spread Sunist values in Inner Mongolia and encouraged him to continue to do so, so that the "union of the five nationalities" could be accomplished. The two men left each other, each one bowing once to the other.[191] A few days later, on February 20, 1934, the Chinese authorities named the Panchen Lama a member of the Republican government.[192]

In this way the Chinese hoped to, at last, create the conditions necessary to control the prelate's activities. The efforts of the Republican government ended up paying off. Although the Panchen Lama could not help himself from returning to Inner Mongolia on August 11, 1934, as of mid-January 1935 he went to the province of Ningxia and on February 8 he inaugurated the first Office of the Emissary in Charge of Spreading Values in the Western Region in Xiangride. From that point on, the office would be operational.

In addition to his roles as ambassador of "values" and informant with regard to the situation in Mongolia and Tibet, the Chinese authorities gave the Panchen Lama a third mission that consisted in creating local annexes of his office and publishing a specialized journal to transmit and further disseminate the Republican government's messages. This journal was published in Tibetan and Chinese. It assembled articles dealing with important Chinese and foreign news, policies of the Republican government, the social situation in the West, and political and religious events taking place in the peripheral regions. It also covered the activities and travels of the Panchen Lama as an emissary of the Chinese government, and was distributed in all the offices of the Panchen Lama and to the armies based at the borders.[193] The covers of the issues I had the pleasure of seeing all had photos of the Tibetan master. Each issue contained thirty or so pages written in Tibetan on the aforementioned themes, including transcriptions of the Panchen Lama's speeches and Buddhist teachings, this was followed by a Chinese translation. In addition to the monthly journal, which was published irregularly between 1935 and 1937, the office of Xiangride published illustrated pamphlets of slogans and small dictionaries sent to associations and monasteries.

The prelate's ambitions went beyond merely representing the Chinese government. In March 1935 the prelate sent a proposal to Huang Musong, the new director of the Mongolian and Tibetan Affairs Commission. In it, he requested the Republican government to give material aid and funding to help the people of Qinghai and Xikang whose misery he described. He then unveiled the key points of his development project for Tibet to be undertaken in partnership with the Chinese authorities. His project primarily involved educational infrastructure and communication networks. Having observed that such infrastructure was nonexistent, he felt the culture of his country was "behind." In order to put his ideas into place, he asked the Republican government to allocate, as soon as possible, no less than 100 million yuan towards the building of schools.

If the Panchen Lama argued in favor of teaching Tibetan to his young fellow-citizens, he also wanted them to learn Chinese because, for him, this was the language of science, itself a synonym of industrial development, a guarantee of economic and social progress, and the improvement of people's standard of living, according to the principles of Sun Yat-sen. The prelate also proposed the creation of post offices equipped with radio transmitters in all the main districts and along newly built roads. Finally, he requested the assistance of Chinese technicians and experts to supervise these partnership projects. For the Panchen Lama, this Tibetan development project symbolized the natural compensation for his country's adherence to the "union of the five nationalities."

On April 24, 1935, the Mongolian and Tibetan Affairs Commission conveyed its response to the Panchen Lama and to the director of the State Council. With regard to the subsidies to help the people of Qinghai and Xikang, the commission stated:

> Although the return of the Panchen to Tibet and the help requested for the needy be of equal importance, priority must be given to the return of the Panchen Lama to Tibet. The issues of funding will be entrusted to an emissary who will go to Qinghai ... However, given the implications, much reflection is necessary before a decision can be made. The amount of subsidies must be first determined in relation to the situation of those in need, so we can bolster the people of the border regions.[194]

The commission may as well have said the inhabitants of Qinghai and Xikang would not receive their much talked-about funding. It further stated that while communication networks and education were extremely important points, current priorities (as well as the state's budget) required that different ministries confer with each other to determine who would take charge of the various aspects of reinforcing the western regions.

Nevertheless, the idea spread among the members of the Republican government because on May 1, 1935, the Chinese State Council entrusted the Mongolian and Tibetan Affairs Commission with cooperating with the ministries of finance, communications, railways, industry, and education to prepare a development project for Tibet.[195] On May 24, 1935, Huang Musong received a report signed by Gao Zhangzhu, an advisor to the Office of General Affairs and Xiong Yaowen, director of the Office of Tibetan Affairs, concerning the adoption by the government ministries of a development project for Tibet based on the Panchen Lama's proposal, although far more modest. Gao Zhangzhu was named as the supervisor for the project.[196] In their report, Gao and Xiong announced that they had organized two meetings, which were attended by representatives of the ministers.

After some debate, the attendees came up with a preliminary development plan for Tibet, which they had submitted to him. In the introduction to the plan, it was explained that it would be unrealistic to begin development in Tibet without first addressing communication and education needs. In this respect, they concurred with the opinion of the Panchen Lama. However, the rest of their recommendations diverged significantly from those of the prelate. Instead of the enthusiasm exuded by the Panchen Lama, we see the cold pragmatism of the Chinese officials:

> Today, the requests of the Great Master Panchen are the following: the repair of roads, the establishment of a postal system, and the creation of schools. In principle, all these proposals are priorities. However, at this time of reduction in public spending, it is difficult to allot significant amounts to these projects. Moreover, the Tibetan situation is special in that we mustn't rush things and arise the suspicions of the Tibetans.

Regarding the establishment of infrastructure in Tibet, Gao Zhangzhu and Xiong Yaowen merely proposed the repair of a road going from Xining to Lhasa. They pointed out that the authorities of Qinghai were already in the process of fixing the road from Xining to Kyégudo (Yushu) within the framework of their military policy. Moreover, the barracks located in the area had been refurbished, allowing the troops stationed there to control the road. They recommended that the Chinese State Council adopt this project and authorize its implementation. The two officials also suggested installing radio transmitters along this road, in addition to those that the telecommunications ministry had already installed in Dartsédo, Kardzé, Bathang, Dergé, and Lhasa, as well as a 500-watt alternator at Tashilhunpo. They also requested that a representative of the Ministry of Telecommunications accompany the Panchen Lama on his return to Tibet.

As for the postal system, based on observation of the gaps in Tibet's existing postal service, the Chinese officials advised that an investigation be undertaken with the local authorities into its public utility. Gao and Xiong also advised that the General Post Office order authorities in Sichuan and Gansu to create a postal road from Bathang to Kardzé and from Kardzé to Qinghai as soon as possible, while also completing the postal road from Kardzé to Chamdo for the purpose of connecting the Tibetan postal roads. Most importantly, they advised that the postal road from Lhasa should fall under the control of China's General Post Office. Regarding educational initiatives, the two Chinese officials reduced these to minimal form, advising that a representative from the Ministry of Education be sent to Tibet to create five primary schools to test the efficiency of the teaching model suggested by the Panchen Lama prior to instituting it more widely. To conclude they stated:

> The budgets of these different projects (with the exception of that concerning the communication networks for which the Ministry of Railways will immediately send

> a representative to speak with the Panchen Lama to prepare a plan for later submission), are to be taken care of by the respective ministries ... Each ministry will send a representative who will examine which development projects can be carried out in terms of industry, commerce, agriculture, geology, and public hygiene works.[197]

On June 28, 1935, Gao Zhangzhu and Xiong Yaowen's proposed development project for Tibet was amended and adopted by the Chinese State Council. The Mongolian and Tibetan Affairs Commission informed the Panchen Lama by letter on July 10. The project proposed by the Republican government had neither the breadth, the ambition, nor the spirit of the Panchen Lama's dream for developing Tibet. Essentially, the development of infrastructure in Tibet and the education program were reduced to next to nothing, and the development works in industry, commerce, agriculture, geology, and hygiene were postponed until preliminary investigations took place. This Republican project sounded the death knell for the economic development the Panchen Lama had hoped to provide for his country.

On March 20, 1936, the State Council authorized the creation in Kyégudo of an Office of the Emissary in Charge of Spreading Values in the Western Region.[198] This was in accordance with a proposal by Dingkyé Rinpoche, one of the reincarnated masters at Tashilhunpo.[199] However, it changed nothing regarding Tibet's development project.

The Republican government supported the Panchen Lama when he propagated its values in Mongolia and Amdo, when he informed local authorities of Chinese policy, and encouraged them to rally behind the "union of the five nationalities." It seemed to appreciate his work as ambassador and informant. However, it systematically abandoned the prelate whenever he took the initiative and got involved with the policies of Mongolia, even though this was behavior that could be considered legitimate with respect to the titles awarded him. The attitude of the Republican government when asked to subsidize or provide tangible help could have easily discouraged the Panchen Lama. This discrepancy between word and deed proves that the Chinese authorities were betting on the Panchen Lama, in case he showed himself capable of producing political miracles. They hoped he would have a better chance of reaching the inhabitants of the border regions, whose psychology and true intentions they had difficulty discerning, but whom they did not, at the same time, take seriously. Although the Panchen Lama remained faithful to the ideas of Sun Yat-sen and the government of Nanjing, it would appear he may not have had much choice, since he found himself in the grip of the Republican government that had become his most powerful donor.

On December 21, 1936, the Panchen Lama learned that Chiang Kai-shek had been kidnapped nine days earlier in Xi'an by troops of his own military representative in the region, Zhang Xueliang. Zhang had switched allegiances and was acting in accord with the Communists. To secure Chiang Kai-shek's release, the kidnappers were demanding the cessation of fighting against the Communists, for the purpose of strengthening resistance efforts against the Japanese so as to protect the nation. As soon as he was informed of these events, the Panchen Lama called for all the monks of Kyégudo monastery to recite prayers for the liberation of Chiang Kai-shek.[200] On December 24, 1936, Chiang Kai-shek was freed after having accepted the creation of a second front united with the Communists against Japan. Two days later, at the announcement of this news, huge festivities were organized at Kyégudo monastery. The Panchen Lama took the opportunity to publicly support President Chiang Kai-shek in a glowing speech. As we will see later, his loyalty was little rewarded.

The Tibetan prelate had not yet finished with his share of disappointment in the Chinese Republicans.

PART THREE

AT THE SINO-TIBETAN MARGINS (1935–1937)

At the end of 1933, the death of the Thirteenth Dalai Lama accelerated the Panchen Lama's return to Tibet. Although the Tibetans were calling for his return, the prelate set down certain conditions. He insisted on the presence of a high Republican official and a Chinese escort in addition to his choice of a return route through Amdo, which complicated negotiations with the Tibetan government to the point that the Chinese and British became involved. In the end, the Panchen Lama's death abruptly resolved the issue definitively. And yet, all did not stop there. His entourage attempted to create an independent state on the Sino-Tibetan border, while Chinese and Tibetans from all sides competed for the possession of his mortal remains.

5

ABORTIVE RETURN TO TIBET

At the end of October 1937, the Panchen Lama was staying at the Kyégu döndrubling monastery in Kyégudo while he waited for the Chinese State Council to choose his place of residence. Actually, in mid-August of the same year the Republican government had suddenly ordered him to stop his advance towards Tibet. Initially the Chinese State Council had designated Kardzé as the Panchen Lama's next destination, per the prelate's wish, but then changed its mind and sent him to Dartsédo. The Panchen Lama complied and prepared to leave Kyégudo on November 22. However, given that he was in poor health, this departure date was uncertain.

At the beginning of November, the Panchen Lama's illness had worsened and his doctor diagnosed him with edema in addition to a problem with his liver. Despite his condition, the Tibetan prelate refused to be examined by a Chinese doctor. Worried, members of his entourage telegraphed the abbots of the three main monasteries in Lhasa to recite long life prayers for him. But nothing seemed to help and the master's health continued to deteriorate. On November 26 a Chinese doctor, who was a member of the Chinese special envoy's office, was finally allowed to examine him. Zhao Shouyu telegraphed Liu Wenhui, the president of the Commission for the Edification of Xikang Province, as well as Dai Jitao requesting that they urgently send a specialist since the health of the Tibetan master had declined further.[1] Premonitory dreams haunted the prelate's mind as he lay dying. He attempted to explain them to his closest associates. He mumbled worrisome things such as "My palanquin is ready, I am leaving this world," and "Look, thousands of birds of colorful plumage invite me to go with them."[2] On December 1, 1937, the Panchen Lama died in Kyégudo at Kyégu döndrubling monastery on the Sino-Tibetan border.[3]

After all is said and done, how could it be that the Panchen Lama never returned to Tibet before his death?[4] The initial conditions the prelate set down for his return to Tashilhunpo provide a partial answer.

CONDITIONS FOR RETURNING TO TASHILHUNPO

First and foremost among the prelate's conditions was that he wanted the Chinese and Tibetan governments to normalize their relations. In January 1929, in a letter addressed to Yan Xishan, then director of the Mongolian and Tibetan Affairs Commission, the Panchen Lama intimated this sentiment.[5] In November

1930 he made this more explicit in a letter sent to Chiang Kai-shek, noting that the time had come "to resolve the Sino-Tibetan conflict." The Panchen Lama explained that a lack of cooperation between the Chinese and Tibetans would only worsen the current situation and constitute a moral obstacle to his return to Tibet. Later in April 1934, according to Kelzang Chönjor who was quoted by a journalist from *Zhongyang ribao*, the Panchen Lama stated that the conditions for his return hinged on the restoration of Sino-Tibetan relations rather than any personal ambitions.[6] By March 1935 the prelate again postponed his return to Tibet, specifically because the absence of any solution to the Sino-Tibetan problem would, he said, obviously lead to skepticism on the part of his compatriots. He encouraged members of the Republican government to re-establish Sino-Tibetan relations, and he also reminded them that, in this affair, the general good of the people must prevail over personal gain.[7]

For the prelate, the normalization of Sino-Tibetan relations consisted in, first, putting an end to the latent conflict involving the Sino-Tibetan borders and, second, obtaining the commitment of Tibet to adhere to the "union of the five nationalities," on the condition that in exchange, the Republican government would establish and finance a development project for modernizing the Land of Snows. In his capacity as Buddhist master, the Panchen Lama saw peace as the prerequisite for the success of such an overall development project. Very early on he expressed himself on the issue, in particular, in an opinion statement of February 1925. Beyond peace, the "union of the five nationalities" was a recurrent theme in his letters and speeches. The prelate brought it up numerous times, as we have seen.[8]

Tangibly, to obtain Tibet's adherence to the "union of the five nationalities," the Tibetan and Chinese governments would, according to the prelate, have to agree on the following points: the definition of the status of the Sino-Tibetan relationship, the organization and administration of Tibet, the resolution of Sino-Tibetan border conflicts, the defense policy and the management of Tibet's foreign relations, the creation of offices of Tibetan representation in China as well as Chinese representation in Tibet, and, finally, the control of religion, including procedures for determining the Thirteenth Dalai Lama's reincarnation and the attribution of the title for the Fourteenth Dalai Lama. The negotiations between the Tibetan and Chinese governments on each of these points were far from easy.

When in July 1931 the Panchen Lama became aware of the violent clashes that had occurred between the Chinese and Tibetan armies on the Kham border that spring, he named Gédun Tashi as director of his office in Dartsédo, giving him the mission to promote peace and end the combat between the Tibetans and Chinese. The effectiveness of Gédun Tashi's action remains difficult to assess due to a lack of original documents. It seems that the fighting ended after the armies of Liu Wenhui and Ma Bufang launched an intensive military offensive against the Tibetan army that obliged the Tibetan authorities to negotiate an unfavorable accord.[9]

As for the development project for Tibet, the Panchen Lama brought it up for the first time in his speech in May 1931 during the opening ceremony of the National People's Convention, and again in his address in December 1932 at the Overseas Chinese Hotel in Nanjing, which was geared for journalists, as much as anyone else. It was not until January 1935, however, that the prelate provided details of the project.[10] Further discussion on the project, particularly with regard to spreading values in Tibet, came in March in a letter to Huang Musong, the Chinese emissary to Tibet.[11]

Resolution of the disagreement regarding normalization of Sino-Tibetan relations was at the very origin of the Panchen Lama's flight to China, but what really put him at odds with Lhasa was his condition that prior to going back to Tibet the Lhasa government return all the goods confiscated in 1923 belonging to the Tashilhunpo monastery and to the aristocratic families living on its lands, as well as the condition that Lhasa recognize Tashilhunpo's legitimate right to administer Namring, Panam, Shigatse, and Nakartsé districts. Further conditions were that Lhasa reimburse all monies taken under the extraordinary tax since 1923, permit Tashilhunpo to control the Tibetan army's soldiers stationed in Tsang and to create a personal guard, and agree to the intervention of a foreign mediator.[12] After learning of the discussions that took place between Ngachen Rinpoche and the Thirteenth Dalai Lama, the Panchen Lama told the newspaper *Zhongyang ribao* that he would not return to Tibet unless these conditions were accepted by the Tibetan government.[13]

The Panchen Lama had, it seems, been quite preoccupied with the uncertainties that surrounded the administration of the districts of Namring, Panam, Shigatse, and Nakartsé as well as the restoration of his political powers in Tsang. In his letters and speeches, he often mentioned prerogatives that were his before 1923. In his September 1931 speech in Hulunbuir, for instance, he spoke of the powers he was forced to leave behind. During speeches in January and October 1933, the prelate stated that he had held spiritual and temporal powers in Tibet for more than thirty years. Following the death of the Thirteenth Dalai Lama, he broadened his claims and expressed his willingness to lead all of Tibet during the vacant period caused by the death of his spiritual master.

The prelate's new attitude can be seen in a May 1934 article in *Zhongyang ribao* in which he confided his intention of returning to Tibet to govern political and spiritual affairs. Two months later, he showed that he was sure of this project and believed he was supported in his approach by Tibetans themselves when he wrote to the director of the Mongolian and Tibetan Affairs Commission saying that the Tibetan government had sent representatives to Nanjing, asking him to return to Tibet to direct all affairs and fulfill the wish of the people.

Was the Panchen Lama being sincere? Had he confused his desires with reality? Effectively, according to the newspaper *Zhongyang ribao,* in April 1934 fifty or so monks representing the three main Gélukpa monasteries did go to Nanjing to try to convince the prelate to return to Tibet before the Thirteenth Dalai

Lama reincarnated. They accompanied Ngachen Rinpoche on his return from his mission to Tibet. During a speech given in Xining to the Qinghai authorities in May 1935, the Panchen Lama reaffirmed that the people of Ü, representing those in the Tibetan province whose capital is Lhasa, hoped he would return soon to take control of the political and spiritual aspects of the country.[14]

Were the demands of the Panchen Lama—that is, the restoration of the powers he had held in Tsang before 1923 and the regency of Tibet after the death of the Thirteenth Dalai Lama—legitimate? At the beginning of the twentieth century, Tashilhunpo had enjoyed relative political autonomy. Logically, when the Panchen Lama wished once again to have authority over his monastery, and thus a major part of Tsang, he believed he was within his rights. In examining the circumstances, he certainly had, without a doubt, every right to these claims.

What about his wish to rule Tibet after the death of the Thirteenth Dalai Lama? Previously the Fourth Panchen Lama had, in fact, taken care of the management of Tibet's state of affairs from September 1844 to May 1845, and if Regent Reting (r. 1934–41) had not been elected to this post by the Tibetan people, the candidacy of the Panchen Lama regarding this precedent was at least equally as legitimate as that of Reting, since before attaining the regency, there was nothing exceptionally brilliant in the regent's political career.[15] In any case, the claims of the Panchen Lama concerning his authority over Tsang and his access to the post of regent were among his conditions for his return to Tibet.

Later the Panchen Lama set as a final condition the successful completion of his mission of "spreading values" in the western regions. In his letter addressed to Huang Musong in March 1935, he expressed regret that he had not yet accomplished this and announced that he would not return to Tibet until he did. According to the prelate, by leaving this work unfinished, he would be disregarding the orders of the Republican government, of which he was a member, and he would be disappointing the people and breaking Buddhist law, which consists in helping the greatest number of people possible. Departing for Tibet without accomplishing his mission would mean breaking his word and commitments, which, for a Buddhist master, is unimaginable. Considering his uncompromising positions on numerous points, did the Panchen Lama really wish to return to Tibet?

At first glance it would seem reasonable to reply in the affirmative. From December 1923 to January 1925, during the early part of his exile in China, the Panchen Lama was seeking donors who might be able to provide him with the funds needed to pay the tax required by the Tibetan government, so he could return in good standing. It seems that at that time, his only ambitions were to free himself from this debt and continue his life at Tashilhunpo.

From 1925–26 on, the prelate's intentions broadened. His belief in Sun Yat-sen's "Three Principles of the People" and his political commitment in favor of the "union of the five nationalities" must have seemed suspicious to the authorities in Lhasa, hindering his hopes for returning to Tibet. But these new difficulties do not seem to have lessened his determination, since at the beginning of 1927 he requested Tsaserkhang, his representative in Kalimpong, to work with the British administration in India to help him return to Tibet.

In May 1927 Tsaserkhang met with Major Bailey, the British political officer in Sikkim. He reminded him of the promise of help given by the Prince of Wales to the Panchen Lama when they met in India in 1905 (twenty-two years prior!), and also gave him a letter from his master. Bailey did try to bring up the subject of the Panchen Lama's return with the Thirteenth Dalai Lama during his visit to Lhasa in 1928, but to no avail.[16] In March the same year, the Panchen Lama had another message transmitted through Tsaserkhang to Charles Bell, who had left India for England a bit earlier. In this letter, the prelate reminded him how highly he considered their bond of friendship, and requested his assistance in returning to Tibet. Bell's reply could only have disappointed him, since he confirmed to the prelate that he was unable to give him the slightest advice.[17] The Panchen Lama, however, did not lose heart.

Two years later in June 1930, once again using the services of Tsaserkhang, the prelate informed Lt. Col. James Leslie Weir, the British official who replaced Bailey, that he was in the process of creating an army to escort himself back to his monastery at Tashilhunpo, and that he needed arms and ammunition (or funds to acquire them).[18] He warned Weir that if the British could not help, he would have to resort to returning to Tibet accompanied by a Chinese guard. This approach bore fruit. In spring 1931 Leslie Weir went to Lhasa where he could meet the Thirteenth Dalai Lama and have him write a letter that E. M. B. Ingram, the chargé d'affaires of the British embassy in China, could then transmit to the Panchen Lama, who was then residing in Nanjing. Disappointed with the content of this letter, the prelate decided to take the initiative of instigating negotiations by sending two representatives, Ngachen Rinpoche and Dangchenwe Tsédor, to Lhasa to begin direct talks with the Thirteenth Dalai Lama concerning his return. He informed his spiritual master through the intermediary of the British.[19]

The Panchen Lama's decision to contact the British requesting they play the role of mediator seems unusual for two reasons. For one thing, the British had systematically declined his advances; and for another, at that time, British officials had little credibility with the Thirteenth Dalai Lama because they had similarly disappointed him several times by refusing to provide military support. This would obviously put the British in an awkward position with the Thirteenth Dalai Lama to be intervening in favor of the Panchen Lama. As could be expected, this first attempt by the prelate to involve the British in his negotiations with Tibetan authorities failed. In fact, it probably furthered his idea of dealing directly with the Lhasa government. The meetings that took place in Lhasa beginning in June 1933 between the representatives of the Panchen Lama and the Dalai Lama, assisted by members of the Tibetan government, quickly came to a halt.[20] The conditions formulated by the prelate constituted too many stumbling blocks, and, in any case, the death of the Thirteenth Dalai Lama that occurred six months later froze all the discussions, which may have been in progress.

Out of desperation, the Panchen Lama turned to the Republican government in June 1934, and began negotiations with various Chinese ministers regarding his return to Tashilhunpo. He gave the director of the Mongolian and Tibetan Affairs Commission a preliminary draft of a proposal, which included a list of arrangements and items necessary for his return. Concerning his travels between Nanjing and Amdo, the prelate requested the Republican government to order the civil and military officials of the provinces that were to be crossed to receive and protect him. He also requested that Chinese authorities ensure the transportation of all his bags and goods, pay his travel expenses, furnish him with a passport, provide him with two armored cars as well as weapons, mortars, and mountain canons, and, finally, support his work in the propagation of values. As for traveling from Amdo to Central Tibet, the intransigence, if not hostility, of the Tibetan government towards him drove the Panchen Lama to take caution and make arrangements to guarantee his security. By his accounts, he would need the presence of two high-level Chinese officials (one civil and one military), the support of an armed escort financed by the Chinese central government, the use of one or two planes to transport his baggage and goods, and the provision of a 500-watt radio transmitter along with radio operators.[21]

It seems implausible that the Panchen Lama would have drafted such a document and undertaken such a project if he did not have a true intention of returning to Tibet.

With the backing of Kang Fu'an, who headed the Office of the Panchen Lama in India and was currently in Lhasa, the Panchen Lama reminded the Chinese government's envoy Huang Musong that he must negotiate with the Tibetan authorities regarding his return to Tashilhunpo.[22] The Tibetan prelate also wanted to be sure that the road he was to travel on was repaired and inspected. He no longer replied to spiritual requests from Mongol princes, in particular that of his disciple and donor, Prince Demchüg Dongrub, since he had obviously decided to head towards Tibet. At the advice of Ma Bufang, the military governor of Qinghai Province, the Panchen Lama sent members of his entourage and their luggage ahead to Xining, which seemed to indicate his imminent departure. Turning his attention once more to corresponding with Huang Musong, who in the meantime had been appointed director of the Mongolian and Tibetan Affairs Commission, the Panchen Lama sent another letter pointing out that he had already provided a list of essential needs for his return to Tibet. Noting that the itinerary for his travel through Amdo had been made one year earlier with the agreement of the Republican government, the Tibetan prelate drew up a list of the most urgent tasks, such as the nomination of a high dignitary who would be in charge of his escort, an immediate budget to cover his travel expenses, and the provision of troops to ensure his security.[23]

At the end of April 1935, the Panchen Lama put additional pressure on the Mongolian and Tibetan Affairs Commission, letting them know he wished to rapidly receive the money necessary for his return and that he had withdrawn his request to the Chinese government for a high dignitary to accompany him to Tibet. He assured the commission that he was determined to return to Tibet as soon as he could, and had set the number of soldiers in his escort at five hundred.[24]

On May 21, 1936, the Panchen Lama gave four reasons that motivated his return to Tibet via Amdo.[25] First, he intended to open an Office of the Great Emissary for the Propagation of Values on the Western Frontier on the lands of the Alashan League; second, he was obliged to look for the reincarnation of the Thirteenth Dalai Lama (we can deduce that at that time, he already believed that the new incarnation of his master would appear in Amdo); third, he desired to thank the former governor Ma Qi and his son Ma Bufang for their hospitality, dating back to the time when he had first left Tibet, as well as to reply to the invitations of local dignitaries and the population; and, finally, he wished to spend time in contemplation in the sacred monastery of Kumbum.[26] These reasons seemed well thought out. Facts show that they are in line with the policy and behavior of the Panchen Lama.

FINAL HESITATIONS BEFORE DEPARTING

In mid-May 1935, the Panchen Lama settled into Kumbum. He concentrated on the task of preparing his return to Central Tibet, wishing to get on the road as soon as he could. Once more, he requested that the Nanjing government provide him funds and an escort. For lack of anything better, he accepted the protection of the army under the military governor of Qinghai Province, Ma Bufang. In fact, the date of his departure had already been pushed back many times. Although, at the time, the prelate's departure date had been set for July 1935, by the end of the month it had been postponed to September. And, when September rolled around, it was pushed to October.[27] But by October, it was no longer possible to travel due to weather and road conditions. What were the reasons for these repeated delays? Once again, did the Panchen Lama truly want to return to Tibet?

At the beginning of June 1935, four trucks, a 100-watt radio transmitter, and 800,000 yuan for travel expenses arrived at Kumbum. The Republican government named Cheng Yun "Special Emissary Responsible for Accompanying the Panchen Lama to Tibet" (*Husong Banchan hui Zang zhuanshi*), and another 220,000 yuan was contributed to the prelate's travel expenses at the beginning of September. Yet the Panchen Lama said he must wait, because he felt the conditions for his departure were still not present. He could not envision leaving without Cheng Yun, who had not yet arrived at Kumbum, and especially without an armed escort. Nevertheless, the Panchen Lama began showing impatience. He ordered Ma Bufang to assemble the camels and yaks necessary to carry his baggage, and he ordered the Chinese government to hasten the arrival of Cheng Yun and to send his escort.[28]

The prelate was forced to wait until December for Cheng Yun to arrive in Kumbum, where his imminent departure made for a feverish atmosphere. The monastery had become a rallying point for all the Buddhists that wished to receive the Panchen Lama's benediction before he left Amdo. The Chinese officials who were to accompany the prelate to Tibet arrived one after another, visiting him and discussing the latest preparations.[29]

The protocol seemed to go on forever, and many Tibetan and Chinese officials henceforth began to lose patience and called for the prelate's departure. Among them, Jiang Zhiyu, the representative of the Chinese government in Lhasa, could not understand why the Panchen Lama had not yet left Kumbum. He began to doubt the sincerity of the prelate who, in a telegram sent to the Tibetan authorities, continued to repeat that he intended to return to Tibet. Jiang began wondering what the Panchen Lama was hiding behind his comments. Would he follow the decisions of the Chinese or the Tibetan government? Was the Republican government manipulating the Panchen Lama, or was it the reverse? From Lhasa's perspective, the Panchen Lama and Cheng Yun were definitely obliged to await the arrival of the escort before leaving for Tibet. The prelate himself made the best of things by devoting himself to his religious activities.[30]

On May 17, 1936, the Panchen Lama finally left Kumbum. From the outset, he adopted a very slow rhythm, stopping to give Buddhist teachings at all the monasteries along the way, seeking out contact with the faithful.[31] And perhaps also seeking funds for his entourage. Or was he perhaps accomplishing the propaganda work the Chinese government had entrusted him, as the reports of Luo Youren and Huang Ju'an suggest?[32] Curiously, everything took place as if the prelate were indecisive regarding his return to Tashilhunpo. The slightest change was used as a pretext to slow his movements toward the high plateau, which only served to irritate both the Chinese and the Tibetan authorities. The route the prelate chose between Kumbum and Labrang trashikhyil followed no logic, other than to visit every monastery in the region.

In hindsight, we can see a striking dissonance between the impatient tone of the letters the Panchen Lama addressed to the Mongolian and Tibetan Affairs Commission, and the zeal in which he exhibited in providing multiple Buddhist teachings. This inevitably leads one to question his motives. Was the man who wrote the imperious letters the same man that was slowly meandering back towards Tibet, stopping his caravan at every possible opportunity all along the way?

It may be that, despite the prelate's pressing demands, neither Cheng Yun nor the promised Chinese escort ultimately accompanied the Panchen Lama when he departed Kumbum. Cheng Yun who had arrived at Kumbum in December 1935 met up with the prelate one month later in Gyengyéthang, accompanied by members of his office and bodyguards, shortly before the prelate arrived at Labrang trashikhyil. As for the Chinese escort, it never showed up in Kumbum. It only met up with the Panchen Lama a year later in Kyégudo, after having undergone various military training exercises in Lanzhou and Xining.[33] Deprived of his escort, it may have been that the Panchen Lama intentionally stalled crossing the Sino-Tibetan border because he did not want to enter Tibetan territory without sufficient protection. In the absence of his deceased master the Thirteenth Dalai Lama, the prelate no doubt feared the vengeance of certain members of the Tibetan government, given his initial refusal to pay the extraordinary tax. Moreover, his hasty departure from Tibet had made the Tibetan government look ridiculous, not to mention the impunity the prelate received by remaining in exile in China, creating a situation that appeared to strengthen his political ambitions. Perhaps it was not fear at all but only that the Panchen Lama felt he had to teach at each monastery he came across, as part of his duties as a traveling religious dignitary.

Having sojourned for more than two months in Labrang trashikhyil, where he conferred numerous Buddhist teachings and initiations from June to August 1936, the Panchen Lama went to Ragya monastery, thus completing the first leg of his trip back to Tibet.[34] On the next part of his trip, he found himself confronted with the rain, wind, and snow of winter 1936–37,[35] which did not stop him from taking the road each morning, ordering members of his procession to recite prayers to alleviate their miserable lot. Would he have made such efforts if he did not want to see his native land again? Most certainly, the Panchen Lama wanted to return to Tibet, and more than any obstacle, it was his faltering health that threatened his project.

To attempt to understand what appears to be contradictory behavior on the part of the prelate, it is necessary to examine in what measure Tibetan and Chinese officials impeded (or facilitated) the Panchen Lama's plans for returning to Tashilhunpo, and, by doing so, attempt to uncover their true intentions.

THE HUANG MUSONG MISSION

The normalization of Sino-Tibetan relations was one of the initial conditions set down by the Panchen Lama for returning to Tibet. For both he and the Republican leaders, this normalization meant Tibet's adherence to the "union of the five nationalities." The Chinese government, who was anxious to resolve the Tibetan question, especially with the convenient pretext of the Panchen Lama's return, began negotiations with its Tibetan counterpart at the end of 1929 and continued throughout until 1935. At first, it was Chiang Kai-shek who took the initiative. He sent Köncho Chungné, the abbot of the Palace of Eternal Harmony, to Lhasa to give the Thirteenth Dalai Lama a letter in which he asked under what conditions Sino-Tibetan relations could be re-established.[36] The letter also addressed such questions as how the Chinese government could "supervise" the Tibetan administration as well as how Tibet's status as an autonomous region would be established, and what its borders would be.[37]

At the beginning of 1934, the Nanjing authorities skillfully used the death of the Thirteenth Dalai Lama to take the opportunity to name Huang Musong the

"Special Emissary in Charge of Presenting the Chinese Government's Sympathies to its Tibetan Counterpart at the Thirteenth Dalai Lama's Funeral." His mission was to go to Lhasa and represent the Republican government at the funeral, as well as give a posthumous title to the Thirteenth Dalai Lama. He was also sent to Lhasa in order to try to reach a political agreement with the regent Reting Rinpoche, and resolve the Sino-Tibetan problem by integrating Tibet into the Chinese administrative structure, conforming to the policy of the "harmonious coexistence of the five nationalities."

For the first time since January 1913, the date of the Thirteenth Dalai Lama's declaration of Tibet's independence, the authorities in Lhasa accepted the arrival of an official Chinese mission on Tibetan soil. In the absence of the Dalai Lama, Huang Musong negotiated with the Council of Ministers (*kashag*) and with the National Assembly (*tsokdu*), as the Panchen Lama would also do later. Reting did not participate in the talks.[38]

For three months, Huang Musong tried everything possible to obtain tangible results. Sincerely interested in Tibetan culture, he made real efforts to try to learn about it. As soon as he departed from Chengdu on his trip towards Lhasa, he showed an aptitude for ethnology as he minutely studied the traditions of the locals that he met, as well as the geography he crossed. But the Chinese State Council, which was perhaps concerned by their special envoy's enthusiasm, or rather as a simple precautionary measure, informed Huang only at the end of his sojourn of the unofficial nature of his negotiations.[39] From its standpoint, the Tibetan authorities had taken advantage of the arrival of Huang Musong in Lhasa to try to recover the southeastern territories of Tibet that had been abandoned to China.

In October 1935 the Chinese State Council detailed a project for the resolution of the Sino-Tibetan question that Cheng Yun, the special envoy in charge of accompanying the Panchen Lama to Tibet, was to present to Tibetan authorities upon his arrival in Lhasa. He was never able do so, given the outcome of the circumstances. This project, which the concerned parties never had the opportunity of discussing, contained the essence of the Chinese position regarding Tibet.[40]

Shortly after the arrival of Huang Musong in Lhasa, the Tibetan authorities, orphaned by the loss of their spiritual and temporal leader, began to protectively call for mediation by the British, all the while maintaining, at all costs, the idea of the chaplain-donor relationship, which as early as 1930 the Thirteenth Dalai Lama had declared would be necessary to serve as the basis for re-establishing connections with China. During a meeting at the Potala, members of the Tibetan National Assembly reaffirmed several times that Tibet was an independent country. Some time later, they indicated to Huang Musong that they clearly refused to participate in the policy of the "harmonious coexistence of the five nationalities," while also demanding that the term "central government" be replaced by "Chinese government." And yet, just prior to the departure of Huang Musong, the National Assembly made a major concession, stating in writing that "in what concerns foreign relations, Tibet would belong to China, but would not be assimilated into a Chinese province," all the while emphasizing their adherence to the chaplain-donor relationship.[41]

Huang Musong, on his part, revealed a certain finesse in his negotiations. First, he quickly swept aside the proposal for British mediation, arguing that the disagreements were internal ones and did not concern a third country. Next, he admitted to the cultural uniqueness of Tibet and did not hesitate to propose that the Tibetan and Chinese governments set up a chaplain-donor relationship, which obviously went in the direction that the Tibetan leaders desired. In the same way, he also declared that the Chinese government considered Tibet an independent country (autonomous?). At the time he wrote in his travel diary that the union between China and Tibet was necessary concerning foreign relations, but pointless for internal Tibetan affairs, confirming therein his personal convictions.[42]

His superiors tempered his ardor. When Huang informed them that the Tibetan attitude had loosened up and that Tibet accepted a dependent relationship towards China, members of the Chinese State Council (who had taken due note of the Tibetan concession and had, of course, assimilated it to a recognition that Tibet belonged to China) reminded him that many points of divergence remained. On October 2, 1935, the Republican government proposed that Tibet and China re-establish "harmonious" relations as had existed before the donor-chaplain system put in place in 1792.[43] But, as the Chinese State Council noted, at the end of November 1934 not all the difficulties had been worked out. To balance out their concession on the foreign affairs issues, the Tibetans were not at all willing to compromise on either their politico-religious system or their administration. Unfortunately for the Tibetans, the Thirteenth Dalai Lama had given Chiang Kai-shek a window of opportunity by replying that he would accept autonomy for the Tibetan region, provided the chaplain-donor relationship was sincerely established for the security of Tibet.

In order to discourage Huang Musong, members of the Tibetan National Assembly insisted on the point that the Chinese government must not interfere in the affairs of Tibet's politico-religious system, which was incompatible with that of the Chinese Republic. They refused to integrate their country into the Chinese political system.[44]

However, it would take more than that to destabilize Huang Musong who, unwavering in his negotiation tactics, began by anesthetizing his counterparts with his commitment that the Chinese government would not interfere in Tibet's domestic affairs.[45] A few days later, he told the Tibetans that his government would not alter the Tibetan administration and would not act against the Tibetan people, but wished that regional autonomy be established.[46] Faced with weak resistance from the Tibetan authorities, he proposed that Tibetan officials receive a salary from the Chinese government. In exchange, the Tibetan government would have to consult the Chinese authorities to name their prime minister and his ministers. Of course, the Council of Ministers and the Tibetan National Assembly refused to allow the Chinese government intervene in the selection of their officials, but they agreed to inform them of the nominations once made. Worse, the Council of Ministers are said to have fallen into the trap of accepting that the Tibetan officials receive government salaries from the Chinese, which would have placed them in an undeniable position of vulnerability by making them dependent on these payments. If this proves to be true, this act would discredit the regency government established after the Thirteenth Dalai Lama's death.[47]

In any case, the Tibetan National Assembly believed it necessary to issue a statement one week later that changed the affair little. Its representatives repeated, as if to reassure themselves, that Tibet would not be assimilated into a Chinese province, that Tibet would respect orders from the Chinese government for the management of domestic and foreign affairs, payments, and so forth on the condition that the Tibetan politico-religious system not be put into question, and that its power over domestic affairs would remain independent as it was at the time. The Tibetan representatives further reiterated that the Chinese government would not intervene in the management of civil affairs, that the Tibetan government would have the responsibility of appointing the regent and high officials (rank of minister and above), conforming to the situation current at that time, and that Chinese residing in Tibet since the Sino-Tibetan war of 1912 would continue under the administration of the Tibetan Department of Agriculture![48]

The harm was done. Certainly, the organization of the Tibetan administrative system remained unchanged, but by paying the officials (it remains to be proven without a doubt whether things actually took place this way) and supervising, in one way or another, their nominations, the Republican government guaranteed its control over the Tibetans, which had been its primary objective. In his travel diary Huang Musong wrote that if the Chinese government accorded autonomy to Tibet, it would not interfere with Tibetan political power and would not modify its traditional politico-religious system. He added, on the other hand, that the Chinese government would administer the appointment of important officials and would send a high Chinese official to reside in Tibet. According to him, this figure would put in place the Chinese government's policies and would verify regional autonomy, but would not interfere in the fields called "autonomous."[49] This having been confirmed, it was left up to Huang Musong to define the content of these "autonomous" fields, which excluded defense policy and the management model for foreign relations that the Republican government would apply in Tibet.

With defense, the Chinese would bring up a sensitive issue that the Tibetans were not ready to let go of. In March 1930 the Thirteenth Dalai Lama had made their task easier by requesting that Chiang Kai-shek provide arms in case of foreign aggression and by emphasizing that if the security of his country was threatened, he would call on the Republican government.[50]

In mid-October 1934, as a precautionary measure, the members of the Tibetan Assembly hastened to warn the Chinese government that it was not to be allowed to open barracks on Tibetan soil.[51] Predictably, Huang Musong began by committing that no Chinese soldier would be stationed in Tibet. However, in exchange, he took pains to demand that no foreigner be stationed in Tibet, hoping, no doubt, to incapacitate the British.[52] Faced with the seemingly accommodating position of the Chinese negotiator, the Tibetan Council of Ministers responded that it would maintain free relations with adjacent countries, that no Chinese soldier was to be stationed in Tibet, and that the Border Defense Army would be trained by the Tibetan government. However these demands fell into the same error that the Thirteenth Dalai Lama had made in his time. The Council of Ministers specified that in case of foreign invasion, Tibet would resist alone, but that if it needed assistance, for logistics or provision of weapons, it would request it from the Chinese government.[53]

Huang Musong needed little more to come up with a counteroffer in which he repeated that no Chinese army would be stationed on the Tibetan borders and that his government would combat any nation that tried to invade Tibet. The Tibetan government would simply be required to consult with its Chinese Republican counterpart before corresponding with other nations.[54] Huang also proposed that five thousand soldiers be selected from those in the Tibetan army and that they make up an army stationed at the borders. According to his plan, the Chinese government would pay for these soldiers, equip, and train them. Among other things, a Chinese official would reside in Lhasa. This official would be furnished with an escort and would control the entire Tibetan army. In this way, Huang Musong once again used a tactic that he had employed with the Tibetan administration, noting that there would be no Chinese soldiers in Tibet, but the Tibetan army would pass under the orders of the Chinese Republican government. Sensing the danger, the Tibetans reacted that same day. Indeed, the Council of Ministers accepted that soldiers be stationed on their borders on condition that they be neither paid nor armed by the Chinese. But for their part, the National Assembly did not see the necessity of putting troops on the borders unless the situation necessitated it. The Council of Ministers reminded the National Assembly that Tibet was independent, and could thus manage its foreign relations. The National Assembly approved and added that the Tibetan government decided to correspond with all nations, including those headed by the British government.

The Council of Ministers and the National Assembly both believed that as Tibet was a fundamentally religious country, no nation would dream of attacking it. If that happened, they would deal directly with the invader without asking for help from the Chinese. Possibly, mutual help between Tibet and China would be foreseeable, but only if deemed necessary.[55]

One week later, the Tibetan National Assembly refined their position. They categorically refused any Chinese military presence on Tibetan land in addition to any interference of the Chinese government in the management of Tibetan military affairs. They were determined to send Tibetan troops to their borders as they had in the past. If reinforcements were deemed necessary in the case of foreign invasion, they would react accordingly and could consult the Chinese government. They, however, relaxed their position concerning foreign relations in a surprising way. While affirming that to ensure stability, Tibet must maintain harmonious relations with adjoining countries, the Tibetans accepted that all treaties negotiated between Tibet and foreign countries be concluded jointly with the Chinese government. Huang Musong could congratulate himself, for the Chinese government could write that it would manage Tibet's international relations, that it would take care of its international treaties signed by Tibet in the past, and that the Land of Snows would sign no more treaties with foreign countries. The Tibetans had just abandoned their own management of foreign affairs to China. Nevertheless, they remained inflexible on the subject of Chinese military presence on their land, which they did not want at any price. Even if in his personal notes, Huang Musong wrote that the Chinese government must take care of Tibet's defense, and even if one year later the Chinese State Council persisted in this approach using an identical phrasing in its resolution project, the Chinese had come up against solid Tibetan determination.[56]

As for the Tibetans, early on they would try to fix the border between Tibet and China, and obtain a resolution of the Sino-Tibetan border conflict. The subject had been close to their hearts since the 1930s, when the Thirteenth Dalai Lama had written to Chiang Kai-shek, saying that the Tibetan regions, which had previously been under Tibetan jurisdiction and were no longer, should come back under the Tibetan government's authority.[57]

During the first official talks that took place in September 1934 between, as usual, Huang Musong and the Tibetan officials (one of whom was Prime Minister Langdun), in the aftermath of the death of the Thirteenth Dalai Lama, the Tibetans took the initiative. They expressed the wish that the Nanjing government recognize the treaty signed in 1932 between Tang Kesan and the General Khyungram, and that they withdraw their troops from the Tsolo and Golok regions in the province of Amdo. This constituted their sole request, aside from their will to involve the British in the negotiations. Shortly afterwards, they renewed their request to see the hotbeds of tension along the southern Sino-Tibetan border quelled and requested that the towns of Kardzé, Nyarong, and Dergé be returned to them. Faced with such determination, Huang Musong could do no less than give his agreement in principle, to satisfy the demands of the Tibetan government by proposing to give back Nyarong, Dergé, and the Golok territories as well as to withdraw Chinese troops stationed in Xining. This did not stop the Chinese government from announcing one month later that at the very most it would consider recognizing the borders as they had been during the time of the Guangxu Emperor (1871–1908), forcing the Tibetans to reiterate their request.

In spite of repeated recriminations by the Tibetan National Assembly that insisted on recovering Bathang, Litang, Nyarong, and the Golok land, Huang

Musong remained unwavering and the Chinese State Council would end the discussions a year later with a mysterious declaration, stating that the Sino-Tibetan border would be established later and that the armies stationed in Kham and Tibet as well as the border authorities busy maintaining the temporary status quo would be used instead to repair the communication networks.[58] It is true that the Republican government had other aims in mind, in particular the creation of an office of Chinese representation in Tibet, and, as it happens, of Tibetan representation in China.

Chiang Kai-shek had opened the discussions in plain terms in 1930 by asking the Thirteenth Dalai Lama if it were true that the Tibetan government had the intention of creating an office in Nanjing, in order to be able to deal with the Republican authorities at any moment. He then wondered if the Chinese government should provide for the expenses of this bureau. Acting in this way, he hoped, on the one hand, to take control of the Tibetan office in Nanjing and, on the other, be able to impose on the Dalai Lama a Chinese representation office in Lhasa, in the name of reciprocity. Five years later, the Chinese position on this subject remained unchanged, since the Republican government envisaged dispatching a high official to Lhasa, who was to reside there to put Chinese policy into place, and in its view, the Tibetan government would have to do the same and send representatives to Nanjing to create an office subsidized by the Chinese government.[59]

As for the Thirteenth Dalai Lama, in his letter to Chiang Kai-shek he had confirmed his intention of creating offices in Nanjing, Beijing, and Kham, and he indicated that he would delegate the task to Köncho Chungné. However, he did not speak about the possibility of opening a Chinese office in Lhasa. According to him, the Nanjing Tibet Office should centralize all correspondence exchanged between the Chinese and Tibetan governments. Concerning the financing of this office by the Chinese government, he refrained from replying.

In the absence of any clear indication handed down from their spiritual and temporal leader on the subject, four years later the Tibetan Council of Ministers found no objection to the Chinese government's proposal to send officials to live in Lhasa, on condition that their number be limited to twenty-five, that they not interfere in Tibetan political affairs, and that they go to Tibet by sea, passing through India.[60] Huang Musong had never hoped for so much. He only wanted one Chinese official in Lhasa to "advise" the Tibetan authorities until the Chinese government felt that Tibet had acquired the capacity to become "autonomous."[61] He also wished all Tibetans of Chinese origin to fall under the jurisdiction of this official. Finally, he hoped that the Tibetan authorities would send a representative to China who would become a member of the Chinese government.[62]

The negotiating strategy used by Huang Musong is well known. The Republican leaders had already used it a few months earlier, on February 20, 1934, when they appointed the Panchen Lama as a member of the Chinese government. By creating a precedent, they made the Tibetans indebted and morally forced them to try and do the same, pushing them to reciprocate and thus to accept the presence of a Chinese official in Lhasa. On the basis of Huang Musong's offer, the Tibetan authorities went back and forth resulting in quite contradictory opinions. In fact, the Council of Ministers would have preferred that no Chinese official reside in Lhasa. If need be, the appointed official should in no case manage the Tibetan army, but he could use an escort of three hundred soldiers, following the Simla Convention, which had not been signed by the Chinese. The Council of Ministers and the Assembly would have, in addition, refused that Tibetans of Chinese origin fall under an official based in Lhasa.[63]

One week later, the Tibetan National Assembly transmitted to Huang Musong a letter whose content was noticeably different. It suggests that only one Chinese official reside in Tibet and that his escort be no more than twenty-five people. This agent should be a sincere practitioner of Buddhism, and no other civil or military person should be sent by the Chinese government. While Chinese officials would be obliged to go to Tibet (for example, for transfers and nominations), they should go by boat and then by road from India and not through Kham. The Chinese official stationed in Lhasa would not have responsibility for his compatriots who had been living in Tibet since the expulsion of Chinese soldiers from Tibet in 1912.[64]

As his sojourn in Tibet was coming to an end, Huang Musong tried a bold move, given that the Tibetan position was showing inconsistencies regarding the presence of Chinese officials in Lhasa and had loosened up on foreign relations. With the official goal of continuing negotiations after his departure, Huang suggested to the Tibetan government that he leave a Chinese official in Lhasa and that they send a Tibetan representative to Nanjing. The Tibetan government, not realizing the trick, naively accepted Huang Musong's offer.

This is how not one, but two Chinese officials equipped with a wireless would come to stay in Lhasa in November 1934 with the hearty approval of the Chinese State Council. Liu Piaocheng and Jiang Zhiyu were those two officials, and had accompanied Huang Musong on his mission.[65] Tangled up in their contradictions, the Tibetans managed to find themselves confronted with the tangible, palpable, and immediate presence of two Chinese observers. In comparison, their obsession of having Chinese officials travel by sea seemed trivial. Chinese officials were already present! In reality, it seemed that the Tibetan authorities preferred to make efforts to save what they could of their religion and their system of reincarnation.

The Tibetan authorities still had serious reasons for mistrusting the Chinese, since in 1930 Chiang Kai-shek had tried to test the resistance of the foundations of the local religious institutions in proposing that the Thirteenth Dalai Lama and the Panchen Lama join the ranks of the Chinese Republic, and in speculating whether the two ecclesiastics would automatically keep their spiritual and temporal positions respectively as in the past or if they wished to modify them.

In essence, Chiang Kai-shek was deliberately trying to turn the master and disciple against each other. In any case, the Thirteenth Dalai Lama, to whom Chiang Kai-shek's message was destined, did not fall into the trap. If he felt it inappropriate to answer the two questions, we can surmise that he must have found them rather stupid, and even perverse.

Subtler still, Huang Musong declared in October 1934 that China could not establish relations with Tibet in the same way that it did with other countries given the Buddhist uniqueness of the Land of Snows. He tried to persuade local leaders that Tibet, as a Buddhist country, could go well together with the Chinese government and help it benefit from its experience in politico-religious matters.[66] That was sufficient for the Tibetans to allow the Chinese government the responsibility of protecting the Buddhist religion and by doing this, set itself up as Tibet's donor.

Did the Tibetans realize that while accepting the Republican government as donor, they exposed themselves to the major risk of enjoying a "protection" that had nothing to do with what they imagined? In any case, this is how Huang Musong proposed to the Tibetan and Chinese governments to set up a relationship of chaplain to donor, in which he had closely calculated his government's interest. However, the Tibetans displayed great lucidity concerning their system of reincarnation, since they insisted on managing the search for the Fourteenth Dalai Lama on their own as well as his enthronement.[67] At the very most, they accepted an obligation to inform the Chinese government of the results of their efforts.[68]

There they remained entrenched in their positions. Huang Musong could affirm in all seriousness that the Chinese government considered Tibet a holy land, that it recognized Tibet's right to have its specific religion and culture, that once the reincarnation of the Thirteenth Dalai Lama was found, they wished to be informed as a first priority so they could offer him a seal and a title, but nothing would steer the Tibetans off the course of their plan.[69] The declaration of the Chinese State Council a year later, specifying that it respected Tibetan Buddhism (within the limits of Chinese legislation), as well as the ranks of the Dalai Lama, Panchen Lama, and the civil and religious officials, changed nothing. The desire of the members of the Tibetan government at the time to preserve Tibetan Buddhism and its unique system of reincarnation was relentless since, as history later shows, after the flight of the Fourteenth Dalai Lama to India in 1959, the Tibetans successfully organized themselves to recreate their system in exile to guarantee its permanence (although things might change following the Dalai Lama's suggestion in 2007 that his successor could be selected through referendum, or while he himself is still alive).

Around 1935, paradoxically, the positions of the Tibetan government and that of its Chinese counterpart were quite close, but at the same time, very far apart. Through his intelligence and talent as a negotiator, Huang Musong managed to coax the Tibetans to admit that his government would be an acceptable donor capable of managing Tibet's foreign affairs. His negotiation strategy was quite repetitive. Huang would begin by putting the other side to sleep through his soothing approach, all the while pretending to accept their demands. Then, he would make a first attack to see how far the other side would go. He compensated for this attack with a minor concession, and while the other side reveled in what they believed to be a victory, he brought in a decisive hit and remained unmoving on his positions. Finally, he let time take care of the rest and would wait patiently for the other side to tire out and end up giving in, bored with fighting. But pockets of resistance remained against the Tibetan government's willingness to join the "union of the five nationalities." The authorities in Lhasa stubbornly refused Chinese military presence on their territory and any form of interference from the Republican government in their religious institutions. Moreover, a significant cultural gap remained between the Tibetans and Chinese, despite Huang Musong's commendable efforts, especially pertaining to the interpretation each side would have regarding the content of the chaplain-donor relationship.

Facts show that the Panchen Lama's dream of seeing Tibet join a great central Asian federation made up of China, Tibet, and Mongolia (as inspired by his interpretation of the "Three Principles of the People" by Sun Yat-sen) would be difficult to achieve. That is why, contrary to what had been announced, the Panchen Lama did not wait for the end of the negotiations regarding Tibet's adherence to the "union of the five nationalities" to try to find a solution to the dispute that locked him in opposition to the authorities in Lhasa, and which constituted one of his explicit conditions for returning to Tibet.

PARTIES INVOLVED IN THE PANCHEN LAMA'S RETURN

Authorities in Lhasa

The demanding attitude of the prelate was met with varying degrees of intransigence and appeasement by the Tibetan government, which followed three distinct phases: January 1924 to December 1933, representing respectively the date of the first letter addressed by the Thirteenth Dalai Lama to his disciple and the death of the Thirteenth Dalai Lama; December 1933 to August 1937, corresponding first with the date of the order given by the Republican government to postpone the prelate's return trip to Tibet up until the prelate's untimely death; and August 1937 and beyond—the aftermath of the Panchen Lama's demise.

During the first phase, the Thirteenth Dalai Lama, whose personality exerted a strong influence over the Tibetan government, remained unchanged. In the three letters he sent to the Panchen Lama in order to encourage the prelate to see things the way he did, the Thirteenth Dalai Lama systematically emphasized the importance of the relationship between master and disciple that united them, and the devotion coupled with respect and strict obedience that, according to the Buddhist tradition, the prelate owed to his master. The Thirteenth Dalai Lama tried to justify his decision to heavily tax Tashilhunpo all the while showing the Panchen Lama that he was acting fairly towards him. He lectured the prelate regarding his hasty departure from Tibet and explicitly asked him to repent. He further called on the prelate's sense of civic duty and reminded him of the political, economic, and religious risks his exile involved for both Tashilhunpo and Tibet. Finally, magnanimously, the Thirteenth Dalai Lama offered to pardon and support his disciple, should he choose to return. However, no concessions were made regarding the Panchen Lama's conditions for his return, and the tone of the letters clearly reveals the Dalai Lama's determination to stand his ground.

In 1928 the Thirteenth Dalai Lama received F. M. Bailey, who was attempting to plead the Panchen Lama's case, but rejected his offer of help and asked the British officer not to interfere in Tibetan domestic affairs.[70] When, two years later, the Dalai Lama answered Chiang Kai-shek's questions concerning the Panchen Lama, he replied that his disciple had no political authority in Central Tibet apart from the management of his monastery, and that he must contribute one-quarter of the country's military expenses. The Dalai Lama left his disciple free to adhere or not to the Nationalist Party. He recognized in the Panchen Lama no authority to resolve those Tibetan affairs that fell within the competence of the Tibetan government.[71]

Only Leslie Weir, who at the time was the British political officer in Sikkim, managed to slightly soften the attitude of the Thirteenth Dalai Lama. By 1931 the spiritual and temporal head of Tibet was forced to relax his position towards the British due to the signature on an agreement unfavorable to Lhasa that ended the Sino-Tibetan conflict, which had broken out in the spring.[72] This conflict had revealed the vulnerability of Tibet's defense, and the Dalai Lama subsequently had been obliged to tighten his relations with the British and had authorized the presence of one of their missions to Lhasa. This is how the Thirteenth Dalai Lama received Leslie Weir, who suggested he free the members of the Panchen Lama's family, who had been imprisoned at the time of his flight, and hasten the return of the Panchen Lama to Tibet.[73] It was after this pressure that the Dalai Lama wrote his third and last letter inviting the prelate to return to Tibet and freed the Panchen Lama's family members.[74]

Independently of the British maneuvers, it seems that the Dalai Lama wished to hasten the return of the Panchen Lama to Tibet for two reasons, thus revealing a contradiction between his intransigence and a sincere belief in the harmful religious consequences of their dispute. First, the end of the fighting on the eastern border of Tibet had not diminished the warring ardor of his people, who were neglecting their religion to focus on war. It was, therefore, urgent that a great master, such as the Panchen Lama, return to Tibet to spread the Buddhist teachings beyond Lhasa. Secondly, the Japanese were encroaching more and more on Inner Mongolian territory and because of the Japanese invasion, the

Panchen Lama was no longer secure in Inner Mongolia, where he spent a good deal of his time.

From a strictly Buddhist point of view, confirmed by all the monks that I interviewed, if the Panchen Lama died without having reconciled with the Dalai Lama, the karmic effects would have been distressing for the reincarnations of the two great masters. Indeed, their relationship of master to disciple would have found itself deteriorated given the law of cause and effect. Also, it is very probable that, despite everything, the Dalai Lama, who was advancing in age, wished to normalize their relations. Yet the interviews the Dalai Lama gave to Ngachen Rinpoche and Dangchenwe Tsédor in Lhasa in June 1933—mandated by the Panchen Lama to discuss the conditions of his return—led to no change in the Dalai Lama's stance.[75] Although the Dalai Lama sent a detachment of twenty-five soldiers to Dingri under the orders of a general (*rupön*) whose mission was to facilitate the trip to Lhasa of Ngachen Rinpoche and Dangchenwe Tsédor's delegation, and although he attributed the title of *da lama* (prior) to Ngachen Rinpoche and the title of *drungchen* (high secretary) to Dangchenwe Tsédor, the Dalai Lama proved to be inflexible concerning the recriminations of the Panchen Lama.[76]

When Ngachen Rinpoche and Dangchenwe Tsédor and the members of their delegation met in Kalimpong with Frederick Williamson, the British political officer in Sikkim, they informed him of the results of their negotiations with the Thirteenth Dalai Lama and the Tibetan National Assembly. According to them, the authorities in Lhasa rejected nearly all the Panchen Lama's demands. They did not grant the prelate the right to administer or appoint the district governors of Dam, Gampa, Lhatsé, Namring, Panam, Phüntsoling, Nakartsé, and Shigatse, and they decided to confiscate two other districts from him. However, they did authorize his collection of taxes from the districts of Dam, Gampa, Lhatsé, Namring, and Phüntsoling. While the National Assembly evaded the subject of the return of the goods confiscated from Tashilhunpo in 1923, it reminded the delegation that it was the responsibility of the Panchen Lama to pay one quarter of the military expenses. The Dalai Lama and the National Assembly also rejected the idea of reimbursing the prelate the amounts received since 1923 under the extraordinary tax. Finally, they refused him control of soldiers from the Tibetan army stationed in Tsang and the creation of a personal guard, and they judged pointless the involvement of a foreign mediator.[77] Worse, they imposed a supplementary condition in the form of a predetermined itinerary for his return—the prelate would have to go by sea and then enter Tibet through Darjeeling.

Six months after the death of the Thirteenth Dalai Lama, the Tibetan authorities changed their attitude. They announced to the members of the vanguard of the Huang Musong mission, who had arrived in Lhasa in May 1934, that they wished to begin official negotiations regarding the return of the Panchen Lama, to whom they decided to send two representatives to try to reason with him. The Tibetan political scene had become orphaned from its head figure and that certainly explains this about-face.[78] Throughout much of Tibetan history, the periods of regency were always unstable and the presence of a second religious dignitary in Tibet would have been highly sought after. That is why from December 1933 to August 1937, the position of the Tibetan authorities regarding the different demands of the Panchen Lama gradually relaxed. Beginning in October 1934, they spoke with Huang Musong about this relaxation in veiled terms, but without much result.[79]

In August 1935 the Tibetan government consented to return the confiscated goods to the officials of Tashilhunpo and on November 14, they proposed to return all the possessions of the Panchen Lama, except those that they had offered to other monasteries and thus could not recover. Finally, the Tibetan ministers offered him the possibility of returning to him all the goods that had belonged to prior incarnations of the line of Panchen Lamas. As for the extraordinary tax on Tashilhunpo, the Tibetan government consented to annul or diminish new taxes and requested the Panchen Lama to make a contribution of one symbolic ounce of silver, or payment in kind, for the revamping of the Tibetan army.[80] Concerning the involvement of a foreign mediator, the approach to negotiations was more nuanced and vacillated, depending on the perception of events. After having turned away the British in 1928, six years later the Tibetan officials asked them to manage the negotiations with Huang Musong, when the special envoy arrived in Lhasa. Then in March 1935, worried about the imminent arrival of the Panchen Lama and his armed Chinese escort, the regent, Reting Rinpoche, invited Frederick Williamson to Lhasa to secure the support of the British in case of conflict between the Chinese and Tibetan armies. But in July 1936 members of the Tibetan National Assembly did not hesitate to reject the proposed resolution drawn up by Basil Gould, British political officer in Sikkim, by informing Raï Bahadur Norbhu Döndup, the British official who had come to Lhasa, that they had sent representatives to the Panchen Lama, who they said were at the point of reaching an agreement with him.[81]

Indeed, on January 30, 1936, ten or so Tibetan officials and representatives from each of the great Gélukpa monasteries in the Lhaṣa region—the abbot Ngawang Gyeltsen for Drépung monastery, the abbot Lozang Gyeltsen for Sera, and the master Tenzin Gyatso for Ganden—had crossed the Sino-Tibetan border in order to meet with the Panchen Lama. Other officials dispatched by the Tibetan government were also responsible for welcoming the Panchen Lama at Kyégudo. The representatives from the three great monasteries met the prelate's caravan in June 1936. Being ecclesiastics, they were highly in favor of his return and asked him to expedite his return. Two months later, on August 27, 1936, Doring Taiji, a representative from the Tibetan government reached Suohe, where the Panchen Lama was residing, and was received by the prelate. Finally, in January 1937 in Dengke, Surkhang Wangchen Tséten, a Tibetan government minister, met Wangdü Norbu, the vicar of the Panchen Lama who was also the director of the accounting department of the special emissary, to try to influence the prelate's opinion.[82] The multiplication of these contacts between envoys of the Lhasa authorities and the Panchen Lama and the members of the prelate's entourage reflects the intensity of the negotiations.

Two points were bitterly debated: the presence of a Chinese escort (including that of a high-ranking Republican official) and the itinerary for the prelate's return. The first point divided those involved for a long time. From the Panchen Lama's perspective, he did have legitimate reasons for mistrusting the reactions of certain radical players among the authorities in Lhasa and he needed to ensure his own protection. The Tibetan government's side also had good reasons to mistrust Chinese soldiers entering their territory, especially since Sino-Tibetan relations had not been clarified. For three years, the Lhasa government had remained entrenched in its position and had invoked the absence of historical precedents to refuse the Panchen Lama permission to return to Central Tibet accompanied by Chinese or Mongols, especially if it entailed a special envoy and armed escort of Chinese.[83] They felt that as an ecclesiastic, the Panchen Lama needed neither arms nor ammunition, and they stipulated that the military equipment of his escort would have to limit itself to hand weapons for individual use. The Panchen Lama then proposed as a compromise that the authorities in Lhasa let him return accompanied by Tibetan members of his entourage, provided they put him under the protection of local soldiers as he traveled from the Sino-Tibetan border to Tashilhunpo. In return, he would ask the special envoy and the Chinese escort to turn back as soon as they reached the border.

Faced with the determination of the Panchen Lama, the Tibetan National Assembly decided to resist his Chinese escort by force and brought arms and ammunition to those places where potential fights might break out. The Tibetan Council of Ministers made its first overture by indicating that if the Panchen Lama returned to Tibet with neither Chinese nor Mongol soldiers, all his demands would be accepted. The National Assembly, on its side, reiterated its threat that Tibetan troops stationed at the border would have orders to engage in combat with the Chinese soldiers accompanying the Panchen Lama.[84] Aware of the gravity of the situation, the prelate requested that his master Phabongka Rinpoche intervene through the abbots of the three great Gélukpa monasteries, asking them to try to reason with the members of the National Assembly. He admitted that the reticence of the authorities in Lhasa was justified, but he added that he had always followed his conscience. Phabongka Rinpoche's response to the prelate's request was:

> The close and less close in the entourage of the master and disciple [The Dalai Lama and the Panchen Lama] have tried to sow discord by falsely showing faith and love. Today, at a time when teaching shines forth and where the powers of accumulated merits blossom, many signs show that doubts are vanishing, just as glaciers melt in springtime.

A few days later, Phabongka informed Reting, by letter, of the Panchen Lama's good intentions, asking him to intervene towards the Tibetan government officials in favor of the prelate's return to his monastery. The regent replied:

> In the letter, which you addressed to me from Cagzam, you clearly indicated to me that after having met the Panchen Lama, you had the feeling that harmony between the master and the disciple had been re-established. You advised me to reflect on the situation with benevolence for the good of religion and politics, for present and future times. You asked me to convince the government to rally to the side of the Panchen Lama. Thank you. Although I personally did all I could towards this end, the Tibetan Assembly could not reach an agreement, because the Panchen Lama is accompanied everywhere he goes by what is called an escort. The members of the Assembly think, therefore, that the master of Tashilhunpo decided to return to his monastery now to take advantage of the Dalai Lama's absence. Their decision is irrevocable. Please excuse me for not being able to convince them.[85]

Indeed, when the prelate was nearing the border at the beginning of 1937, the National Assembly gave orders for Tibetan soldiers to attack his escort.[86] In addition, the Tibetan army forces were increased along the Sino-Tibetan border. Fifteen hundred soldiers normally based in Kham were sent to Rongsum, to the southwest of Dergé, and twelve hundred others armed with five country canons to the northwest of Dergé. Yet, as of December 1935, dissension had appeared between the Council of Ministers and the National Assembly under the pressure of the clergy regarding the counteroffensive ordered towards the advance of the Chinese escort. The abbots of the three great monasteries publicly declared that three hundred Chinese soldiers could not constitute a threat to the country. Six months later, it was the turn of the representatives of the three great monasteries that had joined the Panchen Lama's caravan to inform Cheng Yun, the special emissary, that they were in favor of the prelate's return, but that the "political authorities" in Lhasa still opposed the entry of a Chinese escort into their country. In fact, the main obstacle seemed to come from the Council of Ministers, because in a telegram, Jiang Zhiyu, the permanent envoy of the Chinese Republican government to the Tibetan government, wrote: "the three monasteries and the Assembly ... wish for the rapid return of the Panchen."[87]

Finally in May 1937, the Council of Ministers gave in under heavy pressure from the clergy. It authorized the entry into Central Tibet of the Chinese escort under the condition that it return rapidly to China and that the representatives of the three great monasteries siding with the Panchen Lama give their guarantee.[88] Why such a turnaround?

First, it seems that the Council of Ministers could not resist the will of the sacerdotal community, who desperately needed the presence of the Panchen Lama to quickly find the reincarnation of the Thirteenth Dalai Lama. Next, it is possible that the Council of Ministers became aware of the state of disorganization in which the Tibetan army found itself at that time, as described by Philip Neame, the brigadier who belonged to the British mission headed by Basil Gould, present in Lhasa from August 1936 to February 1937. According to Neame, on the eastern border of Tibet the disorder of the army was such that the four commanders took their orders from Lhasa independently from one another. The Tibetan officers trained in Gyeltsé or Quetta by the British and responsible for, in turn, training their soldiers seemed to have long forgotten what they had learned. In fact, all forms of military training had disappeared since the death of the Thirteenth Dalai Lama; the soldiers were malnourished and rarely paid, and many returned to live at home so as not to waste their ration.[89] To avoid undergoing a bitter defeat and losing face, the Council of Ministers resigned itself to not oppose the Chinese escort, in as much as the Panchen Lama seemed more determined than ever to return home.

As for the insistence that the prelate follow a pre-arranged itinerary, involving travel by boat and then over land through India, it represented little more than a vague hope, even if the Tibetan government fought for it until May 1935, against the demand of the Panchen Lama who wished to return via Amdo. In the end, Lhasa officials authorized the prelate to enter Central Tibet through Amdo, provided that he not be accompanied by Chinese or Mongols.[90]

The Tibetan government never clearly expressed the reasons why it did not want the Panchen Lama to travel through Amdo. By insisting that he use the sea route, Lhasa may have wished to give the British, with whom it was allied, the means to control the prelate's escort. In effect, the port authority in Calcutta could have easily boarded the Panchen Lama's ship to verify his escort and, depending on the intrinsic danger, could refuse authorization to disembark in accordance with any request by the Tibetan government. However, in giving the prelate authorization to travel through Amdo, the authorities in Lhasa took the risk of allowing the Panchen Lama and his escort to arrive at the border without having had the opportunity to inspect their weapons, or to slow them down in case of danger. In addition, it is possible that the Tibetan government feared a circumstantial alliance between the Panchen Lama and the populations of Kham and Amdo, who often showed their lack of allegiance to Lhasa, especially through their propensity for avoiding payment of government taxes and duties. These populations could have even been considered separatists.[91]

From December 1933 to August 1937, the Tibetan government stubbornly resisted the Panchen Lama on several other points. They forbade him to administer the Shigatse district and surrounding areas, to control soldiers from the Tibetan army stationed in Tsang, and to create his own guard based in the monastery compound.[92] After the decision of August 17, 1937, when the Republican government halted the return of the Panchen Lama to Tibet, the Lhasa authorities understood that their hopes of seeing the prelate return to Tashilhunpo were dwindling by the day. The procrastination of the prelate, who seemed resigned to his lot, did not bode well either.

Despite one last disagreement between the National Assembly and the Council of Ministers regarding the attribution of crossing duties and the time frame that the Chinese escort could stay at Tashilhunpo before returning to China, on November 18, 1937, the Tibetan government acceded to the Panchen Lama's final demands. In this way, from the Tibetan side, nothing more could stop the prelate from returning to Tashilhunpo. But these last concessions arrived too late. The Panchen Lama was already in physical agony at Kyégudo monastery.[93]

The Republican Government

The Republican government's reactions to the Panchen Lama's varied demands shifted with time and circumstances. Facts show that during the first ten years of the prelate's exile in China, the authorities in Nanjing took little interest in his vague wishes to return to Tibet. In 1930 Chiang Kai-shek did question the Thirteenth Dalai Lama on how he imagined receiving the Panchen Lama and how he would evaluate the necessity of an escort, but he did not follow up on this.[94]

It was after the death of the Thirteenth Dalai Lama that the Chinese Republicans began to seriously become interested in the question of the Panchen Lama's return to Tashilhunpo. Huang Musong, taking advantage of his presence in Lhasa to try to clarify Sino-Tibetan relations, proposed to the Tibetan authorities that they discuss the subject with him; he highlighted the prestige of the Panchen Lama and the eventual effect on political stability in Central Tibet. Huang Musong suggested that Lhasa invite the Panchen Lama to return quickly, to restore his powers, his role, and his goods, and to ensure his security as well as that of the members of his entourage. If Lhasa agreed, he guaranteed that, in exchange, the Republican government would disarm the prelate.

The fact is that Huang Musong did not manage to convince the Tibetan government. Just before he left Lhasa, he insisted that the Panchen Lama return to Tibet by the northern road and repeated that if the Tibetans decided to protect him, the prelate would be escorted by a small army. But his final efforts turned out to be in vain. Huang Musong could not break the deadlock in the situation, which did not, however, prevent the Republican government from promoting him to the position of director of the Mongolian and Tibetan Affairs Commission in March 1935.[95]

As the months went by, the increasing demands of the prelate brought up growing problems, as evidenced by an incident that occurred at the beginning of April 1935. While the Panchen Lama was going through the province of Ningxia, his baggage, which had been sent from the Bat Khaalga monastery in Inner Mongolia arrived in Kumbum. Upon searching the bags, Chinese officials discovered arms.

Doubt sprang up everywhere. The Tibetan government requested the officials in Amdo to investigate the situation. The Chinese authorities were concerned, because the number of arms they found was much higher than the rifles that

Chiang Kai-shek had given to the Panchen Lama. Furthermore, the models were different from those he had offered the prelate.[96] The Mongolian and Tibetan Affairs Commission questioned the representatives of the Panchen Lama in Nanjing and in Beijing who gave vague, unconvincing explanations. Following this incident, Chiang Kai-shek wondered: Was the Panchen Lama really using his religious power for altruistic goals? Was he creating an army solely for his security during his return to Tibet? Or was he harboring other ambitions?[97] With such hesitations among the authorities in Nanjing, Jiang Zhiyu, the Chinese representative in Lhasa, advised them to limit the number in the Panchen Lama's escort to five hundred soldiers. If the Sino-Tibetan issue was not resolved peacefully, how could he return without risk?[98]

The affair of the clandestine transport of arms did not seem to have influenced the decisions of Huang Musong concerning the Panchen Lama. It is likely that Huang was looking for a way he could exploit the situation to the benefit of the Republican government. Eventually, a few days after the discovery and the turmoil it provoked, the Mongolian and Tibetan Affairs Commission submitted a proposal to the Chinese State Council that was designed to facilitate the return of the prelate to Central Tibet.

The first part of the commission's proposal described the means necessary for the prelate's return. It advised naming a high-ranking official and choosing an armed escort for the Panchen Lama. It saw this action as a way of "stabilizing" the Tibetan situation. In the proposal both parties were advised to make efforts to keep the peace and avoid a situation that could degenerate. Through the proposal, the commission sought to give status to the Panchen Lama's personal guard, after having noticed that under the Qing dynasty nothing had been designated on this subject; it also defined the ideal profile of the high-ranking official who would become the envoy for the Chinese government.

The proposal limited the number of soldiers making up the escort provided by the Republican government for the Panchen Lama to either one thousand or five hundred, in order not to arouse suspicion among the Tibetan people, which might provoke a conflict. It also mandated that the escort's command would follow the orders of the high-ranking official. Next, the proposal set the travel expenses at 1.5 million yuan. Then, it suggested two potential routes for the prelate: one from Amdo to Tibet via Kham, the other via Danglaging, recommending the Panchen Lama take the second route. If an unexpected change were to take place in the process, the proposal stated that the high-ranking official and the Panchen Lama were to consult the Chinese government. In addition, the proposal outlined three precautions that the Chinese State Council should take: first, to classify the proposal as confidential, because it concerned the future relations between China and Tibet; second, to convince the authorities of Qinghai, Sichuan, and Xikang provinces of the importance of the Panchen Lama's return in order to acquire their cooperation; and third, to begin working with the organizations involved in the development project the prelate had designed for Tibet. Finally, the proposal set the mission for the high-ranking official at ten months and suggested that the armed escort stay in Tibet four months.

In the second part of its proposal, the commission described in detail both possible routes for the prelate. Here, the intentions of Huang Musong are discernible. It seems obvious that he hoped to use the pretext of the Panchen Lama's return to Tibet to succeed where he had failed during his visit to Lhasa in 1934; that is, to discretely impose on the Tibetan government the presence of Chinese soldiers on the high plateau.

It was with this in mind that Huang Musong dispatched Cheng Yun, one of the members of his commission, to Lanzhou to support the prelate in his return to Tibet. At the end of April 1935, the Mongolian and Tibetan Affairs Commission informed the Panchen Lama and the Chinese State Council of its opinion. It requested that the government allow an armed escort for the Panchen Lama to ensure his security, and proposed that the prelate's return be treated as a priority. It also made reference to China's past blunders to encourage the Chinese government to name competent officials to deal with the Tibetan prelate.[99]

The Chinese State Council followed Huang's recommendation and entrusted him to set the number of soldiers to escort the Panchen Lama. It also requested him to collaborate with the ministers of finance, communications, railways, industry, and education to prepare the development project for Tibet. Consequently the Mongolian and Tibetan Affairs Commission requisitioned the help of two ministers, Wang Jingwei and Dai Jitao, while in Lanzhou, Cheng Yun continued his discussions with the Panchen Lama.[100]

In response to the categorical refusal of the Tibetan ministers to permit a Chinese or Mongol escort on their territory, the commission did not alter its plans. As the Chinese government prepared to put into place a "Commission for the Edification of Xikang Province" in the Tibetan region of Kham, the authorities in Lhasa hardened their position. The Tibetans were all the more appalled by the fact that the Chinese acted without first discussing this with them.[101] Meanwhile the radio transmitter left in Lhasa by Huang Musong was supposed to allow the two governments to continue their negotiations as to the nature of their relationship in real time. The Tibetans demanded, among other things, that the Chinese representative in Lhasa who Huang Musong had left behind in 1934, Jiang Zhiyu, return to China. But the Chinese government remained firm in its resolve and replied that the prestige of the Panchen Lama and the importance of the Tibetan situation made the establishment of an armed escort and the nomination of a high-ranking official imperative.[102]

Finally, the Chinese State Council set the expense of the trip at 1.6 million yuan, the number of soldiers in the escort at five hundred,[103] and appointed Cheng Yun as "Special Emissary in Charge of Accompanying the Panchen Lama to Tibet."[104] The treatment that it granted Cheng underlined the importance of his mission. Immediately, 200,000 yuan were allocated to him for his trip and the creation of his office. A military police battalion was responsible for his protection. At the end of July 1935, the Chinese government officially named him "Special Emissary to the Panchen Lama," and declared in this way its intent to express its "respect" towards the Tibetan master.

The duties associated with the post of special emissary included protecting the prelate during his return trip to Tibet and establishing *entente cordiale* between both the Tibetan government and the Panchen Lama. During the trip, Cheng Yun's mission was to observe the situation, diffuse the "virtuous" principles of the Chinese Republican government, and "comfort" the people in the border regions. He would have to stay a while in Tibet once his mission was accomplished, which was expected to take ten months, of which eight were to be for the journey itself. The itinerary had already been determined, but the return had yet to be established. The departure date had to be decided jointly by the Panchen Lama and by Cheng Yun, who would have to inform his government. In September 1935 the Chinese State Council launched the operation.[105]

Faced with the concerns of the authorities in Lhasa, Huang Musong reminded the director of the Tibet Office in Nanjing that the nomination of the special emissary and the creation of an armed escort were to ensure the prestige and protection of the Panchen Lama.[106] By doing so, he was hoping to convince him that the Republican government positioned itself as donor of the prelate. He could be satisfied, because this unfolded according to plan.

In November 1935 the Chinese State Council ordered the escort to go with its arms and baggage to Xi'an by train, and then to continue to Amdo. Cheng Yun joined the others as planned at Kumbum monastery where the Panchen Lama was staying.[107] In Lhasa, Jiang Zhiyu, who had asked to be replaced since he was ill, stated in a telegram addressed to the Mongolian and Tibetan Affairs Commission, that the return of the Panchen Lama was a unique opportunity for the Republican government to gain a foothold in Tibet. The commission requested the authorities from Qinghai Province to facilitate the progression of the representatives of the three great Gélukpa monasteries to Kumbum, favorable as they were to the Panchen Lama's plans.[108]

On his side, Cheng Yun took advantage of the unintended rest in Kumbum to complete the guidelines for the return of the Panchen Lama to Tibet, which the Chinese State Council had transmitted to the Mongolian and Tibetan Affairs Commission in February 1936. The special emissary drew up two programs for research and investigation to follow all along the way, destined for his collaborators and members of the armed escort. His goal was to report the situation in the western regions to the Chinese government so that they could reorganize their affairs there. At the same time, he designed an intensive training program for the soldiers of the escort to take place in Lanzhou. Regarding transport, he was obliged to make special arrangements, which took into account the deserted regions they were to cross.[109]

From the Chinese side, everything seemed ready for the departure. However, the Republican government ran up against several obstacles: the persistent opposition by the Tibetan authorities to the Chinese escort; the growing involvement of the British, as we will see; and the lack of funds to pay the soldiers. To overcome the first obstacle, Gao Zhangzhu, the military advisor of the special emissary's decentralized office, suggested that some people be sent to scout ahead in Tibet to negotiate directly with the Tibetan government, which Cheng Yun and the Panchen Lama accepted immediately. To try to minimize the second obstacle, the Chinese minister of foreign affairs, who was under pressure from the British and seemed to doubt the utility of the escort, asked the Mongolian and Tibetan Affairs Commission whether "the day when the Panchen Lama enters Tibet is close, as also is the day when the British ambassador will return to his country, [thus] wouldn't it be better to have the escort protect the Panchen only to the Tibetan border?" The commission replied that the constitution of this escort expressed the will of the Chinese government to "protect Buddhism" and that it conformed to traditional practice.

In order to pay the Chinese soldiers in the escort, Cheng Yun was obliged to request cash from the Mongolian and Tibetan Affairs Commission, which in turn requested 100,000 yuan from the Ministry of Finance. In the end, the ministry ordered its annex in Lanzhou to release 60,000 yuan for Cheng Yun.[110]

Shortly before the caravan took to the road, Huang Musong advised the special emissary to be prudent. He reminded him that the duty of the soldiers in the escort was to be limited to protecting the Panchen Lama, and specified that the emissary must always pay special attention to the peaceful aspect of the mission. Since the Panchen Lama had asked that the escort return to China once it arrived in Tashilhunpo, he recommended that Cheng Yun renegotiate this point with the prelate once they reached Kyégudo. Finally, he insisted on the good impression that the members of the escort must give throughout the voyage in order to facilitate the resolution of the Sino-Tibetan problem.[111]

Huang Musong's immediate concern was not to provoke the Tibetan soldiers nor run into the sensitivity of the Tibetan government because his plan entailed a long-term vision. Huang knew that rallying Tibet to the "union of the five nationalities" was rather complex, and that he imperatively needed the support of an influential Tibetan to help maneuver the recalcitrant members of the regency government. It was possible that Huang Musong felt the Panchen Lama's actions in the western regions were meritorious, but they were politically useless. The prelate would be much more useful to him in Tibet. That is why Huang insisted that the prelate's return go as smoothly as possible. Huang Musong had good reason to be suspicious.

A month and a half after the departure of the caravan, the baggage of the Panchen Lama and those of his entourage crossed the Tibetan border, carried by pack animals. Tibetan soldiers at the border post in Nagchuka searched them and found arms, as we saw earlier.[112] Shortly thereafter, Ma Hetian, the military advisor to Cheng Yun, questioned Liu Jiaju, the general secretary and translator of the Panchen Lama, and Wangdü Norbu, the prelate's vicar about this find. According to Kelzang Chönjor, the seizure of the Panchen Lama's weapons by the Tibetan authorities served as a pretext to harden their position. For Wangdü Norbu, this question was important. In his opinion, the local people would side with the Panchen Lama, and further the Tibetan ministers would not dare affront him.[113]

Should one see a relation of cause and effect, or was it simple coincidence? This incident occurred just when Huang Musong left his position as director of the Mongolian and Tibetan Affairs Commission, without an explanation for his departure and was replaced by Wu Zhongxin.[114]

From that point on, it clearly seems that the Republican government changed its attitude towards the Panchen Lama. One month after the discovery of the arms, Cheng Yun was relieved of his duties and replaced by Zhao Shouyu, a member of the provincial government of Shanxi since 1933. According to the *Bianqiang* review, Cheng Yun had preferred to resign of his own accord, having been unable to gain the confidence of the Panchen Lama and his entourage. It seemed, in fact, that he proved to be incompetent at presenting the Nationalist arguments to the local authorities.[115] In his defense, it must be recognized that the situation surrounding the caravan had quite deteriorated.

Since the beginning of 1936, Chinese Communists, members of the second army of the Long March, had been advancing toward the Tibetan region of Kham where they had cut a route between Dartsédo and Bathang, and had taken the city of Litang. They then approached Kyégudo where the troops of Ma Bufang, the military governor of Qinghai, fiercely resisted. Worried, the Tibetan authorities had placed part of their army at the eastern border of Tibet, but the capacity of their soldiers to fight was not known. The rising number of skirmishes would have frightened Cheng Yun, who feared he was no longer capable of accomplishing his mission of protecting the Panchen Lama, to the point of saying so in a telegram to the Mongolian and Tibetan Affairs Commission. His cautious attitude displeased the Chinese State Council, who in response relieved him of his duties.

As soon as he was named, Zhao Shouyu, the new special emissary, requested supplementary personnel from the Mongolian and Tibetan Affairs Commission. He also took advantage of the situation by demanding a salary triple what had been originally established![116] During this time, at the Labrang trashikhyil monastery, Cheng Yun named Ma Hetian, his military advisor, to the post of interim emissary.[117] One month later, Zhao Shouyu joined the members of his office in Lanzhou. He planned to go as rapidly as possible to Ragya monastery, where the Panchen Lama was residing, but he noticed that the majority of the officials of the office had resigned after Cheng Yun's departure, so he had to replace them. Also, the escort was not yet ready.[118]

Little by little, in the absence of Huang Musong's enthusiasm, the Republican government's interest in the return of the Panchen Lama waned. Indeed, in October 1936, Ma Bufang informed the Mongolian and Tibetan Affairs Commission that the Tibetan army had stationed its forces all along the border (without specifying the importance), and requested that a detachment of soldiers be made available to the Panchen Lama to protect him.[119] This unfortunately was to no avail. On his side, in the following month, Wu Zhongxin, the new director of the Mongolian and Tibetan Affairs Commission, half-heartedly defended the lot of the Chinese escort of the Panchen Lama. Conforming to Huang Musong's initial proposal, which consisted in having the prelate accompanied to his monastery by Chinese soldiers, he envisaged three possible scenarios. First, if the Tibetan troops resisted, both armies would fight; second, the escort accompanying the Panchen Lama would stay from six months to one year in Tibet and its members would take advantage of this period to resolve the Sino-Tibetan issue; and the third scenario was that once the escort arrived in Lhasa, it would return immediately to China.[120]

The last efforts of the representative of the Chinese government in Lhasa, Jiang Zhiyu, to try to break the situation's deadlock changed nothing. These efforts included a proposal to the Mongolian and Tibetan Affairs Commission that a minister from Lhasa go to Nanjing to accelerate the negotiations. Jiang also suggested that, given that the Panchen Lama had planned to leave in June or July 1937, the prelate could postpone his departure a few months to allow a representative from the Tibetan government time to arrive in Nanjing. He added at the end that he wished to be relieved of his functions due to illness.[121] But the Mongolian and Tibetan Affairs Commission requested him to conform to the previous decisions and no longer authorized him to negotiate with the Tibetan ministers. He was requested to stay in Lhasa despite his illness.[122]

In July 1937 the new special emissary Zhao Shouyu and the Chinese escort reached the Panchen Lama at Kyégudo. During discussions with the prelate, Zhao Shouyu expressed concern that the Tibetans had not provided the escort with supplies and actually planned to engage in armed resistance when the Chinese escort entered their territory. The apparent optimism of the Panchen Lama did not seem to reassure him.[123] In mid-August the Mongolian and Tibetan Affairs Commission ordered Zhao Shouyu to wait for the commission to set the date of departure, and two days later, the Republican government gave the Panchen Lama the order to postpone his return to Tibet "to give time to wage war properly against Japan."[124] It also required him to reside in a place that was to be specified at a later date.

The Panchen Lama seems to have had no other choice but to make the best of things. He addressed the following message to Phabongka Rinpoche:

> Here I find the opportunity to practice patience. I think that the most important thing is to not erase the good actions I have been able to accomplish. As times are difficult, I stay at the monastery.[125]

As a matter of anecdotal interest, both biographers of the prelate relate a particular incident that occurred on August 20, while the Panchen Lama was giving a Buddhist teaching in Rabshilungshö monastery. It seems a wall hanging at the entrance to the monastery is said to have torn. All those present saw this as a sign of bad luck. The Panchen Lama immediately requested the monks of the monastery to recite purification prayers to push aside this bad omen.[126]

In fact, foreboding or not, the Republican government manifestly abandoned the prelate. The excuse of the war of resistance against Japan given by the Mongolian and Tibetan Affairs Commission to justify this behavior does not hold up to analysis.[127] It is clear that the five hundred (or one thousand) Chinese soldiers sent to accompany the Panchen Lama were not in a position to make a difference in the strength of forces in the Sino-Japanese war, and the Republican government did not even try to recover them for their use in battle in the following months. Only their arms seemed to interest them.

The true intention behind the abandonment of the prelate by the Chinese authorities lies elsewhere. The most plausible hypothesis seems to be that at the time, independent of his resistance against the Japanese invaders, Chiang Kai-shek had engaged in a merciless fight against the Chinese Communists. To vanquish Mao Zedong, who enjoyed broad support throughout the rural population, he needed Western military support. It is possible that Chiang Kai-shek had given in to demands from the British, who had for months been putting pressure on the Republican government to block the entry of the Panchen Lama's Chinese escort into Tibet. By satisfying the British wish to preserve the independence of Tibet and keep it as a buffer state between their colonial empire and China, Chiang Kai-shek placated the westerners.

The British

Sources show that a subtle game had been established between the Panchen Lama and the authorities in Lhasa, and the Chinese Republican government and British officials who took turns soliciting each other. In less than ten years (1928–37), five British missions went to Lhasa with varying fates. During each one, the subject of the Panchen Lama's return was placed at the heart of the debates, even if the British, reasoning from a long-term perspective, were mainly desirous of establishing a commercial foothold in Tibet.

In 1928 Major F. M. Bailey responded to the pressing calls of the prelate. During his visit to Lhasa, where he was received by the Thirteenth Dalai Lama, he pleaded the cause of the Panchen Lama in vain. The Dalai Lama warned him against any interference. Four years later the British accepted the invitation to come to Lhasa by the Dalai Lama, who was looking to get help from them to reinforce his country's border defense. Leslie Weir, Bailey's replacement as the British political officer in Sikkim, was dispatched to Lhasa with the objective of hastening the Panchen Lama's return to Tibet. At the time, the British thought that the presence of the prelate in China was a menace to peace in Central Asia and that it could harm their commercial interests as well as their relations with the Tibetan government. The British suspected the prelate of having taken sides with Beri monastery during the border conflict in Kham and of having stirred up discord to the benefit of China.

Leslie Weir had more success than F. M. Bailey with the Thirteenth Dalai Lama. He managed, among other things, to convince him to write a letter to his disciple to invite him back to Tibet.[128] He persuaded him to also transmit the letter by the intermediary E. M. B. Ingram, the chargé d'affaires at the British Embassy in China, rather than going through the services of Köncho Chungné, the director of the Nanjing Tibet Office. Doing this, he was able to anchor the idea of British mediation in the Tibetan leader's mind.

In August 1935 the British sent a third mission to Lhasa led by Frederick Williamson, Leslie Weir's replacement. The regent Reting Rinpoche had requested him to visit, since the threat of the arrival of the Panchen Lama's Chinese escort seemed imminent and he wished to obtain a guarantee of British support should things escalate. From his side, Frederick Williamson was particularly responsible for verifying that Jiang Zhiyu and Liu Piaochen, the two Chinese officials who remained in Lhasa after the departure of the Huang Musong mission, had not opened a permanent office. Quickly he reassured his superiors, specifying that Jiang Zhiyu had neither power nor influence in Lhasa and that the Tibetans did not consider the two as a Chinese diplomatic representation. Questioned by the local authorities on the role his government would play if the Tibetan and Chinese armies were to enter into combat, he replied that it was highly unlikely that Great Britain would send reinforcements to help the Tibetans; but he tried to convince them that the Chinese had neither the capacity nor the will to fight because of their domestic problems. At the same time, Williamson was accused by Jiang Zhiyu of inciting the Tibetan authorities to oppose the return of the Panchen Lama accompanied by a Chinese escort. Shortly afterwards, he was contacted by the Panchen Lama, whom he advised to return to Tibet without an armed escort. The prelate asked him to intervene in his favor towards the Tibetan government so they would accept his demands. Frederick Williamson replied that the Tibetan government would commit to satisfying them, except for the creation of a personal army and the control of a greater number of districts.[129] Next, the Panchen Lama wrote to him:

> The Excellent Lonchen Sahib,
>
> The reason for sending this message:
>
> I have duly received your kind message dated the first day of the ninth month [October 28, 1935], which you so kindly sent me through my representatives, Ngagchen Rinpoche and others. In this you inform me that, among my demands there are three points on which the Tibetan government is unable to agree with me. They are: my wish to have control over the whole of the army [in Tsang], my desire to have control of more *dzong*s than before, and my wish to bring Chinese officials and soldiers.

> To avoid all possible trouble in the future I must be frank. I have already told my representatives what they should tell the Tibetan government with regard to my demands. Kindly note that the Tibetan government's statement that I wish to bring Chinese officials and soldiers with me is untrue. This is not one of the points in my demands. Kindly make enquiries as to this. I would request that the British government be kind enough to bring the differences between the Tibetan government and the *labrang* (the Panchen Lama's administration) to a definite settlement in accordance with the list of the demands that I have already made. Kindly let me have a reply by wire so that I may take a definite line of action.[130]

One part of this letter seems unusual in the context of this text, which is the English translation of the original letter written in Tibetan sent by the Panchen Lama to Frederick Williamson. The prelate refutes the statement saying that he wished to bring Chinese officials with him to Tibet and he asks the British to verify this statement. Yet we know that he distinctly asked the Republican government to give him a high-ranking Chinese official to accompany him to Tashilhunpo. Is this incongruity the result of a simple problem of translation? Or did the prelate, in fact, wish to fool the British, as they were not favorites of his? Was he really the author of this letter?

In November 1935 while the Chinese State Council ordered the Panchen Lama's escort to go to Amdo via Xi'an, Sir Alexander Cadogan, the British ambassador in Nanjing, informed Xu Mo, the vice-minister of foreign affairs, that his government opposed the entry of a Chinese army into Central Tibet. He backed up his position with an article from the Simla Convention in which China agreed not to send an army into Central Tibet and not to open a representation office. Xu Mo reminded him that China did not ratify the convention, and specified that the special emissary and his escort were simply responsible for ensuring the protection and prestige of the Panchen Lama. Besides, according to him, it was not a question of an army but of an escort.[131] Facts show that Xu Mo was of bad faith and playing with words.[132]

In any case, the declaration of Cadogan had the merit of clarifying the British position. Frederick Williamson reassured the Tibetan authorities regarding the role his government would agree to play and encouraged them to resist the Chinese escort into Tibet. He died suddenly shortly thereafter. Keith Battye, the British trade agent in Gyeltsé, who succeeded him in Lhasa, met with the Tibetan ministers regarding the conditions given by the Panchen Lama.[133] Clearly, his effort did not manage to convince them of the validity of the attitude of the prelate because they informed him of their intention to continue the tax and the recruitment of soldiers in the province of Tsang, and to refuse to give the prelate the districts of Namring, Nakartsé, Panam, and Shigatse. Despite this, the Tibetan ministers declared themselves satisfied with the actions undertaken by the British in Nanjing, but they despaired at not receiving any military aid.[134]

At the beginning of February 1936, Basil Gould, the new British political officer in Sikkim, found out through Tsaserkhang, the representative of the Panchen Lama in Kalimpong, that the prelate planned to return to Tibet the following summer.[135] During this time, Cadogan reminded Gould that in this affair the main interest for the British was to maintain the integrity and autonomy of Central Tibet, as well as a stable and efficient Tibetan government capable of preserving peace along the Indian border and near other countries where the British were present, such as Bhutan or Sikkim.[136] It is in this state of mind that he met Xu Mo, the Chinese vice-minister of foreign affairs. He proposed that in conformity with the position of the Tibetan government, the Chinese escort must not accompany the Panchen Lama inside Tibet, but must stop at the Sino-Tibetan border. He specified that from there on, the Tibetans would take responsibility for his protection.[137] Xu Mo rejected this proposal and rejected British interference in what he considered to be a domestic affair.[138]

On their side, Basil Gould and the British government in India put together a resolution proposal for the return of the Panchen Lama to Tibet that was addressed to the British government in London.[139] The proposal shows that Cadogan, Britain's ambassador to China, felt that the Tibetan authorities had to make a written request for the mediation of his country. Yet the British minister of foreign affairs raised strong objections concerning the feasibility of such mediation.[140]

According to Gould's wish, the British official Raï Bahadur Norbhu Döndup went to Lhasa in June 1936 to deliver the offer of mediation by the British government, along with the resolution proposal. A few days after his arrival, members of the Tibetan National Assembly rejected British mediation that they judged no longer necessary because of the advances they had made in their own negotiations with the Panchen Lama.

Despite Tibetan refusal to send a written invitation to Basil Gould, the British political officer made his entry into Lhasa in August 1936, as the head of the fifth British mission to Tibet. The mission's objectives were to encourage the Tibetan authorities to oppose the entry of the Chinese escort into Tibet as well as evaluate the capacity of the Tibetan army to resist, propose a sale of arms adapted to the situation, if needed, and verify the level of Chinese presence in Lhasa and its real influence on Tibetan officials.

A month and a half later, given the determination of the Panchen Lama to advance towards the Sino-Tibetan border with his escort, the Tibetan ministers asked Basil Gould to serve as mediator, in case the circumstances required it.[141] Brigadier Philip Neame, who belonged to Gould's mission in Lhasa, drew up a summary of his observations on the Tibetan army. According to Neame, the Tibetan army had been in decline since the death of the Thirteenth Dalai Lama. In response, his superiors made a proposal to the Tibetan Council of Ministers to train their officers in Shillong and provide them with arms for the Tibetan army.[142]

Did the authorities in Lhasa refuse to equip themselves through laxity, disregard for danger, or did they have true funding issues? Why was the effort to modernize the Tibetan armed forces interrupted at the death of the Thirteenth Dalai Lama?

In February 1937 Basil Gould left Lhasa to return to Gangtok, in Sikkim. The British considered his mission a success because he had convinced the Tibetans to continue firmly opposing the entrance of the Panchen Lama's Chinese escort. Also, he had opened the first British office in Lhasa and had received authorization for two members of his mission, Hugh Richardson, the trade agent in Gyeltsé, and Reginald Fox, a radio officer, to stay in Lhasa equipped with a radio transmitter. Their presence in Lhasa counteracted that of Jiang Zhiyu, the Chinese representative.

However, Gould failed on a crucial point, since the Tibetan government declined his offer of (paid) military help.[143] His defeat was unfortunate for two reasons. First, very pragmatically, the British government lost an opportunity to expand its arms business in the region. Secondly, it could no longer count on Tibet to act as a buffer state. Dangerously disarmed, the high plateau was at the mercy of a great predatory power. By wishing to focus on the business side of the situation, and refusing to invest and give the Tibetans valid military support, the British lost their opportunity to transform Tibet into the true buffer state that they had always felt was so important.

Did they feel they were in a position to convince the Chinese Republicans to stop their plans by other means? The fact is that at the moment when the special emissary Zhao Shouyu and the escort arrived in Kyégudo to join the Panchen Lama, and when their departure seemed imminent, consistent with their policies up until then, the British once again expressed disapproval of Chinese soldiers entering Tibet.[144] Effectively, in August 1937 the Republican government clearly stopped the return of the Panchen Lama to Tibet. Had the British influenced their decision? Had they won? Had there been a cause and effect relation between British actions and the decision of the Chinese Republicans? After having encouraged the return of the Panchen Lama when they thought it served their interests, the British may have unwittingly contributed to stopping it.

REASONS FOR THE FAILED RETURN TO TIBET

The politico-commercial imbroglio and struggles for influence in which the Panchen Lama was forced to maneuver around clearly contributed to the failure of his attempted return to Tibet. But were there other factors involved?

The Panchen Lama's insistence (or that of his entourage?) concerning the presence of a high-ranking Republican official with the Chinese escort was, without a doubt, a crucial cause. The incident of the transport of clandestine arms in his baggage (had he been aware of their existence before their discovery?) revealed the extent to which this was a sensitive subject for all the parties concerned. The Panchen Lama feared the members of the Tibetan Council of

Ministers, who themselves feared his entry under Chinese escort on Tibetan land. Having neither a minimum of mutual trust nor a mediator to straighten out the mix-up, the situation became a deadlock. The persistence of the prelate to take the route through Amdo, while the Tibetan government insisted on his traveling by boat to India only made things worse. Faced with so many obstacles, the finesse, open-mindedness, and intelligence of Huang Musong were stymied.

Hindered in his undertakings, the Panchen Lama preferred to occupy himself with his function within the Republican government and to zealously honor his commitment, which consisted in promoting values on the western frontier. All things considered, he respected the orders of the Nanjing authorities to whom he must have felt more or less tied, given the generous gifts that they had given him, as well as the fact that he had linked his ideas so closely with the thought of Sun Yat-sen. But, Chiang Kai-shek was not Sun Yat-sen and it is highly likely that the Tibetan master, full of his knowledge of the science of the mind, easily perceived the difference. During the worst moments, the prelate delved into his religious activities. With the absence of the Thirteenth Dalai Lama, dissension broke out within the Tibetan government in an "opposition-parliament" atmosphere among its mix of lay and religious personalities. This state of affairs only further complicated the negotiations for the prelate's return. The influence exerted by the British on this eclectic theocracy orphaned from its charismatic leader was not accommodating towards the return of the Panchen Lama to Tibet. More preoccupied with the political and economic interests of their empire than with good relations between a "master" and a "disciple," British diplomats and officials tried to dissuade the Nanjing authorities from sending an escort, while persuading those in Lhasa to refuse its entry into Tibet.

Among the causes that stalled the departure of the Panchen Lama was the disingenuousness of the Republican government who committed to providing the travel budget for the mission, but in actual fact, had sent less than promised to the accompanying special emissary.[145] However, the order that the Republican leaders gave to the prelate to postpone his trip contributed decisively to thwarting his return. True, the Panchen Lama was not obliged to obey. The representatives of the three great Gélukpa monasteries and that of the Tibetan government met with the Panchen Lama at Rabshilungshö ganden chökorling monastery to discuss the question.[146] They pressed him to return quickly to Tibet. The Panchen Lama hesitated. He seemed torn between his desire to return to his homeland and to respect orders from the Chinese government. He ended up making a proposal to the Tibetan representatives requesting they send a telegram to their government asking that it accept the Chinese escort and emissary accompanying him to his monastery, with the condition that they would return to China after five months. He also expressed the desire that the unresolved questions be debated during the time of his trip home and that the Tibetans pay him crossing *ulag*. Finally, the prelate informed them that if he did not receive a response from the Council of Ministers in the next ten days, he would obey the Chinese government's orders.[147]

In Lhasa, members of the Assembly and the Council of Ministers accepted these conditions, but their position concerning the crossing corvée that the prelate wanted the Tibetans to pay remained ambiguous. According to some sources, they accepted the idea; other sources indicate otherwise.[148]

Contrary to expectations, despite the insistence of the representatives of the three great Tibetan monasteries, the Panchen Lama (or perhaps his secretaries?) preferred to postpone his departure for Tibet. This change of heart remains difficult to account for. The state of chronic indecision demonstrated by the Panchen Lama seems to be a constant in the behavior of many Tibetan masters. I have had occasion to remark on this several times among Tibetans I have met. Their frequent recourse to divinations is one demonstration of this. This practice, no doubt inherited from pre-Buddhist Tibetan shamanism, is an unusual feature of Tibetan Buddhism. It does not belong to orthodox Buddhist trends. Like others, the Panchen Lama used it. For example in September 1936, when the caravan had just finished its first stage and was resting at Ragya monastery, the prelate undertook a divination that is said to have revealed that the return trip to Tibet was achievable, but that members of the entourage would come across many obstacles. He then asked Tséchokling Rinpoche and Wangdü Norbu, his vicar, to perform similar divinations, which led to identical results. Ceremonies and offerings were immediately undertaken in all the surrounding monasteries, including Labrang trashikhyil and Kumbum.[149] The hesitations of the Panchen Lama during the final negotiations held with the authorities in Lhasa managed to spoil the hopes of those who had been wishing for his return to Tibet. His death ended up definitively settling the question.

Facts show that the Republican government manipulated the Panchen Lama by procuring him an escort that gave them a pretext for sending soldiers into Tibet, all the more so since its own negotiations with Lhasa officials had failed on the crucial point of the defense of the high plateau. On their side, the British manipulated the authorities in Lhasa (and those in Nanjing) according to their own interests. As for the Panchen Lama, at first it seems that he took advantage of the circumstances to acquire an escort by the Republican government. We should remember here that the main reason for the escort was to ensure the physical protection of the prelate. But what did the abbot at Tashilhunpo fear? His *tulku* status signified that he had attained "liberation from samsara," that is, from the cycle of conditioned existences by the force of his karma, such that he was beyond suffering. Is there not a fundamental contradiction between his apparent behavior, as seen in the sources cited here, and his "blessed" state, which would put him above material contingencies? The imperious tone of certain letters and telegrams that are attributed to him and the inflexible attitude that he is said to have had concerning the necessity of an armed escort, don't they stand out from the extemporaneous character seen in so many Tibetan Buddhist masters? Isn't it shocking from a man who the testimonies describe as courteous and gentle? Indeed, did the Panchen Lama make his decisions alone? If not, who influenced him?

ROLE OF THE PANCHEN LAMA'S ENTOURAGE

Clues indicate that the Panchen Lama was surrounded by disreputable individuals, who, reasoning from a short-term perspective, focused on their own personal gain. That was the opinion of the Thirteenth Dalai Lama who had expressed it twice and had characterized the members of the Panchen Lama's entourage as "evil" and "unscrupulous servants." It was also the view of the Tibetan government who judged them "evil."[150]

However, at least one person belonging to the Panchen Lama's entourage seemed to distinguish himself from the others through his good will and abnegation. Ngagchen Rinpoche was one of the reincarnated masters of Tashilhunpo and a disciple of the prelate, as well as one of his traveling companions from the moment he left Tibet with the Panchen Lama in December 1923. He apparently enjoyed the prelate's trust, and was asked twice to go to Lhasa to negotiate directly with the Tibetan government. Indeed, we see him work tirelessly to try to smooth out differences that opposed his spiritual master and the leaders of Tibet. During his first sojourn in the Tibetan capital in June 1933, Rinpoche was received with respect by the Thirteenth Dalai Lama and by the members of the government. Next he went to Tashilhunpo where the monks were looking forward to his visit, eager to have news of their abbot. In Kalimpong on his return trip, he met Frederick Williamson, the British political officer in Sikkim, to whom he gave a verbal account of the results of his negotiations. Given this, one must admit that his attempt was unsuccessful and that the authorities in Lhasa remained inflexible.[151] Ngagchen Rinpoche returned to China empty-handed, passing through India and taking the sea route, perhaps to avoid hurting the sensitivities of the Tibetan leaders, who remained very fussy about the subject.

Upon returning to Nanjing in April 1934, he gave an incantatory speech in which he affirmed that the Thirteenth Dalai Lama had approved the return of the Panchen Lama to Tibet.[152] Was it true? It does seem plausible that the spiritual and temporal leader gave his approval shortly before dying. But, all the same, the Thirteenth Dalai Lama had not given into all the demands of the Panchen Lama. Conscious of the difficulties left to surmount, in his speech Ngagchen Rinpoche called for reason. According to him, the absence of the deceased Thirteenth Dalai Lama made it all the more necessary and urgent that the Panchen Lama return to his monastery, Tashilhunpo. Questioned by a journalist from *Zhongyang ribao*, he affirmed:

> I met the Panchen Rinpoche in Hangzhou and informed him of the welcome that the Tibetans reserve for him. The Panchen Rinpoche wishes whole-heartedly to return to Tibet. Only, the return route has not been set. Will he go over land or by sea? The Tibetans wish that Panchen Rinpoche go by sea and cross India. They will then send people to welcome him. But this trip is particularly long. If the Panchen Rinpoche travels over land, the trip will also be long, requiring five

> or six months of travel. The date of the return to Tibet of the Panchen Rinpoche could be set this year. But the Panchen Rinpoche is old now and I am afraid that in either case the voyage will be too long.[153]

A few days later, Ngagchen Rinpoche spoke out in favor of the Panchen Lama meeting with Chiang Kai-shek in Jiangxi in order to discuss the modalities of his master's return to Tashilhunpo, and to give the Chinese leader presents from the Tibetan government. Next in October, Ngagchen Rinpoche returned to Tibet for his second mission, to again present the demands of the Panchen Lama. Once on site in spring 1935, he sent a telegram to the Mongolian and Tibetan Affairs Commission that his compatriots were eager to see the Panchen Lama return to Tibet.

Without a doubt that was the case, too, for the abbots from the three great Gélukpa monasteries and their constituents. On the other hand, concerning the members of the Council of Ministers, was not Ngagchen Rinpoche exaggerating somewhat?

This time the Tibetan government was better disposed towards the prelate's disciple and the negotiations seemed to make some timid progress. Ngagchen Rinpoche met Captain Keith Battye, the British trade agent in Gyeltsé who had replaced the deceased Frederick Williamson and who confided in him that the Panchen Lama must soften his demands. Probably full of admirable intentions, Ngagchen Rinpoche requested the British government to arrange, as best they could, the affairs between his master and the authorities in Lhasa.

One year later in November 1936, Ngagchen Rinpoche is said to have reported to Basil Gould that his spiritual master was nearly prisoner of the Chinese and that he seemed very influenced by his close associates, themselves paid by the Republican government. It seems he would have been sufficiently well positioned to describe the habits of the entourage of which he was part. Despite his, to say the least, surprising secrets, Ngagchen Rinpoche continued to promote his spiritual master's interests. In December 1936, knowing that a small group of Tibetans still refused the entry of the escort, he suggested that the Panchen Lama announce his intention of sending the escort back to China as soon as he arrived in Tashilhunpo. According to him, this attitude would eliminate the final doubts of the reluctant Tibetans, who would then accept the entry of the escort to Tibet.[154]

This attitude on the part of Ngagchen Rinpoche seems to have damaged his credibility with the Panchen Lama, as was shown in two ways. First, the Panchen Lama chose another mediator from among the members of his entourage. On January 18 (or February 10), 1937, Wangdü Norbu met Surkhang Wangchen Tséten, a minister of the Tibetan government in Dengke. They discussed an agreement on a return route that avoided the cities of Chamdo and Lhasa, and forbade all possibility of the Panchen Lama from participating in the country's political life. On the other hand, Wangdü Norbu affirmed that the prelate had rejected the idea of returning to his monastery without a Chinese escort.[155] If the Panchen Lama had paid attention to the proposal of Ngagchen Rinpoche, would he have let Wangdü Norbu conduct parallel negotiations with a Tibetan minister? Secondly, the Panchen Lama ousted Ngagchen Rinpoche from his functions for having sided too much with the position of the Tibetan government regarding the escort. According to Hugh Richardson, the British representative in Lhasa, the dismissal of Ngagchen Rinpoche would have taken place in March 1937, that is to say well before he reached the Panchen Lama in Kyégudo. This would explain why Ngagchen Rinpoche went back to Nanjing April 7, 1937, instead of going to meet his master in Kyégudo, preferring to stay two or three months in Beijing before going back towards Amdo.[156] He is said to have then left for Japan, looking for new disciples.

By relieving Ngagchen Rinpoche of his functions, didn't the prelate show that beyond simple protection during his return trip to Tashilhunpo, he wished to benefit from the services of the Chinese Republican soldiers permanently, once settled in again in the facilities of his monastery? Did he actually fear that the monks and Tibetan soldiers, appointed by the Tibetan government to welcome him at the border and ensure his security up to his monastery, really had the mission to arrest him and take him to the capital to be judged for his (supposedly) missed past payments? Did he plan to maintain a personal guard at Tashilhunpo, and did he hope to control the soldiers of the Tibetan army stationed in the province of Tsang, as listed among his conditions? Did he decide on the discharge of Ngagchen Rinpoche alone? Who could Ngagchen Rinpoche have disturbed? Apart from the Chinese Republicans who wished to control Tibet and the Panchen Lama who wished to protect himself, who would have been interested in bringing in and maintaining the escort on the high-plateau and why? Before trying to answer these questions, we must examine the personalities of certain members of the Panchen Lama's entourage.

A report written in April 1937 by Gao Zhangzhu, the Chinese chief of staff for the Panchen Lama's escort, and addressed to Wu Zhongxin, the director of the Mongolian and Tibetan Affairs Commission, gives some explanation about the people surrounding the prelate. The simple fact that Gao Zhangzhu wrote this report shows that he wondered about the role played by the Panchen Lama's entourage and sought the opinion of the Nanjing authorities on the subject. According to him, the two people that had the greatest credibility and authority were Lozang Gyeltsen and Lozang Tsültrim. Next came a second group composed of, among others, Wangdü Norbu, Kang Fu'an, Luo Youren, and Dazhuoni.[157] Finally, a third group of less influential people included Ngagchen Rinpoche, Tséchokling Rinpoche, and Kelzang Chönjor.[158]

Lozang Gyeltsen was the Panchen Lama's attendant (*sölpön kenpo*, lit. "head of meals"). He held the post of director of the Panchen Lama's bureau office in Nanjing, then that of director of the Office of the Great Emissary for the Propagation of Values on the Western Frontier.[159] As for Lozang Tsültrim, he was in charge of the Office of the Panchen Lama in Beijing as of 1925, and then he became general manager of the propaganda department for the Great Emissary for the Propagation of Values on the Western Frontier. The occupations of these two men did not involve their being obliged to reside in Nanjing or Beijing, since sources indicate that they were on the road with the prelate most of the time.

Chinese sources frequently mention the name of "Jiansai Luosang." Given that "Jiansai" is the Chinese transcription of the Tibetan term *cansel,* which means "favorite," "Jiansai Luosang" is thus the transcription of Cansel Lozang, that is to say, "Lozang the favorite." In British sources, "Cansel Lozang" is transcribed as "Chense Lobsang," or as "Lo Lama." It seems the British considered Lozang Gyeltsen and Lozang Tsültrim to be one and the same person and mixed them in their biographies.[160] Nothing today allows us to confirm this British conclusion.

Wangdü Norbu served as the Panchen Lama's vicar (*chöpön kenpo,* lit. "head of offerings"). He founded and led the bureau office of the Panchen Lama in Xining for ten years (1926–36), then from 1936, he became director of the Office of the Great Emissary for the Propagation of Values on the Western Frontier in Kyégudo, a post which he held in parallel with that of director of the accounting department at the decentralized office of the Special Emissary in Charge of Accompanying the Panchen Lama to Tibet. Kang Fu'an headed the bureau office of the Panchen Lama in India, and Dazhuoni, that of communications. Luo Youren, the nephew of Lozang Gyeltsen, ran the department of military affairs.[161] However, it remains difficult to know with respect to Gao Zhangzhu, the Chinese chief of staff for the escort, to whom he reported. Was he at the head of the Tibetan guard of the Panchen Lama?

Other members in the escort include Tséchokling Rinpoche, the brother (or twin) of the Panchen Lama, and Kelzang Chönjor, the Panchen Lama's general secretary and translator. Curiously, Gao Zhangzhu does not mention the presence of Garapa Chöken Penkangwang (also called Gédun Rabgyé), the chamberlain (*zimpön kenpo,* lit. "head of the prelate's household"). Did Gédun Rabgyé accompany the prelate when he left Tibet in December 1923? Had the Panchen Lama requested that he stay on site to manage his things left behind? To this day, it is impossible to answer these questions. However, it seems unlikely that Gédun Rabgyé was present among the prelate's entourage during the return trip because his name does not appear in the sources that were consulted, neither Tibetan nor Chinese.

Among the Panchen Lama's entourage, two portraits stand out due to the multiple posts they held: Lozang Gyeltsen and Wangdü Norbu. The following anecdote illustrates this clearly. In April 1937 Xu Tiefeng and Luo Junxia who represented Liu Wenhui, the president of the Commission for the Edification of Xikang Province, asked the Panchen Lama to allow Lozang Gyeltsen and Wangdü Norbu to become advisors within the Commission for the Edification of the Xikang Province.[162] This proposal reflects the importance gradually gained by the two men. Their power was measured according to their degree of proximity to the Panchen Lama and to the positions they occupied in the sphere of influence of the Chinese authorities. By holding the titles of vicar and director of the accounting department of the office of the special Chinese emissary, Wangdü Norbu was in a position to influence the Panchen Lama on how to spend the budget provided by the Republican government. With respect to Lozang Gyeltsen, his family ties to Luo Youren, the director of the department of military affairs, gave him the possibility to orient the usage of all or a portion of the protective troops of the prelate. The fact is that Lozang Gyeltsen benefited from the absolute trust of the Panchen Lama. One proof of this is when in spring 1937 the Panchen Lama accorded him the highest title in the monastic hierarchy of Tashilhunpo, that of general administrator (*kyabying dzasa lama*). This occurred just after the prelate had discharged Ngagchen Rinpoche.[163] Whether Lozang Tsültrim existed or not, does not change anything. Lozang Gyeltsen had clearly become "Lozang the favorite."

However, the appointment of Lozang Gyeltsen to general administrator requires some explanation. It is troubling to note that the discharge of Ngagchen Rinpoche corresponded to the promotion of Lozang Gyeltsen, while in all logic, pushing aside the first had no direct, obvious correlation to the appointment of the second. And if the situation were reversed? Would there be a relation of cause and effect? Could Ngagchen Rinpoche's stance against the indefinite stay of the escort at Tashilhunpo have disturbed Lozang Gyeltsen? The report by Gao Zhangzhu provides an element of response.

The closest associates of the Panchen Lama disagreed regarding the utility of the Chinese escort that was to accompany him to Tibet. Some of them, such as Lozang Gyeltsen, Lozang Tsültrim, Wangdü Norbu, Kang Fu'an, and Kelzang Chönjor, were in favor of using force. They thought that while the Thirteenth Dalai Lama had not dared order his troops to attack the Panchen Lama at the moment of his hasty departure, the same could not be expected of the Tibetan ministers who, now free from the supervision of their deceased leader, would be ready to do anything. They would thus have been in favor of relying on a Chinese escort in Tibetan lands. The others, such as Ngagchen Rinpoche, Tséchokling Rinpoche, and Dazhuoni felt that the Panchen Lama should return respecting the conditions set forth by the Tibetan authorities, which is to say, by sending back the Chinese escort at the border. A disagreement between the two parties seemed, therefore, inevitable.[164] And if we believe the testimony of Gao Zhangzhu, it is highly likely that Lozang Gyeltsen influenced the Panchen Lama to obtain the discharge of Ngagchen Rinpoche, whose opinion he did not share.

All the speculation seems to point to the issue of the escort because by April 1937, it had not yet joined the prelate's caravan. For Lozang Gyeltsen and his friends, did that constitute a risk that went beyond the framework of the Panchen Lama's return to Tibet, whose protection would have been a simple pretext? At this stage of the analysis, it might be useful to remember what the Thirteenth Dalai Lama is said to have written in 1930: "Concerning the return to Tibet of the Panchen Lama, members of his entourage have invented notions of Outer

Tibet and Inner Tibet and want to separate them. They infringe Tibetan law and often act contrary to the interests of their superior."

Did Dong Shufan, the Chinese translator of the letter, stay faithful to the thought of the Thirteenth Dalai Lama?[165] If so, was this just a gratuitous statement by the spiritual and temporal leader? Or was there a true basis behind this declaration?

6

TRANSFER OF MORTAL REMAINS TO TASHILHUNPO

The Panchen Lama passed away on December 1, 1937, at 2:50 a.m. At 4:00 a.m., Kelzang Chönjor announced the news. No one, with the exception of Dingkyé Rinpoche, who had just been named interim minister in the absence of Lozang Gyeltsen, had received authorization to enter the room where the Panchen Lama, although dead, remained sitting in meditation posture.[1]

A disciple of the Panchen Lama, Dingkyé Rinpoche was one of the reincarnated masters of Tashilhunpo who had not immediately followed the prelate when he suddenly left in December 1923. He joined him ten years later, appointed by the monks of the monastery to encourage the Panchen Lama to come back to Tibet. From that moment on, he had accompanied the prelate everywhere and, through the force of circumstance, had become a member of his entourage. Concerned at the death of the Thirteenth Dalai Lama, Dingkyé Rinpoche had taken the initiative of sending a telegram to the Mongolian and Tibetan Affairs Commission to request that the commission accelerate the return of the Panchen Lama. His message read:

> In our humble opinion, the Panchen Lama did not go from Tibet to Nanjing only to spread the Buddhist religion, communicate Tibetan policy, and to fortify the borders of the country; it is therefore not suitable that he stay indefinitively in Nanjing. When he left Tibet, the Panchen Lama said he would return soon. Who would have thought that he would not return for ten years? We await him as farmers caught in a drought wait impatiently for the rain. Recently, a delegation led by Ngagchen Rinpoche came to Lhasa. The Tibetans were reassured and really hoped that the Panchen Lama would come back to Tibet soon and that he would meet with the Thirteenth Dalai Lama: it is their most precious desire. Unfortunately, even before the delegation left Tibet, we learned of the death of the Thirteenth Dalai Lama. The Tibetan people are now orphaned, a people who always considered the Dalai Lama and the Panchen Lama as their father and mother.[2]

The objective of Dingkyé Rinpoche was to put everything in order so that his spiritual master could take up his place at Tashilhunpo monastery again. He was thus involved in organizing the stages of the return journey.[3] The Panchen Lama did give him some means, since in June 1935 he sent him to Kyégudo accompanied by about fifty people to install a radio transmitter provided by the Mongolian and Tibetan Affairs Commission and to represent the Office of the Emissary in Charge of Spreading Values in the Western Region.[4] We do not have confirmation of his participation in the armed strike at Kardzé that was organized by the assembly of reincarnated masters from Tashilhunpo and by the Panchen Lama's guard. Apparently the moment it occurred, Dingkyé Rinpoche was in Dartsédo.[5]

Shortly after the death of his spiritual master, Dingkyé Rinpoche created the Office in Charge of the Official Funeral Ceremonies for the Great Master Panchen (*Banchan da shi zhisang chu*), with the help of Zhao Shouyu, the special emissary of the Chinese government.[6] In the days following the Panchen Lama's death, his body initially remained in an upright meditative pose, according to contemporary testimony. His limbs remained supple, his mouth moist, his complexion as fresh as when he was alive. His head began to tilt forward on December 18.[7]

News of his death spread widely all over Tibet and memorial ceremonies were put in place. Soon, all the Tibetan monasteries in the regions of Kham and Amdo sent their abbots to prepare butter lamp offerings at Kyégudo. The monks of Tashilhunpo, very affected by the news, asked the regent Reting Rinpoche and the abbots of the great Gélukpa monasteries to pray for the rapid return of the Panchen Lama's reincarnation. Lozang Gyeltsen, the Panchen Lama's attendant, suggested that a certain Kyabjé Zhelzang Rinpoche compose a prayer to fulfill this wish. Kyabjé Zhelzang Rinpoche accepted and his prayer was immediately engraved on wooden plaques, printed in many copies, and distributed in all Tibetan monasteries. Then Lozang Gyeltsen had a weaving made on a large piece of fabric of Amitābha, of whom the Panchen Lama is an emanation. Once finished, it was sent to the Dongkar dangchen monastery in Lhatsé in the province of Tsang where it was displayed. Then Lozang Gyeltsen proposed that Kyabjé Dzépa Rinpoche, abbot of the main monastery of Lhatsé, lead prayers at Tashilhunpo. Finally, Drugyal Lozang Rinchen, the general administrator at Tashilhunpo who had been appointed by the Tibetan government following the death in 1928 of the previous administrator Lozang Tenzin, asked the members of the Panchen Lama's entourage to quickly bring the corpse of their master to Shigatse and to participate in the construction of the reliquary where it would be placed.[8]

Tibetans honor their masters whether they are alive or not. The preservation of the mortal remains of a great master in his original monastery is important for worship, while also ensuring the visit of many pilgrims and their offerings. That is why the Panchen Lama's entourage, conscious of the stakes, took pains to see the prelate's body returned to Tashilhunpo.

At first the members of the entourage no longer knew what to do. Originally they planned to head towards the Tibetan region of Amdo, but Ma Bufang, the military governor of Qinghai Province, was Muslim and they feared his reactions. Then, given that Liu Wenhui, the president of the Commission for the Edification of Xikang Province, was Buddhist, and that Kelzang Chönjor, one of his close associates was from Bathang in the Kham region of Tibet, they decided to head towards Kardzé. They informed Zhang Jialin of their choice. Zhang Jialin was the head of Kardzé district and he, in turn, informed Liu Wenhui. In December 1937 members of the entourage requested authorization from the Chinese government to go to Kardzé, but were refused and received orders that the Panchen Lama's body be transported to Dartsédo, so that the funeral ceremony could be held. The reincarnated masters of the entourage then repeated their request, which the Chinese government ended up accepting, all the while insisting that the Panchen Lama's body be transported to Dartsédo afterwards. On their side, the representatives of the Tibetan government and the three great Gélukpa monasteries, who had hoped to convince the Panchen Lama to return to Tibet, realized that the situation was desperate. They felt that not even his body would ever be repatriated to Tibet, and so, they returned to Lhasa.[9]

Alongside the funeral ceremonies, the Mongolian and Tibetan Affairs Commission undertook the dissolution of the offices of the Panchen Lama and attempted to disband his entourage. On December 23, 1937, the Chinese government ordered that the Panchen Lama be given the posthumous title of "Great, Glorious, Enlightened Master Panchen Who Protects the Country and Propagates its Values" (*Huguo xuanhua guanghui yuanjue da shi*). In Dartsédo, they named Dai Jitao, the minister of education and disciple of the Panchen Lama, "Special Envoy in Charge of Paying Respects at the Panchen Lama's Funeral," conforming to the recommendations put forward on December 15 by Wu Zhongxin, director of the Mongolian and Tibetan Affairs Commission. In addition, Dai Jitao put aside a subsidy of 10,000 yuan (Wu Zhongxin had proposed 40,000 yuan) to organize the ceremony.[10] Finally, on December 24, Dai Jitao ordered the Mongolian and Tibetan Affairs Commission to organize a funeral ceremony in memory of the Panchen Lama in Chongqing, where the Chinese Republican government had withdrawn following the Japanese occupation of Nanjing.[11] Shortly thereafter, the one thousand people who made up the Panchen Lama's entourage headed off towards Kardzé. They were protected by two hundred soldiers from the Panchen Lama's private guard, a small troop headed by Zhao Shouyu (the rest of the Chinese escort having already taken leave), and a detachment from Ma Bufang's army.

In mid-January 1938 the procession entered Kardzé.[12] The Panchen Lama's body was placed in Shangkun Rinpoche's residence situated in the town's main monastery. Immediately the funeral rites, which had been interrupted by the trip, resumed. Zhao Shouyu, the special emissary for accompanying the Panchen Lama to Tibet, transmitted a request made by the reincarnated masters in the entourage to the Mongolian and Tibetan Affairs Commission, asking that the Chinese government send soldiers to escort the Panchen Lama's body to his monastery. If necessary, they hoped that Liu Wenhui and Zhao Shouyu would organize the return of the body. They requested that the Chinese government, at the very least, let them take care of things themselves.[13]

At the beginning of March, the Chinese State Council ordered the Mongolian and Tibetan Affairs Commission to recover the firearms held by the members of the Panchen Lama's entourage. The commission, which was responsible for organizing the funeral ceremonies in Chongqing, requested the help of the Office of Tibet and that of the Panchen Lama's bureau office in Nanjing. It planned that prayers be recited for three days in Chinese and Tibetan. The Chinese Buddhist master, Taixu, was to lead the prayers in Chinese and the Changkya Hutuktu would lead them in Tibetan. It was Dai Jitao who finally led the funeral ceremony given in Chongqing in honor of the Panchen Lama. All the members of the various commissions such as Wu Zhongxin, Cheng Yun, Ma Hetian, all the officials above the rank of section manager, the Changkya Hutuktu, and certain members of the entourage such as Zhu Funan and Ngawang Gyeltsen, attended.

That day the Chinese State Council authorized members of the entourage to directly negotiate with the Tibetan authorities the conditions under which the prelate's body would be returned. Some days later, the minister of finance requested that the Mongolian and Tibetan Affairs Commission transfer Zhao Shouyu, the special emissary, and dissolve his office and his escort, made pointless by the Panchen Lama's death. In addition, he proposed to send him 50,000 yuan so he could pay his soldiers. At the time, Zhao Shouyu was not in a position to account for and recover the weapons held by the members of the Panchen Lama's entourage. Actually, Kelzang Chönjor and Dingkyé Rinpoche wanted the Chinese government to set down a ruling on this cache of arms before the entourage divested itself from it. Short of arguments, Zhao Shouyu proposed that the Chinese government require the entourage's managers to draw them up a list of weapons in their possession. He also suggested that the soldiers of the entourage keep their arms for future use. Satisfied with his proposal, the Chinese State Council ordered him to accomplish his mission as rapidly as possible.

On its side, the Military Affairs Commission pushed the Mongolian and Tibetan Affairs Commission to find a way to recover the remaining arms. First, it felt that the arms could be useful for anti-Japanese resistance; and second, it feared that the arms would become a source of incidents along the Sino-Tibetan border, similar to what happened in Dargyé in the spring of 1931. The Military Affairs Commission was all the more worried since it knew that the Chinese government would not have time to put down possible troubles, because its troops were busy elsewhere. It felt that a great part of the Panchen Lama's weapons were stored in Xiangride, a fraction of which had been seized by the Tibetan authorities, and that the rest were still in the hands of the entourage's soldiers.[14]

In April the Chinese State Council decided that Zhao Shouyu and his escort should return to Chongqing after Dai Jitao finished the other funeral ceremonies planned for Dartsédo. Unable to transport the Panchen Lama's body from Kardzé to Dartsédo, Dai Jitao found himself obliged to hold the second ceremony in Kardzé.[15] Did the members of the Panchen Lama's entourage refuse to go that last step from Kardzé to Dartsédo? Most likely, yes. What interest would they have had in distancing themselves from a place where the population supported them, to go to the location of the headquarters of the provincial government of Liu Wenhui, their enemy?

At the time, Wu Zhongxin, the new director of the Mongolian and Tibetan Affairs Commission, proposed a plan concerning the future of the Panchen Lama's offices. According to his proposal, the Office of the Emissary in Charge of Spreading Values in the Western Region would be closed over the next three to six months, but the Panchen Lama's salary, that is 10,000 yuan per month, would be paid until its closure. The ten or so smaller offices connected with the Office of the Great and Glorious Master Panchen Who Protects the Country and Propagates its Values, which in total had about sixty staff, would be preserved, but reorganized.[16] Their running costs would be identical to what they had been, that is, 19,600 yuan per month. The members of these offices would be given the liberty of negotiating the return of the Panchen Lama's body directly with the Tibetan authorities, and would be responsible for the Panchen Lama's goods and soldiers from his personal guard. Once the date for the dispatch of the prelate's body had been set, the Chinese government would name an envoy responsible for the escort to the Sino-Tibetan border. Among the bureau offices opened by the prelate in Nanjing, Beijing, Chengdu, Chongqing, Kham, Amdo, and so forth, the Nanjing and Beijing offices would be subsidized by the Chinese government, the others directly by the Offices of the Great and Glorious Master Panchen Who Protects the Country and Propagates its Values. The Beijing office, having been closed since the occupation of the city by the Japanese, had been immediately dissolved at that time. The offices in Chengdu, Chongqing, Kham, Amdo, and the others were soon to be closed. Only the Nanjing office was saved to become the sole link between the Chinese government and the Tibetan province of Tsang.

With this move, Lozang Gyeltsen, who held the position of director of the Office of the Panchen Lama in Nanjing, clearly received a salary from the Republican government. The school attached to this office, where young Tibetans were trained (it was transferred to Xining soon after the Japanese occupied Nanjing), was to continue its activities and be subsidized by the Chinese government, at a total of 1,480 yuan per month. The three radio transmitters provided to the Office of the Emissary in Charge of Spreading Values in the Western Region would be transferred and kept at the facilities of the Nanjing Office of the Great and Glorious Master Panchen Who Protects the Country and Propagates its Values. Zhao Shouyu's Office of the Special Emissary Responsible for Accompanying the Panchen Lama to Tibet would be dissolved upon the arrival of Dai Jitao in Kardzé. The Commission for the Edification of Xikang Province would take care of the duties that Zhao Shouyu had been unable to achieve. The rest of the Chinese escort would break up at Dai Jitao's arrival.[17]

In April the Chinese State Council ruled on the future of the Panchen Lama's entourage. For the most part, it accepted the recommendations in the proposal of Wu Zhongxin.[18] At the beginning of August, Dai Jitao arrived in Kardzé and settled into Shangkun Rinpoche's residence. As a representative of the Chinese Republican government, he paid tribute to the Panchen Lama at the monastery in Kardzé. The ceremony was identical to that in Chongqing. However, this one was more solemn and serious, since all the members of the Offices of the Great and Glorious Master Panchen Who Protects the Country and Spreads its Values, as well as all those from the Office of the Special Emissary Responsible for Accompanying the Panchen Lama to Tibet and all the monks from the region were present. In addition, Dai Jitao, distraught by the passing away of his master, cried continually; this contributed to the emotion. He did, however, find courage to photograph his master's body.[19] Finally, he paid the total cost of the ceremony as agreed by the Chinese government, which had risen to more than 109,000 yuan. In the days that followed, Dai Jitao made efforts to account for the weapons collected by the Offices of the Great and Glorious Panchen Master Who Protects the Country and Spreads its Values.[20]

As for Dingkyé Rinpoche, he continued making arrangements. He tried, in the name of the assembly of reincarnated masters, to negotiate directly with the Tibetan authorities on the issue of the return of the Panchen Lama's body to Tibet. His calls were unreturned. He sent a telegram to Drugyal Lozang Rinchen, the general administrator of Tashilhunpo, who transmitted his message to the Council of Ministers in Lhasa. Finally, the general administrator of Tashilhunpo, who had been appointed by the Thirteenth Dalai Lama after the Panchen Lama had departed Tibet, informed Dingkyé Rinpoche that the Council of Ministers had accepted the return of the Panchen Lama's body and was prepared for its arrival. Confident in his project, Dingkyé Rinpoche requested the Chinese government to authorize the start of the journey to Tibet. Receiving no reply, he repeated his request. As for the Chinese government, it hesitated, wondering about the legitimacy of according a reply that did not come from the Tibetan authorities. The Chinese seemed to doubt the sincerity of the Tashilhunpo general administrator. Wu Zhongxin, as director of the Mongolian and Tibetan Affairs Commission, then made a decision. Facts showed that the members of the entourage would most likely run into obstacles on a journey back to Tibet to repatriate the body of the deceased, so he requested that Liu Wenhui protect them.[21]

His choice might surprise, given that at that time, Liu Wenhui suspected certain people in the entourage of hoping to divide the province of Kham, and had confronted them openly about the issue.

In January 1939 snow fell unceasingly. Roads were blocked. Members of the entourage were obliged to wait until spring to set off for Tibet. They tried again to contact the Tibetan authorities, but their attempts were unfruitful. They asked the Chinese government to order the Tibetan Council of Ministers to receive the body of the Panchen Lama, to construct a reliquary to house it, and to begin the divinations that would allow the commencement of the search for the prelate's reincarnation. The situation in Kardzé was becoming more and more insecure. The entourage was being harassed by local Chinese civil and military authorities and lacked supplies.[22] Liu Wenhui put stronger and stronger pressure on them.

Two members of the Panchen Lama's entourage (one of whom was a certain Udzin Zimche Debrangpa Purbu Tsering) secretly took possession of the prelate's body in the spring of 1939 and transported it to the monastery of Ragya near Kyégudo, where it was stored safely. They then began to make a replica of the body to display at the Kardzé monastery so no one would realize what they had done.[23]

In December 1939 Liu Wenhui crushed a rebellion organized by the Panchen Lama's entourage. While taking back the positions acquired by the prelate's personal guard, he engaged in acts of pillage in the region of Kardzé, coming upon the replica of the body of the deceased prelate. Since he believed he held the body of the Panchen Lama (which if needed, he could use as a bargaining piece or to rally the local population), Liu dropped his pursuit of the entourage members that were fleeing towards Kyégudo, and then had his men transport the replica of the Panchen Lama's body to Dartsédo. There examining it more closely, the Chinese discovered that they had been fooled. Furious, they immediately abandoned the likeness, leaving it for Dingkyé Rinpoche, who had stayed in Dartsédo during the combat unable to flee with his group, to decide its fate. Given that for Tibetans, any representation of a Buddha or a bodhisattva is precious, Dingkyé Rinpoche brought the very unique replica to the monastery of Kumbum where it was worshipped. Two weeks later, the members of the Panchen Lama's entourage that had fled to Kyégudo gathered around the actual body of their master at Ragya monastery. Apparently Dingkyé Rinpoche and Lozang Gyeltsen were not present. Dingkyé Rinpoche was still in Dartsédo, while Lozang Gyeltsen was in Chongqing.[24]

On February 22, 1940, the Fourteenth Dalai Lama was enthroned in Lhasa in the Potala Palace. Basil Gould, the British political officer in Sikkim, Wu Zhongxin, the director of the Mongolian and Tibetan Affairs Commission, and the representatives from the Nepalese and Bhutanese governments attended the ceremony. When Wu Zhongxin was still in Lhasa, the Mongolian and Tibetan Affairs Commission informed the Tibetan Council of Ministers that the body of the Panchen Lama was located at Kyégudo. The commission proposed that a Chinese escort accompany the prelate's body to the Sino-Tibetan border and that then the Tibetan authorities would take care of its transportation to Tashilhunpo. The Council of Ministers accepted and sent representatives to Kyégudo. It also authorized the entourage to enter Tibet. The Chinese government asked Ma Bufang, the military governor of Qinghai Province, to protect the body of the prelate and the members of his entourage. Ma Bufang named Zhao Shouyu "Special Emissary Responsible for Returning the Mortal Remains of the Panchen Lama to Tibet" (*Husong Banchan hui Zang zhuanshi*).

As for the members of the Panchen Lama's entourage, they wished to leave as soon as possible and awaited Zhao Shouyu's arrival impatiently. As soon as the monks of the delegation from Tashilhunpo had arrived in Lhasa and confirmed that the Panchen Lama's body was clearly located in Kyégudo, they headed towards the Amdo region. In Chamdo, the capital of Kham, Tibetan officials, such as Kenbrön Chesa Lungpa, met up with them and together they traveled towards Kyégudo, escorted by about one hundred soldiers. In August 1940 the prelate's attendant Lozang Gyeltsen and the general administrator of

Tashilhunpo Drugyal Lozang Rinchen suggested that the Mongolian and Tibetan Affairs Commission appoint Ma Bufang to escort the body up to the Sino-Tibetan border because Zhao Shouyu had not yet arrived in Kyégudo. The entire Tibetan delegation entered Kyégudo where it was warmly welcomed by the members of the Panchen Lama's entourage and by Ma Bufang. As soon as they could, the monks from Tashilhunpo and the Tibetan officials went to Lha Hall in Ragya monastery where the body of the Panchen Lama was located, and offered their prostrations fervently. Before his body, they placed a large number of offerings that were then distributed to the monks of the Ragya and Rabshilungshö ganden chökorling monasteries. At the same time, members of the entourage repeated the request that Ma Bufang escort the body until it reached Cagzam, where the Tibetan army would then take over, to which the Chinese government finally agreed. In addition, Liu Wenhui was ordered by the Chinese government to bring back to Kyégudo the goods and ritual objects of the Panchen Lama that had been confiscated by his troops during the attack at Kardzé.[25]

In November 1940 the Panchen Lama's body was transported by members of the entourage to the Sino-Tibetan border, escorted by Ma Bufang and by Zhao Shouyu, who had arrived by then. As agreed, the mission of the two Chinese stopped there. More than two hundred people belonging to the entourage stayed in Kyégudo because they had to go to Xiangride to administer the Office of the Great and Glorious Master Panchen Who Protects the Country and Propagates its Values, which the Chinese government had decided to leave open for the time being.

In Nakchu the body of the Panchen Lama was displayed in Drubkhang Hall in the city's main monastery, which was reserved for the celebration of rites. Then the funeral procession moved on. It bypassed Lhasa, heading directly to Tashilhunpo. Rapidly, the news spread. Everywhere, processions of lay people and monks formed. They all converged on Tashilhunpo. In Shigatse, prayer flags were raised on the roofs of the houses. Auspicious signs were traced in chalk along the road where the funeral procession was to pass. Juniper burned at places all throughout the city. The inhabitants of Shigatse and the monks of Tashilhunpo were greatly moved by the return of the body of their master. The funeral procession proceeded with slow, solemn steps, accompanied by ritual cymbals and horns. Riders, carrying representations of divinities and flags that had been offered by the Qianlong Emperor (r. 1736–95) to the Sixth Panchen Lama (1738–1780) led the way. They were followed by monk musicians. Then came the palanquin adorned with sumptuous yellow fabrics, where the Panchen Lama's body lay. The crowd of disciples and other people who formed the honor guard along the route bowed as he passed. Some held flowers, others incense clasped between their hands in salutation. They piously presented these objects as offerings.

On February 4, 1941, the funeral procession stopped in front of the main door of Tashilhunpo monastery. The riders dismounted and observed a period of silence while the body of the Panchen Lama was taken from the palanquin and placed on the highest throne in his residence, inside the monastery. Then the members of the Tibetan government, the reincarnated masters from the Tashilhunpo colleges, the abbots from the neighboring monasteries, the monks and lay people bowed before the prelate's corpse.[26] The dearest wish of the Panchen Lama had finally been fulfilled. He was back in his native land and in his monastery.

In China, the Mongolian and Tibetan Affairs Commission proposed that the Chinese State Council dissolve the remaining Offices of the Great and Glorious Master Panchen Who Protects the Country and Propagates its Values since the Panchen Lama's body had arrived at Tashilhunpo.[27] As the entourage had lost its income from the offerings received by the Panchen Lama during his sojourn in Inner Mongolia and China (whose value would have amounted to approximately 15 million yuan), its members asked the Chinese Republican government to intervene with Liu Wenhui, requesting that he return the goods (or pay an equivalent sum) and contribute to the construction of the Panchen Lama's reliquary as well as to the expenses of those members of the entourage who were obliged to stay in China to look for the prelate's reincarnation. In May 1941 the Chinese State Council ordered the closure of the offices. Only the Panchen Lama's office in Nanjing was temporarily preserved. The Chinese State Council agreed to contribute to the construction of the reliquary and entrusted to Lozang Gyeltsen, who was still director of the Panchen Lama's bureau office in Nanjing, the task of drawing up a detailed estimate. He was also designated to find the reincarnation of the Panchen Lama.[28] Reassured by the Chinese State Council, Lozang Gyeltsen asked the Mongolian and Tibetan Affairs Commission for authorization to open an office located in the Chinese province of Qinghai, whose members would have the mission of looking for the Panchen Lama's reincarnation.[29]

As of 1940 the regent Reting Rinpoche had already proceeded with divinations, which were said to have indicated that the Panchen Lama had already reincarnated. Lozang Gyeltsen directed his search in the region of Amdo, while Dingkyé Rinpoche led his in the region of Kham. In parallel, other investigations sponsored by the government in Lhasa led them to Central Tibet. Finally, three young children were found. Two of them lived in Central Tibet, while the third resided in the Amdo region. The Tibetan Council of Ministers wanted the three children brought to Lhasa to begin the last tests that would determine, without a doubt, which one was the Tenth Panchen Lama, but they didn't manage to set up the comparison. Of the two candidates found in Central Tibet by the Tibetan government, one was at Drépung monastery and the other at Tashilhunpo. The child found in the province of Amdo by Lozang Gyeltsen (who had the mandate of the Chinese government) had received his first religious education at Kumbum. As it turned out, the Chinese considered him to be the Tenth Panchen Lama. He was enthroned at the monastery in Kumbum on August 10, 1949, without having gone through the final traditional tests.[30] Could the newly enthroned child ever imagine the rocky path that lay before him?

But that is another story . . .

At Tashilhunpo, the construction of the Panchen Lama's reliquary was not finished until 1944. Covered with silver and precious stones, the monument held the embalmed body of the master sitting in a meditation posture on his throne, with his cushion and his ritual objects.[31] It was a peaceful homage, shortly to be destroyed during the pillaging and violence that China's Cultural Revolution brought to Tibet.

CONCLUSION

The Panchen Lama, reincarnated master and abbot of Tashilhunpo monastery, saw his life change radically on December 22, 1923. The main reason for his hasty departure from his monastery that fateful day lies in a dispute between Tashilhunpo's officials and the Tibetan government in Lhasa. This dissension stemmed from new regulations obliging the monastery to pay crossing *ulag* as well as to finance a quarter of Tibet's military expenses. This mandatory contribution, we should remember, originated in the Thirteenth Dalai Lama's evolving political awareness, which had been steadily encouraged (or manipulated?) by the British who wished to establish a buffer state between British India and China. Thus inspired, the Thirteenth Dalai Lama decided to initiate a series of reforms that would modernize Tibet and provide it with an army capable of guaranteeing its sovereignty. As his disciple had spent enormous sums on the construction of a monumental statue of the Buddha Maitreya, the Thirteenth Dalai Lama seemed sure that Tashilhunpo could handle funding one-quarter of the army's budget. However, despite significant agricultural revenue collected each season, and centuries of acquired wealth, the monastery was most likely insolvent. The Panchen Lama would thus have found himself clearly unable to pay the sum of contributions, IOUs, tolls, fines, and debts demanded by the Tibetan government.

We can only imagine that the sudden imposition of this tax on his monastery must have seemed all the more unfair since, until then, Tashilhunpo had enjoyed relative political autonomy due to its physical distance from Lhasa, its economic self-sufficiency, and its *de facto* exemption from tax, not to mention the support it received from the Manchus and the British for its lineage of Panchen Lamas. But we have also seen that although quite independent, Tashilhunpo's administration did not consist of a government nor did it have an army. Consequently, before fleeing, the Panchen Lama was not the head of a sovereign nation (Tsang), which he could have claimed as independent. We must highlight the fact that such a decision would have been in complete contradiction with the state of mind of the prelate. From the very beginning of his public life, he seems to have been afflicted with a wavering and easily-influenced character that led him to commit huge breaches in protocol during both times the Thirteenth Dalai Lama went into exile, but for which, it would seem, the Dalai Lama did not hold him accountable.

The majority of Tibetans, still today, believe that the Panchen Lama and the Dalai Lama are united by an indissoluble and indestructible bond. For them, this link represents a model of unsurpassable faithfulness and devotion. Yet the Ninth Panchen Lama, one of the most tragic figures in the lineage of Panchen Lamas, found himself torn between the loyalty he owed to the Gélukpa order and the budding nationalism initiated by the Thirteenth Dalai Lama, which made the government in Lhasa less tolerant towards such autonomous monastic structures as Tashilhunpo. But to the extent that the Thirteenth Dalai Lama, like the Ninth Panchen Lama, made efforts to preserve the appearance of good relations, it is difficult today to measure the damage caused by their disagreement, which indeed we cannot actually prove existed. Yet it also seems clear that their respective entourages had sown discord between master and disciple, for reasons that seem directly linked to the individual privileges that could be gained. On their side, the last Qing representatives, followed by the Chinese Republicans and the British each jumped at the opportunity to turn the situation to their advantage, using the inexperience of the two ecclesiastics in matters of international politics, as well as the glaring anomaly inherent in the spiritual bond that linked them.

Indeed, one does not have to be a great scholar of Tibetan history to understand that the relationship between a spiritual-temporal leader and his disciple, with a nearly equivalent reputation, exposed them to intrigue and attempts at corruption, especially when the disciple turned out to be as brilliant as the master. The Manchu agents, and even more so the Chinese Republicans, played the hand of the disciple against that of the master in efforts to recover a Tibet that was looking to emancipate itself and confirm its rank as a sovereign nation. But, beyond these undeniable complications that had accumulated between master and disciple, it seems that the Panchen Lama did not fall under the political sway of China, but in reality turned elsewhere to find the means to finance a quarter of the budget of the newly fortified Tibetan army. His flight from Tibet, probably premeditated and put in place by the members of his entourage, was to ensure, above all, that he could find Buddhist Mongol disciple-donors to raise sufficient funds to pay his debts. As he announced in the letter he left behind, he clearly set off for the northwest in the direction of the Republic of Mongolia, a country with a long Buddhist tradition of the Gélukpa school where he had, by definition, more chances than in China of finding a receptive audience for his teachings and, by the same token, donors who would be attentive to and more than willing to help his cause.

The hostile presence of the Russian communists in the Mongolian People's Republic disrupted the prelate's plans and forced him to wander for many months in the province of Gansu. That is why it is difficult to state that the Panchen Lama betrayed his spiritual master and his country for the benefit of China. His primary intention had clearly been to go to the Mongolian People's Republic, as the Thirteenth Dalai Lama had done in 1904. And yet he ended up in Beijing in January 1925, due to a tide of events beyond his control. Moreover, we can see that his interest in the Mongols did not diminish, since a good portion of his time was spent in Inner Mongolia. It is obvious from his frequent returns there that he preferred to live and stay in Mongolia rather than in China.

As of 1925 the Panchen Lama seems, at first glance, to have been buffeted by the muddled winds of fortune, where events were occurring in China at an unbridled pace and where a sequence of varied actors was intervening: warlords, Inner Mongolian princes, disputes within the Republican regime, the Japanese invasion, and the rise of communism. At times, the prelate gives us the feeling that he was behaving as if he were a touring artist, completely absorbed in the exercise of his art: the teaching of Dharma. Perceiving and analyzing the outer world strictly through the prism of Buddhism, he left mundane details up to his entourage, such as the tasks of managing material contingencies, organizing his trips, and making practical decisions for him. This style of "angel-ism," i.e., lack of concern for the pragmatic realm, was particularly dangerous during the troubled times in which he lived. Yet, upon closer examination, we see things were not operating solely on that level.

In reality, as of 1925, the Panchen Lama proved to be set on accomplishing his new mission of encouraging the "harmonious coexistence of the five nationalities" through the "Three Principles of the People" of Sun Yat-sen, whose thought he linked to Buddhist precepts. He thus wished to spur the peripheral regions, notably Inner Mongolia and Tibet, to join the ranks of the Chinese Republic, which would then consist of a grouping of Han, Manchu, Mongol, Tibetan, and Uighur peoples. Progressive and sincerely convinced of the benefits of the bustling industrialized civilization that he discovered in large Chinese cities, he wished to export its foundations and share them with Tibet to wake it up from its medieval lethargy. In order to modernize his country, his objective was to obtain from the Republican government the indispensable means to put into place a development project theoretically linked to a regional autonomy, which Tibet would have by adhering to the coexistence of the five nationalities of the Chinese Republic.

To reach his aims, he established the relation of chaplain-donor with the Republican leaders and enjoyed their material support and protection. He adopted their political program and became their zealous ambassador. This did not oblige him to betray his principles, because, as we have seen, the search for donors is implicit in the approach of reincarnated Tibetan masters and, in addition, the Panchen Lama was absolutely convinced of the validity of the "Three Principles of the People" on which the Nanjing authorities had built their policy. Within the framework of his official program of action, the prelate went to Inner Mongolia several times to attempt to convince the local princes to rally to the "harmonious coexistence of the five nationalities." He also opened offices destined to spread his ideas throughout the territories by means of his magazine, transmitting the political messages of the Republican government, observing the local situations, and reporting back to higher-ups at the Mongolian and Tibetan Affairs Commission.

Without a doubt, this was his state of mind as he prepared his return to Tibet. An out-of-the-ordinary actor on the Chinese political scene, the Panchen Lama was an unhoped-for ally for Chiang Kai-shek and his friends who shamelessly attempted to make him their puppet. Accepting the title of "Propagator of Values," he became the vehicle of morality they so needed for their credibility and for the establishment of their principle of the "well-being of the people." In providing the prelate with an armed escort to take him to Tashilhunpo, they gave themselves, in addition, the means to gain a foothold on the Tibetan plateau.

For his part, the Panchen Lama would have desired the assistance of this escort to protect him from possible vengeance by the most radical members of the Tibetan government, especially since upon the death of the Thirteenth Dalai Lama, he had been deprived of the safeguard that his master's presence had afforded him. It is unrealistic to think that the Panchen Lama would have had the intention of attacking Tibet. His small escort would have been completely outnumbered. What could one thousand soldiers in his escort have done faced with ten thousand men that made up the regular Tibetan army in 1935, even if the latter was under-equipped and badly trained?

As for the hypothesis that the Panchen Lama wanted to use his personal guard supplemented by the Chinese escort to forcefully create an autonomous "Outer Tibet" dependent on China, it does not hold up. Looking at a map of Tibet, we can easily notice that Lhasa (in the Ü region) is located closer to the center of China than is Shigatse (and the region of Tsang). This means that any hypothetical autonomous region of an "Outer Tibet" in the hands of the Panchen Lama and supported by the Republican government would have found itself isolated from China by Ü, the area run by the Dalai Lama's titleholders and supported by the British. In these conditions, how could it have functioned practically? If the Panchen Lama had been the master of Lhasa, or if the Thirteenth Dalai Lama had become an ally of the Chinese Republicans, then a viable "Inner Tibet" might possibly have come into being. But as we have seen, this was not at all the case. As the Panchen Lama was, due to his Buddhist training, an expert in logic, it seems improbable that such a "detail" could have escaped him, even if facts show that his entourage, who manipulated much around him, did entertain separatist ambitions. That is why it is highly unlikely that the prelate would have wished to set up an autonomous "Outer Tibet," which he would have led.

In fact, the Chinese Nationalists got the Panchen Lama on their side and used him to try to obtain unification between Tibet and China, and to send soldiers there to eventually make the Land of Snows a buffer zone between their republic and the British Empire. On their side, the British displayed equivalent objectives. They persuaded the Thirteenth Dalai Lama to create a sufficiently strong army to emancipate his country from Chinese supervision in order to have a buffer state at their disposal to separate them from China. As it turns out, neither the Republican development project for Tibet, so important to the Panchen Lama (yet only half-heartedly supported by the Republican government), nor the dream of an independent Tibet held by the Thirteenth Dalai Lama and encouraged by the British, would see the light of day. In the field, a third, far more radical, solution was on its way: that of Mao's communists.

APPENDIX A

ECCLESIASTICAL LINEAGES AND SUCCESSIONS

PANCHEN LAMAS

Subhūti (Rabjor), disciple of Buddha
Mañjuśrīkīrti (Jampel Drakpa), king of Śambhala
Bhāvyaviveka (Lekden jé), the disciple of Nâgârjuna
Abhayākaragupta (Jigme Chyungnébépa)
Gö Kugpa Latsé, the translator
Sakya Paṇḍita Kunga Gyeltsen
Yungtön Trogyel Dorjépel, the great yogin

1. Kédrub Gélèk Pelzang, Tsongkapa's disciple (1385–1438) (*posthumously*)
2. Sönam Chöki Langpo (1439–1504) (*posthumously*)
3. Ensapa Lozang Döndrub (1505–1566) (*posthumously*)
4. (1) Lozang Chöki Gyeltsen (1567/1570–1662)
5. (2) Lozang Yéshé (1663–1737)
6. (3) Lozang Pelden Yéshé (1738–1780)
7. (4) Lozang Tenpé Nyima (1782–1853)
8. (5) Lozang Pelden Chöki Dragpa Tenpé Wangchuk (1855–1882)
9. (6) Lozang Chöki Nyima Gélèk Namgyel (1883–1937)
10. (7) Lozang Trinlé Lundrub Chöki Gyeltsen (1938–1989)
11. (8) Tenzin Gédun Yéshé Trinlé Püntsok, recognized by the Fourteenth Dalai Lama; Gyeltsen Norbu, recognized by Chinese authorities (1989–present)

Note: The Panchen Lama lineage begins with Subhūti, one of the original disciples of Buddha Śākyamuni and an emanation of Amitāba Buddha. All Panchen Lamas are considered emanations of Ambitāba. Lozang Chöki Gyeltsen was the first Panchen Lama recognized within his lifetime; his three previous reincarnations were posthumously recognized, which accounts for the two different numbering systems.

ABBOTS OF TASHILHUNPO

Panchen Gédun Drub (1391–1474), founder of Tashilhunpo in 1447
Panchen Zangpo Tashi (1410–1478), appointed abbot in 1475
Panchen Lungrik Gyatso (1418–?), appointed abbot in 1478

Panchen Yéshé Tsémo (1433–1510), abbot from 1487 to 1510
Panchen Gédun Gyatso (1476–1542), appointed abbot from 1510 to 1517
Panchen Ngari Lhatsun Lozang Tenpé Nyima Gyeltsen (1471–?), abbot in 1515
Panchen Pelden Takar Pungpa (NA), appointed abbot in 1517
Panchen Lodrö Gyeltsen (1487–?)
Panchen Dönyö Gyeltsen (NA)
Panchen Pashangtön Logrö Lekzang (NA)
Panchen Nenying Chöjé Chöki Gyeltsen (NA)
Panchen Pashangtön Chöpel Gyatso (NA)
Panchen Paphyuk Zhungpa Sönam Gyeltsen (NA)
Panchen Pashangtön Samdrub Pelzang (NA)
Panchen Lozang Chögyen (NA)
Panchen Panyangtön Damchö Yarpèl (NA)
Panchen Panyangtön Lhawang Logrö (NA)
Panchen Lozang Chöki Gyeltsen (1567/1570–1662)

Note: The title "Panchen" was traditionally given to the head abbots of Tashilhunpo who were recognized for their great learning. From the seventeenth century onwards, the successive reincarnations of what came to be recognized as the "Panchen Lama" became the abbots of Tashilhunpo, beginning in 1601 with Lozang Chöki Gyeltsen, who was the first Panchen Lama recognized in his lifetime.

DALAI LAMAS

1. Gédun Drub (1391–1474)
2. Gédun Gyatso (1476–1542)
3. Sönam Gyatso (1543–1588)
4. Yönten Gyatso (1589–1616)
5. Ngawang Lozang Gyatso (1617–1682)
6. Tsangyang Gyatso (1683–1707)
7. Kelzang Gyatso (1708–1757)
8. Jampel Gyatso (1758–1804)
9. Lungtok Gyatso (1805–1815)
10. Tsültrim Gyatso (1816–1837)
11. Kédrub Gyatso (1838–1855)
12. Trinlé Gyatso (1856–1875)
13. Thubten Gyatso (1876–1933)
14. Tenzin Gyatso (1935–present)

Note: All Dalai Lamas are considered emanations of the bodhisattva of compassion, Avalokiteśvara. As bodhisattvas, they are considered spiritual beings who have chosen to be reborn to work for the benefit of all living beings.

HISTORICAL TIES AMONG THE DALAI LAMAS, PANCHEN LAMAS, AND ABBOTS OF TASHILHUNPO

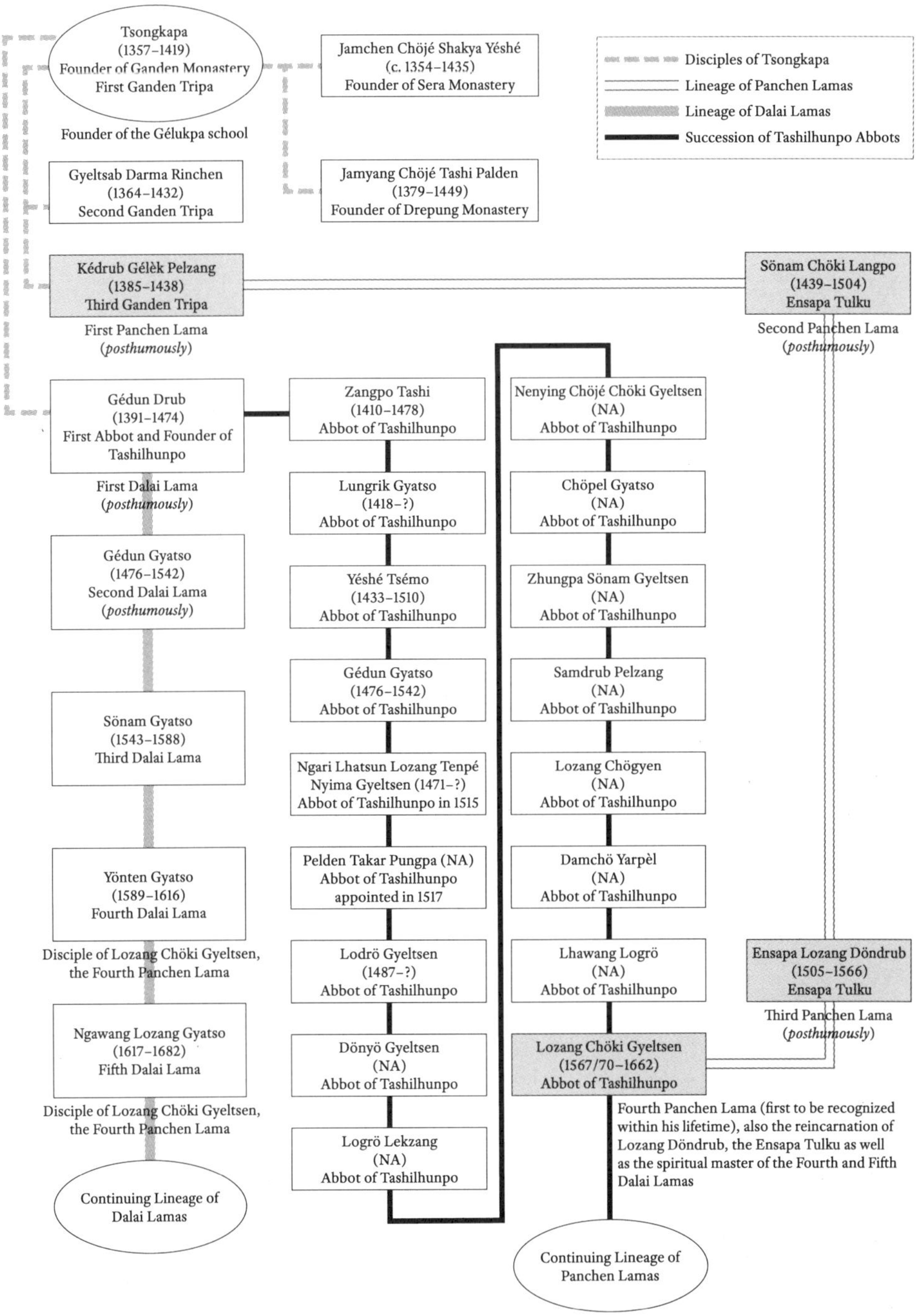

APPENDIX B

POLITICAL ROLE OF THE PANCHEN LAMAS IN TIBET

Historically, the Panchen Lamas have served as political mediators in Tibet's domestic and international affairs. Lozang Chöki Gyeltsen (1567/70–1662) was the Fourth Panchen Lama and the first Buddhist master to hold the title of Panchen Lama. He had undeniable influence since he lived to be more than ninety and was the spiritual master of both the Fourth and Fifth Dalai Lamas. The extraordinary endowment of lands offered him by the Fifth Dalai Lama contributed to establishing his power. It would especially give him the agricultural production capacity synonymous with self-sufficiency and economic power. While he did intervene as a mediator in an isolated conflict opposing Mongol troops at two Tsang military camps, his role was essentially a religious one. It was not the same for his successor Lozang Yéshé (1663–1737), the Fifth Panchen Lama.

Lozang Yéshé was obliged to haphazardly confront a tormented, hectic period in Tibet's history. During his long life, he displayed great finesse, enabling him to survive hostile political circumstances. He had to reach compromises with power-hungry figures such as Sangyé Gyatso, the regent who governed Tibet from 1679 to 1703 and who hid the death of the Fifth Dalai Lama for thirteen years. He also had to negotiate with Lhazang Khan, the grandson of Güshri Khan (1582–1655) and the head of the Mongol Hoshuud tribe who forcefully took full power over Tibet for eleven years (1706–17), as well as with Pholhané Sönam Tobgyé (r. 1728–47), the "king" of Tibet. Under the regency of Sangyé Gyatso, the Fifth Panchen Lama played the role of spiritual master for the young Tsangyang Gyatso (1683–1706), who would later become the Sixth Dalai Lama. He visited him many times, oversaw his novice vows, and gave him religious teachings.[1]

The Manchus suspected Sangyé Gyatso of hiding the death of the Fifth Dalai Lama and of having made an alliance with Galdan Boshugtu Khan, also known as Galdan Taïji (1644–1697), head of the Jüüngar (Dzungar) tribe that was seeking to create a united Mongol empire. They persistently invited the Fifth Panchen Lama to come to Beijing. The prelate refused the first time, using the chicken pox epidemic that was spreading through Tibet as a pretext, and he continued to systematically decline to the point that Emperor Kangxi (1662–1722) believed he was being held by force by the regent.[2] In his autobiography, the Fifth Panchen Lama attests that he wrote of his own accord, explaining to the regent that he did not wish to go to Beijing.[3] As the Sixth Dalai Lama, Tsangyang Gyatso, showed little taste for study or monastic life (preferring to compose songs and poems), the Fifth Panchen Lama was constrained to accept his disciple's (then aged nineteen) renunciation of his vows. During the armed conflict instigated by the youthful indiscretions of the Sixth Dalai Lama and Lhazang Khan, who opposed Sangyé Gyatso, the Fifth Panchen Lama proposed to intervene as mediator, but was pushed aside from the negotiations. In 1703 Lhazang Khan forced Sangyé Gyatso to resign, and four years later assassinated him.[4] Helped by the Manchus, from whom he received the title "Loyal Head and Protector of Buddhist Teaching" (*yifa gongshun han*), Lhazang Khan monopolized full power in Tibet until 1717.[5] In 1705 he decided to force the Sixth Dalai Lama, whose character was far too fanciful for Lhazang Khan's taste, to leave his post and sent him to Beijing, in agreement with the Qing court headed by Emperor Kangxi.[6] On his way, the Sixth Dalai Lama is said to have died under unexplained circumstances.

Lhazang Khan then declared that Tsangyang Gyatso was not the true reincarnation of the Fifth Dalai Lama. He placed a young monk, Pékar Zinpa, on the throne of the Potala Palace and declared him the Sixth Dalai Lama. However, faced with the discontent of the monks and the Tibetan people who did not approve of the substitution, Kangxi sent a grand secretary, La Duhun, to verify the facts. The Fifth Panchen Lama is said to have received La Duhun and to have attested that Pékar Zinpa, enthroned by Lhazang Khan, was the actual Sixth Dalai Lama (thereby renouncing his prior choice of Tsangyang Gyatso as the true reincarnation of the Fifth Dalai Lama). In 1706 Tsangyang Gyatso died, and a child born near Litang, Kelzang Gyatso (1708–1757), showed himself to be his reincarnation. At first, the Fifth Panchen Lama did not recognize him as the Seventh Dalai Lama.[7] For an unknown reason, Kangxi had the child held prisoner in Dergé.

At the beginning of 1713, the Fifth Panchen Lama, who was fifty years old, received the title of "Panchen E'erdeni"[8] from the Manchus who, harassed on their northwest border by the Mongols, did not want to leave full power in the hands of the Mongol Lhazang Khan. Although they had supported Lhazang Khan's arrival in Lhasa in 1705, they gave little credit to his policies and seemed to want to keep a supplementary advantage in the person of the Fifth Panchen Lama, without forgetting the Seventh Dalai Lama they had retained in Dergé before having him enter Kumbum monastery for his studies. Four years later, Lhazang Khan asked the Fifth Panchen Lama to plead his cause to Tséwang Rabten, the head of the Jüüngar Mongols and son of Baatar Khongtaiji who had been allied with Sangyé Gyatso, the assassinated regent. Tséwang Rabten was being solicited by the monks of the three great Gélukpa monasteries to topple the Hoshuud leader, who was then reigning over Tibet. The Fifth Panchen Lama responded positively to the request and came to Lhasa in November 1717. Once there, he is said to have given his moral support to two Tibetan armies that had formed around Lhazang Khan: one coming from Tsang under the direction of Pholhané and the other from Ngari under the command of Khangchené. It is unclear whether the Fifth Panchen Lama had any other options other than to collaborate with the leader of the Hoshuud tribe. In December 1717 Lhazang Khan was defeated and killed by the Jüüngar who deposed Pékar Zinpa, the

Sixth Dalai Lama puppet. The Fifth Panchen Lama is said to have requested the indulgence of the new leader.[9]

In 1720 the Fifth Panchen Lama belatedly recognized the Seventh Dalai Lama, who had been escorted from Kumbum to Lhasa by the Kangxi armies on their way to help Lhazang Khan. Pholhané and Khangchené, who had survived the purge that followed the fall of Lhazang Khan, had managed to drive out the Jüüngar from Lhasa shortly before. In fact, the Jüüngar had become unpopular with the Tibetans by harassing the advocates of the Nyingmapa school, even though they had deposed the Sixth Dalai Lama puppet, gotten rid of Lhazang Khan, and given back the post of regent to a Tibetan. As for the Manchus, they had left a garrison of three thousand soldiers in Lhasa and reorganized the government by reinforcing the power of the four ministers (*kalön*) that made up the Council of Ministers (*kashag*), which had first been placed under the direct control of Yanxin, the commander of the Manchu troops in Tibet. The Manchu commander received the title of third ranked prince (*beile*),[10] while Khangchené received the title of fourth ranked prince (*beizi*)[11] and led the Council of Ministers, all the while remaining governor of Ngari. Three other ministers of inferior rank served as his deputies: Ngaphöpé Dorjé Gyelpo, also governor of the region of Kongpo to the east of Lhasa, Lumpané, who had received the title of prince of the sixth rank (*fuguo gong*),[12] and Charané.[13]

In September 1723 the Fifth Panchen Lama received a mission sent by Yongzheng to officially announce the death of his father, Emperor Kangxi, who died in December 1722, and proclaim his own accession to the throne. The Fifth Panchen Lama seems to have been wooed from all sides at this time, since he also received a visit from Pholhané in December 1721 and another from Khangchené in September 1723.[14] It was also in 1723 that Pholhané became minister, coupling this position with that of governor of Tsang, while at the same moment Yongzheng withdrew the Manchu troops from Tibet, citing economic reasons. In the years that followed, serious dissension appeared within the Council of Ministers, to the point that Ngaphöpé Dorjé Gyelpo, Lumpané, and Charané assassinated Khangchené in 1727, and Pholhané had to flee to Tsang, where he raised an army. The Fifth Panchen Lama tried to intervene between Pholhané's troops and those of the three ministers. According to Shakabpa, he was assisted by the Sakya hierarchy and by a representative of the Seventh Dalai Lama.[15] But all attempts at negotiation failed. Nothing could prevent Pholhané's men from clashing with the troops of the three rebel ministers.

In October 1728 the Fifth Panchen Lama was invited to Lhasa by Jalangga, one of the two Manchu commanders that had directed the army sent to Tibet by Emperor Kangxi, on the pretext of protecting the Seventh Dalai Lama and of putting an end to civil war. At first he tried to refuse, but lacking arguments, the Fifth Panchen Lama left Shigatse in mid-October, to arrive in Lhasa ten days later where he was received by Pholhané and by two Manchu commanders Jalangga and Mailu. A court composed of Jalangga and Mailu assisted the two imperial residents in Tibet, Sengge and Mala, who had just judged the three rebel ministers and condemned them to death.[16] They were executed. In addition, the Manchus decided to exile the Seventh Dalai Lama to Litang, as they felt his father to be the instigator of Khangchené's murder. The forced departure of the Seventh Dalai Lama aided Pholhané, who from then on had full control over Tibet. He won the confidence of the Manchus, who named the two imperial residents to Lhasa, whose posts were to continue until the end of the empire in 1911. The disgrace of the Seventh Dalai Lama reinforced the position of the Fifth Panchen Lama who, at the age of sixty-five, had become a respected and well-known figure. The prelate twice received an official visit in December 1729 and again in December 1731 from Pholhané, who also gave the prelate sumptuous gifts in June 1731. The Fifth Panchen Lama also welcomed a mission of Kukunor princes, who paid tribute to him and offered him numerous gifts.[17]

In 1734 Pholhané, exercising his political power, decided it would be opportune for the Seventh Dalai Lama to return to Lhasa. Accompanied by the Manchu prince Yunli (1688–1755) and the Changkya Hutuktu,[18] who was the spiritual master of the Qing court, the Seventh Dalai Lama returned to the Potala Palace in September 1735.[19] The following year he undertook to visit all of Tibet, escorted by the Changkya Hutuktu. While on the way to Tashilhunpo, the two men requested an interview with the prelate. But the Fifth Panchen Lama, old and sick, refused. He passed away some time later at the end of July 1737 at the age of seventy-four.

Lozang Pelden Yéshé (1738–1780) was recognized as the Sixth Panchen Lama on October 26, 1740, and enthroned at Tashilhunpo on July 13, 1741, with the accord of Emperor Qianlong, who was informed by the Seventh Dalai Lama. The presence of an imperial resident during the ceremony evidenced Qianlong's assent. At just ten years old, the Sixth Panchen Lama was already much solicited. On September 23, 1747, he met Yéshé Tséten, eldest son of Pholhané. On March 9, 1748, he received presents from a Manchu mission and in June the same year, following the death of his father Pholhané in 1747, Gyurmé Namgyel, the new governor of Tibet, and his ministers would make an official visit. On May 25, 1749, at the invitation of the Seventh Dalai Lama, the Sixth Panchen Lama went to Lhasa and stayed one month.[20]

The Sixth Panchen Lama's childhood and adolescence were shaken by the fighting led by Governor Gyurmé Namgyel, who, after establishing his power by executing his older brother and the previous partisans of his father, undertook to end the protectorate of the Qing and obtain the withdrawal of Manchu troops from Tibet. The imperial residents were concerned by this threat and warned the emperor that they wanted to assassinate the Tibetan governor. Indeed, on October 14, 1750, they invited Gyurmé Namgyel to their residence and killed him; in turn, they were executed by the ensuing rioters in Lhasa.[21]

Emperor Qianlong took radical measures regarding Tibet. He sent in an army of one thousand men. Within time the imperial residents' control in Tibet was increased to cover the entire Tibetan administration.[22] In 1757 the Manchus, who still feared the accumulation of powers in one person in Tibet, would try to modify the rules surrounding the choice of regent. From then on, the regent would be a monk chosen by a limited circle of dignitaries, of which the Sixth Panchen Lama was a part. His mandate would obligatorily end at the majority of the Dalai Lama.[23] Thus, at the Seventh Dalai Lama's death in 1757, Demo Ngawang Jampel (r. 1757–77) was named regent after having been designated by the Manchus and recommended by the Sixth Panchen Lama.[24]

Some years later, the Sixth Panchen Lama began to entertain Tibeto-British relations, much to the distress of Lhasa. In 1771 Bhutan went to war with the Indian state Cooch Bihar, capturing its king. The captive subjects called for help to the British, who had recently set up in Bengal. In response, troops of the British East India Company defeated the Bhutanese who requested the Sixth Panchen Lama to intervene in their favor with the British. At the time, the Eighth Dalai Lama was only thirteen years old, so in accordance with the suzerainty that Tibet had held over Bhutan since 1730, the Panchen Lama was the point person for dealing with the British. By letter addressed to Warren Hastings, who had been named governor-general of Bengal in 1772, the Sixth Panchen Lama sought an end to the fighting. He also advised the Bhutanese to free the king of Cooch Bihar. The affair ended on April 25, 1774, with a friendship and trade treaty signed between the East India Company and Bhutan.

Encouraged by this first contact with a Tibetan authority, Warren Hastings sent George Bogle (1746–1781) and Alexander Hamilton on a mission to Tibet. The two men arrived in Shigatse in October 1774 with three principle objectives: to open the trade routes with Tibet, to help the British better establish themselves in different Himalayan countries, and to allow the British to reach Beijing via Tibet (they were unaware at the time that foreigners were not allowed to enter Lhasa).

George Bogle met the Sixth Panchen Lama in the Déchen Rabgyé monastery near Tashilhunpo in November 1774. The two men were able to communicate easily in Hindustani, a language the Sixth Panchen Lama spoke given that his mother was originally from Kashmir. George Bogle requested that the Sixth Panchen Lama intercede with Qianlong in favor of the British, and likewise proposed opening commercial relations between India and Tibet.[25] The Sixth Panchen Lama is said to have responded favorably to the first request, but not to the second. Bogle and Hamilton stayed six months at Tashilhunpo until the Tibetan government, which had refused to allow the two Englishmen to continue further in Tibet, ordered their departure.

As for Qianlong, he wished to receive the Sixth Panchen Lama at his court for his seventieth birthday.[26] In order to speak directly with his guest, the emperor took it upon himself to learn a few words of Tibetan. Attentive to the prelate and fearing that the voyage would be too long and tiring, he ordered the construction of a temple in Chengde (Jehol), the Xumi fushou miao, whose architecture was modeled after Tashilhunpo.[27] The Sixth Panchen Lama arrived in Chengde on August 20, 1780, and met the Manchu emperor for the first time. He reached

Beijing on September 29, 1780, where Qianlong accorded him a second interview the day of his arrival. But in Beijing he ended up dying prematurely of chicken pox on November 2, 1780, at the age of forty-two.

In 1782 in Panam in the region of Tsang, Lozang Tenpé Nyima (1782–1853) was born. He was a cousin of the Eighth Dalai Lama, and was recognized as the reincarnation of the Sixth Panchen Lama by his uncle, the Dalai Lama. Warren Hastings, governor-general of Bengal, was informed of the discovery by Drugpa Hutuktu, the elder brother of the deceased Sixth Panchen Lama. He sent Captain Samuel Turner to Tibet accompanied by Dr. Robert Saunders and Lt. Samuel Davis, who arrived in Shigatse on September 22, 1783.[28] This mission, like the preceding one, was not authorized to go to Lhasa. The representatives stayed a bit in Shigatse and left on December 2, 1783, without having achieved any trade agreement.[29] Captain Turner did, however, have the possibility to pay a courtesy visit to the Seventh Panchen Lama, then just eighteen months old.[30] In 1784 the young Seventh Panchen Lama took his novice vows with the Eighth Dalai Lama, while Qianlong sent him presents in memory of the esteem he had held for his predecessor.[31] One last English mission went to Tashilhunpo in 1785. It was headed by Purangir Gosam, an Indian businessman that also acted as a diplomatic agent in Nepal and Tibet, and who had been part of the Bogle mission. This first Tibeto-British episode had ended after the departure of Warren Hastings from Bengal and the closure of the Tibetan borders at the beginning of 1788, under the menace of the Gurkhas.

The degradation of relations between the Tibetans and Gurkhas had to do with two issues. The first concerned trade relations between the two countries. Since 1751 the Nepalese state, run by the Gurkhas, had progressively replaced the silver in its coins with lead. Nepalese currency thus became devalued in Lhasa and trade exchanges became unbalanced to the profit of the Gurkhas.[32] The Eighth Dalai Lama informed the king of the Gurkhas, Rana Bahadur (r. 1777–99), that the rules, which until then had codified the trade between Tibetan products and Nepalese coins, no longer held. The Gurkhas took offense. The second issue originated in a quarrel at Tashilhunpo surrounding the succession upon the death of the Sixth Panchen Lama, whose half-brother, Shamar Tulku, ninth in the line of the Shamarpa, felt slighted during the distribution of family goods to the profit of his older brother Drugpa Hutuktu, who had been named administrator of Tashilhunpo after the death of the Sixth Panchen Lama. Furious, Shamar Tulku went to the Gurkhas, inciting them to raid Tibet by describing the riches at Tashilhunpo and the profusion of gold and silver mines in Tsang.[33] On September 2, 1788, the Gurkhas defeated the Tibetan and Manchu troops and occupied four districts at Tibet's western border: Nyanang, Rongshar, Kirong, and Purang.[34] The young Seventh Panchen Lama fled to Lhasa. The Gurkhas benefited from their victory by imposing a set of conditions. From that moment on, trade between Nepal and Tibet would occur unilaterally for their profit, and the Tibetans were no longer authorized to cross the Tibeto-Nepalese border.

Further, the Nepalese would not be subject to Tibetan jurisdiction, and the Tibetan government would have to pay an annual tribute of three thousand rupees to the Gurkhas.[35] After the first tribute payment, the Gurkhas returned the four occupied districts to the Tibetans.[36]

In 1791 the Tibetan government refused to pay tribute to the Gurkhas who had annexed Sikkim two years earlier. The reaction of the Gurkhas was swift, and on October 12, 1791, an army of eighteen thousand men entered Tibet once again.[37] On November 6, 1791, Tashilhunpo was pillaged. Shortly thereafter, the Tibetan army and the Manchu general Fukang'an at the head of a ten-thousand strong army managed to push back the Gurkhas and subdue them. The vanquished found themselves obliged to return all the goods stolen from the monastery and to send an ambassador to the Qianlong Emperor every five years.[38]

During the Gurkha raids, the Manchus feared for the lives of the Seventh Panchen Lama and the Eighth Dalai Lama, as testified by voluminous correspondence from that time between Emperor Qianlong and the imperial residents in Tibet. General Fukang'an remained in Tibet until the end of the summer of 1793, and made the most of his stay by participating in a complete reorganization of the Tibetan administration.

Indeed, the Manchus had come to believe that the nepotism that reigned over the great lines of reincarnations in Mongolia, North China, and Tibet led to political intrigue that was detrimental to their interests.[39] In particular, they had observed that the families and close associates of the Dalai Lamas and Panchen Lamas monopolized power in Tibet. At the death of the Seventh Dalai Lama, the Sixth Panchen Lama chose the Eighth Dalai Lama from within a family originating from Tsang. When the Sixth Panchen Lama passed away, his older brother took care of the administration of Tashilhunpo and the Eighth Dalai Lama designated his cousin as the Seventh Panchen Lama.[40] Discovering the unflattering role the half-brother of the Sixth Panchen Lama had played in the Gurkha affair, and noticing that a brother of the Eighth Dalai Lama, responsible for finance and administration of the Potala Palace store house, had been embezzling funds, the Manchus decided at the beginning of 1793 to modify the rules that governed the choice of high reincarnations, both those of the Dalai Lamas and Panchen Lamas. They introduced a system of drawing lots from a golden urn. The name, day, month, and year of birth of the selected children were written on pieces of ivory and put in the urn. The draw had to be done in the presence of imperial residents, as well as the Dalai Lama or the Panchen Lama, according to the case, and the regent. Moreover, for reincarnations of Mongol masters, the draw had to take place in the Palace of Eternal Harmony in Beijing in the presence of the members of the Qing Ministry Ruling the Outer Provinces and of the Changkya Hutuktu, the reincarnated master at the Qing court.[41]

From then on, in the hierarchy established by the Manchus, the imperial residents in Tibet were considered by the emperor as equal in rank to the Dalai Lamas and Panchen Lamas. The two Tibetan prelates were not authorized to communicate directly with Qianlong and had to go through the intermediary of the imperial residents in Tibet.[42] As of November 4, 1788, Qianlong forbade the regent of Lhasa and the administrator of Tashilhunpo to enter into contact or correspond with foreigners.[43] As for the two imperial residents, one had to accomplish inspections in the spring and autumn each year in Tsang, while the other had to stay in Lhasa.

On November 19, 1804, Jampel Gyatso, the Eighth Dalai Lama, passed away at the age of forty-six. Lungtok Gyatso (1806–1815), the Ninth Dalai Lama, was born in 1806, but lived only nine years and died under ambiguous circumstances. Tsültrim Gyatso (1816–1837), the Tenth Dalai Lama, was born in 1816. He had little more luck than his predecessor; he was assassinated, without ever having reigned, twenty-one years later. During this time, the Daoguang Emperor (r. 1821–51) increased favors towards the Seventh Panchen Lama. On May 13, 1837, he sent him a golden seal. On October 4, 1841, the Changkya Hutuktu went to Tashilhunpo to honor him. Finally on June 18, 1842, the Manchus awarded him the title of "Propagator of Values and Pacifier of Borders" (*xuanhua suijiang*). The alleged assassin of the Tenth Dalai Lama was the Regent Tsémönling Ngawang Jampel Tsültrim (1819–1844), who was also accused of terrorizing the Tibetan population and suspected of committing many brutalities. On July 21, 1844, the Seventh Panchen Lama, infuriated by the regent, is said to have addressed a memo to the Daoguang Emperor informing him of the situation.[44] The emperor sent a new imperial resident to Tibet, who was no other than Qishan, the renowned Manchu statesman, with the task of investigating the behavior of Tsémönling. To this end, Qishan created a commission composed of, among others, the Seventh Panchen Lama and Demo Hutuktu, who not long afterwards handed in the findings of their investigation. The regent was found guilty of assassinating the Tenth Dalai Lama, and was relieved of his functions on November 17, 1844.[45] Qishan then proposed that the Seventh Panchen Lama take care of matters of state until a new regent could be appointed.

In this way, the Seventh Panchen Lama ran Tibet for nine months from September 1844 to May 1845. This was the only time in Tibet's history that a Panchen Lama exercised real temporal power over the country. The Seventh Panchen Lama was replaced by Reting Ngawang Yéshé (1845–1862), who succeeded him on May 31, 1845. However, according to L. Petech, Reting exercised limited power. He did not really reign over the region of Ü, while the Seventh Panchen Lama maintained strong influence over his region, Tsang.[46] This situation lasted until 1853, when Lozang Tenpé Nyima, the Seventh Panchen Lama passed away at the age of seventy-one.

In November 1856 the Manchus authorized the search for the Panchen Lama's reincarnation. The choice of the child was made according to the method of drawing lots from the urn, which designated Lozang Pelden Chöki Dragpa Tenpé Wangchuk (1855–1882) as the Eighth Panchen Lama. The child was enthroned in October 1859. His longevity only barely exceeded that of the Eleventh Dalai

Lama (1838–1856) who died, once again, under ambiguous circumstances at the age of eighteen, and that of the Twelfth Dalai Lama (1856–1875) who died at nineteen. Indeed, the Eighth Panchen Lama died prematurely at the age of twenty-seven. During his short life devoted to religious practice, he did not have the opportunity to intervene on Tibet's political scene, which lay in the hands of the exacerbated ambitions of a string of regents. Moreover, as he was the same age as the Twelfth Dalai Lama, it was impossible for him to hold his role as spiritual master for the young Tibetan leader. In addition, the Eighth Panchen Lama would witness an affair that would accelerate deterioration in the relations between Tashilhunpo and Lhasa.

At the end of the nineteenth century, the British were attracted by the unknown geography of the mythical Land of Snows, as could be expected given their cultural penchant for exploration at the time. Driven by their desire to open new commercial routes and by their ambition to make Tibet a buffer state between the Russian Empire and their own, they tried as much as they could to make contact with the Tibetan authorities. Given that the borders of Tibet had been closed to foreigners since 1788, they decided to train natives able to easily cross the Indo-Tibetan border to conduct clandestine information-gathering missions.[47] These explorers, disguised as businessmen or pilgrims, left to study the terrain with a sextant hidden in their prayer wheel to measure the distances by dropping a bead from their rosary every one thousand steps.

Sarat Chandra Das (1849–1917) was one of these men. Born in Bengal, he left for Darjeeling after finishing his studies in civil engineering in Calcutta. He taught English in a school in Calcutta that trained youth from Sikkim for exploration. During his vacation he would visit Sikkim. During each outing he would stay in monasteries where he learned Tibetan and Buddhist philosophy in the company of his friend Ögyen Gyatso. Wishing to know Tibet better, especially since its cultural influence touches all Himalayan countries, he wanted to visit.[48] But the Bengal government refused to give him a permit to leave the territory. Desirous of undertaking his project at all costs, S. C. Das sent his companion Ögyen Gyatso to Tibet, so he could make a passport in his name.

Arriving in Lhasa, Ögyen Gyatso made the request to the local authorities, who would hear nothing of it. Having failed in his mission, Ögyen Gyatso decided to return through Sikkim and on his way he stopped at Tashilhunpo. There he met Drongtséba Sengchen Tulku Lozang Pelden Chöpel, the general administrator of the monastery, who confided his intention of learning Hindustani, the native language of Buddha.[49] Ögyen Gyatso suggested that the administrator take on Sarat Chandra Das as his professor since he knew this language. Sengchen Tulku then gave Ögyen Gyatso a passport for S. C. Das.[50]

With his new Tibetan passport in hand, Sarat Chandra Das easily obtained authorization from his government to go to Tibet. Before leaving India, he was trained in Calcutta in the latest techniques of observation and geographic calculation. In June 1879 he left Darjeeling accompanied by Ögyen Gyatso. On July 7 the two men arrived at Tashilhunpo, where they met the Eighth Panchen Lama and Sengchen Tulku, who gave them the necessary passports to go to Lhasa.[51] Thanks to this precious aid, they were able to visit Tibet for five months before returning to Darjeeling. On November 7, 1881, the two men headed for Tibet again. On December 9 that same year, they arrived at Tashilhunpo disguised as pilgrims. There they once again received help from Sengchen Tulku and one of his cousins, Phalha. In this way they were able to travel throughout Tibet at will, obtain books, and draw up maps of the country. The authorities in Lhasa eventually spotted them and sent agents after them, but S. C. Das and Ögyen Gyatso managed to escape. They returned to Darjeeling on December 27, 1882, safe and sound. Within Tibet, Sengchen Tulku and the members of the Phalha family were severely punished by the authorities in Lhasa for having aided and abetted the two explorers. Sengchen Tulku was condemned to death by drowning;[52] while the Phalha family had its goods confiscated and was forced to pay a heavy fine.[53]

The Eighth Panchen Lama's role in this affair did not go unnoticed by Lhasa officials, although it most certainly did by the Thirteenth Dalai Lama, who was only a child at the time. The Ninth Panchen Lama's role in Tibet's domestic and international dealings would only further increase with time, and his successors were, and continue to be, deeply entwined in Sino-Tibetan affairs and prominent actors on the international scene.

APPENDIX C

CHRONOLOGY OF THE NINTH PANCHEN LAMA'S LIFE

1879 JUN 14: Thirteenth Dalai Lama is enthroned at the Potala Palace, Lhasa.

1882 AUG 28: Eighth Panchen Lama dies at Tashilhunpo monastery, Shigatse.

1883 FEB 19: Samdrub Gyatso, the future Ninth Panchen Lama, is born in Brum gasha village in the Dakpo region.

1887 DEC 23: Three candidates are selected as possible reincarnations of the Eighth Panchen Lama.

1888 FEB 26: Ninth Panchen Lama is chosen by the tradition of drawing lots. The Thirteenth Dalai Lama presides over the ceremony of cutting the Panchen Lama's hair and bestowing his religious name—Jétsun Lozang Chöki Nyima Gélèk Namgyel Pelzangbo.

1892 FEB 1: Ninth Panchen Lama is enthroned at Tashilhunpo monastery and takes novice vows with Demo Hutuktu, the regent of Tibet.

1902 MAY 22: Ninth Panchen Lama takes monastic vows with the Thirteenth Dalai Lama in Lhasa.

1904 AUG 26: Thirteenth Dalai Lama departs for Outer Mongolia due to British raid on Tibet.

1905 SEPT: Ninth Panchen Lama and Captain Frederick O'Connor from the Younghusband Mission meet in Shigatse.
OCT 12: Ninth Panchen Lama departs for India.

1906 JAN 11: Ninth Panchen Lama arrives in Calcutta.

1909 AUG 3: Thirteenth Dalai Lama and Ninth Panchen Lama meet in Nakchu.
SEPT 2: Ninth Panchen Lama returns to Tashilhunpo monastery.
NOV 11: Thirteenth Dalai Lama returns to the Potala Palace, Lhasa.

1910 JAN 3: Thirteenth Dalai Lama departs for India due to Zhao Erfeng's occupation of Lhasa.

1911 JAN: Ninth Panchen Lama visits Lhasa at the invitation of Lian Yu, the imperial resident in Tibet.

1912 JUN: Thirteenth Dalai Lama and the Ninth Panchen Lama meet at Ralung monastery in the Tsang region of western Tibet.

1913 JAN 6: Thirteenth Dalai Lama returns to Lhasa.
JAN 8: Thirteenth Dalai Lama declares Tibet's independence.

1917 Taxation is imposed on the monastic lands of Tashilhunpo in the Gyeltsé district.

1920 JAN–FEB: Ninth Panchen Lama visits Lhasa and meets with the Thirteenth Dalai Lama.

1923 Further taxation is imposed on the entire land holdings of Tashilhunpo monastery.
DEC 22: Ninth Panchen Lama departs Tibet.

1925 JAN 20: Ninth Panchen Lama arrives in China.
JAN 27: Ninth Panchen Lama gives a speech at the preparatory meeting for the National Reconstruction Conference, Beijing.
FEB 1: Ninth Panchen Lama's speech is read by Lozang Gyeltsen, his attendant, at the National Reconstruction Conference, Beijing.
FEB 1: At Mount Wutai, the Ninth Panchen Lama gives the transmission of a Green Tārā Long Life initiation
MAR: Ninth Panchen Lama returns to Beijing and gives the transmission of an Amitāyus and Green Tārā long life initiation at the Palace of Eternal Harmony.
APR: Ninth Panchen Lama gives a teaching on Guru Yoga and presides over a ceremony for Taking Refuge at Lingyin Temple, Hangzhou, where he also gives transmissions of Amitāyus and Green Tārā long life initiations.
APR 29: Ninth Panchen Lama travels to Shanghai at the request of Sun Chuanfang, the military governor of Zhejiang Province.
MAY: Ninth Panchen Lama returns to Beijing; an Office of the Ninth Panchen Lama opens in Beijing.
MAY 6: Ninth Panchen Lama departs for Mount Wutai where he gives a transmission of a White Tārā initiation.
AUG 15: Ninth Panchen Lama returns to Beijing. The Chinese government awards him the title "World Savior who Propagates Orthodoxy."

1926 APR: Ninth Panchen Lama travels to Shanghai by way of Nanjing.
MAY: Ninth Panchen Lama returns to Beijing.
MAY 19: Ninth Panchen Lama gives a transmission of an Amitāyus long life initiation at the Yingtai Palace in the Forbidden City, Beijing.
SEPT: An Office of the Ninth Panchen Lama opens in Xining.
SEPT 15: An Office of the Ninth Panchen Lama opens in Chengdu.
OCT: Ninth Panchen Lama departs Beijing for Shenyang; he then sojourns at the Yellow Temple, Shenyang. An Office of the Ninth Panchen Lama opens in Shenyang.

1927 EARLY: Ninth Panchen Lama meets the deposed Qing emperor Puyi at the Yellow Temple, Shenyang.

1928 APR 15–22: Ninth Panchen Lama gives a transmission of the Kālacakra initiation at the Yangwang monastery located on the territory of Prince Darhan of the Qorcin Banner, Jerim League, Inner Mongolia. This is the first Kālacakra initiation the Panchen Lama gives while in exile from Tibet.
JUN: Ninth Panchen Lama gives a second transmission of the Kālacakra initiation at Jastu monastery on the territory of Prince Jasagt of the Qorcin Banner, Jerim League, Inner Mongolia.

1929 JAN 24: Ninth Panchen Lama sends a letter to Yan Xishan, director of

the Mongolian and Tibetan Affairs Commission, entitled "To the Compatriots of the Five Nationalities of the Chinese Republic."
FEB 28: An Office of the Ninth Panchen Lama officially opens in Nanjing and is recognized by the Republican government.
APR 15: Ninth Panchen Lama gives a third transmission of the Kālacakra initiation at Abaga Beizi monastery in the Kesikten Banner, Juu Uda League, Inner Mongolia.

1930 APR: An Office of the Ninth Panchen Lama opens in Dartsédo.
AUG: Ninth Panchen Lama gives a fourth transmission of the Kālacakra initiation on the lands of the Western Üjümücin Banner, Shilingol League, Inner Mongolia.
NOV 1 (OR 8): Ninth Panchen Lama sends a letter to Chiang Kai-shek.

1931 MAR 17: Ninth Panchen Lama departs Inner Mongolia for Nanjing.
MAY 5: Ninth Panchen Lama meets with Chiang Kai-shek in Nanjing. He also participates in the opening ceremony of the National People's Convention where he gives two speeches: one entitled "I Hope that the Inhabitants of the Country Know Tibet," and the other one entitled "Before Governing the Country, One Must Mend One's Own Ways."
MAY 20: Ninth Panchen Lama gives a speech entitled "Tibet is Part of China's National Territory" at the third session of the Convention of the New Asia Association, Nanjing.
JUN 5: Ninth Panchen Lama gives a transmission of a teaching on the mantra *om mani padme hum* at Longchang Temple in Mount Baohua, Pukou District, Nanjing.
JUL 1: The Chinese government in Nanjing awards the Ninth Panchen Lama the title "Great and Glorious Master Panchen who Protects the Country and Propagates its Values."
JUL 8: Ninth Panchen Lama departs Nanjing for Inner Mongolia.
SEPT 5: Ninth Panchen Lama gives a speech on the lands of the Hulunbuir League, Heilongjiang Province entitled "Let Us Unite Unanimously to Safeguard the National Territory."

1932 MAR 4: Ninth Panchen Lama sends a telegram to the Chinese State Council requesting Chinese authorities to prepare a plan of resistance against the Japanese.
MAY 14: Ninth Panchen Lama's representative Ngachen Rinpoche departs for Tibet to negotiate the conditions for the spiritual master's return.
JUL: Ninth Panchen Lama gives a fifth transmission of the Kālacakra initiation on the lands of the Üjümücin Banner, Shilingol League, Inner Mongolia.
OCT 5: Ninth Panchen Lama departs Inner Mongolia.
OCT 8: Ninth Panchen Lama arrives in Beijing.
OCT 21–24: Ninth Panchen Lama gives a sixth transmission of the Kālacakra initiation at the Hall of Supreme Harmony in the Forbidden City, Beijing.
DEC 12: Ninth Panchen Lama arrives in Nanjing.

DEC 15: Ninth Panchen Lama meets with Lin Sen, the president of the Chinese Republic.
DEC 21: Ninth Panchen Lama gives a speech during a press conference at the Overseas Chinese Hotel in Nanjing entitled "Reflections on the Past, the Present and the Future."
DEC 23: Ninth Panchen Lama gives a speech during a welcome ceremony organized by various members of the Chinese government in Nanjing entitled "The Chinese People Love Peace."
DEC 25: While in Nanjing, the Ninth Panchen Lama is awarded the title "Emissary in Charge of Spreading Values in the Western Region."

1933 JAN: Ninth Panchen Lama organizes and leads a religious ceremony at Longchang Temple in Mount Baohua, Pukou District, Nanjing.
JAN 21: Ninth Panchen Lama gives a speech entitled "The Link Between Tibet's History and the Five Nationalities" on the anniversary of the creation of the Mongolian and Tibetan Affairs Commission, Nanjing.
JAN 30: Ninth Panchen Lama gives a transmission of a Guru Yoga teaching at the Overseas Chinese Hotel in Nanjing.
FEB 7: Ninth Panchen Lama departs Nanjing for Inner Mongolia.
FEB 17: Ninth Panchen Lama arrives at the Baruun monastery of the Darhan Banner, Ulanqab League, Inner Mongolia.
MAR 16: Ninth Panchen Lama sends a telegram to the members of the Nationalist Party, the Republican government, the Military Affairs Commission, and all the major commissions of state describing the Japanese advances in Jehol Province.
MAY 29: An Office of the Ninth Panchen Lama opens in Suiyuan Province.
AUG 7: Ninth Panchen Lama submits a report to the Mongolian and Tibetan Affairs Commission on the state of his propaganda efforts with the western Mongols.
OCT 18: The Republican government gives an encomium praising the Ninth Panchen Lama.
OCT 24: Ninth Panchen Lama gives a speech to the Mongol princes at Baruun monastery in the Darhan Banner, Ulanqab League, Inner Mongolia.
DEC 17: Thirteenth Dalai Lama dies.

1934 JAN 16: Ninth Panchen Lama departs Baruun monastery for Beijing.
JAN 22: Ninth Panchen Lama departs Beijing for Nanjing.
JAN 24: Ninth Panchen Lama arrives in Nanjing.
FEB 2: Ninth Panchen Lama meets with Lin Sen, president of the Chinese Republic, in the Government Reception Hall, Nanjing.
FEB 14: Ninth Panchen Lama organizes and leads religious ceremonies in Nanjing for the funeral of the Thirteenth Dalai Lama.
FEB 20: The investiture of the Ninth Panchen Lama as a member of the Chinese government is held.
APR 25: Ninth Panchen Lama meets with Ngachen Rinpoche who, several

months earlier, had returned from Tibet following an audience with the Thirteenth Dalai Lama just prior to his death in December 1933.

APR 26: Ninth Panchen Lama travels from Nanjing to Hangzhou.

MAY 9: Ninth Panchen Lama gives a speech in Hangzhou at the opening of the Kālacakra ceremony entitled "The Concept of Equality in Buddhism and in the Doctrine Handed Down by Sun Yat-sen."

MAY 13–15: Ninth Panchen Lama gives a seventh transmission of the Kālacakra initiation at Lingyin Temple, Hangzhou.

JUN 6: Ngachen Rinpoche meets with Chiang Kai-shek in Jiangxi.

JUN 30: Ninth Panchen Lama returns to Nanjing and resumes discussions with the Chinese government about his return to Tibet.

JUL 14: Ninth Panchen Lama departs Nanjing for Beijing.

AUG 11: Ninth Panchen Lama departs Beijing.

AUG 17: Ninth Panchen Lama arrives on the lands of the Yeke Juu League, Inner Mongolia.

OCT 5: Ngachen Rinpoche departs once again for Lhasa to continue negotiations regarding the Ninth Panchen Lama's return to Tibet.

1935 JAN 24: Ninth Panchen Lama gives a speech in Ningxia entitled "Reinforce Border Defense by Developing Communication Networks."

FEB 8: An Office of the Emissary in Charge of Spreading Values in the Western Region is established in Xiangride on the lands of the Alashan Banner.

MAR 19: Ninth Panchen Lama sends Huang Musong, director of the Mongolian and Tibetan Affairs Commission, a proposal for a project on the propagation of values in Tibet.

APR 4: An Office of the Emissary in Charge of Spreading Values in the Western Region is established in Nanjing.

APR 11: An Office of the Emissary in Charge of Spreading Values in the Western Region is established in Beijing.

MAY 12: Ninth Panchen Lama gives a speech in Xining entitled "Reasons Why I Will Return to Tibet By Passing Through Qinghai."

JUN: Ninth Panchen Lama gives a transmission of an Amitāyus long life initiation at Kumbum monastery, Amdo (Qinghai Province).

SEPT 12: Ninth Panchen Lama gives an eighth transmission of the Kālacakra initiation at Kumbum monastery.

SEPT 23: Ninth Panchen Lama requests the British to help mediate his return to Tibet by trying to soften the opinions of the members of the Tibetan government.

1936 MAR 20: An Office of the Emissary in Charge of Spreading Values in the Western Region is established in Kyégudo.

MAY 17: Ninth Panchen Lama departs Kumbum monastery to begin his return to Tibet.

JUL 14: Ninth Panchen Lama gives a ninth transmission of the Kālacakra initiation at Labrang trashikhyil monastery, Amdo.

AUG 21: Ninth Panchen Lama departs Labrang trashikhyil monastery.
AUG 30–31: Ninth Panchen Lama gives transmissions of the Avalokiteśvara and Green Tārā initiations on the lands of the Mongol prince Henan.
DEC 26: Ninth Panchen Lama gives a speech at Kyégudo monastery entitled "Support the Revolutionary Leader, Chiang Kai-shek."

1937 JAN: Ninth Panchen Lama meets with Phabongka Rinpoche, the great spiritual master from the Kham region sent by Reting.
MAY 7: Ninth Panchen Lama participates in the search for the reincarnation of the Thirteenth Dalai Lama. He chooses one of the two possible reincarnations of the Thirteenth Dalai Lama.
AUG 16: Ninth Panchen Lama departs Kyégudo and heads towards the Tibetan border.
OCT 11: Ninth Panchen Lama returns to Kyégudo and makes plans to head towards Kardzé.
DEC 1: Ninth Panchen Lama dies in Kyégudo.

1938 JAN 18: Ninth Panchen Lama's mortal remains are transferred to Kardzé.
MAR 8: A funeral ceremony in honor of the Ninth Panchen Lama is presided over by Dai Jitao, education minister of the Chinese government in Chongqing, Sichuan Province.
APR 22: The Offices of the Emissary in Charge of Spreading Values in the Western Region are dissolved.

1940 FEB 22: Fourteenth Dalai Lama is enthroned in the Potala Palace, Lhasa.

1941 FEB 4: Panchen Lama's mortal remains arrive at Tashilhunpo.
MAY 5: All the offices created by the Ninth Panchen Lama are closed, except the Nanjing office.

APPENDIX D

ESTABLISHMENT OF CHINA BUREAU OFFICES OF THE PANCHEN LAMA

1925 MAY
Beijing Office, Fuyou Temple
Founder: Lozang Tsültrim
Director: Li Fangchun

1926 SEPT 15
Chengdu Office
Director: Ngawang Cinpa

SEPT
Xining Office
Founder and Director: Wangdü Norbu
(replaced by Li Jinzhong, June 11, 1936)

1926 Shenyang Office
Director: Dazhuoni Zhong Sulang
(replaced by Luo Zongjia; then replaced by Baxi Kenpo, January 4, 1933)

1929 FEB 20 (OR JAN 20)
Nanjing Office, 13 Qiwang Street
Directors: Lozang Gyeltsen and Zhu Funan

1930 APR 21 (OR JAN)
Dartsédo Office
Director: Ngawang Cinpa
(replaced by Gédun Tashi, February 1931; then replaced by Dianluoyun, January 14, 1935)

1933 MAY 29
Suiyuan Office
Founder and Director: Dingwang Dorjé

1935 FEB 8 (OR MAY 1932)
Xiangride Office, on the lands of the Alashan League
Known as the Office of the Emissary in Charge of Spreading Values in the Western Region

1935 APR 4
Nanjing Office, 293 Jiankang Street
Known as the Office of the Emissary in Charge of Spreading Values in the Western Region
Director: Lozang Gyeltsen

1935 APR 11
Beijing Office, 95 Beichang Street
Known as the Office of the Emissary in Charge of Spreading Values in the Western Region
Director: Lozang Thubten

1936 MARCH 30
Kyégudo Office
Known as the Office of the Emissary in Charge of Spreading Values in the Western Region
Director: Wangdü Norbu (?)

APPENDIX E

ADMINISTRATION OF TASHILHUNPO MONASTERY

INTRODUCTION

Between the seventeenth and nineteenth centuries, the Panchen Lamas, whose reputation was equal to or surpassed that of the Dalai Lamas, took a growing role in the political life of Tibet, particularly as the Manchus and British increasingly made contact with them. The premature deaths of the Sixth, Ninth, Tenth, Eleventh, and Twelfth Dalai Lamas combined with the numerous intrigues of unscrupulous regents amplified this phenomenon. As a result, Tashilhunpo enjoyed relative autonomy up until the beginning of the twentieth century, made possible by several factors: the distance between Shigatse and Lhasa; the monastery's large holdings of arable land, which guaranteed enough agricultural production to establish its economic power base; the tax exemption it seemed to benefit from; and, finally, the high esteem and caution that foreign powers (Manchu and British) maintained towards the lineage of the Panchen Lamas. At the start of the twentieth century, this situation favored the development of the monastery's substantial administration.

Sources are somewhat scant with regard to the administrative structure of Tashilhunpo. Works in Tibetan on Tashilhunpo's history contain little information about its administration.[1] Two articles and one organizational chart that touch on this topic were, however, located. The first article was published in 1991 in *Bod kyi lo rgyus rig gnas dpyad gzhi'i rgyu chab dams bsgrigs* (Historical and Cultural Tibetan Documents). It is part of a collection of testimonies collected during the 1980s from individuals involved in historical events concerning Tibet. The second article is entitled "De snga'i bla brang rgyal mtshan mthon po'i srid 'dzin sgrig gzhi'i spyi'i gnas tshul"[2] (Detailed Presentation of the Former Government of the Residence of Gyeltsen Tönpo).[3] Its authors sLe zur 'Jigs med dbang phyug (Jigme Wangchuk) and bDe zur Rin chen dBang 'dus (Rinchen Wangdü) are both from Tsang aristocratic families. In each case, one of their relatives is said to have entered Tashilhunpo monastery and the private residence of the Ninth Panchen Lama.[4] Their article describes the personnel that made up the monastery's administration, including their functions. As for the organizational chart, it is presented without sources on page 679 in a work entitled *Bod ljongs spyi bzhad* (General Presentation of the Autonomous Region of Tibet) published in 1991 in Lhasa by Mi rigs dpe skrun khang.

Regarding documents written in Chinese, I was able to locate two original and two secondary sources. The original sources are *Wei Zang tongzhi* (Monograph on Central Tibet), particularly chapter 12, published in 1896 by Wei Yuan,[5] and *Da Qing huidian shili* (Imperially Commissioned Collected Regulations and Precedents of the Qing Dynasty), chapter 977, folio 4b to 6b, published in 1899. While these documents reveal how the Manchus perceived the Tibetan administration in Lhasa after 1792, they provide little information on Tashilhunpo. One of the secondary sources, *Xizang de zhengjiao heyi zhi* (The Politico-Religious System of Tibet) was published in 1947, and, likewise, describes with only slight variation the Manchu vision of the Tibetan government, while specifying that Tashilhunpo's administration was modeled after Lhasa's governmental administration.[6] *Zangzu shilue* (The Abridged History of the Tibetan Ethnic Group) published in 1985 provides a brief mention of Tashilhunpo's administration. Since these documents were insufficient to obtain a precise explanation of the inner workings of Tashilhunpo, on-site investigation became necessary. Interviews with members of the Tashilhunpo monastery in Shigatse in June 1993 led to no pertinent information on the subject. Research then turned to the exiled population of monks at the reconstructed Tashilhunpo monastery in Bylakuppe, India. Unfortunately, although there were quite a few aged monks who were direct witnesses to the time period, none had participated in the Ninth Panchen Lama's administration. Finally, a fortunate encounter with Kugo Ngawang Riktröl, a former member of the Tibetan government, was able to shed some light on the question. However, he turned out to be a rather non-objective witness since he had personally taken strong sides on the issue of the Panchen Lama's flight from Tibet.

Examination of the organizational charts drawn up from Tibetan and Chinese sources reveals a great number of differences. According to Tibetan authors, Tashilhunpo's administration melded with that of the Ninth Panchen Lama's private residence. It was placed under the authority of the general administrator (*kyabying dzasa lama*). This appellation *kyabying dzasa lama* breaks down into three titles: *kyabying, dzasa,* and *lama*. The most well-known title is "lama," denoting a knowledgeable Buddhist master. The title *dzasa* comes from the Mongol word *jasak*, which designates a layperson, specifically a hereditary prince governing one of the autonomous Mongol Banners under the Qing.[7] In a religious context, this title was given to religious masters who somehow administered in the context of the Manchu Empire. In Chinese, the title was transcribed in its lay usage as *zhasake*, which became *zhasake da lama* (grand master administrator) in its religious sense.[8] According to Kugo Ngawang Riktröl, the term was synonymous with the Tibetan title *cakzö*, which means "stewards of great monastic estates," such as Tashilhunpo or Kundeling. The title *kyabying* (lit. "protector of the center") was exclusively attributed to the general administrator of Tashilhunpo, in addition to the title of steward. The "center" referred to the Panchen Lama's private residence (*labrang yiktsang*).

The *kyabying dzasa lama* was thus an ecclesiast who administered and protected the private goods of the Panchen Lama. His full title could thus be translated literally as "great master who acts as steward and protector of the private residence."

In fact the translation of "general administrator" implies the idea of administration of property while "general" indicates that the titleholder occupies the highest administrative rank. Kugo Ngawang Riktröl states that the general administrator of Tashilhunpo was of equal rank to the ministers (*kalön*) of the Tibetan government in Lhasa.[9] In their correspondence, the British use the term "prime minister."[10] In February 1924, the Tibetan government appointed Lozang Tenzin as general administrator of Tashilhunpo.[11]

According to Tibetan authors, two departments were under the general administrator's authority: *tsékor lékung* (lit. "Department Concerning the Summit") and *shökor lékung* (lit. "Department Concerning the Base"). It is necessary to point out that in the organization of the Tibetan government, *tsé* was used to describe the religious officials belonging to the branch of government that handled all monastic affairs. *Shö* signified those lay officials who took care of civil affairs (and were helped by monks from the religious branch.) In reality this distinction did not apply to Tashilhunpo's administration because all of its members were religious, with a few rare exceptions. Chinese secondary sources indicate that Tashilhunpo's administration was divided into two separate branches: the private residence and the civil administration. The private residence was placed under the responsibility of three abbots, who additionally served the Panchen Lama directly. The civil administration was directed by the general administrator. It ensured both the running of the monastery and that of the whole province of Tsang. This Chinese description of the Tashilhunpo administration confirms what we find in Chinese geographical works dating from the eighteenth century.[12]

Aside from these differences, it seems useful to compare the information from the various sources consulted to determine the most plausible organizational structure for Tashilhunpo's administration as it existed before the Ninth Panchen Lama left Tibet in 1923. This summary takes into consideration my observations made during visits to working monasteries in Tibet and India.

TASHILHUNPO MONASTERY: ITS STRUCTURE AND PERSONNEL

The lineage of the Panchen Lamas has been attached to the Tashilhunpo monastery since the mid-seventeenth century. As its abbot, the Ninth Panchen Lama, in principle, held spiritual and temporal power. In reality, while he took complete care of spiritual matters, concerning temporal ones he was largely assisted by his general administrator. According to the authors Jigme Wangchuk and Rinchen Wangdü, and given the testimony gathered, it seems that the general administrator who ran the Department Concerning the Summit and the Department Concerning the Base, was the single second-ranked official in the entire Tashilhunpo administration.[13] The members of the first department were in direct service to the prelate while those of the second department ran the monastery's civil affairs. Similarly, that which concerned the Panchen Lama and religious aspects pertained to the "Summit," and that which involved administering civil affairs and lay people came under the "Base." In addition, the clergy belonging to the Department Concerning the Summit made up the Panchen Lama's entourage (*zimchungkak*, lit. "personnel having access to the small residence").[14]

Department Concerning the Summit

A "state secretary" (*drönyer chenmo*) of the fourth rank oversaw the administration of the Department Concerning the Summit.[15] This individual was responsible for the circulation and filing of all documents, reports, decrees, and personal messages destined for the Panchen Lama or sent by the prelate. He had the right to promote, punish, or relieve officials of their duties according to their service. In the absence of the Panchen Lama, he represented him during important ceremonies. Six or seven secretaries (*grönyer*) of the fifth rank assisted him in his tasks. Moreover, he had four monks under his direct orders. They were low-ranking officials who were in charge of maintaining order and discipline during religious ceremonies or when the Panchen Lama was away. The state secretary also headed another department, composed of the manager of the Panchen Lama's palanquin (*phebcamgopa*), assisted by forty porters (*camdekpa*), a dance master (*garpa*), a throne manager (*brempa*), a manager of the offerings of the Panchen Lama's private residence (*drangchöpa*), a stable manager (*chipön chenmo*), a monastery maintenance manager (*gönyer chenmo*), a printing manager (*parpön*), assisted by an employee (*tsédrung* or *létsenpa*),[16] with twenty aids making up the Tashilhunpo and Narthang print shop, and a sweeper (*gepa*) all of the sixth rank, plus two tent managers (*gurpa*) of the seventh rank.

A steward (*dépala*) of the Panchen Lama's private treasury (*tséchyak lékung*) of the fourth rank, aided by two secretaries (*drungyik*) and two assistant stewards (*nyerpa*), was responsible for collecting taxes and took care of the Panchen Lama's personal treasury.

The private college (*kuker dratsang*) or the monastic house (*tségön khangpa*) of the Panchen Lama, called the "Island of Complete Victory over the Three Worlds" (*Sisum Namgyel ling*), was headed by a master teacher (*lopön*) that trained eighty monks who assisted the Panchen Lama during his Buddhist philosophical teachings at Tashilhunpo or elsewhere. One or two tutors (*yongdzin*) taught the sutras and tantras to the Panchen Lama. They were helped by three debate companions (*tshenzhapa*) of the sixth rank chosen from the monks who had passed their Doctor of Theology (*géshé*) exams. The three debate companions taught logic and debating to the Panchen Lama. A monk of the seventh rank, chosen from the most erudite in the monastery, also helped the tutor(s) as master of reading and writing (*chyakpe zhudakpa*) for the Panchen Lama.

The Panchen Lama's personal physician (*lamenpa*) of the sixth rank, helped by a seventh-ranked employee, was responsible for the good health of the prelate and prepared his medicine. He also taught medicine.[17]

Three clergy comprised personal service to the Ninth Panchen Lama (*kucar*, lit. "body personnel"). They included a butler (*sölpön kenpo*, lit. "head of meals"),[18] a chamberlain (*zimpön kenpo*, lit. "head of the household"),[19] and a vicar (*chöpön kenpo*, lit. "head of offerings").[20]

An attendant of the fourth rank (*sölpön kenpo*) ran the cooking (*söltap*, lit. the "Summit's Hearth") and the administration (*sölwa*) of the kitchen. Many people worked under him. The kitchen personnel were responsible for the daily meals served to the Panchen Lama's tutors, members of the entourage, and any visitors. The administrative employees stocked the kitchen and helped in the preparation of banquets. In 1923 the attendant of the Ninth Panchen Lama was Lozang Gyeltsen (1888–?).[21]

A cook of the sixth rank (*machen tsédrung létsenpa*) was in charge of the preparation of the Ninth Panchen Lama's meals and was helped by three cooking assistants (*söltap tsédrung*) of the seventh rank. This cook was also responsible for managing the kitchen personnel, who included a water receiver (*chabsu tsédrung*), a lay person in charge of transporting the water (*chadrel zhelno cawo*), a groom (*lakto*), two well managers (*chuma*), three general helpers (*söltap lakyok drapa*), a sweeper (*trugépa*), a barley grinder (*zhibzöpa*), a fuel manager (*zhinglenpa kyawo*), a lay person in charge of supplies (*söltrum jakmin gopa*), a manager of fresh produce (*zhetsel jakmin gopa*), and a grilled barley flour supply manager (*zhibgyel gopa*).

A kitchen steward ensured the stock of supplies (*söldek tsédrung létsenpa*, lit. "low-ranking religious official in charge of the management of supplies"). Four monks handled the hearth (*zhékar laktselpa drapa*) with the help of two aids (*lakyok*), and two fuel purchasers and two assistant cooks (both referred to as *shinglen tapyok*).

A chamberlain of the fourth rank (*zimkak tripa*), also referred to as "head of those with access to the prelate's dwelling," as well as the favorites (*cansel*) handled the Ninth Panchen Lama's wardrobe. They made up the personnel of the Ninth Panchen Lama's antechamber (*nazagang*).[22] In 1923 the Ninth Panchen Lama's chamberlain was Garapa Chöken Penkangwang and his favorites were Kachen Chöpel and Drongshö Drung Phurbu Tsering.[23]

A vicar of the fourth rank (*chözengpa*), assisted by a junior functionary and a small group of people responsible for offerings, was in charge of preparing the altars for the Ninth Panchen Lama's private residence. In 1923 the Ninth Panchen Lama's vicar was Wangdü Norbu.[24]

Contrary to what one might think by the wording of their titles, field research verified that in active monasteries today the attendant, the chamberlain, and the vicar hold notable power due to their close proximity to the abbot. There is no logical reason why this should not have been the case at the time of the Ninth Panchen Lama. Moreover, if the authors of the Chinese sources underlined the presence of three people to the point of confusing them with the private residence, it reveals the significant role they played on the political scene. In 1792 Emperor Qianlong recognized their importance in deciding that if the post of general administrator of Tashilhunpo fell vacant, the attendant or chamberlain would be promoted to his place.[25]

Department Concerning the Base

The high secretary (*drungyik chenmo*) of the third rank ran the "Department Concerning the Base" and assisted the general administrator. A religious figure, he also held the title of "Grand Master" (*da lama*).[26]

A secretary (*kenchung*) of the fourth rank was at the head of the secretariat for the private residence. He was helped by a young secretary (*drungche kushön*) of the fifth rank, two teachers (*yiktsang gégen*) of the sixth rank, fifteen monk and lay writer clerks (*yiktsang leca drungrik serkya*), and five to six students and two guardians (*yiktsang kunyer*). This secretariat was in charge of all official correspondence; that is to say, of all documents carrying the Ninth Panchen Lama's seal. The secretariat for the private residence delivered all permits and seemed to control all the land holdings. In 1923 the young secretary was Wangchenwa Tsédor.[27]

Two secretaries of the fifth rank were in charge of a particular secretariat known as *nangkang yiktsang* (lit. the "secretariat of the interior and above"). They were backed by two other secretaries (one monk and one lay person) of the sixth rank. This particular secretariat included a Chinese translator (*gyadrung*), three copyists (*yikbri*), and two attendant/messengers (*yikyelpa*) all of the seventh rank. They looked after the daily correspondence.

A low-ranking official (*kenchung*) was in charge of the stables (*chira lékung*). He had one or two employees (*lécadrungrik*) under him, monks or lay people, in addition to two guardians (*nyerpa*). On top of that, ten or so people gathered the hay (*zenpa kyano*), the dried yak dung (*shakpa*) that was used as fuel, and the wood for heating (*kyi tser*). This fuel was used in the Ninth Panchen Lama's kitchens and in those of the general administrator (*tséshö söltap*). It was equally distributed to heat certain prayer halls (*tshokchen*) of the Tantric college (*ngapa dratsang*) and chapels of the monastery.

A monk and a layperson of the fourth rank held the posts of officer attendant (*gönyer*) and were responsible for collecting taxes. They were helped in their tasks by a low-ranking official (of the sixth or seventh rank), eight to nine assistant officers (*nyerdrung*), six tax officers (*bokawa*), and twelve people in charge of weighing the foodstuffs (*bokdépa*).

Once collected, the taxes were deposited in the private residence treasury (*Labrang cakzö*) and guarded by four key bearers (*dechangpa*) of the fifth rank placed directly under the general administrator. Ten or so members of the Ninth

Panchen Lama's entourage helped them in this task. Undoubtedly, they had a discreet surveillance role over the key bearers given the importance of the post.

Two attendants of the seventh rank were responsible for the general administrator's meals. About fifteen people helped them, of which one was a cook (*machen*).[28]

CONCLUSION

Certain points regarding the workings of the Tashilhunpo administration remain unclear, notably the criteria and method of nomination of the officials. In addition, while the four colleges of the monastery and associated monks' residences each had their own administration, it is not clear whether such administration was autonomous or fell under the monastery's administration. Finally, doubt remains as to the extent of the powers of the Tashilhunpo administration. Was the role of the monastery's administration to manage only the lands of the Ninth Panchen Lama's private residence or the entire monastic estate, including the "collective lands?" The present research gives no precise answers. Nevertheless, the large number of officials belonging to the Department Concerning the Base involved in tax collection (six officials, eight or nine assistants, and twelve people in charge of weighing) could indicate that the Tashilhunpo administration held its influence over all the monastic lands, both those of the private residence and those of the "collective lands."

An organizational chart of the administrative structure of Tashilhunpo monastery as it probably existed in 1923 is provided on the next page; it is preceded by an organizational chart of the Lhasa government's administration for comparative purposes. These are followed by personnel charts for the Department Concerning the Summit and the Department Concerning the Base.

ADMINISTRATIVE STRUCTURE OF TIBETAN GOVERNMENT AND TASHILHUNPO MONASTERY

TIBETAN GOVERNMENT

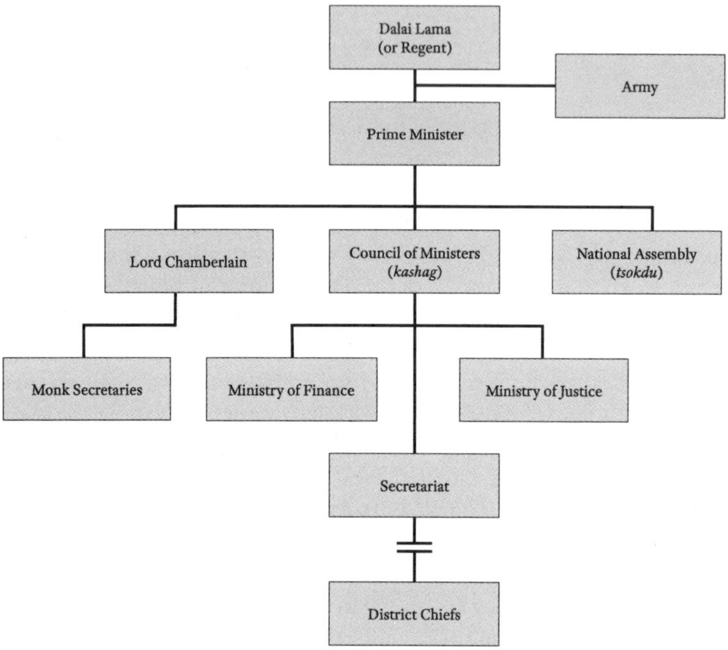

TASHILHUNPO MONASTERY

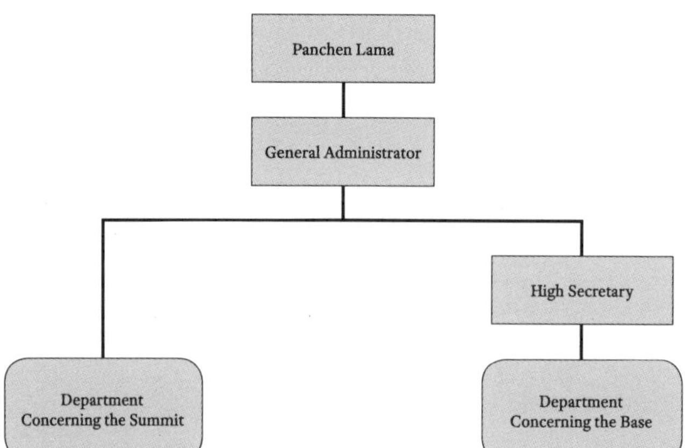

DEPARTMENT CONCERNING THE SUMMIT

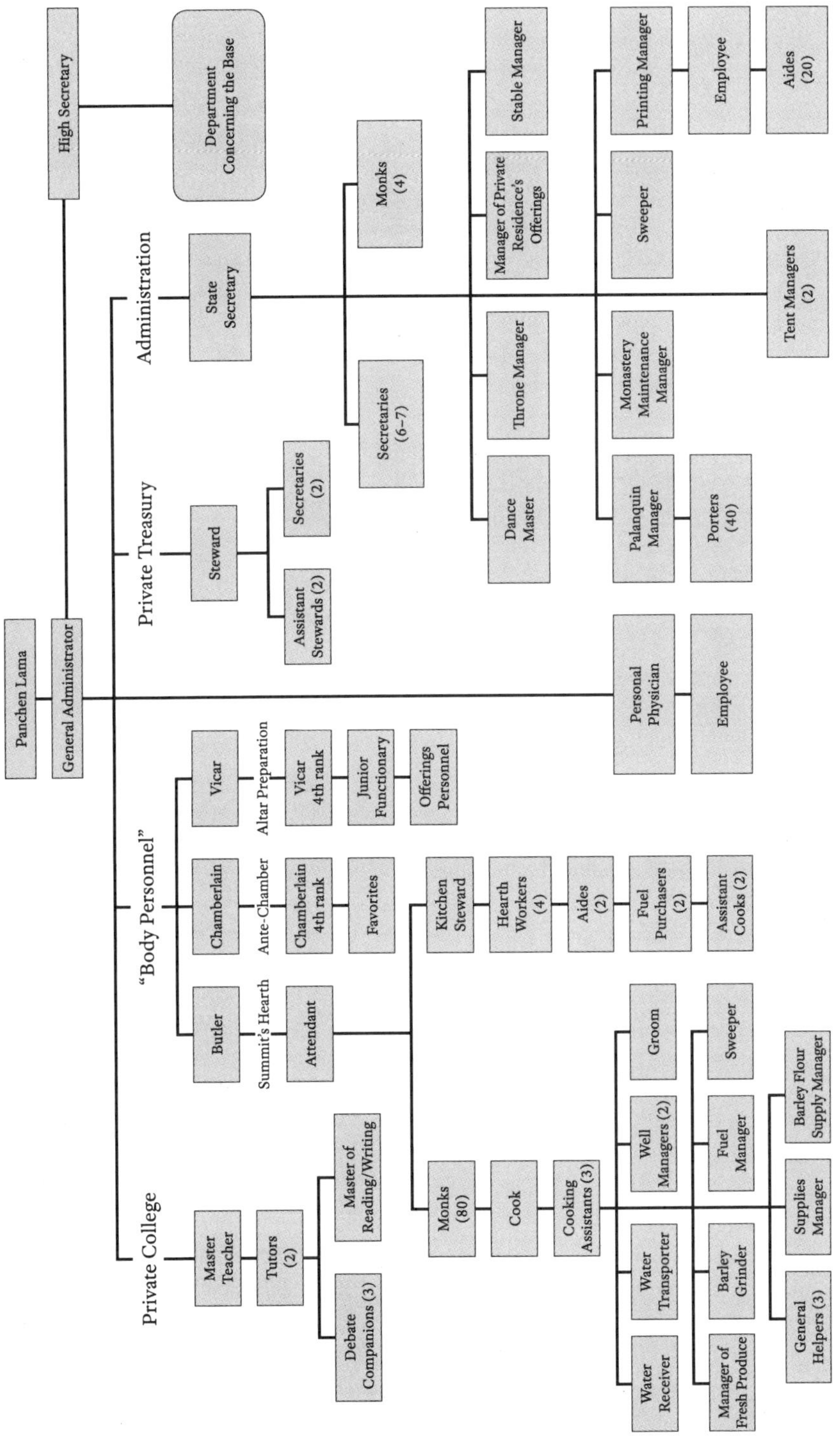

DEPARTMENT CONCERNING THE BASE

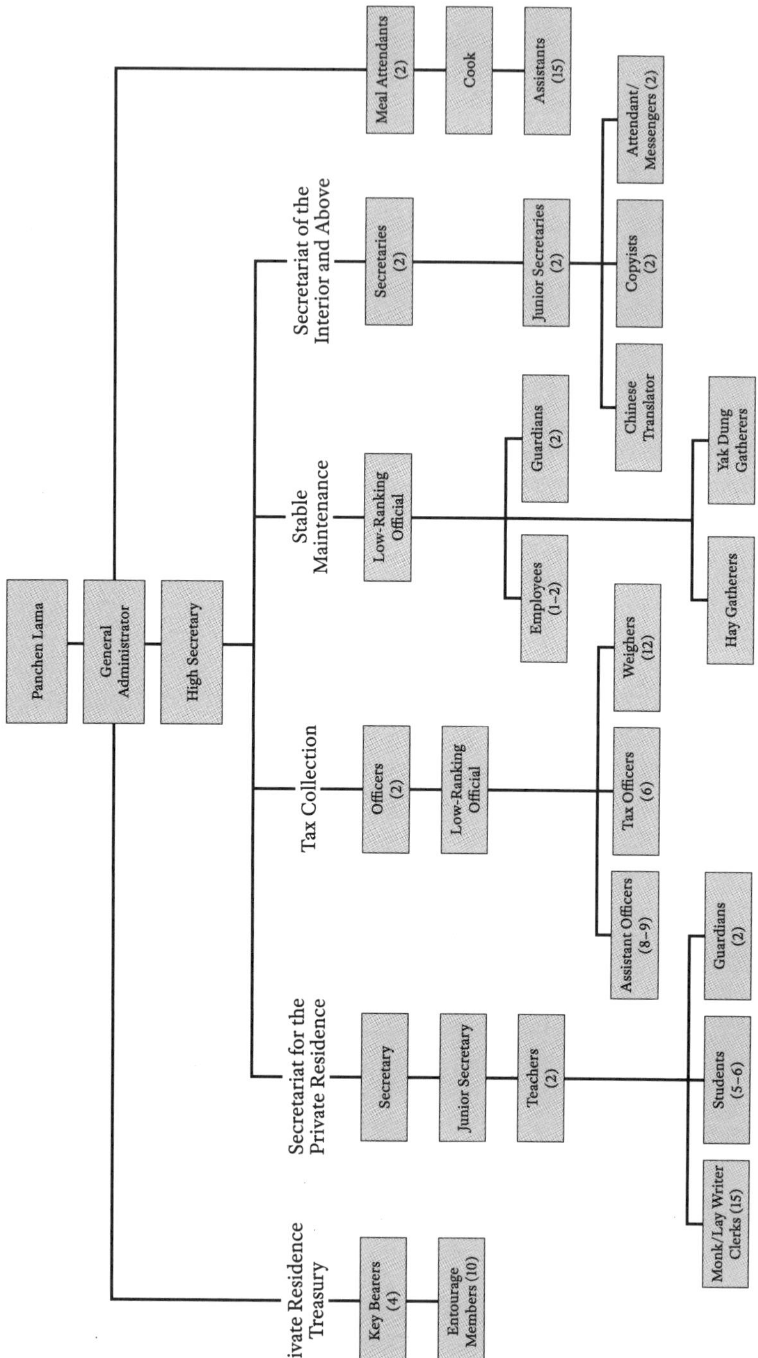

APPENDIX F

TIBETAN PLACE-NAMES

SIMPLIFIED PHONETIC	T. V. WYLIE	PINYIN	CHINESE CHARACTERS
Amdo	A mdo	Anduo	安多
Bathang	'Ba' thang	Ba'an	巴安
Beri	Be ri	Baili	白利
Cagzam	lCags zam	Jiasangka	嘉桑卡
Chamdo	Chab mdo	Changdou	昌都
Coné	Co ne	Zhuoni	卓尼
Dartsédo	Dar rtse mdo	Kangding	康定
Dergé	sDe dge	Dege	德格
Dzayül	rDza yul	Chayu	察隅
Gartok	sGar thog	Gadake	噶大克
Gyeltsé	rGyal rtse	Jiangzi	江孜
Kardzé	dKar mdzes	Ganzi	甘孜
Kham	Khams	Kang	康
Kyégudo	sKye rgu mdo	Yushu	玉樹
Lhasa	lHa sa	Lasa	拉薩
Lhatsé	lHa rtse	Lazi	拉孜
Litang	Li thang	Litang	里唐
Nakartsé	sNa dkar rtse	Nagalaze	納噶拉則
Nakchu	Nag chu	Naqu	納曲
Namring	Ngam ring	Angren	昂仁
Narthang	sNar thang	Nadang	納當
Ngari	mNga' ris	Ali	阿里
Nyarong	Nyag rong	Zhanhua	瞻化
Panam	Pa snam	Bailang	白朗
Phuntsoling	Phun tshogs gling	Pengcuolin	彭錯林
Shigatse	gZhis ka rtse	Rigaze	日噶則
Tashilhunpo	bKra shis lhun po	Zhashilunbu	扎什侖布
Tsang	gTsang	Zang	藏
Tsolo	mTsho lho	Hainan	海南
Ü	dBus	Wei	衛

APPENDIX G

TIBETAN SPELLINGS

SIMPLIFIED PHONETIC	T. V. WYLIE
Amdo	A mdo
babshi lékung	'bab zhib las khung
Bathang	'Ba' thang
Baxi Kenpo	Baxi mkhan po
Beri	Be ri
Bodong gangjong	Bo gdong gangs ljongs
bokawa	'bo kha ba
bokdépa	bogs lded pa
bö ki dönchö	bod gyi don gcod
bö ki gyalpo	bod kyi rgyal po
Brempa	'grems pa
Brönché	gron che
Brum gasha	Brum dGa' sha
bukdam gochen	sbug dam 'go mchan
Cagzam	lCags zam
cakzö	phyag mdzod
cakzöpa	phyag mdzod pa
camdekpa	byams 'degs pa
cansel	spyan bsal
Cenlung	gCen lung
chabsu tsédrung	chab bsu rtse drung
chadrel zhelno cawo	chab drel zhal ngo skya bo
Chamdo	Chab mdo
Champa Tendar	Byams pa bsTan dar
Changchub Gyeltsen	Byang chub rGyal mtshan
Changkya Hutuktu	lCang skya ho thog tu
Changthang	Byang thang
Charané	sByar ra nas
Chenrézi	sPyan ras gzigs
chipön chenmo	chibs dpon chen mo
chira lékung	chibs ra las khung
chökyong	chos skyong
chöné	mchod gnas
Chöpel (Kachen)	Chos 'phel
Chöpel Thubten	Chos 'phel Thub bstan
chöpön kenpo	mchod dpon mkhan po

chöyön	mchod yon
chözengpa	mchod bzhengs pa
Chugoringmo	Chu go ring mo
chuma	chu ma
chyakpe zhudakpa	phyag dpe zhus dag pa
cibgyurdzé	chibs brgyur mdzad
cidzong	spyi rdzong
cikyab	spyi khyab
cinko raluktsa shak	dbyin mkho ra lug rtsa gshag
Coné	Co ne
cushok	bcu shog
Dakpo	Dwags po
Dakpo Rinpoche	Dwags po rin po che
Dalai Lama	Tâ la'i bla ma
da lama	da'a bla ma
Dam	'Dam
Damchö Tsomo	Dam chos mTsho mo
Damchö Yarpèl	Dam chos Yar 'phel
Dangchenwe Tsédor	mDangs chen ba'i rTse rdor
dapön	mda' dpon
Dargyé	Dar rgyas
Dartsédo	Dar rtse mdo
dechangpa	lde chang pa
Déchen Kelzang	bDe chen sKal bzang
Déchen Rabgyé	bDe chen Rab rgyas
Dékilingka	bDe skyid gling ga
Demo Hutuktu	De mo ho thog thu
dépa	sde pa
dépala	sde pa lags
dépön	sde dpon
Dergé	sDe dge
dési	sde srid
Dingkyé Rinpoche	sDing skyes rin po che
Dingri	Ding ri
dingshok	lding shog
Dingwang Dorjé	sDings dbang rDo rje
Dongkar	gDong dkar
Dongkar dangchen	gDong dkar mdangs chen
Dönkhang Kelzang Dékyi	Don khang sKal bzang bDe skyid
Dönyö Gyeltsen	Don yod rGyal mtshan
Doring Taiji	rDo ring Taiji
Dorjé	rDo rje

Dorjé Tsipa	rDo rje rTsis pa
Dorling	rDor gling
Dragkü	Brag khud
drangchöpa	brang mchod pa
Drékang Khenchen Lozang Tenzin	'Bras khang mkhan chen Blo bzang bstan 'dzin
Drépung	'Bras spungs
drokpa	'brog pa
Drölma	Sgrol ma
Drongshö Drung Phurbu Tsering	'Brong shod drung Phur bu Tshe ring
Drongtséba	'Brong rtse ba
Drongtséba Sengchen Tulku Lozang Pelden Chöpel	'Brong rtse ba Seng chen sprul sku bLo bzang dPal ldan Chos 'phel
Drongtsé chöde tarpa lingön	'Brong rtse chos sde thar pa gling dgon
drönyer	mgron gnyer
drönyer chenmo	gron gnyer chen mo
Drubkhang Rinpoche	sGrub khang rin po che
Drubrultsang	Gru brul tshang
Drugpa Hutuktu	'Brug pa ho thog thu
Drugyal Lozang Rinchen	'Brug rgyal bLo bzang Rin chen
drungche kushön	drung che sku gzhon
drungchen	drung chen
drungyik	drung yig
drungyik chenmo	drung yig chen mo
dul	'dul
Dzayül	rDza yul
dzong	Rdzong
Dzongka	rDzong kha
dzongkyel	rdzong skyel
dzongpön	rdzong dpon
Engön	dBen dgon
Ensapa Lozang Döndrub	dBen sa pa Blo bzang Don grub
Gampa	Gam pa
Gampasharmé	Gam pa shar smad
Ganden	dGa' ldan
Ganden chöling püntsok gön	dGa' ldan chos gling phun tshogs dgon
Ganden Podrang	dGa' ldan pho brang
Ganden Tönpo	dGa' ldan mthon po
Ganden Tri Rinpoche	dGa' ldan khri rin po che
Gara Lama	mGar ra bla ma
Garapa Chöken Penkangwang	dGa' rab pa mchod mkhan phan khang dbang

garpa	gar pa
Gartok	sGar thog
Gédun Drub	dGe 'dun Grub
Gédun Gyatso	dGe 'dun rGya mtsho
Gédun Rabgyé	dGe 'dun Rab rgyas
Gédun Tashi	dGe 'dun bKra shis
gélong	dge slong
Gélukpa	dGe lugs pa
gényen	dge bsnyen
gepa	gad pa
Gépèl Kangzang	dGe 'phel Khang bzang
géshé	dge bshes
Géshé Dorjé Tsipa	dGe bshes rDo rje rTsis pa
géshé larampa	dge bshes lha rams pa
gétsul	dge tshul
Gö Kugpa Latsé	'Gos Khug pa Lhas btsas
Golok	mGo log
Gomang	sGo mang
Gromo	Gro mo
grönyer	gron gnyer
Gugé	Gu ge
gurpa	gur pa
gyadrung	rgya drung
Gyamda	rGya mda'
Gyangdochö	Gyang mdo chos
gyashok	brgya shog
gyelchak légyor	rgyal phag las gyor
Gyelchen	rGyal chen
Gyelchung	rGyal chung
gyelkap kyongwé gégen chenpo gyeltsen yongkidagpo tamcé khyenpa	rgyal khab skyong ba'i dge rgan chen po rgyal btsan yongs kyi bdag po thams cad mkhyen pa
gyelkyop tenpel kunkhyen lopön chenpo	rgyal skyob bstan spel kun mkhyen slob dpon chen po
gyelpak léyor	rgyal phag las gyor
gyelpötsap	rgyal po'i tshab
Gyeltsab Darma Rinchen	rGyal tshab Dar ma rin chen
Gyeltsab Tatsag Rinpoche	rGyal tshab rTa tshag rin po che
Gyeltsé	rGyal rtse
Gyeltsen Tönpo	rGyal mtshan mthon po
Gyengyéthang	rGyan gya'i thang
Gyurmé Namgyel	'Gyur med rNam rgyal

Hor	Hor
Jamchen Chöje Shakya Yéshé	'Jam chen chos rje sha kya ye shes
Jampel Drakpa	'Jam dpal grags pa
Jampel Gyatso	'Jam dpal rGya mtsho
Jangpa Chöwang	'Byang pa Chos dbang
Jangpa Thubten	Byang pa Thub bstan
Jédrung	rJe drung
Jétsun Dampa	rJe bstun Dam pa
Jigme Chyungnébépa	'Jigs med 'Byung gnas sBas pa
Jigme Wangchuk	'Jigs med dBang phyug
Jokhang	Jo khang
kachen	dka' chen
Kagyüpa	bKa brgyud pa
Kailash	Gang rin po che
kalön	bka' blon
Kangwa Dzong	rKang ba rdzong
Kardzé	dKar mdzes
Karma Kagyüpa	Kar ma bka brgyud pa
Karmapa	Kar ma pa
Karma Püntsok Namgyel	Kar ma Phun tshogs rNam rgyal
Karma Tenkyong Wangpo	Kar ma bsTan skyong dbang po
Karma Tensung Wangpo	Kar ma bsTan srung dBang po
Kasha	Ka sha
kashag	bka' shag
kashok	bka' shog
Kédrub Gélèk Namgyel Pelzang	mKhas grub dge legs rNam rgyal dPal bzang
Kédrub Gélèk Pelzang	mKhas grub dGe legs dPal bzang
Kédrub Gyatso	mKhas grub rGya mtsho
Kédrub Sangyé Yéshé	mKhas grub Sangs rgyas Ye shes
kel	khal
Kelzang Chönjor (aka Liu Jiaju)	sKal bzang Chos 'byor
Kelzang Gyatso	sKal bzang rgya mtsho
Kenbrön Chesa Lungpa	mkhan mgron Che sa Lung pa
kenchen	mkhan chen
kenchung	mkhan chung
kenpo	mkhan po
Kétsang Rinpoche	sKed tshang rin po che
Kham	Khams
Khampa	Khams pa
Khangchené	Khang chen nas
kharu	mkhar ru
Khyungram	Khyung ram

kitsèr	skyi 'tsher
Köncho Chungné	dKon mchog 'byung gnas
Kongpo	rKong po
Korlam	'Khor lam
korlö gyurwe gyelpo	'khor los sgyur ba'i rgyal po
kucar	sku bcar
kudung	sku gdung
Kugo Ngawang Riktröl	sku sngo Ngag dbang Rig 'khrol
kuker dratsang	sku sger grwa tshang
Kumbum	sKu 'bum
Kundeling	Kun bde gling
Kungyabling	Kun skyab gling
Kunzang Norbu	Kun bzang nor bu
kunzik podrang	kun gzigs pho brang
Kyabjé Dzépa Rinpoche	sKyabs rje mDzes pa rin po che
Kyabjé Zhelzang Rinpoche	sKyabs rje Zhal bzang rin po che
kya bro	skyabs 'gro
kyabying dzasa lama	skyabs dbyings rdza sags bla ma
Kyégudo	sKye rgu mdo
Kyégu döndrubling	sKye rgu'i don grub gling
Kyilkang Lèkshéling	dKyil khang Legs bshad gling
Kyirong	sKyid rong
Kyitseluding	sKyid tshal klu sding
kyi tser	skyi 'tsher
labrang	bla brang
labrang cakzö	bla brang phyag mdzod
Labrang trashikhyil	Bla brang bkra shis 'khyil
labrang yiktsang	bla brang yig tshang
Labzang Tadul	Zla bzang dgra'dul
Lakpa Dorjé	lHag pa rDo rje
lakto	lag to
lakyok	lag g.yog
lama	bla ma
lamenpa	bla sman pa
Lamo	La mo
lamtok	lam thog
lamyik	lam yig
Langdun	gLang mdun
Langtongwa	gLang mthong pa
lécadrungrik	las bya drung rigs
Lekden jé	Legs ldan bjed
Lèn	lHan

Lènlunrab	Lhan lhun rab
létsenpa	las tshan pa
Léu	sLe'u
Lhasa	lHa sa
Lhatsé	lHa rtse
Lhazang Khan	Lha bzang khan
Lhokha	Lho kha
Litang	Li thang
lobur cölthab tagur	glo bur 'byol thabs lta gur
Lodrö Gyeltsen	Blo gros rGyal mtshan
lokar pel né jikten penpa	blo dkar spel nas 'djig rten phan pa
lönchen	blon chen
lopön	slob dpon
Lozang Chögyen	Blo bzang Chos rgyan
Lozang Chöki Gyeltsen	Blo bzang chos kyi rGyal mtshan
Lozang Chöki Nyima Gélèk Namgyel	Blo bzang Chos kyi Nyi ma dGe legs rNam rgyal
Lozang Chöki Nyima Gélèk Nampar Gyelwa Pelzangpo	Blo bzang Chos kyi Nyi ma dGe legs rNam par rGyal ba dPal bzang po
Lozang Döndrub	Blo bzang Don grub
Lozang Dorjé	Blo bzang rDo rje
Lozang Gyatso	Blo bzang rGya mtsho
Lozang Gyeltsen	Blo bzang rGyal mtshan
Lozang Pelden Chöki Dragpa Tenpé Wangchuk	Blo bzang dPal ldan Chos kyi Grags pa bsTan pa'i dBang phyug
Lozang Pelden Yéshé	Blo bzang dPal ldan Ye shes
Lozang Tashi	Blo bzang bKra shis
Lozang Tenpé Nyima	Blo bzang bsTan pa'i Nyi ma
Lozang Tenzin	Blo bzang bsTan 'dzin
Lozang Thubten	Blo bzang Thub bstan
Lozang Thutob	Blo bzang mThu stobs
Lozang Trinlé	Blo bzang 'Phrin las
Lozang Trinlé Lundrub Chöki Gyeltsen	Blo bzang 'Phrin las Lhun grub Chos kyi rGyal mtshan
Lozang Tsültrim	Blo bzang Tshul khrims
Lozang Yéshé	Blo bzang Ye shes
Lozang Yönten	Blo bzang Yon tan
Lukdong	Lug gdong
Lumpané	Lum pa nas
Lungrik Gyatso	Lung rigs rGya mtsho
Lungshar	Lung shar
Lungtok Gyatso	Lung rtogs rGya mtsho

machen	ma chen
machen tsédrung létsenpa	ma chen rtse drung las tshan pa
makang	dmag rkang
makchok	dmag phogs
makdön	dmag don
Makpönri	dMag dpon ri
Mangyül	Mang yul
Méru Lozang Gyeltsen	rMe ru Blo bzang rGyal mtshan
Muchawa	Mu bya ba
Nadong	sNa gdong
Nagchuka	Nag chu ka
Nakartsé	sNa dkar rtse
Nakchu	Nag chu
Nam	rNam
namcu wangden	rnam bcu dbang ldan
Namling	rNam gling
namo guru	na mo gu ru
Namring	Ngam ring
namsé gendzö	rnams sras gan mdzod
namtar	rnam thar
nangkang yiktsang	nang sgang yig tshang
Narthang	sNar thang
nazagang	na bza' sgang
Nenying Chöjé Chöki Gyeltsen	Gnas rnying Chos rje Chos kyi rGyal mtshan
Ngachen Darba Hutuktu (aka Ngachen Rinpoche)	sNgags chen bDar pa ho thog thu
Ngachen Létog Lopa	sNgags chen Las thog Lho pa
Ngachö	lNga mchod
ngapa dratsang	sngags pa grwa tshang
Ngapa Lama	sNgags pa bla ma
Ngaphöpé Dorjé Gyelpo	Nga phod pas rDo rje rGyal po
Ngari	mNga' ris
ngarluk tentsik	sngar lugs gtan tshigs
Ngawang Cinpa	Ngag dbang sByin pa
Ngawang Gyeltsen	Ngag dbang rGyal mtshan
Ngawang Lozang Chöden	Ngag dbang bLo bzang Chos ldan
Ngawang Lozang Gyatso	Ngag dbang Blo bzang rGya mtsho
Ngawang Lozang Tenpé Gyeltsen	Ngag dbang Blo bzang bsTan pa'i rGyal mtshan
Ngawang Lozang Trinlé Rabgyé (Demo Hutuktu)	Ngag dbang Blo bzangs 'Phrin las Rab rgyas

Norbulingka	Nor bu gling kha
nubcok kyongwé gégen chenmo	nub phyogs skyongs ba'i dge rgan chen mo
nubtha tenpel phonya chenmo	nub mtha'a bstan spel pho nya chen mo
Nyanang	gNya' nang
Nyarong	Nyag rong
nyerdrung	gnyer drung
nyerpa	gnyer pa
Nyingmapa	rNying ma pa
nyökhang	nyo khang
Ögyen Gyatso	O rgyan rGya mtsho
Öpamé	Od dpag med
Öyug	'Od yug
Özer Dorjé	'Od zer rDo rje
Pagrong	Phag grong
Panam	Pa snam
Panchen Lama	Pan chen bla ma
Panyangtön Damchö Yarphel	Pa nyang ston Dam chos Yar 'phel
Panyangtön Lhawang Logrö	Pa nyang ston Lha dbang bLo gros
Paphyuk Zhungpa Sönam Gyeltsen	Pa phyug gZhung pa bSod nams rGyal mtshan
Parkang Gyeltsen Püntsok	Par khang rGyal mtshan Phun tshog
parpön	par dpon
Pashangtön Chöpel Gyatso	Pa shangs ston Chos dpal rGyal mtsho
Pashangtön Logrö Lekzang	Pa shangs ston bLo gros Legs bzang
Pashangtön Samdrub Pelzang	Pa shangs ston bSam grub dPal bzang
Pékar Zinpa	Pad dkar 'dZin pa
Pelden Takar Pungpa	dPal ldan 'bras dkar spungs pa
Phabongka Rinpoche	Pha bong kha rin po che
Phakpa Lobrö Gyeltsen	'Phags pa bLo gros rGyal mtshan
Phakri	Phag ri
phebcamgopa	phebs byams 'go pa
phep	phebs
Pholhané Sönam Tobgyé	Pho lha nas bSod nams sTobs rgyas
phreldé cakzö	'phral bde phyag mdzod
Phüntsoling	Phun tshogs gling
Phyongyépa Pèljor Zangpo	'Phyongs rgyas pa dPal 'byor bZang po
Pö	spos
Pome	sPo smad
Potala	Po ta la
Potowa	Po to pa
Püntsok Thubten	Phun tshog Thub bstan
Purang	sPu rangs

Purchok Yongdzin Tulku	Phur lcog Yongs 'dzin sprul sku
Pureng	sPu hreng
Rabjor	Rab 'byor
Rabshilungshö ganden chökorling	Rab shis glung shod dga' ldan chos 'khor gling
Ragya gön	Rwa rgya dgon
Ralung	Ra lung
Ramding	Ram lding
Rampa Sönam Gonkyab	Ram pa bSod rnams mGon skyabs
Reting Rinpoche	Rwa sgreng rin po che
Rimshi Tadrin	rim bzhi rTa mgrin
Rinchentsé	Rin chen rtse
Rinchen Wangdü	Rin chen dBang 'dus
Rinpung	Rin spungs
Riwoché	Ri bo che
Rongshar	Rong shar
Rongsum	Rong gsum
Rongtso	Rong 'tsho
rupön	ru dpon
rushok	ru shog
sadzong lamtok	sa rdzong lam thog
Sagampa	Sa gam pa
Sakyapa	Sa skya pa
Sakya Paṇḍita Kunga Gyeltsen	Sa skya Paṇḍita Kun dga' rGyal mtshan
Samdrub Gyatso	bSam grub rGya mtsho
Samdrub Podrang	bSam grub Pho brang
Samdrubtsé	bSam 'grub rtse
Samkhar Ngawang Shényen	bSam mkhar Ngag dbang bShes gnyen
Samlo	Sam blo
sang	srang
sangcölcé	gsangs 'byol byes
sangpheb	gsangs phebs
Sangyé Gyatso	Sangs rgyas rGya mtsho
Sangyé Menla	sangs rgyas sman bla
Sanpa	San pa
Sarchyung Tséten Wangchuk Dorjé	gSar byung Tshe brtan dBang phyug rDo rje
satsik	sa tshigs
Sengchen Tulku	Seng chen sprul sku
Sera	Se ra
Shab	Zhab
Shakabpa Wangchuk Deden	Zhwa sgab pa dBang phyug bDe ldan

shakpa	shag pa
Shamar Tulku	Zhwa dmar sprul sku
Shang Ganden Rabgyé	Shang dGa' ldan Rab rgyas
Shangkun Rinpoche	Shang kun rin po che
Shar	Shar
Shartsé Samtènling	Shar rtse bSam gtan ling
Shé	bZhas
shébam	she bam
Shédra Peljor Dorjé	bShad sgra dPal 'byor rDo rje
Shérab Senggé	Shes rab Seng ge
Shétongmön shimükang	bZhad mthong smon gzhis mus khang
Shigatse	gZhis ka rtse
shika	gzhis ka
shikachung	gzhis ka chung
Shikasamdrubtsé	gZhis ka bsam grub rtse
shinglen tapyok	shing len thab g.yog
shö	Shod
shökor lekung	shod skor las khung
sikyong	srid skyong
silön	srid blon
sisum namgyel ling	srid gsum rnam rgyal gling
söldek tsedrung létsenpa	gsol 'degs rtse drung las tshan pa
sölpön kenpo	gsol dpon mkhan po
söltap	gsol thab
söltap lakyok drapa	gsol thab lag g.yog grwa pa
söltap tsédrung	gsol thab rtse drung
söltrum jakmin gopa	gsol dkrum ljags smin 'go pa
sölwa	gsol ba
Sönam Chöki Langpo	bSod nams Phyogs kyi gLang po
Sönam Gyatso	bSod nams rGya mtsho
Sönam Rabten	bSod nams Rab brtan
sungbum	gsung 'bum
Surkhang Wangchen Tséten	Zur khang dBang chen Tshe brtan
Tadrin	rTa mgrin
Tanak Rinchentsé	rTa nag Rin chen rtse
Tashi Dzong	bKra shis rdzong
Tashi Lama	bKra shis bla ma
Tashilhunpo	bKra shis lhun po
Tengyeling	bsTan rgyas gling
Tenpa Dargyé	bsTanpa Dar rgyas
Tenzin Chödrak	bsTan 'dzin Chos grags
Tenzin Dalé Gyelpo	bsTan 'dzin Da la'i rGyal po

Tenzin Gédun Yéshé Trinlé Püntsok	bsTan 'dzin dGe 'dun Ye shes 'Phrin las Phun tshogs
Tenzin Gyatso	bsTan 'dzin rGya mtsho
thangka	thang ka
Thösam Norbuling	Thos bsam Nor bu gling
Thubten Gyatso	Thub bstan rGya mtsho
Thubten Sangyé	Thub bstan Sangs rgyas
Thubthob Namgyel	Thub thob rNam rgyal
Thubzang Norbu	Thub bzang Nor bu
Tobgyel	Thob rgyal
Tobshi	Thob gzhis
Tökul dzong	sTod khul rdzong
Trimön Norbu Wangyel	Khri smon Nor bu dBang rgyal
Trinlé Gyatso	'Phrin las rGya mtsho
trugépa	bkru gad pa
tsampa	rtsam pa
Tsang	gTsang
Tsangchen tchuwo	gTsang chen chu bo
Tsangkul dzong	gTsang khul rdzong
Tsangyang Gyatso	Tshang dbyang rGya mtsho
Tsar	Tshar
Tsari	rTsa ri
Tsarong Shape	Tsha rong zhabs pad
Tsarong Wangchuk Gyelpo	Tsha rong dBang phyug rGyal po
Tsaserkhang	Tsaserkhang
tsatsik	rtsa tshig
Tsé	rTse
Tséchokling Rinpoche	rTse mchog gling rin po che
tséchyak lékung	rtse phyag las khung
Tsédong	rTse gdong
tsédrung	rtse drung
tségön khangpa	rtse mgon khang pa
Tségrön	rTse mgron
tsékor lékung	rtse skor las khung
Tsemön(ling)	Tshes mon(gling)
Tsémönling Ngawang Jampel Tsültrim	Tshe smon gling Ngag dbang 'Jam dpal Tshul khrims
tsenzhab	mtshan zhabs
tsenzhapa	mtshan zhabs pa
Tsépamé	Tshe dpag med
tséshö söltap	rtse shod gsol thab
Tséwang Rabten	Tshe dbang Rab brtan

tshokchen	tshogs chen
Tsogo	mTsho sgo
tsokdu	tshogs 'du
Tsolo	mTsho lho
Tsongdü	Tshong 'dus
Tsongkapa	Tsong kha pa
Tsültrim Gyatso	Tshul khrims rGya mtsho
Tsültrim Tenzin	Tshul khrims bsTan 'dzin
Tukwen Rinpoche	Thu'u bkwan rin po che
tulku	sprul sku
Ü	dBus
uchen	dbu chan
Udzin Zimche Debrangpa Purbu Tsering	'bu 'dzin gzim che bDe brang pa Phur bu Tshe ring
Ugyen Wangchuk	U rgyan dBang phyug
Ukpalung	Ug pa lung
ulag	u'lag
umé	dbu med
Wangchen	dBang chen
Wangchenwa Tsédor	mDangs chen ba'i rTse rdor
Wangdü Norbu	dBang 'dus Nor bu
Yarbrok	Yar 'brog
Yarbroktso	Yar 'brog mtsho
Yarlung	Yar klungs
Yatung	Cho mo
Yéshé Dorjé	Ye shes rDo rje
Yéshé Tsémo	Ye shes rTse mo
Yéshé Tséten	Ye shes Tshe brtan
Yikbri	yig 'bri
yiktsang gégen	yig tshang dge rgan
yiktsang kunyer	yig tshang sku gnyer
yiktsang leca drungrik serkya	yig tshang las bya drung rigs ser skya
yikyelpa	yig skyel pa
yönchö	yon mchod
yöndag	yon bdag
yongdzin	yong 'dzin
Yönten Gyatso	Yon tan rGya mtsho
Yungtön Trogyel Dorjépel	gYung ston khro rgyal rDo rje dpal
Zala Nominhan Lozang Döndrub	rdza bla no min han Blo bzang Don grub
Zangpo Tashi	bZang po bKra shis
zen	zan
zenpa kyano	gzan pa skya ngo

zhékar laktselpa drapa	gzhes bsgar lag rtsal pa grwa pa
zhetsel jakmin gopa	bzhes tshal ljags smin 'go pa
zhibgyel gopa	zhib rgyal 'go pa
zhibzöpa	zhib rdzog pa
Zhideling	Zhi bde gling
zhinglenpa kyawo	zhing len pa skya bo
zho	zho
zhung ten pel	gzhung bstan spel
zimchungkak	gzim chung 'gag
zimkak tripa	gzim 'gag khri pa
zimpön kenpo	gzim dpon mkhan po
Zurbuk	Zur sbug

APPENDIX H

CHINESE SINOGRAPHY

Bailing miao	白靈廟
Banchan banshichu	班禪辦事處
Banchan da shi ni jiang lai Hua	班禪大師擬將來華
Banchan da shi zhisang chu	班禪大師治喪處
Banchan E'erdeni	班禪額爾德尼
Banchan zhu Jing banshichu	班禪駐京辦事處
Bangong	辦公
Baotou	包頭
Beile	貝勒
Beiping mi Zang yuan	北平密藏院
Beizi	貝子
bianwei si	邊衛司
bianwu bu	邊務部
Canshi	參事
canyi ting	參議廳
Cao Kun	曹昆
Cejuelin huofo	策覺霖活佛
Chahar	察哈爾
Changchun	長春
Chan zong	禪宗
Chaoyi	超一
Chaozang si	朝藏寺
Chen Daqi	陳大齊
Chengdu	成都
Cheng Yun	誠允
Chen Wenjian	陳文監
Chen Yisun	沉艾孫
Chiang Kai-shek (Jiang Jieshi)	蔣介石
Chongqing	重慶
Cixi, Empress Dowager	慈禧太后
Dagong bao	大公報
Daibeng	戴琫
Dai Jitao	戴季陶
Dazhouni Zhong Sulang	大卓尼鐘蘇郎
da zongtong	大總統
Dengke	鄧柯
Dianluoyun	滇洛雲

Dianshu si 典屬司
difang zizhi 地方自治
difang zizhi qu 地方自治區
dingbeng 定琫
Duan Hongye 段宏業
Duan Qirui 段祺瑞
Duojie Jueba 多傑覺巴
Fafang 法舫
Fang Fanjiu 芳範九
Fazhi weiyuanhui 法制委員會
Fazun 法尊
fei wuzhuang qu 非武裝區
Fengtian 奉天
Feng Yangshan 馮仰山
Feng Yuxiang 馮玉祥
fu doutong 副都統
Fuguo gong 輔國公
Fukang'an 福康安
Fu Mingtai 富明泰
Fuyou si 福佑寺
fu zongcai 副總裁
Fu Zuoyi 傅作義
Gajin Qingpi 噶金傾批
Gangjin 崗金
Gansu 甘肅
Ganzhou 甘州
Gao Erdeng 高爾鄧
Gao Zhangzhu 高長柱
gongshu 公署
Gong Xinzhan 龔心湛
guanding pushan guangci 灌頂普善廣慈
Guangxu 光绪
gulu bai 骨魯拜
Guo Daofu 郭道甫
Guojia 國家
Guominhuiyi 國民會義
Guomin zhengfu weiyuan 國民政府委員
guowu zongli 國務總理
Guwen 顧問
Guyuan 雇員
Hangzhou 杭州
Heilongjiang 黑龍江

Hohhot	呼和浩特
hong ji guangming	宏濟光明
Hou Zang	後藏
Huang Musong	黃慕松
Huang Shaohong	黃紹竑
Huang si	黃寺
Huang Zunxian	黃遵憲
Huayan zong	華嚴宗
Huguo xuanhua guanghui da shi	護國宣化光慧大師
Huguo xuanhua guanghui yuanjue da shi	護國宣化廣慧圓覺大師
Hui	回
Hu Jingyi	胡京翼
Husong Banchan hui Zang zhuanshi	護送班禪回藏專使
Jalangga	查郎阿
Jehol	熱河
jiabeng	甲琫
Jiangsu	江蘇
Jiangxi	江西
Jiang Zhiyu	蔣致余
Jiaotou bao	穚頭堡
Jilin	吉林
Jingtu zong	淨土宗
Jundui	軍隊
junzheng	軍政
Kang ren zhi Kang	康人治康
Kang Zang xuefa tuan	康藏學法團
Kang Zang yuebao	康藏月報
Kongsa Deqinwangmu	孔薩德欽汪姆
Kuomintang (Guomindang)	國民黨
La Duhun	拉都渾
Laiyuan si	徠遠司
Lajia si	拉家寺 or 拉加寺
Lanzhou	蘭州
Leitan	雷壇
Liangzhou	涼州
Lian Yu	聯豫
Liaodong	遼東
Liaoning	遼寧
Li fan yuan	理藩院
Li Jinzhong	李金鐘
Li Shaobai	李少白
Lingcheng	靈櫬

Lingyin si	靈隱寺
Lin Sen	林森
Liu Deng	劉澄
Liu Jiaju (aka Kelzang Chönjor)	劉家駒
Liu Piaocheng	劉朴忱
Liu Wenhui	劉文輝
Lixing si	理刑司
Li Zongren	李宗仁
Longchang si	隆昌寺
Longxi si	龍喜寺
Lou Youren	羅友仁
Lu Entai	陸恩泰
Lu Hongtao	陸洪濤
Luo Junxia	羅君俠
Luo Zongjia	羅宗嘉
Lu Yongxiang	盧永祥
Lu Zhenhua	陸鎮華
Lü zong	律宗
Ma Bufang	馬步芳
Mage	瑪 格
Ma Hetian	馬鶴天
Ma Hongkui	馬鴻逵
Mailu	邁祿
Mala	瑪拉
Man	满
Ma Qi	馬麒
Meng	蒙
Menggu ge meng qi lianhe zhu Jing banshichu	蒙古各盟旗聯合駐京辦事處
Menggu jiuji hui	蒙古救濟會
Menggu meng bu qi zuzhi fa	蒙古盟部旗組織法
Menggu zhu Jing banshichu	蒙古駐京辦事處
Meng min daibiao huiyi	盟民代表會議
Meng qi xuanhua shi	蒙旗宣化使
Meng Zang bu	蒙藏部
Meng Zang jiaoyu weiyuanhui	蒙藏教育委員會
Meng Zang shibao	蒙藏適報
Meng Zang shiwu chu	蒙藏事務處
Meng Zang shiwu ju	蒙藏事務局
Meng Zang weiyuanhui	蒙藏委員會
Meng Zang xueyuan	蒙藏學院
Meng Zang yuan	蒙藏院
Meng Zang yuebao	蒙藏月報

Meng Zang yuekan	蒙藏月刊
minquan zhuyi	民權主義
minsheng zhuyi	民生主義
minzu	民族
minzu tuanjie	民族團結
minzu zhuyi	民族主義
misheng xuehui	密乘學會
Nadang	納當
Nanchang	南昌
Nanjing	南京
neibu	內部
neige xueshi	內閣學士
Nei Menggu zizhi yundong	內蒙古自治運動
Nei Wai Meng lü Ping tongxiang hui	內外蒙旅平同鄉會
neiwu bu	內務部
neiwu zongzhang	內務總長
Nenghai	能海
Ningxia	寧夏
Ningyuan	寧遠
Nuona Lama	諾那喇嘛
Pingfan	平番
Pukou	浦口
Puti xuehui	普提學會
Puyi	溥儀
Qian Zang	前藏
Qiji si	旗籍司
Qin	秦
Qing	清
Qinghai	青海
Qishan	琦善
Qi Xieyuan	齊燮元
Qu Wenliu	屈文六
Rouyuan si	柔遠司
rubeng	如琫
Sengge	僧格
Shanghai	上海
shanhou huiyi	善後會義
Shanxi	山西
Shi Huayan	石華嚴
Shi Qingyang	石青陽
Shunzhi	順治
Suiyuan	綏遠

Sun Chuanfang	孫傳芳
Sun Yat-sen (Sun Zhongshan)	孫中山
Suohe	索河
Taihe dian	太和殿
Taixu	太虛
Taiyuan	太原
Tang Kesan	唐柯三
Tianchi	天池
Tianjin	天津
Tiantai zong	天太宗
Tuguan Hutuktu	土官呼圖克圖
waijiaobu	外交部
Wanghui si	王會司
Wangjie suoma si	王結所瑪寺
Wang Jingwei	汪精衛
Wang Xiaoji	王曉籍
Wang Yiting	王一亭
Wang Yongbin	王用賓
weiren	委任
Wenshi	文碩
Wuhan	武漢
Wu Peifu	吳佩孚
Wutai shan	五太山
Wu Tiecheng	吳鐵城
Wu Zhongxin	吳忠信
wuzu gonghe	五族共和
Xia Chao	夏超
Xi'an	西安
Xiang'erde	香爾德
Xianggen fo	香根佛
Xiangride	香日德
xiantian	先天
Xichui xuanhua shi	西陲宣化使
Xichui xuanhua shi gongshu yuekan	西陲宣化使公署月刊
Xiejian	謝兼
Xikang	西康
Xing'an	興安
xingshu	行署
xingyuan	行院
xingyuan	行轅
Xining	西寧
Xinjiang	新疆

Xiong Yaowen	熊耀文
Xuan cheng ji shi	宣誠濟世
xuanhua suijiang	宣化綏疆
Xumi fushou miao	須彌福壽廟
Xu Mo	徐謨
xunzheng	巡政
Xu Tiefeng	許鐵峰
Xu Xiaotian	許嘯天
Yang Wenhui	楊文會
Yanxin	延信
Yan Xishan	閻錫山
yifa gongshun han	翌法恭順汗
yi lü pingdeng	一律平等
Yingtai	瀛台
Yinguang	印光
Yixi Duoji	益西多吉
yizhangdui	儀仗隊
Yonghe gong	雍和宮
Yongzheng	雍正
Youtai	有泰
Yuan	元
Yuan Shikai	袁世凱
Yunli	允禮
Yunnan	雲南
Yushu	玉樹
Zang	藏
Zangqing dahe	藏青大河
Zhangjia Hutuktu	章嘉呼圖克圖
Zhang Jialin	章家麟
Zhang Xueliang	張學良
Zhang Yintang	張蔭棠
Zhang Zongchang	張宗昌
Zhang Zuolin	張作霖
zhanshe	暫攝
Zhao Erfeng	趙爾豐
Zhao Pilian	趙丕廉
Zhao Shouyu	趙守鈺
Zhao Yanwu	趙炎午
zhaoyin chanhua	召因闡化
Zhejiang	浙江
zhengshi zizhi huiyi	正式自治會義
zhengwu ting	政務廳

zhenshoushi	甘邊寧海鎮守使
Zhi Chan si	殖產司
zhiji	致祭
Zhili	直隶
Zhizhong chanhua	致忠闡化
Zhonghua minguo xunzheng shiqi yuefa	中華民國巡政時期約法
Zhonghua minzu	中華民族
Zhong Ri mijiao yanjiu hui	中日密教研究會
Zhongyang ribao	中央日報
Zhu Funan	朱福南
Zhu Minyi	褚民誼
zhu Qing Kang Zang san bian shichu	西陲宣化使公署駐青康藏三邊事處
zhushi	主事
zhu Zang da chen	駐藏大臣
zizhi zhengfu zuzhi dagang	自治政府組職大綱
zongcai	總裁

NOTES

PREFACE

1. Shakya, *Dragon in the Land of Snows*, 440–47; Jagou, "The Use of the Ritual of Drawing Lots," forthcoming.

2. Jagou, "Une histoire politique du Tibet."

3. Mehra, *Tibetan Polity*; Ya Hanzhang, *Banchan E'erdeni zhuan*; Guo Qing, "Brief Account of the Ninth Panchen Erdeni," 70–82; Goldstein, "A History of Modern Tibet."

4. D. Macdonald, *Twenty Years in Tibet*; Hedin, *Trans-Himalaya*.

5. Jiang Ping, Li Zuomin, and Song Yingting, "Di jiu shi Banchan E'erdeni Quji nima pingzhuan," 12–25; Shi Dongchu, *Zhongguo fojiao jindai shi*.

6. Skinner, *Modern Chinese Society*; Cordier, *Bibliotheca Sinica*; Kuloy and Imaeda, *Bibliography of Tibetan Studies*; Yoshimizu, *Descriptive Catalogue*.

7. This volume of archives is entitled *Waijiao bu* [Ministry of Foreign Affairs] because it contains documents from the end of the Qing to the beginning of the Republic. In reality, it was only in 1912 that the *Waiwu bu* [Foreign Office] became *Waijiao bu*.

8. Chandra, *History of Tibetan Literature*.

9. The current director of the Densapa Library, Lokesh Chandra, confirmed this information in a letter to me, dated March 20, 1995.

10. See Shakya and Tashilhunpo Monastery Historical Research Committee, *sKyabs mgon thams cad mkhyen pa Blo bzang Thub bstan Chos kyi Nyi ma*, 1996, vol. 1, parts 1 and 2, fols. 601–4, 833, 836. This edition was scanned by the Tibetan Buddhist Resource Center in 2003 from a reproduction of the text printed in Tashilhunpo.

11. For a presentation of this work, see Jagou, "Les biographies de maîtres tibétains," 277–82.

12. Tuttle, "Review of *Le 9e Panchen Lama*."

13. lHa mkhar yongs 'dzin bsTan pa rGyal mtshan, *sKyabs mgon rje btsun bla ma Blo bzang Thub bstan Chos kyi Nyi ma*.

14. For further information on *Melong*, see Engelhardt, "Tharchin's Yul-phyogs so-so'i gsar-'gyur me-loṅ."

15. bSam pho bsTan 'dzin Don grub, *Shes bya*, June 1988.

PROLOGUE

1. On the lineage numeration of the Panchen Lamas, see Appendix A.

2. On Lungshar (1881–1940), see Lha klu Tshe dbang rDo rje, "Nga'i pha Lung shar rDo rje Tshe rgyal dran gso byas pa," 93–109; Lhalu Tséwang Dorjé, "Lungshar, My Father," 163–72; Tang Hongbo, "Longxia yu Longxia shijian," 140–47. On Tsogo, see IOR, L/P&S/12/4185 A, Who's Who in Tibet, 76, entry Tso-Ko I; Petech, *Aristocracy and Government in Tibet*, 138–41.

3. The Tibetan reads: "Nga tsho'i lha ma lha red, Lha ma'i chibs pa bya red, Bya la gser sga sgron nas, Nam mkha' dbyings brgyud phep," cited in Goldstein, *History of Modern Tibet*, 120. This information was corroborated by the author's interview with Kachen Lozang Döndrub (monk at Tashilhunpo monastery), Bylakuppe, January 1996.

4. The Tibetan reads: "Lungshar rtsis pa yin ze, rTsis nor thebs nas log byung, Tsogo sha khyi yin ze, Dri snom byas nas log byung," cited in Don khang sKal bzang bDe skyid, "Pan chen sku phreng dgu pa mes rgyal nang khul du gsang phebs kyi snga rjes," 13.

5. Zhwa sgab pa, *Bod kyi srid don rgyal rabs*, 277.

6. Phur lcog yongs 'dzin sprul sku, *Lhar bcas srid zhi'i gtsug rgyan*, vol. 7, fols. 492, 503, 504.

7. IOR, L/P&S/12/4170-File 7, PZ 1922/1933, letter written by Lieutenant-Colonel J. L. R. Weir, dated March 1, 1933.

8. Shétongmön shimükang is a valley located in the Shigatse district. The private residence of Tashilhunpo owned sixty tracts (*kang*) of land here. See Lo Runtshang, *dGa' ldan pho brang ba'i chab*, 372.

9. Don khang sKal bzang bDe skyid, *op. cit.*, 24.

10. The Chinese for these place-names is Nadang, Gangjin, and Zangqing dahe, respectively.

11. Ya Hanzhang, *Banchan E'erdeni zhuan*, 237.

12. Draft of a letter from the minister of foreign affairs to the minister of Mongolian and Tibetan affairs, dated March 21, 1924, citing the memorandum to the minister of foreign affairs from Lozang Gyeltsen in Sichuan sheng dang'an guan, *Jin dai Kang qu dang'an ziliao xuanbian*. In official texts Lozang Gyeltsen is called Lozang, the favorite (Cansel Lozang).

13. On Cao Kun (1862–1938), see Boorman, *Biographical Dictionary of Republican China*, vol. 3, 302–5; Li Shengping, *Zhongguo jin xian dai renming da cidian*, 631; Perleberg, *Who's Who in Modern China*, entry 1331. On Ma Qi (1869–1931), see Lipman, "Ethnicity and Politics in Republican China," 285–316; Qinghai sheng zhi bianzuan weiyuanhui, *Qinghai lishi jiyao*, 674–77.

14. Telegram from the minister of foreign affairs to the commander of the Ma battalion, dated March 25, 1924, in Sichuan sheng dang'an guan, *op. cit.*

CHAPTER 1

1. Twitchett and Fairbank, *Cambridge History of China*, vols. 10–11; Will, "L'ère des rebellions," 45–83.

2. On Shérab Senggé (1382–1445), see Boussemart, *rJe Shes-rab Seng-ge*.

3. Yon tan rGya mtsho, *dGe ldan chos*, 450.

4. bKra shis dgon lo rgyus, *dPal gyi chos*, 18.

5. Boussemart, *rJe Shes-rab Seng-ge*, 102; Gyatso, *dGe ldan chos*, 463; bKra shis dgon lo rgyus, *dPal gyi chos*, 1–47; rdzong rtse Byams pa Thub bstan, *Chos grwa chen po bKra shis lhun po'i chos 'byung*, 35–48.

6. See Appendix A for the reincarnation lineages of the Dalai Lamas and Panchen Lamas.

7. bKra shis dgon lo rgyus, *op. cit.*, 102–5.

8. Yon tan rGya mtsho, *op. cit.*, 466.

9. Zhwa sgab pa, *Bod kyi srid don rgyal rabs*, 386; Yon tan rGya mtsho, *op. cit.*, 466.

10. bKra shis dgon lo rgyus, *op. cit.*, 118.

11. Zhwa sgab pa, *op. cit.*, 403; bKra shis dgon lo rgyus, *op. cit.*, 119.

12. This surely refers to the Shang gaden chökor monastery founded in 1645 at Namling. See Zhang Yisun, *Bod rGya tshig mdzod chen mo*, 2832.

13. Dargyé is located either to the south or to the northeast of the present-day district of Gampa. See Zhang Yisun, *op. cit.*, 1250; "rGya dmar gyi btsen og tu gnas sa'i Bod dang sa 'brel khag gi sa khra" [Map of Tibet and the Tibetan Area Occupied by Communist China], 1/3200 000.

14. If we translate the expression "Ngapa Lama" word by word, it designates either the master (husband) of a community of *Ngapa* or a master of a village that would most likely be Nyingmapa or Bönpo. It could also describe a Ngapa that the villagers had named "Lama" because of his religious activity in the area rather than for his erudition. However, given the context and the original text that provides a list of toponyms, here it is the name of a place. A community of Ngapa resides in Ukpalung in Tsang Province. Finally, although a valley called "Ngapa brama" is located in the Dingri district, we rule out this hypothesis as a spelling error, since the text clearly specifies that the Ngapa Lama lands are located in the Shigatse district. See Lo Runtshang, *dGa' ldan pho brang ba'i chab*, 319; N. Sihlé (anthropologist), in discussion with author, January 13, 1999; C. Ramble (anthropologist), e-mail correspondence with author, January 22, 1999.

15. rdzong rtse Byams pa Thub bstan, *op. cit.*, 622–25.

16. Zhwa sgab pa, *op. cit.*, 398–403; Ahmad, *Sino-Tibetan Relations*, 105–7; Dhondup, *Water-Horse and Other Years*, 1–33; rdzong rtse Byams pa Thub bstan, *gTsang myang smad bSam grub rtse'i.*

17. At the beginning of the twentieth century, Ensa monastery was made up of two buildings. The larger one accommodated 230 monks. In the smaller one was a convent where seventy-two nuns resided. See Kawaguchi, *Three Years in Tibet*, 254. Regarding the Ensa monastery, see Sa byang Tshe dbang rNam rgyal, "En gön gyi chags rabs," 106–15.

18. Ya Hanzhang, *Banchan E'erdeni zhuan*, 1–12.

19. According to the Tibetan tradition, the Dalai Lama is considered the incarnation of Chenrezi (S. Avalokiteśvara), the bodhisattva of compassion. As for the Fifth Dalai Lama, he declared that Panchen Rinpoche Lozang Chöki Gyeltsen was the incarnation of Öpame (S. Amitābha, lit. "infinite light"). Since then, Tibetans see the Panchen Lamas as reincarnations of Öpame. In the Buddhist Mahayana pantheon, Amitābha is one of the five transcendental Buddhas. He reigns over the paradise of the "pure land" and symbolizes wisdom and mercy. He is often represented in a sitting position, surrounded by two standing aides, one of whom is Avalokiteśvara, who represents his active force. Amitābha and Avalokiteśvara can be of mutual spiritual inspiration and instruction to each other.

20. See Schmid, *Saviours of Mankind II*, 10; rdzong rtse Byams pa Thub btan, *Chos grwa chen po bKra shis lhun po'i byung*, 352–587.

21. Tsybikov, *Un pèlerin bouddhiste au Tibet*, 247.

22. Phur lcog yongs 'dzin sprul sku, *Lhar bcas srid zhi'i gtsug rgyan*, vol. 6, fol. 214.

23. The oracle (*chökyong*) of Lamo was linked, at least at one period in time, to the lineage of Panchen Lamas. He gave general indications for finding the Fifth Panchen Lama and was the only oracle that the Panchen Lama consulted regularly all his life.

24. Tobgyel is located in the district of Namling. The Eighth Dalai Lama (1758–1804) and the Eighth Panchen Lama (1855–1882) were born there. See Zhang Yisun, *op. cit.*, 1197; bKra shis dgon lo rgyus, *op. cit.*, 142.

25. Brum is the name of the most important aristocratic family in the region of Dakpo, to the southeast of Lhasa. This name is also written as Phrung pa, sBrum, or Grum. See Petech, *Aristocracy and Government*, 124–27.

26. Phur lcog yongs 'dzin sprul sku, *op. cit.*, vol. 6, fol. 374.

27. Demo Tulku Ngawang Lozang Trinlé Rabgyé was regent from 1886 to 1895.

28. Wenshi held the post of the Manchu imperial resident in Tibet from 1885 to 1888.

29. Excerpt translated from Phur lcog yongs 'dzin sprul sku, *op. cit.*, vol. 6, fol. 373; "Memoir of Wenshi, Manchu Imperial Resident in Tibet to the Emperor Guangxu at the Ministry of Military Affairs, dated April 25, 1888," in *Qing shilu Zangzu shiliao*, 4496; rdzong rtse Byams pa Thub bstan, *Chos grwa chen po bKra shis lhun po'i chos 'byung*, 568–69.

30. Phur lcog yongs 'dzin sprul sku, *op. cit.*, vol. 6, fol. 376; lHag pa tshe ring, "Panchen Chos kyi Nyi ma dgGe legs rNam rgyal gyi gsung 'bum," fol. 343.

31. D. Macdonald, *Twenty Years in Tibet*, 186.

32. Guo Qing, "A Brief Account of the Ninth Panchen Erdeni," 71.

33. D. Macdonald, *op. cit.*, 187. David Macdonald, who mentions some of the auspicious signs that oriented the search for the Ninth Panchen Lama towards the region of Dakpo, was a British trade agent from 1904–24, and stayed in Gromo (Nadong, Chumbi valley).

34. Ibid.; Tsybikov, *op. cit.*, 247–48.

35. Author's interview with Dakpo Rinpoche (monk from Drépung, recognized as a reincarnated lama by the Thirteenth Dalai Lama), Paris, May 1995.

36. Author's interview with the late Kachen Jangpa Thubten (monk from Tashilhunpo), Bylakuppe, January 1996.

37. Guo Qing, *op. cit.*, 71.

38. In Tibet twins are considered bad luck because they are supposed to shorten the lifespan of both parents and children. See Number Two Historical Archives of China (hereafter Nanjing Archives), report by Gao Zhangzhu to the Mongolian and Tibetan Affairs Commission, 1936.

39. D. Macdonald, *op. cit.*, 186–87.

40. On Tséchokling Rinpoche (in Chinese, Cejuelin huofo), see IOR, L/P&S/12/4185A, notes on titles and officials' ranks in Tibet, November 7, 1934.

41. Guo Qing, *op. cit.*, 71; D. Macdonald, *op. cit.*, 187; Wang Chengsheng, "Xizang Banchan jiu shi yisheng shenji," 58.

42. Author's interview with the late Kachen Jangpa Thubten, January 1996.

43. D. Macdonald, *op. cit.*, 187. Numerous coincidences between the lives of those close to the Thirteenth Dalai Lama and the Ninth Panchen Lama seem to corroborate the story related by D. Macdonald. Effectively in 1882, the year the Ninth Panchen Lama was conceived in Brum gasha, Lozang Tashi, the Thirteenth Dalai Lama's second oldest brother, became a religious official. In 1894 he announced that he would take his monk's vows the following year at Tashilhunpo. For thirteen years, he brought gifts offered by the Thirteenth Dalai Lama to the Ninth Panchen Lama. In 1896 he left the order and married a girl from the Brum family. Due to an absence of male heirs, he became the family's head. Damchö Tsomo worked for this same family. In this case, it is possible that the older brother of the Thirteenth Dalai Lama was the father of the Ninth Panchen Lama. See Petech, *op. cit.*, 125–26.

44. Decree from the Guangxu Emperor, dated December 9, 1891, in *Qing shilu Zangzu shiliao*.

45. IOR, MSS EUR F. 80–17, excerpt from the diary of Sir Charles Bell regarding a note on the murder of the father of the present "Tashi Lama" (Panchen Lama), according to information furnished by Lönchen Shatra, dated May 21, 1914. Charles Bell held the post of British political officer in Sikkim from May to November 1904, September 1906 to August 1911, October 1911 to October 1913, September 1914 to April 1918, and January 1920 to January 1921.

46. Richardson, "A Scandal at Tashi Lhunpo," 24–25. Hugh Richardson held the post of British political officer in Sikkim from May to November 1937. He headed the British mission to Lhasa from February to July 1937, from October 1938 to October 1939, from June to September 1944, and from April 1946 to December 1947.

47. Petech, *op. cit.*, 188, 233.

48. lHag pa tshe ring, *op. cit.*, 144; Poster Memorandum by the Tibetan Council of Ministers, 1923.

49. Phur log yongs 'dzin sprul sku, *op. cit.*, vol. 6, fol. 377.

50. Regarding Shigatse, see Tshe ring Don grub, *Bod ljongs spyi bshad*, 84–86; Dai Xinsan, "Rikaze niaokan," 52–62.

51. Tucci, *To Lhasa and Beyond*, 155; David-Neel, *With Mystics and Magicians*.

52. Hedin, *Trans-Himalaya*, 319; Tsybikov, *op. cit.*, 241.

53. Tsybikov, *op. cit.*, 244, 248; author's interview with the late Kachen Jangpa Thubten, January 1996.

54. For further details on Tashilhunpo, see Phur lcog Nga dbang Byams pa, *Grwa sa chen po bzhi dang rgyud pa stod smad chags tshul pad dkar 'phreng ba*, 73–92; bKra shis dgon lo rgyus, *op. cit.*, 16–27; Tshe ring Don grub, *op. cit.*, 157–62; Dai Xinsan, "Zhashelunbu si xiao zhi," 1–8.

55. bKra shis dgon lo rgyus, *op. cit.*, 91–93.

56. Phur lcog yongs 'dzin sprul sku, *op. cit.*, vol. 6, fol. 439.

57. Author's interview with Kachen Lozang Döndrub (monk from Tashilhunpo), Bylakuppe, January 1996.

58. lHa mkhar yongs 'dzin bsTan pa rGyal mtshan, *sKyabs mgon rje btsun bla ma*, vol. 1, fols. 341–418.

59. Author's interview with the late Kachen Jangpa Thubten, January 1996.

60. Phur lcog yongs 'dzin sprul sku, *op. cit.*, vol. 6, fols. 534–35.

61. Members of the private residence of the Thirteenth Dalai Lama are those individuals responsible for his personal services.

62. Phur lcog yongs 'dzin sprul sku, *op. cit.*, vol. 6, fols. 735–45.

63. The private college belonged to the private residence of the Panchen Lama. Monks there wore their robes with two folds to the left side and wore a red cape.

64. Author's interview with the late Kachen Jangpa Thubten, January 1996.

65. Author's interview with Kachen Lozang Döndrub, January 1996.

CHAPTER 2

1. The group accompanying the Panchen Lama as he left Tashilhunpo consisted of ten or so monks; another group of around one hundred joined them a few days later.

2. A telegraph line existed from Kalimpong to Lhasa. It went up to Gyeltsé in 1904 and then on to Lhasa in 1919–20 to allow communication with Bell on his visit in 1920. See Chapman, *Lhasa, The Holy City*, 11; Bell, *Portrait of a Dalai Lama*, 409–10.

3. Don khang sKal bzang bDe skyid, "Pan chen sku phreng dgu pa mes rgyal nas," 8; Blo bzang Tshe brtan, "Ta'a la'i bla ma sku phreng bcu gsum pa," 270.

4. IOR, L/P&S/12/4174 (PZ 1769/24), letter from the Ninth Panchen Lama translated by D. Macdonald, the British trade agent in Gyeltsé, and forwarded to the British political officer in Sikkim, F. M. Bailey, March 1924.

5. Liu Jiaju, *Banchan da shi quanji*, 37.

6. Even if the Thirteenth Dalai Lama had to leave Outer Mongolia due to the jealousy of Jétsun Dampa, nothing confirms that Jétsun Dampa held the same animosity towards the Panchen Lama. See Bell, *op. cit.*, 76.

7. IOR, L/P&S/12/4174 (PZ 6939/32), letter written by the Panchen Lama and translated into English by the British political officer in Sikkim and forwarded to the British government in India, October 19, 1932.

8. F. M. Bailey held the post of British political officer in Sikkim from June 1921 to May 1926 and from December 1926 to October 1928.

9. Don khang sKal bzang bDe skyid, *op. cit.*, 9.

10. On May 22, 1896, Russia managed to acquire the right of passage for the Trans-Siberian railway through Manchuria, so as to obtain access to the Pacific coast. In 1898 the Russians administered Port Arthur, a naval base in Manchuria, which the Japanese had taken two years earlier. Around the same time, China gave the Russians a construction concession to build a new railway, the South-Manchurian, which linked Port Arthur to the Trans-Manchurian branch of the Trans-Siberian. The same year, China made access rights to Manchuria contingent on Russian approval.

11. The Convention of 1886 drew the border between Tibet and Burma. The Convention of 1890 separated Tibet and Sikkim and opened a market on Tibetan land in Gromo. These two conventions were signed between China and Britain with no participation from the Tibetans. For further details on this chapter in Tibetan-British relations and on Younghusband, see Fleming, *Bayonets to Lhasa*; Verrier, *Francis Younghusband and the Great Game*; French, *Younghusband: The Last Great Imperial Adventurer*.

12. Dorjieff, *Chos brgyad gdon gyis zin byas te*; Andreev, *Buddhist Shrine of Petrograd*; Snelling, *Buddhism in Russia*.

13. Dorjieff, *op. cit.*, 4, 19; Andreev, *op. cit.*, 83.

14. Dorjieff, *op. cit.*, 24.

15. Zhwa sgab pa, *Bod kyi srid don rgyal rabs*, vol. 1, 129; Waddell, *Lhasa and its Mysteries*, 169–70; rNam rgyal dBang 'dud, *Bod ljongs rgyal khab chen po'i srid lugs*, 29.

16. Of the fifteen hundred soldiers making up the Tibetan army at Guru, six to seven hundred died in addition to twenty out of the 168 wounded that were cared for by the British. See Chapman, *op. cit.*, 151.

17. Ganden Tri Rinpoche literally means "master and guardian of the Ganden monastery throne." Méru Lozang Gyeltsen was the eighty-sixth successor to Tsongkapa of the Ganden throne. Chosen because of his erudition, he was named as head of the Gélukpa school for seven years (1901–8).

18. Lamb, *The McMahon Line*, 36–51.

19. Article 1 of the Convention. See Van Walt van Praag, *Status of Tibet*, appendix 12, 307–8.

20. As of 1906, Zhao Erfeng controlled the cities of Bathang and Litang. In 1908 he had taken over Dergé. In August 1908 Bathang and Dartsédo became prefectures (*fu*) while Litang and the region of

Sanpa became garrisons (*suo*) under Chinese administration. See Huang Fengsheng, *Zangzu shilüe*, 313–17; Sperling, "Chinese Venture in K'am," 10–36; Bacot, *Le Tibet révolté*.

21. Youtai had held the post of Manchu imperial resident in Tibet from 1902 to 1906. Zhang Yintang held the post of Chinese governor from 1906 to 1908.

22. Andreyev, "Agwan Dorjiev's Secret Work," 12; Zhwa sgab pa, *op. cit.*, 146.

23. The Dalai Lamas and Panchen Lamas visiting Beijing always stayed in the Yellow Temple (*Huang si*), which was composed of two sets of buildings. The one to the east was constructed in 1651. The other, to the west, had been built as a residence for the Fifth Dalai Lama (1617–1682). The Sixth Panchen Lama (1738–1780) stayed there and died in the west wing in 1780. Qianlong had a reliquary built in the temple that still holds the Sixth Panchen Lama's clothes. See Danjiong Rannabanza and Li Decheng, *Ming sha shuang Huang si*.

24. Zhwa sgab pa, *op. cit.*, 151; Chen Qiangyi, "Jianshu shi san shi Dalai rujin," 82–92.

25. Jagou, "The Thirteenth Dalai Lama's Visit to Peking."

26. Ngawang Lozang Tenpé Gyeltsen was the eighty-seventh successor of Tsongkapa to the Ganden throne (1908–14).

27. D. Macdonald, the British trade agent in Gyeltsé, helped the Dalai Lama escape by disguising him as a mailman.

28. Bell, *Tibet: Past and Present*, 111–12.

29. Shortly before his departure, the Thirteenth Dalai Lama requested that Ganden Tri Rinpoche name Dékilingka and Parkang Gyeltsen Püntsok (1863–1939) to the post of minister. Lozang Trinlé (1860–?) and Tsarong Wangchuk Gyelpo (1866–1912), two ministers from the former cabinet, remained in Lhasa after the departure of the Thirteenth Dalai Lama. Zhang Yintang deposed Lozang Trinlé, Dékilingka, and Parkang Gyeltsen Püntsok. He named Tenzin Chödrak, Rampa Sönam Gonkyab (1875–?), and Langtongwa, while Tsarong Wangchuk Gyelpo kept his post. Zhang Yintang also confiscated the property of the Thirteenth Dalai Lama and those of the ministers who had accompanied him to India. See Zhwa sgab pa, *op. cit.*, 183–84.

30. Huang Fengsheng, *op. cit.*, 310–12; Qin Heping, "1912 nian Minguo zhengfu chouzhi Xizang cuoshi shuping," 117–18.

31. Zhwa sgab pa, *op. cit.*, 209–11.

32. Shakabpa, *Tibet: A Political History*, 246–48. Zhwa sgab pa, *op. cit.*, 219–23.

33. Lamb, *The China-India Border*.

34. Zhwa sgab pa, *op. cit.*, 633–35. This treaty signed by the defense minister for the Mongols and by Agvan Dorjieff for the Tibetan side was not ratified by the Thirteenth Dalai Lama or his government. Dorjieff's credentials for signing consisted of a letter that the Thirteenth Dalai Lama is said to have given him. But the Thirteenth Dalai Lama points out that this letter was a request that Dorjieff work for the diffusion of the Buddhist religion; it did not give him the power to sign such a treaty. See Bell, *Tibet: Past and Present*, 151. In his autobiography, Dorjieff states: "Arriving in Mongolia, I offered presents to monks, ministers, and to sKyab mgon rJe btsun dam ba. Later Tibet and Mongolia signed a treaty of alliance" (*Bod Sog phyin chad mthun 'gyur gyi chings yig byans shing*). See Dorjieff, *op. cit.*, fol. 28.

35. The text of this agreement is found in Bell, *Tibet: Past and Present*, 305–6.

36. Lian Yu held the post of Manchu imperial resident in Tibet from 1905 to 1912.

37. Mehra, *Tibetan Polity*, 38.

38. On Yuan Shikai, see Boorman, *Biographical Dictionary of Republican China*, vol. 3, 78–89; IOR, P&EF, 2350/1913, letter from Lu Xingqi to the president and cabinet, dated June 6, 1913, cited in Mehra, *op cit.*, 39. Huang Fengsheng, *op. cit.*, 323. However, none of these sources specify which title was given.

39. IOR, P&EF, 2350/1913, letter from Lu Xingqi to the president and the Council of Ministers, dated July 18, 1913, cited in Mehra, *op. cit.*, 39–40; IOR, L/P&S/11/60-File P3231/1913, copy of a telegram from the viceroy to the secretary of His Majesty's Government in India; Mehra, "Lu Hsing-chi," 43–49.

40. rNam rgyal dBang 'dud, *op. cit.*, 17.

41. *Da Qing huidian shili*, 62/7B–8A; rNam rgyal dBang 'dud, *op. cit.*, 15.

42. Goldstein, *History of Modern Tibet*, 66N2, citing Khreng Ping, "Bod dmag gi lo rgyus mdor bsdus" [Brief History of the Tibetan Army], *Materials on the Culture and History of Tibet* 4 (1984): 182–83.

43. rNam rgyal dBang 'dud, *op. cit.*, 29.

44. Zhwa sgab pa, *op. cit.*, 209–11. Upon the arrival of the Chinese army in Lhasa in 1910, the Thirteenth Dalai Lama left the Tibetan capital and headed for the Sikkim border. During a rest stop in Cagzam, he discovered that a Chinese regiment had been pursuing him and had nearly caught up with him. The Dalai Lama fled Cagzam while certain members of his escort, including Labzang Tadul, stayed to confront the Chinese. The Tibetans defeated the Chinese and after meeting up with the Thirteenth Dalai Lama in India, Labzang Tadul was awarded for his bravery.

45. Surkhang, "Government, Monastic and Private Taxation in Tibet," 30.

46. rNam rgyal dBang 'dud, *op. cit.*, 17–18.

47. Waddell, *op. cit.*, 170.

48. Richardson, *High Peaks, Pure Earth*, 21.

49. IOR, L/P&S/10/344, letter no. 448 EB.

50. IOR, L/P&S/10/344, letter from Tsarong to Charles Bell, dated November 8, 1915.

51. Bell, *Portrait of a Dalai Lama*, 286.

52. Zhwa sgab pa, *op. cit.*, 246, 259; Bell, *Tibet: Past and Present*, 163–64.

53. Zhwa sgab pa, *op. cit.*, 251–324; Teichman, *Travels of a Consular Officer*.

54. In 1929 the British finally accepted a customs tax by the Tibetans on products coming from India, on the condition that it did not exceed 5 percent *ad valorem*. See Goldstein, *op. cit.*, 85.

55. The original letter in which the Thirteenth Dalai Lama gave this news to the Ninth Panchen Lama has yet to be located. However, this information is clearly explained in the following letters: IOR, L/P&S/12/4174, letter, dated November 18, 1922, from D. Macdonald to F. M. Bailey; IOR, L/P&S/12/4174 (PZ 1769/24), letter left by the Ninth Panchen Lama when departing from Tibet, dated December 23, 1923 (translated by D. Macdonald and addressed to F. M. Bailey, March 1924); IOR, L/P&S/12/4174 (PZ 1431/24, letter from the Thirteenth Dalai Lama to the Ninth Panchen Lama, dated February 20, 1924 (enclosed in a letter from F. M. Bailey addressed to His Majesty's Government in India); IOR, L/P&S/12/4174 (PZ6939/32), letter, dated July 1924, from the Ninth Panchen Lama to the Thirteenth Dalai Lama (translated into English by F. M. Bailey and forwarded to His Majesty's Government in India on October 19, 1932).

56. Don khang sKal bzang bDe skyid, *op. cit.*, 1–2; Surkhang, "The Sixth Panchen Lama," 23.

57. Don khang sKal bzang bDe skyid, *op. cit.*, 2.

58. bKra shis dgon lo rgyus, *dPal gyi chos sde chen po bKra shis lhun po*, 147; Liu Jiaju, "Xizang lidai Zang wang ji Dalai Banchan shiyao," 20.

59. David-Neel, *With Mystics and Magicians in Tibet*, 86–87.

60. Dongkar is located in present-day Ngari, in the district of Déchen. See Zhang Yisun, *Bod rGya tshig mdzod chen mo*, (*Zang Han da cidian*), 1349.

61. Dzongka is a town located in the district of Kirong. See Zhang Yisun, *op. cit.*, 2361.

62. The land register of 1830 indicates that Tashilhunpo possessed no land in the Kyirong district.

63. After having put an end to the civil war with the help of the Manchus in 1728, Pholhané headed the newly created government in Lhasa. Pholhané's power was absolute, that of the Seventh Dalai Lama declining, and the control of the Chinese merely nominal. See Petech, *China and Tibet*, 163.

64. rdzong rtse Byams pa Thub bstan, *Chos grwa chen po bKra shis lhun po'i chos 'byung*, 622–25.

65. Huang Fengsheng, *op. cit.*, 250; Petech, *op cit.*, 139.

66. Das, "The Lives of the Panchen-Rinpoches," 115–16.

67. Petech, *op cit.*, 139; Surkhang, "The Sixth Panchen Lama," 22–23, confirms the acquisition of these districts by the Panchen Lama, but he does not specify the circumstances surrounding the acquisition.

68. Das, *op. cit.*, 116. Phakri is located in the Gromo district to the south of Shigatse, and Yarbrok is located in the present-day district of Nakartsé. See Zhang Yisun, *op. cit.*, 1701, 2558.

69. The Chinese terms "Qian Zang" and "Hou Zang" can also be translated as "Anterior Tibet" and "Posterior Tibet." Based on a geocentric Chinese vision, "Inner Tibet" is the region closest to China and "Outer Tibet" the region furthest away. Danzhu Angben, *Da Qing yi tongzhi*, 413/1A; Jagou, "Etude des toponymes choisis."

70. *Da Qing yi tongzhi*, 413/1A.

71. See bKra shis dgon lo rgyus, *op. cit.*, 93.

72. Two land registries were carried out in Central Tibet, one in 1740, and the other in 1830. Minor corrections were made to the second registry in 1831. A revision to the 1830 land registry was then later made in 1864. In that year, the Council of Ministers and the National Assembly chose to list the lands of three districts—Gyeltsé, Nam, and Wangchen—and to include them in the lands of Central Tibet. But as circumstances interrupted the completion of a new land registry, only the 1830 one remained valid for Central Tibet with the exception of the Gyeltsé, Nam, and Wangchen districts, where the 1864 land registry was applied. See Surkhang, "Tax Measurement and *Lag 'don* Tax," 20–25; Surkhang, *"Government, Monastic and Private Taxation,"* 37.

73. See Bell, *The People of Tibet*, 301; D. Macdonald, *The Land of the Lama*, 224; Surkhang, "Tax Measurement and *Lag 'don* Tax," 22. S. C. Das cites two different equivalences for one *kel*: 30 British pounds and 50 British pounds of grain. Cf. Das, *A Tibetan-English Dictionary*, 143; Das, *Journey to Lhasa*, 182.

74. Surkhang, "Tax Measurement and *Lag-'don* Tax," 22.

75. One *kel* of grain equaled seventeen British pounds of roasted barley flour. See Bell, *The People of Tibet*, 301; D. Macdonald, *The Land of the Lama*, 224.

76. Winnington, *Tibet: Record of a Journey*, 167, 170.

77. Petech, *Aristocracy and Government*, 12.

78. *Zhonghua renmin gongheguo fen sheng ditu ji*, 1/400 000, 111.

79. Goldstein, *op. cit.*, 110.

80. bKra shis dgon lo rgyus, *op. cit.*, 92.

81. Ran Hongling, "Xizang siyuan jingji jianlun," 277.

82. Kawaguchi, *Three Years in Tibet*, 250; Tucci, *To Lhasa and Beyond*, 155; Markham, *Narratives of the Mission of Georges Bogle*, 96; Tsybikov, *op. cit.*, 242.

83. Author interviews with Püntsok Thubten (monk from Dakpo monastery), Paris, July 1995; the late Kachen Jangpa Thubten (monk from Tashilhunpo), Bylakkupe, December 1995; Kugo Ngawang Riktröl, (former civil servant with the Tibetan government in Lhasa), Dharamsala, January 1996.

84. One measure of grain equals 1.59–1.94 measures of flour.

85. Tsybikov, *op. cit.*, 241.

86. Tucci, *op. cit.*, 155–56.

87. David-Neel, *op. cit.*, 84.

88. This amount of barley equals roughly 217,500 measures of grain, or an approximate value of 3,262,500 ounces. According to David Macdonald, one measure of grain in 1922 was worth approximately 15 ounces (an imperial unit of measurement). In a letter dated November 18, 1922, Macdonald indicates that the Ninth Panchen Lama wrote him that the Tibetan government was demanding approximately 650,000 rupees, 10,000 maunds of grain estimated at 80,000 rupees, and two thousand boxes of Chinese brick tea estimated at 85,000 rupees. According to Boulnois, one maund equals 37 kg and one measure of grain equals approximately 12–15 kg. From this we can deduce that one maund equaled approximately 2–3 measures of grain. If 10,000 maunds of grain (or approx. 24,750–30,250 measures of grain) are estimated at 80,000 rupees, then that would mean that one measure of grain would be worth from 2.64 to 3.23 rupees (13.2 to 16.15 ounces), or an average value of 14.7 ounces. See IOR, L/P&S/12/4174, letter from D. Macdonald, British trade agent in Gyeltsé, to C. Bell, British political officer in Sikkim, dated November 18, 1922; Boulnois, *Poudre d'or et monnaies d'argent au Tibet*, 126.

89. Don khang sKal bzang bDe skyid, *op. cit.*, 4; *"dPyad mtshams bka' rtsa 'dra bcu gsum pa'i zhal bshas he bag med pa, 1923."*

90. The term *gyelchak légyor* can be translated as "lending a strong hand." The word *lé* literally means "work" and *gyor* means "lend." According to Kugo Ngawang Riktröl, this extraordinary government tax meant that when subjects of one district could not fulfill their obligations due to a natural catastrophe, for example, those of another district would have to assume those obligations without any compensation. In this case, the subjects of the Gyeltsé district had to "lend a strong hand" to those of Phagri.

91. Don khang sKal bzang bDe skyid, *op. cit.*, 4.

92. *Cin* is an abbreviation of *cinji*, a term which signifies "British;" *ko* means "need;" *ra* means "goat;" *luk* "sheep;" *tsa* "fodder;" and *shak* means "share" or "divide" According to Kugo Ngawang Riktröl (interview with author, January 1996), this tax was to be raised on livestock. He says it only applied to northern Tibet. However, the text from the 1923 decree describes the tax being raised in Gyeltsé, thus in southern Tibet. According to Tashi Tsering (interview with author, January 1996), the subjects of Gyeltsé had to provide goats, sheep, and fodder to the British trade agents in Gyeltsé.

93. The crossing *ulag* was further divided into two categories. In the first, when the permit holder had to travel a long distance, those in charge of the *ulag* had to provide at least ten horses and fifteen beasts of burden at each leg of the journey. This was referred to as the "transport *ulag* for one district" (*dzongkyel*). When the army traveled inside the country, soldiers had recourse to this *ulag*. In the second case, when the permit holder was traveling a short distance (e.g., half a day's trip on horseback), those providing the *ulag* had to make available up to ten horses and fifteen beasts of burden at each rest stop. This was referred to as "sojourn *ulag*" (*satsik*). The terms *dzongkyel* and *satsik* were also given to the place where the travelers could change their mounts and get fresh supplies. Only subjects working the collective monastic lands were exempt from the crossing *ulag*. See Surkhang, "Government, Monastic and Private Taxation in Tibet," 24; Goldstein, "Reexamining Choice, Dependency and Command in the Tibetan Social System," 89–90; Sangay "Glossary of 'Government Monastic and Private Taxation in Tibet,'" 42; Carrasco, *Land and Polity in Tibet*, 105.

94. Surkhang, "Government, Monastic and Private Taxation," 31.

95. sLe zur 'Jigs med dBang phyug and bDe zur Rin chen dBang 'dus, "De snga'i bla brang rgyal mtshan mthon po," 138–39.

96. Teichman, *op. cit.* Dzayül is a district located in southeastern Tibet. See Zhang Yisun, *op. cit.*, 2351.

97. Bell, *Portrait of a Dalai Lama*, 284–85.

98. Don khang sKal bzang bDe skyid, who dedicated one of his articles to the life of the Ninth Panchen Lama, briefly mentions this decree without providing the full content of it. See Don khang sKal bzang bDe skyid, *op. cit.*, 5–6; Goldstein, *op. cit.*, 110–12, merely cites the points given by Don khang. Consequently, I was immensely pleased to discover a copy of the original document dating from the same period and conserved at the Library of Tibetan Works and Archives (LTWA) in Dharamsala, in northern India. The copy measures 27 x 8 cm. Its eighty-one pages are folded lengthwise and bound by cotton thread on the upper half. The document opens from the bottom towards the top, as do traditional Tibetan texts. Nothing leads one to believe that it once had a cover protecting it, since the first page, which contains the title (Official Copy of the Thirteen Articles of the Decree) is falling to pieces. Starting from page two, five or six lines of writing follow consecutively with no paragraphs, skipped lines, or other distinguishing features. Only the face of each page has writing, the back remaining blank. The total text is made up of 442 lines. The document has not been authenticated by a seal, which confirms that it is a copy, as indicated by its title. Neither the date of the reproduction nor the name of the copier is noted. The reason Tibetan refugees brought the copy of this decree to Dharamsala remains unknown. The document is written in Tibetan cursive calligraphy (*umé*, lit. "without head"). This script is very different from the one commonly used for official texts (*uchen*, lit. "with head"), and thus made it difficult, if not impossible, for me to read. Luckily, members of the LTWA, notably Tashi Tsering, historian and director of the Amnye Machen Institute, were gracious enough to transcribe the document into letters "with head," making it more accessible. Nevertheless, the content, which includes some of the most obscure administrative and economic

terms, took months of translation time. After having written up a first draft version in French, I had to verify the meaning of many words with former members of the pre-1959 Tibetan government. This was undertaken in January 1996 with Kugo Ngawang Riktröl, who had been a member of the government in Lhasa; Fernand Meyer, director of research at the Centre National de la Recherche Scientifique; and Tenzin Sampel, a Tibetan teacher at the Institut National des Langues et Civilisations Orientales (Inalco). Although several administrative acts are mentioned in this document, it turned out to be impossible to locate them, as the Lhasa archives remain closed to Western scholars.

99. See note 93 for definitions of *dzongkyel* and *satsik*.

100. The Tibetan army's budget in 1917 totaled approximately £150,000. It is interesting and reassuring to note that the figure of £37,500 calculated from Bell's data corroborates that from Macdonald's letter, since £37,500 was equivalent to approximately 500,000 rupees, a figure which is coherent with the 650,000 rupees that Macdonald mentioned for the army's upkeep expenses. See IOR, L/P&S/12/4174, letter from D. Macdonald, British trade agent in Gyeltsé, to C. Bell, British political officer in Sikkim, dated November 18, 1922; Bell, *Portrait of a Dalai Lama*, 187–89.

101. According to Chapman, one British pound was equal to 13.3 rupees in 1936. According to Shakabpa, in 1950, one rupee was equal to five ounces. The exchange rate between the rupee and the ounce stayed quite stable from 1920 to 1950. Thus, in 1923, one British pound was worth around 66.5 Tibetan *sang*. See Chapman, *op. cit.*, 312; Shakabpa, *op. cit.*, 334; Boulnois, *op. cit.*, 172; private letter from H. Richardson, the last head of the British mission in Lhasa, to F. Meyer, dated April 23, 1997.

102. Don khang sKal bzang bDe skyid, *op. cit.*, 2. Here as well, we can see that the figure of 27,000 measures of grain given by Don khang sKal bzang bDe skyid is coherent with that of Macdonald, since 100,000 maunds of grain is equivalent to approximately 27,500 measures of grain. See Don khang sKal bzang bDe skyid, *op. cit.*, 2; IOR, L/P&S/12/4174, letter from D. Macdonald, British trade agent in Gyeltsé, to C. Bell, British political officer in Sikkim, dated November 18, 1922.

103. See, Surkhang, "Government, Monastic and Private Taxation," 25; rNam rgyal dBang 'dud, *op. cit.*, 35–37.

104. "dPyad mtshams bka' rtsa 'dra bcu gsum pa'i zhal bshus he bag med pa, 1923."

105. For further discussion of the political role of the Panchen Lamas historically, see Appendix B.

106. *Da Qing huidian shili*, 677/6A.

107. See IOR, L/P&S/12/4174 (PZ 1769/24), letter written by the Ninth Panchen Lama and left at his monastery prior to his departure from Tibet, dated December 23,1923, and translated by D. Macdonald, March 1924: "Be it known to all the abbots and assistants of the four colleges and also to the acting prime minister and the monk and lay officials of the Tashilhunpo government . . . After due consideration I have appointed the acting prime minister [of Tashilhunpo] to carry on the administration during my absence;" IOR, L/P&S/12/4174 (PZ 1431/24), letter from the Thirteenth Dalai Lama to the Ninth Panchen Lama, sent on January 26, 1924, and translated by F. M. Bailey on February 20, 1924: "You have written to me on many occasions asking me to appoint a Dzasa Lama (prime minister) at Tashilhunpo."

108. *Da Qing huidian shili*, 981/5A.

109. For further details on Tashilhunpo's administration and how its organizational structure compares with that of the Tibetan government, see Appendix E.

110. *Da Qing huidian shili*, 977/5B.

111. Bell, *Portrait of a Dalai Lama*, 110.

112. Macdonald, *op. cit.*, 207; IOR, L/P&S/12/4184, report by F. Williamson concerning his visit to Tibet in 1934.

113. sLe zur 'Jigs med dBang phyug and bDe zur Rin chen dBang 'dus, *op. cit.*, 90.

114. Blo bzang Tshe brtan, *op. cit.*, 2.

115. *Qing shilu*, 533/12B, August 26, 1904.

116. *Qing shilu*, Guangxu, December 21, 1905, report of the advisor Zhang Yintang.

117. Lamb, *The China-India Border*, 21.

118. Alex McKay, personal communication with the author.

119. *Qing shilu*, Guangxu, telegram from the advisor Zhang who forwarded a memo from the officer at Tashilhunpo, dated October 9, 1905.

120. Bell, *Tibet: Past and Present*, 82.

121. Hedin, *Trans-Himalaya*, 321; Bell, *Tibet: Past and Present*, 82; Fang Jianchang, "Di jiu shi Banchan lama dui Yindu de fangwen," 269–75.

122. Letter no. 3575–10/17, dated November 1906 from C. Bell, British political officer in Sikkim, to L. Dane, secretary to His Majesty's Government in India; IOR, Mss Eur F.80/182B, journal of a trip to Shigatse, C. Bell, 17A.

123. Letter no. 3575–10/17, dated November 1906 from C. Bell, British political officer in Sikkim, to L. Dane, secretary to His Majesty's Government in India.

124. *Qing shilu*, Guangxu, 552/4A, January 1, 1906.

125. Bell, *Tibet: Past and Present*, 84.

126. Phur lcog yongs 'dzin sprul sku, *Lhar bcas srid zhi'i gtsug rgyan*, vol. 7, fol. 150–51.

127. Ya Hanzhang indicates that the Thirteenth Dalai Lama and the Ninth Panchen Lama met at Drubkhang monastery. Actually, Drubkhang was the name of the master of the monastery. The monastery itself was called Shab. See Ya Hanzhang, *Biographies of the Dalai Lamas*, 254; Phur lcog yongs 'dzin sprul sku, *op. cit.*, vol. 7, fol. 156.

128. Phur lcog yongs 'dzin sprul sku, *op. cit.*, vol. 7, fol. 153–59; Ya Hanzhang, *op. cit.*, 254, 267–68; Zhwa sgab pa, *op. cit.*, 161–62.

129. Ya Hanzhang, *op. cit.*, 284, citing a memo that Lian Yu, the Manchu imperial resident in Tibet, is to have addressed to the emperor.

130. Phun rab Rin chen rNam rgyal, "gZhung bla'i dbar thog ma'i gal ba yong rkyen," 125–27, cited in Goldstein, *op. cit.*, 62.

131. Zhwa sgab pa, *op. cit.*, 189; D. Macdonald, *Twenty Years in Tibet*, 102; Ya Hanzhang, *Banchan E'erdeni zhuan*, 220.

132. Zhwa sgab pa, *op. cit.*, 191; Liu Jiaju, "Xizang lidai Zang wang ji Dalai Banchan shiyao," 20.

133. Ya Hanzhang, *op. cit.*, 285.

134. D. Macdonald, *Twenty Years in Tibet*, 103.

135. Zhwa sgab pa, *op. cit.*, 191–92.

136. D. Macdonald, *Twenty Years in Tibet*, 103.

137. The original Tibetan is as follows: "bya de skra ka zer ba'i, lus de phyed dkar phyed nag, bya chen khu yug phep nas, bka' mol ga ler zhus chog," cited in Goldstein, *op. cit.*, 63.

138. IOR, L/P&S/11/12-File P.1288/1912, letter from C. Bell, British political officer in Sikkim, to the secretary of His Majesty's Government in India, Gangtok, dated March 9, 1912.

139. IOR, L/P&S/11/18-File P.2102/1912, letter from C. Bell, British political officer in Sikkim, to the secretary of His Majesty's Government in India, Gangtok, dated May 2, 1912.

140. IOR, L/P&S/11/18-File P.2102/1912, letter from C. Bell, British political officer in Sikkim, to the secretary of His Majesty's Government in India, dated May 4, 1912.

141. IOR, L/P&S/11/25-File 2865/1912, telegram no. 42C from D. Macdonald, British trade agent in Gyeltsé, to the secretary of foreign affairs in Simla, dated May 28, 1912; telegram no. 82 from D. Macdonald to the secretary of His Majesty's Government in India, dated June 18, 1912.

142. IOR, L/P&S/11/25-File 2865/1912, telegram from C. Bell, British political officer in Sikkim, to the secretary of His Majesty's Government in India, dated July 5, 1912; telegram no. 415 S, from the secretary of foreign affairs in Simla to D. Macdonald, British trade agent in Gyeltsé, dated July 13, 1912.

143. Phur lcog yongs 'dzin sprul sku, *op. cit.*, vol. 7, fol. 223; Zhwa sgab pa, *op. cit.*, 209. Nothing confirms that the Panchen Lama's entourage was punished.

144. IOR, L/P&S/11/25-File P.2865/1912, telegram from D. Macdonald, British trade agent in Gyeltsé, to Lord Minto, viceroy of India, dated July 22, 1912.

145. Ganden Tri Rinpoche, who was placed at the head of the Tibetan government in the Thirteenth Dalai Lama's absence, had neither political training nor authority.

146. Author interview with Lozang Döndrub (monk from Tashilhunpo), Bylakuppe, January 1996; author interview with Dakpo Rinpoche, (monk from Drépung), Paris, March 1997; letter from the Thirteenth Dalai Lama to the Ninth Panchen Lama, dated May 7, 1918, in Phur lcog yongs 'dzin sprul sku, *op. cit.*, vol. 5, fol. 487.

147. Phur lcog yongs 'dzin sprul sku, *op. cit.*, vol. 5, fols. 484–85, 488–89; Bell, *Portrait of a Dalai Lama*, 240.

148. IOR, L/P&S/12/4174, letter from D. Macdonald, British trade agent in Gyeltsé, to C. Bell, political officer in Sikkim, dated November 18, 1922; IOR, L/P&S/12/4174 (PZ 1769/24), letter from D. Macdonald, British trade agent in Gyeltsé, to C. Bell, political officer in Sikkim, dated March 1924.

149. Letter from the Thirteenth Dalai Lama to the Ninth Panchen Lama, dated November 18, 1919, cited in Phur lcog yongs 'dzin sprul sku, *op. cit.*, vol. 5, fols. 495–97.

150. The "Three Jewels" refers to the three pillars of Buddhism: the Buddha, the Dharma, and the Sangha.

151. Phur lcog yongs 'dzin sprul sku, *op. cit.*, vol. 7, fols. 356–58; Bell, *Portrait of a Dalai Lama*, 241.

152. Phur lcog yongs 'dzin sprul sku, *op. cit.*, vol. 7, fols. 361–62. This visit of the Ninth Panchen Lama to Lhasa is confirmed in a letter from the Thirteenth Dalai Lama to the Panchen Lama, dated July 12, 1920. See Phur lcog yongs 'dzin sprul sku, *op. cit.*, vol. 5, fol. 498.

153. IOR, L/P&S/12/4174 (PZ 1769/24), letter translated by D. Macdonald, British trade agent in Gyeltsé, and addressed to F. M. Bailey, British political officer in Sikkim, dated March 1924.

154. The word "government" only appears in the English translation.

155. IOR, L/P&S/12/4174 (PZ1431/24), enclosure to a letter from F. M. Bailey, British political officer in Sikkim, to His Majesty's Government in India, dated February 20, 1924.

156. IOR, L/P&S/12/4174 (PZ6939/32), letter forwarded in English translation by F. M. Bailey, British political officer in Sikkim, to His Majesty's Government in India, dated October 19, 1932.

157. IOR, L/P&S/12/4174 (PZ6940), letter forwarded in English translation by F. M. Bailey, British political officer in Sikkim, to His Majesty's Government in India, dated October 1, 1932.

158. Lian Yu was the Manchu imperial resident in Tibet from December 1906 to February 1912. He was the only one to hold this post during that time.

159. Zhang Yintang was Chinese governor in Lhasa in 1911. For the Tibetans, both Lian Yu, the previous representative of the Manchu court in Lhasa, and Zhang Yintang were considered of Manchu origin.

160. IOR, L/P&S/12/4174 (PZ 1769/24), letter translated by D. Macdonald, British trade agent in Gyeltsé, and addressed to F. M. Bailey, British political officer in Sikkim, dated March 1924.

161. IOR, L/P&S/12/4174 (PZ6939/32), letter forwarded in English translation by F. M. Bailey, British political officer in Sikkim, to His Majesty's Government in India, dated October 19, 1932.

162. IOR, L/P&S/12/4174 (PZ 1769/24), letter translated by D. Macdonald, British trade agent in Gyeltsé, and addressed to F. M. Bailey, British political officer in Sikkim, dated March 1924.

163. In the second fragment cited by Don khang sKal bzang bDe skyid, the Ninth Panchen Lama does not seem to have addressed himself to his general administrator (whom the British referred to as "prime minister") or to the abbots of the four colleges. He gives a general instruction to watch over the prosperity of the monastery and the good functioning of the monks' studies. See Don khang sKal bzang bDe skyid, *op. cit.*, 9.

164. IOR, L/P&S/12/4174 (PZ1769/24), letter translated by D. Macdonald, British trade agent in Gyeltsé, and addressed to F. M. Bailey, British political officer in Sikkim, dated March 1924.

165. IOR, L/P&S/12/4174 (PZ1431/24), enclosure to a letter from F. M. Bailey, British political officer in Sikkim, to His Majesty's Government in India, dated February 20, 1924.

166. Zhwa sgab pa, *op. cit.*, 277; Srung Kri hru'u, "Panchen sku 'phreng dgu pa dBus gTsang," 118; Don khang sKal bzang bDe skyid, *op. cit.*, 10.

167. Author's interview with the late Kachen Jangpa Thubten, January 1996.

168. See, e.g., Mehra, *Tibetan Polity*; Goldstein, *History of Modern Tibet*; Ya Hanzhang, *Banchan E'erdeni zhuan*; Guo Qing, "Brief Account of the Ninth Panchen Erdeni."

CHAPTER 3

1. Chan, *Religious Trends in Modern China*, 55.
2. Welch, *Buddhist Revival in China*, 94–95, 246–50.
3. Goldfuss, *Vers un bouddhisme du XXe siècle.*
4. Welch, *op. cit.*, 116.
5. Pittman, *Toward a Modern Chinese Buddhism.*
6. Xue Song, *Fojiao faling huibian*, 30–46.
7. Welch, *op. cit.*, 141.
8. Blofeld, *Jewel in the Lotus*, 23, 48. On Feng Yuxiang (1882–1948), see Boorman, *Biographical Dictionary of Republican China*, vol. 2, 37–43; Sheridan, *Chinese Warlord: The Career of Feng Yü-hsiang.*
9. Chan, *op. cit.*, 60–63.
10. Pratt, *Pilgrimage of Buddhism*, 681–89.
11. Fafang, "Zhongguo fojiao de xianzhuang," 22.
12. 'Jam dpal rGyal mtshan, "Khams Ri bo che dgon," 211–20.
13. Thub bstan Sangs rgyas, *rGya nag tu Bod kyi sku tshab*, 11; Xerab Nyima, "From Geshi of Sera Monastery to KMT Attaché," 20; Yao Zhaolin, "Xizang Gunque Zhongni 1924 nian chengwen xi 1924," 79–91.
14. Welch, *op. cit.*, 175.
15. Numerous articles have been written on the subject of the "chaplain-donor" relationship. See, e.g., Ruegg, "Mchod yon, yon mchod and mc̣hod gnas/yon gnas," 441–53; Ruegg, *Ordre spirituel et ordre temporel.*
16. In Buddhism, Kālacakra is a Buddha who reigns over time. The first Kālacakra initiation conferred by the Panchen Lama after his hasty departure from Tibet was held from April 15–22, 1928, at Yangwang monastery on the lands of the Qorcin Banner of the Jerim League, at the request of Prince Darhan. Seventy thousand people are said to have attended (a figure which seems unrealistic); the second occurred in June 1928, at Jastu monastery, on the lands of the Qorcin Banner of the Jerim League at the request of Prince Jasaqt. Liu Jiaju suggests a figure of eighty thousand attendees. Subsequent Kālacakra initiations given by the Panchen Lama were held on April 15, 1929, at Beizi monastery, on the lands of the Kesikten Banner of the Juu Uda League, at the request of the chief of the ten leagues; in August 1930, on the lands of the Üjümücin of the Shilingol League, at the request of Prince Sönam Rabtan; in July 1932, on the lands of the Üjümücin Banner; from October 21–24, 1932, in Beijing, at the Hall of Supreme Harmony in the Forbidden City, at the request of Duan Qirui; from May 13–15, 1934, in Hangzhou, at the Lingyin Temple, at the request of Dai Jitao; in September (or October) 1935 at Kumbum monastery in Amdo, at the request of Dai Jitao; and on July 14, 1936, at Labrang trashikhyil monastery. See Nanjing Archives, telegram from Wangdü Norbu to the Mongolian and Tibetan Affairs Commission, dated September 15, 1935, reproduced in Zhongguo di er lishi dang'anguan, *Jiu shi Banchan nei di*, 482, doc. 7, 7–8; Chen Wenjian, *Banchan da shi dong lai shiwu nian dashiji*, 9–10, 18–20, 61, 73; Liu Jiaju, *Banchan dashi quanji*, 41–43, 58; Ma Hetian, *Gan Qing Zang bianqu kaocha ji*, 109–14; lHa mkhar yongs 'dzin bsTan pa rGyal mtsan, *sKyabs mgon rje btsun bla ma Blo bzang Thub bstan Chos kyi Nyi ma*, vol. 1, fols. 190A–204B, 225A–288A; Hyer and Jagchid, *A Mongolian Living Buddha*, 132–37; A blo ba, *Hwang krin ching Blo bzang Tshe dbang dang kun mkhyen lnga ba chen po*, 140.
17. In Buddhism, Amitāyus (Tib. Tsépamé) is the Saṃbhogakāya aspect of the divinity Amitābha to whom disciples pay homage to obtain a long terrestrial life. Amitāyus is also called the Buddha of eternal life. The first Amitāyus Long Life Initiation was given by the Panchen Lama in March 1925 at the Palace of Harmony in Beijing. This was followed by a second one in April 1925 in Hangzhou at the Lingyin Temple, at the request of Sun Chuanfang, the military governor of Zhejiang Province. Subsequent Amitāyus long life initiations performed by the Panchen Lama occurred on May 19, 1926, at the Yingtai Palace of the Forbidden City in Beijing; in October 1926 at the Yellow Temple

in Shenyang, at the request of Zhang Zuolin and the Mongol princes; and in June 1935 at Kumbum monastery in Amdo. See Chen Wenjian, *op. cit.*, 5–6, 8, 56; Liu Jiaju, *op. cit.*, 38, 40.

18. Tārā (Tib. Drölma) is a Buddha in feminine form. She is considered an emanation of all Buddhas. She has twenty-one different forms, of which the most famous are Green Tārā (associated with the protection of beings) and White Tārā (associated with the longevity of beings). The first Green Tārā long life initiation given by the Panchen Lama was held on February 1, 1925, at Mount Wutai. The prelate's choice of teaching on Mount Wutai was not accidental. It is a prominent Buddhist site from the Northern Wei dynasty (386–534) dedicated to Mañjuśrī, the bodhisattva of knowledge, and is highly venerated in China and elsewhere. Tibetans began pilgrimages to Mount Wutai as early as the thirteenth century. The second long life initiation of Green Tārā took place in March 1925 at the Palace of Eternal Harmony in Beijing. And, a White Tārā initiation was held on May 6, 1925, at Mount Wutai. See *Zhongyang ribao*, March 23, 1925; Chen Wenjian, *op. cit.*, 7; Liu Jiaju, *op. cit.*, 39; Chayet, *Les temples de Jehol*, 147; Arènes, *La déesse Drol-ma*.

19. Bhaiṣajyaguru is the Medicine Buddha. Tibetans refer to him as Sangyé Menla. The Panchen Lama gave a Bhaiṣajyaguru initiation in spring 1933 at the Longchang Temple in Pukou, at the request of Dai Jitao and Shi Qingyang. See Liu Jiaju, *op. cit.* 49.

20. The first guru yoga teaching, which accompanies the tantra, was given by the Panchen Lama in April 1925 at the Lingyin Temple in Hangzhou, at the request of Sun Chuanfang. The second was held on January 30, 1933, in Nanjing at the Overseas Chinese Hotel, at the request of lay Buddhists. See Chen Wenjian, *op. cit.*, 5; Liu Jiaju, *op. cit.*, 49.

21. "Taking refuge" (Tib. *kya bro*) is the act by which a Buddhist places him or herself under the protection of the "Three Jewels." The Panchen Lama gave commentary on this in April 1925 at the Lingyin Temple in Hangzhou, at the request of Sun Chuanfang.

22. The mantra or six-syllable formula *om mani padme hum* literally means "the jewel in the lotus." It evokes the union of method (the jewel) and wisdom (the lotus), enabling access to the full enlightenment of a Buddha, and is associated with Avalokiteśvara, the bodhisattva of compassion. The Panchen Lama taught this mantra in June 1931 at the Longchang Temple in Pukou at the request of Dai Jitao, Wang Yongbin, and Chen Daqi. See Chen Wenjian, *op. cit.*, 12.

23. *Dagong bao*, October 6, 1932.

24. On Duan Qirui (1865–1936), see Boorman, *op. cit.*, vol. 3, 330–35.

25. *Dagong bao*, October 12 and 14, 1932.

26. Hu Jianzhong, "La Cité interdite," 5–6.

27. On Wu Peifu (1874–1939), see Boorman, *op. cit.*, vol. 3, 444–50.

28. On Sun Chuanfang (1885–1935), see Boorman, *op. cit.*, vol. 3, 160–62.

29. On Zhang Xueliang (1898/1901–2001), see Boorman, *op. cit.*, vol. 1, 61–68.

30. On Prince Demchüg Dongrub (1902–1969), see Boorman, *op. cit.*, vol. 2, 6–10. He is also referred to as Prince De (Wang).

31. On the Changkya Hutuktu (1891–1957), see Jiang Zhongzheng, *Hu guo jing jue fojiao da shi Zhangjia Hutuketu shi*.

32. On Dai Jitao (1890–1949), see Boorman, *op. cit.*, vol. 2, 200–5.

33. Chen Wenjian, *op. cit.*, 19–20.

34. Liu Jiaju, *op. cit.*, 5; Chen Wenjian, *op. cit.*, 42; *Zhongyang ribao*, March 22, 1934. On Wang Yiting (1867–1938), see Yu Lingpo, *Zhongguo jin xian dai fojiao renwu zhi*, 346–49.

35. Chen Yisun, "Nan you jishi" in *Banchan dong lai*, 1. This work recounts the different events that the Ninth Panchen Lama participated in during his stays in Hangzhou and Shanghai. Each step of his voyage to these cities is detailed in a corresponding chapter whose pages are renumbered, starting from page one each time. In order to follow the book's original structure, the title of the chapter in addition to the page number is noted each time the book is cited.

36. Chen Wenjian, *op. cit.*, 43; Chen Yisun, "Banchan nan you suicongyuan minglu," in *op. cit.*, 1–3; *Zhongyang ribao*, April 27, 1934.

37. Chen Yisun, "Huanying Banchan fajia lai Hang banfa," in *op. cit.*, 1–3; *Zhongyang ribao*, April 4, 1934.

38. Chen Yisun, "Nan you jishi," in *op. cit.*, 2–3.

39. Ten to twenty thousand people came to welcome the Ninth Panchen Lama at the railway station in Hangzhou. See Chen Yisun, "Nan you jishi," in *op. cit.*, 2; Chen Wenjian, *op. cit.*, 43.

40. *Zhongyang ribao*, April 16–21, 1934.

41. The Kālacakra emblem is a monogram made up of seven letters (Y, R, V, L, M, S, K) and three symbols (sun, moon, and flame), representing "the ten powers" (*namcu wangden*). The letters are written in Lentsa, a Newar adaptation of the Indian Devanāgarī script.

42. *Zhongyang ribao*, April 23, 1934.

43. Chen Wenjian, *op. cit.*, 10; Liu Jiaju, *op. cit.*, 43.

44. Author's interview with Yéshé Dorjé (bodyguard of the Ninth Panchen Lama), Chengdu, November 26, 1992.

45. Author's interview with Lozang Döndrub (monk from Tashilhunpo), Bylakuppe, December 30, 1995.

46. Mongol interest in Buddhism dates back many centuries. The first chaplain-donor relations between Tibetan masters and Mongol authorities was formed between Köden Khan, grandson of Genghis Khan, and Sakya Paṇḍita (1182–1251), and then between Khubilai Khan (1261–1294) and Phakpa Lobrö Gyeltsen (1235–1280), nephew of Sakya Paṇḍita. Moreover, the relationship between the Mongols and the lineage of the Panchen Lamas has always been extremely tight given the geographical proximity between Tashilhunpo monastery and Mongolia, in addition to the presence of many Mongol monks at Tashilhunpo.

47. On the Kālacakra, see Newman, "A Brief History of Kālacakra," 51–90; Vira and Chandra, *Kālacakra Tantra and Other Texts*, introduction. On Shambhala, see Bernbaum, *The Way to Shambhala*; Gar je K'am trül Rinpoche, "A Geography and History of Shambhala," 3–11.

48. Author's interview with Kachen Lakpa Dorjé (monk from Tashilhunpo), Bylakuppe, January 1996. The Palace of the Omniscience and the Palace of the Virtuous belonged to the Panchen Lama and were located in Tashilhunpo. The Kālacakra emblem was on one of the seals that the Ninth Panchen Lama used to stamp his correspondence. See IOR, Mss Eur F. 80–116, correspondence between C. Bell and the Ninth Panchen Lama, 1934–35.

49. Chen Wenjian, *op. cit.*, 44.

50. On Shi Qingyang (1879–1935), see Li Shengping, *Zhongguo jin xian dai renming da cidian*, 90; on Wang Yongbin (1881–1944), see Li Shengping, *idem*, 34.

51. On Zhang Zuolin (1873–1928), see Boorman, *op cit.*, vol. 1, 115–22.

52. Chen Wenjian, *op. cit.*, 8–12; Liu Jiaju, *op. cit.*, 40–44.

53. Huang Zheng, *Duan Qirui yu Wan Xi junfa*, 305.

54. *Dagong bao*, October 21, 1932.

55. Hyer and Jagchid, *op. cit.*, 132–37; Chen Wenjian, *op. cit.*, 18.

56. The Panchen Lama's first trip to Mongolia was in April 1928 where he stayed until March 1931. He made a second trip in July 1931, staying until October 1932; and then on a third trip he stayed from February to October 1933.

57. Hyer and Jagchid, *op. cit.*, 134.

58. Kasuga, "Môko ramabyô chôsa hôkoku," 49–65. Kasuga visited the "Monastery of the Ninth Panchen" in Inner Mongolia in 1944.

59. Liu Jiaju, *op. cit.*, 46.

60. Chen Wenjian, *op. cit.*, 32.

61. Boorman, *op. cit.*, vol. 3, 200; Shi Dongchu, *Dai Jitao xiansheng foxue lunji*, 282.

62. Chen Wenjian, *op. cit.*, 23.

63. Author's interview with Kachen Lakpa Dorjé, January 1996.

64. Blo bzang rDo rje, *Rigs dang dkyil 'khor rgya mtsho'i khyab bdag*, fols. 608A–609B.

65. Author's interview with Dakpo Rinpoche (monk from Drépung), Paris, June 1995.

66. On October 11, 1924, Taixu founded the Buddhist Institute of Tibetan Study (*fojiao Zangwen xueyuan*) within the Ciyin Temple in Beijing. The institute's goal was to prepare Chinese monks to study Buddhism in Tibet with qualified Tibetan masters. Following their studies, the monks would return to China to train other monks, and in this way increase the spread of Buddhism. At the institute, monks studied Tibetan Buddhism with a Chinese layperson. A Chinese monk taught them *tantra* that he had studied in Japan. As for Dorjé Tsipa, the only Tibetan at the institute, he led three daily prayer sessions. In the end, the institute lasted only two years. Ten to twenty students from the single graduating class had the opportunity to go to Tibet. Among them only three made it to Lhasa: Nenghai (1886–1967), Chaoyi, and Fazun (1902–1980). The others studied in the monasteries of Kham. In 1932 Taixu founded the World Buddhist Institute (*shijie fo xueyuan*) in Chongqing thanks to government subsidies. The program of study of this new institute included a four-year seminar on Sino-Tibetan philosophy and religion. Tibetan and Chinese masters taught classic and modern subjects. After four years of study, student monks could choose a subject of specialization. This new institute was more successful than the first, as it remained functioning for eighteen years, during which 248 student monks were trained. See Shi Yinshun, *Taixu fashi nianpu*, 99; Fafang, "Huanying Zang wen xueyuan zhu shi Dong fan hong fa," 2–4; Zhou Guanren, "Goutong Han Zang wenhua," 4–8; Welch, *op. cit.*, 177; Luo Runcang, "Kangzhan qijian Sichuan Zang xue yanjiu gaishu," 12–15.

67. Between 1925 and 1933, the Ninth Panchen Lama created offices in Beijing, Chengdu, Xining, Shenyang, Nanjing, Dartsédo (Kangding), and Suiyuan.

68. See Chen Wenjian, *op. cit.*, 44. Among the local lay Buddhists were Xu Xiaotian, Wang Yiting, Du Yuesheng, Wang Xiaoji, Qu Wenliu, Chen Yuanbai, Zhao Yanwu, and Feng Yangshan. On Wu Tiecheng (1888–1953), see Li Shengping, *op. cit.*, 300.

69. Fafang, "Meng Zang xueyuan yu puti xuehui," 1; Chenkong, "Shanghai puti xuehui zai Wutai Shan chengli banshichu," 8–9.

70. Chen Wenjian, *op. cit.*, 44.

71. *Zhongyang ribao*, June 8, 1934.

72. Fafang, "Meng Zang xueyuan yu puti xuehui," 1–2.

73. Chen Wenjian, *op. cit.*, 64.

74. Chenkong, *op. cit.*, 8–9.

75. Chen Wenjian, *op. cit.*, 64.

76. Chenkong, *op. cit.*, 8–9.

77. Fafang, "Meng Zang xueyuan yu puti xuehui," 1–2.

78. Fazun belonged to the same graduating class as that of Nenghai and Chaoyi. He left for Tibet in 1925 where he spent eight years (five in Kham and three in Lhasa). He returned to Shanghai in June 1933, having passed through India. He was received by the Ninth Panchen Lama in June 1934, shortly before becoming head of the Sino-Tibetan Philosophical and Religious Seminary. See Zhou Guanren, *op. cit.*, 4–8; Fazun, *Wo qu guo de Xizang*, 2–6; Fazun, *Xiandai Xizang*, 133–46; *Zhongyang ribao*, June 26, 1934.

79. Jiang Zhongzheng, *op. cit.*, 33.

80. Chen Wenjian, *op. cit.*, 37.

81. *Zhongyang ribao*, February 13–14, 16, and 19, 1934.

82. Nanjing Archives, telegram from Jiang Zhiyu, Chinese emissary to Tibet in Lhasa, to the Mongolian and Tibetan Affairs Commission, forwarded by the secretary of the Chinese State Council, dated July 4, 1936, reproduced in Zhongguo di er lishi dang'an guan, *Jiu shi Banchan nei di*, doc. 300, 315–16.

83. Chen Wenjian, *op. cit.*, 83.

84. Liu Jiaju, *op. cit.*, 60.

85. Letter from the Fourteenth Dalai Lama addressed to Jiang Zemin, president of the People's Republic of China, dated October 11, 1995, reproduced in *The International Communiqué Ltd.*

CHAPTER 4

1. Chen Wenjian, *Banchan dashi dong lai shiwu nian dashiji*, 5. This meeting was to define the means to achieve the unity of the Chinese nation.

2. Liu Jiaju, *Banchan dashi quanji*, 39; Chen Wenjian, *op. cit.*, 7.

3. Speech by the Ninth Panchen Lama delivered by his attendant Lozang Gyeltsen at the first National Reconstruction Conference held on February 1, 1925, reproduced in Zhongguo di er lishi dang'an guan, *Jiu shi Banchan neidi*, doc. 3, 3–4. A few months after the conference, numerous other conferences took place. They were to define the new organization of the National Assembly and to draw up a provisional constitution. In December 1925 these objectives were achieved, but on April 9, 1926, Duan Qirui was deposed.

4. Letter from the Ninth Panchen Lama to Yan Xishan, director of the Mongolian and Tibetan Affairs Commission, dated January 24, 1929, reproduced in Zhongguo di er lishi dang'an guan, *op. cit.*, doc. 7, 7–8. On Yan Xishan (1883–1960), see Boorman, *Biographical Dictionary of Republican China*, vol. 4, 47–50; Gillin, *Warlord Yen Hsi-shan.*

5. Speech by the Ninth Panchen Lama at the opening ceremony of the National People's Convention, entitled "Before Governing the Country, One Must Mend One's Own Ways" (*Yao zhi guo xian yao xiu ji*), May 5, 1931, in Liu Jiaju, *op. cit.*, 121–22.

6. One of the more recent of several biographies of Sun Yat-sen is that of Bergère, *Sun Yat-sen* (1994), an English translation of which was published in 1998.

7. Speech by the Ninth Panchen Lama entitled "The Concept of Equality in Buddhism and the Doctrine Handed Down by Sun Yat-sen" (*Fojiao yu Zongli yijiao de pingdeng guan*) in Liu Jiaju, *op. cit.*, 146–49. In 1934 the Chinese Buddhist master Taixu invited the Ninth Panchen Lama to teach the Buddhist doctrine and give a Kālacakra initiation at the Lingyin Temple in Hangzhou. The preliminaries began on May 9. It was at the opening ceremony that the Ninth Panchen Lama gave this speech.

8. Xu Wenshan, *Guofu yijiao sanmin zhuyi zongji*; Bergère, *op. cit.*, 400–46.

9. See Ninth Panchen Lama's speech in Hangzhou, May 9, 1934, in Liu Jiaju, *op. cit.*, 146–49.

10. Tuttle, in "Review of *Le 9e Panchen Lama (1883–1937)*," mentions one of the Panchen Lama's speeches that was transcribed into Tibetan in lHa mkhar yongs 'dzin bsTan pa rGyal mtshan, *sKyabs mgon rje btsun bla ma Blo bzang Thub bstan Chos kyi Nyi ma dGe legs rNam rgyal dPal bzang po'i bka 'bum ga pa'i dkar chag rin po che'i phreng ba*, vol. 1, 388–89.

11. Yamagata Aritomo introduced Japan to a political system based on local autonomy that had been developed by Albert Mosse and Omori Shoichi, both of whom had studied with the Prussian Rudolf Gneist (1816–1895). Huang Zunxian (1848–1905), a Cantonese diplomat posted to Japan from 1877 to 1882 introduced the term "autonomous government" (*jichi* in Japanese) into Chinese politics. At the end of the Qing, local autonomy was less a grassroots social movement than a project for political transformation and state expansion. It was primarily ruling class officials and the intelligentsia that advocated for local autonomy. Traditionally having rather limited direct control over localities, the government was obliged to resort to these elite initiatives while, at the same time, submitting them to strict administrative control. Officials thus found a way to increase their powers on a local scale, despite the fact that the masses did not adhere to the idea of "local autonomy." See Kuhn, "Local Self-Government," 257–98; Xiao-Planes, *La société générale d'éducation du Jiangsu*, 305–12.

12. Sun Yat-sen, *Minzu zhuyi*, first lecture on nationalism.

13. Sun Yat-sen, *Minzu zhuyi*, first and third lectures on nationalism.

14. See, e.g., Wang Jingwei, cited in Gasster, *Chinese Intellectuals*, 82; Zhang Binglin, cited in Crossley, "Emperorship and Identity."

15. Speech by the Ninth Panchen Lama delivered by his attendant Lozang Gyeltsen at the first National Reconstruction Conference, February 1, 1925, reproduced in Zhongguo di er lishi dang'an guan, *op. cit.*, doc. 3, 3–4.

16. See speech by the Ninth Panchen Lama given in Hulunbuir, Heilongjiang Province, entitled "Let Us Unite Unanimously to Safeguard the National Territory" (*Yizhi tuantie baoquan lingtu*),

September 5, 1931, in Liu Jiaju, *op. cit.*, 125–26; also reproduced in Zhongguo di er lishi dang'an guan, *op. cit.*, doc. 56, 53–57; and remarks given by the Ninth Panchen Lama in Xining, Qinghai Province on May 12, 1935, in the presence of the governor of the province, Ma Bufang, in which he explains why he chose to return to Tibet by way of Qinghai, in *idem*, 159–60.

17. Letter from the Ninth Panchen Lama to Yan Xishan, director of the Mongolian and Tibetan Affairs Commission, dated January 24, 1929, reproduced in Zhongguo di er lishi dang'an guan, *op. cit.*, doc. 7, 7–9.

18. Speech by the Ninth Panchen Lama at the opening ceremony of the National People's Convention, May 5, 1931, in Liu Jiaju, *op. cit.*, 121–22.

19. Remarks by the Ninth Panchen Lama's to welcoming officials who had come to greet him in Nanjing, December 23, 1932, in Liu Jiaju, *op cit.*, 131–32.

20. Speech by the Ninth Panchen Lama at the anniversary of the founding of the Mongolian and Tibetan Affairs Commission, entitled "The Link Between Tibet's History and the Five Nationalities" (*Xizang lishi yu wuzu zhi lianhe*), January 21, 1933, in Liu Jiaju, *op. cit.*, 126–28; also reproduced in Zhongguo di er lishi dang'an guan, *op. cit.*, doc. 56, 53–57.

21. Speech by the Ninth Panchen Lama in Nanjing during the Third Congress of the New Asia Association (*Xin Yaxiya xuehui*) entitled "Tibet is Part of China's National Territory" (*Xizang shi Zhongguo de lingtu*), May 20, 1931, in Liu Jiaju, *op. cit.*, 123–24. Note that several present-day Chinese government websites cite this speech as given on May 10, 1931. Cf. http://www.china-un.org/eng/zt/xzwt/t28847.htm; http://nz.chineseembassy.org/eng/zt/zgxz/xzfz/t39512.htm; www.china.com.cn/ch-xizang/tibet/serie.../independentframe.html.

22. Speech by the Ninth Panchen Lama at the anniversary of the founding of the Mongolian and Tibetan Affairs Commission, January 21, 1933, in Liu Jiaju, *op. cit.*, 126–28. The Ninth Panchen Lama's view regarding the state of relations between China and Mongolia before 1911 is quite similar to that which he expresses concerning China and Tibet. In 1931 he stated that "in the past, the Chinese and Mongols mutually helped one another ... The Sino-Mongol relations are very close." See, e.g., his speech in Hulunbuir, September 5, 1931, in Liu Jiaju, *op. cit.*, 125–26.

23. Speech by the Ninth Panchen Lama at the anniversary of the founding of the Mongolian and Tibetan Affairs Commission, January 21, 1933, in Liu Jiaju, *op. cit.*, 126–28.

24. Letter from the Ninth Panchen Lama to Yan Xishan, director of the Mongolian and Tibetan Affairs Commission, dated January 24, 1929, reproduced in Zhongguo di er lishi dang'an guan, *op. cit.*, doc. 7, 7–8.

25. On November 1, 1930, the Ninth Panchen Lama reminded Chiang Kai-shek of the existence of the Sino-Tibetan problem in a letter written in his native tongue to which a salutation scarf had been attached. This letter was translated from Tibetan into Chinese by a member of the Mongolian and Tibetan Affairs Commission before being delivered. See Nanjing Archives, letter from the Ninth Panchen Lama to Chiang Kai-shek, delivered to the Office of Civil Affairs by the Mongolian and Tibetan Affairs Commission on November 8, 1930, reproduced in Zhongguo di er lishi dang'an guan, *op. cit.*, doc. 16, 17–19.

26. Letter from the Ninth Panchen Lama to Yan Xishan, director of the Mongolian and Tibetan Affairs Commission, dated January 24, 1929, reproduced in Zhongguo di er lishi dang'an guan, *op. cit.*, doc. 7, 7–8.

27. Nanjing Archives, letter from the Ninth Panchen Lama to Chiang Kai-shek, dated November 8, 1930, reproduced in Zhongguo di er lishi dang'an guan, *op. cit.*, doc. 16, 17–19.

28. Speech by the Ninth Panchen Lama in Hulunbuir, September 5, 1931, in Liu Jiaju, *op. cit.*, 125–26.

29. Speech by the Ninth Panchen Lama at the anniversary of the founding of the Mongolian and Tibetan Affairs Commission, January 21, 1933, in Liu Jiaju, *op. cit.*, 126–28.

30. For example, see the chaplain-donor relations established between the Fifth Dalai Lama and the Shunzhi Emperor in 1652, the Sixth Panchen Lama and the Qianlong Emperor in 1780, and the Thirteenth Dalai Lama and the Guangxu Emperor and the Empress Dowager Cixi in 1908.

31. Speech by the Ninth Panchen Lama in Hulunbuir, dated September 5, 1931, in Liu Jiaju, *op. cit.,* 125–26.

32. Sun Yat-sen, *op. cit.*, sixth lecture on nationalism.

33. National Archives, letter from the Ninth Panchen Lama to Chiang Kai-shek, dated November 8, 1930, reproduced in Zhongguo di er lishi dang'an guan, *op. cit.*, doc. 16, 17–19; report by the Ninth Panchen Lama addressed to the Mongolian and Tibetan Affairs Commission, dated April 17, 1930, reproduced in *idem*, doc. 15, 15–17.

34. Speech by the Ninth Panchen Lama at the opening ceremony of the National People's Convention, May 5, 1931, in Liu Jiaju, *op. cit.*, 121–22.

35. Letter from the Ninth Panchen Lama to Yan Xishan, director of the Mongolian and Tibetan Affairs Commission, dated January 24, 1929, reproduced in Zhongguo di er lishi dang'an guan, *op. cit.*, doc. 7, 7–8.

36. Speech by the Ninth Panchen Lama addressed to Ma Hongkui, military governor of Ningxia Province and all the members of his government, entitled "Reinforce Border Defense by Developing Communication Networks" (*Gonggu bianfang dang yi jiaotong ru shou*), January 24, 1935, in Liu Jiaju, *op. cit.*, 155–56; "Gonggu bianfang dang yi jiaotong ru shou," *Xichui xuanhua shi gongshu yuekan*, 39–40. On Ma Hongkui (1892–1937), see Li Shengping, *op. cit.*, 20.

37. On March 19, 1935, when his departure for Tibet seemed imminent, the Ninth Panchen Lama proposed in a letter to Huang Musong a project for the propagation of values in Tibet. Huang Musong was, at the time, the new director of the Mongolian and Tibetan Affairs Commission. See Zhongguo di er lishi dang'an guan, *op. cit.*, doc. 115, 110–12. On Huang Musong (1885–1937), see Boorman, *op. cit.*, vol. 2, 203–5; Huang Musong, "Xian Xiong Musong shilüe," 1–4.

38. Remarks by the Ninth Panchen Lama in Xining, Qinghai Province, where he explains the reason why he chose to return to Tibet by way of Qinghai, May 12, 1935, in Liu Jiaju, *op. cit.,* 159–60. On Ma Bufang (1903–1975), see Boorman, *op. cit.*, vol. 3, 474–75.

39. Speech by the Ninth Panchen Lama addressed to Ma Hongkui, military governor of Ningxia Province and all the members of his government, January 24, 1935, in Liu Jiaju, *op. cit.*, 155–56.

40. Speech by the Ninth Panchen Lama in Nanjing at the Third Congress of the New Asia Association, May 20, 1931, in Liu Jiaju, *op. cit.*, 123–24.

41. Speech by the Ninth Panchen Lama in Hulunbuir, September 5, 1931, in Liu Jiaju, *op. cit.*, 125–26.

42. Speech by the Ninth Panchen Lama at the anniversary of the founding of the Mongolian and Tibetan Affairs Commission, January 21, 1933, in Liu Jiaju, *op. cit.*, 126–28.

43. Remarks by the Ninth Panchen Lama in Xining, where he explains the reason why he chose to return to Tibet by way of Qinghai, May 12, 1935, in Liu Jiaju, *op. cit.,* 159–60.

44. Speech by the Ninth Panchen Lama addressed to Ma Hongkui, military governor of Ningxia Province and all the members of his government, January 24, 1935, in Liu Jiaju, *op. cit.*, 155–56.

45. Speech by the Ninth Panchen Lama in Hulunbuir, September 5, 1931, in Liu Jiaju, *op. cit.*, 125–26.

46. Remarks by the Ninth Panchen Lama to welcoming officials who had come to greet him in Nanjing, December 23, 1932, in Liu Jiaju, *op. cit.*, 131–32.

47. Speech by the Ninth Panchen Lama in Hangzhou, May 9, 1934, in Liu Jiaju, *op. cit.*, 146–49.

48. Remarks by the Ninth Panchen Lama at the preparatory meeting of the first National Reconstruction Conference, January 27, 1925, in Chen Wenjian, *op. cit.*, 5.

49. Speech of the Ninth Panchen Lama delivered by Lozang Gyeltsen at the first National Reconstruction Conference, February 1, 1925, reproduced in Zhongguo di er lishi dang'an guan, *op. cit.*, doc. 3, 3–4.

50. Speech by the Ninth Panchen Lama at the opening ceremony of the National People's Convention, May 5, 1931, in Liu Jiaju, *op. cit.*, 121–22.

51. Speech by the Ninth Panchen Lama in Hulunbuir, September 5, 1931, in Liu Jiaju, *op. cit.*, 125–26.

52. Nanjing Archives, telegram from the Ninth Panchen Lama to the Chinese State Council, dated March 4, 1932, reproduced in Zhongguo di er lishi dang'an guan, *op. cit.*, doc. 36, 38.

53. Speech by the Ninth Panchen Lama to journalists at the Overseas Chinese Hotel in Nanjing, entitled "Reflections on the Past, the Present and the Future" (*Guoqu xianzai weilai zhi san da ganxiang*), December 21, 1932, in Liu Jiaju, *op. cit.*, 130–31.

54. Speech by the Ninth Panchen Lama addressed to Ma Hongkui, military governor of Ningxia Province and members of his government, January 24, 1935, in Liu Jiaju, *op. cit.*, 155–56.

55. Speech by the Ninth Panchen Lama in Hangzhou, May 9, 1934, in Liu Jiaju, *op. cit.*, 146–49.

56. Speech by the Ninth Panchen Lama in Hangzhou, May 9, 1934, in Liu Jiaju, *op. cit.*, 146–49.

57. Sichuan Archives, draft of a telegram from the minister of foreign affairs to Lu Hongtao, dated April 24, 1924; Chen Wenjian, *op. cit.*, 1. On Lu Hongtao, see Li Shengping, *op. cit.*, 384.

58. Chen Wenjian, *op. cit.*, 1–2; Liu Jiaju, *op. cit.*, 11, 38; Srung Kri hru'u, "Panchen sku 'phreng dgu pa dBus gTsang," 118. The Tibetan term for this title is *zhung ten pel.*

59. Tang Jingfu, "Minguo shiqi lijie Zhongyang zhengfu weihu Xizang zhuquan de cuoshi," 45.

60. Dreyer, *China at War*, 112–16; Sheridan, *Chinese Warlord,* 12.

61. Chen Wenjian, *op. cit.,* 3.

62. On Zhang Zongchang (1881–1932), see Boorman, *op. cit.*, vol. 1, 122–27; on Qi Xieyuan, see Perleberg, *Who's Who in Modern China,* 232.

63. On Lu Yongxiang (1867–1933), see Li Shengping, *op. cit.*, 95.

64. Chen Wenjian, *op. cit.*, 6, 8; Liu Jiaju, *op. cit.*, 40.

65. Dreyer, *op. cit.*, 115–16.

66. Huang Zheng and Chen Zhangde, *Duan Qirui yu Wan Xi junfa*; Ji Yu, *Duan Qirui zhuan*; Sheridan, *op. cit.*; Wang Chaozhu, *Feng Yuxiang he Jiang Jieshi.*

67. For further details of the Changkya Hutuktu, see Appendix B, note 18.

68. Baruun monastery is referred to as Chaozang si in Chinese.

69. Welch, *Buddhist Revival in China*, 174.

70. Jiang Zhongzheng, *Hu guo jing jue fujiao da shi Zhangjia Hutuketu shi*, 33.

71. *Dagong bao*, February 25, 1925.

72. *Minguo ribao*, March 9, 1925.

73. Nanjing Archives, letter no. 156 from the Mongolian and Tibetan Affairs Commission to the Ninth Panchen Lama, dated August 1925, reproduced in Zhongguo di er lishi dang'an guan, *op. cit.*, doc. 4, 5; Chen Wenjian, *op. cit.*, 7; Liu Jiaju, *op. cit.*, 39; Srung Kri hru'u, *op. cit.*, 119. In Tibetan the title "World Savior Who Propagates Orthodoxy" is *lokar pel né jikten penpa.*

74. *Minguo ribao*, April 28, 1925.

75. Chen Wenjian, *op. cit.*, 6.

76. Four army corps were formed. The first was directed by Chiang Kai-shek, the second by Feng Yuxiang, the third by Yan Xishan, and the fourth by Li Zongren.

77. Chen Wenjian, *op. cit.*, 9–10; Liu Jiaju, *op. cit.*, 41–42.

78. Sheridan, *op. cit.*, 252–65; Gillin, *op. cit.*, 118–22.

79. Sheridan, *op. cit.*, 265–67.

80. Chen Wenjian, *op. cit.*, 12; Liu Jiaju, *op. cit.*, 44; *Minguo ribao*, April 16, 1931.

81. On Duan Qirui, see Nathan, "A Constitutional Republic," 283; Boorman, *op. cit.*, vol. 3, 335. On Sun Chuanfang, see Boorman, *op. cit.*, vol. 3, 162; Li Shengping, *op. cit.*, 204.

82. Fletcher, *China's Inner Asian Frontier*; Jagchid, *Essays in Mongolian Studies*, Part 4, "The Inner Mongolian Kuomintang of the 1920s;" Cotton, *Asian Frontier Nationalism.*

83. This party disappeared when it fused with the Chinese National Party in 1927.

84. On Buyantai (Bai Yunti 1894-?), see Boorman, *op. cit.*, vol. 1, 6–9; S. Jagchid, *op. cit.*, 265–66, 276.

85. These two organizations were to be dissolved in 1927 and 1928, respectively. See Boorman, *op. cit.*, vol. 1, 6–9; Jagchid, *op. cit.*, 265–66, 276.

86. Yu Hanhua, "Nei Menggu zizhi yundong zong jiantao," 42–43.

87. Lattimore, *Studies in Frontier History*, 427; Hyer, "Demchugdungrub," 68; Jagchid, "Inner Mongolia under Japanese Occupation," 149–72.

88. On Unenbayin (Wu Heling 1896–1980), see Boorman, *op. cit.*, vol. 3, 353–56.

89. *Meng Zang weiyuanhui jianshi*, 161; Guo Jijiao, *Minguo yilai Zhongyang dui Meng Zang de shizheng*, 12–13; Dong Shufan, *Minguo shi san nian yilai zhi Zhongguo guomindang yu Xizang*, 195–96.

90. Chen Wenjian, *op. cit.*, 8–10; Liu Jiaju, *op. cit.*, 40–43.

91. Letter from the Ninth Panchen Lama to Chiang Kai-shek, forwarded on November 8, 1930, to the Office of Civil Affairs by the Mongolian and Tibetan Affairs Commission, reproduced in Zhongguo di er lishi dang'an guan *op. cit.*, doc. 16, 17–19.

92. Chen Wenjian, *op. cit.*, 12; Liu Jiaju, *op. cit.*, 44; Srung Kri hru'u, *op. cit.*, 119.

93. The condition of my copy of this speech in the work by Liu Jiaju on pages 123 and 124 is unreadable.

94. Liu Jiaju, *op. cit.*, 121–22.

95. Within the title the "Great and Glorious Master Panchen Who Protects the Country and Propagates its Values" (*Huguo xuanhua guanghui da shi*), the literal translation of the Chinese term *xuanhua* (an abbreviation of *xuanchuan wenhua*) is "transmit government orders" or "educate the people." From an etymological point of view, the Chinese term *hua* means "someone who can be transformed by education." Consequently, *hua* means "education" with the implicit sense of "civilize in accordance with Confucian values." If we compare the Chinese title with its Tibetan translation engraved on the Ninth Panchen Lama's seal, which is *gyelkyop tenpel kunkhyen lopön chenpo* (Learned Master Who Propagates Buddhist Teachings and Protects the Country) or *gyelkap kyongwé gégen chenpo gyeltsen yongkidagpo tamcé khyenpa* (Great Master who Protects the Country, Learned Guardian of all the Teachings), it is clear that the Chinese term *hua* is used in the sense of "Buddhist teaching." In this case, the meaning of "education" included in *hua* corresponds to Buddhist teachings given by the Panchen Lama. The Tibetan term *dul* would have been a better choice to translate *hua*, because it has exactly the same meaning as *xuanhua* ("transmit government orders" or "educate the people"). Obviously the Tibetan title corresponded to a Tibetan master better than the Chinese title; this difference in itself has political meaning. See Srung Kri hru'u, *op. cit.*, 119; Ya Hanzhang, *Banchan E'erdeni zhuan*, 563. As for the title "Great Master" (*da shi*), it is a deferential term, which, in principle, is reserved for Buddha, because he represents a model to follow. As of the ninth century, it was awarded to Buddhist monks by the emperor. Its attribution implies a close relationship with the Chinese government. See Forte, "Daishi," 1019–34.

96. Ninth Panchen Lama's speech in Hulunbuir, September 5, 1931, in Liu Jiaju, *op. cit.*, 125–26. Contrary to the Ninth Panchen Lama's statement, we cannot say that the former Qin and Han "had lived in harmony" with the Xiongnu, nor the Tang with the Kitan. We can, however, say that Chinese influence on the Mongols was developed during the Mongol Yuan dynasty.

97. Nanjing Archives, telegram from the office of the Ninth Panchen Lama in Nanjing to the Mongolian and Tibetan Affairs Commission, dated September 22, 1931, reproduced in Zhongguo di er lishi dang'an guan, *op. cit.*, doc. 27, 33.

98. Lattimore, *Nomads and Commissars*, 131–33; Bawden, *Modern History of Mongolia*, 316–18.

99. Atwood, *Revolutionary Nationalist Mobilization in Inner Mongolia*, 127–28.

100. Jagchid, *Essays in Mongolian Studies*, 276.

101. On September 18, 1931, the Japanese bombed the South-Manchurian Railway near the city of Shenyang. They passed off the attack as perpetrated by the Chinese to give themselves the pretext of a self-defense operation that would allow them to advance on Manchuria.

102. Text of the law, reproduced in Guo Jijiao, *op. cit.*, 17–21.

103. Yu Hanhua, *op. cit.*, 44.

104. Bat Khaalga monastery is referred to as Bailing miao in Chinese.

105. Nanjing Archives, telegram from the Ninth Panchen Lama to the Chinese State Council, dated March 4, 1932, reproduced in Zhongguo di er lishi dang'an guan, *op. cit.*, doc. 36, 38.

106. This Chinese title was translated into Tibetan in two different ways. The first as *nubtha tenpel phonya chenmo* or "Great Emissary for the Propagation of Buddhist Teaching on the Western Frontier." The second translation as *nubcok kyongwé gégen chenmo* or "Great Master Who Protects the Western Regions." See Srung Kri hru'u, *op. cit.*, 120; Ya Hanzhang, *op. cit.*, 567.

107. Chen Wenjian, *op. cit.*, 18; Liu Jiaju, *op. cit.*, 46.

108. On Fu Zuoyi (1895–1974), see Boorman, *op. cit.*, vol. 1, 47–51.

109. *Zhongyang ribao*, December 11, 1932; Chen Wenjian, *op. cit.*, 23; Jiang Zhongzheng, *op. cit.*, 33.

110. *Zhongyang ribao*, December 3, 1932; Yu Hanhua, *op. cit.*, 44; Lattimore, *Nationalism and Revolution in Mongolia*, 28.

111. *Zhongyang ribao*, December 17, 1932.

112. *Zhongyang ribao*, December 20, 1932; speech by the Ninth Panchen Lama at the Overseas Chinese Hotel in Nanjing, December 21, 1932, in Liu Jiaju, *op. cit.*, 130–31.

113. *Zhongyang ribao*, December 20, 1932. This newspaper article appeared three days prior to the Panchen Lama's remarks before Chinese officials who had come to welcome him in Nanjing on December 23, 1932. It is likely that the prelate spoke with journalists before the welcoming ceremonies had been organized, and also prior to his speech to them at the Overseas Chinese Hotel on December 21, 1932; see also Liu Jiaju, *op. cit.*, 131–32.

114. Speech by the Ninth Panchen Lama at the anniversary of the founding of the Mongolian and Tibetan Affairs Commission, January 21, 1933, Liu Jiaju, *op. cit.*, 126–28.

115. *Dagong bao*, February 6 and 17, 1933; Chen Wenjian, *op. cit.*, 24–25; Liu Jiaju, *op. cit.*, 49; Srung Kri hru'u, *op. cit.*, 120.

116. Nanjing Archives, telegram from the Ninth Panchen Lama to the Chinese government, dated March 16, 1933, reproduced in Zhongguo di er lishi dang'an guan, *op. cit.*, doc. 57, 57.

117. Huang Shijian, "Riben diguo zhuyi de 'Man Meng zhengce,'" 111; Lattimore, *Studies in Frontier History*, 432. Since March 1933 Xing'an Province was administered directly by the Manchukuo office in Changchun. After having founded the Manchukuo state, the Japanese advanced on the lands of the Inner Mongolia leagues and created a province without a capital, which was joined to Manchukuo. This province, called Xing'an, was the result of an artificial assemblage of the land from three different leagues: Jerim League to the east, Josutu League to the south, and Juu Uda League to the north.

118. Liu Jiaju, *op. cit.*, 50; Chen Wenjian, *op. cit.*, 27–28.

119. Fang Fanjiu, *Menggu gaikuang yu Nei Meng zizhi yundong*, 57.

120. Huang Shijian, *op. cit.*, 115; Yu Hanhua, *op. cit.*, 45.

121. Jagchid, *Essays in Mongolian Studies*, 285–86.

122. Yu Hanhua, *op. cit.*, 45.

123. Huang Shijian, *op. cit.*, 115; Fang Fanjiu, *op. cit.*, 63.

124. Chen Wenjian, *op. cit.*, 32; Liu Jiaju, *op. cit.*, 50.

125. Fang Fanjiu, *op. cit.*, 85.

126. Huang Shijian, *op. cit.*, 114; Chen Wenjian, *op. cit.*, 31.

127. Fang Fanjiu, *op. cit.*, 64.

128. Chen Wenjian, *op. cit.*, 32; Liu Jiaju, *op. cit.*, 51.

129. Chen Wenjian, *op. cit.*, 33.

130. Fang Fanjiu, *op. cit.*, 86; Liu Jiaju, *op. cit.*, 51.

131. Hyer and Jagchid, *A Mongolian Living Buddha*, 140. The biography of Changkya Hutuktu makes no mention of these incidents.

132. Fang Fanjiu, *op. cit.*, 67; Yu Hanhua, *op. cit.*, 46.

133. The Japanese pushed the head of the Shilingol League in the province of Chahar to attend a meeting at Dolonnor. See Huang Shijian, *op. cit.*, 114; Chen Wenjian, *op. cit.*, 33.

134. Chen Wenjian, *op. cit.*, 34.

135. Huang Shijian, *op. cit.*, 115; Fang Fanjiu, *op. cit.*, 67. For the text of this law, see Fang Fanjiu, *op. cit.*, 71–77.

136. Fang Fanjiu, *op. cit.*, 68, 78.

137. Yu Hanhua, *op. cit.*, 46. On Huang Shaohong (1895–1966), see Boorman, *op. cit.*, vol. 2, 205–8.

138. Fang Fanjiu, *op. cit.*, 79–80; Yu Hanhua, *op. cit.*, 46.

139. Fang Fanjiu, *op. cit.*, 68.

140. Fang Fanjiu, *op. cit.*, 68; Yu Hanhua, *op. cit.*, 46.

141. Speech by the Ninth Panchen Lama before the Mongol princes at Bat Khaalga monastery on October 25, 1933, reproduced in Zhongguo di er lishi dang'an guan, *op. cit.*, doc. 75, 72.

142. Fang Fanjiu, *op. cit.*, 69; Yu Hanhua, *op. cit.*, 46.

143. Fang Fanjiu, *op. cit.*, 98; Chen Wenjian, *op. cit.*, 35; Yu Hanhua, *op. cit.*, 46.

144. Fang Fanjiu, *op. cit.*, 100–3; Yu Hanhua, *op. cit.*, 47.

145. Chen Wenjian, *op. cit.*, 36.

146. Fang Fanjiu, *op. cit.*, 99; Chen Wenjian, *op. cit.*, 36.

147. Yu Hanhua, *op. cit.*, 47.

148. Fang Fanjiu, *op. cit.*, 103.

149. *Zhongyang ribao*, March 8, 1934; Yu Hanhua, *op. cit.*, 48; Fang Fanjiu, *op. cit.*, 114–15; Jagchid, *Essays in Mongolian Studies*, 287–88.

150. *Zhongyang ribao*, March 15, 1934, April 13 and 19, 1934, May 11, 1934; *Meng Zang yuebao*, May 25, 1934; Lattimore, *Studies in Frontier History*, 433; Jagchid, *Essays in Mongolian Studies*, 288.

151. Jagchid, *Essays in Mongolian Studies*, 289; Yu Hanhua, *op. cit.*, 51; Lattimore, *Studies in Frontier History*, 438.

152. Nanjing Archives, telegram from the Ninth Panchen Lama to the Chinese State Council, dated September 6, 1934, reproduced in Zhongguo di er lishi dang'an guan, *op. cit.*, doc. 94, 91–93; Chen Wenjian, *op. cit.*, 41, 43, 47–48; Liu Jiaju, *op. cit.*, 54–55.

153. Nanjing Archives, letter no. 156 from the Mongolian and Tibetan Affairs Commission to the Ninth Panchen Lama, dated August 1925, reproduced in Zhongguo di er lishi dang'an guan, *op. cit.*, doc. 4, 5; Chen Wenjian, *op. cit.*, 7; Liu Jiaju, *op. cit.*, 39; Srung Kri hru'u, *op. cit.*, 119; Ya Hanzhang, *Banchan E'erdeni zhuan*, 243. In Tibetan the title "World Savior Who Propagates Orthodoxy" is *lokar pel né jikten penpa.*

154. The court's organization for administering vassals developed with the conquests of the Qing emperors. It acquired its definitive form in 1762 and was composed of an Inner Mongolia office (*qiji si*), an Inner Mongolia reception bureau (*wanghui si*), an Outer Mongolia office (*dianshu si*), an Outer Mongolia reception bureau (*rouyuan si*), a Xinjiang office (*laiyuan si*), and a Justice Office (*lixing si*). See *Qin ding Da Qing huidian shili*, 79/1A–2A. In 1907 two other departments were created: one for colonization (*zhichan si*) and one for border defense (*bianwei si*).

155. The members of the Department of Mongolian and Tibetan Affairs included a director (*zongcai*), a deputy director (*fu zongcai*), two advisors (*canshi*), two secretaries (*mishu*), twelve employees (*zhushi*), four employees serving as chargés d'affaires (*zhishigua*), and several advisors (*guwen/guyuan*).

156. *Meng Zang weiyuanhui jianshi*, 9; Guo Jijiao, *op. cit.*, 12.

157. A director and his deputy headed this ministry, which was composed of an office of advisors (*canshi shi*), office of the secretary (*mishu shi*), a department of general affairs (*zongwu ting*), and two section offices (*di yi, di er liang ci*).

158. *Meng Zang weiyuanhui jian shi*, 14–21.

159. Letter from the Ninth Panchen Lama to Yan Xishan, director of the Mongolian and Tibetan Affairs Commission, entitled "To the Compatriots of the Five Nationalities of the Republic of China," dated January 24, 1929, reproduced in Zhongguo di er lishi dang'an guan, *op. cit.*, doc. 7, 7–8.

160. Nanjing Archives, directive no. 414 from the Republican government, dated February 28, 1929, reproduced in Zhongguo di er lishi dang'an guan, *op. cit.*, doc. 8, 9.

161. Chen Wenjian, *op. cit.*, 10; Liu Jiaju, *op. cit.*, 42; Srung Kri hru'u, *op. cit.*, 121.

162. At the end of the eight sessions of this meeting, which took place from May 8–17, 1931, its members, headed by Dai Jitao, announced the provisional constitution of the Chinese Republic for the "supervisory phase" (*Zhonghua minguo xunzheng shiqi yuefa*).

163. Liu Jiaju, *op. cit.*, 44.

164. *Minguo ribao*, May 4, 1931; Chen Wenjian, *op. cit.*, 12; Liu Jiaju, *op. cit.*, 44. Liu Jiaju states that the Ninth Panchen Lama arrived in Nanjing on May 4, 1931, whereas Chen Wenjian suggests a

date sometime in April 1931. The difference in the accounts of the dates continued from April through June until Liu Jiaju finally stopped trying to establish a specific date. However, the experiences and places visited by the Ninth Panchen Lama follow the same chronology in both biographies. As for the date of May 5, it was chosen to commemorate the day when Sun Yat-sen became president of the Republic of China during the fourth session of the third meeting of the Nationalist Party held in November 1930.

165. *Minguo ribao*, May 5, 1931; *Dagong bao*, May 5, 1931; Chen Wenjian, *op. cit.*, 12; Liu Jiaju, *op. cit.*, 44; Srung Kri hru'u, *op. cit.*, 119.

166. The order to confer this title was made on June 24, 1931. See Nanjing Archives, letter from the Office of Military Advisors Department of Rites to the Office of Civil Affairs, dated June 30, 1931, reproduced in Zhongguo di er lishi dang'an guan, *op. cit.*, doc. 26, 30–32; order from the government, dated July 1, 1931, reproduced in Zhongguo di er lishi dang'an guan, *op. cit.*, doc. 27, 33. Chen Wenjian, *op. cit.*, 15–16, indicates that this title was awarded to the Ninth Panchen Lama on February 24, 1932.

167. Nanjing Archives, letter from the Mongolian and Tibetan Affairs Commission to the Chinese State Council, dated June 21, 1931, reproduced in Zhongguo di er lishi dang'an guan, *op. cit.*, doc. 22, 26–27.

168. The Ninth Panchen Lama would use this seal for the first time on May 5, 1932. See Nanjing Archives, report from the Ninth Panchen Lama to the Chinese government signed with his new seal, dated May 5, 1932, reproduced in Zhongguo di er lishi dang'an guan, *op. cit.*, doc. 46, 45.

169. Liu Jiaju, *op. cit.*, 44.

170. Chen Wenjian, *op. cit.*, 17.

171. Nanjing Archives, order no. 354 of the Chinese State Council, dated April 14, 1932, reproduced in Zhongguo di er lishi dang'an guan, *op. cit.*, doc. 41, 42. Chen Wenjian, however, gives the date of April 19, 1932, based on the directive no. 1042 of the Chinese State Council to the Mongolian and Tibetan Affairs Commission, which transmitted order no. 354. See Chen Wenjian, *op. cit.*, 17.

172. Nanjing Archives, directive no. 1207 from the Chinese Council of State to the Mongolian and Tibetan Affairs Commission, dated April 30, 1932, reproduced in Zhongguo di er lishi dang'an guan, *op. cit.*, doc. 45, 44–45.

173. *Zhongyang ribao*, November 23, 1932; Jiang Zhongzheng, *op. cit.*, 33.

174. *Zhongyang ribao*, December 22, 1932. Lin Sen had been interim president since December 15, 1932, the day when Chiang Kai-shek abandoned power. On Lin Sen (1868–1943), see Boorman, *op. cit.*, vol. 2, 379–82.

175. *Zhongyang ribao*, December 25 and 29, 1932; Chen Wenjian, *op. cit.*, 22; Liu Jiaju, *op. cit.*, 48.

176. Speech by the Ninth Panchen Lama at the anniversary of the founding of the Mongolian and Tibetan Affairs Commission, January 21, 1933, in Liu Jiaju, *op. cit.*, 126–28.

177. *Zhongyang ribao*, February 7–9, 1933.

178. Nanjing Archives, directive no. 1207 from the Chinese State Council to the Mongolian and Tibetan Affairs Commission, dated April 30, 1932, reproduced in Zhongguo di er lishi dang'an guan, *op. cit.*, doc. 45, 44–45.

179. The term *xingshu* is an abbreviation of *xingzheng gongshu* (Decentralized Administrative Office), a term created by the Nationalist government. Since the Tang dynasty, *xingshu* has designated the establishment of a temporary office by an official when he finds himself outside his jurisdiction. See Luo Zhufeng, *Hanyu da cidian*, vol. 3, 915. The word *xingyuan* (行院) refers to a brothel (*jiyuan*) and sometimes to prostitutes (*jinü*). Under the Yuan dynasty, the term referred to a theater director. *Xingyuan* (行院) is thus no doubt the result of a copying error. This word should be replaced by the word *xingyuan* (行轅), which refers to the secondary residence of a high official or the house where he would lodge during a trip. See Luo Zhufeng, *Hanyu da cidian*, vol. 3, 904, 922.

180. Nanjing Archives, letter from the minister of political and military affairs forwarded by the Chinese State Council to the Mongolian and Tibetan Affairs Commission, dated December 31, 1932, reproduced in Zhongguo di er lishi dang'an guan, *op. cit.*, doc. 54, 50–51.

181. Nanjing Archives, report no. 29 of the Mongolian and Tibetan Affairs Commission, dated March 25, 1933, reproduced in Zhongguo di er lishi dang'an guan, *op. cit.*, doc. 59, 58–59.

182. Nanjing Archives, telegram from the Ninth Panchen Lama to the Mongolian and Tibetan Affairs Commission, dated April 1, 1933, reproduced in Zhongguo di er lishi dang'an guan, *op. cit.*, doc. 60, 59.

183. Nanjing Archives, directive no. 217 from the Chinese State Council to the Mongolian and Tibetan Affairs Commission, dated May 27, 1933, reproduced in Zhongguo di er lishi dang'an guan, *op. cit.*, doc. 63, 61–62.

184. Nanjing Archives, telegram from the office of the Shahukou train station to the Mongolian and Tibetan Affairs Commission, dated April 23, 1933, reproduced in Zhongguo di er lishi dang'an guan, *op. cit.*, doc. 61, 59–60.

185. Nanjing Archives, directive no. 217 from the Chinese State Council to the Mongolian and Tibetan Affairs Commission, dated May 27, 1933, reproduced in Zhongguo di er lishi dang'an guan, *op. cit.*, doc. 63, 61–62.

186. Nanjing Archives, letter no. 11 from the Office of the Great and Glorious Master Panchen Who Protects the Country and Propagates its Values to the Mongolian and Tibetan Affairs Commission, dated June 29, 1933, reproduced in Zhongguo di er lishi dang'an guan, *op. cit.*, doc. 64, 62–63.

187. Chen Wenjian, *op. cit.*, 33.

188. Nanjing Archives, government decree congratulating the Ninth Panchen Lama, dated October 18, 1933, reproduced in Zhongguo di er lishi dang'an guan, *op. cit.*, doc. 74, 71.

189. *Zhongyang ribao*, January 13, 1934; Chen Wenjian, *op. cit.*, 37.

190. *Zhongyang ribao*, January 12, 1934.

191. *Zhongyang ribao*, February 2, 1934; Chen Wenjian, *op. cit.*, 39–40.

192. Nanjing Archives, decree naming the Ninth Panchen Lama a member of the Republican government (*Guomin zhengfu weiyuan*), dated February 20, 1934, reproduced in Zhongguo di er lishi dang'an guan, *op. cit.*, doc. 78, 74; *Zhongyang ribao*, February 20 and 21, 1934.

193. Nanjing Archives, letter no. 271 from the Mongolian and Tibetan Affairs Commission to the Office of the Emissary in Charge of Spreading Values in the Western Region, dated January 26, 1935, reproduced in Zhongguo di er lishi dang'an guan, *op. cit.*, doc. 109, 102–7.

194. Nanjing Archives, letter from the Mongolian and Tibetan Affairs Commission to the Ninth Panchen Lama and to the director of the State Council, dated April 24, 1935, reproduced in Zhongguo di er lishi dang'an guan, *op. cit.*, doc. 127, 134–35.

195. Nanjing Archives, confidential order no. 2505 from the Chinese State Council to the Mongolian and Tibetan Affairs Commission, dated May 1, 1935, reproduced in Zhongguo di er lishi dang'an guan, *op. cit.*, doc. 133, 139.

196. On Gao Zhangzhu, see Xu Youchun, *Minguo renwu da cidian*, 740.

197. Nanjing Archives, report by Gao Zhangzhu to the Mongolian and Tibetan Affairs Commission, dated May 24, 1935, reproduced in Zhongguo di er lishi dang'an guan, *op. cit.*, doc. 151, 150–51; letter from the Mongolian and Tibetan Affairs Commission to the Emissary in Charge of Spreading Values in the Western Region, dated July 10, 1935, reproduced in *idem*, doc. 168.

198. Nanjing Archives, directive no. 935 from the Chinese State Council to the Mongolian and Tibetan Affairs Commission, dated March 20, 1936, reproduced in Zhongguo di er lishi dang'an guan, *op. cit.*, doc. 282, 296–97.

199. Nanjing Archives, telegram from Cheng Yun to the Mongolian and Tibetan Affairs Commission, dated March 7, 1936, reproduced in Zhongguo di er lishi dang'an guan, *op. cit.*, doc. 278, 293. The Ninth Panchen Lama would be the source of this proposal, see Chen Wenjian, *op. cit.*, 69.

200. Chen Wenjian, *op. cit.*, 81; Liu Jiaju, *op. cit.*, 59.

CHAPTER 5

1. Nanjing Archives, telegram from Zhao Shouyu to the Mongolian and Tibetan Affairs Commission, dated November 10, 1937, reproduced in Zhongguo di er lishi dang'an guan, *Jiu shi Banchan neidi*, doc. 432, 473. See also Liu Jiaju, *Banchan dashi quanji*, 60–62; Chen Wenjian, *Banchan dashi dong lai shiwu nian dashiji*, 92; 96–97; Ma Hetian, *Gan Qing Zang bianqu kaocha ji*, 642, 651; Srung Kri hru'u, "Panchen sku 'phreng dgu pa dBus gTsang," 1, 125. On Zhao Shouyu (1881–1960), see IOR, L/P&S/12/4186B, PZ 145, telegram from R. G. Howe, counselor of the British Embassy in Beijing to British Minister of Foreign Affairs Anthony Eden, telegram no. 1202 (113/B/1936), dated November 23, 1936. On Liu Wenhui (1895–1976), see Boorman, *Biographical Dictionary of Republican China*, vol. 2, 417–19.

2. Liu Jiaju, *op. cit.*, 62; Ma Hetian, *op. cit.*, 658.

3. Nanjing Archives, telegram from the Office of the Emissary in Charge of Spreading Values in the Western Region to the Mongolian and Tibetan Affairs Commission, dated December 1, 1937, reproduced in Zhongguo di er lishi dang'an guan, *op. cit.*, doc. 434, 474; Chen Wenjian, *op. cit.*, 98; Liu Jiaju, *op. cit.*, 62; Srung Kri hru'u, *op. cit.*, 125; Goldstein, *History of Modern Tibet*, 298.

4. For a chronological account of the Panchen Lama's abortive return to Tibet according to British sources, see Goldstein, *op. cit.*, 252–309.

5. Nanjing Archives, letter from the Ninth Panchen Lama to Yan Xishan, dated January 24, 1929, reproduced in Zhongguo di er lishi dang'an guan, *op. cit.*, doc. 7, 7–9.

6. *Zhongyang ribao*, April 29, 1934.

7. Nanjing Archives, letter from the Ninth Panchen Lama to Huang Musong, dated March 19, 1935, reproduced in Zhongguo di er lishi dang'an guan, *op. cit.*, doc. 115, 110–12.

8. According to the Panchen Lama, the fruitful entry of Tibet into the "union of the five nationalities" required several key points: (i) the participation of both Tibetans and Chinese in this undertaking; (ii) the compassion and sincerity of each; (iii) the commitment of the citizens and leaders to unite to resist the enemy and accomplish the Republican Revolution; and (iv) the allocation of time necessary to achieve such a project. The recurrent theme of the "union of five nationalities" was particularly prominent in the Panchen Lama's speech in Beijing on January 27, 1925; his opinion statement of February 1, 1925; his letter to Yan Xishan of January 24, 1929; his speeches in Nanjing of December 21 and 23, 1932; his speech given at the anniversary of the founding of the Mongolian and Tibetan Affairs Commission on January 21, 1933; his speech in Inner Mongolia on October 24, 1933; his speech in Ningxia on January 24, 1935; his letter to Huang Musong of March 19, 1935; his speech in Xining on May 12, 1935; and his speech in Kyégudo on December 26, 1936.

9. Chen Wenjian, *op. cit.*, 12; Sichuan Archives, provisions for a cease-fire treaty, dated October 8, 1932 (the agreement which concerned the border between Tibet and China's Qinghai Province would be approved by the Nanjing government in July 1933); Zhwa sgab pa, *Bod kyi srid don rgyal rabs*, 269; Fletcher, *China's Inner Asia Frontier*, introduction, 49; Boorman, *op. cit.*, vol. 3, 474–75; Qinghai sheng zhi bianzuan weiyuanhui, *Qinghai lishi jiyao*, 677–81.

10. See speech by the Ninth Panchen Lama addressed to Ma Hongkui, governor of Ningxia Province and all the members of his government, entitled "Reinforce Border Defense by Developing Communication Networks" (*Gonggu bianfang dang yi jiaotong ru shou*), January 24, 1935, in Liu Jiaju, *op. cit.*, 155–56.

11. Letter to Huang Musong, the new director of the Mongolian and Tibetan Affairs Commission, concerning a project for the propagation of values in Tibet, dated March 19, 1935, in Zhongguo di er lishi dang'an guan, *op. cit.*, doc. 115, 110–12.

12. F. Williamson held the post of British political officer in Sikkim from May to December 1926, from April to August 1931, and from January 1933 to November 1935.

13. bKras dgon lo rgyus rtsom 'bri tshogs chung, "sNgags chen bDar pa ho thog thu," 86; IOR, L/P&S/12/4181, telegram from the British political officer in Sikkim to the secretary of foreign affairs of the government of India, dated January 8, 1934; *Zhongyang ribao*, April 4, 1934.

14. *Zhongyang ribao*, May 30, 1934; Nanjing Archives, report from the members of the Office of the Ninth Panchen Lama to the Mongolian and Tibetan Affairs Commission, dated July 21, 1934; *Zhongyang ribao*, April 1, 4, 25, and 29, 1934.

15. Beginning in 1757 the regent was chosen by the Tibetan Council of Ministers (*kashag*) from among a predefined choice of reincarnated masters: Jédrung from Kundeling monastery, Tsemön from Tsémönling, Reting from Zhideling, and Demo from Tengyeling. See Petech, "The Dalais Lamas and Regents of Tibet," 368–94; Wang Xianjun, "Xizang shezheng zhidu taolun," 76–81.

16. F. M. Bailey, British political officer in Sikkim in 1924, proposed himself as mediator between the Thirteenth Dalai Lama and the Ninth Panchen Lama, and offered to transmit letters from the Tibetan government to the Panchen Lama. See IOR, L/P&S/12/4174, letter from F. M. Bailey to His Majesty's Government of India, dated May 5, 1928.

17. Tsaserkhang arrived in Kalimpong from Beijing in March 1927. On March 3, 1928, he left Kalimpong for Darjeeling. At the end of 1938, he returned to Tibet. He died in July 1946. See *Yul phyogs so so'i gsar 'gyur me long*, vol. 2, no. 3, 4; vol. 3, nos. 1–2, 2; vol. 10, no. 4, 3; *Who's Who in Tibet*, Ext. 6867B; IOR, L/P&S/12/4174, note on the Tashi Lama written by F. M. Bailey, dated December 2, 1932; IOR, Mss Eur F.80–90, correspondence from Tsaserkhang concerning the Panchen Lama, dated March 20, 1928; IOR, Mss Eur F.80–90, reply letter, dated April 10, 1928, from C. Bell to a letter from Tsaserkhang, dated March 20, 1928.

18. Weir held the post of political officer in Sikkim from August to October 1911, from October 1928 to April 1931, and from August 1931 to January 1933.

19. IOR, L/P&S/12/4174, letter from Tsaserkhang to Lt. Col. James Leslie Weir, dated June 25, 1930; IOR, L/P&S/12/4170-File 7, PZ 1922/1933, letter no. W1, point no. 10, p. 3, from Lt. Col. James Leslie Weir regarding the visit of the British political officer in Sikkim to Lhasa in 1932, dated March 1, 1933; IOR, L/P&S/12/4174, letter from the Thirteenth Dalai Lama included in the correspondence from Lt. Col. James Leslie Weir to the government of India, dated October 11, 1932; IOR, L/P&S/12/578, letter from E. M. B. Ingram, the chargé d'affaires of the British embassy in China, to John Simon (Foreign Office), paragraph 22, dated January 9, 1933; IOR, L/P&S/12/4174, copies of letters from the Ninth Panchen Lama enclosed in a letter from Lt. Col. James Leslie Weir, addressed to the government of India, dated April 12, 1933; Liu Jiaju, "Xizang lidai Zang wang ji Dalai Banchan shiyao," 91; Fang Qiubi, "Dalai chuanshi yu Banchan fan Zang," 37; bKras dgon lo rgyus rtsom 'bri tshogs chung, "sNgags chen bDar pa ho thog thu," 86; Nanjing Archives, telegram from the Office of the Train Station at Shahukou to the Mongolian and Tibetan Affairs Commission, dated April 23, 1933.

20. Don khang sKal bzang bDe skyid, "Pan chen sku phreng dgu pa mes rgyal nang," 27–29; IOR, L/P&S/12/4181, letter from the British political officer in Sikkim to the secretary of foreign affairs of the government of India, dated January 8, 1934.

21. Chen Wenjian, *op. cit.*, 46; Nanjing Archives, report from the members of the Office of the Ninth Panchen Lama to the Mongolian and Tibetan Affairs Commission, dated July 21, 1934, reproduced in Zhongguo di er lishi dang'an guan, *op. cit.*, doc. 87, 84–85.

22. Huang Musong, *Shi Zang jicheng*, 118, 122.

23. Liu Jiaju, *op. cit.*, 55–56.

24. Nanjing Archives, confidential telegram from Cheng Yun to the Mongolian and Tibetan Affairs Commission, dated April 28, 1935, reproduced in Zhongguo di er lishi dang'an guan, *op. cit.*, doc. 131, 137.

25. *Meng Zang yuekan* 4, no. 4 (1936): 65; Luo Youren, "Banchan da shi zai Qinghai xuanhua jingguo ji," 174.

26. Liu Jiaju, *op. cit.*, 159–60.

27. Chen Wenjian, *op. cit.*, 56; Nanjing Archives, letter from the Ninth Panchen Lama, forwarded by the secretary of the Chinese State Council to the Mongolian and Tibetan Affairs Commission, dated May 21, 1935; telegram from Shao Yuanchong to the Chinese State Council, May 15, 1935; telegram from Ma Bufang forwarded by the Justice Ministry to the Mongolian and Tibetan Affairs Commission, dated May 28, 1935; letter from the Mongolian and Tibetan Affairs Commission to

Chiang Kai-shek, dated September 6, 1935, reproduced in Zhongguo di er lishi dang'an guan, *op. cit.*, doc. 147, 147; doc. 138, 142; doc.154, 155–56, and doc. 184, 192–93, respectively.

28. Nanjing Archives, nomination order by the Chinese State Council forwarded by the Mongolian and Tibetan Affairs Commission to Cheng Yun, dated July 23, 1935. The Panchen Lama was informed of this order on July 27, 1935, see Nanjing Archives, telegram from the Mongolian and Tibetan Affairs Commission to the Ninth Panchen Lama, directive no. 4362 from the Chinese State Council to the Mongolian and Tibetan Affairs Commission, dated August 15, 1935, reproduced in Zhongguo di er lishi dang'an guan, *op. cit.*, doc. 178, 183–88; Chen Wenjian, *op. cit.*, 57, 61.

29. Chen Wenjian, *op. cit.*, 65–66.

30. Nanjing Archives, telegram from Jiang Zhiyu to the Mongolian and Tibetan Affairs Commission, dated January 9, 1936; telegram from Cheng Yun to the Mongolian and Tibetan Affairs Commission, dated January 13, 1936; short letter from the Chinese secretary of state forwarding a copy of a telegram from Jiang Zhiyu to the Mongolian and Tibetan Affairs Commission, dated January 27, 1936, reproduced in Zhongguo di er lishi dang'an guan, *op. cit.*, doc. 236, 245–46; doc. 244, 251–52; Chen Wenjian, *op. cit.*, 70.

31. Chen Wenjian, *op. cit.*, 72.

32. Luo Youren, *op. cit.*, 174; Huang Ju'an, "Banchan da shi you Labuleng zhi Yushu xuanhua jingguo," 163–70.

33. Nanjing Archives, letter from the Mongolian and Tibetan Affairs Commission, dated July 19, 1937, reproduced in Zhongguo di er lishi dang'an guan, *op. cit.*, doc. 386, 426–31; Chen Wenjian, *op. cit.*, 88; Liu Jiaju, *op. cit.*, 60; Ma Hetian, *op. cit.*, 55.

34. The full name of Ragya monastery is Ragya gön ganden tashi chungné. It is referred to in Chinese as Lajia Si.

35. Chen Wenjian, *op. cit.*, 77.

36. On Köncho Chungné, see Xerab Nyima, "From Geshi of Sera Monastery to KMT Attache," 20; Yao Zhaolin, "Xizang Gunque Zhongni 1924 nian chengwen xi," 79–91; Fu Chengyong, "Fu Zang daibiao gui Jing hou tanpian," 6–7.

37. Dong Shufan, *Minguo shi san nian yilai Zhongguo guomindang yu Xizang*, 16–18. Thubten Sangyé, a member of the Tibet Office created in Nanjing by Köncho Chungné under the directive of the Thirteenth Dalai Lama, indicates that Chiang Kai-shek presented ten points to the Dalai Lama, but in his book *The Office of the Tibetan Government in China*, Thubten Sangyé only mentions five: China would have to pay the salaries of the Thirteenth Dalai Lama and the members of the Tibetan government; fund the expenses for the soldiers of the Tibetan army and supply them with necessary arms; come to Tibet's aid in case of foreign invasion; and the Thirteenth Dalai Lama would have to belong to the Nationalist Party, as well as open representation offices (*bö ki dönchö*) in large Chinese cities. See Thub bstan Sangs rgyas, *rGya nag tu Bod kyi sku tshab*, 17–18.

38. The Tibetan Council of Ministers, made up of three lay people and one monk, convened the National Assembly, which was represented by lay officials and monks from the three great Gélukpa monasteries (Drépung, Ganden, and Sera). In principle, the National Assembly neither made decisions nor acted, but gave its opinion to the Council of Ministers who would resubmit the subject to the National Assembly after discussion until consensus was obtained. The ensuing decision was then communicated to the Dalai Lama or the regent for approval, at which time the Council of Ministers would put the decision into action. The Huang Musong mission, as with the question of the Panchen Lama's return to Tibet, revealed that the National Assembly did have a certain amount of independent power and could put forward opinions differing from the Council of Ministers that were, in fact, followed.

39. Huang Musong, *op. cit.*, 154; *Meng Zang yuebao*, July 25, 1934, 28; Nanjing Archives, telegram from the Chinese State Council to Huang Musong, dated November 21, 1934.

40. Nanjing Archives, confidential order no. 3060 from the Chinese State Council to the Mongolian and Tibetan Affairs Commission, dated October 2, 1935, reproduced in Zhongguo di er lishi dang'an guan, *op. cit.*, doc. 203, 209–10.

41. Dong Shufan, *op. cit.*, 16–18; *Yul phyogs so so'i gsar 'gyur me long*, vol. 5, no. 6, November 20, 1930, 3; *Zhongyang ribao*, May 22, 1934, 3; *Meng Zang yuebao*, vol. 1, no. 2, 1934, 42; vol. 1, no. 4, 1934, 28; vol. 1, no. 5, 1934, 27, 29; Nanjing Archives, telegram from Huang Musong to the Chinese State Council, dated September 16, 1934; telegram from Huang Musong to the Chinese State Council, quoting a letter written in Chinese from the Tibetan Council of Ministers that had been forwarded to him, dated October 5, 1934; telegram from Huang Musong to the Chinese State Council, dated October 17, 1934; telegram from Huang Musong to the Chinese State Council, dated October 24, 1934; telegram from Huang Musong to the Chinese State Council, dated November 16, 1934. See also Khung Chin-tsun, "Hong Mu'o sung Bod du bskyod pa'i gnas tshul dngos bkod pa," 149, cited in Goldstein, *op. cit.*, 232; Huang Musong, *op. cit.*, 116, 124.

42. Nanjing Archives, telegram from Huang Musong to the Chinese State Council, dated September 16, 1934; telegram from Huang Musong to the Chinese State Council, dated October 19, 1934, citing a letter he addressed to the Tibetan Council of Ministers; Huang Musong, *op. cit.*, 116, 132.

43. Nanjing Archives, telegram from Huang Musong to the Chinese State Council, dated November 16, 1934; telegram from the Chinese State Council to Huang Musong, dated November 21, 1934; confidential order no. 3060 from the Chinese State Council to the Mongolian and Tibetan Affairs Commission, dated October 2, 1935, reproduced in Zhongguo di er lishi dang'an guan, *op. cit.*, doc. 203, 209–10; Huang Musong, *op. cit.*, 135.

44. Dong Shufan, *op. cit.*, 16–18; *Yul phyogs so so'i gsar 'gyur me long*, vol. 5, no. 6, November 20, 1930, 3; Nanjing Archives, telegram from Huang Musong to the Chinese State Council, dated October 17, 1934.

45. Nanjing Archives, telegram from Huang Musong to the Chinese State Council, dated October 19, 1934, citing a letter he wrote to the Tibetan Council of Ministers.

46. Nanjing Archives, telegram from Huang Musong to the Chinese State Council, dated October 24, 1934.

47. Examining Tibetan administrative documents from that time would be indispensable for confirming veracity; however, I do not have access to these documents.

48. Nanjing Archives, telegram from Huang Musong to the Chinese State Council, dated November 16, 1934.

49. Khung Chin-tsun, *op. cit.*, 155–56, cited in Goldstein, *op. cit.*, 239; Huang Musong, *op. cit.*, 132.

50. Dong Shufan, *op. cit.*, 16–18; *Yul phyogs so so'i gsar 'gyur me long*, vol. 5, no. 6, November 20, 1930, 3.

51. Nanjing Archives, telegram from Huang Musong to the Chinese State Council, dated October 17, 1934.

52. Nanjing Archives, telegram from Huang Musong to the Chinese State Council, dated October 19, 1934, citing a letter he wrote to the Tibetan Council of Ministers.

53. Nanjing Archives, telegram from Huang Musong to the Chinese State Council, dated October 24, 1934.

54. Richardson, *High Peaks, Pure Earth*, 50–52.

55. Khung Chin-tsun, *op. cit.*, 160, cited in Goldstein, *op. cit.*, 240.

56. Nanjing Archives, telegram from Huang Musong to the Chinese State Council, dated November 16, 1934; confidential order no. 3060 from the Chinese State Council to the Mongolian and Tibetan Affairs Commission, dated October 2, 1935, reproduced in Zhongguo di er lishi dang'an guan, *op. cit.*, doc. 203, 209–10; Huang Musong, *op. cit.*, 132.

57. Dong Shufan, *op. cit.*, 16–18; *Yul phyogs so so'i gsar 'gyur me long*, vol. 5, no. 6, November 20, 1930, 3.

58. Nanjing Archives, telegram from Huang Musong to the Chinese State Council, dated September 16, 1934; Huang Musong, *op. cit.*, 116; Khung Chin-tsun, *op. cit.*, 149, 160, cited in Goldstein, *op. cit.*, 232, 241; telegram from Huang Musong to the Chinese State Council, dated October 19, 1934, citing a letter he wrote to the Tibetan Council of Ministers; Richardson, *High Peaks, Pure Earth*, 51–52.

59. Dong Shufan, *op. cit.*, 16–18; Thub bstan Sangs rgyas, *op. cit.*, 17–18.

60. Köncho Chungné founded the three Tibet offices in 1931. He ran the office in Nanjing with the help of Ngawang Gyeltsen. Chöpel Thubten and Wu Mingyuan ran the office in Beijing. Jangpa Chöwang and Tsültrim Tenzin ran the one in Dartsédo. See *Meng Zang shibao*, vol. 9, 1930, 61; *Yul phyogs so so'i gsar 'gyur me long*, vol. 5, no. 6, 1930, 3; vol. 5, no. 9, 1931, 3; Thubs bstan Sang rgyas, *op. cit.*, 29–30; Dong Shufan, *op. cit.*, 16–18.

61. Khung Chin-tsun, *op. cit.*, 155–56, cited in Goldstein, *op. cit.*, 239; Huang Musong, *op. cit.*, 132.

62. Huang Musong, *op. cit.*, 132.

63. Richardson, *High Peaks, Pure Earth*, 51–52.

64. Nanjing Archives, telegram from Huang Musong to the Chinese State Council, dated November 16, 1934.

65. Nanjing Archives, telegram from Huang Musong to the Chinese State Council, dated November 27, 1934.

66. Dong Shufan, *op. cit.*, 16–18; Nanjing Archives, telegram from Huang Musong to the Chinese State Council, dated October 19, 1934, citing a letter he wrote to the Tibetan Council of Ministers.

67. Nanjing Archives, telegram from Huang Musong to the Chinese State Council, dated October 24, 1934.

68. In actual fact, the Chinese Republicans did send a mission to Lhasa to assist in the enthronement of Tenzin Gyatso, the current Fourteenth Dalai Lama.

69. Richardson, *High Peaks, Pure Earth*, 51–52.

70. F. M. Bailey proposed to the Thirteenth Dalai Lama that he help him by serving as a mediator for talks with the Panchen Lama and forwarding the Tibetan government's messages to the prelate. See IOR, L/P&S/12/4174, letter from F. M. Bailey, British political officer in Sikkim in 1924, to His Majesty's Government of India, May 5, 1928.

71. Dong Shufan, *op. cit.*, 16–18.

72. Goldstein, *op. cit.*, 255.

73. IOR, L/P&S/12/4170-File 7, PZ 1922/1933, letter no. W1, point no. 10, from Lt. Col. James Leslie Weir regarding the 1932 visit of the British political officer in Sikkim to Lhasa, dated March 1, 1933.

74. Apparently, the Panchen Lama's stepfather (?) and a nephew had been imprisoned. However, his mother was never married and had taken nun's vows as soon as her son was recognized as the incarnation of the Eighth Panchen Lama. The prelate's brother was a Gélukpa monk, who, was thus also not married and would not have had a child who could have been the Panchen Lama's nephew. I have, therefore, been unable to identify with any certainty who these two people were. We do know, however, that if the Panchen Lama's brother did not leave Tibet in 1923, then he joined the Panchen Lama in China at a later date. See IOR, L/P&S/12/580, letter from F. M. Bailey to His Majesty's Government of India.

75. Liu Jiaju, "Xizang lidai Zang wang ji Dalai Banchan shiyao," 91.

76. Chen Wenjian, *op. cit.*, 29; Liu Jiaju, *Banchan da shi quanji*, 50; bKras dgon lo rgyus rtsom 'bri tshogs chung, "sNgags chen bDar pa ho thog thu," 86.

77. bKra shis dgon lo rgyus rtsom 'bri tshogs chung, "sNgags chen bDar pa ho thog thu," 86; IOR, L/P&S/12/4181, letter from the British political officer in Sikkim to the secretary of foreign affairs of the government of India, dated January 8, 1934.

78. Huang Musong, "Huang zhuanshi baogao ru Zang jingguo," 37; *Zhongyang ribao*, April 13, 1934; Nanjing Archives, telegram sent by Jiang Zhiyu, member of the vanguard to the Huang Musong Mission in Lhasa and to the Office of Transmissions of the Special Envoy in Nanjing who copied it and forwarded it to the secretary of the Chinese State Council, who, in turn, hand-delivered the letter in person to the Mongolian and Tibetan Affairs Commission, dated July 26, 1934; telegram from Jiang Zhiyu forwarded by the Chinese State Council to the Mongolian and Tibetan Affairs Commission, dated July 4, 1934, reproduced in Zhongguo di er lishi dang'an guan, *op. cit.*, doc. 85, 82–83, doc. 89, 87–88; *Zhongyang ribao*, April 1, 1934, 3; April 4, 1934, 2; May 23, 1934, 20; May 30, 1934, 2; June 1, 1934, 3; *Kaifa xibei*, vol. 1, no. 3, 1934, 95; *Meng Zang yuebao*, vol. 3, no. 4, December 31, 1935, 46.

79. Nanjing Archives, telegram from Huang Musong to the Chinese State Council, dated October 12, 1934; Huang Musong, *Shi Zang jicheng*, 125–26.

80. IOR, L/P&S/12/4175 B, report from B. Gould, British political officer in Sikkim, on the 1935 expedition of F. Williamson to Tibet; IOR, L/P&S/12/4186 B, File 22, telegram from Captain Keith Battye to the secretary of His Majesty's Government of India, dated December 16, 1935; IOR, L/P&S/12/4186 B, letter from the British official Raï Bahadur Norbhu Döndup to B. Gould, British political officer in Sikkim, dated July 15, 1936.

81. IOR, L/P&S/12/4174, letter from F. M. Bailey, British political officer in Sikkim to His Majesty's Government of India, May 5, 1928; Nanjing Archives, telegram from Huang Musong to the Chinese State Council, dated September 16, 1934; Huang Musong, *Shi Zang jicheng*, 116; IOR, L/P&S/12/4175 B, report by B. Gould, British political officer in Sikkim, on the 1935 expedition of F. Williamson to Tibet; IOR, L/P&S/12/4186 B, telegram from B. Gould to His Majesty's Government of India, dated August 3, 1936. B. Gould held the post of British political officer in Sikkim from December 1935 to May 1937 and from November 1937 to June 1945.

82. *Kaifa xibei*, vol. 1, no. 6, 1936, 76; *Bianjiang ban yue kan*, vol. 1, no. 6, 1936, 34; Gao Zhangzhu, *Xizang gaikuang*, 63; Hren krung yus and Hren yon ca, "Cang ce hri'i Khrung ching bzhugs sgar gyis Bod kyi gnad don skor la," 289; Nanjing Archives, letter from the Mongolian and Tibetan Affairs Commission to the Chinese State Council, dated June 20, 1936; telegram from Liu Wenhui to the Mongolian and Tibetan Affairs Commission, dated March 4, 1937; Chen Wenjian, *op. cit.*, 66, 72, 75–76.

83. Nanjing Archives, telegram from the Tibet Office in Nanjing to the Mongolian and Tibetan Affairs Commission, dated May 10, 1935, reproduced in Zhongguo di er lishi dang'an guan, *op. cit.*, doc. 135, 140.

84. Nanjing Archives, telegram from the Mongolian and Tibetan Affairs Commission to the Tibet Office in Nanjing, which, in turn, forwarded it to the Tibetan Council of Ministers in Lhasa, dated June 5, 1935; telegram from Jiang Zhiyu to the Chinese State Council, dated September 9, 1935; telegram from the Tibetan Council of Ministers to the Mongolian and Tibetan Affairs Commission, dated September 22, 1935; telegram forwarded by the Tibet Office in Nanjing to the Mongolian and Tibetan Affairs Commission from the Tibetan National Assembly, dated February 7, 1936, reproduced in Zhongguo di er lishi dang'an guan, *op. cit.*, doc. 157, 158–59; doc. 185, 194–96; doc. 194, 202; doc. 256, 272–74.

85. For both Phabongka's response to the Panchen Lama and Reting's response to Phabongka, see Blo bzang rDo rje, *Rigs dang dkyil 'khor rgya*, fols. 610A–610B, 615B, 622B.

86. Nanjing Archives, telegram from Jiang Zhiyu, representative of the Chinese government in Lhasa, forwarded by the secretary of the Chinese State Council to the Mongolian and Tibetan Affairs Commission, dated May 12, 1937, reproduced in Zhongguo di er lishi dang'an guan, *op. cit.*, doc. 373, 410–12.

87. Nanjing Archives, letter from the secretary of the Chinese State Council to the Mongolian and Tibetan Affairs Commission, forwarding a telegram from Jiang Zhiyu that relates the content of a telegram sent by Köncho Chungné, dated December 18, 1935. See also telegram from Cheng Yun to the Mongolian and Tibetan Affairs Commission, dated June 15, 1936, reproduced in Zhongguo di er lishi dang'an guan, *op. cit.*, doc. 223, 231; report from Cheng Yun forwarded by the secretary of the Chinese State Council to the Mongolian and Tibetan Affairs Commission, citing a telegram from Jiang Zhiyu, dated June 26, 1936, reproduced in Zhongguo di er lishi dang'an guan, *op. cit.*, doc. 294, 308.

88. See IOR, L/P&S/12/4186B, letter from Sir Knatchull-Hugessen, British ambassador in Nanjing to His Majesty's Government of India, dated May 15, 1937; telegram from Jiang Zhiyu forwarded by the secretary of the Chinese State Council to the Mongolian and Tibetan Affairs Commission, dated May 15, 1937; telegram from Jiang Zhiyu forwarded by the secretary of the Chinese State Council to the Mongolian and Tibetan Affairs Commission, dated May 20, 1937, reproduced in Zhongguo di er lishi dang'an guan, *op. cit.*, doc. 298, 311–13; doc. 374, 412–13; doc. 375, 413–14.

89. Chapman, *Lhasa, the Holy City*, 233–38.

90. Nanjing Archives, telegram from Jiang Zhiyu to Chiang Kai-shek, reporting on the recent results of the National Assembly's deliberations at the Potala, dated May 17, 1935.

91. Stoddard, *Le mendiant de l'Amdo*, 1985.

92. IOR, L/P&S/12/4186 B, letter from the British official Raï Bahadur Norbhu Döndup to B. Gould, British political officer in Sikkim, dated July 15, 1936.

93. Nanjing Archives, telegram from the Office of the Emissary in Charge of Spreading Values in the Western Region to the Mongolian and Tibetan Affairs Commission, dated November 27, 1937, reproduced in Zhongguo di er lishi dang'an guan, *op. cit.*, doc. 433, 474; Chen Wenjian, *op. cit.*, 96, 98; Liu Jiaju, *op. cit.*, 61; Srung Kri hru'u, *op. cit.*, 125.

94. Dong Shufan, *op. cit.*, 16–18.

95. Richardson, *High Peaks, Pure Earth*, 51–52; Huang Musong, *Shi Zang jicheng*, 116; Nanjing Archives, telegram from Huang Musong to the Chinese State Council, dated September 16, 1934; telegram from Huang Musong to the Chinese State Council, dated November 26, 1934; letter from the Ninth Panchen Lama to the Mongolian and Tibetan Affairs Commission, dated March 19, 1935, reproduced in Zhongguo di er lishi dang'an guan, *op. cit.*, doc. 115, 110–12.

96. Chinese authorities discovered seven thousand rifles each with fifty cartridges, more than twenty sub-machine guns and six (or twelve) country canons. The Republican government had only given the Panchen Lama 1,470 rifles. See Nanjing Archives, letter from the Chinese State Council to the Ninth Panchen Lama, dated March 27, 1935; Chen Wenjian, *op. cit.*, 53.

97. Nanjing Archives, telegram from Chiang Kai-shek to Wang Jingwei and to Huang Musong, reproduced in Zhongguo di er lishi dang'an guan, *op. cit.*, doc. 119, 115.

98. Nanjing Archives, telegram from Jiang Zhiyu to Gao Shibu, director of the Mongolian and Tibetan Affairs Commission, dated April 14, 1935, reproduced in Zhongguo di er lishi dang'an guan, *op. cit.*, doc. 121, 117.

99. Chen Wenjian, *op. cit.*, 55; Nanjing Archives, letter from the Mongolian and Tibetan Affairs Commission to the secretary of the Chinese State Council, dated April 24, 1935, reproduced in Zhongguo di er lishi dang'an guan, *op. cit.*, doc. 127, 134–35.

100. Nanjing Archives, confidential order no. 2505 from the Chinese State Council to the Mongolian and Tibetan Affairs Commission, dated May 1, 1935; telegram from the Mongolian and Tibetan Affairs Commission to Chiang Kai-shek, dated May 1, 1935, reproduced in Zhongguo di er lishi dang'an guan, *op. cit.*, doc. 132, 138; doc. 133, 139.

101. Zhao Erfeng proposed the creation of a province called Xikang after his troops had reached Lhasa in 1910. At first, this province was to occupy an area stretching from the Sichuan border to the banks of the Yangtze, representing territory that would have spanned a large part of the Kham region. In 1912 Hu Jingyi, the Chinese military governor of Sichuan, submitted to Yuan Shikai the idea of reactivating this project. This time, Xikang was not only supposed to cover the entire region of Kham, but also the regions of Dzayül and Pome to the southeast. It would share the Tibetan border at Gyamda. But, under pressure from the British, Yuan Shikai was forced to redraw the Xikang border to follow the banks of the Yangtze. In March 1928 Xikang became a special region. In August the same year, it gained status as a province with no government, and on July 22, 1935, the Chinese government created the Commission for the Edification of the Xikang Province. Finally, the provincial government of Xikang was put in place on January 1, 1939.

102. Nanjing Archives, telegram from the Mongolian and Tibetan Affairs Commission to the Tibetan Council of Ministers forwarded by the intermediary Jiang Zhiyu, dated May 18, 1935; telegram from Jiang Zhiyu to the Mongolian and Tibetan Affairs Commission, dated May 23, 1935, reproduced in Zhongguo di er lishi dang'an guan, *op. cit.*, doc. 149, 149; telegram from the Mongolian and Tibetan Affairs Commission to the Tibet Office in Nanjing, which then forwarded it to the Tibetan Council of Ministers, dated June 5, 1935, reproduced in Zhongguo di er lishi dang'an guan, *op. cit.*, doc. 157, 158–59.

103. Nanjing Archives, telegrams from the Chinese State Council to the Mongolian and Tibetan Affairs Commission, dated June 4 and 18, 1935, reproduced in Zhongguo di er lishi dang'an guan, *op. cit.*, doc. 162, 164–65; Feng Youzhi, *Xikang shi shiyi*, 329. Feng Youzhi was not a direct witness to these events. Given the confidential character (*neibu*) of this publication and that Feng Youzhi seems to have interviewed many people from this time (and was from Dartsédo himself), this document can be considered a primary source.

104. Two men had been approached. The first one, Zhu Minyi, was the Mongolian and Tibetan Affairs Commission secretary. Extremely competent, he had been interested in border problems for many years. The other, Cheng Yun, had held the post of president of the provincial government of Jilin. When the choice was made, he was already in the region of Lanzhou with the Panchen Lama. According to Huang Musong, his experience made him the man for the situation. See Nanjing Archives, letter from the Mongolian and Tibetan Affairs Commission to the Chinese State Council, dated July 10, 1935, responding to a proposal by Chiang Kai-shek, dated June 30, 1935, reproduced in Zhongguo di er lishi dang'an guan, *op. cit.*, doc. 168, 168.

105. Nanjing Archives, an order for a nomination from the Chinese State Council forwarded by the Mongolian and Tibetan Affairs Commission to Cheng Yun, dated July 23, 1935; telegram from the Mongolian and Tibetan Affairs Commission to the Ninth Panchen Lama, dated July 24, 1935; order from the Chinese State Council to the Mongolian and Tibetan Affairs Commission, dated August 10, 1935; directive no. 5094 from the Chinese State Council to the Mongolian and Tibetan Affairs Commission, dated September 27, 1935, reproduced in Zhongguo di er lishi dang'an guan, *op. cit.*, doc. 172, 171; doc. 173, 172–78; doc. 176, 179–82; doc. 200, 206; Gao Zhangzhu, *op. cit.*, 51–52.

106. Nanjing Archives, telegram from the Mongolian and Tibetan Affairs Commission to the Tibet Office in Nanjing, dated July 7, 1935.

107. Nanjing Archives, directive no. 5861 of the Chinese State Council to the Mongolian and Tibetan Affairs Commission, dated November 8, 1935; directive no. 6161 from the Chinese State Council to the Mongolian and Tibetan Affairs Commission, dated November 26, 1935, reproduced in Zhongguo di er lishi dang'an guan, *op. cit.*, doc. 207, 213–14; doc. 212, 219; Chen Wenjian, *op. cit.*, 65; Gao Zhangzhu, *op. cit.*, 54.

108. Nanjing Archives, brief letter from the Chinese State Council secretary to the Mongolian and Tibetan Affairs Commission enclosing a copy of a telegram from Jiang Zhiyu, dated January 27, 1936; telegram from the Mongolian and Tibetan Affairs Commission to Ma Zixiang, the governor of Qinghai Province, dated January 30, 1936, reproduced in Zhongguo di er lishi dang'an guan, *op. cit.*, doc. 244, 251–52; doc. 246, 253–54.

109. Nanjing Archives, the complete guidelines for the return of the Ninth Panchen Lama to Tibet prepared by Cheng Yun and forwarded by the Chinese State Council Secretary to the Mongolian and Tibetan Affairs Commission, dated February 1, 1936, reproduced in Zhongguo di er lishi dang'an guan, *op. cit.*, doc. 250, 250–61.

110. Nanjing Archives, letter from Cheng Yun to the Mongolian and Tibetan Affairs Commission, dated February 18, 1936; telegram from Gao Zhangzhu to the Mongolian and Tibetan Affairs Commission, dated February 20, 1936; letter no. 1823 from the Ministry of Foreign Affairs to the Mongolian and Tibetan Affairs Commission, dated February 27, 1936; telegram from Cheng Yun to the Mongolian and Tibetan Affairs Commission, dated March 1, 1936; telegram from the Mongolian and Tibetan Affairs Commission to the Ministry of Foreign Affairs, dated March 20, 1936, reproduced in Zhongguo di er lishi dang'an guan, *op. cit.*, doc. 262, 279–80; doc. 266, 283–84; doc. 274, 290; doc. 276, 291.

111. Nanjing Archives, cautionary advice from Huang Musong to Cheng Yun, dated April 26, 1936.

112. The arms found in the baggage of the Panchen Lama and his entourage included fifty-eight rifles (originally ninety-six rifles, but the thirty-eight missing ones had already been sent ahead to Tashilhunpo), six hundred grenades, radio transmitters, and gasoline. See Nanjing Archives, telegram from the Chinese official in Lhasa to Jiang Zhiyu, forwarded by the Chinese State Council secretary to the Mongolian and Tibetan Affairs Commission, dated July 4, 1936, reproduced in Zhongguo di er lishi dang'an guan, *op. cit.*, doc. 300, 315–16; IOR, L/P&S/12/4186 B, telegram from the British official in Lhasa, Raï Bahadur Norbhu Döndup, forwarded by His Majesty's Government of India to the secretary of state, dated July 21, 1936.

113. Nanjing Archives, telegram from Ma Hetian to the Mongolian and Tibetan Affairs Commission, dated July 14, 1936, reproduced in Zhongguo di er lishi dang'an guan, *op. cit.*, doc. 303, 319.

114. On Wu Zhongxin (1884–1959), see Li Shengping, *op. cit.*, 296.

115. Nanjing Archives, directive no. 4976 from the Chinese State Council to the Mongolian and Tibetan Affairs Commission, dated August 20, 1936, reproduced in Zhongguo di er lishi dang'an guan, *op. cit.*, doc. 317, 332–33; IOR, L/P&S/12/4186B, PZ 145, telegram from R. G. Howe of the British embassy in Beijing to A. Eden of the British Ministry of Foreign Affairs, no. 1202 (113/5B/1936), dated November 23, 1936; "Banchan hui Zang qingxing," *Bianjiang ban yue kan* 1, no. 6, (1936): 34; Gao Zhangzhu, *op. cit.*, 54–55.

116. Nanjing Archives, telegram from Cheng Yun to the Mongolian and Tibetan Affairs Commission, dated July 24, 1936; letter from Zhao Shouyu to the Mongolian and Tibetan Affairs Commission, dated August 20, 1936, reproduced in Zhongguo di er lishi dang'an guan, *op. cit.*, doc. 307, 323–24; doc. 318, 334–35; Gao Zhangzhu, *op. cit.*, 56.

117. Chen Wenjian, *op. cit.*, 74.

118. Nanjing Archives, report from Zhao Shouyu forwarded by the Chinese State Council secretary to the Mongolian and Tibetan Affairs Commission, dated October 19, 1936, reproduced in Zhongguo di er lishi dang'an guan, *op. cit.*, doc. 330, 351–53.

119. Nanjing Archives, telegram from Ma Bufang to the Mongolian and Tibetan Affairs Commission, dated October 31, 1936, reproduced in Zhongguo di er lishi dang'an guan, *op. cit.*, doc. 333, 355–56.

120. Nanjing Archives, letter from the Mongolian and Tibetan Affairs Commission to the Chinese State Council, dated December 31, 1936, reproduced in Zhongguo di er lishi dang'an guan, *op. cit.*, doc. 343, 368–69.

121. Nanjing Archives, telegram from Jiang Zhiyu forwarded by the Chinese State Council secretary to the Mongolian and Tibetan Affairs Commission, dated March 26, 1937, reproduced in Zhongguo di er lishi dang'an guan, *op. cit.*, doc. 363, 393–95.

122. Nanjing Archives, letter no. 50 from the Mongolian and Tibetan Affairs Commission to the Chinese State Council secretary, dated April 2, 1937, reproduced in Zhongguo di er lishi dang'an guan, *op. cit.*, doc. 366, 399–400.

123. Nanjing Archives, letter from the Military Commission to the Mongolian and Tibetan Affairs Commission, dated July 19, 1937; telegram from Zhao Shouyu to the Mongolian and Tibetan Affairs Commission, dated August 8, 1937, reproduced in Zhongguo di er lishi dang'an guan, *op. cit.*, doc. 386, 426–31, doc. 398, 443–44; Chen Wenjian, *op. cit.*, 88; Liu Jiaju, *op. cit.*, 60.

124. Nanjing Archives, telegram from the Mongolian and Tibetan Affairs Commission to Zhao Shouyu, dated August 17, 1937; directive from the Chinese State Council to the Mongolian and Tibetan Affairs Commission, dated August 19, 1937, reproduced in Zhongguo di er lishi dang'an guan, *op. cit.*, doc. 407, 452; doc. 408, 452.

125. Blo bzang rDo rje, *op. cit.*, fol. 627A.

126. Liu Jiaju, *op. cit.*, 60–61.

127. Gao Zhangzhu, *op. cit.*, 65.

128. IOR, L/P&S/12/4174, letter from F. M. Bailey, British political officer in Sikkim to His Majesty's Government of India, dated May 5, 1928; IOR, L/P&S/12/4170-File 7, PZ 1922/1933, letter no. W1, point no. 10, from Lt. Col. James Leslie Weir regarding the visit of the British political officer in Sikkim to Lhasa in 1932, dated March 1, 1933.

129. Nanjing Archives, telegram from Jiang Zhiyu to the Chinese State Council, dated September 12, 1935, reproduced in Zhongguo di er lishi dang'an guan, *op. cit.*, doc. 407, 452; doc. 188, 198–99; IOR, L/P&S/12/4175 B, report from B. Gould on the 1935 expedition of F. Williamson to Tibet; IOR, L/P&S/12/4186 B-File 22, telegrams from F. Williamson forwarded by His Majesty's Government of India to the secretary of state in India, dated October 14 and 16, 1935; IOR, L/P&S/12/4186 B, telegram from F. Williamson, British political officer in Sikkim, to the government of India, dated October 14, 1935; IOR, L/P&S/12/4186 B, letter from His Majesty's Government of India to the secretary of state in India, dated October 16, 1935.

130. IOR, L/P&S/12/4186 B, file 22, translation of a letter sent by the Ninth Panchen Lama to F. Williamson, dated November 3, 1935.

131. IOR, L/P&S/12/4186 B, telegram from His Majesty's Government of India to F. Williamson,

dated November 11, 1935; IOR, L/P&S/12/4186 B, telegram from the British ambassador in Nanjing to His Majesty's Government of India, dated November 11, 1935; Nanjing Archives, directive no. 6050 from the Chinese State Council to the Mongolian and Tibetan Affairs Commission, dated November 20, 1935; letter from Kong Qingzong to Huang Musong, who forwarded a summary of the contents of an interview held on November 9, 1935, between Xu Mo, the vice-minister of foreign affairs, and A. Cadogan, the British ambassador in Nanjing, dated December 10, 1935, reproduced in Zhongguo di er lishi dang'an guan, *op. cit.*, doc. 407, 452; doc. 208, 214–15; doc. 220, 226–28.

132. On Xu Mo (1893–1956), see Perleberg, *Who's Who in Modern China*, 539; Li Shengping, *op. cit.*, 566.

133. Keith Battye held the post of British trade agent in Gyeltsé from June 20, 1935, to July 20, 1935.

134. IOR, L/P&S/12/4186 B, telegram from His Majesty's Government of India to F. Williamson, dated November 11, 1935; IOR, L/P&S/12/4186 B, File 22, telegram from Captain Keith Battye to the secretary to His Majesty's Government of India, dated December 16, 1935; Nanjing Archives, telegram from Jiang Zhiyu forwarded by the Chinese Ministry of Military Affairs to the Mongolian and Tibetan Affairs Commission, dated November 20, 1935, reproduced in Zhongguo di er lishi dang'an guan, *op. cit.*, doc. 209, 216–17.

135. IOR, L/P&S/12/4186B, copy of telegram no. 7 (1)-P/36 from the British political officer in Sikkim to the secretary of state.

136. IOR, L/P&S/12/4186 B, File 22, telegram from A. Cadogan, British ambassador to China in Beijing, dated January 24, 1936.

137. IOR, L/P&S/12/4186 B, File 22, PZ 1396, telegram from A. Cadogan to His Majesty's Government of India, dated February 11, 1936.

138. Nanjing Archives, letter no. 130 from the Mongolian and Tibetan Affairs Commission to the Ministry of Foreign Affairs, dated February 13, 1936, reproduced in Zhongguo di er lishi dang'an guan, *op. cit.*, doc. 257, 274–75.

139. The general idea behind the resolution proposal was that, since the Panchen Lama truly wished to return to his homeland, his peaceful return would, according to Gould and the British authorities, bolster the Tibetan government and contribute to maintaining Tibet as autonomous and open to the interests of the British Crown. They, therefore, suggested that the prelate be persuaded to accept an escort of Tibetan (instead of Chinese) soldiers in exchange for greater concessions from the Tibetan government. In addition, they proposed sending the British official Raï Bahadur Norbhu Döndup to Lhasa to confirm to the Tibetan authorities that the British ambassador in Nanjing was exerting pressure on the Chinese government regarding the escort. However, their efforts were in vain since the Chinese claimed to have no opposition from the Tibetans. Raï Bahadur Norbhu Döndup also had the duty of informing the Tibetan authorities that if they gave their agreement, Basil Gould would inform the Panchen Lama of the project and recommend that the points of disagreement be settled once he was in Tibet. Raï Bahadur Norbhu Döndup also was to clearly highlight the will of the British government to serve as mediator in resolving the obstacles to the Panchen Lama's return to Tibet. Lastly, Gould and the British government of India put forward the idea of offering favors to the Tibetan government—such as training officers of the Tibetan army in India—to encourage them to relax their stance regarding the Panchen Lama. See IOR, L/P&S/12/4181, letter from His Majesty's Government of India to the British chargé d'affaires in Beijing, cited in Goldstein, *op. cit.*, 274–76.

140. The British minister of foreign affairs asked that certain practical points be spelled out. In particular, he felt it necessary to specify that the mediation did not concern only the Panchen Lama but also that the abandonment of the Chinese escort be *sine qua non*. He further stated that the Panchen Lama should be informed as quickly as possible since, if Basil Gould were to receive him at the Sino-Tibetan border, he would be accompanied by Tibetan (and not British troops), which the prelate had hoped for. He felt that the negotiations with the Tibetan government would have to continue upon the Panchen Lama's arrival in Tibet.

141. IOR, L/P&S/4186 B, telegram from B. Gould to His Majesty's Government of India, dated October 10, 1936.

142. IOR, L/P&S/12/2175, telegram from the Office of Foreign Affairs to the British government in London, dated December 20, 1936; IOR, L/P&S/12/2175, letter from the secretary of state in India to His Majesty's Government of India, dated December 24, 1936; Chapman, *op. cit.*, 233–38; FO 371/20222, recommendations from Neame, cited in Goldstein *op. cit.*, 281–83; Nanjing Archives, report from Gao Zhangzhu to Wu Zhongxin, dated April 1937. Gao Zhangzhu does not provide information on the Tibetan army's arsenal.

143. FO 371/20963, cited in Goldstein, *op. cit.*, 288.

144. Nanjing Archives, letter from the Chinese Ministry of Foreign Affairs to the Mongolian and Tibetan Affairs Commission, dated August 4, 1937, reproduced in Zhongguo di er lishi dang'an guan, *op. cit.*, doc. 395, 441.

145. The lateness of the Chinese soldiers' arrival in Kyégudo where they joined the Panchen Lama could indicate that they were waiting in Xining for their pay before heading off on their mission.

146. The Rabshilungshö ganden chökorling monastery is referred to as Longxi si in Chinese.

147. Nanjing Archives, telegram from Zhao Shouyu to the Mongolian and Tibetan Affairs Commission, dated September 6, 1937, reproduced in Zhongguo di er lishi dang'an guan, *op. cit.*, doc. 411, 454–55; Chen Wenjian, *op. cit.*, 93.

148. Nanjing Archives, telegram from Jiang Zhiyu to the Mongolian and Tibetan Affairs Commission, dated September 21, 1937; letter from the Mongolian and Tibetan Affairs Commission to the Chinese State Council, citing a telegram from the Office of the Ninth Panchen Lama, dated October 12, 1937, reproduced in Zhongguo di er lishi dang'an guan, *op. cit.*, doc. 413, 456; doc. 421, 465–66; Srung Kri hru'u, *op. cit.*, 124; Chen Wenjian, *op. cit.*, 94–95.

149. Chen Wenjian, *op. cit.*, 95, 77.

150. IOR, L/P&S/12/4174 (PZ 6940), letter translated into English and forwarded by F. M. Bailey, the British political officer in Sikkim, to His Majesty's Government of India, dated October 1, 1932; IOR, L/P&S/12/4174, letter from the Thirteenth Dalai Lama included in correspondence from Lt. Col. James Leslie Weir to the government of India, dated October 11, 1932; Nanjing Archives, telegram from Jiang Zhiyu, member of the preparatory team of the Huang Musong mission, to the Office of Transmissions for the Special Envoy in Nanjing, who copied and forwarded it to the secretary of the Chinese State Council who, in turn, hand-delivered it to the Mongolian and Tibetan Affairs Commission, dated July 26, 1934, reproduced in Zhongguo di er lishi dang'an guan, *op. cit.*, doc. 89, 87–88; Dong Shufan, 16–18.

151. IOR, L/P&S/12/4181, telegram from the British political officer in Sikkim to the secretary of foreign affairs of the Indian government, dated January 8, 1934; bKras dgon lo rgyus rtsom 'bri tshogs chung, "sNgags chen bDar pa ho thog," 86; Don khang sKal bzang bDe skyid, *op. cit.*, 27–29; Chen Wenjian, *op. cit.*, 29; Liu Jiaju, *op. cit.*, 50.

152. *Zhongyang ribao*, April 25, 1934.

153. *Zhongyang ribao*, June 1, 1934.

154. Nanjing Archives, telegram from Ngagchen Rinpoche to the Mongolian and Tibetan Affairs Commission, dated April 27, 1935; letter from the Mongolian and Tibetan Affairs Commission to the Chinese State Council, dated December 31, 1936, reproduced in Zhongguo di er lishi dang'an guan, *op. cit.*, doc. 128, 136; doc. 343, 368–69; IOR, L/P&S/12/4175 B, report from B. Gould on the 1935 expedition by F. Williamson to Tibet; IOR, L/P&S/12/4186 B, File 22, telegram from Captain Keith Battye to the secretary of His Majesty's Government of India, dated December 16, 1935; IOR, L/P&S/12/4186 B, telegram no. 2365 of His Majesty's Government of India to the secretary of state, dated November 6, 1936, referring to telegram no. 177 from B. Gould, dated November 4, 1936; *Zhongyang ribao*, June 1 and 3, 1934.

155. Liu Wenhui, president of the Commission for the Edification of Xikang Province attended the interview, assisted by Zheng Shaocheng and by Luo Haikuan, as well as two of his representatives who also attended the meeting. See IOR, L/P&S/12/4186B, letter PZ 2122 from His Majesty's Government of India to the secretary of state, citing a telegram from H. Richardson, dated March 31, 1937; IOR, L/P&S/12/4185A, *Who's Who in Tibet*, 48; Nanjing Archives, report from Gao Zhangzhu to the Mongolian and Tibetan Affairs Commission, dated April 1937, 10; IOR, L/P&S/4186 B,

telegram no. 881 from Sir Knatchull-Hugessen, the British ambassador to China, dated April 23, 1937; Liu Jiaju, *op. cit.*, 59; Chen Wenjian, *op. cit.*, 83; 90; Petech, *Aristocracy and Government*, 151.

156. IOR, L/P&S/12/4186B, letter PZ 2122 from His Majesty's Government of India to the secretary of state, citing a telegram from H. Richardson, dated March 31, 1937; IOR, L/P&S/12/4185 A, *Who's Who in Tibet*, 48; IOR, L/P&S/4186 B, telegram no. 881 from Sir Knatchull-Hugessen, the British ambassador to China, dated April 23, 1937.

157. "Dazhuoni" is a title signifying "secretary." In source material, "Dazhuoni" never appears with a proper name, making it is impossible to provide further identification.

158. Nanjing Archives, report from Gao Zhangzhu to Wu Zhongxin, director of the Mongolian and Tibetan Affairs Commission, dated April 1937.

159. The first Office of the Ninth Panchen Lama to be opened in Nanjing was founded in January or February 1929 at 13 Qiwang Street, and a second office in Nanjing was founded on April 4, 1935, at 293 Jiankang Street.

160. IOR, L/P&S/12/4185 A; *Who's Who in Tibet*, 12; Chen Wenjian, *op. cit.*, 1; Liu Jiaju, *op. cit.*, 38; Taipei Archives, "Zhonghua Minguo waijiao dang'an," Collection Tibet 03.28, Academia Sinica (Zhongyang yanjiuyuan, Taipei), letter from the minister of foreign affairs to the Mongolian and Tibetan Affairs Office, dated March 1924; Thub bstan Sangs rgyas, *op. cit.*, 25.

161. Feng Youzhi, *op. cit.*, 329.

162. Chen Wenjian, *op. cit.*, 84; Liu Jiaju, *op. cit.*, 60; Feng Youzhi, *op. cit.*, 331.

163. IOR, L/P&S/12/4186B, letter PZ 2122 from His Majesty's Government of India to the secretary of state, citing a telegram from H. Richardson, dated March 31, 1937; IOR, L/P&S/12/4185 A, *Who's Who in Tibet*, 48; IOR, L/P&S/4186 B, telegram no. 881 from Sir Knatchull-Hugessen, the British ambassador to China, dated April 23, 1937.

164. Nanjing Archives, report from Gao Zhangzhu to Wu Zhongxin, director of the Mongolian and Tibetan Affairs Commission, dated April 1937.

165. To answer this question, it would be useful to have access to the original Tibetan version of this letter. For the Chinese translation of the letter, see Dong Shufan, *op. cit.*, 16–18.

CHAPTER 6

1. Ma Hetian, *Gan Qing Zang bianqu kaocha ji*, 651; Nanjing Archives, telegram from the Office of the Emissary in Charge of Spreading Values in the Western Region to the Mongolian and Tibetan Affairs Commission, dated December 1, 1937, reproduced in Zhongguo di er lishi dang'an guan, *Jiu shi Banchan neidi*, doc. 433, 474; Chen Wenjian, *Banchan dashi dong lai shiwu nian dashiji*, 98; Liu Jiaju, *Banchan da shi quanji*, 62; Srung Kri hru'u, "Panchen sku 'phreng dgu pa dBus gTsang," 125.

2. Nanjing Archives, telegram from Dingkyé Rinpoche to the Mongolian and Tibetan Affairs Commission, dated May 15, 1934; *Zhongyang ribao*, March 8, 1934; April 25, 1934; Liu Jiaju, *op. cit.*, 52.

3. Chen Wenjian, *op. cit.*, 55; Srung Kri hru'u, *op. cit.*, 122.

4. Chen Wenjian, *op. cit.*, 57. According to Liu Jiaju, *op. cit.*, 57, Dingkyé Rinpoche left Kumbum monastery for Kyégudo monastery on July 19, 1935. Dingkyé Rinpoche's mission was to explain the Republican government's principles of unity and its development projects to local populations in the frontier regions through books printed in Chinese and Tibetan.

5. bsTan 'dzin rGya mtsho, "Panchen bzhugs sgar dang Li'u un hu'i dbar gyi dmag 'khrug," 63.

6. Nanjing Archives, telegram from Zhao Shouyu to the Mongolian and Tibetan Affairs Commission, dated December 1, 1937.

7. Ma Hetian, *op. cit.*, 654, 657.

8. Nor brang O rgyan, "Pan chen sku phreng dgu pa'i sku gdung," 36–37.

9. Nanjing Archives, telegram from members of the Ninth Panchen Lama's entourage to Dai Jitao, dated December 13, 1937; telegram from Wu Zhongxin to Zhao Shouyu, dated December 17, 1937; Liu Jiaju, *op. cit.*, 63; Lai Zuozhong and Deng Junkang, "Ganzi shibian de qianqian houhou," 125–26.

10. Nanjing Archives, telegram from Wu Zhongxin to the Chinese State Council, dated December 15, 1937; order from the Chinese government, dated December 23, 1937.

11. Nanjing Archives, letter no. 262 from the Office of Civil Affairs to the Mongolian and Tibetan Affairs Commission, dated December 24, 1937.

12. Nanjing Archives, telegram from Zhao Shouyu to the Mongolian and Tibetan Affairs Commission, dated December 18, 1937; telegram from Ma Bufang to Wu Zhongxin, director of the Mongolian and Tibetan Affairs Commission, dated December 26, 1937; telegram from Zhao Shouyu to the Mongolian and Tibetan Affairs Commission, dated January 18, 1938; Liu Jiaju, *op. cit.*, 63.

13. Nanjing Archives, telegram from Zhao Shouyu to the Mongolian and Tibetan Affairs Commission, dated February 13, 1938; Liu Jiaju, *op. cit.*, 63.

14. Nanjing Archives, description of a ritual planned by the Department of Rites and forwarded to the Mongolian and Tibetan Affairs Commission on February 15, 1938; directive of the Mongolian and Tibetan Affairs Commission to the Tibet Office and to the Office of the Ninth Panchen Lama, dated February 25, 1938; letter from the Mongolian and Tibetan Affairs Commission to Chen Dingxun, mayor of Chengdu, dated February 25, 1938; telegram from the Chinese State Council to the Mongolian and Tibetan Affairs Commission, dated March 3, 1938; list of the members who would participate in the funeral ceremony, dated March 8, 1938; directive of the Chinese State Council to the Mongolian and Tibetan Affairs Commission, dated March 8, 1938; telegram from the Ministry of Finance to the Mongolian and Tibetan Affairs Commission, dated March 12, 1938; report from the Mongolian and Tibetan Affairs Commission to the Chinese State Council, dated March 14, 1938; order from the Chinese State Council to the Mongolian and Tibetan Affairs Commission, dated March 15, 1938; letter from the Military Affairs Commission to the Mongolian and Tibetan Affairs Commission, dated March 19, 1938.

15. Nanjing Archives, letter from the Chinese State Council to the Mongolian and Tibetan Affairs Commission, dated April 6, 1938. See also Nanjing Archives, "Dai Zhuanxian riji."

16. Nanjing Archives, telegram from Zhao Shouyu to the Mongolian and Tibetan Affairs Commission, dated April 8, 1938.

17. Nanjing Archives, report from the Mongolian and Tibetan Affairs Commission to the Chinese State Council, dated April 12, 1938.

18. The Nanjing State Council dissolved the Office of the Emissary in Charge of Spreading Values in the Western Region, while it kept that of the Office of the Great and Glorious Master Panchen Who Protects the Country and Spreads its Values. The Panchen Lama's office in Nanjing was also kept open. It was decided that the school connected with this office would be managed by the minister of education and the Mongolian and Tibetan Affairs Commission, and that the payments of the Panchen Lama's salary would be suspended. The minister of communications reserved the right to decide how the radio transmitters would be used from the Office of the Emissary in Charge of Spreading Values in the Western Region. The Office of the Special Envoy in Charge of Accompanying the Ninth Panchen Lama to Tibet would be closed upon the arrival of Dai Jitao in Kardzé. See Nanjing Archives, summary by the Chinese State Council to the Mongolian and Tibetan Affairs Commission, dated April 22, 1938.

19. Legend has it that Dai Jitao had such great devotion towards his spiritual guide that later during a long meditation session on a photo of the Panchen Lama, he saw nectar flow from it. Author's interview with Lakpa Dorjé (monk from Tashilhunpo), Bylakuppe, January 1996.

20. Nanjing Archives, "Dai Zhuanxian riji;" telegram from Zhao Shouyu to Wu Zhongxin, dated August 16, 1938; report from the Office of the Special Envoy in Charge of Accompanying the Ninth Panchen Lama to Tibet to the Mongolian and Tibetan Affairs Commission, dated August 20, 1938; report from Dai Jitao to the Republican government, dated November 23, 1938; Liu Jiaju, *op. cit.*, 64; Srung Kri hru'u, *op. cit.*, 126; Feng Youzhi, *op. cit.*, 332–36.

21. Nanjing Archives, telegrams from the Assembly of Abbots (*Banchan kanting*) to the Mongolian and Tibetan Affairs Commission, dated September 7 and 17, 1938; telegram from Kong Qingzong, head of the Tibetan Department of the Mongolian and Tibetan Affairs Commission to Liu Jiaju, dated November 14, 1938; telegram from Wu Zhongxin to Liu Wenhui, dated December 5, 1938.

22. Nanjing Archives, letter from Gao Zhangzhu, a military adviser to Wu Zhongxin, to the Mongolian and Tibetan Affairs Commission, containing two forwarded telegrams from the Office of the Great and Glorious Master Panchen Who Protects the Country and Propagates its Values, dated January 18, 1939.

23. bsTan 'dzin rGya mtsho, *op. cit.*, 61; Nor brang O rgyan, *op. cit.*, 37.

24. Liu Jiaju, *op. cit.*, 64; Srung Kri hru'u, *op. cit.*, 126; bsTan 'dzin rGya mtsho, *op. cit.*, 62–63; Kongsa Yiduo, *op. cit.*, 17; Nor brang O rgyan, *op. cit.*, 39; Yang Xing'an, *op. cit.*, 18.

25. Liu Jiaju, *op. cit.*, 64; Nor brang O rgyan, *op. cit.*, 40–41, 43; Nanjing Archives, telegram from the Mongolian and Tibetan Affairs Commission to the Tibetan Council of Ministers, dated March 16, 1940; telegram from the Tibetan Council of Ministers to the Mongolian and Tibetan Affairs Commission, dated March 30, 1940; telegram from the Military Affairs Commission to the Mongolian and Tibetan Affairs Commission, dated April 29, 1940; telegram from the Office of the Ninth Panchen Lama in Nanjing to the Mongolian and Tibetan Affairs Commission, dated June 29, 1940; telegram from the Office of the Ninth Panchen Lama in Nanjing to the Mongolian and Tibetan Affairs Commission, dated August 26, 1940; telegram from the Mongolian and Tibetan Affairs Commission to Zhao Shouyu, dated September 25, 1940; telegram from the Mongolian and Tibetan Affairs Commission to Liu Wenhui, dated October 4, 1940.

26. Nanjing Archives, telegram from Zhao Shouyu to the Mongolian and Tibetan Affairs Commission, dated December 7, 1940; Liu Jiaju, *op. cit.*, 65; Srung Kri hru'u, *op. cit.*, 127; Nor brang O rgyan, *op. cit.*, 45–46.

27. Nanjing Archives, report from the Mongolian and Tibetan Affairs Commission to the Chinese State Council, dated March 25, 1941.

28. Nanjing Archives, order of the Chinese State Council to the Mongolian and Tibetan Affairs Commission, dated May 5, 1941.

29. Nanjing Archives, telegram from the Office of the Ninth Panchen Lama in Nanjing to the Mongolian and Tibetan Affairs Commission, dated June 8, 1941. On January 20, 1942, the Office of the Prayer Hall of the Panchen Lama (*Banchan tongjing tang*) was created. Its mission was to recognize the reincarnation of the Ninth Panchen Lama. The plan was to dissolve it as soon as the Tenth Panchen Lama was enthroned. See Nanjing Archives, telegram from the Mongolian and Tibetan Affairs Commission to Lozang Gyeltsen, dated January 20, 1942.

30. Dingkyé Rinpoche became the Tenth Panchen Lama's tutor and Lozang Gyeltsen his attendant.

31. Wang Dui, "Wu shi zhi jiu shi Banchan hezang lingta," 134–35.

APPENDIX B

1. Zhwa sgab pa, *Bod kyi srid don rgyal rabs*, vol. 1, 469–71.

2. *Qing shilu*, Kangxi, 171/17A-b; 175/5A-17A; 188/15B-16A.

3. See Shakabpa, *Tibet: A Political History*, 129.

4. Zhwa sgab pa, *op. cit.*, vol. 1, 486–91.

5. Petech, *China and Tibet*, 11; *Qing shilu*, Kangxi 227/24A-25A.

6. *Qing shilu*, Kangxi, 227/28B.

7. *Qing shilu*, Kangxi, 236/17A-18A, 263/4B-5A.

8. *E'erdeni* is a Manchu term designating a reincarnated master. It is translated into Tibetan as "Rinpoche."

9. Petech, *op. cit.*, 30, 34; Zhwa sgab pa, *op. cit.*, vol. 1, 504–11.

10. *Qing shilu*, Yongzheng, 10/18A-19A; Hucker, *Dictionary of Official Titles in Imperial China*, entry 4526.

11. Hucker, *op. cit.*, entry 4546.

12. Brunnert and Hagelstrom, *Present Day Political Organization of China*, entry 445.

13. Petech, "The Missions of Bogle and Turner according to the Tibetan Texts," 66–67.

14. Petech, *China and Tibet*, 72, 76.

15. Zhwa sgab pa, *op. cit.*, vol. 1, 533; Petech, *op. cit.*, 104, 109.

16. Sengge was the imperial resident in Tibet from February 20, 1727, to February 19, 1933. Mala was the imperial resident in Tibet from February 20, 1727 to December 23, 1728, and then again from July 3, 1729 to March 23, 1731.

17. Petech, *China and Tibet*, 144, 148, 150.

18. "Changkya Hutuktu" is a title attributed to reincarnations of a particular lineage. The lineage of the Changkya Hutuktu was created by the Qing emperor Qianlong. Very close bonds united the Mongol master and the Manchu emperor. The origin of the title *hutuktu* remains obscure. It is said to be the translation of the Tibetan term *phakpa*, which means holiness, and is also thought to have been created in honor of Phakpa (1235–1280), the imperial tutor to the Mongol emperor Khubilai (1260–1294). The title might also be a Mongolian transcription of the Tibetan term *tulku*, which means "emanation body" and, consequently, a reincarnated master. The Manchu emperor had conferred this title on eight well-known reincarnations starting in 1691. The title is not hereditary. However, when the lineage is prestigious—as was the case for the Changkya Hutuktu—this appellation is granted nearly automatically to all the previous and later reincarnations. See R. Miller, *Monasteries and Culture Change*, 65; Hyer and Jagchid, *A Mongolian Living Buddha*, 15; Chayet, *Les Temples de Jehol*, 60–64; Wang Xiangyun, "Tibetan Buddhism at the Court of Qing."

19. *Qing shilu*, Yongzheng, 145/8B-9A.

20. Petech, *op. cit.*, 160, 182N3, 184, 187.

21. *Qing shilu*, Qianlong, 374/10A-11A, 376/29B-31A.

22. *Qing shilu*, Qianlong, 377/29B-30A, 385/12B-21B.

23. Several titles were commonly used to designate the Tibetan regents, corresponding to the evolution of the position. From the middle of the seventeenth century to 1747, the regent was the monk or layperson responsible for administrating Tibet's civil affairs during the lifetime of the Dalai Lama who appointed him. At that time he held the title of *cakzöpa* (lit. "officer") or *dési* (lit. "person who reigns over a territory"). The second title to describe the heads of large districts lasted from 1757 to at least the beginning of the twentieth century. Beginning in 1757, the year of the Seventh Dalai Lama's death, the regent (a monk) would manage civil affairs in the absence of and/or during the minority of the Dalai Lamas. From then on he held the title of *gyelpötsap* (lit. the "sovereign's replacement") or that of *sikyong* (lit. "protector of temporal affairs"). He had to leave his duties as soon as the Dalai Lama reached majority. See Petech, "The Dalai Lamas and Regents of Tibet," 368–94; Wang Xianjun, "Xizang shezheng zhidu taolun," 76–81.

24. Rockhill, "The Dalai Lamas of Lhasa," 46; Richardson, *Ch'ing Dynasty Inscriptions at Lhasa*, 27.

25. Markham, *Narratives of the Mission of George Bogle*, lxix; 1–14, 167–68, 195–97, 207–10; Premen Addy, *Tibet on the Imperial Chessboard*, 23.

26. *Qing shilu*, Qianlong, 1072/28A-B.

27. Chayet, *op. cit.*, 48–50.

28. George Bogle died in 1781. Warren Hastings selected Captain Samuel Turner to replace him.

29. Markham, *op. cit.*, lxxiii, lxxv.

30. Turner, *Court of the Teshoo Lama.*

31. *Qing shilu*, Qianlong, 30/2B-3a.

32. Rockhill, *op. cit.*, 50; Imbault-Huart, "Histoire de la conquête du Népal," 348–77.

33. Richardson, *op. cit.*, 30.

34. *Qing shilu*, Qianlong, 140, 7b-9a.

35. Zhwa sgab pa, *op. cit.*, vol. 1, 634–39.

36. Boulnois, *Poudre d'or*, 99–101.

37. *Qing shilu*, Qianlong, 1386/29a-32b; Markham, *op. cit.*, lxxvi; Rockhill, *op. cit.*, 51.

38. Hummel, *Eminent Chinese of the Ch'ing Period*, 254.

39. Chayet, *op. cit.*, 58.

40. Rockhill points out this monopolistic situation in *op. cit.*, 54.

41. *Qing shilu*, Qianlong, 1417/12b-17a, 1424/8a-11b.

42. Richardson, *op. cit.*, 50.

43. *Qing shilu*, Qianlong, 144/17b-21a.

44. *Qing shilu*, Daoguang, 296/13b-14a, 371/44b, 406/5a-5b.

45. Rockhill, *op. cit.*, 67.

46. Petech, *The Dalai Lamas and Regents of Tibet*, 389, specifies that these facts are not mentioned in the Eleventh Dalai Lama's biography.

47. In actuality, some travelers did manage to reach the Tibetan capital. Thomas Manning, a British man, arrived in Lhasa in 1811; the French Lazarist fathers Huc and Gabet traveled to Lhasa in 1846; the Japanese Ekai Kawaguchi and Narita Yasuteru arrived in Lhasa in March and December 1901, respectively; and the Japanese Enga Teramoto in 1904. Other travelers, such as the Frenchman Bonvalot and Prince Henry d'Orléans, were turned back near the border by the Tibetan army before being able to reach the capital.

48. Das, *Tibetan Studies*, introduction.

49. Kyabying Drongtséba Sengchen Tulku Lozang Pelden Chöpel held the post of administrator at Tashilhunpo and of the private estates of the Eighth and Ninth Panchen Lamas from 1881 to 1887. Drongtséba and Sengchen appear to be two titles whose origins are unclear. Drongtséba seems to be the name of an aristocratic family from Drongtséba that disappeared at the end of the eighteenth century. Drongtséba could also refer to the birthplace of Sengchen Tulku Lozang Pelden Chöpel who was, in fact, born in the location of that name. Drongtséba might also be the title held by the lineage of reincarnated masters from the monastery Drongtsé chödé tarpa lingön in Drongtséba to the northwest of Gyeltsé in Tsang Province. Indeed, Drongtséba Sengchen Tulku Lozang Pelden Chöpel lived there. "Sengchen" is thought to be a Chinese appellation meaning the "monk-minister." This name is used for a line of reincarnated masters at Tashilhunpo. Finally, it is not certain whether these titles are systematically used together as in this case, or whether they refer to two or to one and the same lineages of reincarnated masters. See Petech, *Aristocracy and Government in Tibet*, 133; Das, *Journey to Lhasa*, 202; rdzong rtse Byams pa Thub bstan, *Chos grwa chen po bKra shis lhun po'i chos 'byung*, 695; bKra shis dgon lo rgyus, *Dpal gyi chos sde chen po bKra shis lhun po*, 86–87; e-mail correspondence with the late professor Gene Smith, January 20, 1999.

50. Waddell, *Lhasa and its Mysteries*, 7–9.

51. The complete report of C. S. Das and Ögyen Gyatso's mission is comprised of two volumes entitled "Narrative of a Journey to Lhasa in 1881–1882, 1885" and "Lake Yamdo (Palti) and in Lhoka, Yarlung and Sakya in 1882, 1887." One hundred copies were made of each report, and excerpts were published in the following reviews: *Nineteenth Century*, 26 (1889): 681–94; *Asia*, April 1925, 275–85. An abridged version was published in 1882 under the direction of Rockhill. See Das, *Journey to Lhasa and Central Tibet*.

52. The execution took place in June 1887. See Kawaguchi, *Three Years in Tibet*, 15–20.

53. Zhwa sgab pa, *Bod kyi srid don rgyal rabs*, vol. 1, 64–65.

APPENDIX E

1. See, e.g., bKra shis dgon lo rgyus, *bKra shis lhun po dpal gyi sde chen*, 89–90.

2. sLe zur 'Jigs med dBang phyug and bDe zur Rin chen dBang 'dus, "De snga'i bla brang rgyal mtshan mthon po'i srid 'dzin sgrig gzhi'i spyi'i gnas tshul," 102–61. For a Chinese translation of this article, see Machong Mingjiu Duoji, "Zhashelunbu si kanting zuzhi jigou shulüe," 57–68.

3. This is the name of the Panchen Lama's palace that was located within the Tashilhunpo monastic compound. The term also designates the private residence of the Panchen Lama.

4. Author's interview with Kugo Ngawang Riktröl (former member of the Tibetan government), Dharamsala, India, January 10, 1996.

5. *The Monograph of Central Tibet* was written around the end of the eighteenth century, but was not published until 1896.

6. Some other recent works use the Manchu description of Tashilhunpo; for example, Wu Fengpei and Ceng Guoqing, *Qingchao zhu Zang dachen zhidu de jianli yu yange*, 1989.

7. Hucker, *A Dictionary of Official Titles in Imperial China*, 35.

8. Brunnert and Hagelstrom, *Present Day Political Organization of China*, 477; Miller, *Monasteries and Culture Change in Inner Mongolia*, 54.

9. Author's interview with Kugo Ngawang Riktröl (former member of the Tibetan government), Dharamsala, India, January 10, 1996.

10. See, e.g., the use of the term "prime minister" in David Macdonald's translation of the letter left by the Ninth Panchen Lama in his monastery before his departure in 1923. IOR, L/P&S/12/4174 (PZ 1769/4).

11. IOR/L/P&S/12/4170-File 7, PZ 1922/1933, letter from Lt. Col. Weir, dated March 1, 1933.

12. It is important to note a significant divergence in Tibetan and Chinese perceptions of Tibetan space. See page 33.

13. The rankings, determined according to the Chinese system, were introduced into Tibet in 1792. However, the Tibetans only used five of the nine Chinese rankings (from rank 3 to rank 7, inclusive). The second rank was only accorded occasionally. See Petech, *Aristocracy and Government in Tibet*, 8.

14. "Personnel having access to the small residence" (*zimchungkak*) also existed in the case of the Dalai Lamas. A. Macdonald described this for the Fifth Dalai Lama as "Private House." See A. Macdonald, "Un portrait du 5e Dalai Lama," 129. A. Macdonald's translation was not adopted for this present volume since it seems to designate more a department than the personnel comprising it.

15. The title *drönyer chenmo* is often translated as "chamberlain" in English. In French, it can be translated as "high chamberlain" (*grand chambellan*); however, the translation "state secretary" seems more appropriate given the administrative functions of the titleholder, including the fact that he acted by delegation and had to answer directly to the general administrator. See *Petit Larousse illustré*, 927.

16. *Tsédrung* denotes "official monk." *Létsenpa* signifies a low-ranking administrator. See Petech, *op. cit.*, 238–39.

17. sLe zur 'Jigs med dBang phyug and bDe zur Rin chen dBang 'dus, *op. cit.*, 105–16.

18. The translation proposed by A. Macdonald has been employed here. See A. Macdonald, "Un portrait du 5e Dalai Lama," 129.

19. This translation also comes from A. Macdonald.

20. sLe zur 'Jigs med dBang phyug and bDe zur Rin chen dBang 'dus, *op. cit.*, 106.

21. IOR, L/P&S/12/4185a, *Who's Who in Tibet*, confidential dossier corrected in autumn 1937 and completed in February 1938, 6; Perleberg, *Who's Who in Modern China*, 921; Chen Wenjian, *Banchan dashi dong lai shiwu nian dashiji*, 1; Don khang sKal bzang bDe skyid, "Pan chen sku phreng dgu pa mes rgyal nang khul du gsang phebs kyi snga rjes," 8–10; Liu Jiaju, *Banchan dashi quanji*, 36; Srung Kri hru'u, "Panchen sku 'phreng dgu pa dBus gTsang," 117.

22. sLe zur 'Jigs med dBang phyug and bDe zur Rin chen dBang 'dus, *op. cit.*, 106–8.

23. Chen Wenjian, *op. cit.*, 1; Don khang sKal bzang bDe skyid, *op. cit.*, 8–10; Liu Jiaju, *op. cit.*, 36; Srung Kri hru'u, *op. cit.*, 117.

24. Chen Wenjian, *op cit.*, 1; Don khang sKal bzang bDe skyid, *op. cit.*, 8–10; Liu Jiaju, *op. cit.*, 36; Srung Kri hru'u, *op. cit.*, 117.

25. *Da Qing huidian shili*, 1899, 977/5b; *Wei Zang tongzhi*, 1896, 12/9a.

26. sLe zur 'Jigs med dBang phyug and bDe zur Rin chen dBang 'dus, *op. cit.*, 129–30, 134. Regarding the titles "High Secretary" and "Grand Master," see Petech, *op. cit.*, 263.

27. Chen Wenjian, *op. cit.*, 1; Don khang sKal bzang bDe skyid, *op. cit.*, 8–10; Liu Jiaju, *op. cit.*, 36; Srung Kri hru'u, *op. cit.*, 117.

28. sLe zur 'Jigs med dBang phyug and bDe zur Rin chen dBang 'dus, *op. cit.*, 130–36.

BIBLIOGRAPHY

ARCHIVAL COLLECTIONS

Number Two Historical Archives, Nanjing

Collection 141 (Tibet): dossiers 2948; 2950; 2951; 2952; 2956; 2961; 2962; 2966; 2969; 2971; 2972; 2973; 2976; 2977; 2978; 2980; 2981; 2985; 2986; 2988; 2989; 2990; 2996; 2998; 3016; 3864; 3866; 3867; 3870; 3875; 3876; 3877; 3878; 3879; 3880; 3881; 3882; 3889; 3890; 3891.

Oriental and India Office Collection and Records, London

L/MIL/17/14/92 Military report on Tibet
L/P&S/10 Political and Secret Subject Files
L/P&S/11 Political and Secret Annual Files
L/P&S/12 Political and Secret (External) Files and Collections
L/P&S/18 Selected Political and Secret Memoranda
L/P&S/20 Selected Political and Secret Library
Mss Eur F 80 The Bell Collection
Mss Eur F 157 The Bailey Collection
Mss Eur F 197 The Younghusband Collection
Mss Eur E 226 The Bogle Collection
Mss Eur D 722 The Shuttleworth Collection
R/1/4 Selected Indian Foreign Department Personnel Files
V/27/230/54 Summary of the Principal Events and Measures of the Viceroyalty of the Earl of Minto, 1905–1910

Taipei Archives

"Zhonghua Minguo waijiao dang 'an" 中華民國外交檔案: Collection Tibet 03.28.
"Zongli ge guo shiwu yamen Qing dang 'an" 總理各國事務衙門清檔案: Collection Tibet 02.16; 03.16; 04.16.

INTERVIEWS

Kachen Lozang Döndrub (dka' chen Blo bzang don grub): Born in 1924. Entered Tashilhunpo 1938. Testimony on the construction of the Ninth Panchen Lama's reliquary and the arrival of his remains. Bylakuppe, January 1996.

Kachen Jangpa Thubten (dka' chen Byang pa thub bstan): Born in 1904. Monk from Tashilhunpo who received his monk's vows from the Ninth Panchen Lama. Died in 1997. Bylakuppe, December 1995 and January 1996.

Kachen Lakpa Dorjé (dka' chen lHag pa rDo rje): Born in 1907. Monk from Tashilhunpo who received his monk's vows from the Ninth Panchen Lama. Bylakuppe, January 1996.

Tashi Tsering (bKra shis tshe ring): Historian and scholar at the Library of Tibetan Works and Archives, and Director of Amnye Machen Institute, India. Dharamsala, January 1996.

Dakpo Rinpoche (Dwags po Rin po che): Born in 1931. Monk from Drépung monastery in Lhasa. Recognized as a reincarnated lama by the Thirteenth Dalai Lama. Paris, May and June 1995; March 1997.

Liu Shengqi: Chinese-English interpreter at the Office of Chinese Representation in Lhasa, 1940. Beijing, February 1993.

Nyima Gyari (Nyi ma rgya ri): Born in Kardzé. Testimony on events occuring in Kham following the death of the Ninth Panchen Lama. New Delhi, January 1996.
Püntsok Thubten (Phun tshogs thub bstan): Born in 1923. Monk from Dakpo monastery located near the village of Brum gasha, the birthplace of the Ninth Panchen Lama. Paris, July 1995.
W. T. Serga: Born in 1915. Testimony on events occuring in Kham following the death of the Ninth Panchen Lama. New Delhi, January 1996.
Kugo Ngawang Rigköl (sku sngo Ngag dbang rig 'khrol): Civil servant with the Tibetan government in Lhasa. Dharamsala, January 1996.
Yéshé Dorjé (Ye shes rDo rje): Born in 1914. Bodyguard of the Ninth Panchen Lama. Chengdu, November and December 1992.

PERIODICALS

Bengal District Gazetteer, Volume B, Darjeeling District, Statistics 1921–1922 to 1930–1931, Bengal Secretariat Book Depot, Calcutta, 1933
Bianjiang lunwenji 邊疆論文集, Taipei, 2 vols., 1964
Bianshi yanjiu 邊事研究, Chengwen Publishing Co., Nanjing, 1935–1937
Bianzheng gonglun 邊政公論, Nanjing, 1941–1948
China Republic, The, 1932; 1935–1936
China's Tibet, Beijing, 1990–1998
China Today, New York, American Friends of the Chinese People, October 1937–August 1938.
Chinese Republican Studies Newsletter, University of Illinois, Center for East Asian and Pacific Studies, 1976–1983
Dagong bao 大公報, Beijing and Tianjin, 1917–1939
Dalu zazhi 大陸雜志, Taipei, 1950-and following
Dongbei difang shi yanjiu 東北地方史研究, Shenyang, 1988–1992
Dongfang zazhi 東方雜志, Shanghai, 1904 and following
Forward Calcutta, 1923–30
Foxue ban yue kan 佛學半月刊, Foxue Shuju Publishing House, Shanghai, April 1937
Foxue congbao 佛學叢報, Foxue congbao she, Shanghai, vols. 1–12, 1912–1914
Guomin ribao 國民日報, official organ of the Chinese Nationalist Party in the United States, January–February 1933
Haichaoyin 海潮音, Shanghai, Chengdu, and Taipei, vols. 1–33, 1920–1952
Hindustan Times, October 1, 1924; December 31, 1950
Jindai shi yanjiu 近代史研究, Beijing, 1979–2003
Journal of the West China Border Research Society, Chengdu, Canadian Mission Press, 1922–1946
Kaifa xibei 開發西北, Nanjing, 1934 and following
Kang Zang qianfeng 康藏前鋒, Nanjing, 1933–1936
Kang Zang yanjiu 康藏研究, 1947
Lishi yanjiu 歷史研究, Beijing, 1990 and following
Meng Zang shibao 蒙藏適報, Nanjing, 1930–1931
Meng Zang yuebao 蒙藏月報, monthly publication of the Mongolian and Tibetan Affairs Commission, Nanjing, 1934–1940; 1942–1947
Meng Zang yuekan 蒙藏月刊, Nanjing, 1936
Minguo ribao 民國日報, Nanjing, 1916–1932
Minzu yanjiu 民族研究, Beijing, 1990 and following
Minzu zazhi 民族雜志, Beijing, 1990 and following
Pacific Affairs, Institute of Pacific Relations, Honolulu, then New York, 1928 and following
Qinghai sheng zhengfu gongbao 青海省政府公報, Qinghai zhengfu mishu chu, Xining, 1929–1939
Republic of China, The, National Commercial Library Newsletter, Taipei, 1979–1984

Republican China (previously titled *Chinese Republican Studies Newsletter*), University of Illinois, Center for East Asian and Pacific Studies, 1984–1998
Revue nationale chinoise, Shanghai, 1929–1930; 1941
Shen bao 申報, Shanghai, 1872–1949
Shen bao yuekan 申報月刊, Shanghai, June–December 1932
Shengjing shibao 盛京時報, Shenyang, 1906–1944
Shes bya, Dharamsala, 1988 and following
Sichuan yuebao 四川月報, Chongqing, 1932–1937
South China Morning Post, Hong Kong, 1937–1938
Suiyuan wenxian 綏遠文獻, Taipei, 1977; 1987–1995
Tibetan Bulletin, Dharamsala, Information Office of H.H. the Dalai Lama, 1979 and following
Tibetan Review, New Delhi, 1979 and following
Tibet Journal, The, Library of Tibetan Works and Archives, Dharamsala, 1971 and following
Tibet News Review, the Tibetan Community in Britain, London, 1980–1981
Xiandai foxue 現代佛學, Tianjin, 1957
Xibei 西北, Nanjing, 1929–1930
Xibei shidi 西北史地, Lanzhou University, 1981; 1985–1987
Xichui xuanhua shi gongshu yuekan 西陲宣化使公署月刊, Xining, 1935–1937
Xin Menggu 新蒙古, Beijing, 1934–1935
Xin Suiyuan 新綏遠, December 1932–June 1933
Xizang yanjiu 西藏研究, Beijing, 1981–1998
Xizang yanjiu huixun 西藏研究會訊, Taipei, 1986–1993
Yugong 禹貢, Beijing, 1934–1937
Yul phyogs so so'i gsar 'gyur me long, Kalimpong, 1925–1940
Zhongguo bianjiang shi di yanjiu 中國邊疆史地研究, Beijing, 1991–1992
Zhongguo bianzheng 中國邊政, Taipei, 1963–1990
Zhongguo fojiao 中國佛教, Taipei, 1966–1968
Zhongguo fojiao jikan 中國佛教季刊, Beijing, 1943
Zhongguo Xizang 中國西藏, Beijing, 1990 and following
Zhongguo zangxue 中國藏學, Beijing, 1989–1997
Zhongwai zazhi 中外雜志, Taipei, 1969
Zhongyang ribao 中央日報, Nanjing, 1930–1940

HAGIOGRAPHIES, BIOGRAPHIES, AND BIOGRAPHICAL NOTES

Anqin Hutuketu 安欽呼圖克圖. "Banchan fo shiji" 班禪佛事跡 [Biography of the Previous and Current Panchen Lamas]. *Xichui xuanhua shi gongshu yuekan* 西陲宣化使公署月刊 1, nos. 7–8 (1936): 171–74.

bKra shis dgon lo rgyus rtsom 'bri tshogs chung. *dPal gyi chos sde chen po bKra shis lhun po* [The Great Monastery Tashilhunpo]. 3rd ed. Lhasa: Bod rang skyong ljongs mi dmangs dpe skrun khang, 1992.

Boorman, Howard L., ed. *Biographical Dictionary of Republican China*. 5 vols. New York: Columbia University Press, 1967–79.

Ceng Guoqing 曾國慶 and Guo Weiping 郭衛平, eds. *Lidai Zang zu ming ren zhuan* 歷代藏族名人傳 [Biographies of Eminent Figures from the Tibetan Ethnic Group]. Lhasa: Bod rang skyong ljongs mi dmangs dpe skrun khang, 1996.

Chen Wenjian 陳文監. *Banchan dashi dong lai shiwu nian dashiji* 班禪大師東來十五年大事記 [Main Events during the Fifteen Years the Great Master Panchen Spent in the East]. Chongqing, 1943.

Danzhu Angben 丹珠昂奔. *Li bei Dalai Lama yu Banchan E'erdeni nianpu* 歷輩達賴喇嘛与班禪額爾德尼年譜 [Chronological Biography of the Lineages of the Dalai Lamas and the Panchen Lamas]. Beijing: Zhongyang minzu daxue, 1998.

Don khang sKal bzang bDe skyid. "Pan chen sku phreng dgu pa mes rgyal nang khul du gsang phebs kyi snga rjes" [The Whole Story on the Secret Departure of the Ninth Panchen Lama to the Motherland]. *Materials on the Culture and History of Tibet* 4 (1984): 1–32.

Douke Cairang 豆格才讓. "Banchan shixi de chansheng ji lishi Banchan de chuanshi guocheng" 班禪世系的產生及歷世班禪的轉世過程 (shang 上, xia 下) [The Origin of the Panchen Lama Lineage and the Process of Reincarnation of the Panchen Lamas]. *Xizang yanjiu* 1 (1991): 75–85; 3 (1991): 75–86.

Gao Wende 高文德. *Zhongguo minzu shi renwu cidian* 中國民族史人物辭典 [Biographical Dictionary of Figures from the Ethnic Peoples of China]. Beijing: Zhongguo shehui kexue, 1990.

Goldstein, Melvyn C. *A History of Modern Tibet, 1913–1951: The Demise of the Lamaist State*. Berkeley: University of California Press, 1989.

Guo Qing 國慶. "A Brief Account of the Ninth Panchen Erdeni." *Tibet Studies* 1 (1989): 70–82.

———. "Weihu zuguo tongyi, minzu tuanjie de kaimo: Jiu shi Banchan shengping jianshu" 維護祖國統一，民族團結的楷模: 九世班禪生平簡述 [An Example for Safeguarding the Union of the Motherland and the Union of the Nationalities: Abridged Biography of the Ninth Panchen Lama]. *Xizang yanjiu* 4 (1987): 82–87.

Jiang Ping 江平, Li Zuomin 李佐民, and Song Yingting 宋盈亭. "Di jiu shi Banchan E'erdeni Quji nima pingzhuan" 第九世班禪額爾德尼曲吉尼瑪評傳 [A Critical Biography of the Ninth Panchen Lama]. *Zhongguo Zangxue* 3 (1997): 12–25.

Kuan Ren 寬忍. *Fojiao shouce* 佛教手冊 [Manual of Buddhism]. Beijing: Zhongguo wenshi chubanshe, 1991.

lHag pa Tshe ring. "Pan chen chos kyi nyi ma dge legs rnam rgyal gsung 'bum" [Collected Writings of Panchen Chöki Nyima Gélèk Namgyel]. In *gsung 'bum dkar chag* [Index of Collected Writings]. Lhasa: Bod rang skyong ljongs mi dmangs dpe skrun khang, 1990.

lHa mkhar yongs 'dzin bsTan pa rGyal mtshan. *sKyabs mgon rje btsun bla ma Blo bzang thub bstan Chos kyi Nyi ma dGe legs rNam rgyal dPal bzang po'i bka 'bum ga pa'i dkar chag rin po che'i phreng ba* [Collected Writings of the Ninth Panchen Lama Lozang Thubten Chöki Nyima Gélèk Namgyel Pelzangpo]. 1944. Reprint, Shigatse: Tashilhunpo Printing Press, 1974.

Li Shengping 李盛平. *Zhongguo jin xian dai renming da cidian* 中國近現代人名大辭典 [Great Biographical Dictionary of Chinese Figures from Modern and Contemporary Times]. Beijing: Zhongguo guoji changbo, 1989.

Li Youyi 李有義. *Xizang de huofo* 西藏的活佛 [Reincarnated Tibetan Masters]. Beijing: Yanjing shehui kexue, 1948.

Liu Jiaju 劉家駒. *Banchan dashi quanji* 班禪大師全集 [Complete Works of the Great Master Panchen]. Chongqing, 1943.

Mehra, Parshotam. *Tibetan Polity, 1904–1937: The Conflict between the Thirteenth Dalai Lama and the Ninth Panchen Lama*. Wiesbaden: Otto Harrassowitz, 1976.

mKhas btsun bZang po. *Bod du sgrub brgyud shing rta mched brgyad* [Biographical Dictionary of Tibet and Tibetan Buddhism]. 9 vols. Dharamsala: Library of Tibetan Works and Archives, 1973.

rdzong rtse Byams pa Thub bstan. *Chos grwa chen po bKra shis lhun po'i chos 'byung* [Religious History of the Tashilhunpo Monastery]. Dharamsala: Library of Tibetan Works and Archives, 1991.

Shakya dge slong Blo bzang 'Jam dbyangs Ye shes bsTan pa'i rGyal mtshan and Tashilhunpo Monastery Historical Research Committee. *sKyabs mgon thams cad mkhyen pa Blo bzang thub bstan chos kyi nyi ma dge legs rnam rgyal dPal bzang po'i zhal snga nas kyi thun mong pa'i rnam par thar pa Rin chen dpang gi rgyal po'i phreng ba* [Biography of Lozang Thubten Chöki Nyima Gélèk Namgyel Palzangpo, the One Who Protects the People], 1996.

Shes rab. *Nyer mkho'i Bod rim byung mkhas pa'i mdor sdus gzhon nu yid 'phrog* [Biographical Notes of Tibetan Figures from Modern Times]. Xining: Qinghai minzu chubanshe, 1985.

Shi Dongchu 釋東初. *Zhongguo fojiao jindai shi* 中國佛教近代史 [History of Chinese Buddhism in Modern Times]. Taipei: Dongchu chubanshe, 1989.

Sun Caixia 孫彩霞. *Minguo renwu pi zhuanji* 民國人物啤傳集 [Compendium of Biographies of Figures from the Republic of China]. Chengdu: Sichuan minzu chubanshe, 1997.

Sun Wenjing 孫文景. *Zangwen dianji mulu* 藏文典籍目錄 (Tib. *Mi rigs dpe mdzod khang gi dpe tho las gsung 'bum skor gyi dkar chag*) [Catalogue of Old Books and Texts Written in Tibetan and Conserved in the Palace of the Minorities in Beijing]. Beijing: Minzu chubanshe, 1989.

Tang Jingfu 唐景福. *Zhongguo Zang chuan fojiao mingseng lu* 中國藏傳佛教名僧錄 [List of Tibetan Monks]. Lanzhou: Gansu minzu chubanshe, 1991.

Wang Chengsheng 王成聖. "Xizang Banchan jiu shi yisheng shenji" 西藏班禪九世一生神跡 [The Miraculous Life of the Ninth Panchen Lama]. *Zhongwai zazhi* 中外雜志 1, no. 5 (1969): 58–66.

Wang Zhanying 王戰英 and Song Xuewen 宋學文. *Jin xian dai Zhongguo shaoshu minzu ying ming lu* 近現代中國少數民族英名錄 [Biographical Dictionary of Important Figures from China's National Minorities in Modern and Contemporary Times]. Beijing: Huaxia, 1994.

Wuyungaowa 烏雲高娃. "Jiu shi Banchan Nei Menggu zhi xing" 九世班禪內蒙古之行 [The Journey of the Ninth Panchen Lama in Inner Mongolia]. In *Nei Menggu lamajiao jili* 內蒙古喇嘛教紀例 [Chronicles of Lamaist Buddhism in Inner Mongolia], ed. Zhongguo renmin zhengzhi xiegao huiyi, Nei Menggu zizhiqu weiyuanhui wen shi he xuexi weiyuanhui. Hohhot: Nei Menggu wen shi shudian, 1997.

Xu Youchun 徐友春, ed. *Minguo renwu da cidian* 民國人物大辭典 [Biographical Dictionary of Important Figures of Republican China]. Shijiazhuang: Hebei minzu chubanshe, 1991.

Ya Hanzhang 牙含章. *Banchan E'erdeni zhuan* 班禪額爾德尼傳 [Biography of the Panchen Lamas]. Beijing: Minzu chubanshe, 1987.

Yang Guiming 楊貴明 and Ma Jixiang 馬吉祥. *Zang chuan fojiao gao seng zhuanlüe* 藏傳佛教高僧傳略 [Abridged Notes on the Famous Monks of Tibetan Tantric Buddhism]. Xining: Qinghai minzu chubanshe, 1992.

Yon tan rGya mtsho. *dGe ldan chos 'byung gser gyi mchod sdong 'bar ba* [Religious History of the Gélukpa School]. Paris, 1994.

Zhang Erxin 張爾新. *Qing dai si da huofo* 清代四大活佛 [The Four Great Reincarnated Tibetan Masters of the Qing Period]. Beijing: Zhongguo renmin daxue, 1989.

Zhang Yisun 張怡蓀, ed. *Bod rGya tshig mdzod chen mo* (Ch. *Zang Han da cidian* 藏漢大辭典) [The Great Tibetan-Chinese Dictionary]. Beijing: Mi rigs dpe skrun khang, 1985.

Note: These sources are also listed in the general bibliography below. They have been grouped in this section to provide the reader with an easy access list of biographical information on the Ninth Panchen Lama.

GENERAL BIBLIOGRAPHY

Tibetan Sources

A blo ba. *Hwang krin ching Blo bzang Tshe dbang dang kun mkhyen lnga ba chen po sku mched zung gi rnam thar ba rjes su dran pa zag med ye shes kyi me long* [Autobiographical Memoir of Huang Zhengqing Concerning the Master-Disciple Relation that Bound Him to the Fifth 'Jam byang bzhad pa]. Beijing: Minzu chubanshe, 1994.

bDe gzim dPal mgon Tshe ring. "Mes rgyal nang sar bskyod de Pan chen sku phreng dgu pa'i os phrul Bod du gdan zhu'i skor" [Invitation to Tibet from the Reincarnation of the Ninth Panchen Lama Who Had Gone to the Motherland]. *Materials on the Culture and History of Tibet* 4 (1984): 92–122.

bKra shis dgon lo rgyus rtsom 'bri tshogs chung. *dPal gyi chos sde chen po bKra shis lhun po* [The Great Monastery Tashilhunpo]. 3rd ed. Lhasa: Bod rang skyong ljongs mi dmangs dpe skrun khang, 1992.

——. "sNgags chen bDar pa ho thog thu Blo bzang bstan 'dzin 'jigs med dbang phyug gi rnam thar rags bsdus" [Short Biography of Ngachen Rinpoche]. *Materials on the Culture and History of Tibet* 5 (1985): 80–91.

Blo bzang rDo rje. *Rigs dang dkyil 'khor rgya mtsho'i khyab bdag He ru ka 'dpal ngur smrig gar rol skyabs gcig Pha bong kha pa bde chen snying po dpal bzang po'i rnam thar pa don ldan tshangs pa'i dbyangs snyan* [Celestial Melody Endowed with Meaning: Biography of Phabongka, Refuge Manifested in Monks' Robes, Glorious Heruka Lord of the Mandala Ocean of the Five Families]. New Delhi, 1981.

Blo bzang Thub bstan Chos kyi Nyi ma. *gSan yig nor bu'i do shal* [Compilation of Teachings Received by the Ninth Panchen Lama]. New Delhi: Lha mkhar yongs 'dzin bsTan pa rGyal mtshan, 1974.

Blo bzang Tshe brtan. "Ta'a la'i bla ma sku phreng bcu gsum pa Thub bstan rGya mtsho'i dgung tshigs" [Brief Biography of Thubten Gyatso, the Thirteenth Dalai Lama]. *Materials on the Culture and History of Tibet* 2, no. 11 (1989).

Bod kyi lo rgyus rig gnas dpyad gzhi'i rgyu chab dams bsgrigs [Materials on the Culture and History of Tibet]. 1991.

Bod ljongs spyi bzhad [General Presentation of the Autonomous Region of Tibet]. Lhasa: Mi rigs dpe skrun khang, 1991.

Brag dgon pa dKon mchog rGyal mtshan. *mDo smad chos 'byong* [Religious History of Amdo]. Lanzhou: Gansu mi rigs dpe skrun khang, 1981.

bSam pho bsTan 'dzin Don grub. *Shes bya*, June 1988.

bShad sgra dGa ldan dPal 'byor, Chab tshom 'chi med rgyal po, and sReg shing blo bzang don grub. "De snga'i Bod sa gnas srid gzhung gi srid 'dzin sgrig gzhi" [Detailed Study of the Branches of the Tibetan Government]. *Materials on the Culture and History of Tibet* 4 (1991): 1–100.

———. "De snga'i Bod sa gnas srid zhung gis Lha sar yod pa'i Go min tang don gcod khru'i mi sna sogs phyir slog btang ba'i snga rjes kyi lo rgyus dum bu" [The Creation and Dissolution of the Kuomintang Office in Lhasa]. *Materials on the Culture and History of Tibet* 10 (1996) 259–65.

bsTan 'dzin rGya mtsho. "Panchen bzhugs sgar dang Li'u un hu'i dbar gyi dmag 'khrug" [The Civil War between the Panchen Lama and Liu Wenhui Factions]. *Materials on the Culture and History of Tibet* 4 (1982): 44–65.

dka' chen Blo bzang bzod pa. *gDan sa bKra shis lhun po'i khri 'dzin dang dKyil khang legs bshad sgrog pa'i gling gi grwa tshang gi khri 'dzin rnams kyi mTshan byang nor bu'i phreng ba* [List of the Abbots of Tashilhunpo Monastery and of the Kyilkang Lèkshéling College]. New Delhi: Ngawang Sopa, 1979.

Don khang sKal bzang bDe skyid. "Pan chen sku phreng dgu pa mes rgyal nang khul du gsang phebs kyi snga rjes" [The Whole Story of the Secret Departure of the Ninth Panchen Lama Towards his Homeland]. *Materials on the Culture and History of Tibet* 4 (1984): 1–32.

"dPyad mtshams bka' rtsa 'dra bcu gsum pa'i zhal bshas he bag med pa bzhugs gsol, 1923" [Official Copy of the Thirteen Articles of the 1923 Decree]. Housed in the Library of Tibetan Works and Archives, Dharamsala, India.

Dorjieff, Agvan. *Chos brgyad gdon gyis zin byas te rgyal khams don med nyul ba yi, dam chos nor gyis dbul ba'i sprang* [Having Understood the Nature of Worldly Vicissitudes, the Beggar, Gratified by the Wealth of the Pure Doctrine, Wandered about the Kingdom] (autobiography). 1924.

Dung dkar blo bzang phrin las. *Bod gyi chos srid zung 'bral skor bzhad pa* [The Tibetan Politico-Religious System]. Dharamsala: Library of Tibetan Works and Archives, 1981.

Gangs can rig brgya'i sgo 'byed lde mig [Keys That Allow for the Understanding of Tibetan Culture]. Beijing: Minzu chubanshe, 1990.

Guge yongs 'dzin Blo bzang bsTan 'dzin. *Chos grwa chen po bKra shis lhun po'i gsang sngags rgyud pa grwa tshang gi rDo rje slob dpon rnams kyi rtags pa brjod pa dpag bsam ljon pa'i dbang po* [Biographies of the Hierarchs of the Tantric College of Tashilhunpo Monastery]. New Delhi: Ngawang Gélèk Demo, 1980.

Hren krung yus and Hren yon ca. "Cang ce hri'i Khrung ching bzhugs sgar gyis Bod kyi gnad don skor la zhib 'jug byas par dran gso byas pa" [Analysis and Resolution of the Tibetan Problem According to the Chongqing Faction of Chiang Kai-shek]. *Materials on the Culture and History of Tibet* 14 (1992): 273–310.

Kha skong dang mchan bu bKra shis tse ring. *Mi tse'i lo rgyus dang 'brel yod sna tsogs* [Short History of Tibet]. Dharamsala: Library of Tibetan Works and Archives, 1988.

Khe smad bSod nams dBang 'dus. *rGas po' lo rgyus 'bel gtam* [History of Modern Tibet]. Dharamsala: Library of Tibetan Works and Archives, 1982.

Khung Chin-tsun. "Hong Mu'o sung Bod du bskyod pa'i gnas tshul dngos bkod pa" [The Visit of Huang Musong to Tibet]. *Materials on the Culture and History of Tibet* 5 (1985): 109–62.

lHag pa Tse ring. "Pan chen chos kyi nyi ma dge legs rnam rgyal gsung 'bum" [Collected Writings of Panchen Chöki Nyima Gélèk Namgyel]. In *gSung 'bum dkar chag* [Index of Collected Writings]. Lhasa: Bod rang skyong ljongs mi dmangs dpe skrun khang, 1990.

lHa klu Tshe dbang rDo rje. "Nga'i pha Lung shar rDo rje tshe rgyal dran gso byas pa" [Memories of My Father Lungshar Dorjé Tségyel]. *Materials on the Culture and History of Tibet* 2 (1983) 93–109.

lHa mkhar yongs 'dzin bsTan pa rGyal mtshan. *sKyabs mgon rje btsun bla ma Blo bzang Thub bstan Chos kyi Nyi ma dGe legs rNam rgyal dPal bzang po'i bka 'bum ga pa'i dkar chag rin po che'i phreng ba* [Collected Writings of the Ninth Panchen Lama Lozang Thubten Chöki Nyima Gélèk Namgyel Pelzangpo]. 1944. Reprint, Shigatse: Tashilhunpo Printing Press, 1974.

Li Pheng nyan. "Panchen sku phreng dgu pa'i dgongs rdzogs mchod sprin sgrub lugs dang sku phreng bcu pa gser khrir mnga'a gsol tshul skor rags tsam gleng ba" [The Funeral of the Ninth Panchen Lama and the Enthronement of the Tenth Panchen Lama]. *Kong go'i Bod kyi shes rig* 4 (1989): 1–20.

Lo Runtshang, ed. *dGa' ldan pho brang ba'i chab 'bangs dBus gTsang Dwags Kong Rong gag bcas kyi lcags stag zhib gzhung dam 'byar ma'i zhal bshus dge* [Official Sealed Copy of the Land Register from 1830 on Government Subjects in Central Tibet]. Xining, 1989.

Nor brang O rgyan. "Pan chen sku phreng dgu pa'i sku gdung sKye mdo nas bKra shis lhun po dgon du gdan zhu byas pa'i skor" [About the Return of the Mortal Remains of the Ninth Panchen Lama from Kyégudo to Tashilhunpo Monastery]. *Materials on the Culture and History of Tibet* 3 (1990): 35–48.

Panchen Blo bzang Ye shes dPal bzang po. *Chos smra ba'i dge slongs Blo bzang chos kyi rgyal mtshan gyi spyod chul gsal bar ston pa nor bu'i phreng ba* [Biography of the Panchen Lozang Chöki Gyeltsen, the First Panchen Lama]. New Delhi: Ngawang Gélèk Demo, 1969.

——. *dPal ldan bla ma Dam pa rje btsun Blo bzang Ye shes kyis gsung las gsang ba'i rnam thar* [Secret Biography of Panchen Lozang Yéshé, the Fifth Panchen Lama]. Shigatse: Tashilhunpo Printing Press, n.d.

Phren rtsa rTa mgrin rGyal po. "Ngam ring rdzong gi lo rgyus dang bar skabs rdzong sdod 'ga' zhig gi byed phyogs rang nyid las drung byed skabs bcas skor rags bsduds" [Brief Remarks Concerning the History of the Namring District in Addition to Others Dating from the Time I was Secretary]. *Materials on the Culture and History of Tibet* 8 (1994): 67–78.

Phun rab Rin chen rNam rgyal. "gZhung bla'i dbar thog ma'i gal ba yong rkyen" [The Origins of the Dispute between the Panchen Lama and the Tibetan Government]. *Materials on the Culture and History of Tibet* 3 (1984): 123–32.

Phun tshogs Tshe ring. *Bod kyi lo rgyus don chen re'u mig* [Chronological Tables of the History of Tibet]. Beijing: Mi rigs dpe skrun khang, 1991.

Phur lcog Ngag dbang Byams pa. *Grwa sa chen po bzhi dang rgyud pa stod smad chags tshul pad dkar 'phreng ba* [History of the Founding of the Four Great Monasteries and the Two Tantric Colleges]. Lhasa: Bod rang skyong ljongs mi dmangs dpe skrun khang, 1989.

Phur lcog yongs 'dzin sprul sku Thub bstan Byams pa Tshul khrim bsTan 'dzin. *Lhar bcas srid zhi'i gtsug rgyan gong sa rgyal ba bka 'drin mtshungs med sku phreng bcu gsum pa chen po'i rnam thar rgya mtsho lta bu las mdo tsam brjod pa ngo mtshar Rin po che'i phreng ba* [Marvelous Precious Rosary like a Compact Ocean: Biography of the Great Thirteenth Dalai Lama, Victor of Incomparable Goodness, Sovereign Ornament of Sinciput, Nirvana and Samsara, Including the Gods], 7 vols. Sata-Pitaka Series, vols. 287–288. New Delhi: International Academy of Indian Culture, 1981.

rdzong rtse Byams pa Thub bstan. *Chos grwa chen po bKra shis lhun po'i chos 'byung* [Religious History of the Tashilhunpo Monastery]. Dharamsala: Library of Tibetan Works and Archives, 1991.

——. *gTsang myang smad bSam grub rtse'i sde srid gtsang pa rim byung gi mnga' thang 'byor rgud kyi lo rgyus* [History of Fort of Samdrubtsé: The Reign of the Tsang Princes], Dharamsala: Library of Tibetan Works and Archives, 1994.

"rGya dmar gyi btsen og tu gnas sa'i Bod dang sa 'brel khag gi sa khra" [Map of Tibet and the Tibetan Area Occupied by Communist China]. Dharamsala: Amnye Machen Institute, 1998.

rGyal mo 'Brug pa. *Bod kyi lo rgyus gleng ba'i gtam* [Regarding the History of Tibet]. Beijing: Mi rigs dpe skrun khang, 1995.

rje drung 'Jam dpal rGyal mtshan. "Khams Ri bo che dgon dang rje drung sprul sku gong ma mGar ra bla ma bcas kyi lo rgyus rags bsdus" [Short Biographies of Jédrung Tulku Gongma and Gara Lama, Two Reincarnated Masters of Riwoché Monastery]. Article received without reference information.

rNam rgyal dBang 'dud. *Bod ljongs rgyal khab chen po'i srid lugs dang 'brel ba'i drag po'i dmag gi lo rgyus rags bsdus* [Abridged History of the Army and its Relations with the Administration of the Great Country of Tibet]. Dharamsala: Tibetan Cultural Printing Press, 1976.

Sa byang Tshe dbang rNam rgyal. "En gön gyi chags rabs dang En sa Blo bzang Don grub kyi byung bam do tsam brjod pa" [History of the Engön Monastery and Ensapa Lozang Döndrub]. *Bod ljongs zhib 'jug* 2 (1986): 106–15.

Seg shing Blo bzang Don grub. "Go min dang gi 'thus mi Hong Mu'o Taa la'i bcu gsum pa'i dgongs rdzogs mchod sprin spro 'bul du yong ba'i gnas tshul thor bu" [The Huang Musong Mission in Lhasa, 1934]. *Materials on the Culture and History of Tibet* 2 (1983): 73–81.

Shakya dge slong Blo bzang 'Jam dbyangs Ye shes bsTan pa'i rGyal mtshan and Tashilhunpo Monastery Historical Research Committee. *sKyabs mgon thams cad mkhyen pa Blo bzang thub bstan chos kyi nyi ma dge legs rNam rgyal dpal bZang po'i zhal snga nas kyi thun mong pa'i rnam par thar pa Rin chen dpang gi rgyal po'i phreng ba* [Biography of Lozang Thubten Chöki Nyima Gélèk Namgyel Pelzangpo, the One Who Protects the People], vol. 1, parts 1–2, 1996.

Shan kha ba 'Gyur med bSod nams sTob rgyal. *Rang gi lo rgyus lhad med rang byung zangs* [Pure and Spontaneous Autobiography]. Dharamsala: Library of Tibetan Works and Archives, 1989.

Shes rab. *Nyer mkho'i Bod rim byung mkhas pa'i mdor sdus gzhon nu yid 'phrog* [Biographical Notes of Tibetan Figures from Modern Times]. Xining: Mtsho sngon mi rigs dpe skrun khang, 1985.

sKal bzang bKra shis. "mGar ra bla mas Lu'u cun dmag Khams khul 'byor skabs mnyam 'brel dang Go min dang skabs Bod Sog U yon lhan khang gi U yon sogs byas skor" [The Relations of Gara Lama with the Mongolian and Tibetan Affairs Commission at the Time of the Kham War]. *Materials on the Culture and History of Tibet*, 10 (1996): 113–22.

sKal bzang dpal. *Thang ga'i sgyu rtsal* [The Art of Appliqués]. Chengdu: Sichuan meishu, 1992.

sLe zur 'Jigs med dBang phyug and bDe zur Rin chen dBang 'dus. "De snga'i bla brang rgyal mtshan mthon po'i srid 'dzin sgrig gzhi'i spyi'i gnas tshul" [Detailed Presentation of the Former Government of the Residence of Gyeltsen Tönpo]. *Materials on the Culture and History of Tibet* 4 (1991): 102–61.

Srung Kri hru'u. "Panchen sku 'phreng dgu pa dBus gTsang dang zhal bral ba dang dBus gTsang du gyir phebs pa'i skor bshad pa" [The Relations of the Ninth Panchen Lama with Central Tibet during his Trip to Central Tibet]. *Materials on the Culture and History of Tibet* 1 (1984): 115–27.

Thang Khre yan. "mchod yon 'brel ba'i chab srid kyi go don" [The Chaplain-Donor Relation]. *Bod ljongs zhib 'jug* 2 (1985): 46–61.

Thub bstan Sangs rgyas. *rGya nag tu Bod kyi sku tshab don gcod skabs dangs gnyis tshugs stangs skor gyi lo rgyus thabs bral zur lam* [The Office of the Tibetan Government in China]. Dharamsala: Library of Tibetan Works and Archives, 1982.

Tshe ring Don grub. *Bod ljongs spyi bshad* [General Presentation of the Autonomous Region of Tibet]. Lhasa: Bod rang skyong ljongs mi dmangs dpe skrun khang, 1991.

Tshe tan Zhabs drung. *bsTan rtsis kun las btus pa* [Chronological Table of Tibet's History]. Xining: Mtsho sngon mi rigs dpe skrun khang, 1982.

Ya'a Han krang. *Panchen sku phreng rim byon gyi mdze rnam* [Biographies of the Panchen Lamas Lineage]. Lhasa: Bod rang skyong ljongs mi dmangs dpe skrun khang, 1992.

Yon tan rGya mtsho. *dGe ldan chos 'byung gser gyi mchod sdong 'bar ba* [Religious History of the Gélukpa School]. Paris, 1994.

Yul phyogs so so'i gsar 'gyur me long [The Mirror of International News, aka The Tibetan Mirror]. Kalimpong: Thartchin-Polhill Hall, 1925–1940.

Zhang Yisun 張怡孫, ed. *Bod rGya tshig mdzod chen mo* (Ch. *Zang Han da cidian* 藏漢大辭典) [The Great Tibetan-Chinese Dictionary]. Beijing: Mi rigs dpe skrun khang, 1985.

Zhwa sgab pa dBang phyug bDe ldan. *Bod kyi srid don rgyal rabs* [Political History of Tibet]. 2 vols. Kalimpong: Shakabpa House, 1976.

Chinese Sources

Akedachun 阿克達純. "Nei Meng guomindang yuan zai Menggu gongzuo de zhuiyi" 內蒙國民黨員在蒙古工作的追憶 [Memories of Work Done in Mongolia by a Member of the Inner Mongolia Nationalist Party]. *Kaifa xibei* 開發西北 5 (1934): 59–60.

An Qin Hutuketu 安欽呼圖克圖. "Banchan fo shiji" 班禪佛事跡 [Biographical Precedents of the Current Panchen Lama]. *Xichui xuanhua shi gongshu yuekan* 西陲宣化使公署月刊 1, nos. 7/8 (1936): 171–74.

Bai Tianlin 白天霖. "Lüe lun Xizang yong bing xingshi" 略論西藏用兵形勢 [Brief Study Concerning the Tibetan Army]. In *Bianjiang lunwenji* 邊疆論文集, 423–26. Taipei, 1964.

"Banchan ding yue di dao Jing" 班禪定月底到京 [The Panchen Lama Had Planned to Arrive in Nanjing at the Beginning of the Month]. *Meng Zang shibao* 蒙藏適報 7, no. 1 (1931): 5–6.

Banchan E'erdeni 班禪額爾德尼. "Banchan da shi guru gulu fazhishi" 班禪大師古儒古魯法制示 [The Ninth Panchen Lama Transmits the Guru Yoga Teaching]. *Xichui xuanhua shi gongshu yuekan* 1, nos. 4/5 (1936): 121–22.

——. "Xian mi fa yao" 顯密法要 [Exoteric and Esoteric Teaching]. *Xichui xuanhua shi gongshu yuekan* 1, no. 6 (1936): 133–35.

——. "Xizang lishi" 西藏歷史 [History of Tibet]. *Meng Zang yuebao* 蒙藏月報 2, no. 3 (1934): 9–10.

——. "Xizang lishi yu wu zu lianhe" 西藏歷史与五族聯合 [The History of Tibet and the Solidarity of the Five Nationalities]. *Xin Qinghai* 新青海 1, no. 4 (1933): 85–88.

——. "Xizang zhengjiao zhi shimo" 西藏政教之始末 [The Whole Story of the Tibetan Politico-Religious System]. *Kaifa Xibei* 2, no. 1 (1934) 5–7. Reprint, *Xichui xuanhua shi gongshu yuekan* 1, no. 6 (1936): 129–31.

"Banchan hui Zang qingxing" 班禪回藏情形 [Regarding the Return of the Ninth Panchen Lama to Tibet]. *Bianjiang ban yue kan* 邊彊半月刊, June 1, 1936.

"Banchan jin chun fan Zang" 班禪今春返藏 [The Ninth Panchen Lama Will Return to Tibet in Spring of this Year]. *Meng Zang yuebao* 4, no. 4 (1936): 65.

"Banchan juanzhu Zhongshan yiyuan" 班禪捐助中山醫院 [The Ninth Panchen Lama Gave a Donation to the Zhongshan Hospital]. *Xichui xuanhua shi gongshu yuekan* 6, no. 2 (1935): 31.

Beiping tushuguan yu tubu 北平圖書館与圖部. "Bian Zang zuijin zhi wenjian" 邊藏最近之聞見 [Recent News from the Tibetan Border]. *Dongfang zazhi* 東方雜志 8, no. 12 (1912): 7–13.

——. *Bijiao difang zizhi lun* 比較地方自治論 [Comparison of Theories Concerning Regional Autonomy]. Shanghai, 1945.

——. "Kang Zang lunwen suoyin" 康藏論文索引 [Bibliography of Articles Written on Xikang and Tibet]. *Yugong* 禹貢, 12, nos. 6/7 (1937): 113–27.

Bixiao shizhu 避囂室主. "Wo quguo de Xizang" 我去過的西藏 [The Tibet I Visited]. *Haichaoyin* 海潮音 18, no. 3 (1937): 58–64.

Ceng Guoqing 曾國慶 and Guo Weiping 郭衛平, eds. *Lidai Zang zu ming ren zhuan* 歷代藏族名人傳 [Biographies of Eminent Figures from the Tibetan Ethnic Group]. Lhasa: Bod rang skyong ljongs mi dmangs dpe skrun khang, 1996.

Chang shaoru 常少如, ed. *Zang chuan fojiao gu si Yonghe gong* 藏傳佛教古寺雍和宮 [The Palace of Eternal Harmony: An Old Tibetan Buddhist Monastery]. Beijing: Beijing yanshan, 1996.

Chen Baozhu 陳寶珠. "Jiu shi Banchan chuanshi lingtong xunfang rending he shi shi Banchan zuochuang dang'an xuan" 九世班禪轉世靈童尋訪認定和十世班禪坐床檔案選 [Choice of Archived Documents Concerning the Research and Selection of the Reincarnation of the Ninth Panchen Lama and the Enthronement of the Tenth Panchen Lama]. *Minguo dang'an* 民國檔案 1 (1996): 34–45.

Chen Cheng 陳誠. *Xiyu xingchengji, Xi yu fan guo zhi* 西域行程記: 西域番國志 [Travel Report on the Western Border: Monograph of Tribute Paying Countries along the Western Border]. Taipei: Huawen shuju, 1968.

Chen Chongkai 陳崇凱 and Gu Zucheng 顧祖成. "Xizang zai Zhongguo jindai shi zhong de zhongyao diwei" 西藏在中國近代史中的重要地位 [The Important Place Held by Tibet during the Time of Modern China]. *Xizang yanjiu* 西藏研究 4 (1988): 42–50.

Chen Dao 陳道. *Kang Zang souqilu* 康藏搜奇錄 [Journey to Xikang and Tibet at the End of the 1930s]. Hong Kong: Wen-i shu-wu, 1973.

Chen Dengzhi 陳澄之. *Xizang jian wen ji* 西藏見問記 [News from Tibet]. Taipei: Zhengzhong, 1960.

Chen Guangqiang 沉廣強. *Nei Menggu zizhiqu dituce* 內蒙古自治區地圖冊 [Geographical Atlas of the Autonomous Region of Inner Mongolia]. Hohhot: Nei Menggu zizhiqu cehuiju, 1989.

Chen Jianfu 陳健夫. *Xizang wenti* 西藏問題 [The Tibetan Question]. Shanghai: Shangwu yinshuguan, 1937.

Chenkong 塵空. "Shanghai puti xuehui zai Wutai Shan chengli banshichu" 上海菩提學會在五台山成立辦事處 [Shanghai Association of Enlightenment Creates an Office in Wutai Shan]. *Haichaoyin* 17, no. 7 (1936): 8–9.

Chen Qiangyi 陳鏘儀. "Jianshu shi san shi Dalai rujin" 簡述十三世達喇入覲 [Short Description of the Thirteenth Dalai Lama's Audience at the Manchu Court]. *Zhongguo Zangxue* 中國藏學 1 (1988): 82–92.

Chen Wenjian 陳文監. *Banchan da shi dong lai shiwu nian dashiji* 班禪大師東來十五年大事記 [Main Events during the Fifteen Years the Great Master Panchen Spent in the East]. Chongqing, 1943.

Chen Yisun 沉艾孫. *Banchan dong lai* 班禪東來 [The Panchen Lama Came to the East]. Shanghai, 1935.

Chu Junjie 褚俊杰. "Yongzhonglin si gaikuang" 雍仲林寺概況 [A Glance at the Yongzhonglin Monastery]. *Zhongguo Zangxue* 4 (1992): 78–83.

Ci Yang 次央. "Qian tan shi san shi Dalai de xin zheng cuoshi" 淺談十三世達賴的新政措施 [Brief Discussion of the New Policies Undertaken by the Thirteenth Dalai Lama]. *Xizang yanjiu* 3 (1986): 32–36.

Dai Xinsan 戴新三. "Rikaze niaokan" 日喀則鳥瞰 [Overview of Shigatse]. *Bianzheng gonglun* 邊政公論 4, nos. 9/12 (1945): 52–62.

———. "Zhashelunbu si xiao zhi" 扎什倫布寺小志 [Short Monograph of Tashilhunpo Monastery]. *Kang Zang yanjiu* 康藏研究 7 (1947): 1–8.

Dai Yong 戴雍. "Dalai chuanshi yu Banchan hui Zang" 達賴傳世與班禪回藏 [The Reincarnation of the Thirteenth Dalai Lama and the Return of the Ninth Panchen Lama to Tibet]. *Xichui xuanhua shi gongshu yuekan* 9, no. 1 (1937): 49–50.

———. "Wu Zhongxin ru Zang zhuchi di shi si shi Dalai Lama zuochuang dianli dang'an shiliao xuan" 吳忠信入藏主持第十四世達賴喇嘛坐床典禮檔案史料選 [Selected Archival Documents Concerning the Enthronement Ceremony of the Fourteenth Dalai Lama Presided by Wu Zhongxin]. *Minguo dang'an* 4 (1988): 41–55.

Danjiong Rannabanza 丹迥冉納班雜 and Li Decheng 李德成. *Ming sha shuang Huang si, Qingdai Dalai he Banchan zai Jing zhuxi di* 名刹雙黃寺: 清代達喇和班禪在京駐錫地 [The Two Yellow Temples: The Beijing Residences of the Dalai Lamas and the Panchen Lamas during the Qing Era]. Beijing: Zongjiao wenhua chubanshe, 1997.

Danzhu Angben 丹珠昂奔, ed. *Da Qing diguo lishi ditu* 大清帝國歷史地圖 [Geographical and Historical Map of the Great Qing Empire]. Shanghai, 1888.

———. *Da Qing huidian shili* 大清會典事例 [Imperially Commissioned Collected Regulations and Precedents of the Qing Dynasty]. 1872.

———. *Da Qing huidian tu* 大清會典圖 [Map of the Imperially Commissioned Collected Regulations of the Qing Dynasty]. 1872.

———. *Da Qing yitong tianxia quantu* 大清一統天下全圖 [Map of the Entire Territory of the Great Qing]. 1819.

———. *Da Qing yi tongzhi* 大清一統志 [Geography of the Great Qing Empire]. 1902.

———. *Li bei Dalai Lama yu Banchan E'erdeni nianpu* 歷輩達賴喇嘛与班禪額爾德尼年譜 [Chronological Biography of the Dalai Lama and Panchen Lama Lineages]. Beijing: Zhongyang minzu daxue, 1998.

Deng Yanlin 鄧衍林. *Zhongguo bianjiang tu jilu* 中國邊疆圖籍錄 [Bibliography Concerning the Border Regions of China]. Shanghai, 1958.

Donggacang Cairangjia 東噶倉才讓加. "Tang yilai Zangzu diqu siyuan jingji de xingcheng yu fazhan" 唐以來藏族地區寺院經濟的行程与發展 [The Economic Development of Ethnic Tibetan Monasteries during the Tang Dynasty]. *Minzu Yanjiu* 民族研究 3 (1992): 62–70.

Dong Rao 董蕘. *Beiyang xiaoxiong Zhang Zuolin* 北洋梟雄張作霖 [Zhang Zuolin: The Adventurer of the Beiyang Army]. Beijing: Tuanjie chubanshe, 1995.

Dong Shufan 董樹藩. *Minguo shi san nian yilai zhi Zhongguo guomindang yu Xizang* 民國十三年以來之中國國民黨与西藏 [The Chinese Republic and Tibet since 1924]. Taipei: Meng Zang weiyuanhui, 1985.

——. *Xizang shezheng Rezhen Hutuketu yu Zhongyang zhi guanxi* 西藏攝政熱振呼圖克圖與中央之關係 [The Relations between the Regent Reting Rinpoche and the Chinese Central Government]. Taipei: Meng Zang weiyuanhui, 1981.

——. *Zhong gong zhengquan xia Banchan zhengzhi jiaose zhi yanjiu* 中共政權下班禪政治角色之研究 [Study of the Political Role of the Panchen Lama Under the People's Republic of China]. Taipei: Meng Zang weiyuanhui, 1981.

Dong Xiujia 董修甲. *Zhongguo difang zizhi wenti* 中國地方自治問題 [The Question of Regional Autonomy in China]. Shanghai: Commercial Press, 1936.

Douke Cairang 豆格才讓. "Banchan shixi de chansheng ji lishi Banchan de chuanshi guocheng" 班禪世系的產生及歷世班禪的轉世過程 (shang 上, xia 下) [The Origin of the Panchen Lama Lineage and the Process of Reincarnation of the Various Panchen Lamas]. *Xizang yanjiu* 1 (1991): 75–85; vol. 3 (1991): 75–86.

Duojie Caidan 多杰才旦, ed. *Yuan yilai Xizang difang yu Zhongyang zhengfu guanxi dang'an shiliao huibian* 元以來西藏地方与中央政府關系檔案史料匯編 [Compendium of Archival Documents Concerning Sino-Tibetan Relations from the Yuan Era]. Beijing: Zhongguo Zangxue chubanshe, 1994.

Fafang 法舫. "Huanying Zang wen xueyuan zhu shi Dong fan hong fa" 歡迎藏文學院諸師東返宏法 [Welcome to the Masters of the Tibetan Institute Who Have Returned to the East to Teach the Buddhist Doctrine]. *Haichaoyin* 17, no. 8 (1936): 2–4.

——. "Meng Zang xueyuan yu puti xuehui" 蒙藏學院與菩提學會 [The Tibeto-Mongol Institute of Study and the Association of Enlightenment]. *Haichaoyin* 15, no. 9 (1934) 1–3.

——."Shanghai puti xuehui zai Wutai shan chengli banshichu" 上海菩提學會在五臺山成立辦事處 [Association of Enlightenment in Shanghai Creates an Office in Wutaishan] *Haichaoyin* 17, no. 7 (1936): 8–9.

——. "Zhongguo fojiao de xianzhuang" 中國佛教的現狀 [Current Situation of Buddhism in China]. *Haichaoyin* 15, no. 10 (1934): 21–31.

Fan Baoliang 樊保良. *Meng Zang guanxi shi yanjiu* 蒙藏關系史研究 [A Study of the History of Relations between Mongolia and Tibet]. Xining: Qinghai renmin chubanshe, 1992.

Fan Daoqin 范道芹. "Taiwushi bao shi nian lai guanyu Xizang de wenzi suoyin" 泰晤士報十年來關於西藏的文字索引 [Index of Articles from the *Taiwushi bao* Over the Last Ten Years Concerning Tibet]. *Yugong* 6, no. 12 (1937): 129–33.

Fang Borong 方伯榮. *Zhongguo ming zhuan daguan* 中國名傳大觀 [A Biographical Note on Famous Chinese]. Beijing: Yuwen chubanshe, 1995.

Fang Fanjiu 芳範九. *Menggu gaikuang yu Nei Meng zizhi yundong* 蒙古概況与內蒙自治運動 [Overview of Mongolia and the Inner Mongolia Autonomous Movement]. Shanghai: Shangwu yinshuguan, 1934.

Fang Jianchang 房建昌. "Di jiu shi Banchan lama dui Yindu de fangwen (1905 nian 11 yue 8 ri–1906 nian 2 yue 17 ri): Qing chao guanfang wenxian yu Yingguo waijiao mimi dang'an ji qi ta siren jizai bijiao yanjiu" 第九世班禪喇嘛對印度的訪問 (1905 年11 月8日- 1906 年2 月17日) 清朝官方文獻與育英國外交 by 清朝官方文獻與英國外交秘密檔案及其它私人記載比較研究 [Visit of the Ninth Panchen Lama to India (November 8, 1905–February 17, 1906): Analyzed from Qing Archives and Secret Archives of the British Ministry of Foreign Affairs and Individual Diaries]. Paper presented at the *Gudai Zhongwai guanxi shi: xin shiliao de diaocha, zhengli yu yanjiu. Guoji xueshu yantao hui lunwen huibian* 古代中外關係史: 新史料的調查, 整理與研究.國際學術研討會論文匯編. Beijing: Beijing daxue Zhongguo gudai shi yanjiu zhongxin, November 15–16, 2002.

——. "Jianshu Minguo jian youguan Zhongguo bianjiang de jigou yu kanwu" 簡述民國間有關中國邊疆的機構与刊物 [Brief Presentation of Public Institutions and Publications about the Border Regions Published during the Chinese Republican Era]. *Zhongguo bianjiang shidi yanjiu* 2 (1997): 93–105.

Fang Qiubi 方秋筆. "Dalai chuanshi yu Banchan fan Zang" 達賴傳世與班禪返藏 [The Reincarnation of the Thirteenth Dalai Lama and the Return to Tibet of the Ninth Panchen Lama]. *Dongfang zazhi* 7, no. 34 (1937): 109845–109852 [33–40].

Fazun 法尊. *Wo qu guo de Xizang* 我去過的西藏 [The Tibet that I saw]. Chongqing: Han Zang jiaoliyuan, 1937.

——. *Xiandai Xizang* 現代西藏 [Present-day Tibet]. Chengdu: Dongfang shushe, 1943.

Feng Lixia 馮麗霞. "Shi lun Zhang Yintang chaban Zang shi de xingzhi" 識論張蔭棠查辦藏事的性質 [Tentative Analysis of the Characteristics of the Administration of Tibetan Affairs by Zhang Yintang]. *Xizang yanjiu* 4 (1987): 94–99.

Feng Mingzhu 馮明珠. "Di yi ci shijie dazhan qijian Zhong Ying Xizang jiaoshe yu Chuan Zang bian qing (1914–1919)" 弟一次世界大戰期間中英西藏交涉与川藏邊情 (1914–1919) [The Relations between China, Great Britain, and Tibet during the First World War and the Border Situation between Sichuan and Tibet (1914–1919)]. *Xizang yanjiu lunwenji* 4 (1983): 59–98.

——. "Beiyang zhengfu shiqi de Zhongyang Xizang jiaoshe" 北洋政府時期的中央西藏交涉 [Relations between the Central Chinese Government and Tibet under the Beiyang Government]. *Xizang yu Zhongyuan guanxi guoji xueshu taohui* 西藏与中原關係國際學術討會 (1993): 296–338.

Feng Youzhi 馮有志. *Xikang shi shiyi* 西康史拾遺 [Collection of Unedited Facts from the History of Xikang]. Gansu: Zhengxie Ganzi Zang zu zizhizhou weiyuanhui wenshi ziliao weiyuanhui, 1992.

Feng Zhi 馮智. "Wu shi Banchan wei neng jin Jing yuanyin tantao" 五世班禪未能晉京原因探討 [Analysis of the Reasons Why the Fifth Panchen Lama was Blocked from Going to Beijing]. *Zhongguo Zangxue* 4 (1998): 26–33.

Fu Chengyong 傅成鏞. "Xizang tuji lubu" 西藏圖籍錄補 [Supplement to the Bibliography on Tibet]. *Yugong* 4, no. 2 (1935): 65–69.

——. "Fu Zang daibiao gui Jing hou tanpian" 赴藏代表歸京後談論 [Discussions after his Return to Nanjing with the Representative Who Went to Tibet]. *Meng Zang shibao* 47 (1934): 6–7.

Gansu wenshi ziliao xuanji 甘肅文史資料選輯. *Huang Zhengqing yu wu shi Jiamuyang* 黃正清与五世嘉木楊 [Huang Zhengjing and the Fifth Jamyang Shépa]. Lanzhou: Gansu renmin chubanshe, 1989.

Gao Wende 高文德. *Zhongguo minzu shi renwu cidian* 中國民族史人物辭典 [Biographical Dictionary of Celebrities from the Ethnic Groups in China]. Beijing: Zhongguo shehui kexue, 1990.

Gao Zhangzhu 高長柱. *Bianjiang wenti lunwen ji* 邊疆問題論文集 [Compendium of Articles on Border Issues]. Shanghai: Zhengzhong shuju, 1950.

——. *Xizang gaikuang* 西藏概況 [General Overview of Tibet]. Taipei: Mongolian and Tibetan Affairs Commission, 1953.

Gesang Zhuoga 格桑卓嘎. "Shi san shi Dalai Lama Tudan Jiacuo shi zenyang xuanding de" 十三世達賴喇嘛土丹嘉措是怎樣選定的 [How Was Thubten Gyatso, the Thirteenth Dalai Lama, Chosen?]. *Zhongguo Zangxue* 2 (1991): 151–59.

"Gonggu bianfang dang yi jiaotong ru shou" 鞏固邊防當以交通入手 [Reinforce the Defense of the Borders by Developing Communication Networks]. *Xichui xuanhua shi gongshu yuekan*, 1935.

Guang Daodu 光島督. *Guofu quanti* 國父全集 [The Complete Works of Sun Yat-sen]. Taipei: Jindai Zhongguo, 1989.

——. "Yi jiu yi si nian dao yi jiu yi ba nian de chuanbian Han Zang jiufen" 1914 年到1918 年的川邊漢藏糾紛 [The Sino-Tibetan Conflict at the Sichuan Border from 1914 to 1918]. *Xizang yu Zhongyuan guanxi guoji xueshu yanjiu taohui*. Taipei, 1993.

Guojia wenwuju 國家文物局. *Zhongguo wenwu dituji: Qinghai fence* 中國文物地圖集: 青海分冊 [Collection of Geographical Atlases Dedicated to Chinese Cultural Patrimony: Qinghai Volume]. Beijing: Zhongguo ditu chubanshe, 1996.

Guo Jijiao 郭寄嶠. *Minguo yilai Zhongyang dui Meng Zang de shizheng* 民國以來中央對蒙藏的施政 [The Administration of Mongolia and Tibet by the Chinese Central Government since the Creation of the Chinese Republic]. Taipei: Meng Zang weiyuanhui, 1984.

Guo Peng 郭朋. *Taixu sixiang yanjiu* 太虛思想研究 [Research on the Thought of Taixu]. Beijing: Zhongguo shehui kexue chubanshe, 1997.

Guo Qing 國慶. "Weihu zuguo tongyi, minzu tuanjie de kaimo: Jiu shi Banchan shengping jianshu" 維護祖國統一， 民族團結的楷模: 九世班禪生平簡述" [An Example of Safeguarding the Union of the Motherland and theUnion of the Nationalities: A Brief Biography of the Ninth Panchen Lama]. *Xizang yanjiu* 4 (1987): 82–87.

——. "Zhao Erfeng ji qi Batang jingying" 趙爾豐及其巴塘經營 [Zhao Erfeng and His Batang Garrison]. *Xizang yanjiu* 4 (1989): 101–8.

Guo Weiping 郭偉平. "Qing ji shi san shi Dalai Lama chuzou Kulun kao" 清季十三世達賴喇嘛出走庫倫考 [Research on the Flight of the Thirteenth Dalai Lama to Kunlun during the Qing Era]. *Xizang yanjiu* 3 (1986): 37–39.

Gu Zhizhong 顧執中. *Dao Qinghai qu* 到青海去 [Going to Qinghai]. Shanghai: Shangwu yinshuguan, 1937.

Han Jinchun 韓錦春 and Li Yifu 李毅夫. "Hanwen 'minzu' yici de chuxian ji qi chuqi shiyong qingkuang" 漢文民族一詞的出現及其初期使用情況 [The First Appearance of the Term *Minzu* in Chinese and the Context of its Utilization]. *Minzu yanjiu* 2 (1984): 36–43.

He Dong 何東. *Zhongguo gemingshi renwu cidian* 中國革命史人物詞典 [Biographical Dictionary of Chinese Revolutionaries]. Beijing, 1991.

Hong Min 弘憫. *Taixu dashi foxue jingpin* 太虛大師佛學精品 [Spiritual Works and Buddhist Studies of the Great Master Taixu]. Anhui: Anhui chuban she, 1997.

Huang Dingchu 黃定初. "Diguo zhuyi qinlüe xia wo guo bianjiang zhi weiji" 帝國主義侵略下我國邊彊之危機 [Crisis in the Border Regions Caused by the Imperialist Invasion]. *Bianshi yanjiu* 邊事研究 5, no. 2 (1935): 10–27.

Huang Fengsheng 黃丰生. *Bianjiang zhengjiao zhi yanjiu* 邊疆政交之研究 [Study of the Politico-Religious System of Tibet]. Shanghai, 1947.

——. *Meng Zang xinzhi* 蒙藏新志 [New Monograph on Mongolia and Tibet]. Zhonghua shuju, 1938.

——. *Zangzu shilüe* 藏族史略 [Brief History of the Tibetan Ethnic Group]. Beijing: Nationalities Publishing House, 1989.

Huang Ju'an 黃舉安. "Banchan da shi hui Zang yu Xichui guofang" 班禪大師回藏与西陲國防 [Return of the Ninth Panchen Lama to Tibet and the Defense of the Western Regions]. *Xichui xuanhua shi gongshu yuekan* 6, no. 1 (1936): 11–12.

——. "Banchan da shi jianyue yizhangdui shi zhi xunci" 班禪大師檢閱儀仗隊時之巡詞 [Observations Made by the Panchen Lama after He Reviewed the Troops]. *Xichui xuanhua shi gongshu yuekan* 7/8, no. 1 (1936): 1–2.

——. "Banchan da shi you Labuleng zhi Yushu xuanhua jingguo" 班禪大師由拉卜楞至玉樹宣化經過 [Work Done by the Panchen Lama of Propagating Values from Labrang Trashikhyil to Yushu]. *Xichui xuanhua shi gongshu yuekan* 9, no. 1 (1937): 163–70.

Huang Mingxin 黃明信. "Beijing tushuguan Zangwen gu jiu tushu zhulu zanxing jiaoli shuoming" 北京圖書館藏文古舊圖書箸錄暫行條例說明 [Ancient Tibetan Writings Preserved at the Beijing Library]. *Zhongguo Zangxue* 1 (1988): 49.

Huang Musong 黃慕松. "Huang zhuanshi baogao ru Zang jingguo" 黃專使報告入藏經過 [Report of the Mission to Tibet by the Special Envoy Huang]. *Xichui xuanhua shi gongshu yuekan*, May 1935, 35–44.

——. *Huang zhuanshi feng shi Xizang zhiji huguo honghua puci yuanjue da shi Dalai Lama jinian zhaopian* 黃專使奉使西藏致祭護國弘化普慈圓覺大師達賴喇嘛紀念照片 [Photographic Album Commemorating the Funeral Ceremony of the Thirteenth Dalai Lama by Huang Musong]. Nanjing: Huang zhuanshi banshi chu, 1935.

——. *Menggu kaocha baogao* 蒙古考察報告 [Inspection Report from Mongolia]. Beijing, 1913.

——. *Shi Zang jicheng* 使藏紀程 [Mission to Tibet]. Facsimile of a 1964 reproduction. Taipei: Wenhai chubanshe, 1977.

——. "Xian Xiong Musong shilüe" 先兄慕松事略 [Brief History of Venerable Musong]. In *Shi Zang jicheng* 使藏紀程 [Mission to Tibet in 1934]. Taipei: Wenhai chubanshe, 1977.

Huang Shijian 黃時鑒. "Riben diguo zhuyi de 'Man Meng zhengce' he Nei Menggu fandong fengjian shangceng de 'zizhi' 'duli' yundong" 日本帝國主義的滿蒙政策和內蒙古反動封建上層的自治獨立運動 [The Policies of the Japanese Imperialists in Manchuria and in Mongolia and the Independence

Movement for Autonomy of the Reactionary Feudal Lords of Inner Mongolia]. Hohhot: Nei Menggu renmin chubanshe, 1983.

Huang Zheng 黄征 and Chen Zhanghe 陳長河. *Duan Qirui yu Wan Xi junfa* 段祺瑞与皖系軍閥 [Duan Qirui and the Anhui Military Clique]. Zhonghua minguo shi congshu [Republic of China History Series]. Henan: Henan Publishing House, 1992.

Huan Zhenju 還振舉. *Zhongguo de Nei Meng muqu* 中國的內蒙牧區 [The Pastures of Inner Mongolia in China]. Shanghai: Yongxiang, 1953.

Jiangbian Jiacuo 降邊嘉措 and Wu Wei 吳偉. *Shi san shi Dalai Lama 1904 nian Jiangzi zhi zhan* 十三世達賴喇嘛: 1904年江孜之戰 [The Thirteenth Dalai Lama: The 1904 Gyeltsé War]. Beijing: Zhongguo chubanshe, 1985.

Jiang Junzhang 蔣君章, Zhang Guojun 張國鈞, and Yan Zhongmin 嚴重敏. *Zhongguo bianjiang dili* 中國邊彊地理 [Geography of China's Border Regions]. Chongqing, 1944.

Jiang Ping 江平, Li Zuomin 李佐民, and Song Yingting 宋盈亭. "Di jiu shi Banchan E'erdeni Quji nima pingzhuan" 第九世班禪額爾德尼曲吉尼瑪評傳 [Critical Biography of the Ninth Panchen Lama]. *Zhongguo Zangxue* 3 (1997): 12–25.

Jiang Yangni 降央尼. "Banchan Lama yi wei daxi Lama zhi yanjiu" 班禪喇嘛譯為大喜喇嘛之研究 [Study on the Translation of the Title of Panchen Lama into that of Tashi Lama]. *Meng Zang yuebao* 4, no. 4 (1936): 24–34.

Jiang Zhongzheng 蔣中正. *Hu guo jing jue fujiao da shi Zhangjia Hutuketu shi* 護國淨覺輔教大師章嘉呼圖克圖史 [Biography of the Country's Pure, Enlightened Protector Serving the Doctrine, Great Master Zhangjia Hutuketu (Tib. *lCang skya Ho thog thu*)]. Taipei, 1957.

———. "Jieshou Zhangjia Hutuketu zhu Jing banshichu" 接收章嘉呼圖克圖駐京辦事處 [Opening of the Zhangjia Hutuketu (Tib. *lCang skya Ho thog thu*) Office in Nanjing]. *Meng Zang shibao* 4, no. 6 (n.d.): 3.

Jie Xueshi 解學詩. *Wei Manzhouguo shi xinbian* 偽滿洲國史新編 [New Compilation of the History of Manchuria]. Beijing: Peoples Publishing House, 1995.

Jin Liang 金梁. *Yonghe gong zhilüe* 雍和宮志略 [Brief Monograph on the Palace of Eternal Harmony]. Beijing: Zhongguo Zangxue chubanshe, 1994.

Ji Yu 季宇. *Duan Qirui zhuan* 段祺瑞傳 [Biography of Duan Qirui]. Hebei: Anwei renmin chubanshe, 1992.

Juenangdarenate 覺囊達熱那特. *Hou Zang zhi* 後藏志 [Monograph on Outer Tibet]. Lhasa: Bod rang skyong ljongs mi dmangs dpe skrun khang, 1994.

Kaifeng shifan xueyuan dili xi 開封師范學院地理系, ed. *Zhongguo minzu dili ziliao xuanji* 中國民族地理資料選輯 [Choice of Documents on the Geography of China's Ethnic Regions]. Beijing: Shangwu yinshuguan, 1960.

Kang Furong 康敷鎔. *Qinghai zhi* 青海志 [Monograph of Qinghai]. Taipei, 1968.

Kongsa Yiduo 孔薩益多 (Ye shes rDo rje). "Jiu shi Banchan shi weiduizhang de huiyi" 九世班禪侍偉隊長的回憶 [Memories of the Ninth Panchen Lama's Head Escort]. *Zhongguo Xizang* 中國西藏 1 (1989): 50–51.

———. "50 nian qian de Ganzi shibian" 五十年前的甘孜事變 [Fifty Years Ago: The Kardzé Affair]. *Minzu zazhi* 民族雜志 3 (1992): 14–17.

Lai Zuozhong 來作中 and Deng Junkang 鄧俊康. "Ganzi shibian de qianqian houhou" 甘孜事變的前前後後 [The Ins and Outs of the Kardzé Affair]. *Sichuan sheng Ganzi Zangzu zizhizhou wenshi ziliao xuanji* 1 (1982): 125–26.

Lang Depei 郎德沛. "Xizang xian zhengquan yu Yingguo zhi guanxi" 西藏現政權與英國之關係 [The Relations between the Current Tibetan Government and England]. *Bian shi yanjiu* 1, no. 4 (1936): 7–10.

Leng Liang 冷亮. "Guoren duiyu Zang qing ying you zhi jichu zhishi" 國人對於藏情應有之基礎智識 [Indispensible Knowledge to Understanding the Tibetan Situation]. *Dongfang zazhi* 13, no. 34 (1937): 111045–111048 [79–88].

———. "Xizang wenti zhi zhenxiang ji qi jiejue fangfa" 西藏問題之真相及其解決方法 [The Essence of the Tibetan Problem and Ways to Resolve it]. *Meng Zang shibao* 30 (1930): 4–6.

——. "Xizang wenti zhi zhenxiang ji qi jiejue fangfa" 西藏問題之真相及其解決方法 [The Essence of the Tibetan Problem and Ways to Resolve it]. *Dongfang zazhi* 31, no. 9 (1934): 15–26.

Liang Xingliang 梁星亮. *Shaanxi jin xian dai mingren lu* 陝西近現代名人錄 [Catalogue of Celebrities from Shaanxi during the Modern and Contemporary Eras]. Xi'an: Xibei daxue chubanshe, 1994.

Li Desen 李德森. "Fang Zhashilunbu si" 訪扎什倫布寺 [Visit to the Tashilhunpo Monastery]. *Xiandai foxue* 現代佛學 10 (1957): 22–23.

Li Dongyuan 李東園. *Xizang youbi kao* 西藏郵幣考 [Analysis of the Tibetan Postal and Monetary Systems]. Taipei: Zhongguo jiyou ban yue kanshe, 1929.

Lin Enxian 林恩顯. *Jindai Zhongguo bianjiang yanjiu lunzhu mulu* 近代中國邊疆研究論箸目錄 [Bibliography of Writings, Theories, and Studies on China's Border Regions during the Modern Era]. Taipei: Zhengzhi daxue bianzheng yanjiu, 1986.

Lin Jiake 林家可. *Difang zizhi gailun* 地方自治概論 [Introduction to the Local Autonomy System]. Shanghai: Commercial Press, 1933.

Li Pengnian 李鵬年. "Qianxi jiu shi Banchan fan Zang shou zu ji qi yuanyin" 淺析九世班禪返藏受阻及其原因 [Brief Analysis of the Obstacles to the Ninth Panchen Lama's Return]. *Zhongguo Zangxue* 1 (1992): 23–38.

Li Shengping 李盛平. *Zhongguo jin xian dai ren ming dacidian* 中國近現代人名大辭典 [Great Biographical Dictionary of the Well-Known in Contemporary and Modern China]. Beijing: Zhongguo guoji guangbo, 1989.

Li Weihai 李威海, ed. *Dalai, Banchan jin Jing jishi* 達賴班禪晉京紀實 [Historical Narration of the Dalai Lamas and Panchen Lamas's Visits to Beijing]. Beijing: Zhongguo shehui chubanshe, 1996.

Li Yizhuo 李翌灼. *Xizang fojiao lüeshi* 西藏佛教略史 [Brief History of Tibetan Buddhism]. Foxue shuju, 1929.

——. *Xizang fojiao shi* 西藏佛教史 [History of Tibetan Buddhism]. *Zhonghua shuju*, 1933.

Li Youyi 李有義. *Xizang de huofo* 西藏的活佛 [Reincarnated Tibetan Masters]. Beijing: Yanjing shehui kexue, 1948.

Li Yu 李浴. *Kangzhan zhong yujin de Qinghai* 抗戰中邁進的青海 [The Situation in Qinghai during the War of Resistance against Japan]. Xining: Qinghai yinshuaju, 1939.

Liu Huating 劉華庭. *Shuo Han qian chen* 朔漠前塵 [The Gobi Desert's Past]. Shanghai: Shanghai shudian, 1994.

Liu Jiaju 劉家駒 (Kelzang Chönjor). "Alashan Nan si jiyou" 阿拉善南寺紀遊 [Trip to the Southern Monastery in Alashan]. *Xichui xuanhua shi gongshu yuekan* 6, no. 1 (1936): 175.

——. "Banchan Dalai lüeshi" 班禪達賴略史 [Brief History of the Dalai Lamas and Panchen Lamas]. *Kaifa xibei* 1, no. 5 (1934): 57–58.

——. "Banchan da shi guru gulu fa kaishi" 班禪大師古儒古魯法開示 [Guru Yoga Teaching Given by the Ninth Panchen Lama]. *Xichui xuanhua shi gongshu yuekan* 5, no. 1 (1936): 121–22.

——. *Banchan dashi quanji* 班禪大師全集 [Complete Works of the Great Master Panchen]. Chongqing, 1943.

——. "Chang ban Puti xuehui" 倡辦菩提學會 [Project for the Creation of an Association Dedicated to the Bodhi Society]. *Xichui xuanhua shi gongshu yuekan* 5 (1935): 55–57.

——. *Kang Zang* 康藏 [Xikang and Tibet]. Nanjing: Xinyaxiya xuehui, 1932.

——. "Xizang lidai Zang wang ji Dalai Banchan shiyao" 西藏歷代藏王及達賴班禪史要 [Short History of the Kings, Dalai Lamas, and Panchen Lamas of Tibet]. *Kaifa xibei* 5, no. 4 (1935): 15–22. Reprint, *Xichui xuanhua shi gongshu yuekan* 4/5, no. 1 (1936): 86–92.

——. *Xizang zhengjiao shilüe* 西藏政教史略 [A Historical Overview of the History of the Tibetan Politico-Religious System]. Zhongguo bianjiang xuehui, 1948.

Liu Manqing 劉曼卿. *Kang Zang yaozheng* 康藏軺征 [A Ride through Xikang and Tibet]. Changsha: Shangwu pai, 1933–1938.

——. *Xizang* 西藏 [Tibet]. Shanghai: Shangwu, 1934.

Liu Muyan 劉慕燕. "Jiu shi Banchan wei Sun Zhongshan xiansheng feng'an dadian suo zhuan jiwen" 九世班禪為孫中山先生奉安大典所撰祭文 [Funeral Oration for Sun Yat-Sen Written by the Ninth Panchen Lama]. *Minguo dang'an* 2 (1990): 20.

——. "Xizang daibiao chuxi guomin dahui dang'an ziliao" 西藏代表出席國民大會檔案資料 [Archival Documents Concerning the Participation of Tibetan Representatives at the National Conference]. *Minguo dang'an* 3 (1992): 40–58.

——. "Xunfang shi shi Banchan lingtong ji Guan Jiyu zhuchi zuochuang dianli dang'an shiliao xuan" 尋訪十世班禪靈童及關吉玉主持坐床典禮檔案史料選 [Choice of Archival Documents Concerning the Search for the Incarnation of the Tenth Panchen Lama and His Enthronement Ceremony Overseen by Guan Jiyu]. *Minguo dang'an* 2 (1989): 35–68.

Liu Ruizhi 劉銳之. *Xizang mizong qingzuofa gai shuo* 西藏密宗靜坐法概說 [A Look at Esoteric Tibetan Meditative Techniques]. Hong Kong: Xianggang jingang sheng xuehui, 1971.

Liu Shengqi 柳升祺. "1929 nian ban 'Aiqixun tiaoyue' ji di 14 juan he yi you liang zhong butong banben-jianping Ximula huiyi (1913–1914)" 1929 年版艾奇遜條約集第十四卷何以有兩種不同版本 — 兼評西姆拉會議 (1913–1914) [How is it Possible that There Were Two Versions of Chapter 14 of the Qiyisun Treaty Signed in 1929—Critique of the Simla Treaty (1913–1914)]. *Zhongguo Zangxue* 1 (1990): 3.

——. "Liu shi Banchan de lishi gongxian" 六世班禪的歷史貢獻 [The Historical Contribution of the Sixth Panchen Lama]. *Zhongguo Xizang* 1 (1989): 56.

Liu Xi 劉熙. "Xizang zhi zhengzhi yu jiaoyu" 西藏之政治与教育 [The Education and Politics of Tibet]. *Meng Zang yuebao* 5, no. 6 (1936): 3.1–3.6.

Lu Minghui 盧明輝. *Menggu zizhi yundong shimo* 蒙古自治運動始末 [The Whole Story of the Mongol Autonomous Movement]. Beijing: Zhonghua shuju, 1980.

——. "Lun Ying ru qinlüe Xizang" 論英人侵略西藏 [Concerning the Invasion of Tibet by the British]. *Dongfang zazhi* 1, no. 8 (1904): 309–13.

Luo Huirong 羅匯榮. "Yi jiu ling si nian Ronghepeng jin jun Lasa shimo" 一九零四年榮赫鵬進軍拉薩始末 [The Complete Story of the Younghusband's Army's Stay in Lhasa in 1904]. *Dalu zazhi* 大陸雜志 29, no. 7 (1964): 229–35; 29, no. 8 (1964): 267–73; 29, no. 9 (1964): 309–16.

Luo Runcang 羅潤蒼. "Kangzhan qijian Sichuan Zang xue yanjiu gaishu" 康戰期間四川藏學研究概述 [Overview of the Institute of Tibetan Studies of Sichuan during the War of Resistance against Japan]. *Zhongguo Zangxue* 3 (1996): 11–20.

Luo Youren 羅友仁. "Banchan da shi zai Qinghai xuanhua jingguo ji fu La yantu xuanhua qingxing" 班禪大師在青海宣化經過及赴拉沿途宣化情形 [The Ninth Panchen Lama's Propagation of Values in Qinghai and His Planned Journey to Labrang Trashikhyil]. *Xichui xuanhua shi gongshu yuekan* 6, no. 1 (1936): 174.

Luo Zhufeng 羅竹風, ed. *Hanyu da cidian* 漢語大詞典 [The Great Dictionary of the Chinese Language]. 13 vols. Shanghai: Hanyu da cidian, 1994.

Machong Mingjiu duoji 馬沖明久多吉. "Zhashelunbu si kanting zuzhi jigou shulüe" 札什倫布寺堪廳組織機構述略 [Brief Presentation of the Administration of Tashilhunpo Monastery]. *Zhongguo Zangxue* 2 (1995): 57–68.

Ma Hetian 馬鶴天. *Gan Qing Zang bianqu kaocha ji* 甘青藏邊區考察記 [Inspection Journal from the Frontier Regions of Gansu, Qinghai, and Tibet]. Shanghai, 1947.

——. "Meng Zang zhengzhi ying ruhe jianshe" 蒙藏政治應如何建設 [How to Construct Policies in Mongolia and Tibet?]. *Kaifa Xibei* 6, no. 1 (1936): 1–8.

Ma Huiping 馬惠平, ed. *Zhongguo Zangxue shumu* 中國藏學書目 (Tib. *Krung go'i Bod rig pa'i dpe cha'i dkar chag*) [Catalogue of Chinese Publications in Tibetan Studies (1949–1991)]. Beijing: Waiguo yuyan chubanshe, 1994.

Ma Lianlong 馬連籠. "Qi shi Banchan Luosang Badan Jiujian Nima nianpu" 七世班禪羅桑巴丹舊見尼瑪年譜 [Chronological Biography of the Seventh Panchen Lama]. *Xizang yanjiu* 4 (1989): 144–53.

Mei Shuceng 梅恕曾. *Xikang* 西康 [The Province of Xikang]. Nanjing: Zhengzhong, 1934.

Mei Xinru 梅心如. *Xikang* 西康 [The Province of Xikang]. Taipei: Zhengzhong shuju, 1970.

Meng Wei 孟維. *Ta'er si* 塔爾寺 [Kumbum Monastery]. Xining: Qinghai minzu chubanshe, 1994.

Meng Zang weiyuanhui jianshi 蒙藏委員會簡史 [Abridged History of the Mongolian and Tibetan Affairs Commission]. Taipei: Meng Zang weiyuanhui, 1971.

Ming Sanji 明散吉. *Banchan fo shiji jilüe* 班禪佛事跡紀略 [Tracing the Steps of the Panchen Lama]. 1925.

Min Zhengting 民政廳. *Minzu zhuyi yu guojia zhuyi* 民族主義与國家主義 [Nationalism Based on Membership of One Race]. Shanghai: Qianjin shuju, 1927.

——. *Zui jin zhi Qinghai* 最近之青海 [Current Qinghai]. Nanjing: Xinyaxiya xuehui chuban she, 1934.

Nei Menggu jindai shi luncong 内蒙古近代史論叢 [Written Compendium on the Modern History of Inner Mongolia]. Hohhot: Nei Menggu chubanshe, 1983.

"Ni gaishe Xizang xingsheng ce" 擬改設西藏行省策 [Proposals for the Establishment of Tibet as a Province]. *Dongfang zazhi* 3, no. 2 (1906): 33–38.

Nuona jingang shangshi kaishi lu 諾那金剛上師開示錄 [Compendium of Teachings Transmitted by the Tibetan Master Nuona]. 1959.

Peng Dixian 彭迪先. *Liu Wenhui shi hua* 劉文輝史話 [The Words and Biography of Liu Wenhui]. Chengdu: University of Sichuan, 1990.

Peng Yingming 彭英明. "Guanyu wo Guo minzu gainian lishi de chubu kaocha" 關于我國民族概念歷史的初步考察 [Preliminary Observations Concerning the Development of the Concept of Ethnic Groups in China]. *Minzu yanjiu* 2 (1985): 5–11.

Pu Wencheng 蒲文成. *Gan Qing Zang chuanfojiao siyuan* 甘青藏傳佛教寺院 [The Tibetan Monasteries and Institutions of Gansu, Qinghai, and Tibet]. Xining: Qinghai minzu chubanshe, 1990.

Qiabai Cidan Pingcuo 恰白次旦平措, Pingcuo Ciren 平措次仁, and Nuozhang Wujian 諾章吳堅. *Xizang tongshi* 西藏通史 [General History of Tibet]. Lhasa: Xizang guji chubanshe, 1996.

Qin ding Da Qing huidian shili 欽定大清會典事例 [Imperially Commissioned Collected Regulations and Precedents of the Qing dynasty]. 1899.

Qinghai sheng zhi bianzuan weiyuanhui 青海省志編纂委員會. *Qinghai lishi jiyao* 青海歷史紀要 [Chronicle of the History of Qinghai]. Xining: Qinghai minzu chubanshe, 1991.

Qinghai Xikang yipie 青海西康一瞥 [A Look at Qinghai and Xikang]. Shanghai: Shangwu yinshuguan, 1931.

Qing shilu 清實錄. [Veritable Records of the Qing Dynasty]. Beijing: Zhonghua shuju. 1986.

Qing shilu Zangzu shiliao 清事錄藏族事料 [Materials on the Tibetan Ethnic Group from the Qing Dynasty]. Beijing: Xizang renmin chubanshe, 1989.

"Qingzhu Jiang weiyuanzhang chuxian jinian da hui yanci" 慶祝蔣委員長出險紀念大會演詞 [Discourse Given during the Ceremony Commemorating the Liberation of Chiang Kai-shek]. *Xichui xuanhua shi gongshu yuekan* 9, no. 1 (1937): 4.

Qin Heping 秦和平. "1912 nian Minguo zhengfu chouzhi Xizang cuoshi shuping" 1912 年民國政府籌治西藏措施述評 [Presentation of Measures Taken by the Republican Government Regarding Tibet in 1912]. *Zhongguo Zangxue* 4 (1993): 108–22.

Qiu Huaijin 邱懷瑾. "Xizang jingji zhi gaikuang 西藏經濟之概況" [The Economic Situation in Tibet]. *Bian shi yanjiu* 1, no. 4 (1936): 20–22.

Qiu Jiurong 邱久榮. "Shi xi Sun Zhongshan de minzu zhuyi yu minzu guannian" 識析孫中山的民族主義与民族觀念 [Analysis of Sun Yat-sen's Concepts of Nationality and Nationalism]. *Zhongyang minzu daxue xuebao* 中央民族大學學報 1 (1994): 3–10.

Ran Guangrong 冉光榮. *Zhongguo Zang chuanfojiao siyuan* 中國藏傳佛教寺院 [Tibetan Monasteries in China]. Beijing: Zhongguo Zangxue, 1994.

Ran Hongling 冉洪玲. "Xizang siyuan jingji jianlun" 西藏寺院經濟簡論 [Concerning the Monastic Economy in Tibet]. In *Zangzu shilun wenji* 藏族史論文集 [Compendium of Articles on the Tibetan Ethnic Group], 263–80. Chengdu: Sichuan renmin chubanshe, 1988.

Ren Xinjian 任新建. "Kang Zang yanjiushe jieshao" 康藏研究社介紹 [Presentation of Tibetan Research Centers in Kham and Tibet]. *Zhongguo Zangxue* 3 (1996): 21–29.

Rongba zhaxi 戎巴扎西. "Zangzu siyuan jingji fazhan de neizai yuanyou" 藏族寺院經濟發展的內在緣由 [The Internal Causes of Economic Development of the Tibetan Ethnic Group's Monasteries]. *Minzu yanjiu* 4 (1993): 34–39.

Sa Shijiong 薩師炯. *Difang zizhi fagui* 地方自治法規 [Laws and Rules Concerning Regional Autonomy]. Shanghai: Dadong shuju, 1946.

Sha Lanfang 沙蘭芳. "Shan Gan Ning bianqu kaocha baogao" 陝甘寧邊區考察報告 [Inspection Report on the Border Regions of Shaanxi, Gansu, and Ningxia]. *Minguo dang'an*, 2 (1989): 41–44.

"Shao Yuanchong xiansheng fang Banchan Lama" 邵元沖先生訪班禪喇嘛 [Zhao Yuanchong Interviews the Panchen Lama]. *Haichaoyin* 海潮音 16, no. 6 (1935): 130.

Shi Dongchu 釋東初. *Dai Jitao xiansheng foxue lunji* 戴季陶先生佛學論集 [Compilation of Speeches Given by Dai Jitao Regarding Buddhist Study]. Taipei: Zhonghua fojiao wenhuaguan, 1972.

——. *Zhongguo fojiao jindaishi* 中國佛教近代史 [History of Chinese Buddhism in the Modern Era]. Taipei: Dongchu chubanshe, 1989.

Shi Huijiao 釋慧皎. *Gaoseng zhuan* 高僧傳 [Biographies of Distinguished Monks]. Beijing: Zhonghua shuju, 1997.

"Shilun guanding she shou dizi kaishi" 時輪灌頂攝授弟子開示 [Kālacakra Initiation]. *Kaifa Xibei* 2, no. 1 (1934): 5–7. Reprint, *Xichui xuanhua shi gongshu yuekan* 1, nos. 4/5 (1936): 127–30.

Shi Yin 市隱. "Dalai xi shi hou zhi Kang Zang jiufen" 達賴逝世後之康藏糾紛 [The Border Conflict between Kham and Tibet after the Death of the Thirteenth Dalai Lama]. *Dongfang zazhi* 8, no. 31 (1934): 127–28.

Shi Yinshun 釋印順. *Taixu fashi nianpu* 太虛法師年譜 [Chronological Biography of the Buddhist Master Taixu]. Beijing: Zongjiao wenhua, 1995.

Shi Zhenhua 式振華, "Shu Xi fensheng chuyan" 蜀西分省芻言 [A Humble Opinion on the Establishment of a New Province to the West of Sichuan]. *Dongfang zazhi* 5, no. 12 (1908): 161–68.

——, ed. *Xizang diming* 西藏地名 [Tibetan Toponyms]. Beijing: Zhongguo Zangxue, 1995.

Sichuan sheng dang'an guan 四川省檔案館 [Sichuan Archives]. *Jin dai Kang qu dang'an ziliao xuanbian* 近代康區檔案資料選編 [Compilation of Documents Conserved in the Sichuan Archives Concerning the Kham Area during the Modern Era]. Chengdu: University of Sichuan, 1990.

Song Zanliang 宋贊良. "Sela si diaocha" 色拉寺調查 [Investigative Report on Sera Monastery]. *Zhongguo Zangxue* 2 (1991): 134–150; 3 (1991): 81–97; 1 (1992): 108–25.

Sun Caixia 孫彩霞, ed. *Minguo renwu pi zhuanji* 民國人物啤傳集 [Compendium of Biographies of Celebrities of the Chinese Republic]. Chengdu: Sichuan renmin chubanshe, 1997.

Sun Fukun 孫福坤. *Menggu jianshi xinbian* 蒙古簡史新編 [New Essay of the Abridged History of Mongolia]. Beijing: Ziyou chubanshe, 1951.

——. *Minquan zhuyi* 民權主義 [The Principle of Democracy]. Shanghai, 1924.

Sun Wenjing 孫文景. *Zangwen dianji mulu* 藏文典籍目綠 (Tib. *Mi rigs dpe mdzod khang gi dpe tho las gsung 'bum skor gyi dkar chag* [Catalog of Old Tibetan Books and Texts Conserved in the Palace of Minorities in Beijing]. 1989. Reprint, Beijing: renmin chubanshe, 1997.

Sun Yat-sen [Sun Wen] 孫文. *Minzu zhuyi* 民族主義 [The Principle of Nationalism]. Shanghai, 1924.

Sun Yongxin 孫永鑫. "Kang zhan chuqi fojiaotu canjia kang Ri jiuwang huodong shiliao xuan" 抗戰初期佛教徒參加抗日救亡活動史料選(shang 上, xia下) [Choice of Archival Documents Concerning the Resistance Movement against Japan and the Safeguarding of the Fatherland Lead by Devout Buddhists at the Beginning of the War of Resistance against Japan]. *Minguo dang'an* 3 (1996): 35–44; 4 (1996): 28–34.

Sun Zihe 孫子和. "Huang Musong ru Zang shimo" 黃慕松入藏 始末 [The Voyage of Huang Musong to Tibet]. Taipei: Xizang yu Zhongyuan guanxi guoji xueshu yanjiu hui, 1993.

Ta'er si 塔爾寺 [Kumbum Monastery]. Xining: Qinghai minzu chubanshe, 1984.

Taixu 太虛. *Wo de fojiao gaijin yundong lüeshi* 我的佛教改進運動略史 [Abridged History of My Buddhist Reformation Movement]. Nanjing: Jueyinshe, 1941.

Tang Chi'an 湯池安. *Zang Han dianji mulu* 藏漢典籍目錄 (Tib. *Mi rigs dpe mdzod khang gi dpe tho las gsung 'bum skor gyi dkar chag*) [Catalog of Old Tibetan and Chinese Books and Texts Conserved in the Palace of Minorities in Beijing]. Chengdu: Sichuan minzu chubanshe, 1984.

Tang Hongbo 唐洪波. "Longxia yu Longxia shijian" 龍夏与龍夏事件 [Lungshar and the Lungshar Affair]. *Zhongguo Zangxue* 3 (1994): 140–47.

Tang Jingfu 唐景福. "Labuleng si seng ren xue jing zhidu yu jingji laiyuan shulüe" 拉卜楞寺僧人學經制度与經濟來源述略 [Brief Presentation of the Educational System and Economic Resources of Labrang Trashikhyil Monastery]. In *Zangzu shilun wenji*, 248–62. Chengdu: Sichuan renmin chubanshe, 1988.

——. “Minguo shiqi lijie Zhongyang zhengfu weihu Xizang zhuquan de cuoshi” 民國時期歷屆中央政府維護西藏主權的措施 [Measures Taken by the Successive Governments to Preserve Tibetan Sovereignty during the Time of the Republic of China]. *Zhongguo Xizang* 1 (1997): 42–58.

Tan Qixiang 譚其驤. *Jian ming Zhongguo lishi dituji* 簡明中國歷史地圖集 [Historical Atlas of China]. Beijing: Zhongguo ditu, 1991.

Tao Zhong 陶仲. “Yingguo zhi Xizang jun shi qianghua” 英國之西藏軍事強化 [British Military Aid in Tibet]. *Bianshi yanjiu* 1, no. 4 (1936): 23–28.

Tian Jizhou 田繼周. *Zhongguo lidai minzu zhengce yanjiu* 中國歷代民族政策研究 [Study on the Policy Towards Nationalities Held by Past Chinese Dynasties]. Xining: Qinghai renmin chubanshe, 1993.

Tie An 鐵盦. “Xizang wenti” 西藏問題 [The Tibetan Question]. *Bianshi yanjiu* 5, no. 2 (1935): 1–27.

“Tuanjie wu zu bixu zhengjiao jian shi” 團結五族必須政教兼施 [The Union of the Five Nationalities Must Edify Itself Regarding Politics and Religion]. *Xichui xuanhua shi gongshu yuekan* (1935): 1–3.

Wang Chaoguang 汪朝光. “Minguo chunian de Zhong Ying Xizang jiaoshe” 民國初年的中英西藏交涉 [Relations between China, England, and Tibet at the Beginning of the Chinese Republic]. *Xizang yanjiu* 2 (1987): 5–14.

Wang Chaozhu 王朝柱. *Feng Yuxiang he Jiang Jieshi* 馮玉祥和蔣介石 [Feng Yuxiang and Chiang Kai-shek]. Beijing: Zhongguo qingnian, 1994.

——. *Zhang Xueliang jiangjun* 張學良將軍 [General Zhang Xueliang]. Beijing: Zhongguo xiju chubanshe, 1993.

Wang Chengsheng 王成聖. “Xizang Banchan jiu shi yisheng shenji” 西藏班禪九世一生神跡 [The Miraculous Life of the Ninth Panchen Lama]. *Zhongwai zazhi* 中外雜志 1, no. 5 (1969): 58–66.

Wang Dui 旺堆. “Wu shi zhi jiu shi Banchan hezang lingta” 五世至九世班禪合葬靈塔 [The Common Funeral Mausoleum of the Fifth to the Ninth Panchen Lamas]. *Xizang yanjiu* 2 (1990): 134–35.

Wang Gui 王貴. *Zangzu renming yanjiu* 藏族人名研究 [Studies on Tibetan Proper Names]. Beijing: Minzu chubanshe, 1991.

Wang Jinbian 汪今變. *Xizang fengsu zhi* 西藏風俗志 [The Ways and Customs of the Tibetans]. 1931.

Wang Qinyu 王勤堉. *Xizang wenti* 西藏問題 [The Tibet Question]. Shanghai: Shangwu yinshuguan, 1929.

Wang Xianjun 王獻軍. “Xizang shezheng zhidu taolun” 西藏攝政制度討論 [About the Regent System in Tibet]. *Xibei shidi* 西北史地 4 (1998): 76–81.

Wang Xiaochun 王曉春. “Minguo Sichuan Zang zu dang'an shiliao pingjia” 民國四川藏族檔案史料評介 [Critique of the Archival Documents Concerning the Tibetan Ethnic Group in the Province of Sichuan during the Republican Era]. *Xizang yanjiu* 3 (1993): 52–59.

Wang Yigui 王益圭. *Dongbei jiu sheng dizhi* 東北九省地志 [Geographical Monograph of the Nine Northeast Provinces]. Taipei: Zhonghua wenhua, 1958.

Wang Yuping 王玉平. “Huofo chuanshi de chansheng he jinping zhiqian de zhiding” 活佛轉世的產生和金瓶掣簽的制定 [The Process of Reincarnation and the Selection of Reincarnated Beings by Drawing Lots]. *Xizang yanjiu* 1 (1996): 29–33.

Wang Yuanda 王遠大. *Jindai Eguo yu Zhongguo Xizang* 近代俄國与中國西藏 [Russia and Tibet during the Modern Era]. Beijing: Sanlian shudian, 1993.

Wang Zhanying 王戰英 and Song Xuewen 宋學文, eds. *Jin xian dai Zhongguo shaoshu minzu ying ming lu* 近現代中國少數民族英名錄 [Biographical Dictionary of Celebrities from the National Chinese Ethnic Groups during the Modern and Contemporary Eras]. Beijing: Huaxia, 1994.

Wei Guo 魏國. “Guanyu Dalai Lama de fenghao, diwei, zhiquan deng de kaozheng” 關于達賴喇嘛的封號地位職權等的考證 [Critical Study Concerning Titles, Positions, and Political Powers of the Dalai Lama]. *Minzu yanjiu* 5 (1959): 21–28.

Wei Huilin 衛惠林. “Ruhe queli san min zhuyi de bianjiang minzu zhengce” 如何確立三民主義的邊疆民族政策 [How to Construct A Border Policy in Line with the Three Principles of the People]. *Bianjiang lunwenji* 邊疆論文集 1 (1964): 678–81.

Wei Yuan 魏源. *Wei Zang tongzhi* 衛藏通志 [Monograph on Central Tibet]. 1896.

Wu Congzhong 吳從眾. “Yingguo ruqin Xizang dong nan difang shilüe” 英國入侵西藏東南地方史略 [Abridged History of the British Invasion of Southeast Tibet]. *Xizang yanjiu* 3 (1988): 35–42.

Wu Fengpei 吳丰培. "A Bibliography of Studies on Tibetan History. Part II: Chinese Sources." *Xizang yanjiu* (1982): 119.

——. "Tan Minguo shiqi Xizang difang zhengfu yu zhongyang de guanxi" 談民國時期西藏地方政府与中央的關係 [Concerning the Relations between the Chinese Central Government and Tibet under the Chinese Republic]. *Zhongguo Xizang* 1 (1992): 55.

——. "Xizang tujilu" 西藏圖籍錄 [Bibliography of Tibet]. *Yugong* 2, no. 4 (1935): 53–63.

——. "Xizang tujilu sheyi" 西藏圖籍錄拾遺 [Supplement to the Bibliography of Tibet]. *Yugong* 12, no. 6 (1937): 107–11.

Wu Fengpei 吳丰培 and Ceng Guoqing 曾國慶. *Qingchao zhu Zang dachen zhidu de jianli yu yange* 清朝駐藏大臣制度的建立与沿革 [The Creation and Evolution of the System of Imperial Residents in Tibet]. Beijing: Zhongguo Zangxue, 1989.

Wu Heling 吳鶴齡. *Menggu diqu xiandai yanbian tuzhi* 蒙古地區現代演變圖志 [Maps on the Current Evolution of Mongolia]. Taipei: Hongdao wenhua shiye youxian gongsi, 1975.

Wu Yuncen 吳雲岑. "Jinping zhiqian de sheli ji qi yiyi" 金瓶掣簽的設立及其意義 [Creation and Significance of Drawing Lots from the Urn]. *Xizang yanjiu* 1 (1996): 34–42.

Wu Yunian 吳玉年. "Xizang tu jilu" 西藏圖籍錄 [Bibliography of Tibet]. *Yugong* 4, no. 2 (1935): 53–69.

Wu Zhongxin 吳忠信. *Kangzhan yilai zhi Meng Zang* 抗戰以來之蒙藏 [Mongolia and Tibet since the War of Resistance against Japan]. Chongqing: Bianzheng gonglun she, 1944.

——. *Xizang jiyao* 西藏紀要 [Tibetan Chronicle]. Taipei: Zhongyang wenwu gongyin chubanshe, 1953.

Xiao Yi 蕭怡. *Xizang jinxi* 西藏今昔 [Tibet of Yesterday and Today]. Hong Kong: Yazhou chubanshe, 1960.

Xibei yanjiu she 西北研究社. *Kang zhan zhong de Gan Ning Qing* 抗戰中的甘寧青 [Gansu, Ningxia, Qinghai during the War of Resistance against Japan]. 1941.

"Xichui xuanhua shi gongshu zuzhi tiaoli" 西陲宣化使公署阻職條例 [Rules Concerning the Structure of the Office of the Propagator of Values in the Western Region]. *Xichui xuanhua shi gongshu yuekan* (1935): 43–44.

Xie Bin 謝彬. *Xizang wenti* 西藏問題 [The Tibet Question]. Shanghai: Shangwu yinshuguan, 1933.

Xinhai geming Wuchang qiyi jinianguan 辛亥革命武昌起義紀念館. *Xinhai gemingshi dituji* 辛亥革命史地圖集 [Geographical and Historical Atlas of the 1911 Revolution]. Beijing: Zhongguo ditu chubanshe, 1991.

Xining fuzhi 西寧府志 [Monograph of Xining Prefecture]. n.d.

Xining xian xinzhi 西寧縣新志 [New Monograph on the District of Xining]. Taipei: Chengwen chubanshe, 1968.

Xining xianzhi 西寧縣志 [Monograph on the District of Xining]. Taipei: Chengwen chubanshe, 1967.

Xining xinzhi 西寧新志 [New Monograph of Xining]. Beijing: Beijing tushuguan, 2002.

Xin Qinghai 新青海 [The New Qinghai]. Nanjing, 1937.

Xiong Ji 熊季. "Rezheng qi nian shezheng shengya suoyi" 熱振七年攝政生涯瑣議 [Remarks on the Seven Years of the Reting Regency]. *Xizang yanjiu* 4 (1987): 88–93.

Xiong Yaowen 熊耀文. *Zongli duiyu Meng Zang zhi yixun ji Zhongyang duiyu Meng Zang zhi faling* 總理對於蒙藏之遺訓及中央對於蒙藏之法令 [Words Passed on by Sun Yat-sen Concerning Mongolia and Tibet and the Laws and Rules Concerning Mongolia and Tibet, as edited by the Central Chinese Government]. Nanjing: Meng Zang weiyuanhui, 1934.

Xirao Nima 喜繞尼瑪. "Chuyi Minguo shiqi shi san shi Dalai Lama yu Zhongyang zhengfu guanxi" 芻議民國時期十三世達賴喇嘛与中央政府關系 [My Humble Opinion on the Relations between the Thirteenth Dalai Lama and the Chinese Central Government during the Chinese Republican Era]. *Xizang yanjiu* 1 (1993): 60–62.

"Xizang bu neng she xingsheng" 西藏不能設行省 [Impossible to Turn Tibet into a Province]. *Dongfang zazhi* 11, no. 1 (1904): 75.

"Xizang Dalai Lama taodun yuwen" 西藏達賴喇嘛逃遁余聞 [What I Know Regarding the 1910 Flight of the Thirteenth Dalai Lama]. *Dongfang zazhi* 3, no. 7 (1910): 4–6.

"Xizang renwu zhi" 西藏人物志 [Biography of Tibetan Celebrities]. *Kaifa xibei* 3, no. 1 (1934): 95–96.

Xizang xinzhi 西藏新志 [New Monograph on Tibet]. 1912.

Xizang yanjiu 西藏研究 [Studies on Tibet]. Taipei: Zhongguo bianjiang lishi yuwen xuehui, 1960.

Xizang de zhengjiao heyi zhi 西藏的政教合一制 [The Politico-Religious System of Tibet]. Chongqing: Xingzhengyuan, 1947.

Xizang zhi 西藏志 [Monograph on Tibet]. Taipei: Wenhai, 1966.

Xizang zhi 西藏志 [Monograph on Tibet]. Lhasa: Xizang renmin chubanshe, 1982.

"Xizang zhi zhengzhi" 西藏之政制 [The Tibetan Political System]. *Meng Zang yuebao* 2, no. 5 (1935): 4–7.

Xizang zizhiqu cehuiju 西藏自治區測繪局. *Xizang zizhiqu ditu ce* 西藏自治區地圖冊 (Tib. *Bod ljongs sa khra'i deb tho*) [Geographical Atlas of the Autonomous Region of Tibet]. Hebei: Zhongguo ditu chubanshe, 1996.

Xizang zizhiqu ditu 西藏自治區地圖 [Map of the Autonomous Region of Tibet]. Beijing: Zhongguo ditu chubanshe, 1980.

Xue Song 雪嵩. *Fojiao faling huibian* 佛教法令彙編 [Laws and Legislation of Buddhism]. Zhongguo fojiaohui, 1948.

Xu Guangzhi 許廣智. "Zhang Yintang chaban Zang shi shimo" 張蔭棠查辦藏事始末 [The Complete Story of Tibetan Administrative Affairs by Zhang Yintang]. *Xizang yanjiu* 2 (1988): 48–55.

Xu Wenshan 徐文珊. *Guofu yijiao sanmin zhuyi zongji* 國父遺教三民主義總輯 [Compilation of the Three Principles of the People (A Teaching Handed Down by Sun Yat-sen)]. Taipei: Zhonghua yeshu, 1960.

Xu Youchun 徐友春. *Minguo renwu da cidian* 民國人物大辭典 [Biographical Dictionary of Chinese Republican Celebrities]. Shijiazhuang: Hebei renmin chubanshe, 1991.

Ya Hanzhang 牙含章. *Banchan E'erdeni zhuan* 班禪額爾德尼傳 [Biography of the Panchen E'erdeni]. Beijing: renmin chubanshe, 1987.

———. *Dalai Lama zhuan* 達賴喇嘛傳 [Biography of the Dalai Lamas]. 1984. Reprint, Beijing: renmin chubanshe, 1988.

Yang Guiming 楊貴明 and Ma Jixiang 馬吉祥. *Zang chuan fojiao gao seng zhuanlüe* 藏傳佛教高僧傳略 [Short Notes on the Great Monks in Tibetan Buddhism]. Xining: Qinghai renmin chubanshe, 1992.

Yangling Duoji 楊嶺多吉. *Sichuan Zang xue yanjiu* 四川藏學研究 [Research on Tibetan Culture in Sichuan]. Beijing: Zhongguo Zangxue chubanshe, 1994.

Yang Xing'an 楊興安. "Huiyi Ganzi shibian jingguo" 回憶甘孜事變經過 [The Events of the Kardzé Affair]. *Ganzi Chuan wenshi ziliao xuanji* 5 (1986): 1–20.

Yang Xirao 楊希繞. *Qinghai fengtu ji* 青海風土記 [Notes on the Customs of Qinghai]. Nanjing: Xinyaxiya xuehui, 1933.

Yao Zhaolin 姚兆麟. "Xizang Gunque Zhongni 1924 nian chengwen xi" 西藏棍卻仲尼 1924 年呈文析 [Concerning the Nomination of Köncho Chungné as Abbot of the Palace of Eternal Harmony in 1924]. In *Xizang shilun wenji*, 79–91. Chengdu: Sichuan minzu chubanshe, 1988.

Yonghegong gai miao 250 zhou nian wenji 永和宮改廟 250 周年文集 [Academic Papers on the 250th Anniversary of the Yonghegong Lamasery]. Beijing: Zhongguo Zangxue, 1994.

Yonghegong guanlichu 雍和宮管理處. *Jing dou mingsha: Yonghe gong* 京都名刹雍和宮 [Palace of Eternal Harmony: Vestige of Beijing]. Beijing: Zhongguo heping, 1993.

Yuan Yifeng 袁一鋒, ed. *Zhongguo Zongjiao mingsheng shidian* 中國宗教名勝事典 [Dictionary of People, Monuments, and Religious Events in China]. Shanghai: Shanghai renmin chubanshe, 1996.

Yu Hanhua 余漢華. "Nei Menggu zizhi yundong zong jiantao" 內蒙古自治運動總檢討 [Analysis of the Movement for the Autonomy of Inner Mongolia]. *Bianshi yanjiu* 3, no. 4 (1936): 42–43.

Yu Lingpo 于凌波. *Zhongguo jin xian dai fojiao renwu zhi* 中國近現代佛教人物志 [Biographical Dictionary of Buddhist Figures from Modern and Contemporary China]. Beijing: Zongjiao wenhua, 1995.

Yushu diaocha ji 玉樹調查記 [Notes Taken during an Inspection in Yushu (in 1726)]. Taipei: Zhongguo fanzhi congshu, 1968.

Yushu jin shi ji 玉樹近事記 [Notes on the Recent Affairs in Yushu]. Qinghai: Nanbu bianqu jingbei siling bu fushe bianshi yuekan shibian 青海南部邊區警備司令部附設邊事月刊社編, 1933.

Yushu xian zhi kao 玉樹縣志考 [Monograph on Yushu District]. Taipei: Zhongguo fangzhi congshu, 1968.

Yu Yize 余貽澤. "Zang jun fan Kang shulüe" 藏軍犯康述略 [Concerning the Invasion of Xikang by the Tibetan Army]. *Yugong* 12, no. 6 (1937): 53–63.

Zang zu shilüe 藏族史略 [The Abridged History of the Tibetan Ethnic Group]. Beijing: Minzu chubanshe, 1985.

Zhang Erju 張爾駒. *Zhongguo minzu quyu zizhi shigang* 中國民族區域自治史綱 [Broad Historical Outline of the Creation of Autonomy for the Ethnic Groups in China]. Beijing: minzu chubanshe, 1995.

Zhang Erxin 張爾新. *Qing dai si da huofo* 清代四大活佛 [Four Great Reincarnated Tibetan Masters from the Qing Era]. Beijing: Zhongguo renmin daxue, 1989.

Zhang Gengjin 張庚金. *Xizang difang xiangtu* 西藏地方詳圖 [Detailed Map of Tibet]. Shanghai: Zhonghua shuju, 1939.

Zhang Husheng 張虎生. "Qingdai zhu Zang fangjun xi" 清代駐藏防軍析 [Analysis of the Manchurian Army Garrison in Tibet During the Manchu Era]. *Xizang yanjiu* 3 (1996): 68–74.

Zhang Jueren 張覺人. "Lamajiao ji Lama yu Ying E guanxi" 喇嘛教及喇嘛與英俄關係 [Lamaism and the Relations among the Monks, the British, and the Russians]. *Bianshi yanjiu* 3, no. 2 (1935): 89–101.

Zhang Pengyuan 張朋園 and Chen Huaiyu 沉懷玉. *Minguo zhengfu zhiguan nianbiao* (1925–1949) 民國政府職官年表 [Chronological Tables of Members of the Nationalist Government by Administrative Post (1925–1949)]. Vol. 1 (shiliao congkan, 6). [Collection of Materials, 6]. Taipei: Zhongyang yanjiuyuan, Jindai shi yanjiusuo, 1987.

Zhang Qiqin 張其勤. *Xizang diaocha ji* 西藏調查記 [Tibetan Inspection Notes]. Shanghai: Shangwu, 1924.

Zhang Ruide 張瑞德. *Kang zhan shiqi de guojun renshi* 康戰時期的國軍人事 [Military Events during the Xikang War]. Taipei: Zhongyang yanjiuyuan jindaishi yanjiusuo, 1993.

Zhang Wengyan 張翁燕. *Qinghai sheng zhi ziliao* 青海省志資料 [Monograph Documents on Qinghai Province]. Taipei: Guofang yanjiuyuan, 1961.

Zhang Xianwen 張憲文 and Huang Meizhen 黃美真, eds. *Nanjing Guomin zhengfu de jianli* 南京國民政府的建立 [The Creation of the Nanjing Republican Government]. Zhenzhou: Henan renmin chubanshe, 1990.

———. *Duan Qirui yu Wan Xi junfa* 段祺瑞与皖系軍閥 [The Warlords Duan Qirui and Wan Xi]. Zhenzhou: Henan renmin chubanshe, 1990.

Zhang Xingtang 張興唐. *Menggu cankao shumu* 蒙古参考書目 [Bibliography of Reference Works on Mongolia]. Taipei: Zhonghua yeshu weiyuanhui, 1958.

Zhang Yisun 張怡荪, ed. *Zang Han da cidian* 藏漢大辭典 (Tib. *Bod rGya tshig mdzod chen mo*) [The Great Tibetan-Chinese Dictionary]. Beijing: Mi rigs dpe skrun khang, 1985.

Zhang Zhongfu 張中復. "Zhongguo zao qi minzu zhengce zhi yanjiu (1921–1949)" 中國早期民族政策之研究 (1921–1949) [Study on the Policy Held Towards the Nationalities as of the Creation of the Chinese Communist Party (1921–1940)]. *Xizang yanjiu huixun* 西藏研究會訊 12 (1991): 3–10.

Zhao Fuliang 趙富良. "Shilun Zhang Yintang chaban Zang shi ji qi zhi Zang fangzhen" 識論張蔭棠查辦藏事及其治藏方針 [Tentative Analysis of Zhang Yintang's Administration of Tibetan Affairs and Measures He Took for the Governor of Tibet]. *Xizang yanjiu* 2 (1992): 20–25.

Zhao Ruheng 趙如珩. *Difang zizhi zhi lilun yu shiji* 地方自治之理論与實際 [Theories and Realities of Regional Autonomy]. Shanghai: Huatong shuju, 1933.

"Zhashelunbu si" 扎什倫布寺 [The Tashilhunpo Monastery]. *Zhongguo Zangxue* 1 (1988): 10.

Zheng Shan 鄭山, ed. *Xizang fazhan shi* 西藏發展史 [History of the Development of Tibet]. Kunming: Yunnan minzu chubanshe, 1992.

Zheng Yunming 鄭允明. "Xizang tujilu zai bu" 西藏圖籍錄再補 [New Supplement to the Bibliography on Tibet]. *Yugong* 12, no. 6 (1937): 95–105.

Zhongguo bianjiang 中國邊彊 [The Chinese Border Regions]. Chongqing, 1942.

Zhongguo di er lishi dang'an guan 中國第二歷史檔案館 [Second Historical Archives of China]. *Feng shi banli Zang shi baogao shu* 奉使辦理藏事報告書 [Compendium of Documents Concerning the Administration of Tibetan Affairs]. Beijing: Zhongguo Zang xue, 1993.

———. *Jiu shi Banchan neidi huodong ji fan Zang shouzu dang'an xuanbian* 九世班禪內地活動及反藏受阻檔案選編 [Compilation of Documents Preserved in the Nanjing Archives Regarding the Activities of the Ninth Panchen Lama in China and the Obstacles to His Return to Tibet]. Nanjing: Zhongguo Zangxue, 1992.

——. "Jiu shi Banchan wei Sun Zhongshan xiansheng feng'an dadian suo zhuan jiwen" 九世班禪為孫中山先生奉安大典所撰祭文 [Funeral Oration for Sun Yat-sen Written by the Panchen Lama]. Beijing: Zhongguo Zang xue,1990.

——. *Jiu shi Banchan yuanji zhiji he shi shi Banchan chuanshi zuochuang dang'an xuanbian* 九世班禪圓寂致祭和十世班禪轉世坐床檔案選編 [Compilation of Documents Preserved in the Nanjing Archives Concerning the Death of the Ninth Panchen Lama and the Enthronement of the Tenth Panchen Lama]. Nanjing: Zhongguo Zangxue, 1991.

——. "Meng Zang weiyuanhui kaifa Kang Zang jiaotong youdian jihua" 蒙藏委員會開發康藏交通郵電計劃 [The Project of the Mongolian and Tibetan Affairs Commission]. *Minguo dang'an* 3 (1992): 3–5.

——. *Shi san shi Dalai yuanji zhiji he shi si shi Dalai chuanshi zuochuang dang'an xuanbian* 十三世達喇圓寂致祭和十四世達喇轉世坐床檔案選編 [Compilation of Documents Stored in the Nanjing Archives Concerning the Funeral of the Thirteenth Dalai Lama and the Enthronement of the Fourteenth Dalai Lama]. Beijing: Zhongguo Zangxue, 1990.

——. *Zhongguo Kangri zhanzheng shi dituji* 中國抗日戰爭史地圖集 [Historical Atlas of China's War of Resistance against Japan]. Beijing: Zhongguo ditu, 1995.

——. "Zhongguo zhengfu fandui Yingguo soushou Xizang ganshe Zhongguo neizheng de yi jian shiliao" 中國政府反對英國搜手西藏干涉中國內政的一件史料 [Historical Document Showing How the Chinese Government Opposed British Control over Tibet and Interference in Chinese Internal Policy]. *Minguo dang'an* 3 (1990): 34.

Zhongguo renmin zhengzhi xiegao huiyi, Nei Menggu zizhiqu weiyuanhui wen shi he xuexi weiyuanhui 中國人民政治協高會義內蒙古自治區委員會文史和學習委員會. *Nei Menggu lamajiao jili* 內蒙古喇嘛教紀例 [Chronicle of Lamaist Buddhism in Inner Mongolia]. Hohhot: Nei Menggu wen shi shudian, 1997.

Zhongguo shehui kexueyuan minzu yanjiusuo 中國社會科學院民族研究所 [Nationalities Department of the Chinese Academy of Social Sciences] and Xizang zizhiqu dang 'an guan 西藏自治區檔案館. [Tibetan Autonomous Region Archives]. *Xizang shehui lishi Zang wen dang'an ziliao yiwenji* 西藏社會歷史藏文檔案資料譯文集 [Compendium of Archival Documents Translated from Tibetan into Chinese]. Beijing: Zhongguo Zangxue, 1997.

Zhongguo shehui kexueyuan minzu yanjiusuo tushu shi and Xizang shehui kexueyuan hanwen wenxian bianji shi 中國社會科學院民族研究所圖書室，西藏社會科學院漢文文獻編輯室. [Library of the Nationalities Department of the Chinese Academy of Social Sciences, Office of the Translation of Chinese Documents of the Tibetan Academy of Social Sciences]. *Zang shi lunwenxuan* 藏事論文選 [Compendium of Theories on Tibetan Affairs]. Xuchang: Xizang renmin chubanshe, 1985.

Zhongguo Zangxue yanjiu zhongxin 中國藏學研究中心. [China Tibetology Research Center] *Zangxue lunwen xuanji* 藏學論文選集 [Compendium of Articles on Tibetology]. Beijing: Zhongguo Zangxue chubanshe, 1996.

Zhonghua renmin gongheguo fensheng dituji 中華人民共和國分省地圖集 [Provincial Atlases of the People's Republic of China]. Beijing: Zhongguo ditu, 1995.

Zhou Guanren 周觀仁. "Goutong Han Zang wenhua" 溝通漢藏文化 [Help the Chinese and Tibetan Cultures Communicate]. *Haichaoyin* 17, no. 6 (1936): 4–8.

Zhou Kuntian 周昆田. "San min zhuyi zhi bianzheng jianshe" 三民主義之邊政建 設 [The Development of Border Region Policy Following the Three Principles of the People]. *Bianzheng gonglun* 1, no. 1 (1941): 5–20. Reprinted in *Bianjiang lunwen ji* [Collection of Articles on the Border Regions] 1 (1964): 681–87.

——. *Sanmin zhuyi zhi bianjiang zhengce* 三民主義之邊彊政策 [The Development of Border Region Policy Following the Three Principles of the People]. Taipei: Meng Zang weiyuanhui, 1984.

Zhou Qingshu 周清澍. *Nei Menggu lishi dili* 內蒙古歷史地理 [Historical Atlas of Inner Mongolia]. Hohhot: Nei Menggu chubanshe, 1993.

Zhou Xiwu 周希武. *Qinghai Yushu diaocha ji* 青海玉樹調查記 [Inspection Report on Yushu, Qinghai]. Taipei: Huawen shuju, 1968.

Zhou Xiyin 周錫銀. "Zhuming Zangxuejia: Gesang qunjue (Liu Jiaju) et Li Anzhai" 箸名藏學家格桑群覺(劉家駒), 李安宅 [Two Famous Tibetologists: Liu Jiaju and Li Anzhai]. *Xizang yanjiu huixun* 西藏研究會訊 [Tibet Research Newsletter] 15 (1993): 1–8.

Zhou Zhenhe 周振鶴. *Qinghai* 青海 [Qinghai]. Changsha: Shangwu, 1939.
Zhu Shaoyi 朱少逸. *Lasa jianwen ji* 拉薩見聞記 [News from Lhasa]. Shanghai: Shangwu yinshuguan, 1947.

Western Sources

Addy, Premen. *Tibet on the Imperial Chessboard: The Making of British Policy Towards Lhasa, 1899–1925*. Calcutta and New Delhi: Academic Publishers, 1984.
Ahmad, Zahiruddin. *Sino-Tibetan Relations in the Seventeenth Century*. Rome: Ismeo, 1970.
Andreev, A. I. *The Buddhist Shrine of Petrograd*. Ulan Ude: EcoArt Agency, 1992.
Andreyev, A. I. "Agwan Dorjiev's Secret Work in Russia and Tibet." *Tibetan Review* (September 1993): 11–14.
Anonymous. *The Boundary Question between China and Tibet: A Valuable Record of the Tripartite Conference between China, Britain, and Tibet Held in India, 1913–1914*. Beijing, 1940.
Arènes, Pierre. *La déesse Drol-ma (Târâ). Recherches sur la nature et le statut d'une divinité du bouddhisme tibétain*. Louvain: Peters, 1996.
Aris, Michael, ed. *Tibetan Studies in Honour of Hugh Richardson. Proceedings of the International Seminar on Tibetan Studies*. Oxford: Oxford University Press, 1979.
——. *Lamas, Princes and Brigands: Joseph Rock's Photographs of the Tibetan Borderlands of China*. New York: China House Gallery, 1992.
Atwood, Christopher. "National Party and Local Politics in Ordos, Inner Mongolia (1926- 1935)." *Journal of Asian History* 26, no. 1 (1992): 1–30.
——. *The Revolutionary Nationalist Mobilization in Inner Mongolia, 1925–1929*. PhD diss., University of Indiana, Bloomington, 1994.
Aubin, Françoise. "Écrits récents sur le Tibet et les Tibétains. Bibliographie commentée." *Cahiers du CERI* 6, 1993.
——. "Mongolie" *Encyclopedia Universalis*. 4e éd. Vol. 15 (1990): 656–84.
——. "Oïrat." *Encyclopedia Universalis*. 2e éd. Vol. 13 (1984): 432–33.
Aziz, Barbara. *Tibetan Frontier Families: Reflections on Three Generations from D'ing-Ri*. New Delhi: Vikas Publishing House Pvt. Ltd., 1978.
Aziz, Barbara and Mathew Kapstein, eds. *Soundings in Tibetan Civilization. Proceedings of the 1982 Seminar of the International Association for Tibetan Studies Held at Columbia University*. New Delhi: Manohar Publications, 1985.
Bacot, Jacques. *Introduction à l'histoire du Tibet*. Paris: Société Asiatique, 1962.
——. *Le Tibet révolté*. Paris: Peuples du Monde, 1988. First published 1912 by Librairie Hachette et cie.
Batbayar, Tsedendambyn. *Modern Mongolia: A Concise History*. Ulaanbaator: Mongolian Center for Scientific and Technological Information, 1996.
Bawden, Charles. *The Modern History of Mongolia*. London: Kegan Paul International, 1989.
Bell, Charles. "The Dalai Lama: Lhasa 1921." *Central Asian Society* 2 (1924): 36–50.
——. *The People of Tibet*. 1928. Reprint, Oxford: Clarendon Press, 1968.
——. *Portrait of a Dalai Lama: The Life and Times of the Great Thirteenth*. London: Wisdom Publications, 1987. First published 1946 by Wm. Collins.
——. *The Religion of Tibet*. Oxford: Clarendon Press, 1931.
——. *Tibet: Past and Present*. 1924. Reprint, London: Oxford University Press, 1968.
Beresford, M. and B. McFarlane. "Regional Inequality and Regionalism in Vietnam and China." *Journal of Contemporary Asia* 25, no. 1 (1995): 50–72.
Berger, Patricia. *Empire of Emptiness: Buddhist Art and Political Authority in Qing China*. Honolulu: University of Hawai Press, 2003.
Bergère, Marie-Claire. *La bourgeoisie chinoise et la révolution de 1911*. La Haye: Mouton, 1968.
——. *L'âge d'or de la bourgeoisie chinoise, 1911–1937*. Paris: Flammarion, 1986.
——. *La Chine au XXe siècle*. Paris: Fayard, 1989.

——. *Sun Yat-sen*. Paris: Fayard, 1994.

——. *Sun Yat-sen*. Translated by Janet Lloyd. Stanford: Stanford University Press, 1998.

Bernbaum, Edwin. *The Way to Shambhala*. New York: Anchor Books, 1980.

Beyer, Stephan. *The Cult of Tārā: Magic and Ritual in Tibet*. Berkeley: University of California Press, 1973.

Bianco, Lucien. *Les origines de la révolution chinoise 1915–1949*. Paris: Gallimard, 1987.

Bishop, Peter. *The Myth of Shangri-la*. Berkeley: University of California Press, 1989.

Blavatsky, Helena. *The Voice of the Silence: Being Extracts from the Book of the Golden Precepts*. Beijing: The Chinese Buddhist Research Society, 1927.

Blofeld, John. *The Jewel in the Lotus*. London: Sidgwick and Jackson Ltd., 1948.

Blondeau, Anne-Marie. "Les Études Tibétaines." *Journal Asiatique* 261, nos. 1/4 (1973): 153–74.

——. "Les religions du Tibet," In *Encyclopédie de la Pléiade*. 3 vols. Extrait de l'histoire des religions, 233–329. Paris: Gallimard, 1971.

Bogle, Georges. *Mission au Bhoutan et au Tibet*. Traduit de l'anglais, présenté et annoté par J. Thevenet. Paris: Kimé, 1996.

——. *Voyages au Thibet, faits en 1625 et 1626 par le père Andrada, et en 1774, 1784, et 1785 par Bogle, Turner et Pourunguir*. Traduit par J. P. Parraud et J. B. Billecoq. Paris: Imprimerie de Hautbout l'aîné, 1796.

Bogoslovskij, Vassilii. A. *Essai sur l'histoire du peuple tibétain ou La naissance d'une société de classes*. Paris: Klincksieck, 1972.

Boorman, Howard L. *Biographical Dictionary of Republican China*. New York: Columbia University Press, 1967.

Bouillard, Georges. *Les temples de Pékin: Le Temple lamaïste de Yung Ho Kung ou Temple des Lamas*. Beijing, 1924.

Boulnois, Luce. "Contexte politique et économique de la mission de George Bogle en 1774–1775." In *Mission au Bhoutan et au Tibet*, 11–29. Paris: Kimé, 1996.

——. *Poudre d'or et monnaies d'argent au Tibet (XVIIIe s.)*. Paris: CNRS, 1983.

——. *La route de la soie*. Paris: Arthaud, 1963.

Boulnois, L., and H. C. Chen. "Le Népal et la Chine en 1732–1734, à propos de trois lettres des rois Newar à l'empereur de Chine." *Journal Asiatique* 260, nos. 1/2 (1972): 131–54.

Boussemart, Marie-Stella. *rJe Shes-rab Seng-ge (1382–1445)*, mémoire de DEA (Études sur l'Extrême-Orient et l'Asie Pacifique). Paris: Inalco, 1993.

Brunnert, H. S., and V. V. Hagelstrom. *Present Day Political Organization of China*. Translated by A. Beltchenko and E. E. Moran. Shanghai: Kelly & Walsh, 1912.

Buffetrille, Katia. "La restauration du monastère de bSam-yas: un exemple de continuité dans la relation de chapelain-donateur au Tibet?" *Journal Asiatique* 278, nos. 3/4 (1989): 363–411.

Bushell, Stephen W. "The Chinese Silver Coinage of Tibet." *China Review* 6 (1878): 348–49.

——. "The Early History of Tibet from Chinese Sources." *Journal of the Royal Asiatic Society*, New Series 12 (1880): 435–541.

Camman, Spencer. "The Panchen Lama's Visit to China in 1780: An Episode in Anglo-Tibetan Relations." *Far Eastern Quarterly* 9 (1949): 3–19.

Carrasco, Pedro. *Land and Polity in Tibet*. Seattle: University of Washington Press, 1959.

Chan, S. W. *Buddhism in Late Ch'ing Political Thought*. Hong Kong: The Chinese University Press, 1985.

Chan, W. T. *Religious Trends in Modern China*. New York: Columbia University Press, 1953.

Chandra, Lokesh. *Materials for a History of Tibetan Literature*. Sata-pitaka series. Indo-Asian literatures, vols. 28–30. New Delhi: International Academy of Indian Culture, 1963.

Chang, K., et al. *A Regional Handbook on the Inner Mongolia Autonomous Region*. Seattle: Far Eastern and Russian Institute, University of Washington, 1956.

Chang, Y. T. *The Economic Development and Prospects of Inner Mongolia (Chahar, Suiyuan, Ningxia)*. Shanghai: Shanghai Commercial Press, 1933.

Chapman, Spencer. *Lhasa, the Holy City*. London: Readers Union Ltd., 1940.

Chayet, Anne. *Art et archéologie du Tibet*. Paris: Picard, 1994.

——. *La femme au temps des Dalai-Lamas*. Paris: Stock-L. Pernoud, 1993.
——. *Les temples de Jehol et leurs modèles tibétains*. Paris: Éditions du CNRS, 1985.
Chen, K. S. *Buddhism in China*. Princeton: Princeton University Press, 1972.
Chen, T. L., and S. C. Liu. *Tibet and the Tibetans*. Stanford: Stanford University Press, 1953.
Chesneaux, Jean. *Sun Yat-sen*. Paris: Éditions complexes, 1982.
Chinese Ministry of Information, ed., *China Handbook 1937–1943*. New York: The Macmillan Company, 1943.
Clubb, Edmond O. *Twentieth Century China*. New York: Columbia University Press, 1978.
Cordier Henri. *Bibliotheca Sinica: Dictionnaire bibliographique des ouvrages relatifs à l'empire chinois*, 5 vols. Paris: E. Guilmoto, 1904–1922.
Cotton, James. *Asian Frontier Nationalism: Owen Lattimore and the American Policy Debate*. Manchester: Studies on East Asia, Manchester University Press, 1989.
Cressey, Babcock G. "Chinese Colonization in Mongolia: A General Survey." *American Geographical Society*, Special Publications 14 (1932): 273–87.
Crossley, Pamela. "Emperorship and Identity in Qing and Nationalist Thought." Paper presented at Columbia University, February 14, 1991.
——. "Thinking about Ethnicity in Early Modern China." *Late Imperial China* 2, no. 1 (1990): 1–34.
Dargyay, Eva K. *Tibetan Village Communities*. New Delhi: Vikas Publishing House PVT Ltd., 1982.
Das, Sarat Chandra. "Daily Religious Service in the Grand Monastery of Tashi-lhunpo." *Journal of the Buddhist Text Society of India* 1, no. 4 (1893): 13–16.
——. "The Lives of Panchen Rimpoches or Tashi Lamas." In *Tibetan Studies*, ed. A. Chattopadhyaya, 97–141. Calcutta and Delhi: K. P. Bagchi & Co., 1984. First published in 1882 by the *Journal of the Asiatic Society of Bombay*.
——. *Journey to Lhasa and Central Tibet*. New Delhi: Mañjuśri Publications, 1970. First published 1902 by J. Murray.
——. *A Tibetan-English Dictionary with Sanskrit Synonyms*. New Delhi: Academy of Indian Culture and Aditya, 1888; reissued 1992.
——. *Tibetan Studies*. Edited by A. Chattopadhyaya. Calcutta: K. P. Bagchi & Co., 1984.
David-Neel, Alexandra. *With Mystics and Magicians in Tibet*. Paultron (Somerset) and London: Penguin Books Ltd., 1936.
Day, Clarence B. *Popular Religion in Pre-Communist China*. San Francisco: Chinese Materials Center, 1975.
Department of Statistics. *Prices and Wages in India*. Published by the Order of the Governor-General in Council, Superintendant Government Printing, Calcutta, 1923.
Dhamala, R. R. "Political Status of Tibet up to 1950." *The Himalayan Miscellany* (March 1989): 46–56.
Dhondup, K. *The Water-Horse and Other Years: A History of Seventeenth and Eighteenth Century Tibet*. Dharamsala: Library of Tibetan Works and Archives, 1984.
——. *The Water-Bird and Other Years*. New Delhi: Rangwang Publishers, 1986.
Dikotter, Frank. *The Discourse of Race in Modern China*. Hong Kong: Hong Kong University Press, 1992.
——. *The Construction of Racial Identities in China and Japan: Historical and Contemporary Perspectives*. London: C. Hurst, 1997.
Diskalabar, D. B. "Bogle's Embassy to Tibet." *Indian Historical Quarterly* 9, no. 2 (1933): 420–38.
Dittmer, L., and S. S. Kim. *China's Quest for National Identity*. London: Cornell University Press, 1993.
Dreyer, Edward L. *China at War 1901–1949*. London: Longman, 1995.
Eastman, Lloyds E. *The Abortive Revolution: China under Nationalist Rule, 1927–1937*. Cambridge: Harvard University Press, 1990.
——. *Chiang Kai-shek's Secret Past: The Memoir of His Second Wife, Ch'en Chieh-ju*. Boulder: Westview Press, 1993.
——. *Seeds of Destruction: Nationalist China in War and Revolution, 1937–1949*. Stanford: Stanford University Press, 1984.
Eekeln, W. F. "Simla Convention and McMahon Line." *Journal of the Royal Central Asian Society* 54, no. 2 (1967): 179–84.

Ekvall, Robert. *Cultural Relations on the Kansu-Tibetan Border*. Chicago: The University of Chicago Press, 1939.

Engelhardt, Isrun. "Tharchin's Yul-phyogs so-so'i gsar-'gyur me-loṅ." *Sonderheft Nr. 22 der Ostasienabteilung* (2010): 1-22.

Ewing, Thomas E. *Between the Hammer and the Anvil? Chinese and Russian Policies in Outer Mongolia, 1911–1921*. Bloomington: Indiana University Press, 1980.

Fisher, M. W., and L. E. Rose. *England, India, Nepal, Tibet, China 1765–1958: A Synchronistic Table Showing the Succession of Heads of State and Other Political and Diplomatic Personages of Importance in These Countries along with Nepali Tributary Missions to China*. Berkeley: University of California, 1959.

Fleming, Peter. *Bayonets to Lhasa*. Oxford: Oxford University Press, 1961.

Fletcher, Joseph. *China's Inner Asian Frontier: Photographs of the Wulsin Expedition to Northwest China in 1923*, edited by M. E. Alonso, 43–51. Harvard: Harvard University Press, 1979.

——. "Ch'ing Inner Asia c. 1800." In *The Cambridge History of China*. Vol. 10: *Late Ch'ing 1800–1911*, edited by J. K. Fairbank, 351–408. Cambridge: Cambridge University Press, 1978.

Fogel, J. "Race and Class in Chinese Historiography: Divergent Interpretations of Zhang Binglin and Anti-Manchuism in the 1911 Revolution." *Modern China* 3, no. 3 (1977): 346–75.

Forte, Antonio. "Daishi," in *Hôbôgirin*, edited by Anna Seidel, vol. 7. Paris and Tokyo, 1994.

French, Patrick. *Younghusband: The Last Great Imperial Adventurer*. London: Harper Collins, 1994.

French, Rebecca Redwood. *The Golden Yoke: The Legal Cosmology of Buddhist Tibet*. Ithaca and London: Cornell University Press, 1995.

Friedman, Edward. "Reconstructing China's National Identity: A Southern Alternative to Mao-Era Anti-Imperialist Nationalism." *The Journal of Asian Studies* 53, no. 1 (1994): 67–91.

Gaboriau, Marc. *Récit d'un voyageur musulman au Tibet*. Paris, 1973.

Gar Je, K'am trül Rinpoche. "A Geography and History of Shambhala." *The Tibet Journal* 3, no. 3 (1978): 3–11.

Gasster, M. *Chinese Intellectuals and the Revolution of 1911: The Birth of Chinese Radicalism*. Seattle: University of Washington, 1969.

Gelek, S. W. "Government Monastics and Private Taxation in Tibet." *The Tibet Journal* 11, no. 1 (1986): 21–40.

——. "Tibet: The Critical Years (Part II), The Sixth Panchen Lama." *The Tibet Journal* 8, no. 1 (1983): 20–29.

Gillard, David. *The Struggle for Asia, 1828–1914: A Study in British and Russian Imperialism*. London: Methuen & Co., 1977.

Gillin, Donald G. *Warlord Yen Hsi-shan in Shansi Province, 1911–1949*. Princeton: Princeton University Press, 1967.

Gladney, Dru C. "Representing Nationality in China: Refiguring Majority/Minority Identities." *The Journal of Asian Studies* 53, no. 1 (1994): 92–123.

Goldfuss, Gabriele. *Vers un bouddhisme du XXe siècle. Yang Wenhui (1837–1911): réformateur laïque et imprimeur*. Paris: Collège de France, Institut des hautes études chinoises, 2001.

Goldstein, Melvyn C. "The Balance between Centralization and Decentralization in the Traditional Tibetan Political System: An Essay on the Nature of Tibetan Political Macro-Structure." *Central Asiatic Journal* 10, no. 3 (1971): 170–82.

——. "The Circulation of Estates in Tibet: Reincarnation, Land and Politics." *Journal of Asian Studies* 32, no. 3 (1973): 445–55.

——. *A History of Modern Tibet, 1913–1951: The Demise of the Lamaist State*. Berkeley: University of California Press, 1989.

——. *Nomads of Western Tibet: The Survival of a Way of Life*. London: Serindia, 1990.

——. "Reexamining Choice, Dependency, and Command in the Tibetan Social System: 'Tax Appendages' and Other Landless Serfs." *The Tibet Journal* 11, no. 4 (1986): 79–112.

——. "Serfdom and Mobility: An Examination of the Institution of Human Lease in Traditional Tibetan Society." *Journal of Asian Studies* 30, no. 3 (1971): 521–34.

——. *The Snow Lion and the Dragon: China, Tibet, and the Dalai Lama*. Berkeley: University of California Press, 1997.

——. *Tibetan-English Dictionary of Modern Tibetan*. Kathmandu: Ratna Pustak Bhandar, 1983.

Goldstein, Melvyn C., W. Siebenschuh, and T. Tsering. *The Struggle for Modern Tibet: The Autobiography of Tashi Tsering*. Armonk: M. E. Sharpe, 1997.

Goodman, David S. G. "Jinjiluyu in the Sino-Japanese War: The Border Region and the Border Region Government." *The China Quarterly* 140 (1994): 1007–22.

Goswami, P. K. *Indian Currency and Exchange 1835–1940*. New Delhi: Milind Publications Private Limited, 1983.

Guo Qing. "A Brief Account of the Ninth Panchen Erdeni." *Tibet Studies* 1 (1989): 70–82.

Hedin, Sven. *Adventurer in Tibet*. Leipzig: F. A. Brockhams, 1912.

——. *Le Tibet dévoilé*. Paris: Librairie Hachette, 1910.

——. *Trans-Himalaya: Discoveries and Adventures in Tibet, 1909–1913*. London: McMillan & Co., 1910.

Hidden Tradition: Life Inside the Great Tibetan Monastery Tashilhunpo. Beijing: Foreign Languages Press, 1993.

History of Chinese Currency (Sixteenth Century-Twentieth Century AD), A. Hong Kong: Xinhua Publishing House, 1983.

Houn, Franklin W. *Central Government of China 1912–1928: An Institutional Study*. Madison: University of Wisconsin Press, 1959.

Huc, Régis-Evariste. *Souvenirs d'un voyage dans la Tartarie et le Thibet*. Paris: l'Astrolabe-Peuples du Monde, 1987. First published in 2 vols. in 1850 by Le Clere et Cie as *Souvenirs d'un voyage dans la Tartarie, le Thibet et la Chine pendant les années 1844, 1845, et 1846*. Reprinted Beijing: Imprimerie des Lazaristes, 1924.

Hucker, Charles O. *A Dictionary of Official Titles in Imperial China*. Stanford: Stanford University Press, 1985.

Hu Jianzhong. "La Cité interdite, centre du pouvoir politique de la société féodale chinoise." In *La Cité Interdite: Vie publique et privée des empereurs de Chine (1644–1911)*. Paris: Réunion des Musées nationaux, 1996.

Hummel, Arthur W. *Eminent Chinese of the Ch'ing Period*. Taipei: Ch'eng-wen, 1967. First published in 1943 by U.S. Government Printing Office.

Hyer, Paul. "Demchugdungrub: Nationalist Leader in Inner Mongolia's Confrontation with China and Japan." In *30th International Congress of Human Sciences in Asia and South Africa*, edited by Luz M. Martínez Montiel, 64–71. Mexico, D.F.: Colegio de México, 1976.

Hyer, Paul, and Sechin Jagchid. *A Mongolian Living Buddha: Biography of the Kanjurwa Khutughtu*. Albany: State University of New York, 1983.

Imbault-Huart, C. "Histoire de la conquête du Népal par les Chinois sous le règne de Qianlong (1792)." *Journal Asiatique* 7, no. 12 (1878): 348–77

Jagchid, Sechin. *Essays in Mongolian Studies*. Monograph Series, David M. Kennedy Center for International Studies, 3. Provo, Utah: Brigham Young University, 1988.

——. "A Handwritten Letter of Prince Demchughdongrub." In *Mongolian Studies* (1990): 19–45.

——. "Inner Mongolia under Japanese Occupation, 1935–1945: An Eyewitness Report." *Zentralasiatische Studien* 21 (1987): 149–72.

Jagou, Fabienne. "Etude des toponymes choisis par les Mandchous pour définir le territoire tibétain," *Études Tibétaines en l'honneur d'Anne Chayet*, éd. Achard, 127–46. Paris: École Pratique des Hautes Études, 2010.

——. "A Pilgrim's Progress: The Peregrinations of the Sixth Panchen Lama." *Lungta* 10 (1996): 12–23.

——. "Une histoire politique du Tibet, de l'époque du premier Panchen Lama à celle du 7e / 10e (1570 à 1989)," thesis submitted for the Diplôme d'Études Approfondies (D.E.A.), Paris, École des Hautes Études en Sciences Sociales, 1991.

———. "Recherches préliminaires sur les biographies de maîtres tibétains et mongols ayant vécu en Chine à l'époque moderne." *Les Cahiers d'Extrême-Asie* 15 (2005): 277–82.

———. "Review of G. Tuttle's *Tibetan Buddhists in the Making of Modern China*. New York: Columbia University Press, 2005." *Revue d'Etudes Tibétaines* 16 (2009): 83–94.

———. "The Thirteenth Dalai Lama's Visit to Peking in 1908: In Search of a New Kind of Chaplain-Donor Relationship." In *Buddhism between China and Tibet*, ed. M. Kapstein, 349–378. Boston: Wisdom, 2009.

———. "Les traductions tibétaines des discours politiques chinois de Sun Yat-sen sur les Trois Principes du Peuple en tant qu'exemple de traduction moderne d'un texte politique." In *Edition, éditions: l'écrit au Tibet, évolution et devenir*, éds. Chayet et al., 163–83. Munich: Indus Verlag, 2010.

———. "The Use of the Ritual of Drawing Lots for the Selection of the 11th Panchen Lama," forthcoming.

Kapp, R. A. *Szechuan and the Chinese Republic: Provincial Militarism and Central Power, 1911–1938*. New Haven and London: Yale University Press, 1973.

Karma Gelek Yuthok, Venerable. "Dawn of Modern Tibet: The Thirteenth Dalai Lama." In *Zhonghua Minguo Meng Zang xueshu huiyi lunwenji* 中華民國蒙藏學術會議論文集 [World Conference on Mongolian and Tibetan Studies, Republic of China] (some articles in English), edited by Meng Zang xueshu yanjiu zhongxin, Zhongguo wenhua daxue, 651–60. Taipei: Zhongguo wenhua da xue, 1986.

Kasuga, P. "Môko ramabyô chôsa hôkoku" [Report on the Mongol Lamaseries]. *Tôhô Shûkyô* 35 (1970): 49–65. In Japanese.

Kawaguchi, Ekai. *Three Years in Tibet*. London: Theosophical Society, 1909.

———. *Tibetan Materials in the Collection of Kawaguchi Ekai*. Tokyo: Tohoku University, Department of Oriental and Japanese Art History, 1986.

Kimura, Hisao. *Japanese Agent in Tibet*. London: Serindia, 1990.

Klein, D. W., and A. B. Clark. *Biographic Dictionary of Chinese Communism, 1921–1965*. Cambridge: Harvard University Press, 1971.

Kolmas, Joseph. *The Ambans and Assistant Ambans of Tibet (A Chronological Study)*. Prague: The Oriental Institute, 1994.

———. *Chinese Studies on Tibetan Culture*. New Delhi: International Academy of Indian Culture, 1983. A facsimile reproduction of the K'ang-Tsang yen-chiu yüeh k'an.

———. *Tibet and Imperial China: A Survey of Sino-Tibetan Relations up to the End of the Manchu Dynasty in 1912*. Canberra: Australian National University, Centre of Oriental Studies, 1967.

Kuhn, Philip A. "Local Self-Government under the Republic." In *Conflict and Control in Late Imperial China*, edited by F. Wakeman and C. Grant, 257–338. London: University Press of California, 1975.

———. "Ideas behind China's Modern State." *Harvard Journal of Asiatic Studies* 55, no. 2 (1995): 295–338.

Kuleshov, Nicolai. "Agvan Dorjiev: The Dalai Lama's Ambassador." *Asian Affairs* 23, no. 1 (1992): 20–33.

Kuloy, Hallvard K. and Y. Imaeda. *Bibliography of Tibetan Studies*. Narita: Naritasam Shinshoji, 1986.

Kvaerne, Per, ed. "Remarques sur l'administration d'un monastère bon-po." *Journal Asiatique* 258 (1970): 187–92.

Lamb, Alastair. *The China-India Border: The Origins of the Disputed Boundaries*. London: Oxford University Press, 1964.

———. *The McMahon Line: A Study in the Relation between India, China and Tibet, 1904 to 1914*. London: Routledge and Kegan Paul, 1966.

Landon, Parcival. *À Lhasa: la ville interdite*. Paris: Librairie Hachette et cie, 1906.

Landor, Arnold H. *In the Forbidden Land*. London: William Heinemann, 1898.

Lattimore, Owen. "Chinese Colonization in Inner Mongolia: Its History and Present Development." *American Geographic Society* 14 (1932): 288–312.

———. *Inner Asian Frontier of China*. London: Oxford University Press, 1940.

———. *The Mongols of Manchuria: Their Tribal Divisions Geographical Distribution, Historical Relations with Manchus and Chinese, and Present Political Problems*. New York: John Day, 1934.

———. *Nationalism and Revolution in Mongolia*. New York: Oxford University Press, 1955.

———. *Nomads and Commissars: Mongolia Revisited*. New York: Oxford University Press, 1962.

——. *Studies in Frontier History: Collected Papers, 1928–1958.* London: Oxford University Press, 1962.
Lattimore, O., and I. Fujiko. *The Diluv Khutagt: Memoirs and Autobiography of a Mongol Buddhist Reincarnation in Religion and Revolution.* Wiesbaden: Otto Harrassowitz, 1982.
Lee, Wei Kuo. "Tibet in Modern World Politics (1774–1922)," submitted in partial fulfillement of the requirements for the degree of doctor of philosophy. New York, 1931.
Legg, W. and E. T. Williams, eds. *The Dictionary of National Biography, 1941–1950.* Oxford: Oxford University Press, 1959.
Leroi, R. *La politique monétaire anglaise dans l'Inde: pourquoi et comment les Anglais veulent stabiliser la roupie.* Paris: Marcel Giard, 1928.
Lesdain, J. de. "With Tashi Lama in India." *Calcutta Review,* April 1907, 205–28.
——. "Visit to the Court of the Tashi Lama." *Nineteenth Century* 59 (1906): 255–70.
Lessing, Ferdinand D. *Yung-ho-kung, Iconography of the Lamaist cathedral in Peking.* Vol. 1. Stockholm, 1942.
Leung, E. "Regional Autonomy versus Central Authority: The Inner Mongolian Autonomy." *Journal of Oriental Studies* 25, no. 1 (1987): 49–62.
Lhalu Tséwang Dorjé. "Lungshar, My Father." In *The Water-bird Year,* ed. K. Dhondup, 163–172. New Delhi: Rangwang Publishers, 1986.
Ligeti, Louis, ed. *Rapport préliminaire d'exploration fait en Mongolie Chinoise, 1921–1931.* Budapest: Kôrösi-Csoma, 1933.
——. *Proceedings of the Csoma de Köros* [Memorial Symposium]. Budapest: Akademiai Kiado, 1978.
Linebarger, Paul M. A. *The Political Doctrines of Sun Yat-sen: An Exposition of the San Min-chu I.* Westport: Hyperion Press, 1973.
Lipman, Jonathan N. "Ethnicity and Politics in Republican China: The Ma Family Warlords of Gansu." *Modern China* 10, no. 3 (1984): 285–316.
Lipton, B. *Westerners in Tibet, 1327–1950: A Selected Annotated Bibliography.* New York: Newark Museum, 1973.
Li, Tieh-Tseng (Li Tiezheng). *The Historical Status of Tibet.* New York: King's Crown Press, Columbia University, 1956.
——. *Tibet, Today and Yesterday.* New York: Bookman Association, 1960.
Liu, S. "A Memorial to the Ninth Bainqen Lama." *China's Tibet* 2 (1994): 36–37.
Loewe, Michael. "China's Sense of Unity as Seen in the Early Empires." *T'oung pao* 80 (1994): 6–26.
Lowenthal, Rudolph. *The Religious Periodical Press in China.* San Francisco: Chinese Materials Center, 1978.
Macdonald, Alexander W. "Remarks on the Manipulation of Power and Authority in the High Himalaya." *The Tibet Journal* 12, no. 1 (1987): 3–16.
Macdonald, Ariane. "Une lecture des Pelliot 1286, 1287, 1038, 1047 et 1290. Essai sur la formation et l'emploi des mythes politiques dans la religion royale de Srong-bcan sgam-po." In *Études Tibétaines dédiées à la mémoire de Marcelle Lalou,* éd. A. Macdonald, 190–391. Paris: Maisonneuve, 1971.
——. "Un portrait du 5e Dalai Lama avec la collaboration de Dvags-po rimpoche et Yon-tan Rgya-mtsho." In *Essais sur l'art du Tibet,* éd. A. Macdonald and Y. Imaeda, 119–56. Paris: Librairie d'Amérique et d'Orient, 1977.
Macdonald, David. *The Land of the Lama.* London: Seeley Service and Co., 1929.
——. *Twenty Years in Tibet.* London: Seeley, 1932.
Magniac, C. "A Visit to the Court of the Tashi Lama." *Nineteenth Century* 59 (1906): 255–70.
Ma Hetian. *Chinese Agent in Mongolia.* Translated and edited by John de Francis. Baltimore: John Hopkins Press, 1949.
Markham, C. R., *Narratives of the Mission of George Bogle to Tibet and of the Journey of Thomas Manning to Lhasa.* London, 1876. Reprinted, New Delhi: Bibliotheca Himalayica, 1971.
Marshall, Julie. *Britain and Tibet, 1765–1947.* Bundoora: La Trobe University Library, 1977.
Martin, Dan. *Tibetan Histories: A Bibliography of Tibetan-Language Historical Works.* London: Serindia, 1997.

Mathews, Robert H. *Chinese-English Dictionary*. Shanghai: China Inland Mission and Presbyterian Mission Press, 1931.
Mayers, William F. *The Chinese Government*. Shanghai: Kelly and Walsh, 1886.
McCord, Edward A. "Warlordism at Bay: Civil Alternatives to Military Rule in Early Republican China." *Republican China* 17, no. 1 (1991): 38–69.
——. *The Power of the Gun: The Emergence of Modern Chinese Warlordism*. Berkeley: University of California Press, 1993.
McCormack, Gavan. *Chang Tso-lin in Northeast China, 1911–1928: China, Japan, and the Manchurian Idea*. Stanford: Stanford University Press, 1977.
McGovern, William M. *Mon voyage secret à Lhasa*. Translated by V. Marcel. Paris, 1926.
——. *To Lhasa in Disguise: A Secret Expedition through Mysterious Tibet*. Delhi: Book Faith India, 1992. First published 1924 by Grosset & Dunlap.
McKay, Alex. *Tibet and the British Raj: The Frontier Cadre 1904–1947*. London: Curzon, 1997.
Mehra, Parshotam. "Beginnings of the Lhasa Expedition: Younghusband's Own Words." *Bulletin of Tibetology* 4, no. 3 (1967): 9–18.
——. "The Dalai and the Panchen: Tibet's Supreme Incarnate Lamas." *India Quarterly* 15, no. 3 (1959): 262–89.
——. "Lu Hsing-chi: The Simla Conference and After." In *Études tibétaines, Actes du XXIXe Congrès international des Orientalistes, section organisée par Ariane Macdonald*, 43–49. Paris: L'Asiathèque, 1976.
——. *The MacMahon Line and After*. Delhi: Macmillan, 1974.
——. "Tibet and Outer Mongolia *vis-à-vis* China, 1911–1936." *Journal of Indian History* 49 (1964): 727–61.
——. *Tibetan Polity, 1904–1937: The Conflict between the Thirteenth Dalai Lama and the Ninth Panchen Lama*. Wiesbaden: Otto Harrassowitz, 1976.
——. "The Younghusband Expedition: An Interpretation." *Journal of Indian History* 33, no. 2 (1955): 137–62.
Meienberger, Norbert. *The Emergence of Constitutional Government in China (1905–1908)*. Bern: Peter Lang, 1980.
Meisezahl, R. O. "Catalogue des biographies des cinq Panchen Lama et d'autres xylographes tibétains (collection Bacot) conservés au Centre d'études tibétaines du Collège de France, Instituts d'Asie, à Paris." *Oriens* 31 (1988): 240–53.
Meng, C. Y. "Miss Liu's Mission to Tibet." *China Weekly Review* 55 (1930): 22–24.
Michael, Franz H. *Rule by Incarnation: Tibetan Buddhism and Its Role in Society and State*. Boulder, CO: Westview Press, 1982.
Migot, André. *Visages de la Chine éternelle*. Paris: Société continentale d'éditions modernes illustrées, 1964.
Miller, Beatrice. D. "Is there Tibetan Culture(s) without Buddhism?" In *Anthropology of Tibet and the Himalaya*, ed. C. Ramble and M. Brauen, 222–28. Zurick: Ethnological Museum of the University of Zurick, 1993.
——. "A Response to Goldstein's 'Reexamining Choice, Dependency and Command in the Tibetan Social System.'" *The Tibet Journal* 12, no. 2 (1987): 66–67.
Miller, Robert J., *Monasteries and Culture Change in Inner Mongolia*. Wiesbaden: Otto Harrassowitz, 1959.
Montgomerie, T. G. "Journey to Shigatse in Tibet and Return by Dingri, Maidan into Nepaul, in 1871." *Journal of the Royal Geographical Society*, 1875, 330–50.
Morgan, G. *Anglo-Russian Rivalry in Central Asia: 1810–1895*, London: Frank Cass, 1981.
Mortari, Vergera, and G. Beguin, eds. *Demeures des hommes, Sanctuaires des dieux*. Paris: Musée Guimet, 1987.
Nathan, Andrew J. "A Constitutional Republic: The Peking Government, 1916–1928." In *The Cambridge History of China*. Vol. 12, Part 1, *Republican Era 1912–1949*, edited by J. K. Fairbank, 259–83. Cambridge: Cambridge University Press, 1986.
Nations et Nationalismes. Paris: La Découverte, 1995.

Newman, John R. "A Brief History of the Kālacakra." In *The Wheel of Time: The Kālacakra in Context*, edited by Geshe Lhundup Sopa, 51–90. Madison: Deer Park Books, 1985.

Norbu, D. "An Analysis of Sino-Tibetan Relationships, 1245–1911: Imperial Power, Non-Coercive Regime, and Military Dependancy." In *Soundings in Tibetan Civilization. Proceedings of the 1982 Seminar of the International Association for Tibetan Studies held at Columbia University*, edited by B. Aziz and M. Kapstein, 176–95. New Delhi: Manohar Publications, 1985.

Onon, Urgunge, trans. *Mongolian Heroes of the Twentieth Century*. New York: AMS Press, 1976.

Perleberg, Max. *Who's Who in Modern China*. Hong Kong: Ye Olde Printerie, 1954.

Petech, Luciano. *Aristocracy and Government in Tibet, 1728–1959*. Rome: Istituto Italiano per il medio ed estremo oriente, 1973.

——. "China and the European Travellers to Tibet, 1860–1880." *T'oung pao* 62, nos. 4/5 (1976): 219–52.

——. *China and Tibet in the Early Eighteenth Century: History of the Chinese Protectorate in Tibet*. Leiden: E. J. Brill, 1950.

——. "The Dalai Lamas and Regents of Tibet: A Chronological Study." *T'oung pao* 47, nos. 3/5 (1959): 368–94.

——. "The Missions of Bogle and Turner According to the Tibetan Texts." *T'oung pao* 39, nos. 4/5 (1949): 330–46.

——. "Notes on Tibetan History of the Eighteenth Century." *T'oung pao* 52, nos. 4/5 (1965–66): 261–92.

Petit Larousse illustré. Paris: Larousse, 2007.

Pittman, Don A. *Toward a Modern Chinese Buddhism: Taixu's Reforms*. Honolulu: University of Hawai'i Press, 2001.

Poster Memorandum on the Causes of the Departure of Panchen Chöki Nyima, Tibetan Council of Ministers, 1923. In Tibetan.

Pratt, James B. *The Pilgrimage of Buddhism*. London: Macmillan and Co, 1928.

Rahul, Ram. *The Government and Politics of Tibet*. New Delhi: Vikas Publishing House Pvt. Ltd., 1969.

——. "The Government of Tibet." *International Studies* 4, no. 2 (1962): 169–93.

Ray, R. A. "Some Aspects of the Tulku Tradition in Tibet." *The Tibet Journal* 2, no. 4 (1986): 35–69.

Richardson, Hugh, trans. *Ancient Historical Edicts at Lhasa*. London: Royal Asiatic Society, 1952.

——. *Ceremonies of the Lhasa Year*. London: Serindia Publications, 1993.

——. *Ch'ing Dynasty Inscriptions at Lhasa*. Rome: Ismeo, 1974.

——. *High Peaks, Pure Earth, Collected Writings on Tibetan History and Culture*. London: Serindia, 1998.

——. "Ministers of the Tibetan Kingdom." *The Tibet Journal* 2, no. 1 (1977): 10–27.

——. "A Scandal at Tashilhunpo."*Bulletin of Tibetology* 1 (1978): 24–25.

——. "The Sino-Tibetan Treaty Inscription of A.D. 821/823 at Lhasa." *Journal of the Royal Asiatic Society* 2 (1978): 137–62.

——. *Tibet and its History*. 2nd ed., revised and enlarged. Boston: Shambala, 1984. First published 1962 by Oxford University Press.

Rockhill, William W. "The Dalai Lamas of Lhasa and their Relations with the Manchu Emperors of China 1644–1908." *T'oung pao* 11 (1910): 1–104.

——. *Diary of a Journey through Mongolia and Tibet in 1891 and 1892*. Washington: Smithsonian Institution, 1894.

——. *The Land of the Lamas: Notes of a Journey through China, Mongolia, and Tibet*. London: Longmans, 1891.

——. "Tibet: A Geographical Ethnographical and Historical Sketch Derived from Chinese Sources." *Journal of the Royal Asiatic Society of Great-Britain and Ireland* (1891): 1–133, and 185–291.

Rona-Tas, A. "On a Term of Taxation in the Old Tibetan Royal Annals." In *Proceedings of the Csoma de Köros* (Memorial Symposium), edited by L. Ligeti, 357. Budapest: Akademiai Kiado, 1978.

Roux, Alain. *La Chine au XXe siècle*. Paris: Sedes, 1998.

Ruegg, David S. "Mchod-yon, Yon-mchod and mchod-gnas/yon-gnas: On the Historiography and Semantics of a Tibetan Religio-social and Religio-political Concept." In *Tibetan History and*

Language. Studies Dedicated to Uray Géza on His Seventieth Birthday, Wiener Studies zur Tibetologie und Buddhismuskunde, edited by Ernst Steinkellner, 441–53. Wien: Universität Wien, 1991.

——. *Ordre spirituel et ordre temporel dans la pensée bouddhique de l'Inde et du Tibet*. Paris: Collège de France (Institut de Civilisation indienne, quatre conférences au Collège de France, fasc. 64), 1994.

Rupen, Robert A. *Mongols of the Twentieth Century*. Uralic and Altaïc Series, 37. Bloomington: Indiana University, 1964.

Samuel, Geoffrey. *Civilized Shamans: Buddhism in Tibetan Societies*. Washington: Smithsonian Collection, 1993.

Sandjorj, M. *Manchu Chinese Colonial Rule in Northern Mongolia*. London: C. Hurst, 1980.

Sangay, Thubten, comp. and Tsepak Rigzin, trans. "Glossary of 'Government Monastic and Private Taxation in Tibet.'" *The Tibet Journal* 11, no. 1 (1986): 41–47.

Schmid, Tony. *Saviours of Mankind II: Panchen Lamas and Former Incarnations of Amitayus*. The Sven Hedin Foundation, Ethnography 10. Stockholm: Statens Etnografiska Museum, 1964.

Serruhys, Henry. "An Imperial Restoration in Ordos, 1916–1917." *Études Mongoles et Sibériennes* 16 (1985): 51–59.

Shakabpa, Tsepon W. D. *Tibet: A Political History*. New Haven and London: Yale University Press, 1967. Reprint, New York: Potala Publications, 1988.

Shakya, Tsering. *The Dragon in the Land of Snows: A History of Modern Tibet since 1947*. London: Pimlico, 1999.

Shastri, Jampa-Samten, ed. *Catalogue of the Library of Tibetan Works and Archives*. Vol. 1, Historical Works. Dharamsala: Library of Tibetan Works and Archives, 1983.

Shastri, Lobsang, ed. *Catalogue of the Library of Tibetan Works and Archives*. Vol. 2, Historical Works. Dharamsala: Library of Tibetan Works and Archives, 1990.

Sheel, R. N. "The Institution of the Dalai Lama." *The Tibet Journal* 14, no. 3 (1989): 19–32.

Sheridan, James E. *Chinese Warlord: The Career of Feng Yü-hsiang*. Stanford: Stanford University Press, 1966.

——. *China in Disintegration: The Republican Era in Chinese History, 1912–1949*. New York: Free Press, 1975.

Singh, A. K. *Himalayan Triangle: A Historical Survey of British India's Relations with Tibet, Sikkim, and Bhutan 1765–1950*. London: The British Library, 1988.

——. *A Guide to Source Materials in the India Office Library and Records for the History of Tibet, Sikkim and Bhoutan 1765–1950*. London: The British Library, 1988.

Skinner William G. *Modern Chinese Society: An Analytical Bibliography*. 3 vols. Palo Alto, California: Stanford University Press, 1973.

Smith, E. Gene. *The Autobiography of the First Panchen Lama, Blo-bzang Chös-kyi-rgyal-mtshan*. New Delhi: Ngawang Gélèk Demo, 1969.

Smith, Warren W., Jr., *Tibetan Nation: A History of Tibetan Nationalism and Sino-Tibetan Relations*. Boulder: Westview Press, 1996.

Snellgrove, D., and H. Richardson. *A Cultural History of Tibet*. London: Weidenfeld and Nicolson, 1968. Reprint, Boston: Shambala, 1986.

——. *Indo-Tibetan Buddhism*. 2 vols. Boston: Shambala, 1987.

Snelling, John. *Buddhism in Russia: The Story of Agvan Dorzhiev, Lhasa's Emissary to the Tsar*. London: Shaftesbury, 1993.

Sperling, Elliot. "Chinese Venture in K'am, 1904–1911 and the Role of Zhao Erfeng." *The Tibet Journal* 1, no. 2 (1976): 10–36.

Stein, Rolf Aurel. *La civilisation tibétaine*. Paris: Dunod, 1962.

Steinkielner, E., and H. Tauscher, eds. *Contributions on Tibetan Language, History and Culture: Proceedings of the Csoma de Körös Symposium Held at Velm-Vienna, Austria, 13–19 September 1981*. Vienna, 1983.

Stoddard, Heather. "The Long Life of rDo-sbis dGe-bshes Shes-rab rGya-mtsho (1884–1968)." In *Tibetan Studies. Proceedings of the 4th Seminar of the International Association for Tibetan Studies*, edited by Helga Uebach and Jampa L. Panglung, 465–71. Munich: Kommission fur Zentralasiatische Studien, 1988.

——. *Le mendiant de l'Amdo*. Paris: Société d'Ethnographie, 1985.

Suleski, Ronald Stanley. *The Modernization of Manchuria: An Annotated Bibliography*. Hong Kong: The Chinese University Press, 1994.

Sun Yat-sen. *San Min Chu I*. Translated by F. W. Price. Taipei: Government Information Office, 1990.

Surkhang, W. G. "Government, Monastic and Private Taxation in Tibet." *The Tibet Journal* 11, no. 1 (1986): 21–40

——. "Tax Measurement and *Lag-'don* Tax in Tibet." *The Tibet Journal* 9, no. 1 (1984): 20–30.

——. "Tibet: The Critical Years: 'The Regent Reting Rinpoche.'" *The Tibet Journal* 8, no. 2 (1983): 33–39.

——. "Tibet: The Critical Years: 'The Sixth Panchen Lama.'" *The Tibet Journal* 8, no. 2 (1983): 20–29.

——."Tibet: The Critical Years: 'The Thirteenth Dalai Lama.'" *The Tibet Journal* 7, no. 4 (1982): 11–19.

Tada, Takan. *The Thirteenth Dalai Lama*. Tokyo: The Centre for East Asian Cultural Studies, 1965.

Takeuchi, T. "Old Tibetan Loan Contracts." *Memoirs of the Research Department of the Toyo Bunko* 51 (1993): 25–84.

Teichman, Eric. *Travels of a Consular Officer in Eastern Tibet, Together with the History of the Relations between China, Tibet, and India*. Cambridge: Cambridge University Press, 1922.

Thompson, D. "China and Tibet 1911–1961." *The Journal of the Central Asian Society* 49 (1962):

"Tibet Wants Tashi Lama as Regent." *Newsweek*, 1934, 19.

Tien, H. M. *Government and Politics in Kuomintang China, 1927–1937*. Stanford: Stanford University Press, 1972.

Tsao, W. Y. *Constitutional Structure of Modern China*. Melbourne: Melbourne University Press, 1947.

Tsering, Tashi. *A Brief Survey of Fourteen Centuries of Sino-Tibetan Relations*. Dharamsala: Office of Information and International Relations, 1988.

Tsybikov, G. T. *Un pèlerin bouddhiste au Tibet, d'après les journaux de voyage tenus entre 1899 et 1902*. Paris: Peuples du monde, 1992.

Tucci, Giuseppe. *Tibetan Painted Scrolls*. Rome: Istituto Poligrafico e Zecca dello Stato, 1949.

——. *Tibet: Land of Snows*. London: Elek, 1973.

——. *To Lhasa and Beyond*. Rome: Istituto Poligrafico Dello Stato, 1956. Reprint, New York: Snow Lion Publications, 1987, 2nd ed.

Tucci, G., and W. Heissig. *Les religions du Tibet et de la Mongolie*. Translated by R. Sailley. Paris: Payot, 1973.

Turner, Samuel. *An Account of an Embassy to the Court of the Teshoo Lama in Tibet*. London: Nicol, 1800.

——. "An Account of an Interview with Teeshoo Lama and an Account of a Journey to Tibet." *Asia Major*, 1801, 196–220.

——. *Ambassade de M. Samuel Turner auprès du Tashi Lama au Tibet et au Boutan*. Paris, 1877.

——. *Ambassade au Thibet et au Boutan (1783–1784)*. Translated by Jean-Henri Castéra. Paris, 1800.

——. *Voyages au Tibet faits en 1625 et 1626 par le Père Andrade et, en 1774, 1784, 1785 par Bogle, Turner et Pourunguir*, éds. J. Larraud and J. B. Billecoq. Paris: 1796.

Turtle, H. B. *An Outline of Indian Currency*. Calcutta: Thacker, Spink and Co., 1927.

Tuttle, Gray. "Review of *Le 9e Panchen Lama (1883–1937): Enjeu des relations sino-tibétaines* by Fabienne Jagou." *Journal of the International Association of Tibetan Studies*, August 2006, 8.

——. "Tibetan Buddhism in Republican China: Tracing its Support from Private Interests to Government Sponsorship." Unpublished paper presented to the Twentieth Century China Seminar, Harvard University, January 18, 1997.

——. *Tibetan Buddhists in the Making of Modern China*. New York: Columbia University Press, 2005.

Twitchett D., and J. K. Fairbank, eds. *The Cambridge History of China*. Vols. 10–11, *Late Ch'ing 1800–1911*. Cambridge: Cambridge University Press, 1978.

Van Ekelen, P. "The Simla Convention and the McMahon Line." *The Journal of the Central Asian Society* 54 (1967): 179–85.

Van Walt van Praag, Michael C. *The Status of Tibet: History, Rights, and Prospects in International Law*. London: Wisdom Publications, 1987.

Verrier, Anthony. *Francis Younghusband and the Great Game*. London: Jonathan Cape, 1991.

Vira, Raghu, and L. Chandra, eds. *Kālacakra Tantra and Other Texts*. New Delhi, International Academy of Indian Culture, 1966.

Vostrikov, Andreï I. *Tibetan Historical Literature*. New Delhi: Indian Studies Past and Present, 1970.

Waddell, Austin L. *Lhasa and its Mysteries, with a Record of the Expedition of 1903–1904*. London: John Murray, 1905. Reprint, New Delhi: Cosmo Publications, 1996.

Wakeman, F., and C. Grant. *Conflict and Control in Late Imperial China*. London: University Press of California, 1975.

——. *Policing Shanghai, 1927–1937*. Berkeley: University of California Press, 1996.

Waller, Derek J. "The Pundits: British Exploration of Tibet." *Xizang yu Zhongyuan guanxi guoji xueshuyan taolun wenji* (1993): 443–510.

Wang Xiangyun. "Tibetan Buddhism at the Court of Qing: The Life and Work of lCang skya rol pai' rDo rje (1717–1786)." PhD diss., Harvard University, 1995.

Weaver, John R. H. *The Dictionary of National Biography, 1922–1930*. Oxford: Oxford University Press, 1937.

Welch, Holmes. *The Buddhist Revival in China*. Cambridge: Harvard University Press, 1968.

——. *The Practice of Chinese Buddhism 1900–1950*. Cambridge: Harvard University Press, 1967.

Who's Who in Tibet, a confidential dossier prepared by official representatives of the British government for Sikkim, Bhutan, and Tibet, corrected in autumn 1937 and completed in February 1938. Calcutta: Government of India Press, 1938.

Wiley, T. W. "Macro-Exchanges: Tibetan Economics and the Roles of Politics and Religion." *The Tibet Journal* 2, no. 1 (1986): 1–20.

Will, Pierre-Etienne. "L'ère des rebellions et la modernisation avortée." In *La Chine au XXè siècle, d'une révolution à l'autre, 1895–1949*, éds. M. C. Bergère, L. Bianco, and J. Dumas, 45–83. Paris: Fayard, 1989.

Williamson, M. D. *Memoirs of a Political Officer's Wife in Tibet, Sikkim, and Bhutan*. London: Wisdom Publications, 1987.

Wilton, E. C. "The Boundary Provinces of Western China." *The Journal of the Central Asian Society* 3–5 (1916–1918): 27–40.

Winnington, Alan. *Tibet: Record of a Journey*. London: Lawrence and Wishart, 1957.

Woodman, Dorothy. *Himalayan Frontiers: A Political Review of British, Chinese, Indian, and Russian Rivalries*. London: Barne & Rockliff, 1969.

Wright, Mary C. *China in Revolution: The First Phase, 1900–1913*. New Haven: Yale University Press, 1968.

Wylie, Turrel V. "Reincarnation: A Political Innovation in Tibetan Buddhism." In *Proceedings of the Csoma de Köros Memorial Symposium*, edited by L. Ligeti, 579–86. Budapest: Akademiai Kiado, 1978.

Xerab Nyima. "From Geshi of Sera Monastery to KMT Attache." *China's Tibet* 1 (1995): 20–22.

Xiao-Plane Xiaohong. *La société générale d'éducation du Jiangsu et son rôle dans l'évolution socio-politique chinoise de 1905 à 1914*. Paris: EHESS, 2001.

Ya Hanzhang. *The Biographies of the Dalai Lamas*. Beijing: Foreign Languages Press, 1991.

——. *Biographies of the Tibetan Spiritual Leaders: Panchen Erdenis*. Beijing: Foreign Languages Press, 1994.

Yoshimizu, Chizuko, ed. *Descriptive Catalogue of the Naritasan Institute Collection of Tibetan Works*. Kyoto: Naritasan Shinshoji, 1989.

Yu, David C., ed. *Religion in Postwar China: A Critical Analysis and Annotated Bibliography*. London: Greenwood Press, 1994.

Yumiko, I. "On the Dissemination of the Belief in the Dalai Lama as a Manifestation of the Bodhisattva Avalokiteśvara." *Acta Asiatica* 64 (1993): 38–56.

Yuthok, Dorje Yudon. *House of the Turquoise Roof*. New York: Snow Lion Publications, 1990.

INDEX

D

E

F

G

H

I

J

K

L

M

N

O

P

Q

R

S